T0348762

HANDBOOK OF PUBLIC ECONOMICS
VOLUME 4

HANDBOOKS
IN
ECONOMICS

4

Series Editors

KENNETH J. ARROW
MICHAEL D. INTRILIGATOR

N·H

ELSEVIER

Amsterdam • Boston • London • New York • Oxford • Paris
San Diego • San Francisco • Singapore • Sydney • Tokyo

HANDBOOK OF PUBLIC ECONOMICS

VOLUME 4

Edited by

ALAN J. AUERBACH
University of California, Berkeley

and

MARTIN FELDSTEIN
Harvard University

2002

ELSEVIER

Amsterdam • Boston • London • New York • Oxford • Paris
San Diego • San Francisco • Singapore • Sydney • Tokyo

ELSEVIER SCIENCE B.V.
Sara Burgerhartstraat 25
P.O. Box 211, 1000 AE Amsterdam, The Netherlands

First edition 2002

Library of Congress Cataloging in Publication Data
A catalog record from the Library of Congress has been applied for.

British Library Cataloguing in Publication Data
A catalogue record from the British Library has been applied for.

ISBN: 0-444-82315-8
ISSN: 0169-7218 (Handbooks in Economics Series)

⊗ The paper used in this publication meets the requirements of ANSI/NISO Z39.48-1992 (Permanence of Paper).

Printed and bound in the United Kingdom
Transferred to Digital Printing, 2011

INTRODUCTION TO THE SERIES

The aim of the *Handbooks in Economics* series is to produce Handbooks for various branches of economics, each of which is a definitive source, reference, and teaching supplement for use by professional researchers and advanced graduate students. Each Handbook provides self-contained surveys of the current state of a branch of economics in the form of chapters prepared by leading specialists on various aspects of this branch of economics. These surveys summarize not only received results but also newer developments, from recent journal articles and discussion papers. Some original material is also included, but the main goal is to provide comprehensive and accessible surveys. The Handbooks are intended to provide not only useful reference volumes for professional collections but also possible supplementary readings for advanced courses for graduate students in economics.

KENNETH J. ARROW and MICHAEL D. INTRILIGATOR

PUBLISHER'S NOTE

For a complete overview of the Handbooks in Economics Series, please refer to the listing at the end of this volume.

CONTENTS OF THE HANDBOOK

EDITORS' INTRODUCTION TO VOLUME 4

The publication of Volume 3 and this Volume 4 of the Handbook of Public Economics affords us several opportunities: to address lacunae in the original two volumes of this series, to revisit topics on which there has been substantial new research, and to address topics that have grown in importance. Indeed, many of the papers individually encompass all three of these elements. For each chapter related to one from an earlier volume, the new contribution is free-standing, written with the knowledge that the reader retains the opportunity to review the earlier chapter to compare perspectives and consider material that the current author has chosen not to cover. Indeed, such comparisons illuminate the evolution of the field during the roughly two decades that have elapsed since work first began on the chapters in Volume 1. Taken together, the four volumes offer a comprehensive review of research in public economics, in its current state and over the past few decades, written by many of the field's leading researchers.

EDITORS' INTRODUCTION

The field of Public Economics has been changing rapidly in recent years, and the sixteen chapters contained in this Handbook survey many of the new developments. As a field, Public Economics is defined by its objectives rather than its techniques, and much of what is new is the application of modern methods of economic theory and econometrics to problems that have been addressed by economists for over two hundred years. More generally, the discussion of public finance issues also involves elements of political science, finance and philosophy. These connections are evidence in several of the chapters that follow.

Public Economics is the positive and normative study of government's effect on the economy. We attempt to explain why government behaves as it does, how its behavior influences the behavior of private firms and households, and what the welfare effects of such changes in behavior are. Following Musgrave (1959) one may imagine three purposes for government intervention in the economy: *allocation,* when market failure causes the private outcome to be Pareto inefficient, *distribution,* when the private market outcome leaves some individuals with unacceptably low shares in the fruits of the economy, and *stabilization,* when the private market outcome leaves some of the economy's resources underutilized. The recent trend in economic research has tended to emphasize the character of stabilization problems as problems of allocation in the labor market. The effects that government intervention can have on the allocation and distribution of an economy's resources are described in terms of efficiency and incidence effects. These are the primary measures used to evaluate the welfare effects of government policy.

The first chapter in this volume, by Richard Musgrave, presents an historical development of these and other concepts in Public Finance, dating from Adam Smith's discussion in *The Wealth of Nations* of the role of government and the principles by which taxes should be set. The remaining chapters in the Handbook examine different areas of current research in Public Economics.

Analyses of the efficiency and incidence of taxation, developed in Musgrave's chapter, are treated separately in Alan Auerbach's chapter in the first volume and Laurence Kotlikoff's and Lawrence Summers' chapter in the second volume, respectively. Auerbach surveys the literature on excess burden and optimal taxation, while Kotlikoff and Summers discuss various theoretical and empirical approaches that have been used to measure the distributional effects of government tax and expenditure policies.

These general analyses of the effects of taxation form a basis for the consideration of tax policies in particular markets or environments, as is contained in the chapters by Jerry Hausman, Agnar Sandmo, Avinash Dixit, Harvey Rosen, John Helliwell and Terry Heaps, and Joseph Stiglitz.

Hausman discusses the effects of taxation on labor supply, including a treatment of how one empirically estimates such effects in the presence of tax and transfer programs. He also considers the incentive effects of social welfare programs such as unemployment compensation and social security. Sandmo focuses on the other major factor in production, capital, dealing with theory and evidence about the effects of taxation on private and social saving and risk-taking. Dixit shows how the basic results about the effects of taxation may be extended to the trade sector of the economy, casting results from the parallel trade literature in terms more familiar to students of Public Finance. Rosen's chapter brings out the characteristics of housing that make it worthy of special consideration. He considers the special econometric problems involved in estimating the response of housing demand and supply to government incentives. Because of its importance in most family budgets and its relatively low income elasticity of demand, housing has been seen as a suitable vehicle for government programs to help the poor, and Rosen discusses the efficiency and incidence effects of such programs. Helliwell and Heaps consider the effects of taxation on output paths and factor mixes in a number of natural resource industries. By comparing their results for different industries, they expose the effects that technological differences have on the impact of government policies. Stiglitz treats the literature on income and wealth taxation.

The remaining chapters in the Handbook may be classified as being on the "expenditure" side rather than the "tax" side of Public Finance, though this distinction is probably too sharp to be accurate. In Volume 1, Dieter Bös surveys the literature on public sector pricing, which is closely related both to the optimal taxation discussion in Auerbach's chapter and Robert Inman's consideration, in Volume 2, of models of voting and government behavior. The question of voting and, more generally, public choice mechanisms, is treated by Jean-Jacques Laffont in his chapter.

The chapters by William Oakland and Daniel Rubinfeld focus on the provision of "public" goods, i.e., goods with sufficiently increasing returns to scale or lack of excludability that government provision is the normal mode. Oakland considers the optimality conditions for the provision of goods that fall between Samuelson's (1954) "pure" public goods and the private goods provide efficiently by private markets. Rubinfeld surveys the literature on a special class of such goods: local public goods. Since the work of Tiebout (1956), much research has been devoted to the question of whether localities can provide efficient levels of public goods.

The other two chapters in Volume 2 also deal with problems of public expenditures. Anthony Atkinson considers the effects of the range of social welfare programs common in Western societies aimed at improving the economic standing of the poor. Some of these policies are touched on in the chapters by Hausman and Rosen, but the coexistence of many different programs itself leads to effects that cannot be recognized by examining such programs seriatim. Jean Drèze and Nicholas Stern present a unified treatment of the techniques of cost benefit analysis, with applications to the problems of developing countries.

References

Musgrave, R.A. (1959), The Theory of Public Finance (McGraw-Hill, New York).
Samuelson, P.A. (1954), "The pure theory of public expenditures", Review of Economics and Statistics 36:387–389.
Tiebout, C.M. (1956), "A pure theory of local expenditures", Journal of Political Economy 94:416–424.

CONTENTS OF VOLUME 4

Part 5 – INTERGOVERNMENTAL RELATIONS

Part 7 – LABOR MARKET EFFECTS

Chapter 33
Labor Supply Effects of Social Insurance
ALAN B. KRUEGER and BRUCE D. MEYER   2327

Part 4

FISCAL INCIDENCE

Chapter 26

TAX INCIDENCE *

DON FULLERTON

Department of Economics, University of Texas, Austin; and NBER

GILBERT E. METCALF

Department of Economics, Tufts University; and NBER

Contents

* We are grateful for helpful suggestions from Alan Auerbach, Tom Barthold, Leora Friedberg, Michael Keen, and Rob Williams. This paper is part of the NBER's research program in Public Economics. Any opinions expressed in this paper are those of the authors and not those of the National Bureau of Economic Research.

Handbook of Public Economics, Volume 4, Edited by A.J. Auerbach and M. Feldstein

Abstract

This chapter reviews the concepts, methods, and results of studies that analyze the incidence of taxes. The purpose of such studies is to determine how the burden of a particular tax is allocated among consumers through higher product prices, workers through a lower wage rate, or other factors of production through lower rates of return to those factors. The methods might involve simple partial equilibrium models, analytical general equilibrium models, or computable general equilibrium models.

In a partial equilibrium model, the burden of a tax is shown to depend on the elasticity of supply relative to the elasticity of demand. Partial equilibrium models also are used to consider cases with imperfect competition.

In a two-sector general equilibrium model, a tax might be imposed on either commodity, on either factor of production, or on a factor used in one sector. The original use of this model is to analyze the corporate income tax as a tax on capital used only in one sector, the corporate sector. The model can be used to show when the burden falls only on capital or when the burden is shared with labor. The model also has been applied to the property tax, and results of the model have been used to calculate the overall burden on each income group.

Because the total stock of capital is fixed in that model, however, dynamic models are required to show how a tax on capital affects capital accumulation, future wage rates, and overall burdens. Such models might also provide analytical results or computational results. The most elaborate recent models calculate the lifetime incidence of each group. Finally, the chapter reviews the use of such incidence methods and results in the policy process.

Keywords

economic incidence, statutory incidence, tax shifting, distributional effects, payroll taxes, corporate income taxes, personal taxes, sales and excise taxes, general equilibrium models

JEL classification: H22

Introduction

Tax incidence is the study of who bears the economic burden of a tax. Broadly put, it is the positive analysis of the impact of taxes on the distribution of welfare within a society. It begins with the very basic insight that the person who has the legal obligation to make a tax payment may not be the person whose welfare is reduced by the presence of the tax. The statutory incidence of a tax refers to the distribution of tax payments based on the legal obligation to remit taxes to the government. Thus, for example, the statutory burden of the payroll tax in the United States is shared equally between employers and employees. Economists, quite rightly, focus on the economic incidence, which measures the changes in economic welfare in society arising from a tax. The standard view of the economic burden of the payroll tax in the United States is that it is borne entirely by employees.

Economic incidence differs from the statutory incidence because of changes in behavior and consequent changes in equilibrium prices. Consumers buy less of a taxed product, so firms produce less and buy fewer inputs – which changes the net price of each input. Thus, the job of the incidence analyst is to determine how those other prices change, and how those changes affect different kinds of individuals.

Incidence analyses abound in the literature, but they can be roughly classified into a few categories. In particular, when these studies analyze distributional effects of taxes across groups, Atkinson and Stiglitz (1980) note that we economists have used five different ways of dividing taxpayers into groups. First, we can focus on the impact of taxes on consumers as opposed to producers. A partial equilibrium diagram can identify both the loss of consumer surplus and the loss of producer surplus resulting from a tax. Second, we can narrow the focus to analyze the impact of a tax specifically on the relative demands for different factors and the returns to those factors (such as capital, labor, or land). The pathbreaking general equilibrium analysis of Harberger (1962) simply ignores the consumer side by assuming that everybody spends their money the same way, and then he derives the burden of a tax on capital as opposed to labor. Third, we can group individuals by some measure of economic well-being, in order to analyze the progressivity of a tax or tax system. Pechman and Okner (1974) is perhaps the classic analysis of the U.S. tax system that groups taxpayers by annual income, while Fullerton and Rogers (1993) group taxpayers by a measure of lifetime resources. Fourth, taxes can be evaluated on the basis of regional incidence. Such an analysis might focus on regional differences within a country [e.g., Bull, Hassett and Metcalf (1994)], or it might focus on international differences. Finally, taxes can have intergenerational effects. For example, insufficient social security taxes could bring about a transfer from future generations to the current generation. These effects can be captured by the generational accounting approach of Auerbach, Gokhale and Kotlikoff (1991), but see Barro (1974) for a dissenting view.

We begin in Section 1 with some definitions and concepts that will be used throughout this chapter. Next, we turn to a review of static analytical models of tax incidence. We begin with a simple partial equilibrium model, and then proceed to general equilibrium models. While many of the principles and lessons from partial equilibrium analysis carry over to general equilibrium analysis, the latter affords a greater richness and insight than do the partial equilibrium models. In addition, we find a number of instances of results that are "surprising", in the sense that the outcome in the general equilibrium model could not occur in a partial equilibrium model. Along the way, we present examples of empirical incidence analyses with estimates of the burden of the U.S. tax system or individual taxes in the U.S. system. All of these analyses assume perfectly competitive markets, and Section 3 provides a discussion of incidence in imperfectly competitive markets.

In Section 4, we turn to dynamic models. Allowing for endogenous capital accumulation adds both an important type of behavioral change and considerable complexity. Dynamic models also allow the researcher to distinguish between "old" and "new" capital, a source of considerable redistribution in the case of tax reforms. Section 5 continues the analysis in a dynamic framework by investigating the incidence of tax systems over the life cycle. If individuals make consumption decisions on the basis of lifetime income [Modigliani and Brumberg (1954)], then annual income analyses of consumption taxes might be biased towards finding regressivity. Fullerton and Rogers (1993) have looked most thoroughly at this question, and interestingly, they find that the bias predicted by others is not nearly as severe as predicted.

Section 6 focuses on the use of distributional analysis in the policy process. Policy economists face an inherent tradeoff between theoretical rigor and the need for rapid, easily-comprehensible distributional analysis. Economists at several government agencies have refined the available techniques for measuring and reporting incidence impacts of taxes. In this section, we describe both the techniques used to analyze taxes and methods of presenting information to policy makers so that they can make informed decisions. Naturally, other economists have criticized many of the techniques used in the policy process, and we review some of those criticisms here.

Finally, we note that incidence analysis can be more broadly applied than we do in this chapter. We ignore incidence analyses of government spending programs [e.g., Musgrave, Case and Leonard (1974) or McClellan and Skinner (1997)]. Such a spending program can also affect relative prices, and so economic incidence again can differ from statutory incidence. The principles and concepts described in this chapter are not limited to tax analysis and can easily be applied to government spending programs as well.

1. Basic machinery of incidence analysis

In this section we sketch out various concepts and definitions that are commonly used in incidence analysis. We also describe and provide some motivation for analytic techniques that we will use frequently in this chapter.

1.1. Definitions and concepts

A number of concepts are used in incidence analyses. In the introduction, we already drew a distinction between *statutory incidence* (the legal payers of the tax) and *economic incidence* (those who lose real income). We now make further distinctions that are useful to sharpen our understanding of the incidence of various taxes.

To begin, economists might say that a commodity tax is *passed forward,* which means that the consumer price rises and consumers of that good bear the burden. The price received by the supplier might be unchanged. On the other hand, if the consumer price is unchanged when a commodity tax is imposed, then the price received by the supplier must fall. In that case, the burden is *passed backward* onto suppliers (or more precisely, onto labor, capital, or other factors in production). Similarly, a tax that is passed forward to consumers has burdens on the "*uses side*" (depending on how people use their income), while a tax that is passed backward has burdens on the "*sources side*" (because labor and capital are sources of income).

All of these terms must be employed with care. A longstanding principle in tax incidence analysis is that real burdens depend on real allocations, not on the price level or choice of numeraire. Thus, even for a tax on a particular commodity, the true incidence does not depend on whether monetary authorities accommodate by allowing an increase in that price (and thus in the overall price level). Only relative prices matter. Because the price level is irrelevant, however, so must be the question about whether the overall burden is on the uses side or the sources side! Instead, what matters is how changes in relative output prices affect different groups (if some spend more than the average share of income on the taxed good), and how changes in relative factor prices affect different groups (if some earn more than the average share of income from the factor employed intensively in the taxed industry).

Thus, the first job for a complete incidence study is to determine effects on all relative prices. A study might legitimately focus just on the uses side if groups have different spending patterns but all have the same sources of income (or if the taxed industry uses the average capital/labor ratio so that reduced production does not affect relative factor prices). Conversely, a study might focus just on the sources side if all groups spend the same fraction of income on the taxed good (and the taxed industry makes intensive use of labor, capital, or other factors). If the tax affects both output prices and factor prices, then a complete study would divide individuals into groups based on some measure of income, obtain data on all sources of income and all uses of income of each group, and use that data to calculate each group's net economic burden from a tax.

Regardless of how the burden is calculated, for each income group, their relative burdens of a tax can be compared using the ratio of the economic burden to income. A tax is said to be *progressive* if this ratio rises with income, *regressive* if it falls with income, and *proportional* if the ratio is constant. A common misconception is that progressivity is defined by rising marginal tax rates. For example, a flat tax or negative income tax can have a constant marginal tax rate and still be progressive. Let the tax liability (T) be the following linear function of income (Y):

$$T = m(Y - A), \tag{1.1}$$

where m is the marginal tax rate, and $A > 0$ is a family allowance. If income falls below A, then T can be negative (the taxpayer receives a payment from the government)[1]. With this tax system, the average tax rate (T/Y) starts at negative infinity, rises to zero at an income level equal to A, and then continues to rise with income (approaching m asymptotically). This tax is progressive, because the average tax rate rises with income, despite the fact that it has a constant marginal tax rate. For a different example, the Medicare portion of the payroll tax on employees has a constant marginal rate of 2.9%, but this tax is regressive because it applies only to wage income (while non-wage income tends to be concentrated in higher income groups)[2].

Care also is required when we define the incidence experiment. In particular, when we want to determine the distributional effects of raising a particular tax, we need to specify what is done with the revenues. While partial equilibrium incidence analyses often ignore the distribution of the proceeds, a more complete analysis takes into account what is done with the tax revenue. Logically, we have three alternatives. First, *absolute* incidence analysis refers to the assumption that the proceeds of the tax under investigation are simply held by government, but then a full analysis would need to consider the effects of the change in government debt. Second, a *balanced-budget* incidence analysis is one that assumes the revenue is spent, but then the distributional effects depend on how the revenue is spent[3]. Third, a *differential* incidence analysis assumes that the revenue is used to reduce some other tax, but then the distributional effects depend on the effects of the tax being reduced. None of these alternatives isolates the effects of the tax being raised! Still, however, one way to neutralize the effects of the use of the revenue is to assume that the government spends it exactly the same way that consumers would have spent it [as in Harberger (1962)]. This balanced-budget incidence analysis is equivalent to a differential analysis that uses the revenue to reduce lump-sum taxes on consumers – but only if the money goes to exactly the same individuals who were bearing the burden, so that they can spend it the same way

---

[1] The Flat Tax has been proposed in many forms. Perhaps the most well-known variant is due to Hall and Rabushka (1995). Some plans have $T = \max[0, m(Y - A)]$, so taxes are only positive, but $A > 0$ still means that the system is progressive: the average tax rate (T/Y) is zero up to income $Y = A$, and then it starts to rise with Y. Because T can be negative in Equation (1.1), this system is often called a Negative Income Tax.

[2] This statement ignores the benefits arising from the Medicare system, a point we take up below, as well as the employer portion of the tax. However, our statement about the regressivity of the tax is not affected by the fact that employers pay half the tax.

[3] For example, the regressive effects of the social security payroll tax are substantially modified if one includes the effects of using those revenues to provide progressive social security benefits.

they were spending it before the first tax was imposed. Any other use of the revenue with altered spending could itself affect prices.

An advantage of differential incidence analyses with lump-sum tax rebates is that different analyses are additive in the following sense. If one study considers tax proposal A with proceeds used to lower lump-sum taxes by X, and a second study considers tax proposal B with proceeds used to lower lump-sum taxes by X, then the two studies can be combined to analyze the differential incidence of a shift from tax system A to tax system B (or vice versa). Fullerton and Rogers (1997) illustrate how differential tax incidence can modify conventional thinking in the case of a uniform consumption tax. Normally, a uniform consumption tax has the attractive property that no commodity is tax-advantaged[4]. Yet, Fullerton and Rogers note that relative prices still change, and consumers are differentially affected, if the uniform consumption tax is used to replace an existing system that *does* have differential commodity taxes.

Up to now, we have been a bit vague as to the meaning of the *burden* of a tax. A straightforward measure of the burden of a tax is the equivalent (or compensating) variation. The equivalent variation (EV) is the amount of lump-sum income that a person would give up to avoid a particular tax change (such as the imposition of a tax or a complex change to a system of taxes). So long as the taxpayer can take some action to influence the amount of taxes paid (short of tax evasion), the EV will exceed the tax revenue collected from the taxpayer – and the difference is defined as the deadweight loss of the tax. The true economic burden of a tax, therefore, exceeds the revenue loss to the taxpayer unless the tax is lump-sum in nature. Figure 1.1 illustrates. A commodity (X) is provided with perfectly elastic supply, S. The Marshallian demand curve is D^M. Prior to a tax, CF is purchased at a price of 0C. When a tax on X is imposed, the supply curve shifts up to S' (to reflect the cost of production inclusive of the tax). Demand falls to AB and tax revenue of ABDC is collected. The equivalent variation for this tax is the area between the old and new prices to the left of the compensated demand curve (D^C) and equals ABEC. It exceeds the taxes collected by the deadweight loss triangle BDE.

Note the strong informational requirements for this measure of tax burden. The researcher needs to know the utility function (or equivalently the expenditure function) to measure EV[5]. As we shall note below, a number of alternative measures of the burden of a tax are used in practice. A second approach is to measure the change in consumer's surplus. Willig (1976) provides bounds on the income elasticity of demand under which the change in consumer's surplus provides a good approximation of EV. In Figure 1.1, the change in consumer's surplus is ABFC. A third approach is to measure

---

[4] Note, however, that Ramsey (1928) considerations provide no optimal tax rationale for uniform consumption taxation except in certain circumstances.

[5] Hausman (1981) shows how to recover the utility function and thus to derive the EV from observed Marshallian demand functions. While this insight is important, it simply pushes back the information problem from that of specifying the utility function correctly to that of specifying the demand function correctly.

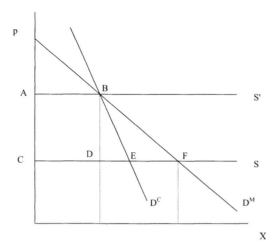

Fig. 1.1. The economic burden of a tax on X.

the tax actually paid (ABDC in Figure 1.1)[6]. This approach ignores the component of the economic burden arising from the deadweight loss. For small taxes, this can provide a good approximation to the true burden of the tax, but for large taxes it can significantly underestimate the true burden. Finally, another common approach is simply to look at the change in net-of-tax prices following tax changes. In Figure 1.1, only the consumer price changes (by AC), and the full burden of the tax is said to be on the consumer.

Before finishing basic concepts and definitions, we have a few other useful terms. A *unit* tax (t) is applied at a particular dollar amount per unit of the good or factor, and so it raises a price from p to $p + t$. An example is a "specific" excise tax. In contrast, an *ad valorem* tax (τ) is some fraction or percentage of the product price, and so it raises a price from p to $p(1 + \tau)$. An example is a local 8% sales tax. Any particular tax law might be worded either way, and it might be analyzed either way so long as the researcher is careful to employ the proper correspondences (such as $\tau = t/p$)[7]. For consistency, we use just *ad valorem* rates below.

Another definitional device useful to incidence analysts is the *unit convention*, which is just a way to define what is one unit of a good. Apples can be priced per pound, per ton, or per bushel, and this choice has no real effect even though the price looks very different. Therefore, we can define a unit as whatever amount costs one dollar (before taxes). Then the initial price is one, and we can focus on tax changes that

---

[6] The EV is the measure of burden in computational general equilibrium (CGE) models discussed below, while the tax actually paid is used as the measure of burden in studies with incidence assumptions [such as Pechman and Okner (1974)]. For taxes paid by businesses, such studies use specific incidence assumptions to allocate the tax burden among income groups.

[7] The different wording of the tax has been shown to matter in particular models, such as those with imperfect competition. See Section 3 below.

may raise that price or lower it. Similarly, if one person buys a car for $20 000 while another buys a car for $10 000, we simply say that the first person has purchased twice as much car. The price they face is the same ($1 per unit). This convention has the added advantage that a one-cent unit tax is the same as a one percent *ad valorem* tax.

Finally, we must be careful about what is in the denominator of the tax rate. A *tax-exclusive* rate is expressed as a fraction of the price excluding tax, while a *tax-inclusive* rate refers to a fraction of the price including tax. An example of the former is a 50% sales tax that raises the price from $1 to $1.50, and an example of the latter is an income tax that takes 33% of all income. These numbers were chosen to make the point that the individual may be indifferent between these two taxes, since government takes one-third of real resources either way. But it matters to the researcher: a 50% sales tax is *not* the same as a 50% income tax! In this chapter, we primarily use a tax-exclusive rate, so the net price is p and the gross price is $p(1 + \tau)$. Similarly, if τ is a wage tax, then the net wage is w and the gross wage is $w(1 + \tau)$. This latter rate needs to be interpreted carefully since it is not the usual income tax rate.

1.2. Log-linearization

Many recent studies of tax incidence have built large-scale computable general equilibrium models that specify particular functional forms for production and for consumer behavior and then calculate the effects of a large tax change on each product price and on each factor return. Such models are necessary in order to capture much detail with many production sectors, consumer groups that own different factors and buy different goods, and large taxes that have non-marginal effects on prices.

On the other hand, many interesting conceptual questions of tax incidence can be addressed using small models that can be solved analytically. Because we address many such questions in this chapter using analytical "log-linearization" methods attributable to Jones (1965), and because we wish to convey the methods of tax incidence analysis to graduate students in economics, we now explain this method quite fully at the outset. The basic point of this method is to be able to specify a set of general non-linear production functions and consumer behavioral relationships, to convert these equations into a set of simpler linear equations, and then to solve these linear equations in a way that shows quite clearly the effect of a tax change on each price and on each quantity.

To explain why it is called *log*-linearization, consider the wage tax example mentioned above where the net wage is w, the gross wage is $w(1 + \tau)$, and the price of consumption is p. Defining W as the real gross wage cost to the firm, we have:

$$W = w(1 + \tau)/p. \tag{1.2}$$

To make this nonlinear equation into a linear relationship, take natural logs of both sides,

$$\ln(W) = \ln(w) + \ln(1 + \tau) - \ln(p), \tag{1.3}$$

and then differentiate:

$$dW/W = dw/w + d\tau/(1+\tau) - dp/p. \tag{1.4}$$

Next, use a "hat" to denote a proportional change, so $\hat{W} \equiv dW/W$ and $\hat{p} \equiv dp/p$. For convenience, every tax rate is treated a little differently, where $\hat{\tau} \equiv d\tau/(1+\tau)$. Using these definitions, we have:

$$\hat{W} = \hat{w} + \hat{\tau} - \hat{p}. \tag{1.5}$$

The nonlinear Equation (1.2) might be part of a system of nonlinear equations that is difficult to solve, but this "log-linearization" technique can be applied to every one of those nonlinear equations to produce a system of linear equations like Equation (1.5)[8]. If the system has N equations with N unknowns, then it is easy to solve (using successive substitution or Cramer's Rule). For example, if the goal is to calculate the effects of a tax change, $\hat{\tau}$, then the relevant unknowns might include changes in equilibrium prices $(\hat{W}, \hat{w}, \hat{p})$ and changes in equilibrium quantities such as labor, capital, and output.

Before getting to a general equilibrium system of such equations, however, we provide a complete illustration of the log-linearization technique for a simple partial equilibrium model of just the labor market. Thus, other prices are fixed (so $\hat{p} = 0$, and $\hat{W} = \hat{w} + \hat{\tau}$). Even this simple model yields important and interesting results, however, regarding the difference between statutory and economic incidence. Because workers receive the net wage w, employers bear the statutory burden and face the gross wage cost $w(1+\tau)$. Depending on labor demand and supply behaviors, however, the burden can be shifted through a change in the equilibrium net wage.

To model such behavior, first consider the definition of the elasticity of labor supply (L^S) with respect to the net wage (w):

$$\eta^S \equiv \frac{dL^S/L^S}{dw/w}. \tag{1.6}$$

Using the hat notation $(\hat{L}^S = dL^S/L^S)$, the nonlinear relationship in Equation (1.6) can be rewritten as $\eta^S \equiv \hat{L}^S/\hat{w}$, and further re-arrangement provides:

$$\hat{L}^S = \eta^S \hat{w}. \tag{1.7}$$

The point here is that we have taken a definition and turned it into a behavioral equation: if the net wage changes by a certain amount, then Equation (1.7) tells us

---

[8] Log-linearization is simply a first-order Taylor series approximation around the initial equilibrium. It is completely appropriate for calculating the effects of a small tax change, but sometimes the method has been applied to a large tax change such as the repeal of a tax – as if all of the derivatives were constant.

how labor supply responds[9]. It is one linear equation for our system. Next, if η^D is the elasticity of labor demand (L^D) with respect to the gross wage (W), then similar rearrangement provides

$$\hat{L}^D = \eta^D(\hat{w} + \hat{\tau}). \tag{1.8}$$

In this model, we assume that $\eta^D \leqslant 0$ and $\eta^S \geqslant 0$ are known parameters. In response to an exogenous tax increase ($\hat{\tau} > 0$), behaviors follow Equations (1.7) and (1.8), but reaching a new equilibrium means that the change in labor demand must equal the change in labor supply:

$$\hat{L}^S = \hat{L}^D. \tag{1.9}$$

We now have a system of three linear Equations (1.7, 1.8 and 1.9) in three unknowns ($\hat{L}^S$, $\hat{L}^D$, and $\hat{w}$). We can solve for $\hat{w}$ in terms of exogenous parameters (η^S, η^D, and $\hat{\tau}$) by setting Equation (1.7) equal to Equation (1.8) and re-arranging:

$$\frac{\hat{w}}{\hat{\tau}} = \frac{\eta^D}{\eta^S - \eta^D}. \tag{1.10}$$

The expression in Equation (1.10) lies between 0 and -1, and it shows what fraction of the tax is shifted from employers to workers[10]. Each side of the market tries to avoid the tax by changing behavior: a larger labor supply elasticity ($\eta^S \gg 0$) in Equation (1.10) means a smaller fall in the net wage to workers ($\hat{w}$)[11]. Or, if employers can be more elastic (larger $\eta^D < 0$), Equation (1.10) implies a larger fall in w (and therefore less increase in the gross wage cost of employers). Certain special cases deserve mention: if labor supply is perfectly inelastic ($\eta^S = 0$), or if labor demand is perfectly elastic (η^D infinite), then the right-hand side of Equation (1.10) is -1, and $\hat{w} = -\hat{\tau}$. Then the net wage w falls by the full amount of the tax, with no change in the gross wage cost to employers.

The principle illustrated in Equation (1.10) extends to a tax in any kind of competitive market. For example, a commodity tax burden will be shared by consumers and producers based on the relative elasticities of demand and supply[12].

---

[9] These elasticity definitions and resulting behavioral equations provide simple examples of log-linearization, but later sections take more care to derive such behaviors from first principles. In Section 2.2, we formally develop the relationship between the labor supply elasticity and primitive preference parameters.

[10] In terms of the measures of "burden" discussed in Section 1.1, this approach uses the price change itself rather than the dollar amount of tax paid or the equivalent variation.

[11] More precisely, η^S must be large relative to $-\eta^D$.

[12] Hines, Hlinko and Lubke (1995) show that when demand and marginal cost curves are linear, both buyers and sellers face the same *percentage* reduction in surplus upon introduction of a commodity tax regardless of demand and supply elasticities. While the burden on consumers may be higher in absolute terms if demand is relatively less elastic than supply, Hines et al. note that the benefits of the market accrue predominantly to consumers (i.e., consumer surplus prior to the tax is greater than producer surplus). The authors interpret this result as support for viewing commodity taxes as flat rate taxes on market surplus, analogous to flat rate income taxes.

We leave as a simple exercise the derivation of the economic incidence of a tax on wage income when the statutory incidence of the tax is on workers rather than on employers [13]. This exercise demonstrates an important principle: in markets with no impediments to market clearing, the economic incidence of a tax depends only on behavior (η^S and η^D) and not on legislative intent (statutory incidence).

We next show some log-linearization techniques that are useful for building a general equilibrium model where supplies and demands are not specified directly, as above, but are instead based on maximizing behavior. Suppose that an output X is produced using both labor L and capital K with constant returns to scale:

$$X = F(K, L). \tag{1.11}$$

This functional form is very general and nonlinear. Differentiate to get:

$$dX = F_K dK + F_L dL, \tag{1.12}$$

where F_K is the marginal product of capital ($\partial F / \partial K$), and F_L is the marginal product of labor ($\partial F / \partial L$). Divide through by X, and we have:

$$\frac{dX}{X} = \frac{F_K K}{X} \cdot \frac{dK}{K} + \frac{F_L L}{X} \cdot \frac{dL}{L}. \tag{1.13}$$

Define θ as the factor share for capital ($rK / p_X X$), where r is the rental price of capital and p_X is the price of X. With perfect competition, where $r = p_X F_K$ and $W = p_X F_L$, the factor share for capital will equal $F_K K / X$ and the factor share for labor will equal $F_L L / X$. And with constant returns to scale, factor shares sum to one, so Equation (1.13) becomes:

$$\hat{X} = \theta \hat{K} + (1 - \theta) \hat{L}. \tag{1.14}$$

While the production function tells us how total labor and capital yield total output, this differential equation tells us how small changes in labor and capital yield changes in output. It is a linear equation in three of the important unknowns ($\hat{X}$, $\hat{K}$, $\hat{L}$).

Finally, for this section, consider the definition of the elasticity of substitution between capital and labor in production (omitting taxes for the moment):

$$\sigma \equiv \frac{d(K/L)/(K/L)}{d(w/r)/(w/r)}. \tag{1.15}$$

If we do the differentiation in the numerator, it becomes

$$\frac{L dK - K dL}{L^2} \cdot \frac{L}{K} = \frac{dK}{K} - \frac{dL}{L} = \hat{K} - \hat{L}. \tag{1.16}$$

---

[13] This exercise would require redefinition of w as the gross wage and $w(1 - \tau)$ as the net wage.

Then, with a similar differentiation of the denominator, we have:

$$\sigma = \frac{\hat{K} - \hat{L}}{\hat{w} - \hat{r}}. \tag{1.17}$$

In fact, many use Equation (1.17) directly as the definition of the elasticity of substitution. A simple rearrangement of the definition turns it into a statement about behavior:

$$\hat{K} - \hat{L} = \sigma(\hat{w} - \hat{r}). \tag{1.18}$$

This procedure converts the complicated nonlinear Equation (1.15) into a linear equation. With the labor tax, where firms react to the gross wage $w(1 + \tau)$, we would have

$$\hat{K} - \hat{L} = \sigma(\hat{w} + \hat{\tau} - \hat{r}). \tag{1.19}$$

For any exogenous tax change (with endogenous change in the wage and interest rate), Equation (1.19) tells us how the firm reacts by changing its use of labor and capital. It is one more linear equation for our system.

   While a computational general equilibrium model must specify a particular functional form for production, such as Cobb–Douglas or Constant Elasticity of Substitution (CES), the production function in Equation (1.11) avoids this limitation. It can be any function with constant returns to scale. However, this log-linearization method is valid only for small changes. It does not require a constant factor share θ (as in Cobb–Douglas) or a constant elasticity of substitution σ (as in CES); instead, it only requires that we know the initial observed θ and σ. In the rest of this chapter, we will use this logic to arrive at equations like (1.14) and (1.19) virtually without explanation.

   The main purpose of this subsection was to define log-linearization and to provide a few examples. That purpose is completed, and so we are ready to start using this method to derive important incidence results.

2. Static analytical models

We begin our survey by looking at static economic models of tax incidence. Such models are particularly good for analyzing taxes that do not affect saving or investment. Many of the insights that we can glean from these models are more general and carry over to richer, complex models with a full specification of saving, investment, and intertemporal optimization.

2.1. Two-sector general equilibrium model

We first turn to the two-sector general equilibrium model with two factors of production (capital, K, and labor, L). Production of two goods (X and Y) occurs in a constant returns to scale environment:

$$X = F(K_X, L_X), \qquad Y = G(K_Y, L_Y). \tag{2.1}$$

Each factor has a fixed total supply but can freely migrate to either sector (with no unemployment). Thus

$$K_X + K_Y = \overline{K}, \qquad L_X + L_Y = \overline{L}. \tag{2.2}$$

Also, since each factor is fully mobile between sectors, it must earn the same after-tax return in both sectors [14]. Harberger (1962) used this model to consider a tax on capital in one sector. Before considering Harberger's specific experiment, we set up the model more generally to consider a number of taxes. In all cases, we return the tax proceeds lump sum to consumers, all of whom are identical. Because all consumers spend their money the same way, we can focus on incidence effects on the sources side [15]. Income for capital is $r\overline{K}$ (where r is the nominal return to capital), while income for labor is $w\overline{L}$ (where w is the nominal wage rate). Since $\overline{K}$ and $\overline{L}$ are fixed, we can focus on changes in the ratio of r to w to see how the burden of the tax is shared.

We develop the model using equations of change, the log-linearization method of Jones (1965) described above. Totally differentiate the equations in (2.2) to get

$$\lambda_{LX}\hat{L}_X + \lambda_{LY}\hat{L}_Y = 0, \qquad \lambda_{KX}\hat{K}_X + \lambda_{KY}\hat{K}_Y = 0, \tag{2.3}$$

where λ_{LX} is the fraction of labor used in the production of X (the original $L_X/\overline{L}$, before the change). The other λ terms are defined similarly.

Production technology can be represented by the elasticity of substitution between K and L for each good (σ_X and σ_Y):

$$\hat{K}_X - \hat{L}_X = \sigma_X \left(\hat{w} + \hat{\tau}_{LX} - \hat{r} - \hat{\tau}_{KX} \right), \qquad \hat{K}_Y - \hat{L}_Y = \sigma_Y \left(\hat{w} + \hat{\tau}_{LY} - \hat{r} - \hat{\tau}_{KY} \right), \tag{2.4}$$

where $\hat{\tau}_{ij} = d\tau_{ij}/1 + \tau_{ij}$ is a tax on factor income ($i = L, K$) in the production of good $j(j = X, Y)$.

---

[14] This model is characterized by the "perfect" assumptions (such as perfect competition, perfect mobility, perfect information, and perfect certainty). Harberger (1962) provided an extremely useful benchmark case that can be solved easily, and he established a research agenda for virtually all of the following incidence literature: what happens with imperfect competition, imperfect mobility, uncertainty, variable factor supplies, unemployment, nonconstant returns to scale, an open economy, some other distortion such as an externality, more than two factors, more than two sectors, or more than one type of consumer?

[15] Harberger assumed homothetic and identical preferences and that government used the revenue to purchase X and Y in the same proportions as do consumers. With either Harberger's assumption or ours, one can ignore uses side effects of the partial factor tax.

Capital is paid the value of its marginal product in competitive markets:

$$p_X F_K = r(1 + \tau_{KX}), \qquad p_Y G_K = r(1 + \tau_{KY}), \tag{2.5}$$

just as labor is paid the value of its marginal product in each industry:

$$p_X F_L = w(1 + \tau_{LX}), \qquad p_Y G_L = w(1 + \tau_{LY}), \tag{2.6}$$

where p_X is the producer price of X and p_Y the producer price of Y. Given Equations (2.5) and (2.6), and constant returns to scale, the value of output in each industry must equal factor payments:

$$p_X X = w(1 + \tau_{LX})L_X + r(1 + \tau_{KX})K_X, \quad p_Y Y = w(1 + \tau_{LY})L_Y + r(1 + \tau_{KY})K_Y. \tag{2.7}$$

Totally differentiate the equations in (2.7) and evaluate at $\tau_{ij} = 0$ to obtain:

$$\begin{aligned}
\hat{p}_X + \hat{X} &= \theta_{KX}\left(\hat{r} + \hat{\tau}_{KX} + \hat{K}_X\right) + \theta_{LX}\left(\hat{w} + \hat{\tau}_{LX} + \hat{L}_X\right), \\
\hat{p}_Y + \hat{Y} &= \theta_{KY}\left(\hat{r} + \hat{\tau}_{KY} + \hat{K}_Y\right) + \theta_{LY}\left(\hat{w} + \hat{\tau}_{LY} + \hat{L}_Y\right),
\end{aligned} \tag{2.8}$$

where the θ's are the factor shares. For example, θ_{KX} is the share of sales revenue in sector X that is paid for capital ($\theta_{KX} \equiv r(1 + \tau_{KX})K_X/(p_X X)$).

In a similar fashion, we can totally differentiate the production functions in Equation (2.1) and use Equations (2.5) and (2.6) to obtain

$$\hat{X} = \theta_{KX}\hat{K}_X + \theta_{LX}\hat{L}_X, \qquad \hat{Y} = \theta_{KY}\hat{K}_Y + \theta_{LY}\hat{L}_Y. \tag{2.9}$$

Note for future reference that the shares of each factor's use add to one,

$$\lambda_{LX} + \lambda_{LY} = 1, \qquad \lambda_{KX} + \lambda_{KY} = 1, \tag{2.10}$$

and that the value shares going to each factor within an industry must add to one:

$$\theta_{KX} + \theta_{LX} = 1, \qquad \theta_{KY} + \theta_{KY} = 1. \tag{2.11}$$

Finally, we can characterize consumer preferences by the elasticity of substitution (in demand) between X and Y (σ_D):[16]

$$\hat{X} - \hat{Y} = -\sigma_D\left(\hat{p}_X + \hat{\tau}_X - \hat{p}_Y - \hat{\tau}_Y\right), \tag{2.12}$$

where the consumer price for X is $p_x(1 + \tau_x)$ and τ_x is an *ad valorem* tax on X. The consumer price for Y is similarly defined.

[16] Consumer behavior is captured by preferences (as represented by the elasticity of substitution between X and Y) and the budget constraint. Equation (2.12) would also hold in a more general model with a labor–leisure choice if leisure is separable and the sub-utility function for X and Y is homothetic. The consumer budget constraint here is unnecessary, as it is implied by Equation (2.7) and the assumption that tax revenues are rebated lump sum to consumers (an example of Walras's Law).

Equations (2.3), (2.4), (2.8), (2.9) and (2.12) are nine equations in the ten unknowns $\hat{X}$, $\hat{Y}$, $\hat{p}_X$, $\hat{p}_Y$, $\hat{w}$, $\hat{r}$, $\hat{L}_X$, $\hat{L}_Y$, $\hat{K}_X$ and $\hat{K}_Y$. Since we focus on real behavior (no money illusion), we must choose a numeraire (fix one of the price changes to zero), giving us nine equations in nine unknowns.

Setting up the system at this level of generality allows us to illustrate a basic equivalency between two tax options. For plan 1, consider an equal tax increase on labor and capital used in the production of X (with no change of tax rates in Y). Define $\hat{\tau}$ as this common increase ($\hat{\tau} \equiv \hat{\tau}_{KX} = \hat{\tau}_{LX}$). Equations (2.3), (2.4), (2.9) and (2.12) are unchanged. Equation (2.8) becomes

$$
\begin{aligned}
\hat{p}_X^1 - \hat{\tau} + \hat{X} &= \theta_{KX}\left(\hat{r} + \hat{K}_X\right) + \theta_{LX}\left(\hat{w} + \hat{L}_X\right), \\
\hat{p}_Y + \hat{Y} &= \theta_{KY}\left(\hat{r} + \hat{K}_Y\right) + \theta_{LY}\left(\hat{w} + \hat{L}_Y\right),
\end{aligned}
\tag{2.8'}
$$

where $\hat{p}_X^1$ is the change in p_X under this plan. As an alternative, consider plan 2 with an output tax on X defined by $\hat{\tau} \equiv \hat{\tau}_X$ (and $\hat{\tau}_Y = 0$), where this $\hat{\tau}$ is the same size as the one above. In this case, Equations (2.3), (2.4), (2.8) and (2.9) are unchanged while Equation (2.12) becomes

$$
\hat{X} - \hat{Y} = -\sigma_D\left(\hat{p}_X^2 + \hat{\tau} - \hat{p}_Y\right).
\tag{2.12'}
$$

Then it is easy to show that the equilibria under the two tax systems are the same: so long as $\hat{p}_X^1 = \hat{p}_X^2 + \hat{\tau}$, then all other outcomes are identical. Basically, $\hat{p}_X^1$ is the change in the price paid by consumers in plan 1 where p_X must rise to cover the tax on factors, while $\hat{p}_X^2 + \hat{\tau}$ is the price paid by consumers in plan 2 when the tax is on output. This points out a basic tax equivalence: an equal tax on all factors used in the production of a good yields the same incidence effects as a tax on output of that industry. Below, we discuss other tax equivalencies noted by Break (1974) and McLure (1975).

Before analyzing this system further, we pause to note that this very simple model is quite flexible and can be used to analyze a number of different problems. In the next section, we consider a special case of this model.

2.2. Special cases: one-sector model

With suitable modifications, the general model can be recast for various interesting special cases. We consider a one-sector model in some detail, in which one good is produced using labor and capital. We interpret the good Y in the Harberger model as leisure produced by the production function $Y = L_Y$. We can now interpret the labor market constraint in Equation (2.2) as a time constraint where time can be spent providing labor (L_X) or leisure ($L_Y = Y$). The price of leisure is the net wage rate ($p_Y = w$). No capital is used in the production of leisure, and all capital is used to produce X ($K_X = \overline{K}$). Thus, K_X is fixed in the short run (though competition among firms in X means that capital continues to be paid the value of its marginal product). The equations defining the system now become

$$\lambda_{LX}\hat{L}_X + \lambda_{LY}\hat{Y} = 0,$$

$$\hat{L}_X = \sigma_X \left(\hat{r} + \hat{\tau}_{KX} - \hat{w} - \hat{\tau}_{LX}\right),$$

$$\hat{p}_X + \hat{X} = \theta_{KX} \left(\hat{r} + \hat{\tau}_{KX}\right) + \theta_{LX} \left(\hat{w} + \hat{\tau}_{LX} + \hat{L}_X\right), \tag{2.13}$$

$$\hat{X} = \theta_{LX}\hat{L}_X,$$

$$\hat{X} - \hat{Y} = \sigma_D \left(\hat{w} - \hat{p}_X - \hat{\tau}_X\right),$$

from which we can solve for $\hat{X}$, $\hat{Y}$, $\hat{p}_X$, $\hat{w}$, $\hat{r}$ and $\hat{L}_X$ (with one numeraire). To begin solving, we can eliminate leisure (Y) from the system and reduce it to market variables only. Solve the first equation of (2.13) for $\hat{Y}$ and substitute into the fifth equation, to get:

$$\hat{L} = \sigma_X \left(\hat{r} + \hat{\tau}_K - \hat{w} - \hat{\tau}_L\right),$$

$$\hat{p} + \hat{X} = \theta_K \left(\hat{r} + \hat{\tau}_K\right) + \theta_L \left(\hat{w} + \hat{\tau}_L + \hat{L}\right), \tag{2.14}$$

$$\hat{X} = \theta_L\hat{L},$$

$$\hat{X} + \phi\hat{L} = \sigma_D \left(\hat{w} - \hat{p} - \hat{\tau}_X\right),$$

where $\phi = \lambda_{LX} / \lambda_{LY}$ is the ratio of labor to leisure. We also drop the subscript X since the system now has only one market good.

The analysis of a tax on capital is very simple. Note that $\hat{r}$ and $\hat{\tau}_K$ always appear together as $\hat{r} + \hat{\tau}_K$ in all equations of (2.14). Therefore, as long as $\hat{r} = -\hat{\tau}_K$ in the first two equations, nothing else is affected. Thus, the tax on capital is borne fully by owners of capital – an unsurprising result since capital is inelastically supplied.

Next consider just a tax on labor. Using Equation (2.14), we can set $\hat{\tau}_K = \hat{\tau}_X = 0$, choose X as numeraire, and solve for $\hat{p}$, $\hat{L}$, $\hat{X}$, $\hat{r}$ and $\hat{w}$ as functions of $\hat{\tau}_L$. Simple manipulation reduces the system to two equations in two unknowns:

$$\left(\frac{\sigma_D}{\phi + \theta_L}\right) \hat{w} = \sigma_X \left(\hat{r} - \hat{w} - \hat{\tau}_L\right), \qquad \theta_K\hat{r} + \theta_L \left(\hat{w} + \hat{\tau}_L\right) = 0. \tag{2.15}$$

Rather than immediately solve for $\hat{w}$ and $\hat{r}$ as functions of $\hat{\tau}_L$, we first rewrite these two equations in terms of labor demand and supply elasticities. From the second equation in (2.15) we have:

$$\hat{r} = - \left(\theta_L / \theta_K\right) \left(\hat{w} + \hat{\tau}_L\right). \tag{2.16}$$

Next, substitute that into the first equation in (2.14) to get

$$\hat{L} = -\frac{\sigma_X}{\theta_K} \left(\hat{w} + \hat{\tau}_L\right) \equiv \eta^D \left(\hat{w} + \hat{\tau}_L\right), \tag{2.17}$$

where η^D is the elasticity of demand for labor with respect to its cost. This equation shows how the general equilibrium model can be used to generate the earlier simple partial equilibrium behavior as a special case.

To derive the elasticity of supply for labor, it is convenient to work with the individual budget constraint. Defining M as non-labor income (i.e., capital income), this budget constraint is

$$pX = wL + M. \tag{2.18}$$

Retaining the output price for the moment, as if we had not yet assigned a numeraire, totally differentiate this constraint to get

$$\hat{p} + \hat{X} = \theta_L \left(\hat{w} + \hat{L} \right) + \theta_K \hat{M}. \tag{2.19}$$

We next combine Equation (2.19) and the fourth equation in (2.14) and rearrange to get an expression for labor supply as a function of prices and income:

$$(\theta_L + \phi)\, \hat{L} = (\sigma_D - \theta_L)(\hat{w} - \hat{p}) - \theta_K \left(\hat{M} - \hat{p} \right). \tag{2.20}$$

Equation (2.20) is a key equation from which we can recover a number of important behavioral parameters. First, note the absence of money illusion. If all prices and nominal incomes change by the same percentage ($\hat{w} = \hat{p} = \hat{M}$), then Equation (2.20) implies no effect on labor supply ($\hat{L} = 0$). Hence, we can operate with or without the numeraire assumption. Second, note that labor supply can be affected by any change in the real wage (w/p) or in real income (M/p). If we hold real non-labor income constant, then the last term in Equation (2.20) is zero, and the labor supply elasticity (η^S) is defined by

$$\hat{L} = \frac{\sigma_D - \theta_L}{\theta_L + \phi}(\hat{w} - \hat{p}) \equiv \eta^S(\hat{w} - \hat{p}). \tag{2.21}$$

This η^S is an uncompensated labor supply elasticity. The first term in its numerator is the substitution effect, while the second term is the income effect. For the incidence analysis below, we assume no initial taxes and that the revenue from the introduction of this labor tax ($\hat{\tau}_L$) is returned to households in a lump-sum fashion. Thus, income effects are not relevant, and we need the *compensated* labor supply elasticity (η_C^S)[17]. From Equation (2.21) it is evident that this elasticity is[18]:

$$\eta_C^S = \frac{\sigma_D}{\theta_L + \phi}. \tag{2.22}$$

---

[17] Note that income effects can be ignored if one starts at a Pareto-optimum. Otherwise, income compensation won't eliminate the full income effect.
[18] The compensated labor supply elasticity can also be derived from an application of Slutsky's Equation.

Using $\hat{L} = \eta_C^S \hat{w}$ together with $\hat{L} = \eta^D(\hat{w} + \hat{\tau}_L)$ from Equation (2.17) yields:

$$\frac{\hat{w}}{\hat{\tau}_L} = \frac{\eta^D}{\eta_C^S - \eta^D}, \tag{2.23}$$

and substituting this into Equation (2.16) yields:

$$\frac{\hat{r}}{\hat{\tau}_L} = \left(\frac{\theta_L}{\theta_K}\right)\left(\frac{-\eta_C^S}{\eta_C^S - \eta^D}\right). \tag{2.24}$$

These two equations are the general equilibrium solution for the effects of the labor tax $\hat{\tau}_L$ on each factor price, expressed in terms of parameters. Yet note the similarity between Equation (2.23) in the general equilibrium model and Equation (1.10) in the partial equilibrium model. The only difference is that the partial equilibrium model ignores the use of the revenue and therefore employs an uncompensated elasticity, whereas the general equilibrium model assumes return of the revenue and therefore uses a compensated elasticity[19].

Finally, for the one-sector model of this section, we turn to consideration of an *ad valorem* tax on output at rate τ_X. Since the producer price is fixed at $p = 1$ (our numeraire), the consumer price $p(1 + \tau_X)$ will rise. And since the real wage is $w/(1 + \tau_X)$, the change in the real wage is $\hat{w} - \hat{\tau}_X$. Using steps similar to the derivation of Equations (2.23) and (2.24), we find how real factor prices adjust to a change in τ_X:

$$\frac{\hat{w} - \hat{\tau}_X}{\hat{\tau}_X} = \left(\frac{\eta_C^S}{\eta_C^S - \eta^D}\right) - 1, \tag{2.25}$$

and

$$\frac{\hat{r} - \hat{\tau}_X}{\hat{\tau}_X} = \frac{\theta_L}{\theta_K}\left(\frac{-\eta_C^S}{\eta_C^S - \eta^D}\right) - 1. \tag{2.26}$$

Again, we see how relative elasticities matter.

This section illustrates the circumstances under which a partial equilibrium model can be viewed as a special case of a general equilibrium model[20]. Anybody who writes down only the simple Equations (1.7) and (1.8) for demand and supply of labor can

---

[19] If the tax revenues were used to finance a government project, which employs some labor L or output X, then earlier equations would have to be re-specified. However, if that government project is separable in the individual's utility function, then the result in Equation (2.23) would be identical to Equation (1.10).

[20] In a model with many consumption goods, the same kind of isolation of the labor market is possible by assuming separability between leisure and consumption and homotheticity in the sub-utility function defined over the consumption goods.

Table 2.1
Two sector–two factor model

$$\left(\hat{X} - \hat{Y}\right) = -\sigma_D\left(\hat{p}_X - \hat{p}_Y\right) - \sigma_D\left(\hat{\tau}_X - \hat{\tau}_Y\right)$$

$$\left(\hat{p}_X - \hat{p}_Y\right) = (\theta_{LX} - \theta_{LY})(\hat{w} - \hat{r}) + \left(\hat{\tau}_{KX} - \hat{\tau}_{KY}\right) + \theta_{LX}\left(\hat{\tau}_{LX} - \hat{\tau}_{KX}\right) - \theta_{LY}\left(\hat{\tau}_{LY} - \hat{\tau}_{KY}\right) \qquad (2.27)$$

$$(\lambda_{LX} - \lambda_{KX})\left(\hat{X} - \hat{Y}\right) = (\sigma_X(\lambda_{LX}\theta_{KX} + \lambda_{KX}\theta_{LX}) + \sigma_Y(\lambda_{LY}\theta_{KY} + \lambda_{KY}\theta_{LY}))(\hat{w} - \hat{r})$$
$$+ \sigma_X(\lambda_{LX}\theta_{KX} + \lambda_{KX}\theta_{LX})\left(\hat{\tau}_{LX} - \hat{\tau}_{KX}\right) + \sigma_Y(\lambda_{LY}\theta_{KY} + \lambda_{KY}\theta_{LY})\left(\hat{\tau}_{LY} - \hat{\tau}_{KY}\right)$$

say it is a *general equilibrium* model with one sector that uses two inputs, where utility is defined over leisure and consumption. A similar procedure, left as an exercise, could develop a model of the market for commodity X with an elasticity of demand for X and supply of X, in order to study the effects of a tax on X. A corresponding general equilibrium model could be constructed to include only two goods in utility (X and Y), one factor like labor that is mobile between production of either good, and another factor that is specific to each industry[21]. Then the elasticity of demand for X would depend primarily on the elasticity of substitution in utility, and the elasticity of supply of X would depend primarily on the elasticity of substitution in production.

Overall, this section has shown how results in the literature that uses a one-sector model can be derived directly from the two-sector model of Harberger (1962).

2.3. Analysis of the two-sector model

We now return to the original model in Section 2.1 with two sectors and two factors. Incidence on the uses side is based on the change in p_X/p_Y, while incidence on the sources side is based on the change in w/r. We therefore simplify the analysis by reducing the system of nine equations to three, where the unknowns are $(\hat{p}_X - \hat{p}_Y)$, $(\hat{w} - \hat{r})$ and $(\hat{X} - \hat{Y})$. We solve for these unknowns in terms of exogenous parameters (like the θ and λ shares) and exogenous tax changes (the various $\hat{\tau}$'s).

The first equation of our system is Equation (2.12), repeated below as the first equation of (2.27), shown in Table 2.1. To get the second equation of our system, substitute Equation (2.9) into (2.8) and then subtract the second equation in (2.8) from the first one. The result is the second equation of (2.27) in Table 2.1.

---

[21] If the production function is $X = F(L_X, K_X)$, where L_X is mobile and K_X is fixed, then the industry will supply more of X as its price rises, by bidding more labor away from the other industry.

Table 2.2
Tax equivalencies

τ_{LX}	and	τ_{KX}	$\rightarrow$	τ_X
and		and		and
τ_{LY}	and	τ_{KY}	$\rightarrow$	τ_Y
$\downarrow$		$\downarrow$		$\downarrow$
τ_L	and	τ_K	$\rightarrow$	τ

To get the third equation, first use Equation (2.9) and subtract its second equation from its first equation. Then use Equation (2.4) to get:

$$\hat{X} - \hat{Y} = \hat{L}_X - \hat{L}_Y + (\theta_{KX}\sigma_X - \theta_{KY}\sigma_Y)(\hat{w} - \hat{r}) + \theta_{KX}\sigma_X\left(\hat{\tau}_{LX} - \hat{\tau}_{KX}\right) - \theta_{KY}\sigma_Y\left(\hat{\tau}_{LY} - \hat{\tau}_{KY}\right).$$
(2.28)

Then Equations (2.3) and (2.4) can be combined to show that

$$\hat{L}_X - \hat{L}_Y = \frac{1}{\lambda_{LX} - \lambda_{KX}}\left(\left(\lambda_{KX}\sigma_X + \lambda_{KY}\sigma_Y\right)(\hat{w} - \hat{r}) + \lambda_{KX}\sigma_X\left(\hat{\tau}_{LX} - \hat{\tau}_{KX}\right)\right.$$
$$\left. + \lambda_{KY}\sigma_Y\left(\hat{\tau}_{LY} - \hat{\tau}_{KY}\right)\right).$$
(2.29)

Substitute Equation (2.29) into (2.28) and simplify to get the third equation in our system (Equation 2.27 of Table 2.1).

The three equations in (2.27) can be solved for the three unknowns ($\hat{p}_X - \hat{p}_Y$, $\hat{w} - \hat{r}$, and $\hat{X} - \hat{Y}$) as functions of the changes in tax rates. Note that the system in Equation (2.27) has not yet assigned a numeraire, and that it includes all possible tax rates. Before solving, we return to the topic of tax equivalencies, and then provide a graphical analysis of a marginal increase in the tax on capital income in sector X [22].

In our initial setup of the two-sector model (at the end of Section 2.1), we noted that a tax on both factors in one industry (with $\hat{\tau}_{LX} = \hat{\tau}_{KX}$) is equivalent to a tax on the output of that industry ($\hat{\tau}_X$). This result appears in the first row of Table 2.2 [23].

Using the equations in this section, we can now explain the first column of Table 2.2, which says that a tax on both industries' use of labor at the same rate is equivalent to a tax on the consumer's labor income. To show this, using our system of three equations, set all $\hat{\tau}_{LX} = \hat{\tau}_{LY}$ and replace those rates with $\hat{\tau}_L$. Then note that the terms $\hat{w} - \hat{r} + \hat{\tau}_L$ appear together throughout the system of three equations, and thus a new equilibrium holds with $\hat{w} = -\hat{\tau}_L$ and with no change in any quantity or in the ratio of the gross wage to the interest rate. The entire burden of this tax falls on labor, because it applies

---

[22] Our graphical analysis is from Atkinson and Stiglitz (1980), but see McLure (1974) for another graphical exposition.

[23] See Break (1974), McLure (1974) and Atkinson and Stiglitz (1980).

at the same rate in both sectors, and labor has fixed total supply. In this model, a tax on a factor in both sectors is a lump-sum tax and affects that factor only.

In the bottom row of Table 2.2, either τ_L or τ_K is a lump-sum tax, so the two together is a lump-sum tax on all income, τ. In the final column, either τ_X or τ_Y alone would change production and impact various prices, but τ_X and τ_Y together at the same rate is equivalent to a lump-sum tax on all income, τ, with no effect on any allocations or relative prices. A simple look at the consumer's budget constraint shows that a tax on both goods at the same rate is the same as a tax on both factors at the same rate.

Next we turn to the graphical analysis of our three equation system (in Equation 2.27). Consider the special case of a tax on capital income in sector X, holding all other tax changes to zero. The first equation in (2.27) relates the relative demand for goods (X/Y) to the ratio of prices (p_X/p_Y). In Figure 2.1, this downward sloping demand equation (D) is graphed in the upper right quadrant[24]. The third equation relates the relative *supply* of goods (X/Y) to relative factor prices (w/r). It is drawn as an upward sloping function in the upper left quadrant of Figure 2.1, for the case where X is relatively labor intensive ($\lambda_{LX} > \lambda_{KX}$). In this case, as the production of X rises relative to the production of Y, the demand for labor rises relative to demand for capital (which raises the wage rate relative to capital return, w/r). Finally, the second Equation (2.27) relates output prices to factor prices. Assuming X is more labor intensive in value ($\theta_{LX} > \theta_{LY}$), an increase in w/r increases the price of X relative to the price of Y. This relationship is graphed in the lower right quadrant of Figure 2.1.

We now use those two curves together to "derive" the supply curve (S) in the upper right quadrant. First, start with a given output price ratio (point A_1 on the horizontal axis). Through the curve in the lower right quadrant, this output price ratio implies a particular factor price ratio (point A_2). Follow this factor price ratio through the 45° line in the lower left quadrant to the upper left quadrant where the factor price ratio (point A_3) implies a particular output ratio. Together with the original output price ratio at A_1, this output ratio gives us a point on a "supply" schedule (A_4). Then, starting at a different output price ratio, (e.g., B_1), we can find another output ratio and thus sketch out the upward-sloping supply schedule (S). The intersection of this supply schedule with the demand curve (the first equation) indicates equilibrium in Figure 2.1.

Next consider how a capital income tax (τ_{KX}) changes the equilibrium (see Figure 2.2). The point E_0 indicates the pre-tax equilibrium, and E_1 indicates the post-tax equilibrium. In the lower right quadrant, the tax on capital in sector X shifts the output price curve to the right, reflecting a higher price for good X (for any given

---

[24] The first equation is a *linear* equation in the form $(\hat{X} - \hat{Y}) = a + b(\hat{p}_X - \hat{p}_Y)$, but this linear equation is derived from a *nonlinear* equation in the form $X/Y = A(p_X/p_Y)^b$. Starting with the latter equation, take the natural log of both sides and differentiate to get the former equation. Thus (X/Y) in Figure 2.1 is a nonlinear function of (p_X/p_Y).

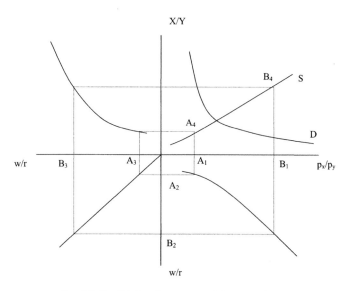

Fig. 2.1. Equilibrium in output and factor markets.

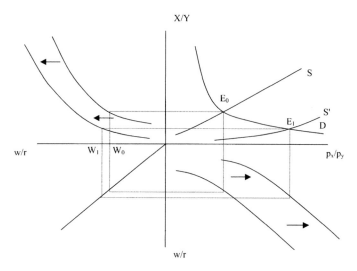

Fig. 2.2. Partial factor tax in general equilibrium.

factor price ratio). Meanwhile, in the upper left quadrant, the tax also shifts the factor demand curve to the left, reflecting a desire to shift out of capital and into labor (for any given output combination). The desired shift from capital to labor raises the wage rate relative to the interest rate (point W_1 relative to W_0).

These new curves can be used to trace out a new "supply" curve in the upper right quadrant that is unambiguously shifted down and to the right, which means an unambiguous increase in p_X/p_Y and an unambiguous decrease in X/Y. The effect on w/r is ambiguous, however. This tax may be borne disproportionately by capital $(\hat{w} - \hat{r} > 0)$, by labor $(\hat{w} - \hat{r} < 0)$, or in proportion to their income shares $(\hat{w} - \hat{r} = 0)$[25]. We now derive the effect on w/r from a change in τ_{KX} (holding all other tax changes to zero). The three-equation system above can be solved to obtain our version of the famous Harberger (1962) equation:

$$\hat{w} - \hat{r} = \frac{1}{D} \left[\sigma_X a_X - \sigma_D \lambda^* \theta_{KX} \right] \hat{\tau}_{KX}, \tag{2.30}$$

where $a_i = \theta_{Ki}\lambda_{Li} + \theta_{Li}\lambda_{Ki}$, $i = X, Y$, $\lambda^* = \lambda_{LX} - \lambda_{KX}$, $\theta^* = \theta_{LX} - \theta_{LY}$ and $D = \sigma_D \lambda^* \theta^* + \sigma_X a_X + \sigma_Y a_Y$. This denominator is unambiguously positive[26]. In the numerator, the first term in brackets is positive, while the sign of the second term depends on the relative capital intensity of the taxed sector. If X is capital intensive $(\lambda_{LX} < \lambda_{KX})$, then this subtracted term is negative, the whole numerator is positive, and τ_{KX} raises w/r (the burden is disproportionately on capital). This case is clear because the tax applies to capital, but only in the capital-intensive sector! If X is labor intensive, however, then the outcome is ambiguous: the tax is a partial factor tax on capital, but it is imposed on the labor-intensive sector.

The impact of a tax on capital in sector X can be decomposed into two components: a substitution effect and an output effect. The first term in brackets on the right-hand side of Equation (2.30) represents the substitution effect and is unambiguously positive (indicating how the burden of the partial capital tax falls on capital). Its magnitude depends on the degree of factor substitution in the taxed industry (σ_X). The second term reflects the fact that the tax applies only in one industry, so it raises the price of that good and thereby induces a shift in demand from X to Y. As capital and labor are shed by the taxed sector, they must be absorbed by the other sector. If sector X is labor intensive $(\lambda_{LX} > \lambda_{KX})$, the wage rate must fall for sector Y to be willing to hire the excess labor. The magnitude of this output effect depends on the elasticity of substitution in demand (σ_D). In this case (and as drawn in Figure 2.2), the output and substitution effects offset, and it is impossible to say whether w/r will rise or fall in response to a tax on K_X.

---

[25] With no change in relative factor prices, burdens cannot differ on the sources side: the tax merely raises the price of the taxed good, relative to factor prices. Capital and labor spend the same fraction of their incomes on the taxed good, so the two factors bear burdens in proportion to their shares of national income. Thus, capital's burden can only be larger than labor's burden if r falls relative to w.

[26] To show that D is positive, first note that all parameters in the second and third terms are positive. Then, to show that the first term is positive, we show that $(\lambda_{LX} - \lambda_{KX})$ and $(\theta_{LX} - \theta_{LY})$ must be of the same sign (either both positive or both negative). We have $\theta_{LX} - \theta_{LY}$ equal to $\theta_{LX}\theta_{KY} - \theta_{KX}\theta_{LY}$, which in turn equals $(wr/(p_X X p_Y Y))(L_X K_Y - K_X L_Y)$. If $\theta_{LX} - \theta_{LY} > 0$, then $L_X K_Y - K_X L_Y > 0$, which implies that $\lambda_{LX}\lambda_{KY} - \lambda_{LY}\lambda_{KX} = \lambda_{LX} - \lambda_{KX} > 0$. However, this result is only guaranteed in a model with no other taxes.

The system of three equations in (2.27) includes many possible tax rates to analyze, but the methods are all similar to the methods just employed to analyze τ_{KX}. We just make one last point about one other tax rate, a tax on the sale of X ($\hat{\tau}_X > 0$). Solving for $\hat{w} - \hat{r}$ as a function of $\hat{\tau}_X$ yields

$$\hat{w} - \hat{r} = -\frac{\sigma_D (\lambda_{LX} - \lambda_{KX})}{D} \hat{\tau}_X, \tag{2.31}$$

where D is as defined above. Note that this is precisely the output effect from the partial factor tax in Equation (2.30). This result follows because either $\theta_{KX} \hat{\tau}_{KX}$ or $\hat{\tau}_X$ equals the change in tax revenue as a fraction of the consumer expenditure on X.

Equation (2.30) can be generalized to allow for non-homothetic preferences and public demand for consumption goods that differs from private demand. Vandendorpe and Friedlaender (1976) have carried out this analysis. Their model also allows for pre-existing distortionary taxation. Consider an experiment in which the partial factor tax on capital used in the production of X is increased, with revenues returned lump sum to consumers. Thus, public demands for X and Y are fixed, while private demands (X^P, Y^P) can change. This more-general model now provides a demand-side force affecting the change in w/r. Equation (2.30) becomes

$$\hat{w} - \hat{r} = \frac{1}{\tilde{D}} \left[\sigma_X a_X - \tilde{\sigma}_D \lambda^* \theta_{KX} + \lambda^* \tilde{\eta} B \right] \hat{\tau}_{KX}, \tag{2.32}$$

where $\tilde{\sigma}_D$ is the elasticity of substitution between X and Y in consumption suitably modified to account for government consumption of a fraction of output,

$$\tilde{\eta} = \left(\frac{X^P}{X} \right) \eta_X - \left(\frac{Y^P}{Y} \right) \eta_Y$$

is the difference in income elasticities weighted by the share of private consumption (X^P, Y^P) in total output (X, Y), and B is a measure of the initial excess burden of pre-existing taxes. This B will be negative to the extent that X is initially taxed more heavily than Y.

Relative to the original Harberger Equation (2.30), the third term inside the brackets in Equation (2.32) is an added demand-side effect. Intuitively, we can track this added effect in three steps, in the case where $B < 0$. First, an increase in taxes on capital used in the production of X increases the relative burden on X and adds to the excess burden of the tax system. This burden effect is first order and constitutes a reduction in real output (and hence income) to society. Second, the term $\tilde{\eta}$ translates this real income loss into a relative shift in demands for X and Y. Imagine that preferences were still homothetic, so that income elasticities equal 1, but that the private share of consumption of X is less than the corresponding share for Y. In that case, $\tilde{\eta} < 0$. The loss in income induces a drop in both private demands (X^P and Y^P), but public demands are fixed. In this case, $(X^P/X) < (Y^P/Y)$ means that the drop in total demand for X will be less than the drop in total demand for Y. Factors must shift over from production of Y to X. Third, λ^* translates the change in relative-output demands into changes in relative-factor demands. If production of X is more labor intensive ($\lambda^* > 0$), the shift in production from Y to X will increase the demand for labor. This will drive the wage rate up relative to the interest rate. Note that $\lambda^* \tilde{\eta} B$ is positive, based on our assumptions in this example, so we get the desired positive effect on $\hat{w} - \hat{r}$. Equation (2.32) indicates precisely how Harberger eliminates this demand-side effect. He assumes homotheticity and that public consumption of X and Y are in the same proportions as private consumption, which together ensure that $\tilde{\eta}$ equals zero.

Recognizing the tremendous usefulness of the basic Harberger model, many economists in the following decades developed many other extensions, generalizations and applications. As one example, Mieszkowski (1972) considers the incidence of the local property tax in an extended model with three factors of production (land, as well as labor and capital). As another example, McLure (1970) considers the effects of imperfect factor mobility. These extensions and generalizations are important, but beyond the scope (and page limits) of this chapter. Readers can find thorough reviews of this literature in McLure (1975) and in Shoven and Whalley (1984).

2.4. The corporate income tax

The original paper by Harberger (1962) uses the general equilibrium model to analyze the corporate income tax. To do this in a two-sector model, he must assume that the whole corporate sector produces only one output (X), and that the corporate income tax is effectively a tax on all capital used in that sector (τ_{KX}). We now turn to some of the special cases of his model, to illustrate the impact of a tax on corporate capital. As in Harberger, we can choose the wage as numeraire ($\hat{w} = 0$) and focus on the return to capital to indicate relative factor returns.

First, when do we know that $\hat{r} < 0$ (the burden of the tax falls disproportionately on capital)? From Equation (2.30), a sufficient condition for this outcome is that the corporate sector is capital intensive. However, a different sufficient condition can be found by a rearrangement of the numerator to include $(\sigma_X - \sigma_D)\lambda_{LX}\theta_{KX}$ as the only term with ambiguous sign. Then $\sigma_X > \sigma_D$ is a sufficient condition for $\hat{r} < 0$. In other words, this tax on capital in X disproportionately burdens capital if firms in X can shift out of capital more readily than consumers can shift out of X. In fact, higher σ_X always raises the burden on capital; as it approaches infinity, the limit of Equation (2.30) is $-\hat{r} = \hat{\tau}_{KX}$ (the rate of return falls by the full amount of the tax). Because the return falls by the full amount of the tax in *both* sectors, the total burden on capital is *more* than the revenue. The cost of capital is unchanged in X, and lower in Y, so labor gains!

Second, we can ask, under what conditions is the tax burden shared equally between labor and capital ($\hat{r} = 0$)? As σ_Y in the denominator of Equation (2.30) approaches infinity, we can see that $\hat{r}$ approaches zero. A large value of σ_Y just means that the untaxed sector can absorb whatever excess capital is no longer used in the taxed sector. Another way to guarantee that $\hat{r} = 0$, from Equation (2.30), is to have

$$\sigma_D (\lambda_{LX} - \lambda_{KX}) \theta_{KX} = \sigma_X (\lambda_{LX} \theta_{KX} + \lambda_{KX} \theta_{LX}). \tag{2.33}$$

Necessary conditions are that the corporate sector is labor intensive ($\lambda_{LX} > \lambda_{KX}$) and that consumers can readily substitute ($\sigma_D > \sigma_X$)[27].

Third, when can this partial tax on capital fall disproportionately on labor? The taxed sector must be very labor intensive for the output effect to dominate the substitution effect and not just to offset part of it.

Fourth, when does the entire burden of the tax fall on capital? This special outcome occurs where $dr(\bar{K}) = -d\tau_{KX}(rK_X)$, which says that the fall in capital income equals the tax revenue collected. For the initial imposition of the tax, where $d\tau_{KX} = \hat{\tau}_{KX}$, this equation can be rewritten as

$$\frac{\hat{r}}{\hat{\tau}_{KX}} = -\lambda_{KX}. \tag{2.34}$$

In the special case where $\sigma_X = \sigma_Y = \sigma_D$, substitution of this single σ into Equation (2.30) shows that it is multiplied times everything in the numerator, and everything in the denominator, so it factors out and disappears. Further rearrangement finds that $D = 1$ in the denominator and that the bracketed expression in the numerator equals λ_{KX}. Thus, the case with all the same elasticities of substitution yields the result that capital bears the entire burden of the corporate income tax. A further special case of this special case is the Cobb–Douglas case where all elasticities of substitution are one[28].

The original paper by Harberger (1962) considered plausible parameter values and likely empirical outcomes. First, he finds that the corporate sector is indeed labor intensive. This result itself is sometimes surprising to those who think about the corporate sector's large manufacturing plants, but remember also the number of workers at those plants: labor intensity is relative, and the non-corporate sector includes a lot of agriculture where a single worker can sit atop a large harvester covering many acres of valuable land (which is part of capital in the aggregation with only two factors). The labor intensity of the corporate sector is important because it means that the burden of this tax on capital might be on labor.

Next, Harberger considers alternative values for the key elasticities of substitution (σ_X, σ_Y, and σ_D). He considers some of the 27 possible combinations that can arise when each of those three parameters can take any of three values (0.5, 1.0, and 1.5).

---

[27] The second condition follows from the fact that $\lambda_{LX} \theta_{KX} + \lambda_{KX} \theta_{LX} = \theta_{KX}(\theta_{LX} - \lambda_{KX}) + \lambda_{KX}$.

[28] In fact, as shown in McLure and Thirsk (1975), the case where all utility and production functions are Cobb–Douglas yields an easy analytical solution for the incidence of a large tax (without using log-linearization techniques that are limited to small changes).

Sometimes capital bears less than the full burden of the corporate income tax (τ_{KX}), and sometimes it bears more than the full burden of the tax, but the main message coming out of his original 1962 paper is that capital is likely to bear approximately the full burden of the corporate income tax, more or less. And capital mobility means that the burden is on all capital, not just corporate capital.

To explain this empirical result, it is important to remember the conceptual result above that capital bears the full burden of the tax anytime the three elasticities are equal ($\sigma_X = \sigma_Y = \sigma_D$). Then, if one of those parameters varies above or below the common value, capital's burden will be somewhat more or less than the full burden of the tax.

Harberger's main focus was the sources side, finding the change in relative factor prices (r/w). He ignored the uses side by assuming that all consumers as well as the government buy X and Y in the same proportions. Although his 1962 paper did not solve for relative goods prices, the same model can also be used to solve for the other unknowns such as $\hat{p}_X$ and $\hat{p}_Y$ (where labor is numeraire). Interestingly, even while capital is bearing the full burden of the tax, τ_{KX} also raises the price of X (thus placing additional burden on those who in fact consume disproportionate amounts of X) and lowers the price of Y (thus providing gains to those who consume more than the average amount of Y). That untaxed industry experiences a fall in their cost of capital, while the wage is fixed at 1.0, so competition among firms in the industry means that the output price must fall. In other words, even though the main effect of this tax is that government confiscates resources *from* the private sector, one of the effects is that some individuals are made better off – anybody who earns most of their income from labor and who spends disproportionately on products of the non-corporate sector.

Many of the empirical studies reviewed below choose to follow the original Harberger (1962) result that all capital income bears approximately the full burden of the corporate income tax, and thus they allocate that tax in proportion to the capital income of each household. However, Harberger assumed (1) a fixed capital stock, (2) a closed economy, (3) no financing decisions, and (4) no uncertainty. We therefore note four challenges to his modeling of corporate tax burdens.

First, in an intertemporal model, the corporate tax might reduce the net rate of return only in the short run, until savings fall enough to reduce the future capital stock and raise the return back up to its long run rate. The smaller capital stock means a lower wage rate, so labor can bear *more* than the full burden of the tax [e.g., Judd (1985a)]. This possibility is discussed in Section 4 below (dynamic models).

Second, in a small open economy with international capital mobility, the corporate tax might just drive capital elsewhere so that domestic savers earn the same net return as before. This drives down the domestic capital stock, and thus the domestic wage rate, so again the burden falls on labor [e.g., Mutti and Grubert (1985)]. Yet Bradford (1978) shows that capital does indeed bear the burden of a local tax on capital, in the aggregate. The tax burden is not on local investors but is spread across all investors worldwide[29].

Third, if investment is financed by debt, then the return is paid as tax-deductible interest. If investment proceeds to the point where the marginal unit just breaks even, with no return above and beyond the interest paid, then no corporate tax applies to the marginal investment. Indeed, as pointed out by Stiglitz (1973), all corporate investment may be financed by debt at the margin. If so, then the corporate tax is a lump-sum tax on infra-marginal investments financed by equity. Then it does not distort the allocation of resources, and it does not affect the return in the non-corporate sector.

Fourth, as pointed out by Gentry and Hubbard (1997), much of the corporate tax applies not just to the risk-free portion of the return to equity-financed investment, but also to a risk premium, to infra-marginal profits, and to lucky windfalls. This has implications for a differential tax incidence analysis of a switch from an income tax to a consumption tax. Such a switch would eliminate the tax only on the first component, and it would continue to tax the other components. Then, since those other components of capital income are concentrated in the top income brackets, they argue that a consumption tax is more progressive than estimated under conventional incidence assumptions. In other words, typical differential incidence studies of a shift from income to consumption taxation err by assuming that the burden of the corporate income tax falls on all capital income, which is disproportionately concentrated in high income brackets, because most of that capital income would still be taxed under a consumption tax. The corporate income tax adds only the burden on risk-free returns, which are not so concentrated in high-income brackets.

2.5. The property tax

Local jurisdictions typically impose a yearly tax on the value of real property – both land and improvements. Alternative "views" of the incidence of this tax have been hotly debated, and general equilibrium analysis has radically changed economists' thinking. First, the property tax has been viewed as an excise tax on housing services that is regressive because housing expenditures are a high proportion of the budgets of low-income families. This "old view" is typically associated with Simon (1943), but it dates back to Edgeworth (1897). Second, the property tax has been viewed as a profits tax on capital income that is progressive because that source of income is a high proportion for high-income families. This view is called the "new view," although it originates with Brown (1924). Perhaps it *is* new relative to Edgeworth (1897)![30]

---

[29] See the discussion in Kotlikoff and Summers (1987). In contrast, Gravelle and Smetters (2001) argue that imperfect substitutability of domestic and foreign products can limit or even eliminate the incidence borne by labor, even in an open economy model. They find that the tax is borne by domestic capital, as in the original Harberger model.

[30] The property tax has also been viewed as a tax on site rents that is shifted to landowners. Marshall (1890) provides an early statement of this "classical" view, but Simon (1943) points out that classical

Mieszkowski (1972) reconciles these views in a Harberger general equilibrium modeling framework. If τ_i is the tax rate on property in community i, we can decompose the rate into two components as $\tau_i = \bar{\tau} + \varepsilon_i$ where $\bar{\tau}$ is the average property tax rate over the entire country, and ε_i is the deviation of the local rate from the national average. By construction, the average of ε_i across all communities is zero. Mieszkowski argues that the first component of τ_i can be viewed as a national tax on housing capital at rate $\bar{\tau}$. Using the Harberger framework, he then argues that this tax burdens *all* capital. The second component, Mieszkowski continues, can be viewed as a differential tax that can be positive or negative. This differential tax might be passed forward to consumers of housing or passed backwards to immobile factors (workers or landowners). Mieszkowski concludes that the bulk of this differential tax is passed forward to consumers.

Even in Mieszkowski's model, note that the regressivity of the tax depends on what sort of tax change is contemplated. A uniform nation-wide increase in property tax would impact capital income, which is progressive under the "new" view. In contrast, a single community's increase in property tax would likely raise that town's cost of housing, which is regressive under the "old" view[31].

Next, Hamilton (1976) articulates a third view, called the "benefit" view, that the property tax is neither regressive nor progressive because it is really no tax at all[32]. Building on Tiebout (1956), Hamilton argues that mobile taxpayers would not live in any jurisdiction that charges a tax higher than the value of its local public goods and services – unless property values adjusted to reflect the differential between the value of services received and taxes paid (the "fiscal surplus"). In other words, house prices would rise by the capitalized value of any positive stream of fiscal surpluses or fall by the capitalized value of any negative stream (where taxes exceed services). If the local property tax becomes a voluntary price paid for those local goods and services, then it is no tax at all. Thus, we have the "old" view, the "new" view, and the "no" view of the property tax[33].

Hamilton's focus is on the efficiency impact of property taxes. He argues that the property tax *per se* has no distributional impact because of capitalization. His story is

---

economists divide the property tax into a portion falling on land rents and a portion falling on improvements.

[31] Part of the early "debate" is published in two papers by Musgrave (1974) and Aaron (1974), but they also point out the importance of institutional detail when doing incidence analyses. Musgrave generally supports the old view, and he notes that many rental markets in urban areas are likely to be imperfectly competitive. Thus, some of the insights from Section 3 below may be useful for thinking about property tax incidence. Aaron generally supports the new view. He notes that, even under the old view, the portion of the property tax falling on rental housing may well be progressive since the ratio of market value to rent rises with rent (more expensive houses have relatively low monthly rent).

[32] Hamilton (1975) first states this argument, but Hamilton (1976) extends it to heterogeneous communities.

[33] Zodrow and Mieszkowski (1983) review this literature, and Zodrow (2001) provides a possible reconciliation of these various views.

not complete yet, as he notes that the value of land is higher when used to construct housing that is below the average value of housing in the community. Because the property tax on such a house would be less than the (uniform) services provided, the fiscal surplus for such a house will be positive, and the landowner can extract those rents when selling the site. This shift in the mix of housing will lead to a shift in the burden of the property tax from owners of below-average-value housing to owners of above-average-value housing. In response, a countervailing political force will limit this shift (zoning or some other form of regulation). The outcome of this political process cannot be predicted in an economic model, and zoning could be so restrictive as to limit the amount of low-value housing to levels that are inefficient (and that lead to a shift of the burden of property tax from high-value homeowners to low-value homeowners). Hamilton concludes that it is impossible to determine the incidence of property taxes until we have a better understanding of the political forces influencing land-use policy.

2.6. Empirical work

Remaining with the property tax for the moment, we note that Oates (1969) first attempts to measure empirically the degree of capitalization of property taxes into property values. This type of measurement turns out to be a complicated statistical exercise, however, and economists continue to disagree about the degree of capitalization. Many economists believe that the benefit view should imply complete capitalization of property taxes (holding public services and other amenities constant). If so, then perhaps an empirical test of capitalization could help us choose between views. Alas, Mieszkowski and Zodrow (1989) point out that property taxes may be capitalized under both the benefit view and the new view. Thus, while capitalization is an important phenomenon in tax incidence theory, it is not useful as an empirical test among views of the property tax.

One interesting study by Carroll and Yinger (1994) looks at property taxes in rental markets rather than homeowner markets. They find that nearly one-half of property tax differentials are passed back to landlords, a result consistent (at least partially) with the new view.

Turning to the corporate income tax, we note the attempt by Krzyzaniak and Musgrave (1963) to estimate the burden econometrically using a time-series regression of the corporate output price on the corporate tax rate and other control variables such as the unemployment rate. They obtain the surprising result that the corporate income tax is "overshifted", meaning that the corporate sector is able to raise prices by *more* than the amount of the tax – and increase their profits. While this overshifting may provide evidence of imperfect competition, as we discuss below, this approach was largely discredited subsequently by considerations of reverse causality. Especially during war years, shortages mean that corporations can raise prices and make profits, which induces Congress to raise the tax rate. We know of no other subsequent attempt to estimate corporate tax incidence econometrically. Thus, while the Harberger model is extremely useful for analysis, the predictions have not exactly been "tested". Debate continues about the incidence of the corporate income tax as well.

Without resolving any of these debates, another empirical approach can apply the theoretical developments just described to find the implications for a large number of households across the income spectrum [Pechman and Okner (1974), Musgrave, Case and Leonard (1974)]. First, this approach must specify how the burden of each tax is shifted (and can specify more than one outcome, for sensitivity analysis). Then, each scenario is applied to micro-data on households' sources and uses of income. Pechman and Okner (1974) merge data files for a sample of 72 000 households. They use information on demographic characteristics such as age and family size, and tax return items such as income from dividends, interest, rent, capital gains, and wages and salaries. They classify households into annual income groups using a measure of economic income that includes transfers, the household's share of corporate retained earnings, and the imputed net rental income from owner-occupied homes. They use tax actually paid as the total burden of each tax to be allocated. Then, for each set of assumptions about the shifting of each tax, they add up the burdens on each household.

Pechman and Okner assume for all cases that the burden of the personal income tax remains with the household, the employee part of the payroll tax remains with the worker, and the burden of sales and excise taxes falls on households according to their consumption patterns. The employer share of the payroll tax is sometimes allocated entirely to workers, and it is sometimes allocated equally between workers and consumers. The property tax is assumed to affect either the return to landowners specifically or all capital owners generally. Finally, for the corporate income tax, they consider several cases with different proportions of the burden on shareholders, capital owners, wage-earners, and consumers. They look only at taxes and ignore the distributional effects of any government spending [34].

For each combination of incidence assumptions, Pechman and Okner calculate the effective tax rate on each household, defined as the total tax burden as a fraction of economic income. Their results indicate that the most progressive set of assumptions do not yield markedly different results than the least progressive set of assumptions. In either case, the overall U.S. tax system is roughly proportional over the middle eight deciles. The effective tax rate is higher, however, at the top and bottom tails of the income distribution. At very low-income levels, any positive consumption implies a positive sales tax burden divided by a small income in the denominator. At the other end of the distribution, the rate is high because of the progressive personal income tax and assumed corporate tax burdens from disproportionate holding of corporate stock.

---

[34] Thus, when they allocate the burdens of payroll taxes, they ignore the distributional effects of using those revenues to provide social security benefits. This treatment is most troublesome if a marginal increase in benefits is tied to a marginal payment of tax, because then only the difference is really a "burden".

This finding of rough proportionality has shaped tax policy debates for the past two decades[35]. The general consensus is that the progressive effects of the personal income tax and the corporate income tax are more or less offset by the regressive impacts of payroll taxes, sales taxes, and excise taxes. Musgrave, Case and Leonard (1974) reach similar conclusions. In contrast, however, Browning and Johnson (1979) find that the U.S. tax system as a whole is highly progressive. They assume that sales and excise taxes raise product prices, but government transfers are indexed to provide the same real benefits, thus protecting low-income transfer recipients. These taxes do not fall on consumption generally, but only on consumption out of factor income.

These studies all have three problems. First, they classify households by annual income rather than by income over some longer time period (such as an entire lifetime)[36]. Second, they assume the allocation of a total tax burden equal to tax actually paid, not a burden based on each group's change in consumer welfare (such as the equivalent variation, EV). Third, they use results from different kinds of models to guide their assumptions about the incidence of each tax, but they do not calculate these effects in a single model.

To address the first such problem, Davies, St. Hilaire and Whalley (1984) construct lifetime histories of earnings, transfers, inheritances, savings, consumption, and bequests. Using Canadian survey data, they measure lifetime income and use it to classify households, and then add up each household's lifetime burdens under each set of incidence assumptions. Thus, they extend the approach of Pechman and Okner to a lifetime context. They find that personal income taxes are less progressive in a lifetime context, while sales and excise taxes are less regressive, so the Canadian tax system is as mildly progressive in the lifetime framework as it is in the annual framework[37].

In a different approach to this first problem, Slemrod (1992) notes that a "snapshot" of one year suffers from fluctuations, while a lifetime income perspective requires

---

[35] The 1966 data used by Pechman and Okner (1974) were updated by Pechman (1985). There, he finds that progressivity fell due to an upward trend in payroll taxes and downward trend in corporate taxes. Browning (1986) indicates that the new data understate transfers and overstate labor income for the poorest groups, and that appropriate adjustments to the data would make the 1985 tax system appear no less progressive than the 1966 system. Pechman (1987) corrects his data and finds virtually no change in progressivity at the low end of the income distribution, but he still finds reduced progressivity at the very top of the income distribution (due to reduced taxes on capital).

[36] An individual at a given percentile of a particular year's annual income distribution may appear at a different place in the lifetime income distribution, both because annual income is volatile and because it tends to rise systematically and then fall with age. Tax incidence across lifetime income groups may also be affected by the shape of the earnings profile: if those with higher lifetime incomes have earlier peaks in their earnings profiles, then they must save more for retirement and bear more burden from taxes on capital.

[37] Poterba (1989) classifies households by current consumption, as a proxy for lifetime income, and he therefore finds that consumption taxes are less regressive than when using annual income to classify households. Lyon and Schwab (1995) use data from the PSID in a life-cycle model, finding that cigarette taxes are just as regressive when using lifetime income rather than annual income as the classifier. They find that alcohol taxes are slightly less regressive.

heroic data assumptions. Slemrod argues that a "time-exposure" of about seven years may be a reasonable compromise. He compares 1967–73 to 1979–85. While annual income inequality has risen substantially over those decades, Slemrod finds less increase in time-exposure income inequality. However, the effect of taxes on inequality is the same in both cases.

To address the last two problems, other researchers have built explicit computational general equilibrium (CGE) models that can calculate the effect of all taxes simultaneously on all prices and quantities, from which they can calculate utility-based measures of consumer welfare. For example, Ballard, Fullerton, Shoven and Whalley (1985) specify production functions for 19 industries that use both primary factors and intermediate inputs. Each tax may affect the demand for each factor in each industry. They also specify 12 income groups that receive different shares of income from labor, capital, and indexed government transfers. Assuming utility maximization, they calculate demands for each good by each group that depend on product prices and on after-tax income, while factor supplies depend on net factor returns. The imposition of any tax may then affect prices, and they calculate the EV to measure the burden of each group [38].

A different type of general equilibrium model is built by Auerbach, Kotlikoff and Skinner (1983) and fully described in Auerbach and Kotlikoff (1987). Auerbach and Kotlikoff sacrifice intragenerational heterogeneity to concentrate on intergenerational redistribution. Their model has only one sector but allows for 55 overlapping generations with life-cycle savings decisions. Instead of calculating the incidence of a tax across 12 income groups, they calculate the incidence across age groups. In particular, they find that the switch from an income tax to a wage tax would reduce the burden on the elderly, while the switch to a consumption tax would substantially raise tax burdens on the elderly.

Auerbach and Kotlikoff provide the first computational model of lifetime tax incidence for different age groups, but cannot calculate progressivity across different income groups. Later efforts proceed to calculate lifetime tax incidence for different income groups at each age [Fullerton and Rogers (1993), Altig, Auerbach, Kotlikoff, Smetters and Walliser (2001)]. All of these computational general equilibrium models can calculate the incidence of each tax using explicit production functions and utility-

---

[38] This type of CGE model captures many behaviors and employs utility-based measures of welfare rather than accounting measures, but it does not capture some other behaviors and effects on utility. Mulligan and Philipson (2000) have a unique "reverse" view of the effect of some redistributive tax policies and other programs. For an example, consider a hypothetical tax credit for health insurance. Under the usual "accounting" approach to tax incidence, this tax credit would seem to be progressive since it provides a flat dollar benefit that is a higher fraction of a poor family's income. They point out that this "merit" good is provided because the rich want for the poor to purchase more health care. If the rich have positive "willingness to pay" for the government to induce the poor to buy more health care, then the program makes the rich better off. It also contrains the choices of the poor more than of the rich. Thus, under this reverse view, such a program is regressive rather than progressive.

based measures of welfare (such as EV), but computational feasibility requires some aggregation across households – such as considering only 12 income groups.

In contrast, the approach based on Pechman and Okner (1974) must assume the incidence of each tax without utility or production functions, but can employ detailed micro data on many thousands of households. This detailed approach also allows calculations of incidence across dimensions other than income (by region, race, gender, or other demographic characteristics). For these reasons, several recent efforts also build upon the original approach of Pechman and Okner. For example, Kasten, Sammartino and Toder (1994) combine data from the Labor Department's Consumer Expenditure Survey, the Commerce Department's Census Bureau, and the Treasury Department's tax returns. Instead of trying to construct a "full" measure of economic income, however, they classify households by a measure of realized cash income. They calculate federal income taxes and payroll taxes for each household, and they assign corporate taxes and federal excise tax burdens according to assumptions about their incidence (but they omit all state and local taxes on income, sales, and property). Despite major changes in federal tax policy between 1980 and 1993, they find virtually no change in the overall level of taxation or in the distribution of burdens, except a slight decline in the effective tax rate for those in the top one percent of the income distribution.

As another example, Gale, Houser and Scholz (1996) use data from the Survey of Income and Program Participation (SIPP) and classify households by "expanded" income that includes some imputations (e.g., employer-provided health insurance) but not others (e.g., imputed rental income from owner-occupied homes). They consider federal and state income taxes, corporate taxes, and payroll taxes, but not federal excise taxes, state sales taxes, or local property taxes. They do consider transfer income. Like prior authors, they find that the current tax system is progressive.

While the three studies mentioned above appear quite similar, it is important to note that they differ in subtle but important ways that can affect the incidence results obtained: each such study makes its own choices about where to get the data, whether to use individual taxpayers or families, which set of taxes to put in the numerator of the effective tax rate (ETR) calculation, and what definition of income to use to classify taxpayers (and to put in the denominator of the ETR calculation). Even once the ETR is calculated at each income level, these studies could choose from among many measures of progressivity[39].

We now turn to empirical tests of these incidence assumptions. First, for the payroll tax, virtually all applied incidence studies assume that both the employee share and the employer share are borne by the employee (through a fall in the net wage by the full

---

[39] Kiefer (1984) reviews indices of progressivity. For example, the Pechman and Okner (1974) index is calculated as the Gini coefficient after taxes minus the Gini coefficient before taxes, all divided by the latter $((\text{Gini}_{AT} - \text{Gini}_{BT})/\text{Gini}_{BT})$. Other measures such as the Suits Index [Suits (1977)] are based on the tax concentration curve.

amount of payroll tax). This assumption has been tested and confirmed repeatedly, going back to Brittain (1971) who used a 1958 cross-section of 13 industries in 64 nations and found full burdens on labor. Gruber (1997) reviews other more recent empirical studies that use both cross-section and time-series data, consistently finding full burdens on labor. Gruber (1997) himself uses data from a survey of manufacturing plants in Chile over the 1979–86 period to estimate the effects of dramatic 1981 cuts in that country's payroll tax, and finds that "the reduced costs of payroll taxation to firms appear to have been fully passed on to workers in the form of higher wages ..." (p. S99)[40].

Second, for sales and excise taxes, the standard assumption is that burdens fall on the consumers of taxed products (through higher prices). For example, Fullerton (1996) and Metcalf (1999) employ a model with constant returns to scale and perfect competition, such that the long-run supply curve is flat, and any product tax logically must be passed on to purchasers. They then use input–output evidence on each industry's purchases of taxed products to calculate the increase in the cost of production of each industry – and thus the increase in each equilibrium output price. Finally, data on consumer expenditures can be used to indicate which consumers pay those higher prices[41].

This assumption, too, has been tested, but results are mixed. If the flat supply curve in the above analysis is replaced by an upward-sloping supply curve, then the burden of an excise tax might be shared in any proportions between consumers and producers, such that product price rises by *less* than the tax. In contrast, several studies reviewed by Poterba (1996) find "overshifting", such that the product price rises by *more* than the tax. In his own analysis, however, Poterba uses city-specific clothing price indices for 14 cities during 1925–39 (finding less-than-complete forward shifting) and eight cities during 1947–77 (finding mild, if any, overshifting). On the other hand, Besley and Rosen (1999) point out that overshifting is perfectly consistent with several models of imperfect competition (as discussed more in the next section). They find substantial overshifting for more than half of the 12 goods they study in 155 cities. This result would make excise taxes even more regressive than conventionally thought.

Finally, for the personal income tax, applied studies have consistently assumed that economic incidence is the same as statutory incidence – on the taxpayer – even though this assumption has never been tested.

In summary, few of the standard assumptions about tax incidence have been tested and confirmed (e.g., payroll tax). Most others have never been reliably tested (the

---

[40] In a survey of all labor economists at top-40 U.S. institutions, Fuchs, Krueger and Poterba (1998) find that the median belief about the payroll tax is that 20% of the burden is borne by employers.

[41] Metcalf (1999) uses the methodology of Caspersen and Metcalf (1994) to compute a measure of lifetime income for each household, and thus can calculate the incidence of these excise taxes across lifetime income groups or across annual income groups. He finds that excise taxes on fuels are regressive when measured annually by themselves, but can be slightly progressive when measured on a lifetime basis if the revenue is used to reduce payroll and personal income taxes in a progressive fashion.

personal income tax, corporate income tax, and local property tax). The standard assumption about the corporate income tax that the burden falls 100% on capital remains the standard assumption even though it is commonly believed to be false (because of international capital mobility and endogenous saving)[42]. The standard assumption about sales and excise taxes is that the burden is shifted 100% to consumers, and this assumption has been tested several times. Some of these studies cannot reject 100% shifting to consumers, while others find significantly less than 100% shifting, and still others find significantly more than 100% shifting.

Many general equilibrium simulation studies "calculate" the incidence of each tax based on carefully-articulated theories, and many data-intensive studies use these results to "assume" the incidence of each tax. But competing theories are rarely tested, and so econometric estimation remains fertile ground for new research.

3. Imperfect competition

In this section, we consider the effects of taxation in imperfectly competitive markets. The analysis, for the most part, is partial equilibrium in nature, and we consider both *ad valorem* and specific taxes on output[43]. Imperfectly competitive markets can appear in a wide variety of forms, and the tax analyst faces the difficult task of determining which model is appropriate in each application (see Tirole (1988) for an excellent discussion of different models). Broadly speaking, we can first classify models on the basis of whether they consider homogeneous or heterogeneous products. Models with different firms producing identical products include the Bertrand oligopoly and the Cournot–Nash oligopoly model. Those with heterogeneous goods include the monopolistic competition models [e.g., Dixit and Stiglitz (1977) and Spence (1976)], location models [e.g., Hotelling (1929) and Salop (1979)], and models of vertical differentiation [e.g., Gabszewicz and Thisse (1979) and Shaked and Sutton (1982)]. Whether products are homogeneous or heterogeneous, we will find that the impact of taxes on prices works through both direct and indirect channels (with the indirect channels differing across models).

3.1. Oligopolies

Let us first turn to the case of Bertrand oligopoly with identical firms and a constant returns to scale production function. Bertrand competition is a Nash equilibrium

---

[42] Fuchs, Krueger and Poterba (1998) surveyed public finance economists at top-40 U.S. institutions and found that the median belief about the corporate income tax is that 40% of the burden is borne by capital.

[43] Unlike perfect competition, the incidence impact of equal revenue *ad valorem* and specific taxes differs in imperfectly competitive markets. See Delipalla and Keen (1992) for a comparison of these two taxes.

concept in which firms compete in prices. The price equilibrium is quite simple: firms compete by lowering prices until all firms set price equal to their common marginal cost. No firms earn economic profits, leaving no incentive for entry or exit. The effects of a unit tax on output in such a model is straightforward. Since the producer price cannot fall below marginal cost, the entire tax is passed forward to consumers. More generally, even with a positive aggregate supply elasticity, the Bertrand model and perfect competition produce the same equilibrium outcome.

We next turn to the Cournot–Nash oligopoly model in which identical firms compete by choosing levels of output conditional on their expectations of their competitors' output levels. We proceed in two steps: first by fixing the number of firms in the market at N and then by allowing free entry. To simplify matters, we will assume firms are identical and that the equilibrium is symmetric[44].

Consider firm i in the market. Its profit function is given by

$$\pi_i(q_i) = (1 - \tau_v)p(q_i + Q_{-i})q_i - c(q_i) - \tau_s q_i, \tag{3.1}$$

where q_i is the output of the ith firm, Q_{-i} is the output of all other firms in the market, and $p(Q)$ is the inverse demand function for market demand Q. The cost function is $c(q_i)$, and τ_v and τ_s are *ad valorem* and specific taxes on q with statutory incidence on the firm.

The first order condition for the ith firm is given by

$$(1 - \tau_v)p'q_i + (1 - \tau_v)p - c' - \tau_s = 0, \tag{3.2}$$

where a prime indicates a first derivative. Second order conditions are

$$(1 - \tau_v)p''q_i + 2(1 - \tau_v)p' - c'' < 0, \tag{3.3}$$

or

$$\frac{\tilde{p}'}{N}(\eta + N + Nk) < 0, \tag{3.4}$$

where $\tilde{p} \equiv (1 - \tau_v)p$ is the producer price, $\eta = Qp''/p'$ is the elasticity of the slope of the inverse demand function and $k = 1 - \frac{c''}{\tilde{p}'}$ measures the relative slopes of the demand and marginal cost curves. Since $p' < 0$, the second order conditions require $\eta + N + Nk > 0$.

---

[44] The Cournot–Nash assumption is that firm i optimizes assuming that other firms do not adjust output in response. An alternative approach is to apply a conjectural variation assumption. Let $\lambda = \mathrm{d}Q/\mathrm{d}q_i - 1$ be the conjectured response in output of all other firms as firm i increases output by 1 unit. The Cournot–Nash assumption is equivalent to assuming that λ equals 0. Papers that employ the conjectural variations approach include Katz and Rosen (1985), Seade (1985) and Stern (1987). They also consider tax incidence in a Cournot model with a fixed number of firms.

In a symmetric equilibrium, we need only solve for p and q using the two equations:

$$p = p(Nq), \tag{3.5}$$

and

$$(1 - \tau_v)p'(Nq)\,q + (1 - \tau_v)p(Nq) - c'(q) = \tau_s. \tag{3.6}$$

Differentiating Equation (3.6) with respect to τ_s and rewriting, we get:

$$\frac{dq}{d\tau_s} = \frac{1}{\tilde{p}'(\eta + N + k)}. \tag{3.7}$$

It follows directly that

$$\frac{dQ}{d\tau_s} = \frac{N}{\tilde{p}'(\eta + N + k)}, \tag{3.8}$$

and

$$\frac{d\tilde{p}}{d\tau_s} = (1 - \tau_v)p'\left(\frac{dQ}{d\tau_s}\right) = \frac{N}{\eta + N + k}. \tag{3.9}$$

If second-order conditions hold, then $\eta + N + Nk > 0$. And, if $\eta + N + k > 0$, then output falls and the tax is (to some extent) passed forward to consumers. The degree of forward shifting of the unit tax on output depends on the elasticity of the slope of the inverse demand function (η), the number of firms (N), and the relative slopes of the marginal cost and inverse demand functions (k).

Overshifting occurs when the producer price rises by more than the excise tax. As we showed in an earlier section, this outcome is impossible in perfectly competitive markets. Once imperfectly competitive markets are allowed, overshifting becomes a possibility and can be guaranteed in some model specifications. Overshifting can occur because of the existence of market power and strategic behavior among firms. Firms recognize that forward shifting of the tax will decrease demand for their product. Thus, under some circumstances, they will wish to raise the price more than the increase in tax to compensate for the revenue loss from decreased demand[45].

By definition, overshifting occurs if the derivative in Equation (3.9) is greater than 1, which means that $\eta + k < 0$. If costs are linear in output, then $c'' = 0$ and $k = 1$, so a necessary and sufficient condition for overshifting ($d\tilde{p}/d\tau_s > 1$) is that $\eta < -1$. Consider a constant elasticity demand function with demand elasticity $\varepsilon < 0$. In that

---

[45] Note that overshifting does not imply an increase in profits for the firm. In fact, if demand is Cobb–Douglas, profits are unaffected by a marginal increase in a specific tax despite the existence of overshifting.

case, $\eta = (1 - \varepsilon)/\varepsilon < -1$ for all $\varepsilon < 0$. Overshifting will *always* occur, and it increases as demand becomes less elastic (as η increases in absolute value).

Producer prices rise with an increase in an *ad valorem* tax as follows:

$$\frac{d\tilde{p}}{d\tau_v} = \frac{Np(1 + 1/\varepsilon)}{\eta + N + k}, \tag{3.10}$$

where $\varepsilon < 0$ is the price elasticity of demand. Overshifting of an *ad valorem* tax occurs when the percentage change in the producer price exceeds 100%, and it occurs in this model when $-N < \eta + k < N/\varepsilon$.

Having analyzed tax incidence in the fixed-N Cournot oligopoly, analysis of monopoly markets is straightforward (simply set $N = 1$) [46]. Assuming no pre-existing *ad valorem* tax, a monopolist can shift more than 100% of an excise tax (τ_s) when $1/(\eta + 1 + k) > 1$, or $-1 < \eta + k < 0$. With linear costs, overshifting occurs when $-2 < \eta < -1$. Overshifting cannot occur in the simple case of linear demand and linear costs (because $\eta = 0$ and $k = 1$). From Equation (3.9), $d\tilde{p}/d\tau_s$ equals 1/2 in the linear demand/cost case. On the contrary, if demand is of the constant elasticity type, and costs are linear, then overshifting will always occur in the monopoly model. Thus, the two models most typically assumed (constant slope or constant elasticity) each impose a particular incidence pattern in the monopoly model with constant marginal costs of production [see, for example, Musgrave (1959)].

Returning to the general oligopoly model with fixed number of firms, note that N does not affect the overshifting condition for excise taxes but does affect the degree of overshifting. Again, we consider the case with no pre-existing *ad valorem* tax. Assume that $-N < \eta + k < 0$ (so that $d\tilde{p}/d\tau_s > 1$). Then $d^2\tilde{p}/d\tau_s dN < 0$. In other words, for given values of η and k, overshifting is maximized for a monopolist and disappears as N approaches infinity.

Now allow for free entry in the Cournot model. In addition to Equations (3.5) and (3.6), we need a third equation to pin down the equilibrium number of firms. Firms will enter until the marginal firm earns zero profits. With identical firms, the zero profit condition becomes

$$(1 - \tau_v)p(Nq)q - c(q) - \tau_s q = 0. \tag{3.11}$$

Equations (3.5), (3.6) and (3.11) determine p, q, and N. We now limit our discussion to changes in excise taxes and assume τ_v equals zero. Thus, $\tilde{p}$ equals p, and

$$\frac{dp}{d\tau_s} = \frac{N(k + 1)}{\eta + N + Nk}. \tag{3.12}$$

With a linear cost function ($k = 1$), $dp/d\tau_s > 1$ iff $\eta < 0$. We now have a wider class of aggregate demands for which overshifting will occur [see Besley (1989) for a fuller

---

[46] See Bishop (1968) for an early treatment of *ad valorem* and unit taxes under monopoly.

analysis of this point]. The indirect effect of the tax on industry structure contributes to overshifting (where structure here means the number of firms). To see this, note that

$$\frac{\mathrm{d}N}{\mathrm{d}\tau_s} = \frac{N}{p'q} \left(\frac{\eta + k + 1}{\eta + N + Nk} \right),\tag{3.13}$$

and $\mathrm{d}N/\mathrm{d}\tau_s < 0$ if $\eta + k + 1 > 0$. With a positive fixed cost and constant marginal cost, then the equilibrium number of firms will fall in the range of η between -2 and zero. This decrease in firms tends to drive up prices, and the effect is that overshifting occurs for η between -1 and 0 in the variable-N case but not in the fixed-N case. Note that this overshifting does not lead to increased economic rents for producers: in the free-entry model, profits are always zero, so the effect of the unit tax is to drive up costs of production and to induce exit if aggregate demand is sufficiently elastic.

More generally,

$$\frac{\mathrm{d}p}{\mathrm{d}\tau_s} - \frac{\mathrm{d}p}{\mathrm{d}\tau_s} \bigg|_N = \left(\frac{p - c - t}{\eta + N + k} \right) \left(-\frac{\mathrm{d}N}{\mathrm{d}\tau_s} \right).\tag{3.14}$$

Entry and exit affect the degree of forward shifting through changes in the equilibrium number of firms. Assuming $\eta + N + k > 0$ (consumer prices rise with a unit tax in the fixed-N case), then consumer prices rise more as the equilibrium number of firms falls so long as some market power is in effect ($p - c - t > 0$). This indirect price effect arises because the decrease in the equilibrium number of firms yields increased market power for the remaining firms. Interestingly, if we start at an efficient equilibrium with no market power, then taxes have no indirect effect on prices. The result that part of the incidence impact of a tax occurs through changes in the equilibrium number of firms is a result that will occur in a number of models of imperfectly competitive firms, as we shall see later.

Delipalla and Keen (1992) show that in both the Cournot–Nash and free-entry oligopoly models, *ad valorem* taxes are less likely to lead to overshifting than unit taxes. Venables (1986) notes that *ad valorem* taxes dampen the impact of output changes on prices and thus make the market act more like a perfectly competitive market. Applying that insight here, *ad valorem* taxes will have an impact more like taxes in perfectly competitive markets and so should lead to less overshifting than unit taxes.

Support for overshifting in imperfectly competitive markets appears in a number of empirical studies. Karp and Perloff (1989) econometrically estimate the conjectural variations parameter ($\lambda = \mathrm{d}Q/\mathrm{d}q_i - 1$) in the Japanese market for televisions. They find evidence for imperfectly competitive markets and, based on that conclusion, derive the incidence of a domestic luxury tax on televisions. They find more than 100% forward shifting. Their conclusions depend heavily on the structural assumptions imposed in their model. Harris (1987) analyzed the 1983 increase in the U.S. federal excise tax on cigarettes from \$.08 to \$.16 per pack[47]. He finds that the \$.08 tax increase led to a consumer price rise of \$.16 per pack. As mentioned in the previous section, Besley and Rosen (1999) investigate the impact of changes in state and local sales taxes on product prices for a highly disaggregated set of commodities[48]. They employ quarterly data for 12 goods in 155 cities over a nine-year period (1982–1990), about 4200 observations per commodity. They find overshifting for a number of commodities, including bread, shampoo, soda, and underwear. They cite evidence by Anderson (1990) for market power in many local grocery markets, and estimated markups that are 2.355 times price for retail trade, from Hall (1988).

Poterba (1996), in contrast, finds no evidence for overshifting of sales taxes. The major difference between the Besley and Rosen study and the Poterba study is the level of disaggregation; it is possible that any overshifting in the latter study is obscured by changes in composition of the items in the bundles studied[49]. Doyle (1997) also finds evidence of overshifting in the new car market, where a onc-dollar increase in tax is associated with a price increase ranging from \$2.19 for luxury cars to \$2.97 for trucks.

3.2. Differentiated products

The oligopoly models discussed above suffer from the restrictive assumptions that goods are identical and that no distinction can be made between different brands. In some markets (e.g., agricultural commodity markets), this may be a reasonable assumption. In most other markets, however, producers go to great length to differentiate their products. Product differentiation creates some monopoly power, and the results in the fixed-N oligopoly model indicate that the ability to pass taxes forward depends importantly on the number of competitors in the market. In this section, we consider several models of differentiated products and examine the relationship between product competition and tax incidence.

We begin with Dixit and Stiglitz (1977) and their model of monopolistic competition. This is a somewhat special model in that each product competes with all other products, and the main thrust of the model is to illustrate the benefits of product variety. It is useful to begin with this model, however, as it highlights the importance of product differentiation – a feature left out of the homogeneous-good oligopoly model. Consider the following simplified Dixit–Stiglitz model of product variety based on Krugman (1980). Consumers are identical and maximize a utility function

$$U(x_1, x_2, \ldots, x_N) = \frac{1}{\theta} \sum_{i=1}^{N} x_i^{\theta}, 0 < \theta < 1. \tag{3.15}$$

---

[47] The increase was first temporary but was made permanent in 1986. See Harris (1987) for details.

[48] They consider such items as a three-pound can of Crisco, a dozen large Grade-A eggs, a 200-count box of Kleenex facial tissues, and (naturally) the board game Monopoly.

[49] The studies also differ by cities and time periods examined and econometric specifications employed.

Consumption goods enter utility symmetrically but are not perfect substitutes (unless θ equals 1). Individuals maximize utility subject to the budget constraint that (exogenous) income (M) equals expenditures:

$$\sum_{i=1}^{N} p_i x_i = M,$$ (3.16)

where p_i is the consumer price of the ith good. From the first-order conditions, we can derive the demand functions:

$$x_i = \lambda^{-\varepsilon} p_i^{-\varepsilon}, \varepsilon = \frac{1}{1 - \theta} > 1,$$ (3.17)

where λ is the private marginal utility of income. If N is large, we can assume that the pricing decisions of an individual firm will have negligible effect on λ and demand can be written as

$$x_i = A p_i^{-\varepsilon},$$ (3.18)

and is of the constant elasticity variety.

Firms maximize profits, and we assume that costs are linear of the form $cx_i + F$, where c is marginal cost and F is fixed cost. Letting $\tilde{p} \equiv (1 - \tau_v)p$ be the producer price with an *ad valorem* tax (τ_v), the firm's pricing rule is given by the standard monopolist's pricing rule:

$$\tilde{p} = \left(\frac{\varepsilon}{\varepsilon - 1}\right)(c + \tau_s).$$ (3.19)

For either an excise or *ad valorem* tax applied to a particular industry only, we can differentiate Equation (3.19). Thus,

$$\frac{d\tilde{p}}{d\tau_s} = \frac{\varepsilon}{\varepsilon - 1} > 1,$$ (3.20)

and

$$\frac{d\tilde{p}}{d\tau_v} = 0.$$ (3.21)

The insights from monopoly model in the last section carry forward: an excise tax is more than 100% forward shifted (constant elasticity and linear cost result), while an *ad valorem* tax has no impact on the producer price but is entirely shifted forward to consumers.

A disadvantage of the Dixit–Stiglitz model is that all products are treated as equal competitors with other products. A quick look at any number of markets indicates that this assumption is untenable. We next turn to a model of spatial competition where firms locate themselves in product space to capture maximal customers in a simultaneous entry game. We use the Salop (1979) circle model as developed to analyze *ad valorem* and excise taxes by Kay and Keen (1983)[50]. The virtue of the circle model is that it explicitly allows for modeling of the number of firms in equilibrium [unlike the linear model of Hotelling (1929)]. Following Salop, we assume N identical firms simultaneously deciding whether to enter a market where consumers are located uniformly around the circle, and where each consumer wishes to purchase 1 unit of the product. Firms that enter locate equidistantly around a unit circle. Thus, in equilibrium, each firm will face demand of $1/N$ (assuming the market is covered). Each individual will purchase at most one unit of the good, and each prefers to purchase the good of quality or location x that is as close as possible to their most-preferred quality (x^*). Specifically, the consumer's cost of the good is the purchase price (p_i) plus a "transport cost" that is assumed to be a constant h times the distance from their location $|x - x^*|$. Utility for a consumer who purchases a unit of x obtains utility equal to

$$U = \bar{s} - p - h|x - x^*|,\tag{3.22}$$

where $\bar{s}$ is an arbitrary constant sufficiently large to ensure $U > 0$.

Consider a consumer located at $\hat{x}$, between 0 and $1/N$ from firm i. That consumer will be indifferent between purchasing from firm i and firm $i+1$ if

$$p_i + h\hat{x} = p + h(1/N - \hat{x}),\tag{3.23}$$

where p_i is the price charged by the ith firm, and p is the price charged by other firms. For that price p_i (making the consumer at $\hat{x}$ indifferent), demand for the ith firm's good, $D(p_i, p)$, will be equal to $2\hat{x}$. Solve Equation (3.23) for $\hat{x}$ and double it, to get:

$$D(p_i, p) = \frac{p - p_i}{h} + \frac{1}{N}.\tag{3.24}$$

The firm maximizes profits by choosing price. It faces an *ad valorem* tax rate τ_v and a unit tax rate τ_s. Profits are given by

$$\pi_i = ((1 - \tau_v)p_i - c - \tau_s)\left(\frac{p - p_i}{h} + \frac{1}{N}\right) - F,\tag{3.25}$$

---

[50] Anderson, de Palma and Kreider (2001) provide a more general analysis that incorporates the Kay and Keen model as a special case. These authors stress the similarity of results under a Bertrand–Nash environment with differentiated products to the Cournot–Nash setting with homogeneous products analyzed by Delipalla and Keen (1992). Metcalf and Norman (2001) extend the Kay and Keen model to allow for price discrimination and costly re-anchoring of product types in response to entry.

where c is marginal cost and F is fixed cost. Take the derivative, set it equal to zero, and set p_i equal to p (assuming identical firms have equal price in equilibrium), to yield:

$$p_i = \frac{h}{N} + \frac{c + \tau_s}{1 - \tau_v}. \tag{3.26}$$

We can rewrite this in terms of the producer price ($\tilde{p}$):

$$\tilde{p} = \frac{(1 - \tau_v)h}{N} + c + \tau_s. \tag{3.27}$$

Thus, unit taxes are fully passed forward in the sense that the producer price rises by the full amount of the tax[51]. Strictly speaking, this statement is only true if the equilibrium number of firms is unaffected by changes in the excise tax.

We need a second equation to pin down the equilibrium number of firms. A zero-profit condition for the marginal firm does this. In equilibrium, each firm covers $1/N$ of the market. Plug this supply into the profit function and set profits equal to zero, to get:

$$((1 - \tau_v)p_i - c - \tau_s)\left(\frac{1}{N}\right) = F. \tag{3.28}$$

Substituting Equation (3.26) into (3.28) and solving for N, we get:

$$N = \sqrt{\frac{(1 - \tau_v)h}{F}}. \tag{3.29}$$

While a change in the excise tax does not affect the equilibrium number of firms, a change in the *ad valorem* tax does.

Ad valorem tax incidence can be decomposed into two components: a direct effect and an indirect effect through the change in the equilibrium number of firms. Fixing N,

$$\frac{\partial \tilde{p}}{\partial \tau_v}\bigg|_N \equiv \frac{\partial (1 - \tau_v)p}{\partial \tau_v}\bigg|_N = -\frac{h}{N}. \tag{3.30}$$

The complete incidence is given by

$$\frac{\partial \tilde{p}}{\partial \tau_v} = -\frac{1}{2}\sqrt{\frac{Fh}{1 - \tau_v}} = -\frac{1}{2}\frac{h}{N}, \tag{3.31}$$

exactly half the incidence in Equation (3.30) where N is fixed. In other words, firm exit cuts the burden on producers in half (and raises the burden on consumers)[52].

---

[51] From Equation (3.26), the consumer price rises by more than the unit tax in the presence of an *ad valorem* tax. The increase in price by the firm to cover the unit tax must also cover an increase in *ad valorem* tax collections. It is not the case, however, that the unit tax is more than 100% passed forward.

[52] Firms exit because an increase in *ad valorem* taxation is equivalent (from the firm's point of view) to an increase in fixed cost relative to revenue. See Kay and Keen (1983) for details.

Some of the theories described in this section have also been incorporated into computable general equilibrium models with imperfect competition. For example, Harris (1984) builds an open-economy trade model of Canada with 29 different industries, of which 20 are potentially noncompetitive. He specifies a fixed cost for each plant within an industry, free entry, and two alternative models (with and without product differentiation). He finds that "the estimated welfare gains from trade liberalization are substantial in the industrial organization model and on the order four times larger than the gains estimated from the competitive model" (p. 1031). In terms of incidence, internationally-mobile capital in his model means that capital-owners are unaffected, but his Table 2 (p. 1028) reveals that the gain in labor productivity from trade liberalization can be four to six times higher in the imperfectly competitive models.

Once we allow for heterogeneous products, we see new avenues for taxes to affect equilibrium prices. Consider a duopoly model with heterogeneous goods in which firms compete over price, and product quality is endogenous. Cremer and Thisse (1994) present a model of vertical product differentiation and show that a uniform *ad valorem* tax applied to both firms *reduces* the consumer price in equilibrium. Part of the price decrease arises from a decrease in quality and hence reduction in marginal (and average) production costs. But the authors note that the price decrease exceeds the cost reduction. A reduction in quality differences sharpens price competition and reduces monopoly power of firms.

A general point can be made here. With differentiated products, taxes can affect prices over additional avenues, whether through the degree of product variety as in the Kay and Keen model or through the distribution of product quality as in the Cremer and Thisse model. Non-price competition can substantially affect the degree to which output taxes are passed forward to consumers and can lead to counterintuitive results, as in the Cremer and Thisse model[53].

4. Dynamic models and incidence

Models with intertemporal optimization allow for endogenous saving and investment. The essential engine of long-run incidence in these models is the impact of taxes on capital–labor ratios (and thus factor prices). We shall also see, however, that short-run inelastic capital supply plays an important role through asset price revaluations in response to tax policy. Anticipations also become important.

Beginning in the 1960s, research on factor taxation in a dynamic setting used neoclassical growth models either with exogenously-specified savings functions or with

---

[53] In the Cremer and Thisse model, the impact of *ad valorem* taxes on market power has obvious welfare implications. They show that a small increase in a uniform *ad valorem* tax from a no-tax equilibrium is always welfare improving. See Auerbach and Hines (2002) in Volume 3 of this Handbook for further discussion.

overlapping generations (OLG models). In a two-period setting, OLG models have been extensively discussed by Kotlikoff and Summers (1987) and Kotlikoff (2002), and we refer the reader there for more detail. Here, we briefly discuss capital income taxation in a growing economy using a model due to Feldstein (1974). We then turn to perfect-foresight models in which savings behavior follows explicitly from consumer preferences. This provides a link between the savings function and the pure rate of time preference that is lacking in the previous literature. Finally, we turn to asset-pricing models and transition dynamics.

4.1. Taxation in a growing economy

Static models of tax incidence cannot easily capture the impact of changes in the capital-labor ratio on factor prices. Consider a simple linearly-homogeneous production function $y = f(k)$, where output per worker (y) is a function of the capital–labor ratio (k). With competitive pricing, each factor price will be a function of k:

$$r(k) = f'(k), \tag{4.1}$$

$$w(k) = f(k) - kf'(k), \tag{4.2}$$

where r is the rental rate of capital and w the wage rate. As k grows, the rental rate decreases and the wage rate increases. If net capital income is taxed at rate τ, and r is the net rental rate, then the marginal product of capital is equal in equilibrium to $(1 + \tau)r$. Feldstein (1974) develops a model to analyze the long-run incidence of a capital income tax and concludes that much (if not all) of the burden of the tax is shifted to workers in the form of lower wages resulting from a decline in the capital–labor ratio. He notes that a change in the tax on capital income per person (rk) has two components:

$$\frac{\mathrm{d}(rk)}{\mathrm{d}\tau} = k\frac{\mathrm{d}r}{\mathrm{d}\tau} + r\frac{\mathrm{d}k}{\mathrm{d}\tau}. \tag{4.3}$$

He argues that the second term should not be viewed as a burden of the tax, but rather as a shift in the timing of consumption. Thus, Feldstein measures the long-run burden of a new capital income tax as the ratio of the loss to capitalists ($-k\mathrm{d}r$) to the new tax revenue ($rk\mathrm{d}\tau$); the burden on owners of capital from an increase in tax is the ratio of ($-k\mathrm{d}r$) to the loss in real income ($-(k\mathrm{d}r + \mathrm{d}w)$).

The conclusions from the model are particularly stark in a two-class world in which all savings is from capital income only. Assuming that the savings rate s is a function of the net rate of return ($s = s(r)$), then saving per person equals $s(r)rk$. In the long-run steady state, the capital stock must grow at the rate of growth of the population (n), and equilibrium in capital markets requires

$$s(r)rk = nk. \tag{4.4}$$

The net rate of return (r) is a function of the growth rate of the population (n) only, and is unaffected by a change in the capital income tax rate. Thus, capital owners bear none of the burden of the tax in the steady state. Even if the savings rate out of labor income is positive, much of the burden of the capital tax can be shifted to labor [54].

Once saving is endogenous, other "standard" results can also be reversed. For example, because land is inelastically supplied, many presume that a tax on land is borne by the landowner. In a model where land serves not only as a factor of production but also as an asset, however, Feldstein (1977) shows that a tax on land rent then induces investors to increase holdings of other assets in their portfolios. The resulting increase in reproducible, physical capital can then lead to an increase in the wage rate and a decrease in the return to physical capital. Hence, part of the tax on land rent is shifted to capital, with wage rates rising in response to the greater capital–labor ratio.

Boadway (1979) points out that focusing on the steady state provides an incomplete picture of the impact of a capital income tax. He takes Feldstein's (1974) model and parameter assumptions and carries out simulations of a marginal increase in capital income taxation that finances a reduction in labor income taxation. In steady state, labor is made worse off by the shift, with wage rates falling over 7% in the long run [55]. But Boadway shows that the wage rate first rises before falling, and in fact is higher for 65 years in his simulation [56]. A complete picture of the burden would have to discount and add up the workers' gains and losses over time.

One simple way to measure the burden shift would be to compute the present discounted value of the change in wage income assuming some given discount rate. We note four problems with this approach. First, the discount rate is exogenous rather than being linked to consumer preferences. Second, it would be preferable to have some dynamic measure of compensating or equivalent variation for the tax shift. Third, the savings rate $s(r)$ does not follow from consumer preferences. Fourth, it depends only on current information with no anticipations. For example, an announcement today of a temporary surtax on capital income for ten years that would begin five years from now should have an impact on capital accumulation over the next five years. The models of Feldstein, Grieson, and Boadway cannot capture this effect. We turn next to a model based on Judd (1985a) that addresses all four of these concerns.

4.2. Taxation in a perfect foresight model

The essential departure in the model of Judd (1985a) is the assumption of perfect foresight by an infinitely-lived individual. Perfect foresight is an extreme assumption and perhaps should be viewed as one end of a continuum; it has the attractive quality

---

[54] Feldstein presents an example with Cobb–Douglas production. With equal savings rates for labor and capital, he calculates that 1/3 of the tax is shifted to labor. With a savings rate for capital twice that for labor, half the tax is shifted.

[55] Grieson (1975) also shows that a shift from wage to capital income taxation can make workers worse off in the long run through a decrease in the steady-state capital-labor ratio.

[56] He also reports results where the wage rate rises for over 75 years.

of allowing individuals to look forward and thus to make decisions today on the basis of beliefs about the world in the future.

Consider a very simple world with only two people: a capitalist and a worker, each of whom lives forever [57]. The capitalist earns income only from the rental of capital, while the worker earns income only from labor supply (fixed at one unit). Workers do not save, and the only purpose of taxation is to redistribute income from capitalists to workers [58]. If τ is the tax rate on capital income, we can consider policy experiments of the form $d\tau = \varepsilon h(t)$ where ε is small and $h(t)$ is used to represent the timing of the policy under consideration. For example, $h(t) = 1$ for $t \geqslant 0$ would be an immediate permanent increase in capital income taxation, while $h(t) = 1$ for $t \geqslant T$ would be a permanent increase beginning at some date T in the future (but announced at time 0). Finally, a temporary tax increase could be modeled by $h(t) = 1$ for $0 \leqslant t \leqslant T$, and $h(t) = 0$ for $t > T$.

Output is produced according to a concave production function $f(k)$ which gives output per worker in terms of capital per worker. The produced good is taken as the numeraire good and can be used for consumption or investment. In equilibrium, factor prices are given by

$$r_t = f'(k_t), \tag{4.5}$$

$$w_t = f(k_t) - k_t f'(k_t), \tag{4.6}$$

where r_t is the rental rate for capital and w_t is the wage paid to the worker.

Whereas neoclassical growth models [e.g., Feldstein (1974), Grieson (1975), Boadway (1979) and Bernheim (1981)] do not directly link savings behavior to key utility parameters (in particular, the pure rate of time preference), Judd models savings behavior directly from the intertemporal optimization problem of capitalists [59]. Specifically, the capitalist maximizes an additively-separable utility function of the isoelastic form:

$$U^k = \int_0^\infty e^{-\rho t} \frac{(c_t^k)^{1-\beta}}{1-\beta} dt, \tag{4.7}$$

by choosing a time path of consumption (c_t^k) and capital (k_t) subject to the constraint

$$c_t^k + \dot{k}_t = (1 - \tau) r k_t, \tag{4.8}$$

and some given level of the capital stock at time zero (k_0). The pure rate of time preference (ρ) is fixed (and the same both for the capitalist and the worker). A dot

---

[57] The infinitely-lived consumer assumption can be justified in terms of the dynastic model of Barro (1974).

[58] These assumptions are all innocuous. See Judd (1987) for discussion of endogenous labor supply and other generalizations.

[59] To avoid confusion about who is a worker as opposed to a capitalist, Judd specifies that the worker does not save anything. Consumption for the worker is simply the wage received plus a transfer from the government, financed by the capital income tax.

over a variable indicates a time derivative. The parameter β is the elasticity of the marginal utility of consumption. We assume that utility is concave in consumption so that $\beta > 0$. Along an optimal path, the capitalist trades off a unit of consumption today against the benefit of increased consumption in the future from investing the unit and receiving a net return in the future:

$$u'(c_t^k) = (c_t^k)^{-\beta} = \int_t^\infty e^{-\rho(s-t)}(1-\tau)\,ru'(c_t^k)\,ds = \int_t^\infty e^{-\rho(s-t)}(1-\tau)\,r(c_t^k)^{-\beta}ds.$$

(4.9)

The optimal time path of consumption for the capitalist is determined by differentiating Equation (4.9) and substituting in Equation (4.5):

$$\dot{c}^k = \frac{-(\rho - (1-\tau)f'(k))\,c^k}{\beta},$$

(4.10)

where we have omitted the time subscripts. Capital accumulation is given by

$$\dot{k} = (1-\tau)\,kf'(k) - c^k.$$

(4.11)

Equations (4.10) and (4.11) are the equations of motion for the system.

In the steady state, Equation (4.10) shows that the net return to capital is constant and equal to ρ. This suggests that capital taxes are shifted entirely to workers through adjustments in the capital–labor ratio. While the net return is fixed in the long run, however, it can vary along a transition path to the new steady state, and redistribution can occur along this transition path. For a complete picture, as we shall see, it is important to focus not only on the steady state but on the entire transition path.

We now entertain a change in capital income taxation where a policy of the form $d\tau = \varepsilon h(t)$ is announced as of the present time ($t = 0$). Thus, the equations of motion become

$$\dot{c}^k = \frac{-(\rho - (1 - \tau - \varepsilon h(t))f'(k))\,c^k}{\beta},$$

(4.10′)

and

$$\dot{k} = (1 - \tau - \varepsilon h(t))\,kf'(k) - c^k.$$

(4.11′)

Consumption and capital (as well as their time derivatives) are now functions of ε as well as time. Let $c_\varepsilon^k(t) \equiv \frac{\partial c_t^k}{\partial \varepsilon}$, evaluated at $\varepsilon = 0$ (and similarly for other variables). Judd differentiates Equations (4.10′) and (4.11′) with respect to ε, evaluating the derivatives at $\varepsilon = 0$ and at the initial steady-state level of capital. Defining $\mu > 0$ as

$$\mu = \frac{\rho}{2}\left(1 - \frac{\theta_L}{\sigma} + \sqrt{\left(1 - \frac{\theta_L}{\sigma}\right)^2 + \frac{4\theta_L}{\beta\sigma}}\right), \tag{4.12}$$

where θ_L is labor's share of output and σ is the elasticity of substitution between labor and capital in production, Judd shows that the initial shock to consumption of the capitalist equals [60]

$$c_\varepsilon^k(0) = H(\mu)\frac{\rho}{1-\tau}\left(\frac{\rho - \mu\beta}{\rho}\right)\frac{c^k}{\beta}, \tag{4.13}$$

where $H(\mu)$ is the Laplace transform of $h(t)$ evaluated at μ. For any discount rate s, $H(s) = \int_0^\infty e^{-st}h(t)\,dt$ is the present value of the policy function $h(t)$. It is easy to show that $\mu > \rho$ iff $\beta < 1$. Also, Judd shows that $\mu\beta < \rho$ iff $\beta < 1$. Thus, capitalists may immediately increase or decrease their consumption in response to an announced increase in capital income taxation. Increased future capital income taxation has an income effect that works to reduce present consumption. On the other hand, the substitution effect works to shift consumption from the future to the present. If $\beta < 1$, the substitution effect dominates and consumption increases. For $\beta > 1$, the preference for smooth consumption makes the income effect dominant. The role of the policy duration appears in $H(\mu)$, where $H(\mu)$ increases with the duration of the tax increase. Thus, consumption at time zero falls more for a longer duration tax increase (in present value terms) when the income effect dominates ($\beta > 1$). Note that consumption falls now, even if the start of the tax increase is delayed. But the drop in consumption is attenuated as a tax hike of fixed duration is put further off into the future.

To determine the degree to which the tax and transfer scheme benefits workers, we need to know how the consumption path for workers changes in response to an increase in capital income taxation. Consumption for the worker is given by

$$c_t^w = f(k) - kf'(k) + (\tau + \varepsilon h(t))kf'(k), \tag{4.14}$$

where the first two terms are wage income and the last term is the transfer financed by capital income taxation. Define $c_\varepsilon^w(t) \equiv \frac{\partial c_t^w}{\partial \varepsilon}$ evaluated at $\varepsilon = 0$, and B_ε^w as the

---

[60] Judd solves the linear differential equation system by first taking Laplace transforms. See Judd (1985b) for details on this derivation.

discounted increase in lifetime utility measured in time zero consumption arising from the tax increase,

$$B_{\mathcal{E}}^w = \frac{\int_0^\infty e^{-\rho t} u'(c_t^w) c_{\mathcal{E}}^w(t)\, dt}{u'(c_0^w)}. \tag{4.15}$$

Judd shows that

$$B_{\mathcal{E}}^w = kf'H(\rho) \left(1 - \frac{\left[1 - \beta + \frac{H(\mu)}{H(\rho)} \left(\frac{\mu\beta}{\rho} - 1 \right) \right] \left[\left(\frac{\tau}{1-\tau} \right) \frac{\sigma}{\theta_L} + 1 \right]}{1 - \beta} \right). \tag{4.16}$$

We can now specify the policy experiments and evaluate the impact on consumers.

4.2.1. Immediate temporary tax increase

A short-lived tax increase put into place at time zero can be modeled as $h(t)$ equaling 1 for small t and 0 otherwise. If dt is the length of the time the temporary tax increase is in place, then $H(\mu) = H(\rho) = dt$ and $H(\mu)/H(\rho)$ is one (approximately). Thus,

$$B_{\mathcal{E}}^w = kf'H(\rho) \left(1 + \underbrace{\frac{\beta}{1-\beta} \left(1 - \frac{\mu}{\rho} \right) \left(\frac{\tau}{1-\tau} \frac{\sigma}{\theta_L} + 1 \right)}_{(A)} \right). \tag{4.17}$$

Recall that $\beta < 1$ iff $\mu > \rho$. Thus, the term in parentheses in Equation (4.17) labeled A is negative and workers are better off from this temporary incremental tax hike if this term is less than 1 in absolute value. If the initial capital income tax is sufficiently low, then workers are better off. This follows from the continuity of $B_{\mathcal{E}}^w$ in τ and the fact that this expression evaluated at $\tau = 0$ is

$$B_{\mathcal{E}}^w = kf'H(\rho) \left(1 + \frac{\rho - \mu\beta}{\rho(1-\beta)} \right), \tag{4.17'}$$

as well as the fact that $\beta < 1$ iff $\rho > \mu\beta$. For pre-existing τ sufficiently large, $B_{\mathcal{E}}^w$ will be negative, and so workers do not always benefit from an increase in the capital income tax. Essentially, the worker would like to save some of the large transfer but is precluded from doing so by high transactions costs or other institutional barriers; in that case, the worker would prefer capital income to be left with the capitalist who will invest it (and so make a portion of it available to the worker in the future through future taxes and transfers).

4.2.2. Immediate permanent tax increase

Now consider a permanent tax increase implemented at time zero. Thus, $h(t)$ equals 1 for all t. The function $H(s) = s^{-1}$ and B_ε^w now equals

$$B_\varepsilon^w = \frac{kf'}{\rho} \frac{\beta}{1-\beta} \left(1 - \frac{\rho}{\mu\beta}\right) \left(\frac{\tau}{1-\tau} \frac{\sigma}{\theta_L} + 1\right). \tag{4.18}$$

Again, B_ε^w is positive for small τ but becomes negative for τ sufficiently large. Equation (4.18) can be contrasted to the measures of burden in Feldstein (1974) and Boadway (1979). While Boadway makes the point that wages may initially increase as a result of redistributive taxation, he does not provide a utility-based measure of the gains from the tax shift. Equation (4.18) is just such a measure.

4.2.3. Announced permanent tax increase

Finally, consider the announcement today of a permanent tax increase to be put into effect at some later time. Thus, $h(t)$ equals 0 for $t < T$ and equals 1 for $t > T$. The ratio $H(\mu)/H(\rho)$ now equals $\frac{\rho}{\mu} e^{-(\mu-\rho)T}$ and goes to zero as T gets large if $\mu > \rho$ (and explodes if $\rho > \mu$). Now the benefit of redistributions to the worker depends critically on the value of β. If $\beta < 1$, then $\mu > \rho$, and B_ε^w is zero if τ equals zero (and negative if $\tau > 0$). Thus, the worker is made worse off from an announced future increase in capital income taxation, starting at a positive level of taxation, even with the proceeds transferred to the worker. The decrease in the capital stock along the path prior to the enactment of the tax increase will reduce wages, which in present value terms are more valuable than any future increase in transfers.

In the case that $\beta > 1$, then $\rho > \mu$, and $H(\mu)/H(\rho)$ dominates in Equation (4.16). The terms including $H(\mu)/H(\rho)$ will be positive (since $\mu\beta > \rho$), and workers benefit from a tax increase. Highly concave utility (high β) implies strong intertemporal smoothing of consumption and slow capital stock adjustment to new tax rates. Thus, future tax increases will not lead to immediate and rapid reductions in the capital stock (which would hurt the worker). While 100% shifting of the tax eventually occurs, the burden shift can occur quite slowly, allowing a period during which labor benefits from the higher tax[61].

4.2.4. The role of anticipations

The last result indicates the importance of anticipation in perfect foresight models. We can make this point more emphatically by considering policy changes designed in such a way that they lead to no change in the consumption of the capitalist at time

---

[61] This focus on anticipations distinguishes this analysis from that of other neoclassical growth models with workers and capitalists.

zero. Given the desire to smooth intertemporal consumption in the additively-separable utility function, any deviation from a steady-state consumption path at time zero must arise from a surprise in tax policy. Thus, a policy that leads to $c_\varepsilon^k(0) = 0$ is a policy that is perfectly anticipated by capitalists. From Equation (4.13), $c_\varepsilon^k(0) = 0$ equal to zero implies that $H(\mu)(1 - \frac{\mu\beta}{\rho})$ equals zero, and so

$$B_\varepsilon^w = -H(\rho)\,kf'\,\frac{\tau}{1-\tau}\,\frac{\sigma}{\theta_L}, \tag{4.19}$$

which is zero if τ is zero and negative otherwise. In other words, workers cannot benefit from a tax policy that is perfectly anticipated by capital owners. It is the surprise at time zero along with an inelastic short-run supply of capital that generates a benefit for workers from a tax and transfer scheme.

The Judd model illustrates a number of key points. First the incidence of a tax in a dynamic model can have strong effects through changes in saving and investment and consequently the capital–labor ratio. Both the perfect-foresight model and the neoclassical growth model make this point clearly. The perfect-foresight model, however, illustrates the importance of anticipations and surprises and suggests the possibility of lump-sum taxes on existing capital at the time of the announcement of a new tax regime ("old" capital) [62]. Because of the importance of anticipations and lump-sum characteristics of some tax policies, we pursue this further by developing a model in which taxes affect welfare through changes in asset prices. This model will make clear the distinction between "old" and "new" capital and the role of anticipations.

4.3. Incidence and the market value of capital

We present a simple partial equilibrium model of capital investment that emphasizes the importance of costs of adjustment in changing the capital stock. In the Judd (1985a) model previously described, capital accumulation depended on preferences and, in particular, the concavity of the utility function. Costs of adjusting the capital stock played no role. However, firms can incur significant costs during the process of major investment projects [63]. Summers (1985) presents a simple model to illustrate how corporate tax policy can affect investment as well as the market value of capital in place.

Costs of adjustment are captured in a simple capital–supply relationship. Consider a good that is produced with capital, K, according to the concave production function $F(K)$. Let the price of this good as well as the market price of capital

---

[62] Auerbach and Kotlikoff (1987) also emphasize the normative possibilities associated with taxing old capital in a lump-sum fashion.
[63] Large-scale urban transportation projects are a good example of investment projects that generate large-scale costs to businesses and residents in the urban area (for example, the Big Dig in Boston).

equal 1[64]. Firms wish to invest when the market value of the firm's capital exceeds its replacement cost at the margin. Investment is costly, however, and so firms adjust their capital stock towards some desired level slowly according to the function

$$\dot{K} = \left(g\left(\frac{V}{K} \right) - \delta \right) K, \tag{4.20}$$

where V is the value of the firm, δ is the rate of depreciation, and a dot indicates a time derivative. The function g has the property that $g(1) = 0$ and $g' > 0$. Defining $q = V/K$, Equation (4.20) is a standard Tobin investment function [Tobin (1969)].

Firms finance investment out of retained earnings, and the opportunity cost of funds for equity-holders equals ρ. Thus, if equity-holders are to receive a return equal to ρ, the value of the firm must evolve over time according to the relation

$$\rho = \frac{D}{V} + \frac{\dot{V}}{V}, \tag{4.21}$$

where D is the dividend paid to equity-holders. Dividends are equal to

$$D = F'(K)K - \tau(F'(K) - \delta)K - g(q)K, \tag{4.22}$$

where τ is the tax rate on income net of economic depreciation. Combining Equation (4.21) and (4.22), the value of the firm evolves as

$$\dot{V} = \rho V - F'(K)K + \tau(F'(K) - \delta)K + g(q)K. \tag{4.23}$$

We can re-express the change in value of the firm in terms of the change in value per dollar of existing capital $(\dot{q})$:[65]

$$\dot{q} = (\rho + \delta - g(q))\, q + g(q) - (1 - \tau)F'(K) - \tau\delta. \tag{4.24}$$

Equations (4.20) and (4.24) form the equations of motion for our system in terms of K and q. In the steady state (with $\dot{K} = 0$ and $\dot{q} = 0$), q takes the value q^* such that $g(q^*) = \delta$, and the steady-state capital stock (K^*) is defined by

$$(1 - \tau)(F'(K^*) - \delta) = \rho q^*. \tag{4.25}$$

Net of depreciation and tax, the return on capital must equal ρ, the return available on other investments. We illustrate the movements of K and q through the use of a phase diagram (Figure 4.1). The diagram breaks the $q - K$ space into four regions bounded

---

[64] We abstract from inflation.
[65] Differentiate $q = V/K$ to get $\dot{q} = \dot{V}/K - q(\dot{K}/K)$. Then substitute Equation (4.20) for $\dot{K}$ and Equation (4.23) for $\dot{V}$.

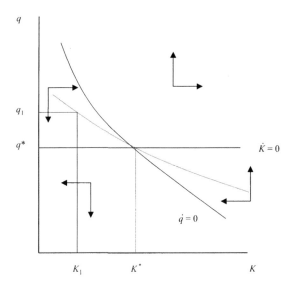

Fig. 4.1. Asset price model phase diagram.

by the $\dot{q} = 0$ and $\dot{K} = 0$ loci. Above the $\dot{K} = 0$ locus, the capital stock grows (depicted in the NE and NW quadrants with a horizontal arrow pointing to the right). Below this locus, the capital stock declines. To the right of the $\dot{q} = 0$ locus, q grows (depicted by the arrows pointing upward) while to the left, q falls. The intersection of these two lines is the steady-state.

The capital stock can only adjust slowly in response to shocks, but q can adjust instantaneously to any level. The dotted line is the saddle-point path moving to the steady-state from either the NW or SE. Consider some catastrophe that reduces the capital stock from K^* to K_1 (an earthquake, say). With perfect foresight, the value of the remaining capital (per unit of K) would immediately jump from q^* to q_1. With q now greater than q^*, investment would exceed depreciation, and the capital stock would slowly return to K^*. With myopic expectations, by contrast, q would jump immediately up further to the $\dot{q} = 0$ locus, as investors do not anticipate the capital loss that follows when new capital comes on line. Such a movement would not be sustainable (in the sense of q moving continuously back to q^*), as movement from the $\dot{q} = 0$ locus would be horizontally to the right, into a region where q and K both increase. This is a region of speculative bubbles, which must collapse at some point (with the price dropping back to the saddle-path).

Along the saddle-path, owners of capital would receive the normal rate of return. While the dividend yield exceeds the required rate of return, the investor incurs a capital loss as new net investment drives down the market price of capital. The only beneficiaries of the destruction of part of the capital stock are the owners of the undestroyed capital who earn a windfall capital gain at time zero.

We first use the model to illustrate a basic point about tax capitalization. Consider an increase in the corporate tax rate (τ). This shifts the $\dot{q} = 0$ locus to the left but

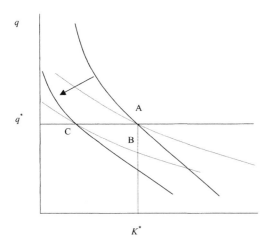

Fig. 4.2. An increase in the corporate tax rate.

leaves the $\dot{K} = 0$ locus unchanged. See Figure 4.2. The result is an immediate drop in the value of capital (a movement from A to B in Figure 4.2). All of the burden of the tax has been capitalized into a price drop at the time of enactment. No future capital owners will be affected, as the return on capital equals ρ along the saddle-path from B to C. Capitalization of taxes into asset prices complicates incidence analysis considerably[66].

The model can also be used to make an important point about the distinction between old and new capital. Old capital is capital in place at the time of a change in tax policy. Consider the enactment of a tax credit for the purchase of new capital. Because of the reduction in taxes, this might ordinarily be viewed as advantageous to all capital owners. To use this model to analyze this policy change, Equation (4.20) must be modified to account for the fact that the price of capital has been reduced from 1 to $1 - s$, where $s < 1$ is the level of the investment tax credit.

$$\dot{K} = \left(g\left(\frac{q}{(1-s)} \right) - \delta \right) K. \tag{4.20'}$$

The reduction in taxes increases the funds available to pay out as dividends. Equation (4.24) is accordingly modified:

$$\dot{q} = \left(\rho + \delta - g\left(\frac{q}{1-s} \right) \right) q + (1-s) g\left(\frac{q}{1-s} \right) - (1-\tau) F'(K) - \tau\delta. \tag{4.21'}$$

As s is increased from zero, both the $\dot{q} = 0$ and the $\dot{K} = 0$ loci move. See Figure 4.3. The $\dot{K} = 0$ locus shifts down from q^* to $(1-s)q^*$. Simultaneously, the $\dot{q} = 0$ locus

[66] See Aaron (1989) for a discussion of this point along with other issues that complicate the analysis of tax policy.

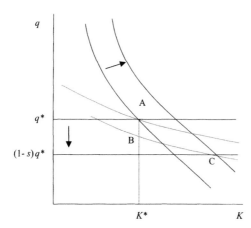

Fig. 4.3. An investment tax credit.

shifts to the right. The immediate impact on q is indeterminate. On the one hand, the rightward shift in the $\dot{q} = 0$ locus operates to create a windfall gain to owners of old capital: any future capital they purchase will be less expensive, and so dividends can be increased. On the other hand, the downward shift in the $\dot{K} = 0$ locus operates to generate a windfall loss: old capital must now compete with new capital that is less expensive. As drawn, the second effect dominates. Prior to the increase in the investment tax credit, the economy is at point A with $q = q^*$. The investment tax credit leads to an immediate drop in q from A to B. Over time, q drops further as the economy moves from B to C. This move does not imply a further loss in value, because the capital loss is exactly offset by an above-normal dividend yield so that investors along the path from B to C receive the normal rate of return (ρ). The tax credit has the desired effect of increasing the capital stock but the unexpected effect of burdening the owners of old capital with a windfall loss at the time of enactment. We leave it as an exercise for the reader to work out the price path for an announcement at time zero of an investment tax credit to be implemented at a given future date.

Dynamic incidence modeling has evolved considerably in the past twenty-five years. With increased computer power, it has become possible to create large-scale computational general equilibrium (CGE) models to evaluate tax policy over the lifetime, as well as to consider questions of capital accumulation and intergenerational redistributions. We turn now to models of lifetime tax incidence analysis, and we consider how these models provide new light on old issues.

5. Lifetime tax incidence

Up to this point, we have focused only indirectly on the relevant time frame for our incidence analysis. To classify households from rich to poor, most of the applied studies reviewed in Section 2.4 use income from one year, but others use income from an

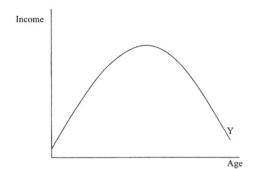

Fig. 5.1. Income over the lifetime.

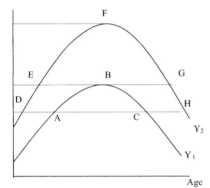

Fig. 5.2. Lifetime income heterogeneity.

entire lifetime. Intermediate choices also are possible, as Slemrod (1992) uses "time exposure" income from a period of seven years.

We now turn to models of lifetime tax incidence and begin with a very simple example to illustrate the importance of the time horizon. Consider a world with *identical* individuals such that one person of each age is alive at any given time. Figure 5.1 illustrates the income profile of each individual throughout life. Income is low at the beginning of life and increases to a peak before decreasing as the individual approaches retirement. Annual income at any given age is measured by the height of the curve, and lifetime income is the area under the curve.

Given our assumptions about identical individuals and the pattern of births and deaths, Figure 5.1 can also be interpreted as the distribution of income in the economy at any given point of time. Young and old have low annual income, while the middle-aged have high annual income. An annual tax incidence analysis using this snapshot of income would give the erroneous impression of considerable income inequality in this economy, despite the fact that everyone is identical. On the basis of the lifetime, the economy has no income inequality at all.

Now let us complicate the economy slightly and allow for two types of people with different lifetime income profiles (see Figure 5.2). Individuals with profile Y_1 earn

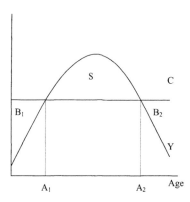

Fig. 5.3. Lifetime income and consumption.

less income at any age than do those with profile Y_2. Now the comparison gets more complicated. An annual income analysis will rank the person at F as the richest person in the economy, followed by the three individuals B, E and G. It then ranks individuals at A, C, D, and H as the poorest. This classification inappropriately groups a lifetime-poor person at the peak of earnings (point B) with lifetime-rich individuals at either the beginning or end of their earnings profiles (E and G).

A lifetime incidence analysis can yield a sharply different conclusion about the progressivity of any given tax as compared to an annual income analysis. Returning to our simple model of identical individuals, one of whom is alive at any given time, consider a consumption-smoothing model as posited by Modigliani and Brumberg (1954). In Figure 5.3, income is hump-shaped as above, and consumption is constant throughout life. At ages below A_1, individuals borrow to finance consumption. Between A_1 and A_2, they repay debt and start to save. In retirement (after A_2), individuals draw down savings to finance consumption. In the absence of bequests, the areas B_1 and B_2 are equal to S (in present value).

An annual incidence analysis of a tax on consumption would compare the average effective tax rate (tax as a percentage of income) across different annual income groups. Consider a flat consumption tax with no exemptions. For the young and the elderly, this tax as a fraction of annual income could be quite high (and possibly exceed 100%). The average tax rate would be lowest for those individuals at the peak of their profile, those whose earnings exceed consumption. Thus, a consumption tax would look highly regressive. On a lifetime income basis, however, the average tax rate (lifetime consumption taxes divided by lifetime income) would simply equal the tax rate on consumption. Then the tax is strictly proportional.

A bit of thought leads to the conclusion that differences in the degree of progressivity between lifetime and annual income analyses will vary depending on the tax under investigation. Continuing with our simple economy, consider a tax equal to a fixed percentage of wage income. On a lifetime basis this tax is proportional, but on an annual basis it will look somewhat regressive since capital income is left out of the tax base. However, the degree of regressivity implied in an annual income analysis will be sharply lower than in the case of our simple consumption tax, because the average tax rate can never exceed the statutory tax rate on wages.

Analyses of lifetime tax incidence have been carried out in a number of fashions. One approach is to build an overlapping generations (OLG) computable general equilibrium (CGE) model of an economy with a representative agent in each cohort [see, for example, Auerbach, Kotlikoff and Skinner (1983) or Auerbach and Kotlikoff (1987)]. Such models are very useful for understanding the intergenerational incidence of government policies [Kotlikoff (2002)]. They are not well suited, however, to studying the intragenerational redistribution brought about by government policies. A second approach is to jettison the CGE analysis of age cohorts, but instead focus on lifetime heterogeneity using incidence assumptions in the style of Pechman and Okner (1974). An example is the Davies, St. Hilaire and Whalley (1984) lifetime model based on Canadian data. A third approach is to combine both intertemporal and intratemporal heterogeneity. Fullerton and Rogers (1993) were one of the first to build a complete CGE model of this type.

Empirical incidence analyses from a lifetime perspective suffer from the lack of data on the entire lifetime income and consumption patterns of households. Thus, any attempt to apply the lifetime approach requires heroic assumptions. In the Davies et al. model, for example, all income streams are exogenous and the consumption path is based on an additive isoelastic utility function. Interest and growth rates are predetermined based on Canadian data, and the model calculates life-cycle consumption, income, tax payments, and government transfers[67].

Other empirical studies use annual data to construct a proxy for lifetime income. Poterba (1989) invokes the Modigliani and Brumberg (1954) consumption-smoothing story to study U.S. federal excise taxes. With perfect life-cycle consumption smoothing, and individuals identical except for lifetime income levels, current consumption is proportional to lifetime income. Thus, Poterba uses current consumption to categorize individuals by lifetime income. For alcohol, fuel, and tobacco taxes, he finds striking differences between annual and lifetime incidence. Metcalf (1994) applied a similar idea to the system of state and local sales taxes in the United States and finds that a case can be made for viewing this system of taxes as progressive, contrary to accepted wisdom. The shift to a lifetime perspective is one important factor blunting the regressivity of state and local sales taxes. In addition, most states exempt a variety of goods with low income elasticities, thereby adding to the progressivity of the system.

Other efforts to carry out lifetime incidence analysis using (primarily) annual data include Lyon and Schwab (1995), Caspersen and Metcalf (1994), Gale, Houser and Scholz (1996) and Feenberg, Mitrusi and Poterba (1997), among others. Caspersen

---

[67] They find that the incidence of the overall Canadian tax system is mildly progressive under either a lifetime or an annual incidence framework. Personal income taxes look less progressive, while consumption taxes look less regressive under the lifetime incidence framework.

and Metcalf use data from the Panel Study on Income Dynamics (PSID) to estimate age–earnings profiles for individuals based on variables that exist in both the PSID and the Consumer Expenditure Survey (CEX). The PSID has excellent data on income across households and years, so it is a good source for estimating age–earnings profiles that can be used to construct measures of lifetime income. Unfortunately, the PSID has minimal consumption data, which precludes distributional analysis of consumption taxes. The CEX, on the other hand, has excellent consumption data but poor income data. Hence, Caspersen and Metcalf use the PSID to predict age–earnings profiles for households in the CEX. For the introduction of a value added tax (VAT) in the United States, they find that a lifetime incidence analysis sharply reduces regressivity.

In another effort to capture life-cycle considerations, Gale, Houser and Scholz (1996) carry out an analysis in which they restrict their sample to married families with the head between the ages of 40 and 50, arguing that this approach reduces the inappropriate comparisons between people either at the beginning or end of their earnings career with people at the peak of their earnings. They find that this approach does not alter their conclusions about the distributional implications of a shift from income to consumption taxation[68].

5.1. A lifetime utility model

These studies all measure changes in tax liabilities rather than changes in welfare. As we discussed in the introduction, changes in tax liabilities misrepresent the change in welfare for various reasons. An advantage of a general equilibrium model (whether analytical or numerical) is that the researcher can make assumptions about the form of utility and explicitly measure changes in welfare in dollar terms (typically using the equivalent variation). Fullerton and Rogers (1993) construct a lifetime computable general equilibrium model to study the U.S. tax system[69]. We sketch out this model and compare its lifetime results to the classic annual results of Pechman and Okner (1974).

Fullerton and Rogers build a model with consumers of different ages and different lifetime incomes. All have the same lifetime utility function, but differ in labor

---

[68] Metcalf (1999), however, carries out an incidence analysis of an environmental tax reform using the lifetime methodology of Caspersen and Metcalf (1994) and also using a cohort analysis similar to Gale et al. He finds that the two approaches give very different answers, suggesting that the cohort approach is not a good proxy for a more complete lifetime analysis. One possible reason follows from the permanent income hypothesis [Friedman (1957)]. If people make decisions on the basis of permanent rather than annual income, then any deviations between the two will magnify the perceived regressivity of a consumption tax. Lifetime income approaches are less likely to suffer from this measurement problem.

[69] Other results from this model are presented in Fullerton and Rogers (1991, 1995, 1996, 1997).

productivity (and hence wage rate). Lifetime utility is a nested-CES function with the top-level allocating consumption and labor across time:

$$U = \left[\sum_{t=1}^{T} a_t^{1/\varepsilon_1} x_t^{(\varepsilon_1 - 1)/\varepsilon_1} \right]^{\varepsilon_1/(\varepsilon_1 - 1)}, \tag{5.1}$$

where T is length of life (known with certainty), x_t is the amount of the composite commodity consumed at time t, ε_1 is the intertemporal elasticity of substitution, and a_t is a weighting parameter that reflects the consumer's underlying rate of time preference. Economic life is 60 years, from ages 20 to 79. Lifetime utility is maximized subject to the lifetime budget constraint

$$\sum_{t=1}^{T} x_t \left(\frac{q_t}{(1+r)^{t-1}} \right) = I_d, \tag{5.2}$$

where q_t is the composite price of x_t, r is the net-of-tax rate of return, and I_d is the present value of lifetime discretionary income [70]. The composite price, q_t, is implicitly defined by Equation (5.2) and will turn out to be a weighted average of the prices of the components of x_t. A benefit of the nested-CES utility structure is that the demand functions can be solved sequentially beginning at the top nest of the utility function. Defining $\tilde{q}_t = q_t/(1+r)^{t-1}$, then the maximization of Equation (5.1) subject to Equation (5.2) yields standard CES demands in terms of prices $\tilde{q}_t$. In an important simplification, Fullerton and Rogers assume that these prices can be calculated from the current interest rate. These "myopic expectations" mean that each equilibrium period can be calculated before proceeding to the next period, sequentially, whereas perfect foresight would require endogenous calculation of all periods' prices and interest rates simultaneously.

Lifetime income includes bequests received. Rather than model endogenous bequest behavior, Fullerton and Rogers assume that each individual must bequeath the same level bequest at death as received at birth, after adjusting for economic and population growth. Bequests received (and left) as a fraction of income are calibrated to data from Menchik and David (1982).

At the next level of the nest, consumers choose between purchased consumption goods and leisure according to the sub-utility function:

$$x_t = \left[\alpha_t^{1/\varepsilon_2} \bar{c}_t^{(\varepsilon_2 - 1)/\varepsilon_2} + (1 - \alpha_t)^{1/\varepsilon_2} \ell_t^{(\varepsilon_2 - 1)/\varepsilon_2} \right]^{\varepsilon_2/(\varepsilon_2 - 1)}, \tag{5.3}$$

where $\bar{c}_t$ is a composite commodity consumed at time t, ℓ_t is leisure at time t, ε_2 is the elasticity of substitution between consumption and leisure, and α_t is a weighting

---

[70] They use a Stone–Geary sub-utility function with minimum required expenditures, so I_d is net of the cost of required expenditures. Only discretionary consumption (in excess of required consumption) is available for lifetime smoothing, so x is defined as discretionary consumption.

parameter. The time endowment is fixed at 4000 hours per year, and the wage rate per effective labor unit is constant, but wage rates can vary across individuals based on individual labor productivity. The individual chooses leisure and labor (L_t) based on maximization of the sub-utility function in Equation (5.3) subject to the budget constraint

$$\bar{p}_t \bar{c}_t + w_t \ell_t = q_t x_t, \tag{5.4}$$

This maximization yields demands for ℓ_t and $\bar{c}_t$. Then composite consumption is modeled as a Stone–Geary function of individual consumption goods (c_{it}):

$$\bar{c}_t = \prod_{i=1}^{N} (c_{it} - b_{it})^{\beta_{it}}. \tag{5.5}$$

The model includes 17 consumer goods ($N - 17$), minimum required consumption (b_{it}), and marginal share parameters (β_{it}). The Stone–Geary function is a parsimonious specification that allows consumption shares to vary across income, and across age groups, as is observed in the data. It also dampens consumption fluctuations, thereby making savings less sensitive to changes in the interest rate[71].

Using the Consumer Expenditure Survey, Fullerton and Rogers estimate 408 parameters: b_{it} and β_{it} for 17 goods for each of 12 different 5-year age brackets. Thus, taxes will affect income groups differentially on the sources side because of different relative factor incomes and on the uses side because of different observed spending shares. And yet the modelers need not assume that the rich are fundamentally different from the poor, in terms of preferences. Here, the fundamental difference between rich and poor is simply their income levels. All 12 groups in the model have the same utility function, with the same 408 parameters, but low-income groups spend much of their money on the minimum required purchases while other groups spend more in proportions given by the marginal expenditure shares.

Next, Fullerton and Rogers convert the vector of 17 consumer goods (C) to a vector of 19 producer goods (Q) using the Leontief transformation $C = ZQ$, where Z is a 17 by 19 transformation matrix. Finally, they distinguish corporate (Q^c) and non-corporate (Q^{nc}) output using another sub-utility function

$$Q_j = \left[\gamma_j^{1/\varepsilon_3} \left(Q_j^c \right)^{(\varepsilon_3 - 1)/\varepsilon_3} + \left(1 - \gamma_j \right)^{1/\varepsilon_j} \left(Q_j^{nc} \right)^{(\varepsilon_3 - 1)/\varepsilon_3} \right]^{\varepsilon_3/(\varepsilon_3 - 1)}, \tag{5.6}$$

where ε_3 is the elasticity of substitution, and γ_j is a weighting parameter for industry j. This function explains the co-existence of corporate and non-corporate production within a single industry, and it explains differences in production patterns across

---

[71] See Starrett (1988) for a discussion of the sensitivity of savings to changes in the interest rate in Stone–Geary and isoelastic utility functions.

industries. Maximization subject to the budget constraint ($p_j^c Q_j^c + p_j^{nc} Q_j^{nc} = p_j^Q Q_j$) yields demands for Q_j^c and Q_j^{nc} that depend on relative prices – which, in turn, depend on differential taxation of the corporate sector.

Whereas the corporate and non-corporate prices are observable, the various price indices are not. Fullerton and Rogers take the Lagrangian multiplier from this last maximization and invert it, to obtain

$$p_j^Q = \left(\gamma_j (p_j^c) + (1 - \gamma_j) (p_j^{nc})^{1-\varepsilon_3} \right)^{1/(1-\varepsilon_3)}. \tag{5.7}$$

Knowing these prices, they use the transition matrix Z to recover consumer prices ($p_i = \sum p_j^Q Z_{ji}$). Then, the reciprocal of the Lagrangian multiplier from the maximization of the Stone–Geary utility function is the price of the composite commodity:

$$\bar{p}_t = \prod_{i=1}^{N} \left(\frac{p_i}{\beta_{it}} \right)^{\beta_{it}}, \tag{5.8}$$

and finally,

$$q_t = \left(\alpha_t \bar{p}_t^{1-\varepsilon_2} + (1 - \alpha_t) w^{1-\varepsilon_2} \right)^{1/(1-\varepsilon_2)}. \tag{5.9}$$

With an explicit utility function, Fullerton and Rogers can measure the equivalent variation (EV) associated with any change in the tax system. They carry out differential tax incidence experiments where they replace a particular tax with a proportional tax on lifetime labor endowments. If U^0 is lifetime utility under the old tax regime, and U^1 is lifetime utility under the new tax regime, then

$$EV = (U^1 - U^0) P^0, \tag{5.10}$$

where P^0 is a price index on the lifetime bundle $\{x_t\}$ calculated at old prices.

Production in each of the 19 industries is based on a similar nested structure. At the top level, value added is combined with intermediate goods from other industries in a Leontief production function. Value added is a CES function of labor (L) and a capital aggregate ($\bar{K}$), where σ_1 is the elasticity of substitution. Aggregate capital is then a CES combination of five capital types, where σ_2 is the elasticity of substitution, to capture differential tax treatment of equipment, structures, land, inventories and intangibles.

Note that production is constant returns to scale, so firms earn zero profits in a competitive environment. This is a common assumption in many CGE models used to measure tax incidence. Firms solve a simple one-period optimization problem, in contrast to consumers who solve an intertemporal maximization problem. Dynamics are not ignored, however, in that interest rates affect capital accumulation.

The government engages in three activities in this model. First, it makes transfer payments that vary according to age and income. Second, it produces goods and services sold in the market place. In this regard, the government is simply one more producer using capital, labor and intermediate goods for production. Third, government buys goods and services for a public good that enters utility in a separable fashion.

The treatment of taxes in the Fullerton and Rogers model is similar to that of Ballard, Fullerton, Shoven and Whalley (1985). Personal income taxes are specified as a linear function of consumer income, with a constant slope and an intercept that varies across lifetime income categories and age. The slope measures the marginal tax rate, while the intercept captures various deductions and exemptions that vary across consumers. Payroll taxes are treated as *ad valorem* taxes on the use of labor services by industry [72]. Retail sales taxes are treated as *ad valorem* taxes on consumer goods, while excise taxes are *ad valorem* taxes on producer goods. Business tax provisions are incorporated using the cost-of-capital approach of Hall and Jorgenson (1967). This includes corporate taxes at both the federal and state level, property taxes, investment incentives, and depreciation deductions. These tax provisions affect the demand for capital by firms, which affects the interest rate used both in the consumer's problem and in the firm's cost of capital.

Finally, Fullerton and Rogers group households into lifetime income categories through a two-step procedure. Using data from the PSID, they estimate lifetime profiles for wages, taxes and transfers. They estimate wage rate rather than wage income regressions, since labor supply is endogenous in their model. These wage rates vary on the basis of age, education, race and sex. Using the estimated coefficients, they forecast and backcast wages of each individual to create a lifetime wage profile. An initial measure of lifetime income (LI) is then given by the equation

$$\mathrm{LI} = \sum_{t=1}^{60} \frac{4000 \cdot w_t}{(1+r)^{t-1}}, \tag{5.11}$$

where r is a discount rate, and w_t is the actual wage for any year in the sample, or an estimated wage for any other year [73]. In the second step of the procedure, individuals are sorted into 12 groups on the basis of this initial measure of lifetime income [74]. For each group, the log of the wage rate is again regressed on age, age squared, and age cubed. This 2-step procedure allows wage profiles to differ across income groups. Differences in the wage profiles will create differences in savings patterns

---

[72] No distinction is drawn between the employer and employee share of the payroll tax, under the assumption that statutory incidence does not affect the economic incidence.

[73] The lifetime income measure is adjusted for taxes and transfers. For couples, each individual is given the average income for the two spouses.

[74] They first divide the sample into ten deciles. They then subdivide the top decile into the top 2% and next 8%, and the bottom decile into the bottom 2% and next 8%.

Fig. 5.4. Wage profiles.

across groups, which will play an important role in determining the incidence of capital income taxation.

Figure 5.4 shows estimated wage profiles for different lifetime income groups. Both the curvature of the wage profiles and the location of the peak varies across groups. More sharply curved wage profiles mean individuals must engage in more saving to smooth consumption. An earlier peak also means more savings – for consumption in later years.

Table 5.1 shows the burden of all U.S. taxes in 1984, as measured by the lifetime EV benefit as a percentage of lifetime income of a switch from the existing tax system to a proportional lump-sum labor-endowment tax. Except for the first group (the bottom 2% of the distribution), every income group gains. These benefits are roughly flat from the second through tenth income groups and then rise sharply in the highest two income groups (top ten percent of the population). This pattern of proportionality across the middle of the income distribution with progressivity at the top end matches the findings of Pechman and Okner (1974) and Pechman (1985) in their annual income incidence analyses. Fullerton and Rogers's results differ from Pechman's at the bottom of the income distribution. The former find progressivity at the lowest end, while the latter finds regressivity.

The table shows distributional results in the new steady state. The sum of the 12 groups' gains from shifting to the lump-sum tax is large, measuring 3.5% of their aggregate lifetime income. This large gain comes about, in part, through a substantial tax on endowments of older generations during the transition. In present value terms, the gains are less than half, reflecting the fact that losses accrue to living generations while gains primarily accrue to future generations.

While the degree of progressivity in the U.S. tax system appears similar in either annual or a lifetime incidence analyses, important differences remain for particular

Table 5.1
Lifetime incidence of US tax system in 1984[a]

Lifetime income category	EV as a percentage of lifetime income
1	−0.06
2	3.13
3	1.41
4	2.37
5	3.58
6	1.39
7	3.46
8	2.51
9	2.95
10	3.01
11	5.55
12	11.10
All, in steady state	3.52
PV(EV)/LI	1.29

[a] Source: Fullerton and Rogers (1993, Table 7-15).

taxes. Perhaps the most important difference is that Pechman finds that corporate taxes are progressive because of the sources side of income. Since high-income people disproportionately earn capital income, they are most impacted by a capital income tax. In contrast, Fullerton and Rogers find that the corporate tax does not appreciably affect factor prices (because the statutory corporate rate is largely offset in 1984 by the investment tax credit and accelerated depreciation allowances). Instead, the corporate tax affects relative output prices (because some industries have larger corporate sectors and get more credits and allowances). Thus, it primarily affects individuals on the uses side of income. For the lower part of the distribution, the tax is regressive because the poor tend to spend greater fractions of incomes on goods produced in the corporate sector. At the top end of the distribution, the tax is progressive because of the nature of the replacement tax. The proportional tax on labor endowments does not tax inheritances, and the rich receive larger inheritances, so they benefit from the tax on labor endowment.

Another important finding of the model is that sales and excise taxes continue to be regressive when measured on a lifetime basis – whereas previous work by Poterba (1989) and others hypothesized that consumption taxes would look roughly proportional on a lifetime basis. Fullerton and Rogers note two reasons. First, the utility structure that they employ does not specify a minimum required leisure expenditure. The lifetime poor must spend a greater share of their income on required goods, so

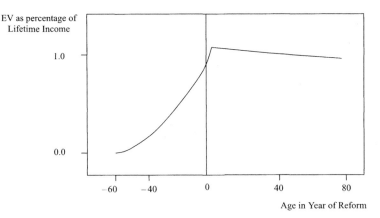

Fig. 5.5. Intergenerational transfers.

they pay more sales tax as a fraction of lifetime income. Thus, some regressivity is built into the model structure. Second, goods with high tax rates tend to be goods with high estimated minimum required purchases (alcohol, tobacco, and gasoline).

Another advantage of lifetime models is the ability to capture intergenerational transfers. Consider sales and excise taxes, for example. Figure 5.5 groups individuals by age of birth, rather than by lifetime income, and it shows the equivalent variation as a percent of lifetime income (for the replacement of sales and excise taxes by a proportional tax on labor endowment). The EV as a fraction of income for the entire population is 0.44%. The figure shows how the EV varies across cohorts. For those born after the tax reform goes into effect (individuals to the right of the vertical line in the middle of the graph), EV is roughly 1% of lifetime income. For those born prior to the reform, EV is substantially lower and approaches zero for the oldest groups. This picture tells a complicated incidence story. Older generations get less of a benefit from the tax shift because the replacement tax is a tax on their time endowment – which translates, for the elderly, into a tax on their leisure time.

Lifetime incidence models can be constructed to focus on both intergenerational and intragenerational redistribution. The Fullerton and Rogers model focuses on both types of redistributions, but assumes myopic expectations about future prices as well as ad hoc bequest behavior. Auerbach and Kotlikoff (1987) construct a dynamic model with a perfect foresight equilibrium[75], but they have a representative agent in each cohort and thus focus only on intergenerational redistribution arising from fiscal policy[76]. Altig, Auerbach, Kotlikoff, Smetters and Walliser (2001) build

---

[75] An early published version of the model was in Auerbach, Kotlikoff and Skinner (1983). For a brief history of the model's development, see Kotlikoff (2000).

[76] The Auerbach–Kotlikoff model also has only one type of good and makes no distinction between corporate and non-corporate production, thus limiting its ability to provide meaningful incidence results for the existing tax system.

on the Auerbach–Kotlikoff model, but follow Fullerton and Rogers in adding intragenerational heterogeneity. They use the new model to measure the utility gains and losses from different types of fundamental tax reforms. But because their replacement tax is different from the one in Fullerton and Rogers, results from the two models cannot easily be compared.

5.2. Generational accounts

As noted earlier, a complete picture of the incidence of government fiscal policy would take into account transfers as well as taxes [Browning (1985, 1993)]. Auerbach, Gokhale and Kotlikoff (1991) develop "generational accounts" to measure the fiscal impact of government taxes and transfers over each cohort's lifetime. A generational account is simply a measure of a cohort's net tax payments (taxes less transfers) from today until all members of the cohort die. For a cohort born in year k, its account in year t is defined as

$$N_{t,k} = \sum_{s=\upsilon}^{k+D} \frac{T_{s,k} P_{s,k}}{(1+r)^{(s-\upsilon)}}, \tag{5.12}$$

where $T_{s,k}$ is the net tax for cohort k in year s, $P_{s,k}$ is the population weight for cohort k in year s (accounting for mortality and immigration), r is the discount rate, $\upsilon = \max(t, k)$, and D is maximum length of life. For generations already born ($k < t$), the account $N_{t,k}$ is the present value of all future net tax payments discounted back to year t. For future generations ($k > t$), $N_{t,k}$ discounts net tax payments back to year k. For generations alive at time t, net tax payments into the future are based on current law and government projections of changes in tax and transfer programs. For years beyond government projections, taxes and transfers are assumed to grow at the growth rate assumed for the whole economy, thereby keeping net tax payments fixed relative to income. To assess net tax payments for future cohorts, we begin with the government intergenerational budget constraint:

$$\sum_{k=t-D}^{t} N_{t,k} + \frac{\sum_{k=t+1}^{\infty} N_{t,k}}{(1+r)^{k-t}} = \sum_{s=t}^{\infty} \frac{G_s}{(1+r)^{s-t}} - W_t^g. \tag{5.13}$$

Equation (5.13) states that the government budget constraint must be balanced over time. Future net tax payments (left-hand side of Equation 5.13) must equal the present value of future government consumption (G_s) less net government wealth in year t (W_t^g). The first term on the left-hand side is the stream of remaining net tax to be paid by cohorts alive at year t. The second term is the net tax paid by future cohorts. Assuming some path for future government purchases, as well as knowledge of the current net wealth stock, the right-hand side of Equation (5.13) is fixed. The first term on the left-hand side is also known, leaving the second term as a residual. Finally,

Table 5.2
Net tax payments (present value in thousands of $ 1995)[a]

Generation's age in 1995	Male	Female
0	77.4	51.9
20	182.2	115.0
40	171.2	99.0
60	−25.5	−52.0
80	−77.2	−90.2
Future generations	134.6	90.2

[a] Source: Gokhale, Page and Sturrock (1999, Tables 21.1, 21.2).

for these residual net tax payments to be divided across different future cohorts, it is assumed that average per capita tax payments grow at the same rate as productivity growth. Thus, for future generations, net tax liability relative to lifetime income is constant[77]. Table 5.2 gives an example of the calculation of net tax payments, from Gokhale, Page and Sturrock (1999).

Ignoring the newborn for the moment, net tax payments are highest for the young and decline with age. This reflects the fact that the current elderly will pay little in taxes relative to the benefits they receive in future years. Of course, the elderly in 1995 had paid taxes prior to 1995, but the table does not take account of those past taxes. Following Equation (5.12), it focuses only on future net tax liabilities. Women have lower net tax liabilities, reflecting both their smaller tax payments and higher benefit receipts (largely due to social security and mortality differences between men and women). The newborn have a lower net tax liability since their taxes and transfers, for the most part, will not begin for some time into the future and so in present value terms are smaller[78]. For future generations, we see the current fiscal imbalance: taxes will have to be raised on future generations in order to bring the government's budget into balance.

Net tax payments in the tables above cannot be compared for any cohorts other than newborns and future generations, since net tax payments are only computed over a portion of the lives of generations currently alive in 1995. To compare all cohorts both living and not yet born, net tax liabilities can be computed for each cohort over their entire lifetime and discounted back to time zero for each cohort. Similarly, lifetime income can be calculated and discounted back to time zero. Then an average tax liability can be calculated as the ratio of lifetime taxes to lifetime income[79]. Table 5.3

---

[77] Other assumptions can be made, depending on the experiment under consideration.

[78] Gokhale, Page and Sturrock (1999) use a discount rate of 6%. Adjusting for the fact that newborns enter the work force roughly 20 years in the future, the corresponding net tax payment would be 248.2, which is 36% higher than that of people born in 1975.

[79] This calculation is similar to the methodology of Fullerton and Rogers.

Table 5.3
Lifetime net tax rates [a]

Year of birth	Net tax rate	Gross tax rate	Gross transfer rate
1900	23.9	28.0	4.0
1920	29.6	36.4	6.7
1940	32.5	40.3	7.8
1960	33.3	44.1	10.8
1980	30.8	43.0	12.2
1995	28.6	41.7	13.1
Future generations	49.2	–	–

[a] Source: Gokhale, Page and Sturrock (1999, Table 21.3).

shows lifetime net tax rates for living and future generations, from Gokhale, Page and Sturrock (1999).

For generations born from 1900 to 1960, the increase in net tax rates reflects the growth of government over the first half of the century (see gross tax rates in the middle column). The decline in net tax rates since 1960 reflects longer life expectancies and the rapid increase in medical transfers (see transfers in the last column). The bottom row indicates that the current policy cannot persist. Net tax rates will have to increase from 28.6% (for people born in 1995) to 49.2%, an increase of 72%.

The calculation of these generational accounts is in the spirit of the Pechman and Okner analysis rather than the CGE models of Fullerton and Rogers or Auerbach and Kotlikoff. It takes fiscal policy as given, and it allows neither for behavioral responses nor for changes in factor prices in response to government policies. Fehr and Kotlikoff (1999) compare net tax burdens using both generational accounting and the Auerbach–Kotlikoff CGE model described above. They find that the generational accounts methodology works well for closed economies and for economies with minimal capital adjustment costs.

Generational accounting has been used to look at Social Security and Medicare policy [Auerbach, Gokhale and Kotlikoff (1992)] as well as to compare tax and transfer systems in various countries around the world [Auerbach, Kotlikoff and Leibfritz (1999)].

6. Policy analysis

Applied incidence analysis plays an important role in tax policy making, as the results of government studies help determine the course of actual reform. Most such studies use recent incidence theory, as described above, to allocate the burden of each tax among income groups using much data about the sources and uses of income in each group [as in Pechman and Okner (1974) or Gale, Houser and Scholz (1996)]. This

Table 6.1
Distributional effects of repeal of federal communications excise tax: calendar year 2003 [a]

Income category	Change in federal taxes		Effective tax rate	
	Millions ($)	Percent	Present law	Proposal
Less than $10000	−324	−4.3	9.3%	8.9%
10000 to 20000	−621	−2.3	7.4%	7.2%
20000 to 30000	−608	−0.9	12.4%	12.3%
30000 to 40000	−572	−0.6	16.0%	16.0%
40000 to 50000	−490	0.4	17.4%	17.3%
50000 to 75000	−920	−0.3	19.9%	19.9%
75000 to 100000	−531	−0.2	22.4%	22.3%
100000 to 200000	−421	−0.1	25.1%	25.1%
200000 and over	−371	−0.1	28.6%	28.6%
Total: all taxpayers	−4858	−0.3	21.5%	21.5%

[a] Source: U.S. Joint Committee on Taxation (2000).

approach forms the foundation for analyses undertaken by the U.S. Congressional Budget Office (CBO), the Office of Tax Analysis (OTA) of the U.S. Department of the Treasury, and the U.K. Office for National Statistics [80]. We focus here primarily on the incidence analysis by the staff of the Joint Committee on Taxation (JCT) of the U.S. Congress [81].

6.1. The distributional table

A key tool used by policy makers in their consideration of changes to the tax system is the distributional table. Table 6.1 presents a distributional table for the repeal of the federal communications excise tax for the calendar year 2003. The first column indicates the income categories over which the tax is distributed. This column has a number of features. First, the unit of observation is the tax-filing unit, so a data point in any of the income categories may be a single taxpayer or a couple filing jointly. Thus, if a married couple each earn $17000 and file separately, they show up

---

[80] See Bradford (1995) for a discussion and critique of this type of analysis in the United States. For the United Kingdom, Lakin (2001, p. 35) reports figures that are very similar in nature to those for the USA: "The proportion of gross income paid in direct tax by the top fifth of households is almost double that paid by those in the bottom fifth: 24% compared with 13%. Indirect taxes have the opposite effect to direct taxes taking a higher proportion of income from those with lower incomes". We cannot know whether the similarity of results is because of similar methodology or because of similar policies.

[81] See U.S. Joint Committee on Taxation (1993). Cronin (1999) describes the OTA methodology, while Kasten, Sammartino and Toder (1994) describe work at CBO.

in this table as two data points in the second row of the table. If they file jointly, however, they appear in the fourth row[82]. Second, the annual time frame is used for measuring income. Third, the JCT uses a measure of income called "expanded income". This measure is defined as adjusted gross income (AGI) plus tax-exempt interest, employer contributions for health plans and life insurance, the employer share of payroll taxes, worker's compensation, nontaxable Social Security benefits, the insurance value of Medicare benefits, alternative minimum tax preference items, and excluded income of U.S. citizens living abroad. This measure is an effort to conform more closely to a Haig–Simons definition of income[83]. It is by no means a close proxy for economic income, however, nor is it a close proxy for lifetime income. One advantage of expanded income is its explicit recognition that factor income by itself is inadequate for measuring income, and another advantage is its easy calculation from readily-available data, primarily tax returns. These features help make the measure more readily understandable to policy makers, many of whom have limited economics education[84]. Fourth, the number of tax filing units differs across the income categories. In 1995, for example, the number of tax returns filed in the $10 000 to $20 000 AGI category was roughly 20 times the number in the over-$200 000 AGI category[85]. Fifth, taxpayers are grouped into income categories on the basis of year 2000 income, the first year of analysis in this report. Any changes in income due to either transitory fluctuations or trends do not shift taxpayers across brackets.

The second column of Table 6.1 shows the aggregate change in federal taxes for each income category, while the third column shows the change as a percentage of expanded income. The essential point to understand about this measure is that it is an estimate of the change in tax payments, not the change in tax burden. Figure 6.1 illustrates the distinction for a simple case where supply is perfectly elastic. Consider an existing tax that shifts the supply curve from S_0 to S_1, and an increase that shifts the supply curve from S_1 to S_2. The tax increase will raise revenue by an amount equal to A–F, but the increased tax burden is area A + B. These are quite different sizes, and they may even differ in sign. Depending on the price elasticity of demand, the higher tax rate may increase or decrease tax revenue (area A may be less than area F). However, the increased tax burden given by the area A + B is unambiguously positive[86]. Thus, the use of tax revenue as a proxy for burden can lead to the incorrect

---

[82] OTA uses the family as the unit of observation, combining tax returns of all members of the family.

[83] OTA uses a measure called Family Economic Income (FEI) that is more comprehensive and therefore closer in spirit to Haig–Simons income. In addition to data from tax returns, FEI requires imputations of certain income sources. See Cronin (1999) for details.

[84] The need for a simple income measure may help explain why imputed rental income for owner-occupied housing is excluded.

[85] U.S. Bureau of the Census (1999, Table 559). Note that these AGI categories do not correspond exactly to the expanded income categories in Table 6.1.

[86] Here we ignore distinctions between the change in consumer surplus and equivalent or compensating variation.

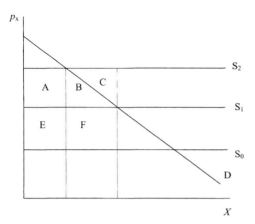

Fig. 6.1. Measuring tax burden for policy analysis.

conclusion that a higher tax rate could reduce tax burden. As discussed below, the Joint Committee on Taxation reported distribution tables based on tax burdens rather than tax revenues for a brief while. OTA reports burden estimates, but only reports area A as the increased burden, ignoring the deadweight loss (area B)[87].

Finally, for each income category, the table reports effective tax rates (the ratio of tax payments to expanded income) under current law and under the proposed policy change. The proposal portrayed in Table 6.1 would be characterized as progressive, since average tax rates fall the most for lower income groups.

This approach is subject to a number of criticisms[88]. In addition to the issues highlighted above, another problem is the failure to take account of asset price changes and implicit taxation. In Section 4.3 above, we made the point that tax capitalization complicates the task of identifying who bears the burden of a tax. Subsequent owners are observed to pay a tax, in distributional tables, but they may not bear any burden if they bought the asset for a reduced amount. Distributional analyses also ignore implicit taxation, which occurs when a tax-favored asset pays a lower rate of return than a comparable non-favored asset. Consider, for example, state and local municipal debt that is exempt from federal tax[89]. If the taxable rate is 8% and the tax-exempt rate is 6%, then the implicit tax on municipal debt is 25%. Distributional tables ignore this implicit tax, despite its equivalence to an explicit 25% tax that is used to pay those who now benefit from the reduced rate on municipal debt[90].

---

[87] See Cronin (1999) for a discussion of other issues associated with measuring burden.

[88] See, for example, Graetz (1995) and Browning (1995).

[89] State and local debt is often exempt from state taxation also.

[90] Gordon and Slemrod (1983) find that the rich benefit from tax-exempt municipal debt through lowered taxes payments, while the poor benefit from increased expenditures made possible by the lower borrowing rate paid by communities.

6.2. Suggested changes

In 1993, the Joint Committee on Taxation made significant changes in their methodology for distributing the burden of taxes, as described in U.S. Joint Committee on Taxation (1993) as well as Barthold and Jack (1995)[91]. Despite the fact that many of the changes were short-lived, they are worth discussing because they illustrate a creative effort to apply economic theory to the policy process. In making the changes, the JCT attempted to adhere to three broad principles: 1) to make calculations on the basis of the economic incidence rather than the statutory burden of a tax, 2) to be consistent in the treatment of taxes expected to have the same economic incidence (regardless of the statutory incidence), and 3) to use a methodology that allows comparisons of unrelated tax proposals.

In addition to the choice of the "expanded income" measure described above, the JCT made two other significant conceptual changes. First, they measured burden from tax changes rather than just distributing tax payments across groups. Above, we noted that using changes in tax revenue as a proxy for changes in burden can lead to the anomalous result that a tax increase is beneficial to the taxpayer (ignoring the use of proceeds from the tax). Like OTA, the JCT did not propose to measure the change in consumer surplus, but rather to use a proxy that could easily be estimated from existing data. Unlike OTA, however, the JCT measured burden by the change in tax revenue that would occur if behavior were fixed. Thus, in Figure 6.1, the JCT's measure of the burden from a tax increase would be the area $A + B + C$.

Second, the JCT chose to measure the burden of a tax proposal over a five-year window[92]. Prior to that time, the JCT measured burdens within a single year. The second principle noted above was violated in cases where some or all of the burden of a tax fell outside of the one-year window. Shifting to a five-year window does not solve this problem but reduces its impact since less of a tax is likely to fall outside a five-year window (and because the present value of tax changes five years out is lower than the present value one year out). The JCT chose not to go to an infinite window for a number of reasons. Results are sensitive to the choice of discount rate in an infinite-horizon model, and economic forecasting of key variables required for revenue estimation become increasingly unreliable for years further into the future. Furthermore, it is simply not credible to assume that tax policy will remain unchanged into the distant future. Thus, a shorter time horizon was chosen.

The JCT then reports an annuitized measure that accounts for economic growth. To illustrate the idea, we take an example from U.S. Joint Committee on Taxation (1993). Assume a discount rate of 10%, and economic growth of 5%, and consider three proposals. First, consider a permanent tax reduction of $100 per year beginning immediately. The JCT assumes that the value of the tax reduction will grow at the

---

[91] Also, see Barthold, Nunns and Toder (1995) for a comparison of the new JCT methodology and the OTA and CBO methodologies.

[92] The five-year window is similar to the "time-exposure" measure of Slemrod (1992).

Table 6.2
Annuitization of taxes in Joint Committee on Taxation (JCT) methodology

Proposal	Year					Total
	1	2	3	4	5	
Immediate permanent tax reduction of $100/year	100	105	110	116	122	553
Immediate temporary tax reduction of $100	22	23	24	25	26	120
Postponed permanent tax reduction of $100/year	18	19	20	21	22	100

overall rate of economic growth and so will be worth $105 next year and $110, $116, and $122 in subsequent years. The JCT calculates an annuity equivalent for year one that is also assumed to grow at the overall rate of economic growth. In this case, the annuity equivalent is $100 for year one (followed by 105, 110, 116, and 122). Second, consider an immediate tax cut of $100 that lasts only one year, with a present value of simply $100. The five-year annuity equivalent would be $22 in year one (an amount that could grow at five percent per year over the five-year window and be discounted at 10% to yield a present value of $100). For a final example, take a permanent $100 per year tax cut that is postponed for four years, so that the first year of benefits occurs in the last year of the five-year window. The value in the last year is $122, which in present value terms equals $83. The annuity equivalent would be $18 in the first year. Table 6.2 shows the tax reductions that the JCT would report in a five-year window.

The third proposal (with a permanent $100/year tax cut) looks very much like the second proposal (with a $100 tax cut in only one year), because only the first year of the delayed permanent tax cut is counted. A one-time tax reduction in year five would give the same annuity equivalent as is recorded in this third row of Table 6.2. Comparing rows 2 and 3, it is clear that an immediate tax reduction of $100 is worth more than a postponed reduction of $122, a result that follows because the 10% discount rate exceeds the 5% growth rate.

Two other issues described in the 1993 JCT publication relate to the treatment of a broad-based consumption tax such as a national retail sales tax. The first issue is whether the general price level rises (to accommodate forward shifting of the tax) or remains unchanged (in which case taxes are shifted backward in the form of lower factor incomes). Real factor prices are the same in either case, and the status of the general price level would appear to have no impact on the measured distribution of the tax burden, but government transfer programs complicate the analysis [Browning and Johnson (1979)]. Some transfers to the poor are stated in nominal dollars, so a consumption tax shifted forward into higher prices will reduce the real purchasing power of these transfers. If the consumption tax is shifted backwards into lower factor prices, however, recipients of these government transfers are not affected[93]. Whether the general price level rises or not depends importantly on monetary policy and cannot be predicted beforehand. But the price level response may have an important impact on the outcome of the analysis, especially as it relates to households with the lowest incomes[94].

The second issue about the consumption tax is when to allocate the tax. We can allocate a consumption tax when consumption occurs, or when the income that finances that consumption is earned. The advantage of the latter approach is that the analysis then conforms to the third principle above, namely, to use techniques that allow analysts to combine proposals. In particular, the JCT says that it facilitates the comparison of consumption taxes to income taxes (the predominant type of tax analyzed by the JCT).

The distinction between allocating consumption taxes when consumption occurs or when the income is earned is only relevant with any saving or dissaving. This, in fact, is the main reason for using lifetime measures of income for consumption tax analysis, as discussed above. Since life-cycle changes in net wealth can be quite large, over periods of more than five years, the JCT measure of the burden of a consumption tax can still be quite different from the burden measured in a lifetime analysis.

Rather than allocating the consumption tax, the JCT converts a broad-based consumption tax into a combined tax on wage income and old capital. To see the equivalence, consider the budget constraint of an individual with k years remaining in life at the time a consumption tax is imposed:

$$W_0 + \sum_{t=0}^{k} \frac{w_t L_t}{(1+r)^t} = \sum_{t=0}^{k} \frac{(1+\tau) C_t}{(1+r)^t}, \tag{6.1}$$

where W_0 is the person's net wealth at time 0, $w_t L_t$ is wage income in year t, C_t is consumption, τ is the consumption tax rate, and r is the rate of return available to the individual. The JCT approach works by defining a tax at rate $\tilde{\tau}$ on old capital (W_0) and wage income such that $1 - \tilde{\tau} = 1/(1+\tau)$. Then Equation (6.1) becomes

$$(1-\tilde{\tau}) W_0 + \sum_{t=0}^{k} \frac{(1-\tilde{\tau}) w_t L_t}{(1+r)^t} = \sum_{t=0}^{k} \frac{C_t}{(1+r)^t}. \tag{6.2}$$

From the individual's point of view, the consumption tax is equivalent to a tax on wage income plus a capital levy[95].

---

[93] They would be affected if policy makers reduced transfers in nominal terms, which seems unlikely.

[94] Many transfers in the USA are indexed, including social security, food stamps, and in-kind health care, but other non-indexed transfers are received by the lowest income bracket, as discussed below. Also, the price-level problem and the response of the Federal Reserve to the imposition of a tax is not, in principle, limited to general consumption taxes. Consider an income tax that is assumed to be shifted backwards to labor and capital. The Federal Reserve could increase the monetary supply and allow nominal prices to rise, to keep nominal factor prices from changing (even though real factor prices still fall).

[95] The lump-sum component of a consumption tax with no transition rules is a major source of efficiency gain from a consumption tax relative to a wage tax. See Auerbach and Kotlikoff (1987) for more on

Table 6.3
Distributional impact of a 5% comprehensive consumption tax (as a percentage of pre-tax income)

Income class	(p, C)	(p, Y)	(w, Y)	(w, C)
$0–$10 000	3.70	3.69	2.84	2.85
10 000–20 000	2.66	2.68	2.86	2.83
20 000–30 000	2.90	3.00	3.10	2.99
30 000–40 000	2.92	3.04	3.20	3.07
40 000–50 000	2.94	3.10	3.26	3.10
50 000–75 000	2.77	2.97	3.21	2.99
75 000–100 000	2.63	2.88	3.01	2.74
100 000–200 000	2.50	2.84	2.92	2.57
200 000 and over	1.76	2.78	2.86	1.76

[a] Source: U.S. Joint Committee on Taxation (1993, Table 3, p. 55).

These two issues give rise to four possible ways of distributing a consumption tax. Following the JCT's notation, we can distinguish:

(p, C) prices allowed to rise and burden assigned as consumption occurs;

(p, Y) prices allowed to rise and burden assigned as income occurs;

(w, C) factor prices fall and burden assigned as consumption occurs;

(w, Y) factor prices fall and burden assigned as income occurs.

Our Table 6.3, taken from JCT (1993), shows the impact of the four different approaches on the distribution of a comprehensive 5% tax on consumption.

As noted above, whether prices are allowed to rise primarily affects the burden of the tax at the very low end of the income distribution (because some transfers are not indexed). On the other hand, the timing of the tax burden affects the very top of the income distribution (because they undertake most savings). The measured burden of a consumption tax in the highest-income group is roughly one percent of pre-tax income higher when allocated on the basis of income rather than consumption[96].

The first column of Table 6.3 (labeled (p, C)) is the traditional method for distributing consumption taxes, and it makes consumption taxes look sharply regressive. If the (w, Y) method were used to distribute consumption taxes, they would look nearly proportional. Instead, the JCT favors the (p, Y) approach, on the basis of some empirical evidence that the introduction of value added taxes in Europe led to at-least-

this point. As an aside, individuals who have negative net wealth at the time of the imposition of a consumption tax receive a lump-sum subsidy equal to $\tilde{\tau}W_0$. Thus, the consumption tax redistributes from lenders to those in debt (relative to a tax just on wages).

[96] A dollar of saving receives relief from a full dollar of a consumption tax when the tax is allocated as consumption occurs, but it only receives relief equal in value to the annuity that a dollar buys when the consumption tax is allocated as income is earned.

partial forward shifting into higher consumer prices, combined with the JCT's wish to adhere to their third principle of tax comparability.

The JCT used the approach outlined in U.S. Joint Committee on Taxation (1993) for a brief while, but it then reverted to an approach that distributes tax payments rather than burdens, on a year-by-year basis instead of using five-year windows. In particular, the analysis in Table 6.1 accords with current JCT policy.

Both U.S. Joint Committee on Taxation (1993) and Cronin (1999) illustrate creative efforts to bridge the gap between economic theory and real-world policy analysis. In addition to theoretical rigor, policy analysts need measures that are easily constructed from readily-available data and easily understood both by the public and by policy makers. The retreat at the JCT from the innovations described in U.S. Joint Committee on Taxation (1993) is perhaps discouraging, particularly in light of the tentative nature of the steps towards a more-comprehensive lifetime measure of economic burden arising from changes in tax policy. But it should be recognized that much of the policy process occurs in an informal give-and-take between policy makers and staff economists; it may be in this latter environment that incidence theory can be most effective[97].

7. Conclusion

The field of incidence analysis has progressed dramatically in the past twenty years, as new research has yielded fresh insights into the burden of taxes in imperfectly competitive models and in intertemporal models. The increase in computing power and the availability of large-scale data sets have also enriched our understanding of tax incidence. Moreover, the power of recent analytical models and of new data sets is evident in recent attempts by government economists to bring state-of-the-art incidence analysis to policymakers.

Yet, the basic tools of log-linearization in simple two-sector models are just as useful today as they were in Harberger's classic 1962 paper. These techniques are still frequently used in studies of new taxes, externalities, imperfect competition, and other non-tax distortions. Such analytical models can yield important insights that do not follow directly from complicated computable general equilibrium models. In fact, many researchers now combine both approaches within a single paper, as they find it useful to push the analytical results as far as is possible, for intuition, before turning to numerical methods to determine likely magnitudes. Using all of these techniques, the topic of tax incidence will continue to be an area of productive research yielding further insights in the years to come.

---

[97] But see Graetz (1995) for a more pessimistic viewpoint.

References

Aaron, H.J. (1974), "A new view of property tax incidence", American Economic Review 64:212–221.

Aaron, H.J. (1989), "Politics and the professors revisited", American Economic Review 79:1–15.

Altig, D., A.J. Auerbach, L.J. Kotlikoff, K. Smetters and J. Walliser (2001), "Simulating fundamental tax reform in the United States", American Economic Review 91:574–595.

Anderson, K.B. (1990), A Review of Structure-Performance Studies in Grocery Retailing (Bureau of Economics, Federal Trade Commission, Washington, DC).

Anderson, S.P., A. de Palma and B. Kreider (2001), "Tax incidence in differentiated product oligopoly", Journal of Public Economics 81:173–192.

Atkinson, A.B., and J.E. Stiglitz (1980), Lectures on Public Economics (McGraw-Hill, New York).

Auerbach, A.J., and J.R. Hines Jr (2002), "Taxation and economic efficiency", in: A.J. Auerbach and M. Feldstein, eds., Handbook of Public Economics, Vol. 3 (Elsevier, Amsterdam) pp. 1347–1421.

Auerbach, A.J., and L.J. Kotlikoff (1987), Dynamic Fiscal Policy (Cambridge University Press, Cambridge).

Auerbach, A.J., L.J. Kotlikoff and J. Skinner (1983), "The efficiency gains from dynamic tax reform", International Economic Review 24:81–100.

Auerbach, A.J., J. Gokhale and L.J. Kotlikoff (1991), "Generational accounts: a meaningful alternative to deficit accounting", Tax Policy and the Economy 5:55–110.

Auerbach, A.J., J. Gokhale and L.J. Kotlikoff (1992), "Social security and Medicare policy from the perspective of generational accounting", Tax Policy and the Economy 6:129–145.

Auerbach, A.J., L.J. Kotlikoff and W. Leibfritz, eds (1999), Generational Accounting Around the World (University of Chicago Press, Chicago, London).

Ballard, C.L., D. Fullerton, J.B. Shoven and J. Whalley (1985), A General Equilibrium Model for Tax Policy Analysis (University of Chicago Press, Chicago).

Barro, R.J. (1974), "Are government bonds net wealth?", Journal of Political Economy 82:1095–1117.

Barthold, T.A., and W. Jack (1995), "Innovations in the JCT distribution methodology", in: D.F. Bradford, ed., Distributional Analysis of Tax Policy (AEI Press, Washington, DC) pp. 148–163.

Barthold, T.A., J.R. Nunns and E. Toder (1995), "A comparison of distribution methodologies", in: D.F. Bradford, ed., Distributional Analysis of Tax Policy (AEI Press, Washington, DC) pp. 96–110.

Bernheim, B.D. (1981), "A note on dynamic tax incidence", Quarterly Journal of Economics 96: 705–723.

Besley, T.J. (1989), "Commodity taxation and imperfect competition: a note on the effects of entry", Journal of Public Economics 40:359–367.

Besley, T.J., and H.S. Rosen (1999), "Sales taxes and prices: an empirical analysis", National Tax Journal 52:157–178.

Bishop, R.L. (1968), "The effects of specific and ad valorem taxes", Quarterly Journal of Economics 82:198–218.

Boadway, R. (1979), "Long-run tax incidence: a comparative dynamic approach", Review of Economic Studies 46:505–511.

Bradford, D.F. (1978), "Factor prices may be constant but factor returns are not", Economics Letters 1:199–203.

Bradford, D.F., ed. (1995), Distributional Analysis of Tax Policy (American Enterprise Institute Press, Washington, DC).

Break, G.F. (1974), "The incidence and economic effects of taxation", in: A.S. Blinder, R.M. Solow, G.F. Break, P.O. Steiner and D. Netzer, eds., The Economics of Public Finance (Brookings Institution, Washington, DC).

Brittain, J.A. (1971), "The incidence of social security payroll taxes", American Economic Review 61:110–125.

Brown, H.G. (1924), The Economics of Taxation (Holt, New York).

Browning, E.K. (1985), "Tax incidence, indirect taxes, and transfers", National Tax Journal 38:525–533.

Browning, E.K. (1986), "Pechman's tax incidence study: a note on the data", American Economic Review 76:1214–1218.

Browning, E.K. (1993), "Transfers and tax incidence theory", Public Finance 48:138–141.

Browning, E.K. (1995), "Tax incidence analysis for policy makers", in: D.F. Bradford, ed., Distributional Analysis of Tax Policy (AEI Press, Washington, DC) pp. 164–180.

Browning, E.K., and W.R. Johnson (1979), The Distribution of the Tax Burden (American Enterprise Institute, Washington, DC).

Bull, N., K.A. Hassett and G.E. Metcalf (1994), "Who pays broad-based energy taxes? Computing lifetime and regional incidence", Energy Journal 15:145–164.

Carroll, R., and J. Yinger (1994), "Is the property tax a benefit tax? The case of rental housing", National Tax Journal 47:295–316.

Caspersen, E., and G.E. Metcalf (1994), "Is a value added tax regressive? Annual versus lifetime incidence measures", National Tax Journal 47:731–746.

Cremer, H., and J.-F. Thisse (1994), "Commodity taxation in a differentiated oligopoly", International Economic Review 35:613–633.

Cronin, J.A. (1999), U.S. Treasury Distributional Analysis Methodology (Office of Tax Analysis, Washington, DC).

Davies, J.B., F. St. Hilaire and J. Whalley (1984), "Some calculations of lifetime tax incidence", American Economic Review 74:633–649.

Delipalla, S., and M. Keen (1992), "The comparison between ad valorem and specific taxation under imperfect competition", Journal of Public Economics 49:351–367.

Dixit, A.K., and J.E. Stiglitz (1977), "Monopolistic competition and optimum product diversity", American Economic Review 67:297–308.

Doyle, M.P. (1997), The Effects of Interest Rates and Taxes on New Car Prices (Board of Governors of the Federal Reserve System, Washington, DC).

Edgeworth, F.Y. (1897), "The pure theory of taxation", The Economic Journal 7:46–70.

Feenberg, D.R., A.W. Mitrusi and J.M. Poterba (1997), "Distributional effects of adopting a national retail sales tax", Tax Policy and the Economy 11:49–90.

Fehr, H., and L.J. Kotlikoff (1999), "Generational accounting in general equilibrium", in: A.J. Auerbach and L.J. Kotlikoff, eds., Generational Accounting around the World (University of Chicago Press, Chicago).

Feldstein, M. (1974), "Incidence of a capital income tax in a growing economy with variable savings rates", Review of Economic Studies 41:505–513.

Feldstein, M. (1977), "The surprising incidence of a tax on pure rent: a new answer to an old question", Journal of Political Economy 85:349–360.

Friedman, M. (1957), A Theory of the Consumption Function (Princeton University Press, Princeton, NJ).

Fuchs, V.R., A.B. Krueger and J.M. Poterba (1998), "Economists' views about parameters, values, and policies: survey results in labor and public economics", Journal of Economic Literature 36: 1387–1425.

Fullerton, D. (1996), "Why have separate environmental taxes?", Tax Policy and the Economy 10:33–70.

Fullerton, D., and D.L. Rogers (1991), "Lifetime versus annual perspectives on tax incidence", National Tax Journal 44:277–287.

Fullerton, D., and D.L. Rogers (1993), Who Bears the Lifetime Tax Burden? (Brookings Institution, Washington, DC).

Fullerton, D., and D.L. Rogers (1995), "Distributional effects on a lifetime basis", in: D.F. Bradford, ed., Distributional Analysis of Tax Policy (AEI Press, Washington, DC) pp. 262–294.

Fullerton, D., and D.L. Rogers (1996), "Lifetime effects of fundamental tax reform", in: H.J. Aaron and W.G. Gale, eds., Economic Effects of Fundamental Tax Reform (Brookings Institution Press, Washington, DC) pp. 321–347.

Fullerton, D., and D.L. Rogers (1997), "Neglected effects on the uses side: even a uniform tax would change relative goods prices", American Economic Review 87:120–125.

Gabszewicz, J.J., and J.-F. Thisse (1979), "Price competition, quality and income disparities", Journal of Economic Theory 20:340–359.

Gale, W.G., S. Houser and J.K. Scholz (1996), "Distributional effects of fundamental tax reform", in: H. Aaron and W. Gale, eds., Economic Effects of Fundamental Tax Reform (Brookings Institution, Washington, DC) pp. 281–315.

Gentry, W.M., and R.G. Hubbard (1997), "Distributional implications of introducing a broad-based consumption tax", Tax Policy and the Economy 11:1–47.

Gokhale, J., B.R. Page and J.R. Sturrock (1999), "Generational accounts for the United States: an update", in: A.J. Auerbach, L.J. Kotlikoff and W. Leibfritz, eds., Generational Accounting around the World (University of Chicago Press, Chicago) pp. 489–517.

Gordon, R.H., and J. Slemrod (1983), "A general equilibrium simulation study of subsidies to municipal expenditures", Journal of Finance 38:585–594.

Graetz, M.J. (1995), "Distributional tables, tax legislation, and the illusion of precision", in: D.F. Bradford, ed., Distributional Analysis of Tax Policy (AEI Press, Washington, DC) pp. 15–78.

Gravelle, J.G., and K. Smetters (2001), "Who bears the burden of the corporate tax in the open economy", Working Paper (NBER, Cambridge, MA).

Grieson, R.E. (1975), "The incidence of profit taxes in a neo-classical growth model", Journal of Public Economics 4:75–85.

Gruber, J. (1997), "The incidence of payroll taxation: evidence from Chile", Journal of Labor Economics 15:S72-101.

Hall, R.E. (1988), "The relationship between price and marginal cost in U.S. industry", Journal of Political Economy 96:921–947.

Hall, R.E., and D.W. Jorgenson (1967), "Tax policy and investment behavior", American Economic Review 57:391–414.

Hall, R.E., and A. Rabushka (1995), The Flat Tax (Hoover Institution Press, Stanford).

Hamilton, B.W. (1975), "Zoning and property taxation in a system of local governments", Urban Studies 12:205–211.

Hamilton, B.W. (1976), "Capitalization of intrajurisdictional differences in local tax prices", American Economic Review 66:743–753.

Harberger, A.C. (1962), "The incidence of the corporation income tax", Journal of Political Economy 70:215–240.

Harris, J.E. (1987), "The 1983 increase in the federal cigarette excise tax", Tax Policy and the Economy 1:87–111.

Harris, R. (1984), "Applied general equilibrium analysis of small open economies with scale economies and imperfect competition", American Economic Review 74:1016–1032.

Hausman, J.A. (1981), "Exact consumer's surplus and deadweight loss", American Economic Review 71:662–676.

Hines Jr, J.R., J.C. Hlinko and T.J.F. Lubke (1995), "From each according to his surplus: equi-proportionate sharing of commodity tax burdens", Journal of Public Economics 58:417–428.

Hotelling, H. (1929), "Stability in competition", The Economic Journal 39:41–57.

Jones, R.W. (1965), "The structure of simple general equilibrium models", Journal of Political Economy 73:557–572.

Judd, K.L. (1985a), "Redistributive taxation in a simple perfect foresight model", Journal of Public Economics 28:59–83.

Judd, K.L. (1985b), "Short-run analysis of fiscal policy in a simple perfect foresight model", Journal of Political Economy 93:298–319.

Judd, K.L. (1987), "A dynamic theory of factor taxation", American Economic Review 77:42–48.

Karp, L.S., and J.M. Perloff (1989), "Estimating market structure and tax incidence: the Japanese television market", Journal of Industrial Economics 37:225–239.

Kasten, R., F. Sammartino and E. Toder (1994), "Trends in federal tax progressivity, 1980–93", in: J. Slemrod, ed., Tax Progressivity and Income Inequality (Cambridge University Press, Cambridge) pp. 9–50.

Katz, M., and H.S. Rosen (1985), "Tax analysis in an oligopoly model", Public Finance Quarterly 13:3–19.

Kay, J.A., and M. Keen (1983), "How should commodities be taxed?", European Economic Review 23:339–358.

Kiefer, D.W. (1984), "Distributional tax progressivity indexes", National Tax Journal 37:497–513.

Kotlikoff, L.J. (2000), "The A-K Model – its past, present, and future", in: G. Harrison, S.E. Hougaard Jensen, L.H. Pedersen and T.H. Rutherford, eds., Using Dynamic CGE Models for Policy Analysis (North Holland, Amsterdam).

Kotlikoff, L.J. (2002), "Generational policy", in: A.J. Auerbach and M. Feldstein, eds., Handbook of Public Economics, Vol. 4 (Elsevier, Amsterdam) Chapter 27, this volume.

Kotlikoff, L.J., and L.H. Summers (1987), "Tax incidence", in: A.J. Auerbach and M. Feldstein, eds., Handbook of Public Economics, Vol. 2 (Elsevier, Amsterdam) pp. 1043–1092.

Krugman, P. (1980), "Scale economies, product differentiation, and the pattern of trade", American Economic Review 70:950–959.

Krzyzaniak, M., and R.A. Musgrave (1963), The Shifting of the Corporation Income Tax (Johns Hopkins Press, Baltimore).

Lakin, C. (2001), "The effects of taxes and benefits on household income, 1999–2000", Economic Trends 569:35–74.

Lyon, A.B., and R.M. Schwab (1995), "Consumption taxes in a life-cycle framework: are sin taxes regressive?", Review of Economics and Statistics 77:389–406.

Marshall, A. (1890), Principles of Economics, 8th Edition (Macmillan and Co., London).

McClellan, M., and J. Skinner (1997), "The incidence of Medicare", Working Paper (National Bureau of Economic Research, Cambridge, MA).

McLure Jr, C.E. (1970), "Taxation, substitution, and industrial location", Journal of Political Economy 78:112–132.

McLure Jr, C.E. (1974), "A diagrammatic exposition of the Harberger model with one immobile factor", Journal of Political Economy 82:56–82.

McLure Jr, C.E. (1975), "General equilibrium incidence analysis: the Harberger model after ten years", Journal of Public Economics 4:125–161.

McLure Jr, C.E., and W.R. Thirsk (1975), "A simplified exposition of the Harberger model, I: Tax incidence", National Tax Journal 28:1–27.

Menchik, P.L., and M. David (1982), "The incidence of a lifetime consumption tax", National Tax Journal 35:189–203.

Metcalf, G.E. (1994), "The lifetime incidence of state and local taxes: measuring changes during the 1980s", in: J. Slemrod, ed., Tax Progressivity and Income Inequality (Cambridge University Press, Cambridge) pp. 59–88.

Metcalf, G.E. (1999), "A distributional analysis of green tax reforms", National Tax Journal 52:655–681.

Metcalf, G.E., and G. Norman (2001), "Oligopoly deregulation and the taxation of commodities", Working Paper (Tufts University, Medford, MA).

Mieszkowski, P.M. (1972), "The property tax: an excise tax or a profits tax?", Journal of Public Economics 1:73–96.

Mieszkowski, P.M., and G.R. Zodrow (1989), "Taxation and the Tiebout model: the differential effects of head taxes, taxes on land rents and property taxes", Journal of Economic Literature 27(3):1098–1146.

Modigliani, F., and R. Brumberg (1954), "Utility analysis and the consumption function: an interpretation of cross-section data", in: K.K. Kurihara, ed., Post-Keynesian Economics (Rutgers University Press, New Brunswick) pp. 388–436.

Mulligan, C.B., and T.J. Philipson (2000), "Merit motives and government intervention: Public finance in reverse", Working Paper 7698 (National Bureau of Economic Research, Cambridge, MA).

Musgrave, R.A. (1959), The Theory of Public Finance (McGraw-Hill, New York).

Musgrave, R.A. (1974), "Is a property tax on housing regressive?", American Economic Review 64: 222–229.

Musgrave, R.A., K.E. Case and H. Leonard (1974), "The distribution of fiscal burdens and benefits", Public Finance Quarterly 2:259–311.

Mutti, J., and H. Grubert (1985), "The taxation of capital income in an open economy: the importance of resident–nonresident tax treatment", Journal of Public Economics 27:291–309.

Oates, W.E. (1969), "The effects of property taxes and local public spending on property values: an empirical study of tax capitalization and the Tiebout hypothesis", Journal of Political Economy 77:957–971.

Pechman, J.A. (1985), Who Paid the Taxes: 1966–85? (Brookings Institution Press, Washington, DC).

Pechman, J.A. (1987), "Pechman's tax incidence study: a response", American Economic Review 77: 232–234.

Pechman, J.A., and B.A. Okner (1974), Who Bears the Tax Burden? (Brookings Institution Press, Washington, DC).

Poterba, J.M. (1989), "Lifetime incidence and the distributional burden of excise taxes", American Economic Review 79:325–330.

Poterba, J.M. (1996), "Retail price reactions to changes in state and local sales taxes", National Tax Journal 49:165–176.

Ramsey, F.P. (1928), "A contribution to the theory of taxation", The Economic Journal 37:47–61.

Salop, S.C. (1979), "Monopolistic competition with outside goods", Bell Journal of Economics 10: 141–156.

Seade, J.E. (1985), Profitable Cost Increases and the Shifting of Taxation: Equilibrium Responses of Markets in Oligopoly (University of Warwick, Warwick).

Shaked, A., and J. Sutton (1982), "Relaxing price competition through product differentiation", The Review of Economic Studies 49:3–13.

Shoven, J.B., and J. Whalley (1984), "Applied general equilibrium models of taxation and international trade: an introduction and survey", Journal of Economic Literature 22:1007–1051.

Simon, H.A. (1943), "The incidence of a tax on urban real property", Quarterly Journal of Economics 59:398–420.

Slemrod, J. (1992), "Taxation and inequality: a time-exposure perspective", Tax Policy and the Economy 6:105–127.

Spence, A.M. (1976), "Product selection, fixed costs, and monopolistic competition", Review of Economic Studies 43:217–235.

Starrett, D.A. (1988), "Effects of taxes on savings", in: H.J. Aaron, H. Galper and J.A. Pechman, eds., Uneasy Compromise: Problems of a Hybrid Income-Consumption Tax (Brookings Institution Press, Washington, DC) pp. 237–268.

Stern, N.H. (1987), "The effects of taxation, price control and government contracts in oligopoly and monopolistic competition", Journal of Public Economics 32:133–158.

Stiglitz, J.E. (1973), "Taxation, corporate financial policy, and the costs of capital", Journal of Public Economics 2:1–34.

Suits, D.B. (1977), "Measurement of tax progressivity", American Economic Review 67:747–752.

Summers, L.H. (1985), "The asset price approach to the analysis of capital income taxation", in: G.R. Feiwil, ed., Issues in Contemporary Macroeconomics and Distribution (Macmillan, London) pp. 429–443.

Tiebout, C.M. (1956), "A pure theory of local expenditures", Journal of Political Economy 64:416–424.

Tirole, J. (1988), The Theory of Industrial Organization (The MIT Press, Cambridge, MA).

Tobin, J. (1969), "A general equilibrium approach to monetary theory", Journal of Money, Credit and Banking 36:227–239.

U.S. Bureau of the Census (1999), Statistical Abstract of the United States: 1999 (U.S. Government Printing Office, Washington, DC).

U.S. Joint Committee on Taxation (1993), Methodology and Issues in Measuring Changes in the Distribution of Tax Burdens (U.S. Congress, Washington, DC).

U.S. Joint Committee on Taxation (2000), Distributional Effects of the Chairman's Amendment in the Nature of a Substitute to H.R. 3916 (Repeal of the Federal Communications Excise Tax) for Markup by the Committee on Ways and Means on May 17, 2000 (U.S. Congress, Washington, DC).

Vandendorpe, A.L., and A.F. Friedlaender (1976), "Differential incidence in the presence of initial distorting taxes", Journal of Public Economics 6:205–229.

Venables, A.J. (1986), "Production subsidies, import tariffs, and imperfectly competitive trade", in: D. Greenaway and P.K.M. Tharakan, eds., Imperfect Competition and International Trade (Wheatsheaf, Sussex).

Willig, R. (1976), "Consumer's surplus without apology", American Economic Review 66:589–597.

Zodrow, G.R. (2001), "The property tax as a capital tax: a room with three views", National Tax Journal 54:139–156.

Zodrow, G.R., and P.M. Mieszkowski (1983), "The incidence of the property tax: the benefit view vs. the new view", in: G.R. Zodrow, ed., Local Provision of Public Services: The Tiebout Model after Twenty-Five Years (Academic Press, New York) pp. 109–129.

Chapter 27

GENERATIONAL POLICY *

LAURENCE J. KOTLIKOFF

Boston University; The National Bureau of Economic Research

Contents

* I thank Alan Auerbach, Martin Feldstein, Liqun Liu, Karl Shell, and Guido Tabellini for very helpful comments. I thank Boston University and the National Institute of Aging for research support.

Handbook of Public Economics, Volume 4, Edited by A.J. Auerbach and M. Feldstein

Abstract

Generational policy is a fundamental aspect of a nation's fiscal affairs. The policy involves redistributing resources across generations and allocating to particular generations the burden of paying the government's bills. This chapter in Volume 4 of the *Handbook of Public Economics* shows how generational policy works, how it is measured, and how much it matters to virtual as well as real economies.

The chapter shows the zero-sum nature of generational policy. It then illustrates the difference between statutory and true fiscal incidence. It also illuminates the arbitrary nature of fiscal labels as well as their associated fiscal aggregates, including the budget deficit, aggregate tax revenues, and aggregate transfer payments. Finally, it illustrates the various guises of generational policy, including structural tax changes, running budget deficits, altering investment incentives, and expanding pay-as-you-go-financed social security.

Once this example has been milked, the chapter shows that its lessons about the arbitrary nature of fiscal labels are general. They apply to any neoclassical model with rational economic agents and rational economic institutions. This demonstration sets the stage for the description, illustration, and critique of generational accounting. The chapter's final sections use a simulation model to illustrate generational policy, consider the theoretical and empirical case for and against Ricardian Equivalence, discuss government risk sharing and risk making, and summarize lessons learned.

Keywords

generational policy, generational accounting, tax incidence, deficit, debt, efficiency, Ricardian Equivalence, time consistency, the government's intertemporal budget constraint, generational balance, deficit accounting

JEL classification: H2, H5, H6

1. Introduction

Generational policy – the government's treatment of current and future generations – is a fundamental aspect of a nation's fiscal affairs. The policy involves two actions – redistributing resources across generations and allocating to particular generations the burden of paying the government's bills. Taking from one generation to help another or forcing one generation to pay for another's public goods raises a host of ethical as well as economic questions. How much of the government's bills should future generations be forced to pay? How should the government treat today's elderly versus today's young? Should those born in the future pay more because they will benefit from improved technology? Can the government redistribute across generations? If so, how does this work? Does relieving current generations of fiscal burdens let them consume more and, thereby, reduce or *crowd out* national saving and domestic investment? Should the government try to pool risks across generations?

Generational morality is the province of philosophers. But the positive questions surrounding the treatment of the old, the young, and unborn have captivated economists since the birth of the discipline. Their work has firmly embedded the analysis of generational policy within the broader theory of fiscal incidence [1]. This theory has three central messages. First, those to whom the government assigns its bills or designates its assistance are not necessarily those who bear its burdens or enjoy its help. Second, the incidence of policies ultimately depends on the economic responses they invoke. Third, apart from changes in economic distortions, generational policy is a zero-sum game in which the economic gains to winners (including the government) equal the economic losses to losers [2].

Because the gulf between policy goals and policy outcomes can be so large, incidence analysis is both important and intriguing. This is particularly true for generational policy where a range of private responses can frustrate the government's initiatives. These include intra-family intergenerational redistribution, private changes in saving and labor supply, and the market revaluation of capital assets.

The admonishment of incidence theory that policy descriptions bear no necessary relationship to policy outcomes is particularly apt in considering the traditional measure of generational policy, namely official government debt. Notwithstanding its common use, official government debt is, as a matter of neoclassical economic theory, an artifice of fiscal taxonomy that bears no fundamental relationship to generational policy.

In contrast to deficit accounting, which has no precise objective, a relatively new accounting method, *Generational accounting,* attempts to directly assess generational

---

[1] For surveys of tax incidence see Kotlikoff and Summers (1987) and Fullerton and Metcalf, Chapter 26, this volume.

[2] Changes (including reductions) in economic distortions include policy-induced changes in the economy's degree of risk sharing to the extent that marginal rates of substitution and production are not equated across states of nature.

policy. Specifically, it tries to measure the intergenerational incidence of fiscal policy changes as well as understand the fiscal burdens confronting current and future generations under existing policy.

Generational accounting represents but one way of trying to quantify the economic impacts of generational policy. Another is computer simulation. Each passing year sees the development of ever more sophisticated and carefully calibrated dynamic computer simulation models. These virtual environments are simplifications of economic reality. But they allow economists to conduct stylized controlled experiments in studying the dynamic impacts of generational policies.

This chapter shows how generational policy works, how it is measured, and how much it matters to virtual as well as real economies. To make its points as quickly and simply as possible, the chapter employs a two-period, overlapping generations model. This model is highly versatile. It illustrates the central controversies surrounding generational policy, including its potential impact on national saving and its potential impotency due to *Ricardian Equivalence.* It exposes the vacuity of deficit accounting. And it elucidates the government's intertemporal budget constraint that provides the framework for generational accounting.

Section 2 begins the analysis by presenting the two-period life-cycle model, defining generational incidence, and showing the zero-sum nature of generational policy. Section 3 illustrates generational policy with a simple example, namely a policy of redistributing, in a non-distortionary manner, to the contemporaneous elderly from the contemporaneous young as well as all future generations. This example clarifies the difference between statutory and true fiscal incidence. It also illuminates, as described in Section 4, the arbitrary nature of fiscal labels as well as their resultant fiscal aggregates, including the budget deficit, aggregate tax revenues, and aggregate transfer payments. Finally, it illustrates the various guises of generational policy, including structural tax changes, running deficits, altering investment incentives, and expanding pay-as-you-go-financed social security.

Once this example has been fully milked, the chapter shows that its lessons about fiscal labels are general. They apply when fiscal policy, in general, and generational policy, in particular, is distortionary, when it is uncertain, when it is time inconsistent, and when segments of the economy are credit constrained. Indeed, they apply to any neoclassical model with rational economic agents and rational economic institutions (including the government). This demonstration sets the stage for Section 5's description, illustration, and critique of generational accounting. This section also lays out the implications of generational policy for monetary policy.

Because generational policies play out over decades rather than years and can have major macroeconomic effects, understanding their impacts is best understood through computer simulation analysis. Section 6 presents results from simulating two major generational policies – changing the tax structure and privatizing social security. The messages of this section are that generational policies can have significant effects on the economy and the well-being of different generations, but that such policies take a long time to alter the economic landscape.

Having illustrated generational policy, its measurement, and the potential magnitude of its effects, the Chapter turns, in Section 7, to Ricardian Equivalence – the contention that generational policy, despite the government's best efforts, just does not work. The alleged reason is that parents and children are altruistic toward one another and will use private transfers to offset any government attempts to redistribute among them. Ricardian Equivalence has been assailed by theorists and empiricists. These attacks have paid off. As Section 7 discusses, there are very good theoretical and empirical reasons to doubt the validity of Ricardian Equivalence, at least for the United States. Section 8 considers the government's role in improving or worsening intergenerational risk sharing. The final Section 9 summarizes and concludes the chapter.

To conserve space, the chapter makes no attempt to survey the voluminous literature on generational policy. But any discussion of the modern analysis of generational policy would be remiss if it failed to identify the four major postwar contributions to the field, namely Samuelson's (1958) consumption-loan model, Diamond's (1965) analysis of debt policies, Feldstein's (1974) analysis of unfunded social security, and Robert Barro's (1974) formalization of Ricardian equivalence. These papers and their hundreds, if not thousands, of offspring collectively transformed the field from a collection of intriguing, but poorly posed questions to an extremely rich and remarkably clear set of answers.

2. The incidence of generational policy

2.1. The life-cycle model

Consider a two-period, life-cycle model in which agents born in year s have utility U_s defined over consumption when young, c_{ys}, consumption when old, c_{os+1}, leisure when young, l_{ys}, and leisure when old, l_{os+1}.

$$U_s = u\left(c_{ys}, c_{os+1}, l_{ys}, l_{os+1}\right). \tag{1}$$

For this dynamic economy, consumption and leisure from a point in time, say the beginning of time t, onward is constrained by a constant returns production function satisfying

$$F\left(c_{ot} + c_{yt} + g_t, c_{ot+1} + c_{yt+1} + g_{t+1}, \ldots, l_{ot} + l_{yt} - 2T, l_{ot+1} + l_{yt+1} - 2T, \ldots, k_t\right) = 0, \tag{2}$$

where g_s is government consumption in year s, k_t is the capital stock at the beginning of time t (before time-t production or consumption occurs), and T is the time endowment available to each generation in each period[3]. Since there are two generations alive at

---

[3] To keep the notation simple, this presentation abstracts from uncertainty in leaving out subscripts that denote state of nature. Indexing commodities by the state of nature is straightforward.

each point in time, the aggregate time endowment in each period is $2T$. The arguments of Equation (2) are the net (of endowments) demands for consumption and leisure at time t and in all future periods plus the beginning of time t endowment of capital.

Output is non-depreciable and can be either consumed or used as capital. Since there are no future endowments of capital, only the time-t endowment of capital enters Equation (2). The fact that all of the leisure being demanded in a given period enters as a single argument independent of who enjoys this leisure implies that the amounts of labor supplied by different agents are perfect substitutes in production. Finally, the fact that the aggregate time endowment (T) is constant through time reflects the simplifying assumption that each cohort is of equal size – the value of which is normalized to unity.

Using the constant returns-to-scale property, the production function can be written as:

$$
\begin{aligned}
&\left(c_{ot} + c_{yt} + g_t\right) + R_{t+1}\left(c_{ot+1} + c_{yt+1} + g_{t+1}\right) + \cdots + w_t\left(l_{ot} + l_{yt}\right) \\
&+ R_{t+1}w_{t+1}\left(l_{ot+1} + l_{yt+1}\right) + \cdots \quad = \frac{k_t}{R_t} + w_t 2T + R_{t+1}w_{t+1}2T + \cdots,
\end{aligned}
\tag{3}
$$

where R_{s+1} is the marginal rate of transformation of output in period s into output in period $s+1$ (the cost of an extra unit of output in period $s+1$ measured in units of output in period s); i.e.,

$$
R_{s+1} \equiv \frac{F_{cs+1}}{F_{cs}},
\tag{4}
$$

and w_s is the marginal rate of transformation of output in period s into leisure in period s (the cost of an extra unit of leisure in period s measured in units of output in period s), i.e.,

$$
w_s \equiv \frac{F_{ls}}{F_{cs}}.
\tag{5}
$$

The terms R_{s+1} and w_s – the respective time-s marginal products of capital at time $s+1$ and labor at time s – are referenced below as pre-tax factor prices.

Equation (3) is the economy's intertemporal budget constraint. It requires that the value of current and future consumption and leisure, all measured in units of current consumption, not exceed the value of the economy's current and future endowments, also measured in units of current consumption.

In choosing their consumption and leisure demands, agents born in year $s \geqslant t$ maximize Equation (1) subject to:

$$
c_{ys} + R_{s+1}c_{os+1} + w_s l_{ys} + R_{s+1}w_{s+1}l_{os+1} = w_s T + R_{s+1}w_{s+1}T - h_{ys} - R_{s+1}h_{os+1},
\tag{6}
$$

where h_{os} is the net payment of the old at time s.

Those agents born in $t-1$ maximize their time-t remaining lifetime utility subject to:

$$c_{ot} + w_t l_{ot} = \frac{a_{ot}}{R_t} + w_t T - h_{ot}. \tag{7}$$

In Equations (6) and (7), h_{ys} is the net payment to the government by the young at time s, and a_{ot} represents the net worth of the initial elderly at the beginning of time t.

2.2. The government's intertemporal budget constraint

Substitution of Equations (6) and (7) into the economy-wide budget constraint (3) yields the government's intertemporal budget constraint:

$$
\begin{aligned}
h_{ot} + h_{yt} &+ R_{t+1}\left(h_{ot+1} + h_{yt+1}\right) + R_{t+1}R_{t+2}\left(h_{ot+2} + h_{yt+2}\right) + \cdots \\
&= g_t + R_{t+1}g_{t+1} + R_{t+1}R_{t+2}g_{t+2} + \cdots + \frac{a_{ot} - k_t}{R_t}.
\end{aligned}
\tag{8}
$$

The right-hand side of Equation (8) is the government's bills – the present value of its current and future projected consumption plus its net debt, which equals the difference between total private-sector net worth and the economy's aggregate capital stock, $(a_{ot} - k_t)/R_t$. The government's intertemporal budget constraint requires that either current or future generations pay for the government's bills, where its bills represent the sum of its projected future consumption plus its initial net debt. As discussed below, different ways of labeling government receipts and payments will alter h_{ot} (the remaining lifetime net payment, or *generational account*, of the time-t elderly) and $(a_{ot} - k_t)/R_t$ by equal amounts. In contrast, the lifetime net payments (the generational accounts) facing initial young $(h_{yt} + R_{t+1}h_{ot+1})$ and future generations $(h_{ys} + R_{s+1}h_{os+1}$, for $s > t)$ are invariant to the government's vocabulary; i.e., the fiscal burden on current and future newborns is well defined, whereas the government's net debt is not.

2.3. The incidence of generational policy

Suppose that at time t the government changes policy. The policy change will affect the generation born at time $t-1$ (the initial elderly), the generation born at time t (the initial young), and all generations born after time t (the future generations). The incidence of the policy for an affected generation born in year s is found by differentiating Equation (1):

$$dU_s = u_{cys}dc_{ys} + u_{cos+1}dc_{os+1} + u_{lys}dl_{ys} + u_{los+1}dl_{os+1}. \tag{9}$$

For the initial elderly, $s = t-1$, and $dc_{yt-1} = 0$ and $dl_{yt-1} = 0$, since consumption and leisure that occurred before the policy changed is immutable.

The incidence experienced by each generation born at $s \geqslant t$ can be expressed in units of consumption when young by dividing Equation (9) by the marginal utility of consumption when young.

$$\frac{\mathrm{d}U_s}{u_{cys}} = \mathrm{d}c_{ys} + \frac{u_{cos+1}}{u_{cys}}\mathrm{d}c_{os+1} + \frac{u_{lys}}{u_{cys}}\mathrm{d}l_{ys} + \frac{u_{los+1}}{u_{cys}}\mathrm{d}l_{os+1}. \tag{10}$$

Equation (10) traces generational incidence to changes in each generation's consumption and leisure when young and old valued in terms of their consumption when young. In the case of the initial elderly, the change in utility can be normalized by the marginal utility of consumption when old.

2.4. The zero-sum nature of generational policy

Policy-induced changes in consumption and leisure experienced by the various generations alive at time t and thereafter must satisfy Equation (11), which results from differentiating Equation (2).

$$
\begin{aligned}
&\left(\mathrm{d}c_{ot} + \mathrm{d}c_{yt} + \mathrm{d}g_t\right) + R_{t+1}\left(\mathrm{d}c_{ot+1} + \mathrm{d}c_{yt+1} + \mathrm{d}g_{t+1}\right) + \\
&R_{t+1}R_{t+2}\left(\mathrm{d}c_{ot+2} + \mathrm{d}c_{yt+2} + \mathrm{d}g_{t+2}\right) + \cdots + w_t\left(\mathrm{d}l_{ot} + \mathrm{d}l_{yt}\right) + \\
&R_{t+1}w_{t+1}\left(\mathrm{d}l_{ot+1} + \mathrm{d}l_{yt+1}\right) + R_{t+1}R_{t+2}w_{t+2}\left(\mathrm{d}l_{ot+2} + \mathrm{d}l_{yt+2}\right) + \cdots = 0.
\end{aligned} \tag{11}
$$

Let E_t stand for the sum over all generations alive from time t onward (including the initial elderly born in $t-1$) of policy incidence measured in units of time-t consumption.

$$E_t = \frac{\mathrm{d}U_{t-1}}{u_{cot}} + \frac{\mathrm{d}U_t}{u_{cyt}} + R_{t+1}\frac{\mathrm{d}U_{t+1}}{u_{cyt+1}} + R_{t+1}R_{t+2}\frac{\mathrm{d}U_{t+2}}{u_{cyt+2}} + \cdots \tag{12}$$

Using Equations (10) and (11), rewrite Equation (12) as

$$
\begin{aligned}
E_t =\ &\left(R_{t+1}^n - R_{t+1}\right)\mathrm{d}c_{ot+1} + R_{t+1}\left(R_{t+2}^n - R_{t+2}\right)\mathrm{d}c_{ot+2} + \cdots\ \left(w_{ot}^n - w_t\right)\mathrm{d}l_{ot} \\
&+ \left(w_{yt}^n - w_t\right)\mathrm{d}l_{yt} + \left(w_{ot+1}^n R_{t+1}^n - w_{t+1}R_{t+1}\right)\mathrm{d}l_{ot+1} + R_{t+1}\left(w_{yt+1}^n - w_{t+1}\right)\mathrm{d}l_{yt+1} \\
&+ R_{t+1}\left(w_{ot+2}^n R_{t+2}^n - w_{t+2}R_{t+2}\right)\mathrm{d}l_{ot+2} + R_{t+1}R_{t+2}\left(w_{yt+2}^n - w_{t+2}\right)\mathrm{d}l_{yt+2} \\
&+ \cdots - \mathrm{d}g_t - R_{t+1}\mathrm{d}g_{t+1} - R_{t+1}R_{t+2}\mathrm{d}g_{t+2} - \cdots,
\end{aligned} \tag{13}
$$

where

$$R_s^n \equiv \frac{u_{cos}}{u_{cos-1}},\ w_{ys}^n \equiv \frac{u_{lys}}{u_{cys}},\ \text{and } w_{os}^n \equiv \frac{u_{los}}{u_{cos}}. \tag{14}$$

There are two sets of terms on the right-hand-side of Equation (13). The first set involves differences between marginal rates of substitution (MRS) and marginal rates of transformation (MRT) multiplied by a) the change in the economic choice being distorted, and b) a discount factor. These MRS–MRT wedges arise from distortionary fiscal policies and are often referred to as marginal tax wedges. This first set of terms is related, but not strictly identical to, the present value of the marginal change in economic efficiency (the change in excess burden) arising from the policy. The second set of terms measures the present value of the policy-induced change in the time-path of government consumption.

Thus, Equation (13) shows that fiscal-policy incidence summed over across all current and future generations equals a) the present value of the time-path of terms related to policy-induced changes in excess burden, and b) the increase in the present value of government consumption. Thus, apart from efficiency effects, any change in government consumption must be fully paid for in terms of reduced welfare experienced by current or future generations. If the policy entails no efficiency change and no change in government consumption, E_t equals zero, and the policy simply redistributes fiscal burdens across generations. Hence, ignoring efficiency effects, policy changes are, generationally speaking, zero-sum in nature. Either current or future generations must pay for the government's spending and holding government spending fixed, any improvement in the well-being of one generation comes at the cost of reduced well-being of another generation.

It is important to note that Equation (13) takes into account policy-induced changes in the time-path of factor prices. Apart from efficiency considerations, Equation (13) tells us that *all* intergenerational redistribution, be it direct government intergenerational redistribution, arising from changes in the constellation of net payments it extracts from various generations, or indirect intergenerational redistribution, arising from policy-induced changes in the time-path of factor prices, is zero-sum in nature. Stated differently, the benefits to particular generations arising from policy-induced changes in wage and interest rates are exactly offset by losses to other generations from such factor-price changes.

Although the first set of terms in Equation (13) involving MRS–MRT wedges arise only in the presence of economic distortions, their sum represents a precise measure of the change in excess burden only if the policy being conducted compensates all generations for the income effects they experience. To show how this compensation could be effected, take the case of a policy change that a) does not alter the time-path of government consumption, b) compensates members of each generation by keeping them on their pre-policy-change budget constraints, and c) does not require resources from outside the economy (i.e., leaves the economy on its intertemporal budget constraint)[4].

Since each generation remains on its initial budget constraint (defined in terms of its slope and intercept) the policy serves only to alter the choice of the position on that constraint. This change in the consumption/leisure bundle arises because of the

---

[4] This is a Slutsky compensation in an intertemporal setting.

policy's alteration in relative prices (i.e., because of changes in incentives). Hence, each generation's change in utility arises due to a change in how it allocates its budget, rather than a change in the size of its budget. The resulting change in utility is a pure change in economic distortion. Because these utility changes are measured in units of time-t output, adding them up, as Equation (13) does, across all current and future generations indicates the amount (positive or negative) of time-t output that could be extracted from the economy by engaging in the policy, but using generation-specific non-distortionary net payments that keep each generation at its pre-policy change level of utility.

To keep each generation on its initial budget constraint, the government must alter the net amounts it takes from each generation when young and old to offset all policy-induced income effects, including those arising from changes in relative prices of consumption and leisure when young and old. Assuming, without loss of generality, that the amount of distortionary net payments made by each generation are offset by non-distortionary net payments of equal magnitude, the only income effects to be offset are those arising from changes in relative prices. This means setting dh_{ot} such that

$$dh_{ot} = dw_t T - dw_t l_{ot}, \tag{15}$$

and setting dh_{ys} and dh_{os+1} for $s \geqslant t$ such that

$$\begin{aligned} dh_{ys} + R_{s+1} dh_{os+1} = dw_s T &+ d \left(R_{s+1} w_{s+1} \right) T - dR_{s+1} h_{os+1} - dR_{s+1} c_{os+1} \\ &- dw_s l_{ys} - d \left(R_{s+1} w_{s+1} \right) l_{os+1}. \end{aligned} \tag{16}$$

Does this compensation policy satisfy the government's intertemporal budget constraint? The answer is yes. To see why, take the differentials of Equations (3), (6) and (7). These equations plus (15) and (16) generate the differential of the government's budget constraint. Intuitively, the constant-returns property of the production function implies that factor-price changes are zero-sum in nature. Hence, the government can redistribute resources from generations experiencing beneficial factor-price changes to those experiencing adverse factor-price changes. This leaves each generation on its initial budget frontier, although, potentially, at a different point on that frontier.

When one applies Equations (15) and (16) in conjunction with a policy change that leaves government spending unchanged, the resulting consumption and leisure differentials in Equation (13) are compensated ones. For discrete, as opposed to infinitesimal, policy changes, one can integrate E_t over the range of the policy change. The resulting expression will be the present value sum of each period's Harberger excess burden triangle, if there are no initial distortions in the economy[5].

---

[5] Were one to expand the above analysis to incorporate uncertainty about future states of nature, all commodities at a particular point in time would be indexed by their state of nature and the discrepancies between marginal rates of substitution and marginal rates of transformation would capture the absence of risk-sharing arrangements associated with incomplete insurance markets.

3. Illustrating generational policy

3.1. A Cobb–Douglas example

A very simple Cobb–Douglas two period life-cycle model suffices to illustrate how generational policy works and why it cannot be uniquely described with conventional fiscal taxonomy. Let the utility of the young born at time s, U_s, be given by:

$$U_s = \alpha \log c_{ys} + (1 - \alpha) \log c_{os+1}. \tag{17}$$

In Equation (17), we make the assumption that labor supply is exogenous. Specifically, the young work full time and the elderly are retired. Also let the production function for output per worker satisfy:

$$y_s = A k_s^\beta. \tag{18}$$

Each cohort has N members, so there is no population growth. Finally, assume that the government takes an amount $\bar{h}$ from each member of each young generation and hands the same amount to each member of the contemporaneous old generation.

At any time $t + 1$, capital per old person equals capital per worker, k_{t+1}, because the number of old and young are equal. The amount of capital held at $t + 1$ by each old person is what she accumulated when young; i.e.,

$$k_{t+1} = w_t - \bar{h} - c_{yt}. \tag{19}$$

Given that consumption when young equals a share, α, of lifetime resources, we can write Equation (19) as:

$$k_{t+1} = w_t - \bar{h} - \alpha \left(w_t - \frac{r_{t+1} \bar{h}}{1 + r_{t+1}} \right). \tag{20}$$

Finally, using the fact that factor prices equal marginal products, we can express Equation (20) as:

$$k_{t+1} = (1 - \beta)(1 - \alpha) A_t k_t^\beta - \bar{h} + \alpha \left(\frac{\beta A_{t+1} k_{t+1}^{\beta-1} \bar{h}}{1 + \beta A_{t+1} k_{t+1}^{\beta-1}} \right). \tag{21}$$

Equation (21) represents the transition equation for the capital labor ratio. Knowing the value of k_t, one can solve (by nonlinear methods) for the value of k_{t+1}.

3.2. The crowding out of capital

Consider introducing the policy at time 0. Because α is between zero and one, the derivative of k_{t+1} for $t = 0$ with respect to $\bar{h}$ is negative evaluated at $\bar{h}$ equals zero.

Hence, if we assume the policy is introduced at time 0, it reduces the economy's capital stock at each future date. What is the explanation for this crowding out of capital? The answer is the increased consumption of those who are old at the time of the reform – time 0. This cohort receives $\bar{h}$ for free; i.e., without being forced to hand over $\bar{h}$ when young. And the cohort immediately increases its consumption by $\bar{h}$ per person. This present value gain to the initial old is offset by a present value loss to the initial young and future generations of interest on $\bar{h}$; i.e., if one discounts, at the time path of the marginal product of capital, the sum of all the losses of interest on $\bar{h}$ by the initial young and future generations, the total equals $-\bar{h}$.

If the losses to the current young and future generations are equal in present value to the gains to the initial old, why is there an initial (time 0) net increase in consumption and a decline in national saving? The answer is that the increased consumption by the elderly at time 0 is only partially offset by the reduced consumption of the contemporaneous young. As just indicated, the contemporaneous young pay for only a small portion of the transfer to the initial elderly. Moreover, their propensity to consume, α, is less than one – the propensity to consume of the initial elderly. So the positive income effect experienced by the initial elderly exceeds in absolute value the negative income effect experienced by the initial young, who, in any case, have a smaller propensity to consume. Hence, consumption of the initial elderly rises by more than the consumption of the initial young falls, thereby reducing national saving and investment.

Although all future generations will be forced to reduce their consumption once they are born, that does not matter to the time-0 level of national consumption and saving. Moreover, the reason this policy has a permanent impact on the economy's capital stock is that there are always generations coming in the future whose consumption has not yet been depressed because of the policy; i.e., at any point in time, say t, the cumulated policy-induced net increase in the economy's aggregate consumption from time 0 through time t is positive. Another way to think about the policy is to note that as of time 0 the old are the big spenders, whereas the young and future generations are the big savers. Indeed, future generations have a propensity to consume at time 0 of zero. So the policy redistributes resources at time 0 from young and future savers to old spenders.

3.3. The policy's incidence

The incidence of the policy can be described as follows. The elderly at time 0 receive $\bar{h}$, and since factor prices at time 0 are unchanged, they experience no reduction in the return they earn from their capital. Hence, the policy unambiguously makes the initial elderly better off. Next consider the young at time 0. They give up $\bar{h}$ when young, but receive the same amount when old. On balance, they lose interest on the $\bar{h}$. This reduction in lifetime income is somewhat counterbalanced by the fact the policy drives up the return they receive on their savings. The reason is that the policy reduces k_1 relative to what it would otherwise have been. (Note that while the policy alters k_1

and subsequent levels of capital per workers, it does not change k_0, which means it does not change the wage earned by the initial young.) Finally, consider those born at time 2 and thereafter. Each of these generations loses interest on $\bar{h}$. In addition, each earns a lower wage on its labor supply and a higher rate of return on its saving than in the absence of the policy. On balance, these factor price changes make these generations worse off.

Since there is neither government consumption nor economic distortions in this example, the policy, according to Equation (13), is zero-sum across generations with respect to welfare changes. Now the derivative of each generation's utility has two components – the change due to raising $\bar{h}$ (above zero) and the change due to policy-induced factor price changes. If we measure these two components in present value (in units of time-0 consumption) and add them up across all generations, Equation (13) tells us that their sum is zero. However, as indicated above, the sum across all initial and future generations of the first component – the utility changes from raising $\bar{h}$ is, by itself, zero[6]. Hence, the present value sum of the utility changes experienced by initial and future generations from factor-price changes must also sum to zero. In concrete terms, this means that the gain to the initial young from receiving a higher rate of return in old age, measured in units of time-0 consumption, equals the sum of the net losses, measured in time-0 consumption, incurred by subsequent generations from receiving a lower real wage when young plus a higher return when old.

4. Deficit delusion and the arbitrary nature of fiscal labels

In presenting generational policy in the Cobb–Douglas model, no use was made of the terms "taxes", "transfer payments", "interest payments" or "deficits". This section points out that there are an infinite number of equally uninformative ways to label the above policy using these words. Each of these alternative sets of labels use the words "taxes", "transfers", "spending", and "deficits" in conventional ways. Consequently, no set of labels has a higher claim to relevance than any other.

The choice of a particular set of fiscal labels to use in discussing the model (the choice of fiscal language) is fundamentally no different than the choice of whether to discuss the model in English or French. The message of the model lies in its mathematical structure. And no one would presume that that message would differ if the model were discussed in English rather than French.

Showing that fiscal labeling is, from the perspective of economic theory, arbitrary, establishes that the "deficit" is not a well defined measured of generational or, indeed, any other aspect of fiscal policy. It establishes the same point with respect to "taxes", "transfer payments" and "spending", where spending consists of "transfer payments"

---

[6] Recall that the present value sum of the loss of interest on $\bar{h}$ by the initial young and future generations equals $\bar{h}$ – the gain to the initial elderly.

and "interest payments on government borrowing". Since the "deficit", "taxes", "transfer payments" and "spending" are, from the perspective of economic theory, content free, so too are ancillary fiscal and national income accounting constructs like "debt", "national income", "disposable income", "personal saving" and "social security". Given the ubiquitous use by governments and economists of these verbal constructs to discuss, formulate, and evaluate economic policy, the import of this point cannot be overstated.

4.1. Alternative fiscal labels

Consider first labeling the payment of $\bar{h}$ by members of the initial young and future generations as a "tax" and the labeling of the receipt of $\bar{h}$ by the initial and subsequent elderly as a "transfer payment". With these words, the government reports a balanced budget each period since "taxes" equal "spending". This is true despite the fact that the government is running a loose fiscal policy in the sense that it redistributes toward the initial old from the initial young and future generations. Furthermore, the budget remains in balance regardless of whether the policy is extremely loose ($\bar{h}$ is very large) or extremely tight ($\bar{h}$ is negative and very large in absolute value).

As a second example, let the government (1) label its payment of $\bar{h}$ to the elderly at time 0 as "transfer payments", (2) label its receipt of $\bar{h}$ from the initial young and subsequent generations as "borrowing", and (3) label its net payment of $\bar{h}$ to each elderly generation from time $s = 1$ onward as "repayment of principal plus interest in the amount of $(1 + r_s)\,\bar{h}$ less an old age tax of $r_s\bar{h}$". While each old person starting at time 0 still receives $\bar{h}$ and each young person still hands over $\bar{h}$, with this alternative set of words the government announces that its running a deficit of $\bar{h}$ at time 0 since time-0 spending on transfer payments equals $\bar{h}$ and time-0 taxes equal zero. At time 1 and thereafter, the deficit is zero since the old age tax equals the government's interest payments (the only government spending). Hence, the stock of debt increases from 0 to $\bar{h}$ at the beginning of time 1 and stays at that value forever.

The above two examples are special cases of the following general labeling rule: 1) label the receipt from the young of $\bar{h}$ as net borrowing from the young of $m\bar{h}$ less a net transfer to the young of $(m - 1)\bar{h}$, 2) label the payment of $\bar{h}$ to the initial old as a transfer payment, and 3) label the payment of $\bar{h}$ to the old in periods $s \geqslant 1$ as return of principal plus interest of $m(1 + r_s)\,\bar{h}$ less a net old age tax of $(m - 1)\bar{h} + mr_s\bar{h}$. Note that in the first example, m equals 0. In the second, m equals 1. Also note that regardless of the value of m, the government, on balance, extracts $\bar{h}$ from the young each period and hands $\bar{h}$ over to the old each period.

The government's reported deficit at time 0 is $m\bar{h}$. At time $s \geqslant 1$, the reported deficit equals government spending on interest payments of $mr_s\bar{h}$ plus net transfer payments of $(m - 1)\bar{h}$ minus government net taxes of $(m - 1)\bar{h} + mr_s\bar{h}$; i.e., the reported deficit in $s \geqslant 1$ is zero. Hence, from time 1 onward, the stock of government debt is $m\bar{h}$. Since m can be any positive or negative integer, the government can choose language to make its reported debt for $s \geqslant 1$ any size and sign it wants.

For example, if the government makes m equal to $-30\,000$, it will announce each period that it is "taxing the young $30\,001\,\bar{h}$ and lending the young $30\,000\,\bar{h}$ and, in each period $s \geqslant 1$, that it is "receiving from the old principal and interest payments of $30\,000\,(1 + r_s)\,\bar{h}$ and making a transfer payment to the old of $30\,001\,\bar{h} + 30\,000\,r_s\bar{h}$. In this case, the government reports a surplus at time 0 of $30\,000\,\bar{h}$.

Thus, each choice of m corresponds to a different choice of fiscal language. And since the government and private sector are always fully repaying those payments and receipts that are described as "government borrowing" and "government loans", one choice of m is no more natural than any other from the perspective of everyday parlance. From the perspective of economic theory, the choice of m is completely arbitrary as well; i.e., the equations of the model presented above do not contain m.

In addition to not pinning down the choice of m at a point in time, the model's equations provide no restrictions on changes in the choice of m through time. Let m_s stand for the choice of m applied to the receipt of $\bar{h}$ from the young at time s as well as the receipt of $\bar{h}$ by the old at time $s + 1$. So m_s references the language used to describe the fiscal treatment of generation s. In this case, the deficit at time s will equal the quantity $(m_s - m_{s-1})\,\bar{h}$.

To summarize, regardless of the true size and nature of generational policy as determined by the size and sign of $\bar{h}$, the government can announce any time-path of deficits or surpluses it chooses. For example, the government can choose a sequence of m_s that makes its reported debt grow forever at a faster rate than the economy. This means, of course, that the debt to GDP ratio tends to infinitely. It also means that the invocation in economic models of a transversality condition, which limits the ratio of debt to GDP, is a restriction about permissible language, not a restriction on the economy's underlying economic behavior.

At this point, an irritated reader might suggest that the above is simply an exercise in sophistry because as long as the government chooses its fiscal language (its m) and sticks with it through time, we'll have a meaningful and consistent language with which to discuss fiscal policy.

This is not the case. Even if the government were to choose an m and stick with it through time, the resulting time path of government deficits would have no necessary connection to actual fiscal policy. As we've seen in the above example, if the government chooses a large (in absolute value) negative value of m to label the $\bar{h}$ policy, it will announce over time that it has a huge level of assets, despite the fact that it is conducting loose policy. Moreover, the government's choice of fiscal labels is not sacrosanct. The fact that the government has chosen a particular time-path for the value of m does not preclude each individual in society from choosing her or his own time-path of m_s in describing the country's past and projected future fiscal affairs. Each of these alternative time paths has the same claim (namely zero) to explaining the government's actual past, present, and future fiscal position. Indeed, those who wish to show that deficits crowd out capital formation need only define a time path of m_s that produces a negative correlation between investment and the deficit. And those who wish to show the opposite can choose a time path of m_s that produces a positive correlation.

Finally, unless the government's fiscal policy is described in label-free terms, there is no way for the public to know what m the government has chosen or whether it is maintaining that choice through time. In our simple model, the reported deficit depends on the current period's choice of m, the previous period's choice of m, as well as the size of $\bar{h}$. Without independent knowledge of $\bar{h}$, the public cannot tell if the deficit is changing because of changes in fiscal fundamentals or simply because of changes in fiscal labels. Nor can the public tell if the same labels are being used through time.

4.2. Other guises of generational policy

In the above discussion, we've indicated that the our $\bar{h}$ intergenerational redistribution policy can be conducted under the heading "pay-as-you-go" social security", "deficit-financed transfer payments" or "surplus-financed transfer payments", where the deficits or surpluses can be of any size. This is not the limit of the language that could be used to describe the policy. The policy could also be introduced under the heading of "structural tax reform". To see this, suppose the government initially has in place a consumption tax that it uses to make transfers to the young and old which precisely equal their tax payments. Now suppose the government switches from consumption to wage taxation as its means of collecting the same amount of revenue to finance the transfer payments. Since the initial elderly are retired and pay no wage taxes, they will be relieved of paying any net taxes over the rest of their lives. Hence, this reform redistributes to them from the initial young and future generations. These latter generations find that the present value (calculated when young) of their lifetime net tax payments has been increased.

Our final example of fiscal linguistic license is particularly artful. As discussed in Auerbach and Kotlikoff (1987), it involves the government engineering a stock market boom and, thereby, raising the price at which the elderly sell their capital assets to the young. In so doing, the government can claim that market revaluation, rather than government policy, is responsible for improving the well-being of the initial elderly at the cost of lower welfare for the initial young and future generations. Since we want to describe this outcome as a particular labeling of our $\bar{h}$ policy, we need to clarify the difference between capital assets and consumption goods. The difference arises not in the physical property of the two, since our model has only one good, but rather in the date the good is produced. The economy's capital stock at time t consists of output that was produced prior to time t. And the government can tax or subsidize the purchase of output produced in the past differently from the way it taxes or subsidizes output produced in the present.

In terms of the equations of our model, $\bar{h}$ stands for the higher price of capital (measured in units of consumption) that the young must pay to invest in capital. It also stands for the higher price (measured in units of consumption) that the old receive on the sale of their capital to the young.

How can the government engineer a stock market boom of this kind? The answer is by announcing a tax on the purchase of newly produced capital goods by the young. Since the young can either invest by buying new capital goods or by buying old capital from the elderly (the capital valued in the stock market), this will drive up the price of the capital the elderly have to sell to the point that the young are indifferent between the two options. To avoid the government retaining any resources, we can have it return to the young the equivalent of their investment tax payments, but in a lump-sum payment (a payment that is not related to the level of that investment. This, plus a couple of additional elements that leave the effective tax rate on capital income unchanged, will make the "investment tax policy" differ in name only from conducting our benchmark policy under the alternative headings "pay-as-you-go social security", "deficit-financed transfer payments to the elderly", "surplus-financed transfer payments to the elderly" and "structural tax change" [7].

4.3. Generalizing the point that the deficit is not well defined

The above illustration of the arbitrary nature of deficit accounting was based on a simple framework that excluded distortionary policy, economic as well as policy uncertainty, and liquidity constraints. Unfortunately, none of these factors provide any connection between the measured deficit and fiscal fundamentals.

4.3.1. Distortionary policy

To see that distortionary policy has no purchase when it comes to connecting deficits with fiscal fundamentals, consider again the general model that includes variable first period and second period leisure and net payments from the young and old in period t to the government of h_{yt} and h_{ot}. To introduce distortionary fiscal policy, we simply let h_{yt} and h_{ot} depend on how much generation t decides to consume and work when young and old, respectively. In maximizing its lifetime utility function subject to (6)

---

[7] To make this policy fully isomorphic to our benchmark policy, we need to include six elements: (1) a subsidy to capital income received by generation s when old that is levied at the same rate as the tax generation s pays when young on new investment; (2) a lump sum transfer paid to the elderly equal to the subsidy to capital income; (3) a lump sum transfer to the young equal to the proceeds of the investment tax; (4) the setting of the investment tax rate each period to ensure that the net cost of purchasing the capital rises by exactly $\bar{h}$; (5) if the elderly consume their own capital, the government provides them a subsidy at the same rate as the investment tax; and (6) if the young invest their own capital (the output they receive as wages), they will be forced to pay the investment tax. Element 1 ensures that there is no change in the effective rate of capital income taxation under this description of the policy. Elements 2 through 4 ensure that the budget constraints of the young and old each period are precisely those of the benchmark policy. Element 5 guarantees that the elderly are indifferent between consuming their own capital or selling it to the young, and element 6 guarantees that the young are indifferent between investing their own wages, purchasing new capital for investment from other young people, or purchasing the capital owned by the elderly.

or (7), agents take into account the marginal dependence of h_{yt} and h_{ot+1} on their consumption and leisure demands and this marginal dependence helps determine the marginal prices they face in demanding these commodities.

Our model with distortionary policy thus consists of a) government-chosen time-paths of the h_{yt} and h_{ot} functions and g_t (government consumption demands) that satisfy the government's intertemporal budget constraint, household demands for consumption and supplies of labor, and firms supplies of output and demands for capital and labor inputs. Market clearing requires that, in each period along the economy's dynamic transition path, a) firms' aggregate output supply cover the consumption demands of households and the government plus the investment demand of firms, and b) labor supply equals labor demand.

The fact that we can formulate and discuss our model of distortionary fiscal policy making no use whatsoever of the words "taxes", "transfer payments", or "deficits" in itself tells us that the deficit has no connection to policy, even if that policy is distortionary. But to drive home the point, consider labeling h_{yt} as "government borrowing" of $m_t h_{yt}$ from the young at time t less a "net transfer payment" to the young at time t of $(m_t - 1) h_{yt}$. The corresponding labeling of the payment by the old of h_{ot+1} would be labeled as "repayment of principal and interest" of $-m_t h_{yt}(1 + r_{t+1})$ (which is negative, because the government is doing the repaying) plus a "net tax payment" of $h_{ot+1} + m_t h_{yt}(1 + r_{t+1})$. Notice, that regardless of the size of m_t, the net payments of generation t when young and old are h_{yt} and h_{ot+1}, respectively and its generational account is $h_{yt} + R_{t+1} h_{ot+1}$. Thus, the choice of the time path of the m_ts makes no difference to economic outcomes, although it leads to a sequence of "official" deficits, d_t, of

$$d_t = m_t h_{yt} - m_{t-1} h_{yt-1}. \tag{22}$$

To make this math more concrete, suppose that the government finances its possibly time-varying consumption each period based on a net payment from the young of h_{yt}, which distorts each generation's first-period labor supply[8]. How can observer A report that the government is taxing only the labor earnings of the young from time 0 onward and always running a balanced budget? How can observer B report that the government runs a deficit of h_{y1} at time 0? And how can observer C report that the same government runs a surplus of h_{y1} at time 0?

The answer is that observer A sets m_s equal to zero for all s; observer B sets m_0 equal to zero and m_1 equal to 1; and observer C sets m_0 equal to zero and m_1 equal to -1. Observer A describes the government as taxing generation 1 *when it is young* on the amount it earns when young. Observer B describes the government as taxing generation 1 *when it is old* on the accumulated (at interest) amount it earns *when young*. Observer C describes the government as taxing generation 1 *when it is young*

---

[8] In this example, the net payment of the old each period is assumed to equal zero.

on its labor supply by more than the amount needed to cover government spending. Observer C also describes the government as subsidizing generation 1 *when it is old* based on the accumulated (at interest) amount it earned *when young*. The key point here is that, although all three observers report different time-0 deficits, all three report that the government is imposing the same tax, at the margin, on labor supply *when young*.

The labels of observers B and C may, at first, seem a bit strained because they entail stating that the government is collecting revenue or making subsidies in one period based on economic choices made in another. There are, however, multiple and important examples of such elocution. Take 401k, IRA, and other tax-deferred retirement accounts. The tax treatment of these accounts is expressly described as taxing in old age the amount earned when young plus accumulated interest on those earnings. Another example comes from the Social Security System, which provides social security benefits in old age based on the past earnings of workers in a manner that connects marginal benefits to marginal past contributions. A third example is the U.S. federal income tax which taxes social security benefits and thus, indirectly, taxes in old age the labor supplied by retirees when they were young.

Moreover, such cross-period references are not essential. Take B's observation that generation 1 pays zero taxes when young and $(1 + r_2) h_{y1}$ taxes when old. B can describe the zero taxes that generation 1 pays when young as "revenues from a tax on labor supply *when young* less a lump-sum transfer payment made to the young at time 1 of equal value". And B can describe the taxes generation 1 pays when old as a "lump sum tax"[9].

Although the model discussed above has only a single type of agent per generation, the argument about the arbitrary nature of fiscal labels is equally valid if agents are heterogeneous. In this case, the net payments to the government, h_{yt} and h_{ot}, will differ across agents. If the government cannot observe individual characteristics, like innate talent, these functions will be anonymous. On the other hand, the labeling convention – the choice of m_t can be individual specific; i.e., we are each free to describe our own and our fellow citizens' net payments to the government with any words we like.

Ghiglino and Shell (2000) point out that if the government were restricted in its choice of words to, for example, announcing only anonymous tax schedules, those restrictions might, in light of limits on reported deficits constrained the government's policy choices. This point and their analysis, while very important, is orthogonal to the one being made here, namely that whatever is the government's policy and however the government came to choose that policy, it can reasonably (in the sense of using standard

---

[9] Recall that, according to observer B, this second-period lump-sum tax is offset by the second-period repayment of principal plus interest on the government's borrowing, so that the agent makes no net payment in the second period. Thus, if the agent dies prior to reaching the second period, observer B can claim that the agent's estate used the proceeds of the debt repayment to pay the second-period lump-sum tax.

economic terminology) be described by men and women, who are not encumbered by government censors, as generating any time path of deficits or surpluses.

4.3.2. Liquidity constraints

Another objection to the above demonstrations that "deficit" policies are not well defined is that they ignore the possibility that some agents are liquidity constrained. If some young agents cannot borrow against future income how can they be indifferent between a policy that involuntarily "taxes" them and one that voluntarily "borrows" from them? There are two answers.

First, the government can compel payments with words other than "taxes". For example, government's all around the world are currently "reforming" their social security pension systems by forcing workers to "save" by making contributions to pension funds, rather than by making social security "tax" contributions. The governments are then "borrowing" these "savings" out of the pension funds to finance current social security benefit payments. When the workers reach retirement, they will receive "principal plus interest" on their compulsory saving, but, presumably, also face an additional tax in old age to cover the government's interest costs on that "borrowing". While this shell game alters no liquidity constraints, it certainly raises the government's reported deficit.

The point to bear in mind here is not that governments may, from time to time, opt for different words to do the same thing, but, rather that any independent observer can, even in a setting of liquidity constraints, reasonably use alternative words to describe the same fundamental policy and, thereby, generate total different time-paths of deficits.

The second reason why liquidity-constrained agents may be indifferent between "paying taxes" and "lending to the government" is due to Hayashi (1987). His argument is that private-sector lenders are ultimately interested in the consumption levels achieved by borrowers since the higher those levels, the greater the likelihood that those who cannot repay will borrow and then default. When the government reduces its "taxes" on liquidity-constrained borrowers, private lenders reduce their own loans to those borrowers to limit the increase in their consumption. Instead of lending as much as it did to its borrowers, the private lenders make loans to the government. Indeed, in equilibrium, the private lenders voluntarily "lend" to the government exactly the amounts the liquidity-constrained agents were otherwise sending the government in "taxes". Hence, the borrowers find their private loans cut back by precisely their cut in taxes (i.e., they find their "tax cuts" being used to buy government bonds) and end up with the same consumption. Thus, changing language will not alter the degree to which any agent is liquidity constrained since these constraints will themselves be determined, fundamentally, by the unchanged level and timing of the agents' resources net of their net payments to the government.

4.3.3. Uncertainty

A third objection to the proposition that fiscal labels are economically arbitrary involves uncertainty. "Surely", the objection goes, "future transfer payments and taxes are less certain than repayment of principal plus interest, so one cannot meaningfully interchange these terms". In fact, the risk properties of government payments and receipts provide no basis for their labeling; i.e., the deficit is no better defined in models with uncertainty than it is in models with certainty. The reason is that any uncertain payment (receipt) $\tilde{X}$, where the refers to a variable that is uncertain, can be relabeled as the combination of a certain payment (receipt) $\bar{X}$ plus an uncertain payment (receipt) $\tilde{X} - \bar{X}$. So a net payment when young of h_{yt} and an uncertain receipt when old of $\tilde{h}_{ot+1}$ can be described as a net payment when young of h_{yt} plus a certain old age receipt of h_{yt}/R_{t+1} less an uncertain receipt of $\tilde{h}_{ot+1} - h_{yt}/R_{t+1}$. Regardless of what one calls the uncertain component of this receipt, there are, as we've seen, an infinite number of ways to label the certain payment when young and the certain receipt when old. More generally, whatever are the risk properties of net payments that are labeled "borrowing" and "interest and principal repayment", these same net payments can be labeled as "taxes" and "transfer payments".

Take, as an example, Barsky, Mankiw, and Zeldes' (1986) demonstration that "a tax cut coupled with a future income tax increase (that pays off the associated borrowing) can stimulate consumer spending" and that "the marginal propensity to consume out of a tax cut, coupled with future income tax increases, can be substantial under plausible assumptions". In their two-period life-cycle model, agents' second period earnings are uncertain. According to the way they label their equations, the government cuts taxes by an amount T when workers are young and repays its borrowing by taxing workers when old in proportion to their earnings. Since agents have no way to insure their risky earnings, the policy provides an element of intragenerational risk sharing and, thereby, lowers precautionary saving and raises consumption when young. Barsky, Mankiw and Zeldes view this increase in consumption in response to the "tax cut" as a Keynesian reaction to a Ricardian policy.

While the points Barsky, Mankiw, and Zeldes make about consumption under uncertainty are impeccable, their findings have nothing to do with "tax cuts", "deficit finance" or "the timing of taxation". One can equally well describe their equations as showing that there is a sizeable and very non-Keynesian consumption response to a tax hike of size T. How? By labeling the policy as "raising taxes on the young by T and making a loan to the young of T". When the young are old, the government "receives loan repayments of T plus interest" but makes a "transfer payment" of $2T$ less an amount that is proportional to earnings at the same rate described by Barsky, Mankiw and Zeldes (1986) as the tax rate.

4.3.4. Time consistency

Another question about the alleged arbitrary nature of fiscal labels is whether the timing of "taxes" is better defined in a setting in which government policy is subject to time-consistency problems[10]. One way to demonstrate that it is not is to show that time inconsistent policy can be modeled with no reference to "taxes", "transfers" or "deficits". Take, for example, an economy consisting of a generation that lives for two periods and is under the control of a time inconsistent government in both periods. Specifically, suppose the government has a social welfare function $W_y(u_1, u_2, \ldots, u_n)$ that represents its preferences over the lifetime utilities of agents 1 through n when they are young. Let $W_o(u_1, u_2, \ldots, u_n)$ represent the government's preferences when the agents are old. Further, assume that agent i's utility is a function of her consumption when young and old, c_{iy} and c_{io}, her leisure when young and old, l_{iy} and l_{io}, and her enjoyment of public goods when young and old, g_y and g_o. Thus, $u_i = u_i(c_{iy}, c_{io}, l_{iy}, l_{io}, g_y, g_o)$. When the cohort is old, the government will maximize W_o taking as given the consumption and leisure and public goods that each agent enjoyed when young.

If the $W_o(\ ,\ ,\ )$ and $W_y(\ ,\ ,\ )$ functions differ, the government's preferences will be time inconsistent. In this case, the young government (the government when the cohort is young), will realize that the old government will exercise some control over the consumption and leisure that agents will experience when old and use that control to generate undesirable outcomes. Consequently, the young government will use dynamic programming to determine how the old government will make its decisions and the ways in which it can indirectly control those decisions.

The government, both when it is old and young, can use non-linear net payment schedules to redistribute across agents and extract resources from agents. If the government is not able to identify particular agents, these net payment schedules will be anonymous. If government favors agents with particular unobservable characteristics, such as low ability, it will condition its net payments schedules on observables, such as earnings, that are correlated with those characteristics, and face self-selection constraints as in Mirrlees (1971).

The government's second-period optimization is also constrained by the amount of second-period output, which depends on the economy's second-period capital stock as well as agents' second-period labor supplies. The solution to this problem includes the choice of g_o and as well as agent-specific second-period values of consumption and leisure. These choices are functions of second-period capital, and these functions are used by the young government in setting policy; i.e., the young government considers how its net payment schedules will affect the economy's capital in the second period and, thereby, the consumption, leisure, and the public goods enjoyed by different agents when old. In recognizing that the old government will control second-period outcomes, the young government formulates a time-consistent policy.

---

[10] Note that time consistency problems can be potentially resolved by having successive governments purchase consistent behavior from their predecessors. See Kotlikoff, Persson and Svensson (1988).

4.3.5. An example

To make this point concrete, consider a simple model with two agents, a and b, both of whom would earn w when young and old were they to work full time. The young government supplies $2g_y$ and the old government $2g_o$ in public goods. The two governments differ with respect to their preferences over the utilities of the two agents, u_a and u_b. Specifically, assume that $\alpha > .5$ and that

$$W_o = \alpha u_a + (1 - \alpha) u_b, \tag{23}$$

$$W_o = (1 - \alpha) u_a + \alpha u_b. \tag{24}$$

Suppose that utility is separable in public goods, consumption, and leisure and that the utility of consumption and leisure is given by

$$u_i = \log c_{iy} + \log l_{iy} + \theta (\log c_{io} + \log l_{io}) \quad \text{for } i = a \text{ and } b. \tag{25}$$

It is easy to show using dynamic programming that the consistent solution entails

$$\frac{c_{ao}}{c_{ay}} = \frac{\alpha R \theta}{(1 - \alpha)(1 + \theta)}, \tag{26}$$

$$wl_{ay} = c_{ay}, \tag{27}$$

$$wl_{ao} = c_{ao}, \tag{28}$$

$$c_{ay} = \frac{(1 - \alpha) \left(w + \frac{w}{R} - g_y - \frac{g_o}{R}\right)}{1 + \theta}, \tag{29}$$

where R stands for 1 plus the rate of return. A symmetric set of equations holds for the consumption and leisure of agent b with α replaced by $(1 - \alpha)$ and $(1 - \alpha)$ replaced by α. These government choices for consumption and leisure can be compared with the private choices that would arise in the absence of government policy. Those private demands are found by setting α, g_y, and g_o to zero. Compared to the no-policy setting, the interaction of the two governments distorts the intertemporal allocation of consumption and leisure of the two agents. Agent a (b) ends up with higher (lower) ratios of consumption when old to consumption when young and leisure when old to leisure when young. The reason, of course, is that the old government redistributes toward agent a, while the young government redistributes toward agent b.

Having worked out the best lifetime allocations that it can achieve given the old government's ultimate control of second-period outcomes, the young government needs to implement this time-consistent solution. Because it can announce non-linear as well as non-differentiable net payment schedules, the above allocation can be decentralized in an infinite number of ways. One way is to announce agent-specific lump-sum payments, h_a and h_b, plus agent-specific payments per unit of expenditure on old-age consumption and leisure, p_a and p_b. In this case, the agents will perceive the following lifetime budget constraints:

$$\left(c_{ay} + wl_{ay}\right) + \frac{p_a(c_{ao} + wl_{ao})}{R} = w + \frac{w}{R} - h_a, \tag{30}$$

$$\left(c_{by} + wl_{by}\right) + \frac{p_b(c_{bo} + wl_{bo})}{R} = w + \frac{w}{R} - h_b, \tag{31}$$

where

$$h_a = (2\alpha - 1)\left(w + \frac{w}{R}\right) + 2(1 - \alpha)\left(g_y + \frac{g_o}{R}\right), \tag{32}$$

$$h_b = (1 - 2\alpha)\left(w + \frac{w}{R}\right) + 2\alpha\left(g_y + \frac{g_o}{R}\right), \tag{33}$$

$$p_a = \frac{1 - \alpha}{\alpha}, \tag{34}$$

$$p_b = \frac{\alpha}{1 - \alpha}. \tag{35}$$

Note that the two lump-sum payments add up to the present value of the government's purchase of public goods. Also note that since $\alpha > 0.5$, agent a faces a lower marginal payment on second-period expenditures than does agent b. It is easy to show that the marginal payments generate no net resources to the government.

The fact that one can, as just shown, model time-inconsistent government preferences without resort to the terms "deficit", "taxes" or "transfer payments" indicates that whatever are the policies that arise in the model just described or in similar models, they can be labeled any way one wants. Indeed, models of time consistency that cannot be relabeled freely may be predicated on fiscal irrationality. Consider, in this respect, Fischer's (1980) classic analysis of time-inconsistent capital-income taxation.

Fischer's model also features a single generation that consumes and works when young and old and a government that wants to provide public goods. But unlike the above model, all generation members are identical. Fischer permits his government to levy only proportional taxes on labor earnings when young and old and a tax on capital holdings when old. These restrictions may seem benign, but they are not. Why? Because Fischer is saying that the old government can levy what, from the perspective of the second period, is a non-distortionary tax on capital, but that it *cannot* levy the same non-distortionary tax as part of a non-linear second-period earnings tax in which inframarginal earnings are taxed at a different rate than are marginal earnings [11].

---

[11] Suppose, for example, that Fischer's old government levies a tax of 50 units of the model's good on capital and a 15% proportional tax on labor earnings. From the perspective of second-period agents, this is no different from a policy under which the government announces that it will not tax capital at all, but instead assess a 50 unit tax on the first dollar earned and a 15% tax on each dollar earned thereafter.

If one drops Fischer's restriction and allows non-linear net payment schedules, his model collapses to the above model with $\alpha = .5$. In this case, the young and old governments agree and extract inframarginal net payments to pay for public goods. Hence, Fischer's economy ends up in a first-best equilibrium, in which no margins of choice are distorted. This is a far cry from the third-best equilibrium Fischer proposes – an equilibrium in which the government can only tax second-period earnings in a distortionary manner and to avoid doing so, places very high, and possibly confiscatory taxes on agents' capital accumulation. Agents naturally respond by saving little or nothing.

Do Fischer's restrictions, which he does not justify, reflect economic considerations, or are they simply a subtle manifestation of fiscal illusion? One economic argument in their behalf is that the governments he contemplates do not have the ability to observe individual earnings or capital holdings and are forced to collect net payments on an anonymous basis. For example, the governments might be able to collect net payments from firms that are functions of the firms' aggregate capital holdings and aggregate wage payments, but not be able to collect net payments from individual agents. This does not immediately imply the absence of inframarginal labor earnings taxes since the governments could, in addition to taxing the firms' total wage bill at a fixed rate, levy a fixed payment per employee on each firm, assuming the government can observe the number of employees. But, for argument's sake, let us assume the government cannot observe the number of employees.

In this case, can one still re-label fiscal flows in Fischer's model without changing anything fundamental? The answer is yes. Take the first of Fischer's two third-best equilibria. It entails a first-period proportional labor-earnings tax, a second-period proportional capital levy, and no second-period labor-earnings tax. Now starting from this tax structure, suppose the government wants to "run" a smaller surplus. It can do so by labeling first-period labor-income taxes of T_y as "a first-period loan" to the government of T_y plus a "second-period tax" of $(1 + r) T_y$, where r is the rate of interest. Since this second-period tax is calculated as a function of labor earnings when young, the re-labeling alters no incentives to work when young. Nor does it change the government's cash flows, since the government still receives T_y in the first period as a "loan" and uses the $(1 + r) T_y$ second-period "tax" receipt to repay "principal plus interest" on its first-period "borrowing". The government has no reason to either a) renege on repaying this debt, or b) tax these debt holdings because in the second period it is getting all the receipts it needs from its non-distortionary capital levy[12].

---

[12] If the government wants, instead, to announce a larger first-period surplus, it can raise the first-period labor-income tax, lend the additional proceeds back to the young, and provide a second-period subsidy on first-period labor earnings paid for with the proceeds of the loan repayment. Again, the old government has no reason to renege on this second-period subsidy because it is already collecting all the resources it needs via the non-distortionary capital levy. Alternatively, it can collect the second-period capital-income tax in the form of a first-period tax on the acquisition of assets and then lend these additional first-period receipts back to the young. This leaves the net payment of the young unchanged,

If the government is effecting its transactions through firms, it can borrow from firms in the first period, repay the firms in the second period, and assess a tax in the second period on the firms based on their first-period wage payments. In this case, the firms will withhold and save enough of the worker's first-period pre-tax wages so as to be able to pay these extra second-period taxes. The firms will invest in the government bonds and use the proceeds of those bonds to pay off the additional taxes.

Fischer's alternative third-best tax structure entails a confiscatory tax on all physical capital accumulated for old age and positive first- and second-period labor-earnings taxes. Can the government, also in this setting, postpone its taxes on first-period labor earnings and get the young, or the firms on behalf of the young, to lend it what it would otherwise have collected as first-period taxes? The answer is yes. If the government reneges on its debt repayment in the second-period, by either repudiating the debt or levying a tax on holdings of debt, the old, or the firms on their behalf, will not be able to repay the taxes that are due in the second-period on first-period labor earnings unless the government violates Fischer's stricture against taxing second-period earnings at other than a fixed rate that is independent of the level of earnings. To see this, note that taxes levied on first-period labor earnings are, from the perspective of the second period, lump-sum since first-period labor supply decisions have already been made. So paying off the debt has no efficiency implications because the proceeds of this debt repayment are immediately handed back to the old government in the form of a lump-sum tax. If the government were to renege on its debt and also tax first-period labor earnings in the second period, it would force the old (the firms) to pay additional taxes from the proceeds of their second-period labor earnings (their second-period wage payments). This would require a non-linear tax, which, again, is something that Fischer seems to have ruled out a priori. The non-linear tax in this case would be a fixed payment, independent of second-period labor earnings, plus a payment based on the level of second-period labor earnings.

4.3.6. Voluntary vs. involuntary payments

A final issue is whether the voluntary nature of private purchases of government bonds makes debt labels meaningful. This proposition is indirectly advanced in a very interesting article by Tabellini (1991) on the sustainability of intergenerational redistribution. In his model, the government wants to finance uniform transfer payments to young parents by extracting payments from a subset of them, namely those that are rich. Unfortunately, Tabellini's government cannot observe endowments, and were it to force all young parents to make the same payment, it would defeat its purpose. Instead, the government "borrows" from young parents, with the result that only those young parents with large endowments voluntarily "lend" to the government.

---

and the second-period repayment of principal plus interest on the loan gives the government the same second-period net receipts it has under its initial wording.

Tabellini notes that these loans will be repaid when these rich parents are old. Why? Because their children will join with them in voting for debt repayment since much of that repayment will come from the children of the poor. In the course of showing that intragenerational distribution considerations can help enforce intergenerational redistribution, Tabellini claims that this same policy could not be implemented through a social security system, because a social security tax would be compulsory.

I disagree for the simple reason that social security tax payments need not be compulsory. Instead of announcing that it is "borrowing", Tabellini's government could equally well announce a payroll tax that is the same function of the young parents' endowment as is their debt purchases. The government would also announce social security benefit payments that are set equal to the tax contributions plus the market rate of return that would otherwise be paid on government bonds. True, the government cannot force the parents, when they are young, to pay social security taxes because the government cannot observe the parent's initial endowments. But there is no need to enforce the tax collection; the same parents who would otherwise have purchased debt will want to pay the tax because it will ensure them an old age social security benefit in a setting in which they have no other means to save for old age.

Note that in many countries, payroll tax payments are in large part voluntary. Workers can choose to work in the formal sector and pay those taxes or they can choose to work in the informal sector and not pay. Another way to think about "enforcing" the "tax" is for the government to announce a penalty, namely, disqualification from receipt of the old-age transfer payment, so that formal-sector workers could choose not to contribute without the fear of being sent to jail. Note also that with this alternative labeling, the children of the rich will want to enforce the payment of social security benefits because their parents will otherwise lose out to the benefit of the children of the poor.

With Tabellini's fiscal labels (case a), the government reports a deficit when the parents are young. Under mine (case b), it reports a balanced budget. If it wanted to report a surplus, it could announce a social security tax schedule that was, say, double what it would announce in case b, but also announce that it would make loans to all tax payers equal to one half of their tax contributions. When old, in this case c, the parents would get twice the social security benefits that they'd get in case b, but they would have to pay back their loans with interest. If the government in Tabellini's model wants to report an even larger deficit (case d), it could borrow twice as much and announce that it would provide a special transfer payment to its lenders equal to, say, one half of the loans they provide. When old, these lenders would face an extra tax, equal to the special transfer plus interest, with the proceeds of this tax subtracted out of the government's repayment to the lenders.

In each of these cases, the net flows between each parent and the government in each period is the same, so the voting choices of the young will not change. The only change is the government's reported deficit/surplus.

4.4. Implications for empirical analyses of deficits, personal saving, and portfolio choice

The above demonstration that government debt and deficits are not well defined has serious implications for the vast time-series literature that purports to connect these aggregates to consumption, interest rates, and other macroeconomic variables. This literature is reviewed in Elmendorf and Mankiw (1998). The problem with these studies is that they use wholly arbitrary measures of deficits and debts, which could just as well be replaced by other equally arbitrary measures that have the opposite correlation with the dependent variable. Moreover, in the absence of any theoretical ground rules for measuring the deficit, Eisner and Pieper (1984) and other economists have felt free to "correct" the U.S. federal deficit in ways that substantiate their priors about the impact of deficits on the economy.

Empirical analysis of personal saving suffers from the same shortcoming. The measurement of personal saving is predicated on the measurement of personal disposable income, which, in turn, depends on the measurement of taxes and transfer payments. Since taxes and transfer payments can be freely defined, the nation's personal saving rate can be anything anyone wants it to be. This fact casts a pall on studies like those of Bosworth, Burtless and Sabelhaus (1991) and Gale and Sabelhaus (1999) that purport to "explain" or, at least illuminate, changes over time in the nation's rate of personal saving.

Finally, if government debt is not well defined, then the division of private portfolios between stocks and bonds, including government bonds, is a matter of opinion, not fact. This calls into question studies that purport to identify risk preferences and other portfolio determinants based on the shares of portfolios invested in bonds versus stocks.

5. Generational accounting

Generational accounting was developed by Auerbach, Gokhale and Kotlikoff (1991) in response to the aforementioned problems of deficit accounting. The objective of generational accounting is to measure the generational incidence of fiscal policy as well as its sustainability and to do so in ways that are independent of fiscal taxonomy. Generational accounting compares the lifetime net tax bills facing future generations with that facing current newborns. It also calculates the changes in generational accounts associated with changes in fiscal policies. Both of these comparisons are label-free in the sense that they generate the same answer regardless of how government receipts and payments are labeled.

Although academics have spearheaded development of generational accounts, much of the work has been done at the governmental or multilateral institutional level. The U.S. Federal Reserve, the U.S. Congressional Budget Office, the U.S. Office of Management and Budget, H.M. Treasury, the Bank of Japan, the Bundesbank, the

Norwegian Ministry of Finance, the Bank of Italy, the New Zealand Treasury, the European Commission[13], the International Monetary Fund, and the World Bank have all done generational accounting. Much of the interest in generational accounting by these institutions stems from the projected dramatic aging of OECD countries coupled with the commitments of OECD governments to pay very high levels of social security and health care benefits to the elderly.

Generational accounting has also drawn considerable interest from academic and government economists. Haveman (1994), U.S. Congressional Budget Office (1995), Cutler (1993), Diamond (1996), Buiter (1997), Shaviro (1997), Auerbach, Gokhale and Kotlikoff (1994), Kotlikoff (1997), Raffelhüschen (1998), and others have debated its merits.

Much of the interest in generational accounting is motivated by the extraordinary aging of industrial societies that will, over the next few decades, make almost all of the leading countries around the world look like present-day retirement communities. Population aging per se is not necessarily a cause for economic concern, but population aging in the presence of high and growing levels of government support for the elderly makes early attention to the long-term fiscal implications of aging imperative.

While generational accounting is a natural for old and aging countries, developing countries, like Mexico and Thailand, which do not face aging problems, have their own reasons for examining generational accounting. In particular, they realize that their relative youth means they have more current and future young people to help bear outstanding fiscal burdens and that viewed through the lens of generational accounting, their fiscal policies might look much more responsible relative to those of the developed world.

This section lays out generational accounting's methodology, shows alternative ways of measuring generational imbalances, stresses the importance of demographics in generational accounting, discusses practical issues in constructing generational accounts, shows examples of generational accounts and measures of generational imbalances, points out the connection between generational accounting and traditional tax incidence analysis, and mentions, along the way, a variety of concerns that have been raised about this new form of fiscal appraisal.

5.1. The method of generational accounting

Equation (36) rewrites the government's intertemporal budget constraint (Equation 8) in terms of the generational accounts of current and future generations.

$$\sum_{s=1}^{\infty} N_{t,t+s} P_{t,t+s} (1+r)^{-s} + \sum_{s=0}^{d} N_{t,t-s} P_{t,t-s} = \sum_{s=0}^{\infty} G_{t+s} (1+r)^{-s} + D_t. \qquad (36)$$

---

[13] The European Commission has an ongoing project to do generational accounting for EU member nations under the direction of Bernd Raffelhueschen, Professor of Economics at Freiburg University. See Raffelhüschen (1998).

In Equation (36), $N_{t,k}$ stands for the per capita generational account in year t of the generation born in year k. For generations currently alive, $N_{t,k}$ denotes per capita remaining lifetime net taxes discounted to the current year t. For generations not yet born, $N_{t,k}$ refers to per capita lifetime net taxes, discounted to the year of birth. The term $P_{t,k}$ stands for the population in year t of the cohort that was born in year k. This first summation on the left-hand side of Equation (36) adds together the generational accounts of future generations, discounted at rate r to the current year t. The second summation adds the accounts of existing generations. In actual applications of generational accounting, separate accounts are calculated for males and females, but this feature is omitted from Equation (36) to limit notation.

The first term on the right-hand side of Equation (36) expresses the present value of government purchases. In this summation the values of government purchases in year s, given by G_s, are also discounted to year t. The remaining term on the right-hand side, D_t^g, denotes the government's explicit net debt – its financial liabilities minus the sum of its financial assets and the market value of its public enterprises based on whatever arbitrary language conventions the government has adopted.

5.1.1. The precise formula for generational accounts

The generational account $N_{t,k}$ is defined by:

$$N_{t,k} = \sum_{s=\max(t,k)}^{k+D} T_{s,k} \frac{P_{s,k}}{P_{t,k}} (1+r)^{-(s-t)}, \tag{37}$$

where $\kappa = \max(t,k)$. The term $T_{s,k}$ stands for the projected average net tax payment to the government made in year s by a member of the generation born in year k.

The term $P_{s,k}/P_{t,k}$ indicates the proportion of members of cohort k alive at time t who will also be alive at time s[14]. Thus, it represents the probability that a particular member of the year-k cohort who is alive in year t will survive to year s to pay the net taxes levied, on average, in that year on year-k cohort members. Hence, $N_{t,k}$ is an *actuarial* present value. It represents the average value in the present of the amount of net taxes that members of cohort k will pay in the future, where the averaging is over not just net tax payments, but also survivorship.

5.1.2. What do generational accounts exclude?

Note that generational accounts reflect only taxes paid less transfer payments received. With the exception of government expenditures on health care and education, which

---

[14] The population weights $P_{s,k}$ incorporate both mortality and immigration, implicitly treating immigration as if it were a "rebirth" and assigning the taxes paid by immigrants to the representative members of their respective cohorts. This approach does not, therefore, separate the burdens of natives and immigrants. See Ablett (1999) and Auerbach and Oreopoulos (2000) for applications of generational accounting that make that separation as well as study a variety of fiscal issues associated with immigration.

are treated as transfer payments, the accounts do not impute to particular generations the value of the government's purchases of goods and services. Why not? Because it is difficult to attribute the benefits of such purchases. Therefore, the accounts do not show the full net benefit or burden that any generation receives from government policy as a whole, although they can show a generation's net benefit or burden from a particular policy change that affects only taxes and transfers. Thus, generational accounting tells us which generations will pay for the government spending not included in the accounts, rather than telling us which generations will benefit from that spending. This implies nothing about the value of government spending; i.e., there is no assumption, explicit or implicit, in the standard practice of generational accounting concerning the value to households of government purchases [15].

5.1.3. Assessing the fiscal burden facing future generations

Given the right-hand side of Equation (36) and the second term on the left-hand-side, generational accountants determine, as a residual, the value of the first term on the left-hand side – the collective payment, measured as a time-t present value, required of future generations. Given this amount, one can determine the average present value lifetime net tax payment of each member of each future cohort under the assumption that these lifetime net tax payments rise for members of each successive future cohorts at the economy's rate of labor productivity growth, g. Now, if labor productivity grows at g percent per year, so will real wages. Hence, the lifetime labor income of each new cohort will be g percent larger than that of its immediate predecessor. So, in assuming that each successive cohort pays lifetime net taxes that are g percent larger than those of its predecessor, one is assuming that each successive future cohort pays the same share of its lifetime labor income in net taxes; i.e., one is assuming that each future cohort faces the same lifetime net tax rate.

Let $\bar{N}$ stand for the growth-adjusted generational account of future generations. $\bar{N}$ is the amount each member of a future cohort would pay in lifetime net taxes if her lifetime labor income were the same as that of a current newborn. The actual amount the cohort born in year $t+1$ will pay is $\bar{N}(1+g)$. The actual amount the cohort born in year $t+2$ will pay is $\bar{N}(1+g)^2$. The actual amount the cohort born in year $t+3$ will pay is $\bar{N}(1+g)^3$, and so on. Equation (38) can be used to solve for $\bar{N}$.

$$\sum_{s=0}^{D} N_{t,t-s} P_{t,t-s} + \sum_{s=1}^{\infty} \bar{N}(1+g)^s P_{t,t+s}(1+r)^{t-s} = \sum_{s=t}^{\infty} G_s(1+r)^{t-s} + D_t. \tag{38}$$

$\bar{N}$ is the lifetime net tax payment of future generations adjusted for growth, so it is directly comparable to that of current newborns, $N_{t,t}$. This comparison is also label-free because alternative labeling conventions leave unchanged lifetime net payments.

---

[15] Raffelhüschen (1998) departs from this conventional approach to generational accounting of not allocating the benefits of government purchases. Instead, he allocates these purchases on a per-capita basis.

If $\bar{N}$ equals $N_{t,t}$, generational policy is balanced. If $\bar{N}$ exceeds (is smaller than) $N_{t,t}$, future generations face larger (smaller) growth-adjusted lifetime net tax burdens than do current newborns.

The assumption that the generational accounts of all future generations are equal, except for a growth adjustment, is just one of many assumptions one could make about the distribution across future generations of their collective net tax payments to the government. One could, for example, assume a phase-in of the additional fiscal burden (positive or negative) to be imposed on future generations, allocating a greater share of the burden to later future generations and a smaller share to earlier ones. Clearly, such a phase-in would mean that generations born after the phase-in period has elapsed would face larger values of lifetime burdens (the $N_{t,k}$'s) than we are calculating here.

5.1.4. Alternative ways to achieve generational balance

Another way of measuring the imbalance in fiscal policy is to ask what immediate and permanent change in either a) government purchases, or b) a specific tax (such as the income tax) or transfer payment (such as old-age social security benefits) would be necessary to equalize the lifetime growth-adjusted fiscal burden facing current newborns and future generations. Because such policies satisfy the government's intertemporal budget constraint, they are also sustainable.

To be more precise about this type of calculation, suppose one wants to find the immediate and permanent percentage reduction in government purchases needed to achieve generational balance. Denote this percentage reduction by z. Next, use Equation (39) to solve for z under the assumption that $\bar{N}$ equals $N_{t,t}$.

$$\sum_{s=0}^{D} N_{t,t-s} P_{t,t-s} + \sum_{s=1}^{\infty} \bar{N}(1+g)^s P_{t,t+s}(1+r)^{t-s} = \sum_{s=t}^{\infty} (1+z) G_s (1+r)^{t-s} + D_t.$$

(39)

As a second example, consider the immediate and permanent percentage increase in income taxes needed to achieve generational balance. Call this percentage increase v [16]. To determine the size of v, try different immediate and permanent income tax hikes until you find the one with the following property: given the new values of generational accounts (the values inclusive of the tax hike), the calculated value of $\bar{N}$ equals $N_{t,t}$. In contrast to the calculation of z, in this calculation of v, $N_{t,t}$, the generational account of current newborns, is not held fixed. Like the accounts of all other existing generations, $N_{t,t}$ is higher because of the increase in the income tax. Consequently, so is $\bar{N}$.

---

[16] To introduce v in Equation (4) we would have to express the generational accounts of current generations as a) the present value of their future tax payments minus b) the present value of their future transfer payments and simply multiply the expression for the present value of future tax payments by $(1+v)$.

5.1.5. The role of demographics

As can be seen in Equations (23–26), demographics play a central role in determining the size of the imbalance in generational policy. Other things being equal, the larger the population sizes of future generations, the smaller will be the size of $\bar{N}$, and, therefore, the smaller will be the imbalance of generational policy. Ceteris paribus, larger population sizes of current generations will raise or lower $\bar{N}$ depending on the sign of the generational accounts these population totals are multiplying. For example, if the generational accounts of those over age 65 are negative, larger numbers of older people will make the calculated value of $\bar{N}$ larger. A negative account means that the government will, under current policy, pay more to a generation in transfer payments than it receives in taxes. Negative generational accounts for older generations is the norm in industrialized countries because these generations receive more in state pension, health, and other benefits over the remainder of their lives than they pay in taxes.

What is the impact of the large number of baby boomers on generational imbalance? Since these generations typically still have positive generational accounts, they are contributing, on balance, to lowering the size of $\bar{N}$ and, thus, the imbalance in generational policy. On the other hand, since these generations are close to receiving large net transfers from the government, the current values of their generational accounts are quite small. Hence, the contribution they are making toward lowering $\bar{N}$ is small. This is the channel through which the very sizable benefits that are due to be paid in retirement to the enormous baby boom generation in industrialized countries constitute a fiscal burden on young and future generations.

5.1.6. Inputs to generational accounting

Producing generational accounts requires projections of population, taxes, transfers, and government purchases, an initial value of government net debt, and a discount rate. Since generational accounting considers all levels of government – local, state, and federal – the measures of taxes, transfers, and government purchases must be comprehensive. Government infrastructure purchases are treated like other forms of purchases in the calculations. Although such purchases provide an ongoing stream, rather than a one-time amount, of services, they still must be paid for. Generational accounting clarifies which generation or generations will have to bear the burden of these and other purchases. Government net debt is calculated net of the current market value of state enterprises. This value is determined by capitalizing the net profits of those businesses. In contrast to the treatment of the market value of state enterprises, government net debt does *not* net out the value of the government's existing infrastructure, such as parks, highways, and tanks. Including such assets would have no impact on the estimated fiscal burden facing future generations because including these assets would require adding to the projected flow of government purchases an exactly offsetting flow of imputed rent on the government's existing infrastructure.

Taxes and transfer payments are each broken down into several categories. The general rule regarding tax incidence is to assume that taxes are borne by those paying the taxes, when the taxes are paid: income taxes on income, consumption taxes on consumers, and property taxes on property owners. There are two exceptions here, both of which involve capital income taxes. First, as detailed in Auerbach, Gokhale and Kotlikoff (1991), one should, data permitting, distinguish between marginal and infra-marginal capital income taxes. Specifically, infra-marginal capital income taxes should be distributed to existing wealth holders, whereas marginal capital income taxes should be based on future projected wealth holdings. Second, in the case of small open economies, marginal corporate income taxes are assumed to be borne by (and are therefore allocated to) labor. The general rule for allocating transfer payments is to allocate them to those who directly receive them.

The typical method used to project the average values of particular taxes and transfer payments by age and sex starts with government forecasts of the aggregate amounts of each type of tax (e.g., payroll) and transfer payment (e.g., welfare benefits) in future years. These aggregate amounts are then distributed by age and sex based on relative age-tax and age-transfer profiles derived from cross-section micro data sets. For years beyond those for which government forecasts are available, age- and sex-specific average tax and transfer amounts are generally assumed to equal those for the latest year for which forecasts are available, with an adjustment for growth.

Equation (40) helps clarify the method of distributing annual tax or transfer aggregates in a particular year to contemporaneous cohorts. Again, to simplify the presentation we abstract from the distinction between sexes that we consider in the actual calculations.

$$H_t = \sum_{s=0}^{D} T_t, R_{t,t-s} P_{t,t-s}. \tag{40}$$

In Equation (40), H_t stands for an aggregate tax or transfer amount in year t. Let us assume it stands for total income tax payments to make the example concrete. The term T_t, is the average amount of income tax paid in year t. $R_{t,t-s}$ is the relative distribution profile for income taxes in year t. Specifically, it stands for ratio of the average income tax payment of members of the cohort born in year $t - s$ to the average income tax payment in year t. Finally, $P_{t,t-s}$ stands for the number of people in year t who were born in year $t - s$, i.e., it is the population size of the age $t - s$ cohort. Given H_t and the values of the $R_{t,t-s}$ and $P_{t,t-s}$ terms, one can use Equation (41) to solve for T_t. To form $T_{t,t-s}$, the terms that enter Equation (37) that are used to calculate each current generation's account, note that

$$T_{t,t-s} = T_{t,t} R_{t,t-s}. \tag{41}$$

5.1.7. *Discount rates and uncertainty*

For base-case calculations, generational accountants typically use a real rate of discount around 5%, a rate that exceeds the real government short-term borrowing rate in most developed countries. This rate seems justified given the riskiness of the flows being discounted. However, the "right" discount rate to use is in sufficient question to merit presenting results based on a range of alternative discount rates – a practice routinely followed by those constructing generational accounts.

The appropriate discount rate for calculating the present value of future government revenues and expenditures depends on their uncertainty. If all such flows were certain and riskless, it would clearly be appropriate to discount them using the prevailing term-structure of risk-free interest rates. However, even in this simple and unrealistic case, such discounting could be problematic since it would require knowing the values of this term structure. To discern these values, one might examine the real yields paid on short-term, medium-term, and long-term inflation-indexed government bonds. But this presupposes the existence of such bonds. Many countries do not issue indexed bonds, and those that do do not necessarily issue indexed bonds of all maturities.

In the realistic case in which countries' tax revenues and expenditures are uncertain, discerning the correct discount rate is even more difficult. In this case, discounting based on the term structure of risk-free rates (even if it is observable) is no longer theoretically justified. Instead, the appropriate discount rates would be those that adjust for the riskiness of the stream in question. Since the riskiness of taxes, spending, and transfer payments presumably differ, the theoretically appropriate risk-adjusted rates at which to discount taxes, spending, and transfer payments would also differ. This point carries over to particular components of taxes, spending, and transfer payments, whose risk properties may differ from those of their respective aggregates[17]. Moreover, if insurance arrangements are incomplete, the appropriate risk adjustments would likely be generation-specific. Unfortunately, the size of these risk adjustments remains a topic for fortune research. In the meantime, generational accountants have simply chosen to estimate generational accounts for a range of discount rates.

5.2. Illustrating generational accounts – the case of the USA

In their recent calculation of U.S. generational accounts, Gokhale, Page, Potter and Sturrock (2000) used the latest long-term projections of The Congressional Budget

---

[17] To see this, consider a government policy in the two-period life-cycle model of borrowing from the young at time t and using the proceeds to purchase stock from the young. When the young are old the government repays the principal it borrowed by selling its shares and making up the difference between its interest obligations and the return (including capital gain) on its stock as a net tax payment. This entire set of transactions entails no net payments from the government to generation t either when it is young or old. However, net tax payments will, on average, be negative when generation t is old, since stocks average a higher return than bonds. If one discounts the safe and risky components of the net tax payments at their appropriate and different risk-adjusted discount rates, the present value of future net tax payments will be zero. This is what one would want generational accounting to show, since the policy simply involves the government borrowing stock from the young and returning it (including its return) when they are old; i.e., the policy entails no increase in lifetime net payments. But were one to mistakenly discount the total of expected net taxes in old age at a single discount rate, the value of the change in the generational account would be non zero.

Table 1A
Composition of male US generational accounts [a,b]

Age in 1998	Net tax payment	Tax payments				Transfer receipts [c]			
		Labor income taxes	Capital income taxes	Payroll taxes	Excise taxes	OASDI	MEDC	MEDD	Welfare
0	249.7	128.3	61.8	107.3	93.4	45.2	24.0	58.1	13.7
5	256.4	136.3	66.0	114.1	97.4	48.0	35.9	58.9	14.6
10	272.3	147.1	71.8	123.1	102.1	51.7	44.2	60.2	15.8
15	291.4	158.4	77.9	132.8	105.9	55.4	50.5	60.6	17.1
20	318.7	171.2	85.4	143.8	107.5	59.0	51.9	59.9	18.3
25	327.3	174.5	91.6	145.7	102.4	61.2	52.5	55.2	17.8
30	313.7	167.8	98.2	138.1	95.9	64.6	55.2	49.9	16.5
35	279.2	153.9	104.5	124.3	89.4	69.4	63.7	45.0	14.9
40	241.4	137.1	110.0	108.9	83.2	76.4	67.4	40.4	13.5
45	194.2	116.1	113.0	91.2	75.5	85.5	67.9	35.9	12.3
50	129.7	93.0	112.4	71.8	65.6	95.6	75.4	31.0	11.1
55	66.2	65.5	108.4	50.4	56.0	108.1	69.7	26.3	10.0
60	−5.8	38.0	100.5	29.1	46.4	123.1	66.1	21.8	9.0
65	−77.5	16.6	89.5	12.7	37.2	138.5	69.3	17.7	8.0
70	−91.0	6.8	76.3	5.1	28.4	129.7	56.2	14.8	7.0
75	−75.1	3.3	61.3	2.4	20.8	106.5	38.2	12.5	5.7
80	−56.3	1.4	46.1	1.2	14.6	85.7	20.2	9.7	4.0
85	−42.4	0.5	33.0	0.5	10.1	67.0	9.0	8.0	2.6
90	−25.6	0.4	28.5	0.4	7.9	51.7	3.1	6.0	2.0

[a] Table assumes a 4% real discount rate and 2.2% growth rate. Present values in thousands of 1998 dollars.
[b] Growth-adjusted net tax payment of future generations: 361.8; Lifetime net tax rate on future generations: 32.3%; Lifetime net tax rate on newborns: 22.8%; Generational imbalance: 41.7%.
[c] Abbreviations: OASDI, Old Age Survivior and Disability Insurance; MEDC, MEDICARE; MEDD, MEDICAID.

Office (CBO) with one modification. They assumed that U.S. federal discretionary spending would grow with the economy. Table 1 reports generational accounts on this basis, constructed using a 4.0% real discount rate and assuming a 2.2% rate of growth of labor productivity. This discount rate is roughly the current prevailing rate on long-term inflation-indexed U.S. government bonds, and the productivity growth rate is the one currently being projected by the CBO. The accounts are for 1998, but are based on the CBO projections available as of January 2000.

Table 1 shows, for males and females separately, the level and composition of the accounts. Recall that the accounts are present values discounted, in this case, to 1998.

Table 1B

Composition of female US generational accounts [a,b]

Age in 1998	Net tax payment	Tax payments				Transfer receipts [c]			
		Labor income taxes	Capital income taxes	Payroll taxes	Excise taxes	OASDI	MEDC	MEDD	Welfare
0	109.6	67.8	21.6	64.1	89.0	42.3	24.6	44.0	22.0
5	104.6	72.1	23.0	68.2	92.7	45.0	38.3	44.7	23.4
10	104.6	77.9	25.1	73.7	97.0	48.7	48.8	46.1	25.6
15	105.4	84.1	27.2	79.6	99.9	52.4	57.9	46.9	28.2
20	113.7	91.0	29.8	86.2	100.9	56.4	61.1	46.9	29.9
25	112.3	91.5	31.8	86.4	96.6	58.9	63.7	45.2	26.2
30	95.6	85.1	33.9	79.9	91.2	61.9	68.0	43.2	21.3
35	65.6	75.6	35.9	70.8	85.7	65.7	78.6	41.1	17.0
40	37.9	66.0	37.9	62.0	79.7	71.4	83.7	39.3	13.3
45	7.9	55.4	39.2	52.1	72.7	78.8	84.7	37.6	10.4
50	−37.7	42.2	39.6	39.6	64.4	87.7	94.1	33.5	8.2
55	−73.9	28.3	39.1	26.6	55.2	99.0	87.5	29.8	6.8
60	−115.0	15.6	37.4	14.7	46.0	112.7	84.0	26.2	5.8
65	−157.6	6.6	34.6	6.1	36.9	124.6	89.3	22.6	5.2
70	−155.9	2.5	30.8	2.2	28.7	116.8	78.7	20.0	4.6
75	−131.8	0.9	26.3	0.9	21.3	100.0	59.6	17.9	3.8
80	−99.2	0.3	21.5	0.3	15.3	82.1	36.9	14.5	3.1
85	−70.5	0.2	16.9	0.1	11.1	63.4	20.6	12.5	2.4
90	−44.4	0.1	14.1	0.1	8.3	47.3	9.0	8.9	1.8

[a] Table assumes a 4% real discount rate and 2.2% growth rate. Present values in thousands of 1998 dollars.
[b] Future generations: 158.8.
[c] Abbreviations: OASDI, Old Age Survivior and Disability Insurance; MEDC, MEDICARE; MEDD, MEDICAID.

As an example, consider the $112 300 account of 25 year-old males in 1998. This amount represents the present value of the net tax payments that 25 year-old males will pay, on average, over the rest of their lives.

The generational accounts for both males and females peak at age 25 and become negative for females at age 50 and for males after age 60. The accounts for those younger than age 25 are smaller because they have a longer time to wait to reach their peak tax-paying years. The accounts are also smaller for those above age 25 because they are closer in time to receiving the bulk of their transfer payments. By age 10 for males and age 30 for females, Medicare and Social Security benefits are the two most important forms of transfer payments, if one uses the government's fiscal taxonomy.

The only figures in this table that are not a function of labeling conventions are the lifetime net tax rate of future generations and of newborns. The denominators in these lifetime tax rates are the present value of lifetime earnings. And they are constructed by pooling the net tax payments and labor earnings of males and females. In the case of future generations, the present value to 1998 of all future net taxes of all future generations is divided by the present value to 1998 of the labor earnings of all future generations.

5.2.1. The imbalance in US generational policy

For newborns the lifetime net tax rate is 22.8%. For future generations it is 32.3%. So future generations face a lifetime net tax rate that is 41.6% higher than that facing current newborns [18]. Stated differently, future generations, according to current policy, are being asked to pay almost a dime more per dollar earned than are current newborns.

In thinking about the magnitude of the U.S. generational imbalance, it is important to keep in mind that the lifetime net tax rate facing future generations under current policy assumes that *all* future generations pay this same rate. If, instead, one were to assume that generations born, say, over the next decade are treated the same as current newborns, the net tax rate for generations born in 2010 and beyond would be higher than 32.3%.

5.2.2. Policies to achieve generational balance in the USA

Table 2 considers five alternative policies that would achieve generational balance in the U.S. The first is a 31% immediate and permanent rise in federal personal and

Table 2
Alternative policies to achieve generational balance[a] in the USA

Policy	Immediate and permanent percentage change in policy instrument	Equalized lifetime net tax rate
Raise all taxes	12.0	27.5
Raise Federal income taxes	31.3	27.3
Cut all transfers	21.9	26.5
Cut all governmental purchases	21.0	22.8
Cut federal purchases	66.3	22.8

[a] Generational imbalance is the percentage difference in lifetime net tax rates of newborns and future generations.

---

[18] This is a very sizeable imbalance, but it's nevertheless smaller than the imbalance estimated in the early 1990s. The decline in the imbalance reflects policy changes and much more optimistic long-term fiscal projections.

corporate income taxes. Had the U.S. adopted this policy in 2000, the federal surplus reported by the government for that year would have more than doubled. Hence, based on the government's fiscal language, the year-2000 surplus was far too small compared to that needed to achieve generational balance.

Rather than raising just federal income taxes, one could raise all federal, state, and local taxes. In this case, an across-the-board tax hike of 12% could deliver generational balance. Cutting all Social Security, Medicare, Medicaid, food stamps, unemployment insurance benefits, welfare benefits, housing support, and other transfer payments by 21.9% is another way to eliminate the generational imbalance. Two final options considered in the table are immediately and permanently cutting all government purchases by 21% or cutting just federal purchases by 66.3%.

Cutting government purchases to achieve generational balance would leave future generations paying in net taxes the same 22.8% share of lifetime earnings as current newborns are expected (under current policy) to pay. In contrast, either raising taxes or cutting transfer payments would mean higher lifetime net tax rates for those now alive. As Table 2 indicates, these alternative policies would leave newborns and all future generations paying roughly 27 cents out of every dollar earned in net taxes. This net tax rate is over 4 cents more per dollar earned than newborns are now forced to pay. The payoff from having newborns as well as everyone else who is currently alive pay more in net taxes, is a reduction in net tax rate facing future generations by 5 to 6 cents per dollar earned.

5.2.3. Achieving generational balance in 22 countries

The United States is certainly not alone in running imbalanced generational policies. Table 3, abstracted from Kotlikoff and Raffelhüschen (1999), reports alternative immediate and permanent policy changes that would achieve generational balance in 21 countries. According to the second column in the table, 13 of the 22 countries need to cut their non-educational government spending by over one fifth if they want to rely solely on such cuts to achieve generational balance. This group includes the United States and Japan and the three most important members of the European Monetary Union: Germany, France and Italy. Four of the 13 countries – Austria, Finland, Spain and Sweden – need to cut their non-education purchases by more than half, and two countries – Austria and Finland – need to cut this spending by more than two thirds! Bear in mind that generational accounting includes regional, state, local, and federal levels of government. So the cuts being considered here are equal proportionate cuts in all levels of government spending.

Not all countries suffer from generational imbalances. In Ireland, New Zealand, and Thailand future generations face a smaller fiscal burden, measured on a growth-adjusted basis, than do current ones given the government's current spending projections. Hence, governments in those countries can spend more over time without unduly burdening future generations. There are also several countries in the list, including Canada and the United Kingdom, with zero or moderate generational

Table 3
Alternative ways to achieve generational balance in 22 countries[a]

Country	Cut in government purchases	Cut in government transfers	Increase in all taxes	Increase in income tax
Argentina	29.1	11.0	8.4	75.7
Australia	10.2	9.1	4.8	8.1
Austria	76.4	20.5	18.4	55.6
Belgium	12.4	4.6	3.1	10.0
Brazil	26.2	17.9	11.7	74.0
Canada	0.1	0.1	0.1	0.2
Denmark	29.0	4.5	4.0	6.7
Finland	67.6	21.2	19.4	50.8
Germany	25.9	14.1	9.5	29.5
Ireland	−4.3	−4.4	−2.1	−4.8
Italy	49.1	13.3	10.5	28.2
Japan	29.5	25.3	15.5	53.6
Netherlands	28.7	22.3	8.9	15.6
New Zealand	−1.6	−0.6	−0.4	−0.8
Norway	9.9	8.1	6.3	9.7
Portugal	9.8	7.5	4.2	13.3
Spain	62.2	17.0	14.5	44.9
Sweden	50.5	18.9	15.6	41.9
Thailand	−47.7	−114.2	−25.0	−81.8
France	22.2	9.8	6.9	64.0
United Kingdom	9.7	9.5	2.7	9.5
United States	21.0	21.9	12.0	31.3

[a] Sources: Kotlikoff and Leibfritz (1999), Raffelhüschen (1998), Gokhale and Kotlikoff (2001).

imbalances as measured by the spending adjustment needed to achieve perfect balance. What explains these tremendous cross-country differences? Fiscal policies and demographics differ dramatically across countries. The U.S., for example, has experienced and is likely to continue to experience rapid health-care spending. Japan's health care spending is growing less rapidly, but it is aging much more quickly. The United Kingdom has a policy of keeping most transfer payments fixed over time in real terms. Germany is dealing with the ongoing costs of reunification.

One alternative to cutting spending is cutting transfer payments. In Japan, education, health care, social security benefits, unemployment benefits, disability benefits, and all other transfer payments would need to be immediately and permanently slashed by

25%. In the U.S., the figure is 20%. In Brazil, it is 18%. In Germany, it is 14%. And in Italy it is 13%. These and similar figures for other countries represent dramatic cuts and would be very unpopular.

So too would tax increases. If Japan were to rely exclusively on across-the-board tax hikes, tax rates at all levels of government (regional, state, local, and federal) and of all types (value added, payroll, corporate income, personal income, excise, sales, property, estate, and gift) would have to rise overnight by over 15%. In Austria and Finland, they'd have to rise by over 18%. If these three countries relied solely on income tax hikes, they had to raise their income tax rates by over 50%! In France and Argentina, where income tax bases are relatively small, income tax rates would have to rise by much larger percentages. In contrast, Ireland could cut its income tax rates by about 5% before it needed to worry about over-burdening future generations. The longer countries wait to act, the harder will be their ultimate adjustment to fiscal reality. As an example, the United Kingdom needs to raise income taxes by 9.5% if it acts immediately. But if it waits 15 years, the requisite income tax hike is 15.2%.

5.2.4. How well does generational accounting measure true fiscal incidence?

One concern about generational accounting is the accuracy of its implicit incidence assumptions. Fehr and Kotlikoff (1997) use the Auerbach–Kotlikoff (1987) dynamic general equilibrium life-cycle model, described below, to compare changes in generation accounts with true fiscal incidence. Tables 4 and 5, taken from their paper, use the closed-country version of the Auerbach–Kotlikoff model to illustrate the relationship between changes in generation's utilities, measured in units of current consumption, and changes in their generational accounts. The tables consider the effect of a shift in the tax structure. Specifically, the economy switches from having a 20%

Table 4
Structural tax reform in the Auerbach–Kotlikoff model[a]

Year	Capital	Labor	Output	Wage	Interest rate	Consumption tax rate	Saving rate
1	89.9	19.2	25.7	1.000	0.071	0.000	0.035
2	89.9	19.5	25.9	0.997	0.072	0.064	0.054
3	90.4	19.5	25.9	0.998	0.072	0.064	0.053
4	90.8	19.5	25.9	1.000	0.071	0.064	0.052
5	91.3	19.4	26.0	1.001	0.071	0.064	0.051
10	91.7	19.4	26.0	1.003	0.071	0.063	0.050
20	95.5	19.3	26.1	1.015	0.068	0.061	0.042
60	97.2	19.2	26.1	1.021	0.067	0.061	0.037
∞	97.3	19.2	26.1	1.021	0.067	0.061	0.037

[a] Source: Fehr and Kotlikoff (1997).

Table 5
Comparing changes in generation's utility and their generational accounts[a]

Generation's year of birth	Change in generational account[b]	Change in utility[b]
−54	−2.39	−2.41
−50	−2.13	−2.03
−45	−1.64	−1.60
−40	−1.16	−1.22
−35	−0.72	−0.87
−30	−0.36	−0.55
−25	−0.06	−0.26
−20	0.17	−0.01
−15	0.32	0.21
−10	0.40	0.37
−5	0.41	0.49
0	0.37	0.55
5	0.36	0.68
10	0.35	0.80
20	0.34	0.94
50	0.33	1.04
∞	0.33	1.05

[a] Source: Fehr and Kotlikoff (1997).
[b] Changes are expressed as percent of remaining lifetime economic resources.

income tax to having a 15% income tax plus a consumption tax where the revenue loss from lowering the income-tax rate is covered by the consumption tax. Government spending on goods and services is held fixed per capita in the simulation.

In the first year of the economy's transition the consumption tax rate is 6.4%. Over time it drops to 6.1%. In the long run, the economy's capital stock, wage rate, and interest rate end up 8.2% higher, 2.1% higher, and 5.6% lower, respectively. This crowding-in of the capital stock reflects the shift in the tax burden from initial young and future generations to initial older generations. Table 5 shows how key economic variables evolve over time in the model.

Table 5 compares changes in generational accounts with the true policy incidence. As is clear from the table, generational accounts, in this case, do a very good job in capturing the general pattern of the generation-specific utility changes. They do less well for certain generations in capturing the precise magnitude of their welfare changes. The changes in generational accounts match up fairly closely to the changes in utility for those initially over age 25. For younger and future generations, the match is much less good. In this simulation, generational accounting provides a lower bound estimate of the absolute change in welfare of those born in the long run. The reason is that policies that raise the economy's capital stock are generally policies that redistribute from the initial old to the initial young and future generations. Since a higher long-run degree of capital intensity means a higher long-run wage, the direct redistribution from those alive in the long run, captured by generational accounting, will understate the improvement in welfare of those born in the long run. In addition to missing this long-run general equilibrium action, Fehr and Kotlikoff show that generational accounting, as conventionally applied, omits the efficiency gains and losses arising from fiscal reforms. For particular reforms these efficiency effects can be important components of the policy's overall incidence effects. Fehr and Kotlikoff conclude that the incidence assumptions used in generational accounting needs to be augmented to incorporate both efficiency and general equilibrium feedback effects.

5.2.5. Generational accounting and monetary policy

One of the net taxes that are allocated in forming generational accounts is the seignorage the government collects from the private sector in printing and spending money. When it prints and spends money, the government acquires real goods and services, but it also precipitates a rise in the price level that would not otherwise have occurred. This real gain to the government is a loss to the private sector that comes in the form of a reduction in the real value of their holdings of money.

The government can also garner resources from the private sector by deflating the real value of its official nominal liabilities as well as implicit nominal transfer payment obligations. On the other hand, it can lose resources by deflating away the real value of tax receipts that are fixed in nominal terms. Finally, governments can use the printing of money and its associated inflation to reduce the real value of their spending on goods and services to the extent this spending is fixed in nominal terms. Each of the ways in which governments use monetary policy as a fiscal instrument can and have been incorporated in generational accounting. For example, the hidden seignorage tax is allocated across cohorts by using data on average real money balances by age and sex.

Generational accounting can also be used to help determine the likely course of future monetary policy. Countries with very large generational imbalances are countries that are likely to have to print large quantities of money to help "pay" their bills. Indeed, generational accounting can be used to determine the amount of money creation needed to achieve a generationally balanced and sustainable policy. Hence, generational accounting should be of as much importance and interest to monetary authorities as it is to fiscal authorities.

6. Simulating generational policy

The advent of high-speed computers has transformed generational policy analysis. Today researchers around the world are constructing large-scale dynamic simulation models to assess how policy changes would affect macroeconomic outcomes as well as the intra- and intergenerational distributions of welfare [19]. This section illustrates the effects of two generational policies – the wholesale shift from income to consumption taxation and the wholesale privatization of social security, with the accrued liabilities of the old system financed via a consumption tax. Both of these policies effect major redistributions across generations. Indeed, it is hard to contemplate policies with greater potential to redistribute across generations.

There are three key questions that these and similar simulations address. First, how large are the macroeconomic effects of policies of this magnitude? Second, how long does it take for these effects to occur? Third, how large are the welfare changes visited on different generations as well as on particular members of those generations?

The illustration is based on the Auerbach–Kotlikoff–Smetters–Walliser (AKSM) model. The AKSM model descended from the Auerbach–Kotlikoff (1987) (AK) model. The AK model featured 55 overlapping generations with a single representative agent in each cohort. Unlike the steady-state and myopic transition models developed by Miller and Upton (1974), Kotlikoff (1979), Summers (1981), Seidman (1983), Hubbard and Judd (1987), and others, the AK model solved for the economy's perfect foresight transition path. The solution is found using an iterative convergence algorithm that begins by guessing the time-paths of factor demands, endogenous tax rates, and other key endogenous variables. The algorithm then uses these guesses to generate the time-path of factor prices and marginal net prices. These variables are fed into the supply side of the model where households determine how much to save and work. These micro decisions, when aggregated, deliver a time-path of economy-wide factor supplies that is compared with the initial guess of the time-path of factor demands. If the supply of factors equals the demand for factors each period, a dynamic equilibrium has been determined. Otherwise, the algorithm averages the initial guessed time-path of factor demands and the associate time-path of factor supplies to form a new guess of the time-path of factor demands, and the iteration continues.

The AKSM model uses the same solution technique of the original AK model, but it differs in two important respects [20]. First, it follows the lead of Fullerton and Rogers (1993) by incorporating intra- as well as intergenerational inequality. Specifically, the model posits 12 different earnings groups within each cohort. The groups are labeled 1 through 12, with earnings higher for groups referenced with a higher number. Groups 1 and 12 represent the lowest and highest 2% of earners. Groups 2 and 11 are the

---

[19] Hamann (1992), Arrau and Schmidt-Hebbel (1993), Raffelhüschen (1989, 1993), Huang, İmrohoroğlu and Sargent (1997), İmrohoroğlu, İmrohoroğlu and Joines (1995, 1998, 2001), Altig and Carlstrom (1996), Heckman, Lochner and Taber (1997, 1998), Hirte and Weber (1998), Schneider (1997), Fougère and Merette (1998, 2000), Merette (1998), Lau (2000), Rutherford (2000) and Schmidt-Hebbel (2002) are examples in this regard.

[20] There is also a new demographic version of the AKSM model [Kotlikoff, Smetters and Walliser (2002)], not used here, that provides a much more realistic modeling of fertility and lifespan than in the original AK model and that can initiate simulations from non steady-state positions.

next lowest and next highest sets of earners, but each constitutes 8% of earners. And groups 3 through 10 each constitute 10% of earners. The new model also approximates U.S. fiscal institutions much more closely. Second, it includes an array of tax-base reductions, a progressive Social Security system, and a Medicare system.

6.1. Switching from income to consumption taxation

Tables 6 and 7, extracted from Altig, Auerbach, Kotlikoff, Smetters and Walliser (2001), show some of the AKSW model's results from simulating the complete replacement of the current U.S. personal and corporate federal income taxes with an equal revenue proportional consumption tax. Given the above discussion of deficit delusion, it is important to point out that the term "revenue" here is based on the U.S. federal government's fiscal language. Under alternative labeling conventions, reported tax revenue would be dramatically larger or smaller than what the government says it is collecting and a "revenue-neutral" switch in tax bases, which did not try to preserve the same changes in generational accounts and economic incentives, would have different economic effects. That said, the tax reform considered here entails a major redistribution across generations because it confronts those rich and middle class retirees alive at the time of the reform with a much greater remaining lifetime net tax burden than would otherwise be the case. Low-income retirees are, on the other hand, largely insulated from the policy because their social security benefits are adjusted in the model to retain their original purchasing power.

Table 6 reports macroeconomic effects, while Table 7 shows welfare effects for five of the twelve lifetime earnings classes. Note that income class 1 refers to the poorest members of each cohort (those with the smallest endowment of human capital), and income class 12 refers to the richest members of each cohort (those with the largest endowment of human capital.) The horizontal axis locates cohorts by their years of birth measured relative to the reform, which occurs in year zero. The welfare changes are measured as equivalent variations, specifically the percentage change in full remaining lifetime economic resources that an agent living under the old policy regime (living in the initial steady state) would need to achieve the same level of remaining lifetime utility as she/he experiences under the new policy.

The macroeconomic effects of the tax reform are significant. In the long run, the economy's capital stock, labor supply, and output are larger by 25.4%, 4.6%, and 9.4%, respectively. However, getting reasonably close to this new steady state takes a while. For example, achieving half of the ultimate increase in the capital stock takes about 15 years. The policy's capital deepening raises pre-tax wages by 4.6% and lowers the pre-tax return to capital by 100 basis points. The expansion of the economy permits a decline in the consumption tax rate from an initial rate of 16.6% to a final rate of 14.5%. Measured on a wage-tax equivalent basis, the long-run consumption tax rate is 12.7%. This is substantially below the initial steady-state's 21.4% average marginal tax rate on wage income. It is even further below the 34.0% peak marginal wage tax faced by those in the top earnings class.

Table 6
Impact of proportional consumption-tax reform on macro variables

Variable	1996	1997	2010	2145
Aggregates				
National income index	1.000	1.044	1.063	1.094
Capital stock index	1.000	1.010	1.108	1.254
Labor supply index	1.000	1.063	1.054	1.046
Net saving rate	0.051	0.073	0.067	0.059
Wage rates, interest rates, and asset values				
Before-tax wage index	1.000	0.987	1.013	1.046
After-tax wage	0.775	0.817	0.843	0.881
Interest rate	0.083	0.079	0.076	0.073
Federal consumption and payroll tax rates				
Consumption tax rate	0	0.166	0.160	0.145
Payroll tax rate	0.146	0.140	0.140	0.141

[a] Source: Altig, Auerbach, Kotlikoff, Smetters and Walliser (2001).

Table 7
Welfare effects of proportional consumption-tax reform [a]

Lifetime earnings class	Cohort (year of birth)				
	−54	−30	0	30	∞
1	1.01	0.97	0.94	0.95	0.96
3	1.00	0.99	0.98	0.99	0.99
6	1.00	1.00	1.00	1.01	1.01
9	0.99	1.0	1.01	1.02	1.02
12	0.99	1.02	1.03	1.04	1.04

[a] Source: Altig, Auerbach, Kotlikoff, Smetters and Walliser (2001)
Welfare is measured relative to the no-reform equilibrium. A value, for example, of 0.97 means that the group in question experiences a welfare change from the reform that is equivalent to their experiencing a 3% decline in consumption and leisure at each age under the initial fiscal structure.

As Table 7 shows, the tax reform effects a major redistribution across generations, but one that differs markedly for the lifetime poor and rich. In forcing rich (e.g., earnings class 12) initial retirees to pay a high consumption tax rate, the policy, in effect, taxes their accumulated wealth. This lowers their remaining lifetime utility[21]. In contrast, members of this earnings class that are born in the new long-run steady state experience a 4% increase in their lifetime utilities measured relative to their welfare in the absence of the reform. For the lowest earnings class, the generational incidence pattern is the opposite. The initial poor retirees experience a small welfare improvement, but future members of this class are worse off. The reason is that the consumption-tax structure is much less intragenerationally progressive than the original income-tax structure. The generational incidence pattern for the other earnings groups in the top (bottom) half of the earnings distributions is similar, but less pronounced than that for earnings group 12 (1).

6.2. Social Security's privatization

The U.S. Social Security System faces a grave long-term financial crisis, the full dimension of which is not well known. Paying out benefits on an ongoing basis requires an immediate and permanent increase of roughly 50% in the OASDI payroll tax rate[22]. The United States is now embarked in a national debate about how to save Social Security. Options here include cutting benefits, raising the payroll tax, and privatizing all or part of the system by allowing people to contribute to individual accounts. The key issues in this debate are how any policy, including maintaining the status quo, will affect the macro economy as well as rich and poor members of current and future generations.

Table 8 extracted from Kotlikoff, Smetters and Walliser (2002), illustrates the A–K OLG Model's analysis of the effects of social security's privatization. The table

Table 8
Privatizing social security with consumption-tax transitional finance[a]

Macro variable	Percentage change relative to initial steady state for year of transition:			
	5	10	25	150
National income	0.6	1.3	4.9	13.0
Capital stock	1.8	4.1	12.8	39.0
Labor supply	0.3	0.4	2.4	5.5
Before-tax wage	0.4	0.9	2.4	7.1
Interest rate	−1.1	−2.7	−6.9	−18.9

[a] Source: Kotlikoff, Smetters and Walliser (2002).

[21] The simulated model includes capital adjustment costs, which limit the economic losses to initial elderly generations. The reason is that they own much of the economy's existing capital stock and this capital experiences a rise in its relative price because it is a relatively scarce factor with respect to installing additional capital.

[22] See Gokhale and Kotlikoff (2001).

Table 9

Privatizing social security: percentage change in remaining lifetime utility for selected income classes by cohort[a]

Class	Cohort year of birth relative to initial steady state						
	−54	−25	−10	1	10	25	150
1	0.7	−2.1	−0.6	0.5	1.3	3.2	6.0
3	−0.4	−2.0	0.0	1.2	2.1	4.2	7.4
6	−0.9	−1.7	0.3	1.6	2.6	4.8	8.0
9	−1.2	−1.6	0.5	1.7	2.7	4.9	8.1
12	−1.5	−2.5	−1.8	−1.0	−0.1	1.7	4.4

[a] Source: Kotlikoff, Smetters and Walliser (2002).

considers privatizing the U.S. system and financing the 45-year transition, during which social security benefits are gradually phased out, with a consumption tax. The policy generates sizeable long-run increases of 39% and 13% in the economy's capital stock and output, respectively. But the half-life of the policy is 30 years, roughly twice the half-life of the tax reform just considered. The transition takes longer because the policy phases in gradually over time.

Table 9 shows that these long-run gains are not free. They come at the price of lower utility to initial older and middle-aged generations. All those alive in the long run, including the richest (group 12) and poorest (group 1) agents, are better off. Since the system being privatized features a highly progressive benefit schedule, but also a highly regressive tax schedule (due to the ceiling on taxable earnings), the fact that the long-run poor are better off is particularly interesting. It shows that paying off the existing system's benefit liabilities in a more progressive manner (by making initial rich and middle income elderly contribute to that cause) outweighs the loss the long-run poor incur from not receiving benefits based on social security's progressive benefit schedule.

The long-run poorest earnings group experiences a 6.0% rise in lifetime utility. This is a substantial welfare change; it means that were social security not to be privatized, providing this group with the same welfare improvement would require a 6% increase in their consumption and leisure in each year they are alive. The long-run richest earnings group enjoys a 4.4% improvement in its lifetime utility. The biggest winners from the reform are those in the upper middle classes (groups 6 though 9) alive in the long run. Their welfare gains are roughly 8%. Like their poorer contemporaries, these groups enjoy the higher real wages delivered by the privatization. But the removal of social security means more because, compared with their contemporaries, they faced the highest rate of lifetime net social security taxation. The costs of delivering these long-run welfare gains are visited on the initial middle-class and high-income elderly as well as all initial workers. The largest losses amount to about 3% of remaining lifetime resources.

The two simulations just presented provide a sense of the maximum potential macroeconomic and redistributive effects of generational policy. The reasons are a) the policies are radical, b) they entail major intergenerational redistribuiton, and c) they significantly improve marginal economic incentives to work and save. But as described in Altig, Auerbach, Kotlikoff, Smetters and Walliser (2001) and Kotlikoff, Smetters and Walliser (2002), the benefits available to future generations from tax reform or social security's privatization can easily be dissipated by providing transition relief to early generations. In the case of consumption-tax reform, such relief could come in the form of exempting the initial elderly from paying taxes when they purchase consumption with existing assets[23]. In the case of privatizing social security, transition relief could come in the form of the delaying the imposition of a new tax to cover the loss of revenues arising from having workers make their social security contributions to private accounts. Such a policy permits workers close to retirement to gain at the expense of subsequent generations.

7. Ricardian equivalence

Ricardian equivalence refers to the proposition that private intergenerational transfers will undo government intergenerational transfers making generational policy entirely ineffectual and generational accounting a waste of time. The proposition is appropriately attributed to David Ricardo who, in discussing whether to borrow or tax to finance a war, wrote that "in point of economy, there is no real difference in either of the modes ..."[24] More precisely, in comparing a one-time war tax of £1 000 and a perpetual tax of £50 to pay interest on borrowing of £1 000, Ricardo said that "if he (the payee) leaves his fortune to his son, and leaves it charged with this perpetual tax, where is the difference whether he leaves him £20 000, with the tax, or £19 000 without it?"[25]

While Ricardo realized that bequests could be raised or lowered to undo government intergenerational redistribution, he was skeptical that such behavior would arise in practice. For in his next sentence he says: "The argument of charging posterity with the interest on our debt, or of relieving them from a portion of such interest, is often used by otherwise well informed people, but we confess we see no weight in it"[26].

---

[23] If consumption taxation was instituted (i.e., labeled) by the government as a tax on income with 100% expensing of new investment/saving (i.e., as taxing output minus saving, which equals consumption), transition relief could come in the form of grandfathering the investment incentives provided to existing capital under the prior tax structure.

[24] Ricardo (1951, 4:185–6). Also see O'Driscoll's (1977) discussion of why Ricardo rejected Ricardian equivalence as an empirically relevant phenomenon.

[25] Ricardo (1951, 4:187).

[26] Ibid.

7.1. Barro's proof of the irrelevance proposition

Ricardo would presumably have included Robert Barro (1974) in the category of "otherwise well informed people", notwithstanding the latter's elegant and influential derivation of the former's irrelevance proposition. Barro's derivation begins by positing that the utility of one generation depends not only on the goods (including leisure) it consumes over its lifetime, but also the utility of its children. In the two-period model, this function is

$$u_t = u\left(c_{yt}, c_{ot+1}, l_{yt}, l_{ot+1}, u_{t+1}\right). \tag{42}$$

Writing the corresponding expression for u_{t+1} and substituting into Equation (42) and then doing the same for u_{t+2} and all other future utility functions leads to the following infinite horizon utility function whose arguments consist of all future values of consumption and leisure:

$$u_t = u\left(c_{yt}, c_{ot+1}, l_{yt}, l_{ot+1}, c_{yt+1}, c_{ot+1}, l_{yt+1}, l_{ot+2}, \dots\right). \tag{43}$$

Thus, Barro's simple and seemingly quite natural formulation of intergenerational altruism has the striking implication that those alive today will care not only about their own levels of consumption and leisure, but also the consumption and leisure of their children, grandchildren, and all subsequent descendants. The generation alive at time t takes its inheritance, b_t, as given and chooses consumption when young and old as well as bequests (or intervivos transfers) when old, b_{t+1}, to maximize Equation (43) subject to

$$c_{yt} + w_t l_{yt} + R_{t+1}\left(c_{ot+1} + w_{t+1}l_{ot+1} + b_{t+1}\right) = b_t + w_t T + R_{t+1}\left(h_{t+1} + w_{t+1}T\right), \tag{44}$$

where R_{s+1} discounts flows at time $s+1$ to time s.

To make Barro's point about the irrelevance of generational policy, Equation (44) includes a policy, announced at time t, of giving an amount h_s at time $s \geqslant t+1$ to the contemporaneous old and taking that same sum from the contemporaneous young. The generation alive at time $t+1$ faces the analogous budget constraint, except it includes the receipt when young of the government's net payment.

$$\begin{aligned} c_{yt+1} + w_{t+1}l_{yt+1} + R_{t+2}\left(c_{ot+2} + w_{t+2}l_{ot+2} + b_{t+2}\right) \\ = b_{t+1} - h_{t+1} + w_{t+1}T + R_{t+2}\left(h_{t+2} + w_{t+2}T\right). \end{aligned} \tag{45}$$

If one solves for b_{t+1} in Equation (45) and substitutes for that variable in Equation (44), the terms involving h_{t+1} drop out. The resulting expression now involves b_{t+2}, which can be eliminated by solving for b_{t+2} from the time $t+2$ version of Equation (45).

Doing so leads h_{t+2} to drop out. Proceeding indefinitely in this manner leads to the extended family's infinite horizon constraint:

$$
\begin{aligned}
c_{yt} + w_t l_{yt} &+ \frac{c_{ot+1} + w_{t+1} l_{ot+1}}{1 + r_{t+1}} + c_{yt} + w_t l_{yt} + \frac{c_{ot+1} + w_{t+1} l_{ot+1}}{1 + r_{t+1}} + \cdots \\
&= b_t + w_t T_t + \frac{w_{t+1} T}{1 + r_{t+1}} + \cdots
\end{aligned}
\tag{46}
$$

The extended family maximizes Equation (43) subject to Equation (46). Since all the terms involving the government's generational policy have dropped out of Equation (46), generational policy has no impact whatsoever on the economy. Operationally, the extended family nullifies generational policy by raising its bequests at time $s \geqslant t + 1$ by h_s. Note that h_s can be positive or negative. Generations that receive a positive net payment when old bequeath these receipts to their children. The children, in turn, use this inheritance to make their net payments to the government; i.e., the children's payment to the government is given to their parents who hand it back to the children. Since bequests can be negative as well as positive, we can also describe the change in bequests as the children reducing their own private transfers to their parents. If the government's net payment to the elderly is negative, the elderly will respond by cutting back on their bequests to their children; alternatively, their children will hand the positive net payment they receive from the government to their parents.

7.2. Theoretical objections to the Barro framework

Barro's model ignores four interrelated issues whose consideration undermines, if not vitiates, his result. First, the model ignores marriage. Second, it ignores differences in preferences among extended family members. Third, it assumes symmetric information across family members about each others' incomes. Fourth, it ignores uncertainty.

The fact that it takes two to tango means that marriage entails at least two sets of parents, both of which may be altruistically linked to the married couple, but may have no particular interest in each other. One way to model intergenerational transfers in this context is to assume that each set of in-laws takes the other's transfers to their children as given. But as shown in Kotlikoff (1983) and Bernheim and Bagwell (1988), this Nash assumption implies the effective altruistic linkage of the two sets of in-laws. And if the in-laws have other children, the original in-laws will become altruistically linked with the all of the other children's in-laws as well. Hence, if altruism were as widespread as Barro posits, essentially everyone would be altruistically interlinked with everyone else around the world as a consequence of marriage within groups and intermarriage across racial, ethnic, religious, and national lines.

The resource sharing arising from altruistic linkage means that each interlinked household's consumption and leisure is determined by the collective resources of all extended family members. State differently, the distribution of resources across extended family members makes no difference to the distribution of consumption and leisure of those members. Thus, the Barro model implies that the consumption of a randomly chosen person in Nashville, Tennessee should depend on the income of a randomly chosen person in Almati, Kazakhstan.

The source of this patently absurd prediction is the assumption that each extended family takes the transfers of other extended family members as given. The difficulty with this assumption becomes apparent if one compares two parties who each care so strongly about each other that each wants to transfer to the other. Taking each other's transfers as given may lead to an infinite handing back and forth of funds between the two parties; i.e., the problem may have no solution. Of course, in the real world, such situations are handled by would-be recipients simply refusing to receive the funds they are handed. As Kotlikoff, Razin and Rosenthal (1990) point out, the power to refuse a transfer if it is too big or, indeed, if it is too small, as well as the power to refuse to make a transfer if someone else's transfer is too small or too large, changes the bargaining game fundamentally. In particular, threat points matter and Ricardian Equivalence no longer holds because when the government redistributes across generations, it alters their threat points.

Conflicts over who loves whom and by how much may also lead parties to withhold information about their economic positions. Kotlikoff and Razin (1988) point out that altruistic parents trying to transfer to children whose abilities and labor efforts are unobservable will condition their transfers on their children's earnings. In this setting, government redistribution between parents and children can modify the self-selection constraints under which parents operate in establishing their earnings-related transfer functions. In this case, the policy will be non-neutral.

Feldstein (1988) raised another important theoretical objection to the Barro model, namely that, in the context of uncertainty, Ricardian equivalence will only hold if transfers are operative in all states of nature in which the government's redistribution occurs. Take parents who are altruistic, but whose altruism is not strong enough to lead them to make transfers to their children if their children end up with higher incomes than their own. Then government redistribution from children to parents will generate no private offset in the form of higher bequests or intervivos gifts in those states of nature in which the children would otherwise be better off than the parents. In developed economies in which per capita incomes grow through time, one would expect Feldstein's point to be particularly applicable.

7.3. Testing intergenerational altruism

As mentioned, the Barro Model of intergenerational altruism predicts that the consumption of altruistically linked individuals is independent of the distribution of resources across those individuals. This implication has been tested in a variety of ways with a variety of data. Boskin and Kotlikoff (1985) took the Barro model as the null hypotheses and used dynamic programming to determine the level of annual consumption that would be demanded by Barro dynasties given earnings and rate of return uncertainty. They estimated their model on postwar U.S. time series data and tested whether the cross-cohort distribution of resources matters to aggregate consumption given the level of consumption predicted by the Barro Model. The authors report a very strong dependence of aggregate consumption on the intergenerational distribution of resources.

Abel and Kotlikoff (1994) pointed out that altruistically linked households will automatically share risk and, therefore, experience identical shocks (Euler errors) to their marginal utilities of consumption. They also showed that changes in the average Euler error by cohort would share this property if, as Barro believed, the economy was dominated by intergenerational altruists. Abel and Kotlikoff aggregated by cohort U.S. consumer expenditure data to test for the commonality of Euler errors. Their test strongly rejects intergenerational altruism; cohorts that experience positive income shocks spend, rather than share, their good fortune.

Altonji, Hayashi and Kotlikoff (1992) and Hayashi, Altonji and Kotlikoff (1996) use Panel Study of Income Dynamics data on the consumption of extended family members to test whether a) the distribution of consumption of extended family members depends on the distribution of resources among those members, and b) whether extended family members share risk – an implication not simply of altruism, but also selfish risk sharing. The data strongly reject both propositions. Another study by the three authors [Altonji, Hayashi and Kotlikoff (1997)] considers the subset of extended PSID families who were actively making transfers among themselves. They showed that taking a dollar from a child and giving it to a parent who is giving the child money results in an increase in transfers to the child of only 13 cents – an amount that is not only small, but also insignificantly different from zero.

Additional compelling evidence against the Barro view is provided by Gokhale, Kotlikoff and Sabelhaus (1996). This article documents that the dramatic postwar decline in U.S. saving has been the result of an equally dramatic increase in intergenerational transfers to the elderly that have led to an enormous increase in their absolute and relative consumption. Since 1960 the consumption of the elderly, on a per person basis, has roughly doubled relative to that of young adults. A related finding, developed in Auerbach, Gokhale, Kotlikoff, Sabelhaus and Weil (2001),is the dramatic postwar increase in the annuitization of the resources of the elderly. This increased annuitization has been engineered primarily by the government, which provides the elderly substantial resources in old age in the form of cash and medical benefits that continue until they die, but are not bequeathable. If Barro were right, and the elderly were altruistic, they would have responded to their being forced to acquire more annuities by purchasing more life insurance. In fact, the life insurance holdings of the elderly have not increased in the postwar period as a share of their remaining lifetime resources. They've declined.

8. The government's role in intergenerational risk sharing

Samuelson's (1958) classic consumption-loan model pointed out the inherent incompleteness in markets arising from the fact that agents alive at one point in time cannot contract with those who will be born well after those agents are deceased. This market failure is manifest primarily in the area of risk sharing. Were they able to contract, agents alive today and those born in the future could form risk-sharing arrangements by buying or selling state-contingent contracts of various kinds. The question raised by these missing markets is whether the government can redistribute across generations to emulate, if not replicate, the risk-sharing arrangements that members of different cohorts would privately conclude.

As shown in Kotlikoff (1993), it is an easy matter to extend the two-period model of Section 3 to include uncertainty both with respect to the economic environment and government policy. Kotlikoff (1993) considers uncertain technology, specifically the coefficient of total factor productivity, as well as uncertain (i.e., state-contingent) government net payments each period from the young to the old. The role for government intergenerational risk sharing in this model is to transfer resources from the contemporaneous young to the contemporaneous old at time t if the technology at time t is better than at time $t-1$. The degree of redistribution would also be conditioned on the economy's time-t capital stock.

The fact that government's can pool risks across generations does not mean they necessarily do so. Indeed, governments may exacerbate the degree of uncertainty facing generations by randomly distributing among them. As Auerbach and Hassett (1999) point out, this manufacturing of uncertainty may come in the form of simply delaying the decision of who will pay the government's bills. Take, as an example, the current failure of the U.S. government to determine how it will close the very sizeable imbalance in U.S. generational policy. The government can either place a larger fiscal burden on the current elderly, on middle-aged baby boomers, on the current young, or on future generations. The size of the bill is reasonably clear. But in failing to specify immediately which generations will pay what, the U.S. government is generating uncertainty for all generations, where none intrinsically exists.

Can one say whether the government is, on balance, pooling risk across generations? Yes and no[27]. Abel and Kotlikoff (1994) stress that their study tests and strongly rejects intergenerational risk sharing, no matter whether that risk sharing is arising from a) altruistic extended family behavior, b) selfish extended family arrangements, c) the purchase of contracts and securities in private insurance and financial markets, or d) government policy. But Abel and Kotlikoff's study does not tell us the precise role, if any, played by the government in frustrating or improving intergenerational risk sharing.

---

[27] Note that the government may pool risks within generations at the same time it generates risks across generations. Hubbard, Skinner and Zeldes (1995) and Eaton and Rosen (1980) are two important studies of government intragenerational risk sharing.

9. Conclusion

Generational policy – the question of which generation will pay the government's bills – lies at the heart of most fiscal policy debates. The importance of this issue has stimulated a prodigious amount of theoretical, empirical, and simulation research. This research has delivered some important findings. First, which generation pays the government's bills is, apart from efficiency considerations, a zero-sum game. Second, generational policy works not just by redistributing resources directly across generations, but also by redistributing resources indirectly via policy-induced general equilibrium changes in factor prices. Third, the same generational policy can be conducted under a variety of headings and operate through surprising channels, including asset markets. Fourth, notwithstanding its ubiquitous use, the budget deficit is not a well-defined measure of generational or any other aspect of economic policy. The same is true of taxes and transfer payments as well as their associated constructs, such as disposable income and personal saving. Fifth, generational accounting represents an important, but far from perfect method of assessing generational policy. Sixth, generational policies in non-altruistic economies can effect major redistribution across generations and major changes in the long-run values of key macroeconomic variables. Seventh, generational policies take a fairly long time to effect the economy. Eighth, intergenerational altruism can nullify the impact of generational policy, but the theoretical conditions under which it would arise are highly unlikely to prevail. Ninth, there is a plethora of evidence, at least for the U.S., that intergenerational redistribution, be it across cohorts or between older and younger members of the same extended families, materially raises the well-being to those receiving the transfers and materially harms those making the payments. Tenth, at least in the U.S., government policy does not achieve intergenerational risk sharing. Indeed, U.S. government policy may, on balance, be an important, if not the primary source of generational risk. Finally, and most important, a variety of countries around the world are running generational policies that will dramatically reduce the economic well-being of their future generations. Achieving generational balance in those countries requires immediate, major, and highly painful policy responses.

References

Abel, A., and L.J. Kotlikoff (1994), "Intergenerational altruism and the effectiveness of fiscal policy: new tests based on cohort data", in: T. Tachibinachi, ed., Savings and Bequests (Michigan University Press, Ann Arbor, MI) pp. 167–196.

Ablett, J. (1999), "Generational accounting in Australia", in: A.J. Auerbach, L.J. Kotlikoff and W. Leibfritz, eds., Generational Accounting Around the World (Chicago University Press, Chicago) pp. 141–160.

Altig, D., and C.T. Carlstrom (1996), "Marginal tax rates and income inequality in a life-cycle model", Working Paper (Federal Reserve Bank of Cleveland).

Altig, D., A.J. Auerbach, L.J. Kotlikoff, K. Smetters and J. Walliser (2001), "Simulating fundamental tax reform", The American Economic Review 91(3):574–599.

Altonji, J.G., F. Hayashi and L.J. Kotlikoff (1992), "Is the extended family altruistically linked?" The American Economic Review 82(5):1177–1198.

Altonji, J.G., F. Hayashi and L.J. Kotlikoff (1997), "Parental altruism and inter-vivos transfers: theory and evidence", Journal of Political Economy 105(6):1121–1166.

Arrau, P., and K. Schmidt-Hebbel (1993), "Macroeconomic and intergenerational welfare effects of a transition from pay-as-you-go to fully funded pensions", Policy Research Dept., Macroeconomics and Growth Division (World Bank, Washington, DC).

Auerbach, A.J., and K.A. Hassett (1999), "Uncertainty and the design of long-run fiscal policy", Working Paper 7036 (NBER, Cambridge, MA).

Auerbach, A.J., and L.J. Kotlikoff (1987), Dynamic Fiscal Policy (Cambridge University Press, Cambridge, UK).

Auerbach, A.J., and P. Oreopoulos (2000), "The fiscal impact of U.S. immigration – a generational accounting perspective", Tax Policy and the Economy 14 (MIT Press, Cambridge, MA) pp. 123–156.

Auerbach, A.J., J. Gokhale and L.J. Kotlikoff (1991), "Generational accounts: a meaningful alternative to deficit accounting", in: D. Bradford, ed., Tax Policy and the Economy 5 (MIT Press, Cambridge, MA) pp. 55–110.

Auerbach, A.J., J. Gokhale and L.J. Kotlikoff (1994), "Generational accounting: a meaningful way to assess generational policy", The Journal of Economic Perspectives 8(1):73–94.

Auerbach, A.J., J. Gokhale, L.J. Kotlikoff, J. Sabelhaus and D. Weil (2001), "The annuitization of Americans' resources: a cohort analysis", in: L.J. Kotlikoff, ed., Essays on Saving, Bequests, Altruism, and Financial Planning (MIT Press, Cambridge, MA) pp. 93–132.

Barro, R.J. (1974), "Are government bonds net wealth?", Journal of Political Economy 48(6):1095–1118.

Barsky, R.B., N.G. Mankiw and S.P. Zeldes (1986), "Ricardian consumers with Keynesian propensities", The American Economic Review 76(4):676–691.

Bernheim, B.D., and K. Bagwell (1988), "Is everything neutral", Journal of Political Economy 96(2):308–338.

Boskin, M.J., and L.J. Kotlikoff (1985), "Public debt and U.S. saving: a new test of the neutrality hypothesis", Carnegie-Rochester Conference Series on Public Policy, Autumn.

Bosworth, B., G. Burtless and J. Sabelhaus (1991), "The decline in saving: evidence from household surveys", The Brookings Papers on Economic Activity 1:183–242.

Buiter, W.H. (1997), "Generational accounts, aggregate saving and intergenerational distribution", Economica 64:605–626.

Cutler, D.M. (1993), "Review of generational accounting: knowing who pays, and when, for what we spend", National Tax Journal 46(1):61–76.

Diamond, P.A. (1965), "National debt in a neoclassical growth model", The American Economic Review 55:1126–1150.

Diamond, P.A. (1996), "Generational accounts and generational balance: an assessment", National Tax Journal 49(4):597–607.

Eaton, J., and H.S. Rosen (1980), "Labor supply, uncertainty, and efficient taxation", Journal of Public Economics 14:365–374.

Eisner, R., and P.J. Pieper (1984), "A new view of the federal debt and budget deficits", The American Economic Review 74:11–29.

Elmendorf, D.W., and N.G. Mankiw (1998), "Government debt", Working Paper 6470 (NBER, Cambridge, MA).

Fehr, H., and L.J. Kotlikoff (1997), "Generational accounting in general equilibrium", FinanzArchiv 53(4):1–27.

Feldstein, M. (1974), "Social security, induced retirement, and aggregate capital accumulation", Journal of Political Economy 82:905–926.

Feldstein, M. (1988), "The effects of fiscal policy when incomes are uncertain: a contradiction to Ricardian equivalence", The American Economic Review 1:14–23.

Fischer, S. (1980), "Dynamic inconsistency, cooperation, and the benevolent dissembling government", Journal of Economic Dynamics and Control 2:93–107.

Fougère, M., and M. Merette (1998), "Economic dynamics of population aging in Canada: an analysis with a computable overlapping-generations model", Paper presented at the Canadian Public Economics Study Group, Ottawa, Canada, May 1998.

Fougère, M., and M. Merette (2000), "Population aging, intergenerational equity and growth: analysis with an endogenous growth, overlapping generations model", in: G.W. Harrison, S.E. Hougaard Jensen, L. Haagen Pedersen and T.F. Rutherford, eds., Using Dynamic Computable General Equilibrium Models for Policy Analysis (Elsevier, Amsterdam).

Fullerton, D., and D.L. Rogers (1993), Who Bears the Lifetime Tax Burden? (The Brookings Institution, Washington, DC).

Gale, W.G., and J. Sabelhaus (1999), "Perspectives on the household saving rate", The Brookings Papers on Economic Activity 1:181–214.

Ghiglino, C., and K. Shell (2000), "The economic effects of restrictions on government budget deficits", Journal of Economic Theory 94(1):106–137.

Gokhale, J., and L.J. Kotlikoff (2001), "Family assumptions: the crack in the budget facade", The Milken Review 3(1):24–32.

Gokhale, J., L.J. Kotlikoff and J. Sabelhaus (1996), "Understanding the postwar decline in U.S. saving: a cohort analysis", The Brookings Papers on Economic Activity 1:315–390.

Gokhale, J., B.R. Page, J. Potter and J.R. Sturrock (2000), "Generational accounts for the U.S. – an update", The American Economic Review 90(2):293–296.

Hamann, A.J. (1992), "A quantitative assessment of the effects of inflationary finance in an overlapping generations model", Ph.D. Dissertation (Boston University).

Haveman, R. (1994), "Should generational accounts replace public budgets and deficits?" Journal of Economic Perspectives 8(1):95–111.

Hayashi, F. (1987), "Tests for liquidity constraints: a critical survey and some new observations", in: F. Truman Bewley, ed., Advances in Econometrics. Fifth World Congress, Vol. 2 (Cambridge University Press, Cambridge, UK).

Hayashi, F., J.G. Altonji and L.J. Kotlikoff (1996), "Risk-sharing between and within families", Econometrica 64(2):261–294.

Heckman, J.J., L. Lochner and C. Taber (1997), "Explaining rising wage inequality: explorations with a dynamic general equilibrium model of labor earnings with heterogeneous agents", Mimeo, November 1997 (University of Chicago).

Heckman, J.J., L. Lochner and C. Taber (1998), "Evaluation of education and training programs in a general equilibrium setting", Mimeo (University of Chicago).

Hirte, G., and R. Weber (1998), "Pareto-improving transition from a pay-as-you-go to a fully-funded system – is it politically feasible?", FinanzArchiv.

Huang, H., S. İmrohoroğlu and T. Sargent (1997), "Two computational experiments to fund social security", Mimeo (University of Southern California); Macroeconomic Dynamics, forthcoming.

Hubbard, R.G., and K.L. Judd (1987), "Social security and individual welfare: precautionary saving, borrowing constraints, and the payroll tax", The American Economic Review 77(4):630–646.

Hubbard, R.G., J. Skinner and S.P. Zeldes (1995), "Precautionary saving and social insurance", Journal of Political Economy 103(2):360–399.

İmrohoroğlu, A., S. İmrohoroğlu and D.H. Joines (1995), "A life cycle analysis of social security", Economic Theory 6:83–114.

İmrohoroğlu, A., S. İmrohoroğlu and D.H. Joines (1998), "Social security in an overlapping generations economy with land", Mimeo (University of Southern California).

İmrohoroğlu, A., S. İmrohoroğlu and D.H. Joines (2001), "The effect of tax-favored retirement accounts on capital accumulation", The American Economic Review, forthcoming.

Kotlikoff, L.J. (1979), "Social security and equilibrium capital intensity", Quarterly Journal of Economics 93(2):233–253.

Kotlikoff, L.J. (1983), "Altruistic extended family linkages – a note", Mimeo (Boston University); also published in 1989, in: L.J. Kotlikoff, What Determines Savings? (MIT Press, Cambridge, MA) pp. 86–87.

Kotlikoff, L.J. (1993), "From deficit delusion to the fiscal balance rule: looking for an economically meaningful way to assess fiscal policy", Journal of Economics 7:17–41; reprinted in 1999, in: A.J. Auerbach, L.J. Kotlikoff and W. Leibfritz, eds., Generational Accounting Around the World (University of Chicago Press, Chicago) pp. 9–30.

Kotlikoff, L.J. (1997), "Reply to Diamond's and Cutler's reviews of 'Generational accounting' ", The National Tax Journal L(2):303–314.

Kotlikoff, L.J., and W. Leibfritz (1999), "An international comparison of generational accounts", in: A.J. Auerbach, L.J. Kotlikoff and W. Leibfritz, eds., Generational Accounting Around the World (Chicago University Press, Chicago) pp. 73–102.

Kotlikoff, L.J., and B. Raffelhüschen (1999), "Generational accounting around the globe", The American Economic Review, 161–166.

Kotlikoff, L.J., and A. Razin (1988), "Making bequests without spoiling children: bequests as an implicit optimal tax structure and the possibility that altruistic bequest are not equalizing", Working Paper 2735 (NBER, Cambridge, MA); also published in 2001, in: L.J. Kotlikoff, Essays on Saving, Altruism, Bequests, and Financial Planning (MIT Press, Cambridge, MA) pp. 303–312.

Kotlikoff, L.J., and L.H. Summers (1987), "Tax incidence", in: A.J. Auerbach and M.S. Feldstein, eds., Handbook of Public Economics, Vol. 2 (North Holland, Amsterdam) pp. 1043–1088.

Kotlikoff, L.J., T. Persson and L.E.O. Svensson (1988), "Social contracts as assets: a possible solution to the time-consistency problem", The American Economic Review 78(4):662–677.

Kotlikoff, L.J., A. Razin and R. Rosenthal (1990), "A strategic altruism model in which ricardian equivalence does not hold", The Economic Journal 100(403):1261–1268.

Kotlikoff, L.J., K. Smetters and J. Walliser (2002), "Distributional effects in a general equilibrium analysis of social security", in: M. Feldstein and J. Liebman, eds., The Distributional Effects of Social Security and Social Security Reform (University of Chicago Press, Chicago) pp. 327–370.

Lau, M.I. (2000), "Assessing tax reforms when human capital is endogenous", in: G.W. Harrison, S.E. Hougaard Jensen, L. Haagen Pedersen and T.F. Rutherford, eds., Using Dynamic Computable General Equilibrium Models for Policy Analysis (North Holland, Amsterdam) pp. 203–222.

Merette, M. (1998), "The effects of debt reduction on intergenerational equity and growth", Mimeo (Statistics Canada, Ottawa) Miles Corak, ed.

Miller, M., and C. Upton (1974), Macroeocnomics: A Neoclassical Introduction (Irwin, Homewood, IL).

Mirrlees, J. (1971), "An exploration in the theory of optimum income taxation", in: Symposium on Public Finance, The Review of Economic Studies 38(2):175–208.

O'Driscoll Jr, G.P. (1977), "The ricardian nonequivalence theorem", Journal of Political Economy 85(1):207–210.

Raffelhüschen, B. (1989), "Anreizwirkungen des Systems der Sozialen Alterssicherung. Eine Dynamische Simulationsanalyse", Mimeo (Frankfurt).

Raffelhüschen, B. (1993), "Funding social security through Pareto-optimal conversion policies", in: B. Felderer, ed., Public Pension Economics, Journal of Economics/Zeitschrift für Nationalökonomie 7(Suppl.):105–131.

Raffelhüschen, B. (1998), "Aging, fiscal policy and social insurances: a European perspective", Mimeo (Albert-Ludwigs-University of Freiburg, Germany; and University of Bergen, Norway).

Ricardo, D. (1951), The Works and Correspondence of David Ricardo (Cambridge University Press, Cambridge, UK), edited by Piero Sraffa.

Rutherford, Thomas F. (2000), "Carbon abatement, technical change, and intergenerational burden sharing", in: G.W. Harrison, S.E. Hougaard Jensen, L. Haagen Pedersen and T.F. Rutherford, eds., Using Dynamic Computable General Equilibrium Models for Policy Analysis (North Holland, Amsterdam) pp. 79–118.

Samuelson, P.A. (1958), "An exact consumption-loan model of interest with or without the social contrivance of money", Journal of Political Economy 66(6):467–482.

Schmidt-Hebbel, K. (2002), "Pension reform, informal markets, and long-term income and welfare", in: Pension Systems: From Crisis to Reform (The World Bank, Washington, DC).

Schneider, O. (1997), "Dynamic simulation of pension reform", Mimeo (Charles University, CERGE-EI, Prague).

Seidman, L.S. (1983), "Taxes in a life cycle model with bequests and inheritances", American Economic Review 73(3):437–441.

Shaviro, D.N. (1997), Do Deficits Matter? (University of Chicago Press, Chicago).

Summers, L.H. (1981), "Capital taxation and accumulation in a life cycle growth model", American Economic Review 71(4):533–544.

Tabellini, G. (1991), "The politics of intergenerational redistribution", Journal of Political Economy 99(2):335–357.

U.S. Congressional Budget Office (1995), Who Pays and When: An Assessment of Generational Accounting (U.S. Government Printing Office, Washington, DC).

Part 5

INTERGOVERNMENTAL RELATIONS

Chapter 28

INTERNATIONAL TAXATION *

ROGER H. GORDON

University of California – San Diego; and NBER

JAMES R. HINES JR

University of Michigan; and NBER

Contents

* We would very much like to thank Alan Auerbach and Joel Slemrod for comments on an earlier draft.

Handbook of Public Economics, Volume 4, Edited by A.J. Auerbach and M. Feldstein

Abstract

The integration of world capital markets carries important implications for the design and impact of tax policies. This paper evaluates research findings on international taxation, drawing attention to connections and inconsistencies between theoretical and empirical observations.

Diamond and Mirrlees (1971a,b) note that small open economies incur very high costs in attempting to tax the returns to local capital investment, since local factors bear the burden of such taxes in the form of productive inefficiencies. Richman (1963) argues that countries may simultaneously want to tax the worldwide capital income of domestic residents, implying that any taxes paid to foreign governments should be merely deductible from domestic taxable income.

Governments do not adopt policies that are consistent with these forecasts. Corporate income is taxed at high rates by wealthy countries, and most countries either exempt foreign-source income of domestic multinationals from tax, or else provide credits rather than deductions for taxes paid abroad. Furthermore, individual investors can use various methods to avoid domestic taxes on their foreign-source incomes, in the process avoiding taxes on their domestic-source incomes.

Individual and firm behavior also differs from that forecast by simple theories. Observed portfolios are not fully diversified worldwide. Foreign direct investment is common even when it faces tax penalties relative to other investment in host countries. While economic activity is highly responsive to tax rates and tax structure, there are many aspects of behavior that are difficult to reconcile with simple microeconomic incentives.

There are promising recent efforts to reconcile observations with theory. To the extent that multinational firms possess intangible capital on which they earn returns with foreign direct investment, even small countries may have a degree of market power, leading to fiscal externalities. Tax avoidance is pervasive, generating further fiscal externalities. These concepts are useful in explaining behavior, and observed tax policies, and they also suggest that international agreements have the potential to improve the efficiency of tax systems worldwide.

Keywords

fiscal externalities, foreign direct investment, international taxation, multinational corporations, tax avoidance, transfer pricing, tax havens

JEL classification: H87, H25, F23, H21, F32

1. Introduction

The design of sensible tax policies for modern economies requires that careful attention be paid to their international ramifications. This is a potentially daunting prospect, since the analysis of tax design in open economies entails all of the complications and intricacies that appear in closed economies, with the addition of many others, since multiple, possibly interacting, tax systems are involved. These complications are no less harrowing for a researcher interested in studying the impact of taxation in open economies. Fortunately, the parallel development of theoretical and empirical research on taxation in open economies offers straightforward and general guidance for understanding the determinants and effects of tax policies, as well as their normative significance. The purpose of this chapter is to review the analysis of international taxation, drawing connections to research findings that are familiar from the analysis of taxation in closed economies.

The rapid development of open-economy tax analysis in the last fifteen or so years differs sharply from previous patterns, when the bulk of the academic research on taxation posited that the national economy was closed. In this literature the implications for tax policy of international trade and international factor movements typically consisted of a short discussion at the conclusion of a long analysis. In studies of closed economies, real and financial activity cannot cross international borders, so that prices clear each national market separately. This restriction to a closed economy characterized not only much of the theoretical work on optimal tax policy but also most of the general equilibrium models of the effects of taxes, e.g., Fullerton, Shoven and Whalley (1978) or Auerbach and Kotlikoff (1987), and even most of the econometric studies of tax policy and behavior.

To be fair, the assumption of a closed economy was widely thought to have been an adequate approximation of at least the American economy over much of the postwar period. As seen below, this assumption also succeeded in eliminating many complications that otherwise must be faced in thinking about tax policy. However, with the growing importance not only of international trade in goods and services but also of multinational corporations, together with increasing integration of world capital markets, it is becoming more and more important to rethink past work on tax policy in an open economy setting.

As described in Section 2 below, many aspects of tax policy analysis are affected by the openness of the economy. For example, while in a closed economy it does not matter whether a proportional tax is imposed on income from saving or income from investment (since aggregate saving equals aggregate investment), in an open economy this equivalence no longer holds. Furthermore, taxpayer responses to policy changes can look very different once the implications of an open economy are taken into account. In a closed economy, the analysis of the incidence of a tax on saving or investment depends on its effect on the market clearing interest rate, which in equilibrium depends on the price elasticities of both individual savings and firms' factor demand for capital. In contrast, in a small open economy, the interest rate is determined by the world capital market, so is unaffected by a tax. Similarly, the incidence of commodity taxes becomes simpler in a small open economy, since the relative prices of at least tradable goods are again set on world markets and therefore do not respond to tax changes[1]. Results on factor price equalization even suggest that market wage rates should not be affected by tax policy, in spite of the lack of mobility of people across borders. In all of these cases, the absence of price changes means that quantity changes will be larger, generally raising the implied efficiency costs of tax distortions.

A greater complication is that the range of behavioral responses to tax policy becomes broader in an open economy setting. This paper explores in detail the types of behavioral responses that theory forecasts, and that appear in practice. Differential income tax rates on profits earned by different industries can change the pattern of trade flows, leading to increased exports from industries receiving more favorable tax treatment. The location decisions of firms earning above normal profits are likely to be particularly sensitive to tax differentials. Individual investors not only choose among domestic debt and equity securities but can also invest in equivalent securities abroad. Similarly, taxes can affect the financial as well as operational behavior of multinational firms. Not only do tax rates affect choices of where to locate foreign affiliates, but taxes also influence the optimal scale of foreign operations, the location of borrowing, research activity, exports, and a host of other decisions. A multinational firm has a certain degree of discretion in choosing the prices used to conduct transactions between members of its affiliated group, allowing it to report accounting profits in tax-favored locations.

All of these aspects of behavior depend on the tax systems of home and foreign countries. A country's tax base and even its comparative advantage therefore depend on differences between tax structures across countries. As a result, in any analysis of policy setting, the nature of interactions among tax policies in different countries becomes an important issue. To the extent that international tax competition makes tax policies in one country a function of those in other countries, the importance of such interactions is magnified.

Any analysis of tax policy in an open economy setting must reconcile the frequent inconsistency of observed behavior with the forecasts from simple models. Standard models of portfolio choice, for example, forecast that risk-averse investors will hold diversified portfolios of equities issued worldwide, yet observed portfolios tend to be heavily specialized in domestic equity. The standard assumption of costless mobility of capital across locations appears to be inconsistent with the evidence that domestic savings is highly correlated with domestic investment. As seen below, the behavior of multinational firms is also frequently inconsistent with the forecasts of standard

---

[1] World markets greatly dampen the price effects of tax changes from the standpoint of a small open economy, but since these price changes apply to a very large world economy, their net effect on world welfare need not be negligible.

models. Furthermore, observed tax policies often deviate sharply from those predicted by standard models. As the chapter argues in section five, some of the added considerations that have been used to explain observed individual and firm behavior may also help explain observed tax policies.

Section 2 of this chapter reviews the theory of optimal tax-setting in open economies, starting with the problems faced by governments of small countries. Section 3 generalizes these implications to a more realistic setting. Section 4 focuses on taxes and portfolio choice, in an attempt to reconcile the theory with the observed "home bias". Section 5 surveys evidence of the impact of taxation on the activities of multinational firms, while Section 6 offers a reconciliation of the evidence of behavior of taxpayers and governments in open economies.

2. Optimal income taxation in an open economy

This section considers the implications of optimal tax theory for the design of taxes in open economies. For additional detail on optimal tax structures, see Auerbach and Hines (2002) in Volume 3 of this Handbook.

The nature of optimal tax policy often depends critically on whether the economy is open or closed. The importance of this distinction is evident immediately from the difference that economic openness makes for tax incidence. In a closed economy, the incidence of a tax on the return to capital depends not only on the elasticity of saving with respect to the interest rate but also on the elasticity of factor demands and the elasticity of consumer substitution between capital-intensive and labor-intensive goods. The presumption has been that, for plausible elasticities, the burden of a corporate income tax falls primarily on capital owners.

In a small open economy, in contrast, a tax on the return to domestic capital has no effect on the rate of return available to domestic savers[2], since the domestic interest rate is determined by the world capital market. Domestic investment falls in response to higher tax rates. For firms to continue to break even, in spite of the added tax, either output prices must rise or other costs must fall by enough to offset the tax. When output prices are fixed by competition with imports, the tax simply causes the market-clearing wage rate to fall. As a result, the burden of the tax is borne entirely by labor or other fixed domestic factors. While a labor income tax would also reduce the net wage rate, it would not in contrast distort the marginal return to capital invested at home vs. abroad. Following Diamond and Mirrlees (1971a,b), a labor income tax dominates a corporate income tax, even from the perspective of labor[3]. As a result, one immediate and strong conclusion about tax policy in an open economy setting is

---

[2] This follows from the standard assumptions that capital is costlessly mobile internationally and there is no uncertainty.
[3] Dixit (1985) provides a detailed and elegant development of this argument.

that a "source-based tax" on capital income should not be used since it is dominated by a labor-income tax.

2.1. Choice of tax instrument

It is useful to illustrate this finding in a simple setting in which the government has access to various tax instruments, at least including a source-based tax on capital, a payroll tax, and consumption taxes on any nontraded goods. The country is small relative to both the international capital market and the international goods markets, so takes as given the interest rate, r^*, on the world capital market, and the vector of prices, p^*, for traded goods.

Resident i receives indirect utility equal to $v_i(p^* + s, p_n + s_n, r^*, w(1 - t)) + V_i(G)$, where p_n represents the vector of prices for nontraded goods, s and s^* respectively represent the sales tax rate on tradables and nontradables, r^* represents the rate of return to savings available on the world capital market, w equals the domestic wage rate, t is the tax rate on labor income, and G is a vector of government expenditures.

Each dollar of capital employed by domestic firms faces a tax at rate τ. Domestic firms have constant returns to scale, and operate in a competitive environment, so must just break even in equilibrium. Therefore, the unit costs for firms in each industry must equal the output price in that industry. Using c and c_n to denote the costs of producing traded and nontraded goods, respectively, equilibrium requires that, for traded goods[4], $c(r^* + \tau, w) \geq p^*$, while for nontraded goods $c_n(r^* + \tau, w) = p_n$. Since the country is assumed to be a price taker in both the traded goods market and the capital market, it follows immediately that firms in the traded sector continue to break even when τ increases only if the wage rate falls by enough to offset the added costs due to the tax. This implies that

$$\frac{\mathrm{d}w}{\mathrm{d}\tau} = -\frac{K}{L}, \tag{2.1}$$

in which K/L is the equilibrium capital/labor ratio in these firms[5]. Hence, the effect of taxation on domestic factor prices is determined by competition in traded goods industries.

For firms selling nontradables, the market-clearing price of their output must adjust to ensure that these firms continue to break even. The break-even condition is given by $p_n q_n = K_n(r^* + \tau) + L_n w$, in which q_n is the quantity of nontraded output, and K_n

---

[4] This equation is satisfied with an equality whenever the good is produced domestically.
[5] Note that this implies specialization in one particular industry, since this condition cannot simultaneously be satisfied for different industries selling tradables that have different capital/labor ratios. In equilibrium, a higher tax rate will cause the country to specialize in a less capital-intensive industry. See Lovely (1989) for further discussion.

and L_n are quantities of capital and labor used in its production. Differentiating this condition, and imposing Equation (2.1), implies that

$$\frac{\mathrm{d}p_n}{\mathrm{d}\tau} = \frac{L_n}{q_n}\left(\frac{K_n}{L_n} - \frac{K}{L}\right). \tag{2.2}$$

Prices rise in sectors of the economy that are more capital intensive than the traded goods sector, and fall in sectors that are more labor intensive.

Consider the government's choice of τ. By increasing τ, individuals are affected only indirectly, through the resulting drop in the market-clearing wage rate and through changes in the market-clearing prices of nontradables[6]. The same changes in effective prices faced by individuals could equally well have been achieved by changing appropriately the payroll tax rate t, and the sales tax rates s_n. From an individual's perspective, an increase in τ is equivalent to changes in the payroll tax rate, t, and the sales tax rates s_n, that generate the same changes in after-tax wages and prices.

Since these alternative policies are equivalent from the perspective of individual utility, holding G fixed, it is possible to compare their relative merits by observing what happens to government revenue as τ rises, while the payroll tax rate t, and the sales tax rates s_n are adjusted as needed to keep all consumer prices unaffected. Given the overall resource constraint for the economy, the value of domestic output, measured at world prices, plus net income from capital exports/imports must continue to equal the value of domestic consumption and saving plus government expenditures. Therefore[7],

$$p_g G = p^* \left[f\left(S + K_m, L_a\right) - (C + S)\right] - r^* K_m, \tag{2.3}$$

in which p_g measures the production cost of each type of government expenditure, $f(\cdot)$ is the economy's aggregate production function, S measures the net savings of domestic individuals, C is their consumption, K_m measures capital imports/exports, and L_a is aggregate labor supply.

If τ increases, but its effect on consumer prices is offset through suitable readjustments in the payroll tax and in sales tax rates, then S, C, and L will all remain unaffected. Welfare is maximized if the tax rates are chosen so that the resulting value of K_m maximizes the value of resources available for government expenditures. Given the aggregate resource constraint, this implies that $p^* f_K = r^*$. Firms would choose this allocation, however, only if $\tau = 0$. Under optimal policies, therefore, there should be no source-based tax on capital. Any capital tax prevents the country from taking full advantage of the gains from trade.

---

[6] Note that individual returns to saving are unaffected by τ, since this is a tax on investment in the domestic economy, while returns to saving are fixed by the world capital market.
[7] The discussion is simplified here by ignoring government purchases of nontradables. Tax changes do affect the prices of nontradables, but they imply equal changes in both government revenue and expenditures, so that these price changes have no net effect on the government budget.

The choice of tax instrument carries implications for optimal levels of government expenditure. Since the use of source-based capital taxes entails a higher welfare cost than does the alternative of raising revenue with wage and sales taxes, it follows that welfare-maximizing governments constrained to use capital taxes will generally spend less on government services than will governments with access to other taxes. Of course, one might wonder why an otherwise-optimizing government would resort to capital taxes in a setting in which welfare-superior alternatives are available. A number of studies put this consideration aside, constraining the government to use capital taxes, in order to analyze the implications of tax base mobility for government size[8].

In cases in which individual utility functions are additively separable in private and public goods, optimal government spending levels are lower with capital taxes whenever marginal deadweight losses increase with tax levels. This conclusion follows directly from the preceding analysis, since at any given individual welfare level capital taxation generates less tax revenue than does wage and sales taxation. Optimal government spending requires that the marginal cost of raising additional revenue equal the marginal benefits of government services. Consequently, if the marginal cost of raising revenue is an increasing function of tax levels, then moving from wage to capital taxation entails lower utility levels, higher marginal costs for any given spending level, and therefore reduced government spending. While there are odd circumstances in which the marginal cost of raising revenue falls at higher tax rates[9], more standard cases entail rising marginal costs, and therefore smaller government if funded by capital taxes.

This model can also be used to analyze the optimal tax rate on income from savings. Analysis of the optimal taxation of capital income in a closed economy [reviewed by Auerbach and Hines (2002)] is largely unaffected when cast in a small open economy. Since the before-tax interest rate is unaffected by the tax, the incidence of the tax now falls entirely on capital owners. As a result, the change in savings due to a tax change can be larger than in a closed economy, but wage rates will be unaffected. The same distributional considerations that might lead a government to tax savings in a closed economy may justify such a tax as well in an open economy.

The results derived by Diamond and Mirrlees (1971a,b) still imply that production will be efficient under an optimal tax system, as long as there are no relevant restrictions on the types of commodity taxes or factor taxes available. As a result, under such a "residence-based tax" on capital, residents should face the same tax rate on their return to savings regardless of the industries or countries in whose financial securities they invest[10]. These results also imply that foreign investors in the domestic

---

[8] See, for example, Wilson (1986), Zodrow and Mieszkowski (1986) and Hoyt (1991).

[9] See, for example, Atkinson and Stern (1974), and the discussion in Auerbach and Hines (2002) in Volume 3 of this Handbook.

[10] Naito (1999) shows, however, that these results no longer necessarily hold once one drops the assumption that different types of workers are perfect substitutes in production. Without this assumption,

economy should not be taxed – in a small open economy domestic workers would bear the burden of the tax.

Another immediate implication of the findings of Diamond and Mirrlees concerning productive efficiency under an optimal tax system is that a small open economy should not impose differential taxes on firms based on their location or the product they produce. This not only rules out tariffs but also differential corporate tax rates by industry. As shown by Razin and Sadka (1991b), this equilibrium set of tax policies implies that marginal changes in tax policy in other small countries will have no effects on domestic welfare. Behavioral changes in some other small economy can induce marginal changes in trade patterns or capital flows. Such changes in behavior have no direct effect on individual utility by the envelope condition. They therefore affect domestic welfare only to the degree to which they affect government revenue. Under the optimal tax system, however, marginal changes in trade patterns or capital imports also have no effect on tax revenue. Therefore, there are no fiscal spillovers under the optimal tax system, and the Nash equilibrium tax structure among a set of small open economies cannot be improved on through cooperation among countries.

2.2. Taxation of foreign income

The taxation of foreign income under an optimal residence-based tax system has received particular attention. When host countries impose source taxation on income earned locally by foreign investors, the use of residence-based taxation in capital exporting countries raises the possibility that foreign investment income might be double taxed. From a theoretical standpoint it is tempting to discount this possibility, since while countries may well choose to tax the income from savings that individuals receive on their worldwide investments, they should not find it attractive to impose source-based taxes on the return to capital physically located within their borders. In practice, however, all large countries impose corporate income taxes on the return to capital located therein. As a result, cross-border investments are taxed both in host and home countries. The combined effective tax rate could easily be prohibitive, given that corporate tax rates hovered near 50% in the recent past. To preserve cross-border investments, either the home or the host government must act to alleviate this double taxation. While the theory forecasts that such prohibitive tax rates would not arise because host governments would not tax this income, what instead happens is that home governments have offered tax relief of some sort on the foreign income earned by resident firms and individuals.

The modern analysis of this issue started with the work of Peggy Richman (1963), who noted that countries have incentives to tax the foreign incomes of their residents while allowing tax deductions for any foreign taxes paid. This argument reflects

---

a marginally higher tax rate on capital in industries employing primarily skilled labor, for example, will be borne primarily by skilled workers, providing a valuable supplement to a nonlinear income tax.

incentives to allocate capital between foreign and domestic uses, and can be easily illustrated in a model in which firms produce foreign output with a production function $f^*(K^*, L^*)$ that is a function of foreign capital and labor, respectively, and produce domestic output according to $f(K, L)$, a function of domestic capital and labor. All investments are equity financed, and the foreign government taxes profits accruing to local investments at rate τ^*. From the standpoint of the home country, the total returns (the sum of private after-tax profits plus any home-country tax revenues[11]) to foreign investment are:

$$\left[f^*(K^*, L^*) - w^* L^* \right] (1 - \tau^*),$$ (2.4)

while total returns to domestic investment are:

$$[f(K, L) - wL].$$ (2.5)

For a fixed stock of total capital ($\bar{K}$), the allocation of capital between domestic and foreign uses that maximizes the sum of Equations (2.4) and (2.5) subject to the constraint that $(K^* + K) \leqslant \bar{K}$ satisfies:

$$\frac{f_k}{f_k^*} = (1 - \tau^*).$$ (2.6)

If the home country imposes a tax on domestic profits at rate τ, then to preserve the desired allocation of capital expressed by Equation (2.6), it must also tax foreign profits *net of foreign taxes* at the same rate τ. Denoting the residual home country tax on foreign profits by τ_r, a firm receives $[f^*(K^*, L^*) - w^* L^*](1 - \tau^* - \tau_r)$ from its investment in the foreign market, and $[f(K, L) - wL](1 - \tau)$ from its investment in the domestic market; profit-maximizing capital allocation therefore implies:

$$\frac{f_k}{f_k^*} = \frac{1 - \tau^* - \tau_r}{1 - \tau}.$$ (2.7)

Equation (2.7) is consistent with Equation (2.6) only if $\tau_r = \tau(1 - \tau^*)$, which means that the home government subjects after-tax foreign income to taxation at the same rate as domestic income. The logic of this outcome is that, from the standpoint of the home country government, foreign tax obligations represent costs like any other (such as wages paid to foreign workers), and should therefore receive analogous tax treatment.

---

[11] This formulation treats private income and government tax revenue as equivalent from a welfare standpoint, which is sensible only in a first-best setting without other distortions. Horst (1980), Slemrod, Hansen and Procter (1997), Keen and Piekkola (1997) and Hines (1999b) evaluate the impact of various tax and nontax distortions on the optimal tax treatment of foreign income.

In practice, most tax systems do not in fact tax foreign income in this way. Richman offers the interpretation that governments may adopt policies designed to enhance world rather than national welfare. She notes that, from the standpoint of home and foreign governments acting in concert, the appropriate maximand is the sum of pre-tax incomes:

$$\left[f^* \left(K^*, L^* \right) - w^* L^* \right] + \left[f \left(K, L \right) - wL \right]. \tag{2.8}$$

Maximizing the sum in Equation (2.8) subject to the capital constraint yields the familiar condition that $f_k^* = f_k$, which, from Equation (2.7), is satisfied by decentralized decision makers if $\tau_r = (\tau - \tau^*)$. As will be described shortly, this condition is characteristic of the taxation of foreign income with full provision for foreign tax credits, a policy that broadly describes the practices of a number of large capital exporting countries, including the United States.

3. Tax complications in open economies

This section considers extensions of the simple model of optimal taxation in open economies. These extensions incorporate the difficulty of enforcing residence-based taxation, the optimal policies of countries that are large enough to affect world prices or the behavior of other governments, the time inconsistency of certain optimal policies, and the effects of fiscal externalities.

3.1. Increased enforcement problems in open economies

The analysis in Section 2 assumes that tax rules can be costlessly enforced. While this assumption can of course be questioned even in a closed economy, the potential enforcement problems in an open economy are much more severe. Consider, for example, the enforcement of a tax on an individual's return to savings. This return takes the form primarily of dividends, interest, and accruing capital gains. Enforcement of taxes on capital gains is particularly difficult, but even taxes on dividends and interest face severe enforcement problems in an open economy.

In a closed economy, taxes on dividend and interest income can be effectively enforced by having firms and financial intermediaries report directly to the government amounts paid in dividends and interest to each domestic resident [12]. Without this alternative source of information to the government, individuals face little incentive to report their financial earnings accurately and enforcement would be very difficult.

---

[12] With a flat tax rate on the return to savings, the government can simply withhold taxes on interest and dividend payments at the firm or financial intermediary level, with rates perhaps varying with the nationality of the recipient.

In an open economy, however, individuals can potentially receive dividends and interest income from any firm or financial intermediary worldwide. Yet governments can impose reporting requirements only on domestic firms and intermediaries. As a result, individuals may be able to avoid domestic taxes on dividends and interest they receive from foreign firms and intermediaries. This is true even if the dividends or interest originate from domestic firms, if the recipient appears to be foreign according to available records [13]. Furthermore, states competing for foreign investment accounts have incentives to help individual investors maintain secrecy and therefore hide their foreign investment income from the domestic tax authorities. Of course, individuals would still have incentives to report all interest payments and tax losses, so on net the attempt to tax capital income should result in a loss of tax revenue [14].

Based on the presumed ease of evasion through this use of foreign financial intermediaries, Razin and Sadka (1991a) forecast that no taxes on the return to savings can survive in an open economy. Any taxes would simply induce investors to divert their funds through a foreign financial intermediary, even if they continue to invest in domestic assets. Of course, use of foreign financial intermediaries may not be costless. The main costs, though, are likely to be the relatively fixed costs of judging how vulnerable the investment might be due to differing regulatory oversight (in practice as well as in law) in the foreign country. Individuals with large savings would still likely find it worth the fixed cost to find a reliable foreign intermediary, so that the tax would fall primarily on small savers. Enforcement problems therefore give the tax unintended distributional features and higher efficiency costs (by inducing individuals to shift their savings abroad as well as to reduce their savings). As the costs of using foreign intermediaries drop over time due to the growing integration of financial markets, these pressures to reduce tax rates become larger. There is considerable controversy in interpreting recent European tax developments, but some argue that tax rates within Europe are falling in response to such international pressures [15].

A uniform tax on the return to savings, consistent with the results in Diamond and Mirrlees (1971a,b), should tax accruing capital gains at the same rate as dividends and interest. The taxation of capital gains, however, is an administrative problem even in a closed economy. In a closed economy, financial intermediaries may have information on the sales revenue from most assets sales for each domestic resident, but they would rarely have information about the original purchase price. Therefore, a tax on *realized* capital gains is difficult to enforce. Even if it were enforceable, it is not equivalent to a tax on capital gains at accrual, since investors can defer tax liabilities until they

---

[13] Note that the optimal tax policies analyzed in Section 2 would exempt foreigners from domestic taxation.

[14] See, for example, Gordon and Slemrod (1988), Kalambokidis (1992), or Shoven (1991) for evidence that the U.S. tax system lost revenue from attempting to tax capital income, at least in the years analyzed (1975–1986).

[15] See, for example, the papers collected in Cnossen (2000).

choose to sell their assets [16]. The practice has instead been to tax accruing capital gains primarily at the firm level by imposing corporate taxes on retained earnings that generate these capital gains [17]. The lower is the effective tax rate on realized capital gains at the individual level, the higher would be the appropriate tax rate on accruing gains at the firm level.

Under the equivalent tax system in a small open economy, the government would need to tax corporate retained earnings to the extent that shares are owned by domestic residents. Such taxes are inconsistent with current international tax practice. Imposing instead a higher tax rate at realization on foreign-source capital gains would be difficult, since the government cannot learn directly about the sale of an asset if the investor uses a foreign financial intermediary, and again the high rate generates a costly "lock-in" effect.

One method of addressing these enforcement problems is for countries to establish bilateral information-sharing agreements that provide for exchange of information to aid in the enforcement of domestic residence-based taxes. However, these agreements have been undermined by various tax havens that enable domestic investors to acquire anonymity when they invest, facilitating avoidance of residence-based taxes on capital income. As Yang (1996) notes, as long as there is one country that remains completely outside this network of information-sharing agreements, then evasion activity would in theory be left unaffected – all savings would simply flow through the sole remaining tax haven. Recent sharp efforts by the OECD (2000) to encourage all countries to share information on foreign bank accounts and investment earnings of foreign investors are intended to prevent their use to avoid home-country taxes.

Gordon (1992) and Slemrod (1988) argue that an international agreement to impose withholding taxes on any financial income paid to tax haven intermediaries, at a rate equal to the maximum residence-based income tax rate, would be sufficient to eliminate the use of tax havens to avoid taxes on income earned elsewhere. Again, however, any one country on its own would not have an incentive to impose such a withholding tax on payments made to tax haven financial intermediaries, so an international agreement among all countries would be necessary to implement such a policy.

Some countries attempt to enforce their tax systems by preventing individuals from purchasing foreign securities while still allowing domestic multinationals to establish foreign operations [18]. The benefit of imposing such controls is that enforcement

---

[16] In principle, the tax rate paid at realization can be adjusted to make the tax equivalent to a tax at accrual. See Auerbach (1991) or Bradford (1996) for further discussion. No country has attempted such a compensating adjustment in tax rate, however. Many countries, though, have imposed a reduced rate on realized capital gains, to lessen the incentive to postpone realizations, thereby further lowering the effective tax rate on capital gains compared to that on dividends and interest.

[17] In some countries, most notably the United States, profits rather than retained earnings have been taxed, subjecting dividend income to double taxation. Many countries, though, have adopted dividend imputation schemes that rebate corporate taxes collected on profits paid out as dividends.

[18] During the 1980's, controls of roughly this form existed in such countries as Australia, France, Italy, Japan, and Sweden. See Razin and Sadka (1991a) for a theoretical defense of this approach.

problems are much less severe when taxing domestic firms than when taxing domestic individuals on their foreign-source incomes. Under existing tax conventions domestic governments have the right to tax retained earnings accruing abroad to domestic multinationals, even if they cannot tax these retained earnings when individuals invest abroad. In addition, multinationals need to submit independently audited accounting statements in each country in which they operate, providing tax authorities an independent source of information about the firms' earnings that is not available for portfolio investors. If multinational firms can be monitored fully and portfolio investment abroad successfully banned[19], then this approach solves the enforcement problem. Since multinationals can take advantage of the same investment opportunities abroad that individual investors can, the models do not immediately point out any efficiency loss from such a channeling of investments abroad through multinationals. Capital controls can therefore provide an effective means of making avoidance of domestic taxes much more difficult, facilitating much higher tax rates on income from savings. Gordon and Jun (1993) show that countries with temporary capital controls also had dramatically higher tax rates on income from savings during the years in which they maintained the capital controls. For example, Australia had capital controls until 1984. Until then, the top personal tax rate on dividend income was 60%. By 1988, taking into account both the drop in the top tax rate and the introduction of a dividend tax credit, Australia's net marginal tax rate had fallen to eight percent. Similarly, Sweden had capital controls until 1988. At that date, the top marginal tax rate was 74%, but two years later it had fallen to 30%. Capital controls are difficult and costly to enforce, however, and can prevent individuals from taking advantage of sound economic reasons for investing in foreign assets. As a result, many countries have abandoned capital controls in recent years, reopening the problem of enforcing a tax on the return to savings.

3.2. Countries that affect market prices

The models described above made strong use of the assumption that a country is a price taker in world markets. There are several reasons, however, for questioning this assumption.

The first possibility, discussed at length by Dixit (1985), is that a country may have a sufficiently dominant position in certain markets that its exports or imports can have noticeable effects on world prices. Yet unless the domestic industry is monopolized, the country will not take advantage of this market power without government intervention. Therefore, tariffs can be used to gain at the expense of foreign producers and

---

[19] Enforcement of taxes discouraging or banning portfolio investment in foreign assets remains difficult, however. Gros (1990) and Gordon and Jun (1993) both report evidence of substantial ownership of foreign financial assets by investors in countries with capital controls, held through foreign financial intermediaries.

consumers[20]. As a simple example, assume that the domestic production cost of some exportable good, X, is $p(X)$, while the revenue received in world markets from the export of X equals $q(X)X$. Then the exporting country's desired value of X satisfies $p' = q + Xq'$. It follows that $q > p'$, so price exceeds marginal cost. This allocation can be achieved by use of an export tariff at rate t satisfying $t = -Xq'$.

Similarly, if a country is large relative to world capital markets, so that the size of its capital exports and imports affects world interest rates, then the country has an incentive to intervene to take advantage of its market power. If it is a net capital importer, then it would want to restrict imports in order to lower the rate of return required on the world market. One approach to restricting imports is to impose a withholding tax on payments of dividends or interest to foreign investors in the domestic economy. Conversely, a capital exporter would want to restrict exports, e.g., by imposing a surtax on financial income received from abroad. These implications are apparent from differentiating the country's budget constraint (2.3) with respect to K_m, permitting the world interest rate r^* to be a function of K_m. The first-order condition for budget (and thus welfare) maximization becomes:

$$p^* f_K = r^* + K_m \frac{\mathrm{d}r^*}{\mathrm{d}K_m}. \tag{3.1}$$

This condition characterizes private sector economic activity if the government imposes a tax on interest payments (or a subsidy on interest receipts) at a rate equal to the elasticity of the world interest rate with respect to capital imports $\left(\frac{\mathrm{d}r^*}{\mathrm{d}K_m} \frac{K_m}{r^*} \right)$.

While net capital flows from the largest countries have the potential to affect world interest rates[21], tax policy in these countries has not changed in the ways forecast when net capital flows changed. For example, the United States did not increase withholding taxes on financial payments to foreign investors when it became a large capital importer in the 1980's – in fact, it eliminated its withholding tax on portfolio interest income in 1984. Withholding tax rates are also quite similar in capital exporting and capital importing countries. Apparently, a country's effects on world interest rates are too small to generate any noticeable response.

When the return to capital invested in different countries is uncertain, with outcomes not fully correlated across countries[22], then even small countries may have some

---

[20] In an intertemporal context, Gordon (1988) argues that countries will also have incentives to reduce their current account deficits or surpluses in efforts to maintain the optimal quantity of exports period by period. Summers (1988) provides evidence that countries do in fact attempt to limit their current account deficits and surpluses.

[21] For example, the extra capital demand in the United States following its tax cuts in the early 1980's, and in Germany following reunification, are contemporaneous with higher world interest rates. See, e.g., Sinn (1988).

[22] Random differences in weather patterns, in demand patterns by domestic residents, or in technology (assuming incomplete information flows across borders), would all generate such idiosyncratic risk patterns. Adler and Dumas (1983) in fact document a very low correlation in equity returns across countries.

market power in world capital markets. Each country's securities provide investors a source of diversification not available elsewhere, and as a result, exhibit downward sloping demand curves. For example, if returns across countries are independent, then a CAPM-type model would imply that the expected rate of return, r^e, that investors require in order to be willing to invest an extra unit of capital in country n equals:

$$r^e = r^* + \rho K_{ni} \sigma_n^2, \tag{3.2}$$

in which σ_n is the standard deviation of the return to a unit of capital invested in country n, K_{ni} is the amount of capital in country n owned by investor i, r^* is a risk-free opportunity cost of funds, and ρ measures the investor's risk aversion.

Rather than facing a fixed cost, r^*, per unit of capital acquired from abroad, Equation (3.2) instead implies that the marginal cost of acquiring funds on the world market is an upward sloping function of the total volume of funds acquired. Each domestic firm, however, would take the cost of funds, r^e, as given in making its investment decisions, and therefore ignore the effects of its extra investment on the cost of funds faced by other domestic firms. Based on standard optimal tariff considerations, it follows that a country has an incentive to intervene to reduce the amount of domestic equity acquired by foreign investors[23].

This intervention might take the form of corporate taxes on the return to domestic capital supplemented by an additional withholding tax on dividends and capital gains paid to foreign owners[24]. Hines and Willard (1992) document that, while many countries impose significant withholding taxes on dividend payments to foreign owners, it is much less common to impose large withholding taxes on interest payments. This is as would be expected if countries have little ability to affect the net-of-tax interest rate paid on "risk-free" assets[25]. With this explanation for withholding taxes, it is no longer surprising that countries change them very little in response to changes in net capital flows.

As with other uses of tariffs, the gains to country n from imposing withholding taxes come at the expense of investors from other countries, who earn lower rates of return on their investments in country n's securities. These losses to nonresidents would not be considered by the government of country n in setting its policies, implying that the policies chosen in equilibrium by each government will not be Pareto optimal from the perspective of the governments jointly. As a result, there would potentially be a mutual gain from agreements to reduce tariffs[26]. In fact, bilateral treaties to reduce

---

[23] See Gordon and Varian (1989), Werner (1994), Huizinga and Nielsen (1997) and Gordon and Gaspar (2001) for alternative derivations of the optimal tax policies in this setting.

[24] See Gordon and Gaspar (2001) for a formal derivation.

[25] Huizinga (1996) offers evidence that higher withholding taxes raise pretax interest rates, but that the availability of foreign tax credits offered by creditor countries mitigates this effect.

[26] As always, if countries are sufficiently asymmetric, then side payments may be needed to assure that each government gains from these mutual tariff reductions.

withholding taxes on cross-border financial payments are common, as documented by Hines and Willard (1992).

3.3. Time inconsistency of the optimal tax system

Another important aspect of simple models of optimal tax policy is that individuals own no assets initially, thereby removing the possibility of implementing a nondistorting (lump-sum) tax on initial asset holdings. If individuals do own assets at the time tax policy is being determined, then the model implies that one component of the optimal tax policy will be to seize any initial assets, since such actions raise revenue without distorting future decisions. Not only does this seizure have no efficiency cost, but it may also be attractive on distributional grounds to the extent that the owners are rich or foreign[27]. While such lump-sum taxes are seldom observed, unexpected taxes on capital investments also raise revenue from the initial owners of assets, so can serve much the same purpose[28].

These policies would not be time-consistent, however. The optimal policy involves no such seizure of assets in later periods, yet the government will have an incentive according to the model to impose such a "lump-sum" tax in the future whenever it reconsiders its tax policy. Investors might then rationally anticipate these seizures in the future, thereby discouraging investment and introducing distortions that optimal tax policies would otherwise avoid.

As a result, governments have incentives *ex ante* to constrain themselves not to use such time-inconsistent policies in the future. Laws can be enacted, for example, providing full compensation in the event of an explicit expropriation. Existing assets can also be seized indirectly, however, by unexpected tax increases, assuming investments already in place have become irreversible. Given the inevitable uncertainties about future revenue needs, a commitment never to raise taxes in the future would not be credible. At best, governments can attempt to develop reputations for not imposing windfall losses on existing owners of assets by grandfathering existing assets from unexpected tax increases.

This problem of time inconsistency is present even in a closed economy. The incentive to renege on any implicit commitment is much stronger, however, when foreigners own domestic assets. If foreign investors can impose a large enough penalty *ex post* on any government that seizes foreign-owned assets (directly or indirectly), then a government would not find it attractive to seize these assets and the time consistency

---

[27] As emphasized by Huizinga and Nielsen (1997), the government will be more inclined to seize assets owned by foreigners, since their welfare is of no consequence to the government. Faced with this threat, however, firms have incentives to reduce the share of their assets held by foreigners, a point emphasized in Olsen and Osmundsen (2001).

[28] In fact, a commitment to using distorting rather than lump-sum taxes may provide a means for the government to promise credibly not to impose too high a tax rate *ex post*, due to the resulting efficiency costs.

problem disappears[29]. Governments would therefore find it in their interests to make it easier for foreign investors to impose such penalties. By maintaining financial deposits abroad that can be seized in retaliation for any domestic expropriations, for example, governments can implicitly precommit not to expropriate foreign-owned assets, though at the cost of making these financial deposits vulnerable to seizure by the foreign government. These approaches are unlikely to be effective against unexpected increases in tax rates, however.

How can a government induce foreign investment in the country, given this difficulty of making a credible commitment not to raise taxes on these investments in the future? If foreign investors expect the government to impose an extra amount T in taxes in the future due to these time consistency problems, then one approach the government might take initially is to offer investors a subsidy of T if they agree to invest in the country[30]. Alternatively, governments might offer new foreign investors a tax holiday for a given number of years, yet still provide thcm government services during this period. Since firms commonly run tax losses during their first few years of business, however, given the large deductions they receive initially for their start-up investments, Mintz (1990) shows that such tax holidays may not in fact be very effective at overcoming the time consistency problem.

3.4. Fiscal externalities

As tax systems deviate from the pure residence-based structure predicted by the simple theory, the result that the Nash equilibrium in tax policies generates no fiscal externalities is lost. In general, changes in tax policy in any one country can affect welfare in other countries, effects that would be ignored in setting tax policies independently. In particular, when a single country raises its tax rate, individuals have incentives to reallocate taxable income into other jurisdictions, providing positive externalities to these other jurisdictions. Conversely, when countries use taxes to exploit their power in international markets, or to seize foreign assets irreversibly invested in the local economy, then they impose negative externalities on investors in other countries. Given these externalities, there is potential for mutual gains from coordinating tax policies.

In order to illustrate these effects, assume that the economies in other countries have the same general structure as the domestic economy analyzed in Section 2. In particular, the utility of each foreign individual equals $v_i^*(p^* + s^*, p_n^* + s_n^*, r^*, w^*(1 - t^*)) + V_i(G^*)$, where the superscript "*" denotes "foreign". The foreign government's budget constraint implies that $p_g^* G^* = \tau^* K^* + s^* Q^* + s_n^* Q_n^* + t^* w^* L^*$, in which Q^* and Q_n^*, respectively, denote consumption of tradables and nontradables by consumers in the

---

[29] See Eaton and Gersovitz (1981) for an exploration of the form such penalties can take.
[30] Doyle and van Wijnbergen (1994), for example, note that the government can contribute T towards the initial costs of the investment.

foreign country. If the domestic country raises its tax rate τ, then capital leaves and is invested elsewhere[31]. This can affect welfare abroad for a variety of reasons. To begin with, if the remaining capital invested in the domestic economy is "sunk", then existing capital owners now earn lower after-tax returns, at least until the capital stock depreciates to the new equilibrium level. To the extent this capital was owned by foreign investors, they suffer windfall losses on their savings.

In addition, the increase in τ causes K to fall. Since total savings should remain unaffected, assuming no nonnegligible changes in r^*, capital simply shifts abroad, raising K^*. The extra capital raises welfare abroad first due to the extra resulting tax revenue, $\tau^* \Delta K^*$. In addition, this extra investment will tend to raise the wage rates in these foreign countries, and slightly lower the world interest rate. These price changes will be attractive to many governments on distributional grounds, and would normally induce people to work more, generating an efficiency gain due to the tax revenue on the extra earnings[32].

Changes in rates of capital income taxation therefore create a variety of externalities on foreigners, some negative but most positive. If on net these externalities are positive, then the Nash equilibrium choices for τ will be too low from an international perspective, and conversely. In spite of the potential gains from tax coordination it does not then follow that tax harmonization measures, even if wisely implemented, necessarily will be welfare-enhancing for all participating countries. Differences between country sizes [as analyzed by Bucovetsky (1991) and Wilson (1991)], to say nothing of differences in consumer preferences or other endowments, create heterogeneous welfare effects of tax harmonization when individual countries can affect world prices. This is evident by comparing the implications of Equation (3.1) for countries of differing sizes, in a setting in which the world capital market guarantees that dr^*/dK_m is the same for all countries. The direction in which a country prefers the world interest rate, and therefore capital tax rates, to move then depends critically on its level of K_m, which must differ between countries unless none are capital importers.

Of course, taxes other than those on capital income are capable of generating fiscal externalities. Bucovetsky and Wilson (1991) note that international capital mobility implies that similar fiscal externalities appear with wage taxation. In their model of tax competition between symmetric countries with wage and capital tax instruments, governments set inefficiently low wage tax rates because they ignore their impact on other countries. Higher wage tax rates generally reduce labor supply (if aggregate labor supply is an increasing function of after-tax wages), increasing the pretax cost of labor and causing capital outflow. This process stimulates greater labor demand in capital-importing countries, thereby enhancing efficiency to the extent that foreign countries also tax labor income.

---

[31] Note that total savings would remain unchanged, as long as the interest rate is unaffected.

[32] See Gordon (1983) for a more complete tabulation of the many forms that these cross-border externalities can take, and Wilson (1999) for a useful survey of tax competition models.

A second type of fiscal externality appears with indirect taxation. For example, when value-added tax (VAT) rates vary by country, and are imposed on an origin basis, then consumers have incentives to travel in order to buy goods in countries with low VAT rates. While transportation costs have limited the volume of cross-border shopping in the past, cross-border shopping is likely to become far more important in the future with the growth of mail-order houses and more recently of internet sales. When goods physically cross borders, governments have at least the potential to impose a VAT at the border, preventing evasion. Monitoring at the border is costly, however, which is why it has been abandoned within the European Union. When goods do not physically cross borders, e.g., when information is transferred electronically over the internet or when financial services create no detectable cross-border transfer of funds, then consumers can easily take advantage of differences in VAT rates across countries. A reduced VAT rate in one country then imposes fiscal externalities on other countries. As a consequence, there is the potential for welfare-improving agreements between countries to coordinate VAT rates [33].

Differences in the timing of income taxes and value-added taxes can also generate fiscal externalities through migration. Individuals have incentives to work in countries with low tax rates on labor income, but to retire to countries with low VAT rates. Differences in capital gains tax rates also create incentives for individuals to move before selling assets with large accumulated capital gains. The quality of publicly-provided schools, hospitals, and safety-net programs can differ substantially across countries, inviting migration in anticipation of heavy use of these government services. Use of debt finance invites inmigration when debt issues substitute for taxes, but outmigration when the debt is repaid.

While multilateral agreements to coordinate tariff policies are common, there have been few such attempts to coordinate tax policies across countries. Giovannini and Hines (1991) point out the gains from coordinating income tax policies within the European Union. They observe that one way to enforce residence-based tax rates on capital income within Europe is to impose equal source-based taxes on capital income at the highest European rate, permitting capital owners to claim rebates for any differences between the European tax rate and those imposed by their home governments. Enforcement costs fall as a result, since it is far easier to monitor the return to capital physically located in the country than to monitor the income accruing internationally to each domestic resident. However, such source-based taxes can be maintained in equilibrium, according to the models, only if the governments explicitly coordinate among themselves, since each government in isolation has an incentive to eliminate its source-based tax [34]. In spite of much discussion, there have been no such agreements within the European Union.

[33] See, for example, Mintz and Tulkens (1986), Trandel (1992) and Kanbur and Keen (1993).

[34] The mechanism described by Giovannini and Hines might require intercountry resource transfers if there are uneven capital flows within Europe. See Gammie (1992) for a more recent detailed examination of the options for coordination of corporate tax structures within the European Union.

Countries do commonly have bilateral tax treaties that set withholding tax rates on payments of dividends, interest, and capital gains between signatories. The agreements on withholding tax rates almost always involve *reductions* in these rates, however, suggesting that negative externalities, e.g., through exercise of market power, outweigh any positive externalities generated by tax competition[35]. In addition, these treaties deal only with withholding tax rates, whereas domestic personal and corporate income taxes can also generate tax spillovers to other countries.

Another source of coordination is the OECD convention that member countries adopt some mechanism to avoid the double-taxation of foreign-source income, either through a crediting arrangement or through exempting foreign-source income. Either arrangement is contrary to the forecast from the initial theory that countries would seek to impose residence-based taxes, so the OECD requirement does help to explain the existence of crediting and exemption arrangements for foreign-source income. Under an exemption system, however, corporate taxes are precisely source-based so that the Nash equilibrium set of tax rates is zero in small open economies. Therefore, this convention does not serve to internalize tax spillovers.

Under the crediting system, there is not even a Nash equilibrium set of tax policies with trade in capital[36]. Gordon (1992) points out, however, that the crediting system might make sense if the capital exporters coordinate and act as a Stackelberg leader. Given this crediting system, capital-importing countries will have incentives to match the tax rate chosen by the capital exporters. In particular, under such a tax credit system, the net-of-tax income accruing to a foreign subsidiary in some country c equals[37] $\pi_c[1 - \tau_c - \max(\tau_h - \tau_c, 0)] = \pi_c[1 - \max(\tau_c, \tau_h)]$, where π_c equals the pretax taxable income of the subsidiary, τ_c is the tax rate in the host country, and τ_h is the tax rate in the home country offering a tax credit. As long as $\tau_c \leqslant \tau_h$, any increase in τ_c leaves firms unaffected yet collects additional revenue for the host country; therefore, the host country has an incentive to raise τ_c up to τ_h[38].

Knowing this response of any host government, capital-exporters can induce tax rates to rise point for point in host countries when they increase their own domestic tax rates. As a result, domestic residents would face the same tax increase abroad that they face at home when the home country raises its tax rate, so can no longer avoid the tax by shifting operations abroad. From the perspective of the firm, the tax

---

[35] The link between reductions in withholding tax rates and information-sharing agreements also suggests that countries may reduce their withholding tax rate simply because they no longer need such a high tax rate to prevent domestic investors from shifting their assets offshore.

[36] See, e.g., Bond and Samuelson (1989) or Gordon (1992) for further discussion.

[37] Under existing crediting schemes, firms can receive credits for any foreign taxes paid up to the amount of domestic taxes due on foreign income. When foreign tax payments exceed domestic tax liabilities on this income, the firm has "excess foreign tax credits", since it has potential credits it cannot use. If instead the firm owes residual domestic taxes on foreign income, then it has what is known as "deficit foreign tax credits".

[38] By prior arguments, it would not want to raise τ_c further, since doing so is simply a source-based tax on capital.

has become a residence-based tax[39]. Gordon (1992) shows that use of this tax credit may be attractive to the capital-exporting country, even without OECD requirements, if investors can otherwise avoid a residence-based tax at some cost. Without such a tax-crediting scheme, equilibrium capital income tax rates instead equal zero.

Under this argument, however, capital exporters are attempting to induce capital-importing countries to raise their tax rates on capital imports so as to discourage capital flight. This is contrary to the observation in tax treaties that governments attempt to *reduce* the taxes host governments impose on capital imports. In addition, all countries except New Zealand that offer a credit against their domestic taxes for foreign tax payments allow multinationals to defer their domestic tax liabilities until profits are repatriated. With deferral, host countries still have incentives to impose withholding taxes on dividend repatriations to parent firms. Corporate taxes, however, are now dominated by withholding taxes[40]. Furthermore, many countries allow firms to pool their repatriations from abroad, so that excess foreign tax credits from one country can offset domestic taxes otherwise owed on repatriations from other countries. Firms can then arrange their investments and repatriations so that no taxes are due in the home country on foreign operations. If no domestic taxes are due, then any taxes paid abroad become source-based taxes, which remain unattractive.

Given the availability of both worldwide averaging and deferral of tax until repatriation, it is difficult to argue that tax-crediting arrangements have much effect on equilibrium corporate tax rates in host countries. Therefore, there is no plausible theoretical expectation as well as no direct evidence of coordination of tax policies.

4. Taxes and portfolio capital flows

This section considers the effect of taxation on the demand and supply of international portfolio capital flows. Such capital flows are characterized by the absence of mutual controlling interest between transacting parties, so that they might take the form of bank loans to unrelated firms, or individual purchases of shares of stock in foreign companies. Most international capital movements take the form of portfolio capital flows, and while there are features of portfolio capital flows that carry standard implications for international tax policies, there are also some observed aspects that are difficult to reconcile with standard theories.

4.1. Uniform income taxation

The most analytically straightforward type of international capital flow is that involving debt contracts between unrelated parties, since simple capital market arbitrage

---

[39] From the perspective of the governments, however, the outcome is not equivalent to a residence-based tax, since the tax payments made by domestic residents on their investments abroad go to the foreign rather than the domestic government.

[40] A corporate tax now discourages investment because the credit is delayed in time, and therefore of less value.

implies that investors must face identical risk-adjusted after-tax real interest rates for all transactions. International borrowing and lending entail at least two important complications that distinguish them from purely domestic transactions. The first is that borrowers and lenders experience gains or losses resulting from movements in the relative values of foreign and domestic currencies. The tax treatment of these gains and losses then affects the desirability of borrowing and lending in currencies in which exchange gains and losses are possible. The second complication is that governments may impose withholding taxes on cross-border payments of interest. These issues are considered in turn.

Interest rates in international capital markets adjust in reaction to anticipated nominal price changes, though the extent of this adjustment is affected by the tax regime. This point is illustrated most clearly in the case of a small open economy. The expected after-tax net return to foreign lenders $(r_{n,w})$ loaning money to a borrower in the small open economy is:

$$r_{n,w} = (1 - \theta^*)r + (1 - g^*)\dot{e}^*, \tag{4.1}$$

in which θ^* is the foreign tax rate on interest receipts from abroad (inclusive of any withholding taxes), r is the home (small) country nominal interest rate, g^* is the foreign tax rate on exchange rate-related gains and losses, and $\dot{e}^*$ is the anticipated appreciation (in foreign currency) of domestic assets held by foreign lenders. We assume exchange rates to be determined by purchasing power parity (PPP) in the goods market, which implies $\dot{e}^* = \pi^* - \pi$ (in which π^* is the foreign inflation rate, and π is the domestic inflation rate)[41]. A small open economy must offer foreign lenders an after-tax rate of return equal to returns available elsewhere[42]. Consequently, capital market equilibrium implies that $\frac{dr_{n,w}}{d\pi} = 0$, and differentiating Equation (4.1) with respect to π implies:

$$\frac{dr}{d\pi} = \frac{(1 - g^*)}{(1 - \theta^*)}, \tag{4.2}$$

in which it is implicit that $\frac{d\pi^*}{d\pi} = 0$. If foreign tax systems treat exchange rate-related gains and losses in the same way as ordinary income, so that $g^* = \theta^*$ [43], then $\frac{dr}{d\pi} = 1$,

---

[41] While this assumption is fairly standard, it is important to note that the literature suggests that PPP is best understood as a long-run phenomenon. See, for example, Parsley and Wei (1996) and Froot, Kim and Rogoff (1995).

[42] Strictly speaking, capital market equilibrium requires that risk-adjusted after-tax returns must be equalized. In the certainty framework used here, risk considerations are absent and capital market equilibrium requires only that after-tax returns be equalized. For an explicit consideration of the implications of risk for the analysis, see for example Gordon and Varian (1989).

[43] In practice, the capital exporting countries whose tax systems are described by the Commission of the European Communities (1992, pp. 235–303) generally set $g^* = \theta^*$. For the issues that arise when these tax rates differ, see Levi (1977) and Wahl (1989).

consistent with much of the empirical work on the relationship between interest rates and inflation[44].

While this change in r in response to an increase in inflation leaves foreign investors unaffected, the rate of return available to domestic investors falls. In particular, domestic investors receive real returns of $r(1 - \theta) + (1 - g)(\pi - \pi^*) - \pi$ on their investments in bonds from any given country (including their own). An increase in the domestic inflation rate, π, then reduces the after-tax return on all bonds, both domestic and foreign, as viewed from the standpoint of domestic lenders. The reason is that lenders must pay taxes on the purely nominal component of their investment returns. If, instead, domestic nominal interest rates were to respond to inflation so that $\frac{dr}{d\theta} = \frac{1}{(1-\theta)}$, then (taking $g = \theta$), lenders would experience no change in their after-tax real returns; this is the basis of Feldstein's (1976) argument that nominal interest rates should rise more than one-for-one with inflation in closed economies.

What distinguishes foreign and domestic investors is that foreign lenders are able to deduct against their taxable incomes any foreign exchange losses (or reduced foreign exchange gains) created by domestic inflation, while domestic savers are unable to deduct the real losses they incur as a result of domestic inflation. Perfect indexation of domestic tax systems would of course eliminate this difference, but in practice, most countries do not provide such indexation. Foreign exchange gains are taxable, and foreign exchange losses are deductible, simply by virtue of the convention of measuring taxable income in units of home currencies.

This tax treatment of exchange rate gains and losses then also influences the effect of inflation on the demand for capital investment in domestic economies. Tax systems that are not perfectly indexed permit inflation to affect investment incentives through the use of historic cost depreciation and inventory valuation, the taxation of nominal capital gains, and the ability to deduct nominal interest payments[45]. While all of these considerations appear in closed economies, what makes the open economy different is the attenuated reaction of nominal interest rates to changes in inflation. Since nominal interest rates react only one-for-one to changes in inflation, the real after-tax interest rate falls as inflation rises. Then to the extent that debt finance is used at the margin, and more generally that investment is affected by the cost of capital, domestic investment should rise in reaction to a reduced cost of borrowing[46]. The net

---

[44] Unless $g = \theta$ in all countries, however, then r cannot respond to changes in π in a way that leaves all investors indifferent, a point emphasized by Slemrod (1988). In this case, without some addition to the model, e.g., short-sales constraints as in Gordon (1986) or risk considerations as in Gordon and Varian (1989), there will no longer be an equilibrium.

[45] See Feldstein (1980). Auerbach and Hines (1988) note, however, that over the postwar period, U.S. depreciation schedules appear to have been informally indexed by regular legislative adjustments to compensate for inflation.

[46] See Hartman (1979) for a development of this argument. For evidence of the responsiveness of saving and investment to the after-tax cost of capital, see Bernheim (2002) and Hassett and Hubbard (2002) in Volume 3 of this Handbook.

effect of inflation on capital demand then depends on the relative importance of this consideration and others including the nonindexation of depreciation deductions[47].

The preceding analysis ignores the impact of withholding taxes on cross-border interest payments. In practice, many governments impose such taxes, which might take the form of requiring domestic borrowers to withhold a tax equal to 5% of any interest paid to foreign lenders. These withholding taxes are formally the obligation of those receiving interest payments, so lenders can claim foreign tax credits for withholding taxes. But since some lenders are ineligible to claim foreign tax credits (because their home governments do not permit them), and others are unable to take full advantage of additional foreign tax credits (due to tax losses, excess foreign tax limits, or a decision not to report the income), it follows that at least some fraction of withholding tax liabilities are borne by lenders and should therefore be reflected in higher nominal interest rates. Huizinga (1996) offers evidence that pre-tax borrowing rates are increasing functions of local withholding tax rates, though there is some indication that the potential creditability of withholding taxes mitigates this effect. Papke (2000) reports volumes of loans from foreigners to American borrowers are negatively affected by withholding tax rates on interest payments from the United States.

It is possible to broaden this analysis to consider the effect of taxation on individual portfolios containing differentiated assets. The starting point in thinking about taxes and portfolio choice is the observation that taxes have no effect on equilibrium portfolios if all countries impose residence-based taxes on income from savings at the same rate for all forms of savings, even though these rates are not identical across countries. To see this, assume there are I possible assets, where any asset i yields a before-tax real returns of r_i. Assume that each country k imposes a uniform residence-based income tax at rate m_k. Then in equilibrium investors are indifferent among all the different assets if and only if they yield the same risk-adjusted after-tax return:

$$r_i\,(1 - m_k) = r_j\,(1 - m_k)\ \forall\,i,j,k. \tag{4.3}$$

In equilibrium, it must be that $r_i = r_j\ \forall\,i,j$, and there are no tax distortions to portfolio choice.

4.2. Nonuniform income taxation

In practice, tax rates on investment income commonly differ by type of asset, with rules differing by country. For example, relative tax rates on interest, dividends, and

---

[47] Gordon (1982) attempts to measure the sizes of these terms, finding that the reduced value of depreciation allowances is likely to be more than offset by the induced decline in the real cost of debt and equity finance. Desai and Hines (1999b) analyze the magnitude of the welfare costs of inflation-associated saving and investment distortions, finding that the welfare costs of inflation in open economies have the potential greatly to exceed the costs of inflation in closed economies.

capital gains differ by country; and the returns to certain assets are tax-exempt in some countries but not in others. Denote the tax rate on the return to asset i in country k by m_{ik}. Then investors from that country are indifferent between holding any two assets i and j if and only if $r_i(1 - m_{ik}) = r_j(1 - m_{jk})$. As emphasized by Slemrod (1988), this equality can hold simultaneously for investors from different countries for only a very restrictive set of relative tax rates, yet actual tax structures are much more variable. Equilibrium portfolios are therefore distorted, given existing tax structures. In fact, without some additional factors limiting portfolio choice (such as restrictions on short sales) there is no equilibrium. It is therefore important to consider the implications of nonuniform taxation of asset income, and the factors that might reconcile them with observed portfolios.

The preceding analysis of the effect of inflation takes foreign exchange gains and losses to be taxed at the same rates as ordinary income. As emphasized by Gordon (1986), additional portfolio distortions are introduced if capital gains and losses resulting from changes in exchange rates are not taxed at accrual – as is, for example, characteristic of equity investments that generate unrealized capital gains, or when tax systems fail to implement appropriate discount rules for long-term bonds. In particular, bonds issued in countries with a high inflation rate might need to pay a high nominal interest rate to compensate for the capital loss that investors experience due to the inflation. When the required addition to the nominal interest rate is taxed at a higher rate than applies to the associated capital loss due to inflation, the size of the increase in the interest rate needed to compensate for inflation will be higher the higher the tax rate of the investor. As a result, these bonds will be purchased primarily by investors facing low tax rates. If exchange rates were riskless, then a costless form of tax arbitrage becomes feasible, with investors in high tax brackets borrowing in countries with a high inflation rate and investing in bonds from countries with a low inflation rate, and conversely for investors in low tax brackets.

When different types of assets face different tax rates, their pretax rates of return will adjust in equilibrium to compensate for the differences in tax treatment, so that heavily taxed assets offer the highest pretax rates of return. This observation has interesting implications for tax policy. For a country raising capital from abroad, the pretax rate of return it has to pay to foreign investors will be higher if the financial asset used will face higher domestic tax rates in the investors' home countries. By this argument, bond finance should be more expensive than equity finance, at least after controlling for risk. However, when interest but not dividend payments are deductible under the corporate tax, firms may prefer debt to equity finance – due to the deductibility of interest payments, debt finance can be cheaper to the firm even when it is more expensive for the country as a whole. The government absorbs the extra costs through the fall in tax revenue, and so has a strong incentive to reduce or eliminate the tax advantage to debt finance[48]. Similarly, when domestic investors have a tax incentive to buy equity

---

[48] For further discussion, see Gordon (1986).

or other more lightly taxed assets, the pretax return they earn is reduced, which again would be reflected in a fall in government tax revenue. This pressure towards equal tax treatment of different type of assets is an example of the gains from productive efficiency described in Diamond and Mirrlees (1971a,b).

4.3. Home bias

The standard approach in the finance literature to explain portfolio choice is to assume that investors are risk averse and that the returns to different assets are risky, with the return on each asset having at least some idiosyncratic elements. Without taxes, standard portfolio models forecast full diversification of portfolios worldwide. The difficulty is that this forecast is clearly counterfactual, since the data show that a large fraction of the equity and debt issued in any country is held directly by residents of that country. This phenomenon is known as "home bias"[49], and its source is not entirely understood. One possibility is that tax systems may be responsible for at least part of observed "home bias".

Introducing taxes into a standard portfolio model generates the prediction that investors will tend to specialize in those securities where they face relatively favorable tax treatment compared with other investors. For example, if investors in country k face a tax rate m_k on income from bonds and a rate αm_k on income from equity, with $\alpha < 1$, where for simplicity α does not vary across countries, then the fraction of portfolios held in equity should be an increasing function of m_k. This model implies that the portfolios of American investors should contain smaller fractions of equity following the U.S. personal tax rate reduction in 1986[50]. As documented by Scholes, Wolfson, Erickson, Maydew and Shevlin (2002), foreign investors (primarily foreign multinational firms) increased their equity investments in American firms after 1986, which is consistent with the forecast of this model.

Taxes have the potential to affect portfolio choices, and some of the forecasted effects appear in the data. However, the above forecasts with taxes still do not explain the observed specialization in portfolios, suggesting important omissions from this model. One important omission is the possibility of tax evasion on income from foreign securities through use of foreign financial intermediaries. This potential ease of evading personal income taxes on portfolio income through use of foreign financial intermediaries has strongly influenced some of the discussion of equilibrium tax policy in the theoretical literature. If "capital flight" were an important empirical phenomenon, then a large fraction of the funds invested in the United States should appear to be coming from "nonresidents", as residents try to disguise themselves as nonresidents in order to avoid domestic taxes. Consistent with this forecast, an

---

[49] See Adler and Dumas (1983) and French and Poterba (1991) for evidence.
[50] The tax change in fact raised α by increasing the relative tax rate on capital gains, reinforcing this forecast.

unusually large volume of funds enters the United States from Switzerland, the Netherlands Antilles, and other tax havens. The same process, however, implies that domestic investors will appear to be foreign in the data, so that observed portfolios should have a "foreign-bias" rather than a "home-bias", which is inconsistent with reported patterns.

There are at least some elements of the tax law that result in higher effective tax rates on holdings of *foreign* equity. For example, countries commonly impose withholding taxes on dividends and capital gains received by foreign investors. While many investors receive credits for these withholding taxes against their domestic income tax liabilities, this is not true for all investors[51]. Those investors whose tax liabilities are increased by withholding taxes would in response reduce their equity investments[52].

In addition, many countries have dividend imputation schemes. Under a dividend imputation scheme, when a domestic shareholder in country j receives a dividend d from a domestic firm, he owes personal taxes of $d(m_j - \tau_c)/(1 - \tau_c)$ on this income, where τ_c is the domestic corporate income tax rate[53]. In contrast, when the investor receives a dividend d from a foreign firm, he owes personal taxes of dm_j[54]. Therefore, the scheme gives domestic investors a powerful incentive to favor domestic equity[55]. Foreign investors, in contrast, normally do not qualify for the rebate of corporate taxes under the dividend imputation scheme[56].

Under these dividend imputation schemes, however, individual investors could simply shift to investing abroad through domestic multinational companies. The investor would then potentially qualify for the dividend imputation scheme on the dividends paid by the domestic parent firm regardless of whether the underlying income was earned at home or abroad[57]. As a result, domestic taxes would no longer distort

---

[51] Since the foreign tax credit is limited to domestic tax liabilities, investors in low tax brackets are unable to take full advantage of them. Foreign tax credits are of least value to tax-exempt investors such as pension funds, though some tax treaties do exempt foreign pension funds from withholding tax liabilities.

[52] When countries have market power in world equity markets, then the intent of these withholding taxes may well have been to reduce foreign holdings of domestic equity.

[53] The intent of these schemes is to tax the pre-corporate-tax income at the personal tax rate m_j. In particular, a local firm needs to earn $d/(1 - \tau_c)$ before corporate taxes on its local investments to finance this dividend. While it pays $\tau_c d/(1 - \tau_c)$ in corporate taxes on this income, the shareholder receives this amount as a rebate, so on net he faces an effective tax rate of m_j on the underlying corporate income.

[54] This assumes that investors do not evade domestic taxes on the dividends they receive from foreign firms. If taxes on foreign but not domestic dividends are evaded, then the dividend imputation scheme provides an incentive to specialize in domestic equity only if $m_j < \tau_c$.

[55] See Boadway and Bruce (1992) for further discussion.

[56] The U.K. is one exception, allowing foreign investors to receive the same rebate of U.K. corporate taxes.

[57] In an attempt to restrict the rebate to domestic-source income, dividends are commonly eligible for the dividend imputation scheme only to the extent that they are less than reported domestic-source income,

the international composition of portfolios, though in many countries they strongly favor multinational investments over portfolio investments.

While these tax distortions may explain some part of the observed portfolio specialization, they are far too small to rationalize the substantial specialization in portfolios observed in the data[58]. As a result, a large literature has developed exploring a variety of possible explanations for the observed "home bias" in portfolios[59]. The question from a tax perspective is the implications of the resulting home bias for both positive and normative models of taxes on income from capital.

A natural inference from observed home bias is that aggregate demand for domestic equity is much less elastic than would be implied by standard models of portfolio choice. As a result, the incidence of a tax on the return to domestic equity falls more heavily on the owners of this equity (both foreign and domestic) than would be true in standard portfolio choice models that forecast more balanced portfolios. This less elastic behavior then may help explain the substantial tax rates that apply to income from domestic capital, in spite of the forecasts from simpler models that there should be no "source-based" taxes on capital.

Surprisingly, perhaps, the attempts to date to confirm this intuition by reexamining optimal tax rates in an explicit model potentially capable of rationalizing specialized portfolios do not support this intuition. Gordon and Bovenberg (1996), for example, analyze tax policy in a model in which specialized portfolios result from asymmetric information across investors from different countries – investors are assumed to be much better informed about domestic securities than about foreign securities, so may overpay for foreign securities. In this model, the resulting "lemons" problem leads to too little trade in equity. Domestic owners of equity gain at the margin from greater foreign demand, since it consists of more poorly informed customers that potentially can be overcharged. In a small open economy, however, it is still true that the incidence of any subsidies or taxes on income from domestic capital falls entirely on domestic residents. As a result, the government in a small open economy has an incentive to subsidize foreign purchases of domestic equity until the resulting gains to domestic owners are just offset by the costs of the marginal subsidy. Rather than leading to

---

requiring that $d(\pi_d + \pi_f) \leqslant \pi_d$, where d is the dividend payout rate and where π_d (π_f) equals domestic-source (foreign-source) income. This constraint therefore requires that $d < \pi_d/(\pi_d + \pi_f)$. Given typical dividend payout rates, this constraint is likely to bind for only a few highly international companies. [Hines (1996b) notes, though, that payout rates seem to be higher on foreign-source income.]

[58] See French and Poterba (1991), for example, for an attempt to calculate the size of the relative advantage to domestic equity needed to rationalize observed behavior.

[59] For example, French and Poterba (1991) and Tesar and Werner (1994) both conclude that higher transactions costs on investments abroad cannot be the explanation. Eldor, Pines and Schwartz (1988) hypothesize that domestic equity helps hedge against risks in labor income; Hartley (1986) suggests that it may hedge against risks from nontraded assets; while Gordon and Gaspar (2001) focus on a hedging role against random consumer prices. Bottazzi, Pesenti and van Wincoop (1996) provide some empirical support for the first such hedging role, while Pesenti and van Wincoop (2002) provide evidence against the second such hedging role.

positive tax rates on domestic capital, this model forecasts subsidies at least to foreign purchasers of domestic capital.

Gordon and Gaspar (2001) analyze optimal tax policy under the alternative assumption that investors specialize in domestic equity because it offers a hedge against uncertainty in the price of domestic consumer goods. Their results suggest that introducing this hedging role for domestic equity lowers rather than raises the optimal tax rates on domestic capital. An important reason is that hedging lowers the fraction of domestic shares owned by foreigners, thereby reducing the extent to which any tax burden is shifted abroad.

Other possible explanations for observed "home bias" could well have yet different implications for optimal tax policy. In the absence of a compelling explanation for observed "home bias", it is difficult to characterize optimal tax policy even in a small open economy.

5. Taxes and the behavior of multinational firms

Multinational corporations play a dominant role in international capital flows and international trade, so it is essential in analyzing the effects of taxation in an international context to focus on their implications for the behavior of multinationals. In particular, it is useful to consider empirical evidence of the effect of taxation on the activities of multinational firms, and the extent to which these responses are consistent with theoretical forecasts. Important differences between actual and predicted behavior have the potential to suggest useful modifications to the theory of multinational firms, which in turn may carry implications for optimal tax design. This section takes these issues in turn, first reviewing the evidence, then assessing its theoretical implications[60].

5.1. Behavioral evidence

International tax rules and the tax laws of other countries have the potential to influence a wide range of corporate and individual behavior, including, most directly, the location and scope of international business activity, but also including domestic operations that are connected to foreign operations through various international tax provisions[61]. A sizable and growing literature is devoted to measuring behavioral responses to international tax rules. In so doing, this literature identifies behavioral patterns that are important to understanding the responses to domestic taxation as well. These patterns

---

[60] The following section relies heavily on Hines (1997, 1999a).

[61] There are numerous indirect ways in which international taxation affects domestic economies, such as by influencing the nature and extent of competition from imports and from foreign multinational firms. This section follows virtually all of the literature in focusing on the direct effects of international tax rules, since indirect effects are extremely difficult to identify with available data.

include investment behavior as well as various financial and organizational practices used to avoid taxes.

5.1.1. Foreign direct investment

Cross-border investment by controlling entities has acquired a special name, foreign direct investment, and an associated acronym, FDI. What defines such investment is not only that owners reside in a different country than the site of investment, but also that ownership is of a controlling form, typically defined as 10% or more of total ownership in the local investing entity[62].

Tax policies are obviously capable of affecting the volume and location of FDI, since, all other considerations equal, and in the absence of countervailing effects, higher tax rates reduce after-tax returns, thereby reducing incentives to commit investment funds. In practice, FDI is affected by commercial and regulatory policies, characteristics of labor markets, the nature of competition in product markets, the cost and local availability of intermediate supplies, proximity to final markets, and a host of other attributes that influence the desirability of an investment location. The importance of these other considerations suggests to observers such as Markusen (1995) that any effect of taxes on FDI will be unnoticeable in practice. The most reliable FDI studies indicate, however, the existence of statistically significant and quantitatively important tax effects. These findings are important not only because they demonstrate the ability of the data to identify tax effects against a background of many other variables affecting FDI, but also because there are at least two additional reasons why one might anticipate not finding an important empirical relationship between taxes and FDI. The first is that firms may be able to use creative financing and other methods so effectively that they costlessly avoid all taxes on their international income. The second is that governments imposing high tax rates may indirectly compensate firms with difficult-to-measure investment incentives such as worker training and infrastructure.

The empirical literature on the effect of taxes on FDI considers almost exclusively U.S. data, either the distribution of U.S. direct investment abroad, or the FDI patterns of foreigners who invest in the United States[63]. The simple explanation for this focus is not only that the United States is the world's largest economy, but also that the United States collects and distributes much more, and higher-quality, data on FDI activities than does any other country.

The available evidence of the effect of taxation on FDI comes in two forms. The first is time-series estimation of the responsiveness of FDI to annual variation in after-tax

---

[62] FDI consists of changes in the ownership claims of controlling foreign investors. For example, an American parent firm that establishes a wholly-owned foreign affiliate with $100 million of equity and $50 million of loans from the parent company thereby creates $150 million of FDI. In order for foreign investment to count as FDI, the American investor must own at least 10% of the foreign affiliate. FDI is the sum of parent fund transfers and American owners' shares of their foreign affiliates' reinvested earnings, minus any repatriations to American owners. Reported FDI typically represents book values.

[63] Devereux and Freeman (1995) and Hines (2001) are recent exceptions.

rates of return in host countries[64]. Studies of this type consistently report a positive correlation between levels of FDI and after-tax rates of return at industry and country levels[65]. The implied elasticity of FDI with respect to after-tax returns is generally close to unity, which translates into a tax elasticity of investment of roughly –0.6. The estimated elasticity is similar whether the investment in question is American direct investment abroad or FDI by foreigners in the United States.

Much of this literature is highly aggregate, evaluating, for example, the correlation between annual movements in after-tax rates of return earned by FDI in the United States and annual changes in FDI flows to the United States. Aggregate FDI data distinguish investment financed by retained earnings of foreign affiliates from FDI financed by transfers of parent funds (debt plus equity). Studies that estimate separate (and independent) equations for these two sources of FDI typically find that FDI financed by retained earnings is more strongly influenced by host country after-tax rates of return[66].

It can be difficult to interpret such evidence. Estimated tax effects in aggregate time-series studies are identified by yearly variation in taxes or profitability that may be correlated with important omitted variables. As a result, it is almost impossible to distinguish the effects of taxation from the effects of other variables that are correlated with tax rates.

Two of the time-series studies exploit cross-sectional differences that offer the potential for greater explanatory power. Slemrod (1990) distinguishes FDI in the United States by the tax regime in the country of origin. Investors from countries (of which Slemrod analyzes data for Japan and the United Kingdom) with tax systems similar to that used by the United States receive foreign tax credits for taxes paid to the United States. Investors from certain other countries (of which Slemrod analyzes data for Australia, Canada, France, Germany, and the Netherlands) are more or less exempt from home-country taxation of any profits earned in the United States. Consequently, investors from France and Germany have stronger incentives to invest in the United States during low-tax years than do investors from Japan and the United Kingdom, since Japanese and British investors are eligible to claim tax credits for any U.S. taxes they pay. In his analysis of data covering 1962–1987, Slemrod finds no clear empirical pattern indicating that investors from countries that exempt U.S. profits

---

[64] Implicit in this estimation is a q-style investment model in which contemporaneous average after-tax rates of return serve as proxies for returns to marginal FDI. In theory, these specifications should also control for after-tax rates of return available elsewhere, though in practice this is infeasible.

[65] See, for example, Hartman (1984), Boskin and Gale (1987), Newlon (1987), Young (1988), Slemrod (1990) and Swenson (1994).

[66] For example, Hartman (1984) reports elasticities with respect to after-tax returns of 1.4 for FDI financed by retained earnings and 0.5 for FDI financed by transfers of parent funds. Similarly, Young (1988) reports elasticities with respect to after-tax returns of 1.89 for FDI financed by retained earnings and close to zero for FDI financed by transfers of parent funds. Boskin and Gale (1987) likewise obtain results that are very similar to Hartman's.

from home-country taxation are more sensitive to tax changes than are investors from countries granting foreign tax credits. This evidence suggests either that home-country tax regimes do not influence FDI, or that time series variation in tax rates is inadequate to identify tax effects that are nonetheless present.

Swenson (1994) considers the tax determinants of industry-level FDI in the United States over the 1979–1991 period. U.S. tax changes often affect industries to differing degrees, based largely on the assets in which they invest; this was particularly true of tax legislation enacted in 1981 and 1986. Swenson finds that industries in which the (U.S.) after-tax cost of capital rose the most after passage of the U.S. Tax Reform Act of 1986 were those in which foreign investors concentrated their FDI in the post-1986 period. This is consistent with the tax incentives of foreign investors from countries granting foreign tax credits, since such investors are the least affected by U.S. tax provisions – but it is also possible that foreign investors chose to concentrate in such industries for any of a number of non-tax reasons. Auerbach and Hassett (1993) lend credence to the latter interpretation with their finding that investors from countries granting foreign tax credits were no more likely than were other foreign investors to concentrate their FDI in tax-disadvantaged industries after 1986.

Other studies of investment location are exclusively cross-sectional in nature, exploiting the very large differences in corporate tax rates around the world to identify the effects of taxes on FDI. Grubert and Mutti (1991) and Hines and Rice (1994) estimate the effect of national tax rates on the cross-sectional distribution of aggregate American-owned property, plant and equipment (PPE) in 1982. PPE differs from FDI in that PPE represents (the book value of) real productive assets held by American-owned affiliates, while FDI equals the annual change in the book value of ownership claims of controlling foreign investors[67]. Grubert and Mutti analyze the distribution of PPE in manufacturing affiliates in 33 countries, reporting a −0.1 elasticity with respect to local tax rates. That is, controlling for other observable determinants of FDI, ten percent differences in local tax rates are associated with one percent differences in amounts of local PPE ownership in 1982. Hines and Rice consider the distribution of PPE in all affiliates in 73 countries, reporting a much larger −1 elasticity of PPE ownership with respect to tax rates. Altshuler, Grubert and Newlon (2001)

---

[67] The distinction between FDI and PPE ownership of foreign affiliates is perhaps best illustrated by an example. Consider two American-controlled foreign affiliates, each with $100 million of assets entirely invested in PPE. One affiliate is 100% owned by its American parent, while the other is 60% owned by the parent company and 40% owned by investors in its host country. Both affiliates account for $100 million of PPE. Establishing the first affiliate with $100 million of debt and equity from the parent company represents $100 million of outbound FDI from the United States, while establishing the second with parent funds represents $60 million of FDI. If half of the affiliate financing represented funds borrowed from local banks, then establishing the affiliates would represent $50 million and $30 million of FDI, respectively. To the degree that the affiliates' assets were not entirely invested in PPE, then the PPE figures could change without any corresponding change in FDI. Of the two measurement concepts, PPE more closely corresponds to capital stock notions implicit in most economic models than does the stock of accumulated FDI.

compare the tax sensitivity of PPE ownership in 58 countries in 1984 to that in 1992, reporting estimated tax elasticities that rise (in absolute value) from −1.5 in 1984 to −2.8 in 1992. Hines (2001) compares the distribution of Japanese and American FDI around the world, finding Japanese investment to be concentrated in countries with which Japan has "tax sparing" agreements that reduce home country taxation of foreign income. The estimated FDI impact of "tax sparing" is consistent with the tax elasticity of PPE reported by Hines and Rice.

Harris (1993) uses firm-level data to consider the effect of the Tax Reform Act of 1986 on direct investment abroad by American companies. One of the consequences of the 1986 Act was to remove many of the benefits previously enjoyed by taxpayers investing in equipment located in the United States. Harris finds that American firms with higher equipment/structures ratios invested abroad more heavily after 1986, suggesting that the tax change encouraged them to substitute foreign for domestic investment. This evidence is no more than suggestive, however, since unobserved firm characteristics that are correlated with high equipment/structures ratios could also be responsible for greater outbound FDI after 1986.

A number of cross-sectional studies consider the effects of subnational taxes on the geographic pattern of FDI within the United States[68]. Foreign investors must pay state corporate income taxes, at rates that vary from zero to close to 15%. Coughlin, Terza and Arromdee (1991) estimate the determinants of new plant location by foreign investors during 1981-1983, reporting insignificant effects of local tax rates after controlling for other variables. Ondrich and Wasylenko (1993) analyze a larger sample of new plant establishments over a longer time span (1978–1987), finding significant effects of state tax rates on the location of new plants. Ondrich and Wasylenko fit a model of the probability of locating plants in each state; their estimates imply an elasticity of the number of new plants with respect to state tax rates equal to −0.6. Swenson (2001) estimates separate regressions for differing types of transactions (such as the establishment of new plants, plant expansions, mergers and acquisitions, and joint ventures) undertaken by foreign investors in the United States. The results indicate that tax effects vary with transaction type: high state tax rates are negatively correlated with the establishment of new plants and with plant expansions, while they are positively correlated with acquisitions by foreign investors.

---

[68] There is also a small literature analyzing the effects of Puerto Rico's special tax status. Prior to legislative changes enacted in 1993, mainland American firms were effectively exempt from U.S. corporate tax on profits earned in Puerto Rico, though they were subject to Puerto Rican tax. Bond (1981) identifies significant effects of expiring Puerto Rican tax holidays on decisions of mainland firms to exit the garment industry over the 1949–1972 period. Grubert and Slemrod (1998) find that mainland firms with attributes associated with intangible assets – such as high R&D and advertising intensities – are the most likely to invest in Puerto Rico. Grubert and Slemrod note that this pattern may reflect the ability of firms with intangible assets to shift profits into their affiliates in low-tax jurisdictions, thereby increasing the attractiveness of locating investment in Puerto Rico.

One of the difficulties facing all cross-sectional studies of FDI location is the inevitable omission of many important determinants of FDI that may be correlated with tax rates and therefore bias the estimation of tax elasticities. This consideration makes it attractive to use empirical specifications that include locational fixed effects, but then the question becomes how it is possible simultaneously to identify the impact of tax differences on investment.

Hines (1996a) incorporates state fixed effects in comparing the distributions of FDI within the United States of investors whose home governments grant foreign tax credits for federal and state income taxes with those whose home governments do not tax income earned in the United States. The inclusion of fixed effects implicitly controls for hard-to-measure state attributes (such as those that make Silicon Valley or midtown Manhattan "special"), as long as the effect of these attributes does not vary systematically between investors from countries with differing home-country tax regimes. Tax effects are identified by comparing, for example, the extent to which investments from Germany (which exempts from tax foreign-source income earned in the United States) tend to be located in lower-tax states than are investments from the United Kingdom (which provides foreign tax credits for state income taxes paid). The evidence indicates that one percent state tax rate differences in 1987 are associated with ten percent differences in amounts of manufacturing PPE owned by investors from countries with differing home-country taxation of foreign-source income, and three percent differences in numbers of affiliates owned. Taken as a structural relationship, the estimates imply a tax elasticity of investment equal to −0.6. It is worth bearing in mind, however, that this estimate reflects the effect of taxation on the identity of ownership of capital as well as on the volume of investment.

The econometric work of the last fifteen years provides ample evidence of the sensitivity of the level and location of FDI to its tax treatment. Indeed, given the pervasiveness of this finding, this research is perhaps too greatly focused on an earlier question – do tax policies influence FDI? – and not enough on more subtle variants such as the role of tax policy in affecting the form that FDI takes, the possible importance of tax policy credibility and enforcement, and the relationship between tax and non-tax determinants of FDI.

Hines (1991) and Collins and Shackelford (1995) consider more dramatic reactions to high tax rates in which firms relocate their corporate homes to countries with more attractive tax climates. They estimate the tax savings available to firms that move from countries (such as the United States) with worldwide tax systems to countries that exempt foreign earnings from taxation. It is striking that, in spite of the appeal of low tax rates, very few multinational firms actually relocate their corporate homes to tax havens. In part, this reflects the tax and regulatory costs of doing so, but in part it also reflects the unwillingness of governments to impose excessively heavy tax burdens that encourage widespread departures.

5.1.2. Tax avoidance

International investors often have at their disposal numerous alternative methods of structuring and financing their investments, arranging transactions between related parties located in different countries, and returning profits to investors. These alternatives have important tax implications, and there is considerable evidence that tax considerations strongly influence the choices that firms make.

Sophisticated international tax avoidance typically entails reallocating taxable income from countries with high tax rates to countries with low tax rates, and may also include changing the timing of income recognition for tax purposes. Many of these methods are quite legal, and closely resemble those used by domestic taxpayers. Dramatic examples of international tax avoidance that qualify as evasion – such as knowingly underreporting income to tax authorities, or filing false documents – are thought to be uncommon among large corporate taxpayers, though possibly more common among individual taxpayers. Very little is known about the determinants or magnitude of international tax evasion, since the self-reported data that serve as the basis of analysis not surprisingly reveal nothing about it.

The financing of foreign affiliates presents straightforward opportunities for international tax avoidance. If an American parent company finances its investment in a foreign subsidiary with equity funds, then its foreign profits are taxable in the host country and no taxes are owed the U.S. government until the profits are repatriated to the United States. The alternative of financing the foreign subsidiary with debt from the parent company generates interest deductions for the subsidiary that reduce its taxable income, and generates taxable interest receipts for the parent company.

Simple tax considerations therefore often make it attractive to use debt to finance foreign affiliates in high-tax countries and to use equity to finance affiliates in low-tax countries[69]. The evidence is broadly consistent with these incentives. Hines and Hubbard (1990) find that the average foreign tax rate paid by subsidiaries remitting nonzero interest to their American parent firms in 1984 exceeds the average foreign tax rate paid by subsidiaries with no interest payments, while the reverse pattern holds for dividend payments. Grubert (1998) estimates separate equations for dividend, interest, and royalty payments by 3467 foreign subsidiaries to their parent American companies (and other members of controlled groups) in 1990, finding that high corporate tax rates in countries in which American subsidiaries are located are correlated with higher interest payments and lower dividend payout rates.

Firms face certain tax and regulatory limits on their abilities to select among alternative methods of financing their foreign and domestic operations. Many host countries limit the extent to which interest payments to foreign parent companies can

---

[69] Hines (1994) identifies exceptions to this rule that stem from the benefits of limiting equity finance in affiliates located in countries with very low tax rates in anticipation of reinvesting all of their after-tax profits over long periods.

be used to reduce the taxable incomes of local affiliates. Cross-border payments of interest, dividends and royalties are commonly subject to special withholding taxes that can be reduced by the terms of bilateral tax treaties. And, in the years since 1986, American companies with foreign operations have not been permitted to deduct all of their domestic interest expenses in calculating their U.S. tax liabilities. Instead, firms may deduct a fraction of their U.S.-incurred interest expenses in determining taxable U.S. income, with the remainder of their interest expenses used to reduce any U.S. tax liabilities on *foreign*-source income. In practical terms, what this means is that, in the years after 1986, American multinational companies with excess foreign tax credits (those whose foreign income is taxed at rates exceeding the U.S. tax rate) receive only partial interest deductions for their domestic borrowing expenses, the fraction being a function of the ratio of foreign to total assets. American multinational firms with deficit foreign tax credits (those whose foreign income is taxed at rates less than the U.S. tax rate) receive the full benefits of interest deductions for domestic borrowing, since any interest expenses allocated against their foreign-source incomes nevertheless reduce U.S. tax liabilities that they would otherwise incur.

Collins and Shackelford (1992) examine financial responses to the introduction of the interest-allocation rules by considering changes in preferred stock issuances by multinational firms after 1986. Preferred stock is a natural substitute for debt, but U.S. law does not treat payments to holders of preferred stock as interest, making such payments nondeductible and also not subject to allocation to foreign source under the terms of the Tax Reform Act of 1986. Collins and Shackelford find that, among the Fortune 100, firms with higher ratios of foreign to domestic assets – for whom higher fractions of interest expense are allocated against foreign income – are more likely than others to issue preferred stock after 1986. Since these issuances coincide with changing tax incentives, they are likely to represent reactions to changing tax rules, but this does not rule out the possibility that at least some of these large multinational firms may have issued preferred stock for reasons unrelated to tax considerations in the years after 1986.

Altshuler and Mintz (1995) examine confidential information provided by eight American multinational firms, finding a high correlation between tax costs imposed by interest allocation and propensities to borrow abroad after 1986. Since foreign and domestic borrowing are substitutes, this correlation is consistent with the results reported by Collins and Shackelford, and suggests that firms respond to higher domestic borrowing costs by actively pursuing financial substitutes.

Froot and Hines (1995) analyze a sample of 416 large American multinationals, finding that firms most adversely affected by the 1986 tax change do the least borrowing (as a fraction of assets) after 1986. They distinguish firms with foreign operations located in high-tax countries from firms with foreign operations located in low-tax countries. For all firms, the 1986 change reduces interest deductions allocated against domestic income and increases interest deductions allocated against foreign income. This reallocation has no effect on taxes paid to foreign governments, while it increases domestic tax liabilities if firms have excess foreign tax credits. In the absence of changing tax incentives, there is no particular reason to expect firms in these two groups to exhibit differing borrowing patterns around 1986. The estimates imply that firms with excess foreign tax credits and half of their assets abroad borrow five percent less annually after 1986 than do firms without excess foreign tax credits. Affected firms also exhibit slower rates of accumulation of plant and equipment after 1986, and are more likely than other firms to lease plant and equipment after 1986.

Contractual arrangements between related parties located in countries with different tax rates offer numerous possibilities for sophisticated (and unsophisticated) tax avoidance. It is widely suspected that firms adjust transfer prices used in within-firm transactions with the goal of reducing their total tax obligations. Multinational firms typically can benefit by reducing prices charged by affiliates in high-tax countries for items and services provided to affiliates in low-tax countries. OECD governments require firms to use transfer prices that would be paid by unrelated parties, but enforcement is difficult, particularly when pricing issues concern unique items such as patent rights. Given the looseness of the resulting legal restrictions, it is entirely possible for firms to adjust transfer prices in a tax-sensitive fashion without even violating any laws.

The evidence of tax-motivated transfer pricing comes in several forms. Grubert and Mutti (1991) and Hines and Rice (1994) analyze the aggregate reported profitabilities of U.S. affiliates in different foreign locations in 1982. Grubert and Mutti examine profit/equity and profit/sales ratios of U.S.-owned manufacturing affiliates in 29 countries, while Hines and Rice regress the profitability of all U.S.-owned affiliates in 59 countries against capital and labor inputs and local productivities. Grubert and Mutti report that high taxes reduce the reported after-tax profitability of local operations; Hines and Rice find considerably larger effects (one percent tax rate differences are associated with 2.3% differences in *before*-tax profitability) in their data.

The reported low profit rates of foreign-owned firms in the United States over the last 20 years is a source of concern to observers who suspect foreign investors of transferring profits earned in the United States to low-tax jurisdictions offshore. Grubert, Goodspeed and Swenson (1993) use firm-level tax return data to compare the tax liabilities of foreign-owned firms in the United States with the tax liabilities of otherwise-similar American-owned firms in 1987. They report that approximately 50% of the difference in the reported U.S. tax obligations of foreign and domestic firms is explainable on the basis of observable characteristics such as firm sizes and ages. The other 50% may reflect the use of aggressive transfer pricing by those foreign investors with stronger incentives than American firms to shift taxable income out of the United States, though it may also simply capture the effect of important omitted variables.

Harris, Morck, Slemrod and Yeung (1993) report that the U.S. tax liabilities of American firms with tax haven affiliates are significantly lower than those of otherwise-similar American firms over the 1984–1988 period, which may be indirect evidence of aggressive transfer-pricing by firms with tax haven affiliates. As Grubert and Slemrod (1998) observe, it is difficult to attach a structural interpretation to this pattern, since firms endogenously select the locations of their foreign affiliates; nevertheless, this evidence suggests an important role for tax havens in facilitating international tax avoidance. Collins, Kemsley and Lang (1998) analyze a pooled sample of U.S. multinationals over 1984–1992, finding a similar pattern of greater reported foreign profitability (normalized by foreign sales) among firms facing foreign tax rates below the U.S. rate. The reduction in the U.S. statutory corporate tax rate from 46% in 1986 to 34% in 1988 offers another method of identifying propensities to shift reported profits internationally. Klassen, Lang and Wolfson (1993) find that American multinationals report book returns on equity in the United States that rose by 10% over this time period relative to reported book returns in their foreign operations. The very limited nature of publicly available data on even the location of foreign operations makes it difficult, however, to discern the extent to which this change is attributable to changing economic conditions in the United States and abroad.

Patterns of reported profitability are consistent with other indicators of aggressive tax-avoidance behavior, such as the use of royalties to remit profits from abroad and to generate tax deductions in host countries. Hines (1995) finds that royalty payments from foreign affiliates of American companies in 1989 exhibit a −0.4 elasticity with respect to the tax cost of paying royalties, and Grubert (1998) also reports significant effects of tax rates on royalty payments by American affiliates in 1990. Clausing (2001) finds that reported trade patterns between American parent companies and their foreign affiliates, and those between foreign affiliates located in different countries, are consistent with transfer-pricing incentives. Controlling for various affiliate characteristics, including their trade balances with unaffiliated foreigners, Clausing finds that ten percent higher local tax rates are associated with 4.4% lower trade surpluses with parent companies. This pattern is suggestive of pricing practices that move taxable profits out of high-tax jurisdictions.

Multinational firms can adjust the timing of their dividend repatriations from foreign subsidiaries to reduce the associated tax liabilities, and there is considerable evidence that they do. Many countries, including the United States, tax the income of foreign subsidiaries only when repatriated as dividends, so multinational firms are able to defer home country taxation by reinvesting their profits abroad. Hines and Hubbard (1990) examine tax return information for the foreign subsidiaries of American firms in 1984, finding that only 16% paid positive dividends to their parent companies in that year. Foreign subsidiaries were more likely to pay dividends to parent companies if the associated tax costs were low and if parent companies also paid sizable dividends to their common shareholders. Altshuler and Newlon (1993) report similar findings in their analysis of tax return data for 1986. Desai, Foley and Hines (2001) compare the behavior of American-owned foreign subsidiaries, whose dividend repatriations may trigger U.S. tax liabilities, with the behavior of American-owned foreign branches, whose income is taxable by the United States whether or not it is repatriated as dividends. Foreign subsidiaries in low-tax locations are significantly less likely to repatriate dividends than are either branches in the same countries or subsidiaries in high-tax locations; the results indicate that one percent higher repatriation taxes are associated with one percent lower dividend payments. Altshuler, Newlon and Randolph (1995) find transitory tax costs to have much larger effects on dividend payments than do permanent tax costs in their panel of American-owned foreign subsidiaries in 1980, 1982, 1984, and 1986. This estimated difference between the effects of transitory and permanent tax costs is consistent with Hartman's (1985) insight that, while transitory tax costs should affect the timing of dividend repatriations, permanent costs should not, since permanent costs must be paid ultimately and are not reduced by deferral. It remains an open question, however, to what extent permanent tax costs can be accurately identified in a panel covering four years.

The form of a business organization can affect its tax obligation, thereby creating incentives for tax avoidance through the endogenous selection of organizational forms. The U.S. Tax Reform Act of 1986 introduced an important distinction between the tax treatment of income received from majority-owned foreign affiliates of American companies and income received from foreign joint ventures owned 50% or less by Americans. After 1986, Americans were required to calculate separate foreign-tax-credit limits for dividends received from each minority-owned joint venture. This change greatly reduces the attractiveness of joint ventures, particularly those in low-tax foreign countries. Desai and Hines (1999a) report that American participation in international joint ventures fell sharply after 1986, in spite of rising joint venture activity by non-American multinational firms. The drop in American joint venture activity is most pronounced in low-tax countries, which is consistent with changing tax incentives, and for which there is no obvious non-tax explanation. Moreover, joint ventures in low-tax countries use more debt and pay greater royalties to their American parents after 1986, reflecting their incentives to economize on dividend payments.

The location and intensity of R&D activity also appears to reflect tax avoidance incentives. Hines (1993) compares changes in the growth rate of R&D spending from 1984–1989 by firms with and without excess foreign tax credits in a sample of 116 multinational companies. The U.S. R&D expense allocation rules are similar to those for interest: multinational firms with excess foreign tax credits faced higher tax costs of performing R&D in the United States after 1986, while firms without excess foreign tax credits were unaffected. What distinguish firms in these two groups are their average foreign tax rates, which are more or less randomly distributed (in the sense of being uncorrelated with R&D spending in the years before 1986). R&D spending levels of firms in the first group grew more slowly than those of firms in the second group, the implied elasticity of demand for R&D lying between −0.8 and −1.8 in alternative specifications of the R&D demand equation.

International differences in royalty withholding taxes offer evidence of the substitutability of R&D in different locations. Higher royalty taxes raise the cost of imported technology, which in turn stimulates local R&D if imported technology and local R&D are substitutes, and discourages local R&D if they are complements. Hines (1995) finds that American-owned foreign affiliates are more R&D-intensive if located in countries that impose high withholding taxes on royalty payments, and similarly, that foreign firms investing in the United States are more R&D-intensive if they are subject to higher royalty withholding tax rates. These results suggest that imported technology and locally produced technology are substitutes, and that multinational firms respond to tax rate differences by undertaking such substitution. Hines and Jaffe (2001), however, find that American multinational firms for which the tax cost of performing R&D in the United States became most expensive after 1986 exhibited the slowest subsequent growth in foreign patenting, which suggests a complementary relationship between domestic and foreign research.

International tax avoidance is evidently a successful activity. The reported profitability of multinational firms is inversely related to local tax rates, a relationship that is at least partly the consequence of tax-motivated use of debt financing, the pricing of intrafirm transfers, royalty payments, and other methods. It is important not to lose sight of the fact that, in spite of the demonstrated ability of multinational firms to arrange their affairs to avoid taxes, these large corporations nevertheless pay enormous sums in taxes each year. Tax avoidance appears to be limited by available opportunities and the enforcement activities of governments.

5.2. Reconciling theory and evidence

This section considers the degree to which the behavior of multinational firms is consistent with the implications of theoretical models, an exercise that serves to identify useful and promising directions in which to extend existing theory.

5.2.1. Multinationals as financial intermediaries

Consider first a model in which multinationals are simply vehicles through which domestic residents can invest abroad. In particular, assume that multinationals possess the same technology as other firms, operate in a competitive environment, cannot avoid reporting to the tax authorities their true incomes from investments in each location, and face no uncertainty.

If multinationals serve simply as financial intermediaries, then individuals will invest abroad through multinationals rather than through portfolio investment if the transactions costs of doing so are cheaper, there are tax savings from use of multinationals, or multinationals are better able to locate the most profitable investments. For example, when countries have dividend imputation schemes, then investors face strong tax incentives to invest abroad through multinationals. Rather than exploring the relative advantages of portfolio investments vs. direct investments, however, we take as given here the total amount invested abroad through multinationals and focus instead on the location of this investment. By assumption, multinationals have access to the same constant-returns-to-scale technology as other firms, so that their investments are equivalent to the purchase of equity in local firms. It is useful to consider whether this model's implied pattern of multinational behavior is consistent with the observations summarized in the previous section.

If the corporate tax in all countries simply taxed the return to capital physically located in that country, then in equilibrium the rate of return on capital net of local corporate tax rates should be equilibrated across countries[70]. More formally, $f_k^i(1 - \tau_i)$ should be the same for all i, where f_k^i is the marginal product of capital in country i and τ_i is the corporate tax rate in that country. This condition reflects the impact of international mobility of portfolio capital. Based on tax considerations alone, therefore, all multinationals would be indifferent to where they locate, regardless of their home countries.

Many capital exporting countries include any income from foreign subsidiaries in the parent firm's taxable corporate income, and in compensation offer credits for income and withholding taxes paid to foreign governments[71]. It is worth considering whether this complication explains observed investment patterns. In order to simplify the setting, and at the expense of some realism, suppose that the home country taxes foreign income at accrual rather than at repatriation, and also that foreign tax credits are applied only against tax liabilities created by the income stream associated with the credits. Then if the marginal product of capital net of local corporate tax is equated across countries, so that $f_k^i(1 - \tau_i)$ is the same for all i (and therefore can be denoted r), the availability of the foreign tax credit implies that the net-of-corporate-tax return to a multinational investor from country j equals $f_k^i(1 - \max(\tau_i, \tau_j)) = r - \max(\tau_j - \tau_i, 0)$. This condition implies that a multinational firm will earn a return r in all countries with corporate tax rates above the firm's home country tax rate, but will face domestic tax surcharges and therefore earn a lower rate of return when investing in countries with lower corporate tax rates. With a sufficient number of available investments earning r, multinationals should be indifferent among countries with higher tax rates than the domestic rate, and avoid investing in countries with a corporate tax rate below the domestic rate. This forecast is clearly counterfactual, given the evidence that FDI is a declining function of tax rates in host countries.

With a sufficient volume of investment abroad by multinationals from countries with high corporate tax rates, it is possible that some FDI will be located in lower tax rate countries despite the tax penalty. Specifically, the equilibrium might include multinationals from country k investing in countries with tax rates above some τ_j, with $\tau_j < \tau_k$. For all host countries with $\tau < \tau_k$, the pretax return to capital in equilibrium will be the same as that available in country k, despite their lower tax rates, in order to be able to attract FDI from these multinationals. Portfolio investors from country k, however, then have a tax advantage over multinationals when investing in these

---

[70] In particular, the local wage rate must drop by enough to compensate for a higher corporate tax rate, so that firms can still pay investors the same after-corporate-tax rate of return available elsewhere.

[71] This foreign tax credit can be used to offset taxes due on foreign-source income but cannot be used to offset any taxes due on domestic-source income. Home-country taxation of the income of separately-incorporated foreign subsidiaries is typically deferred until the income is repatriated in the form of dividends.

countries with $\tau < \tau_k$, since they do not face the corporate surtax at repatriation[72]. Also, local investors in these host countries would earn a higher after-tax return at home than in countries with higher corporate tax rates. Only under extreme conditions, however, would this theory be able to explain why FDI is located in tax havens.

With worldwide averaging of repatriated profits, these forecasts need to be modified. If a multinational now invests K_l in a country with a low corporate tax rate, say τ_l, it simply needs to invest enough in some country with high corporate rate, say τ_h, so that the excess credits received from taxes paid in the high-tax country at least offset any domestic taxes due on the investments in the low-tax country. This occurs if $\tau_h K_h f_k^h + \tau_l K_l f_k^l \geqslant \tau_j [K_h f_k^h + K_l f_k^l]$ where τ_j is the home country tax rate. If all investments earn r net of local taxes, then this investment strategy earns r net of all taxes. Now FDI can occur in tax havens, but only if matched by enough FDI in high-tax countries.

The evidence indicates, however, that multinational investments are concentrated in countries with low corporate tax rates, and that the rate of investment is a declining function of the local corporate tax rate. This evidence is therefore inconsistent with forecasts of models in which multinational firms are simply financial intermediaries.

One possible explanation for the existence of FDI in low-tax countries was proposed by Hartman (1985). He notes that standard models focus on foreign investments financed by funds provided by parent firms, even though most FDI is financed by retained earnings of existing subsidiaries. When an existing subsidiary considers whether to repatriate a dollar of profits now or reinvest this dollar and repatriate profits later, it will choose whichever option generates the highest present value of repatriations. If the new investment earns the going rate of return, and the repatriation tax rate is constant over time, then Hartman shows that the firm will be indifferent between the two[73]. The key insight, drawn from the model of dividend behavior of Auerbach (1979) and Bradford (1981), is that the opportunity cost of the investment to the parent firm and the future profits earned on the investment are both equally reduced by the repatriation tax, so that the required rate of return on the investment is unaffected by the size of the repatriation tax. As a result, once a subsidiary is located in a low-tax-rate country, it has no incentive to move.

It is useful to examine the properties of this model of the firm, since they illustrate several aspects of the behavior of profit-maximizing multinational firms[74]. Consider the incentives of a firm that produces output with a concave production function $Q = f(K_t^*)$, in which K_t^* is the capital stock employed by the subsidiary in year t, and the $f(\cdot)$ function subsumes profit-maximizing choices of labor and other inputs. Q is output net of capital depreciation, and home and host countries' tax systems apply

---

[72] For evidence that portfolio investment does to some degree crowd out multinational investments in such countries, see Gordon and Jun (1993).

[73] If the repatriation tax rate varies over time, then the model forecasts that the incentive to invest is high when the repatriation tax rate is high, while repatriations will be high when the tax rate is low.

[74] The following analysis relies on Hines (1994).

true economic depreciation for tax purposes. Output is sold locally at an unchanging price taken to be unity and parametric to the firm.

The parent firm chooses the real and financial policies of its subsidiary to maximize the present value of the parent's after-tax cash flow. Let β represent the (annual) factor used to discount future after-tax cash flows (in the hand of the parent corporation). Denote by D_t the dividend payment from the subsidiary to the parent in period t; by definition, $D_t \geqslant 0$. Home-country taxation of foreign-source income, together with provision of foreign tax credits, reduces the after-tax value of a dividend payment of D_t to $D_t(1 - \tau)/(1 - \tau^*)$. For firms with mature foreign investments that use accumulated foreign profits to finance dividends paid to the parent company and any future foreign investments, the value (V_a) of their interest in the foreign affiliate is given by:

$$V_a = \left(\frac{1 - \tau}{1 - \tau^*} \right) \sum_{t=0}^{n} \beta^t D_t. \tag{5.1}$$

From Equation (5.1), it is clear that the policies that maximize V_a are identical to those that would maximize the present value of dividends in the absence of home-country taxation. Specifically, firms have incentives to reinvest foreign profits in their foreign operations up to the point that the after-foreign tax rate of return equals the opportunity cost of funds, or $f_k^*(1 - \tau^*) = \frac{1-\beta}{\beta}$. Since the repatriation tax is unavoidable to a firm financing investments out of foreign retained earnings, then its presence does not affect repatriation policies. This argument is identical to that in the corporate tax literature on "trapped equity" models of corporate dividends [see Auerbach (2002), Chapter 19 in Volume 3 of this Handbook]. As in the corporate tax literature, firms would incur unnecessary tax costs if they were simultaneously to inject equity funds from the parent company while remitting from subsidiaries dividends on which net home country tax liabilities are due.

Of course, repatriation taxes reduce the after-tax value of foreign investments, and thereby tend to reduce *ex ante* investment levels, since firms demand higher pre-tax rates of return in settings with significant repatriation taxes. In selecting initial foreign investment levels, forward-looking firms that anticipate future repatriation taxes have incentives to keep the capitalization of foreign affiliates at modest levels, since doing so prolongs the period before dividends are paid and home country taxation incurred. Sinn (1993) and Hines (1994) generalize the Hartman model to include this consideration, and Hines (1994) notes that this initial underinvestment makes it profitable for multinational firms to use significant levels of debt finance, even in low-tax countries. Of course, this consideration applies only to the extent that multinational firms actually incur repatriation taxes, since, as Hines and Rice (1994), Weichenrieder (1996) and Altshuler and Grubert (2002) note, there may be a large supply of attractive foreign investment opportunities to which foreign retained earnings might be devoted. Hines (1988, 1994) and Leechor and Mintz (1993) further generalize the Hartman model to situations in which home-country taxation uses a different tax base definition than does taxation by foreign governments. In this setting, marginal foreign investments have the potential to affect home-country taxation of inframarginal dividends received from abroad, and therefore repatriation taxes may influence repatriation patterns. Illustrative calculations presented by Hines (1988) suggest that this effect may be sizable enough to remove much of the value of popular foreign investment incentives such as accelerated depreciation.

There are a number of other clear inconsistencies between this initial theory and data on multinationals. If investments in equilibrium all yield the same rate of return r, net of source-based taxes, then the pre-tax rate of return in a country should be higher when the local corporate tax rate is higher. Yet, as described above, reported pretax rates of returns of subsidiaries appear to be a *decreasing* function of the local corporate tax rate, with particularly high rates of return reported in tax havens. Another important inconsistency is that the simple model cannot easily explain why countries have adopted such tax systems. Worldwide averaging produces outcomes in which the allocation of capital might be the same as would have arisen with source-based corporate taxes in each country, in spite of home-country attempts to tax income at repatriation. Yet such source-based taxes remain inconsistent with the forecasts from the Diamond–Mirrlees (1971a,b) framework.

5.2.2. Multinationals as corporate tax avoiders

The most striking inconsistency between this initial theory and observation is the very high reported rates of return in "tax havens". As noted above, the evidence suggests that multinationals actively make use of their abilities to reallocate taxable income from subsidiaries in countries with high corporate tax rates to those in countries with very low corporate tax rates. There are several possible methods of reallocating income, including judicious choices of prices, interest rates, and royalty rates used for transactions between related parties, substitution between debt and equity finance, and careful consideration of where to locate investments that might become unusually profitable.

The following framework is useful in understanding the empirical work on tax-motivated profit shifting, since much of this work relies on the premise that the stringency of government enforcement of international tax rules is a function of the extent to which reported profits differ from those actually earned in each jurisdiction. Consider the case in which a multinational firm earns true profits $\rho_i > 0$ in location i, but arranges transfer prices in order to report an additional profit of ψ_i in the same location (in which ψ_i might be negative). The firm incurs compliance costs equal to $\gamma \frac{\psi_i^2}{\rho_i}$, with $\gamma > 0$. Consequently, reported profits in jurisdiction i equal:

$$\pi_i = \rho_i + \psi_i - \gamma \frac{\psi_i^2}{\rho_i}. \tag{5.2}$$

The firm chooses ψ_i to maximize worldwide profits:

$$\sum_{i=1}^{n} (1 - \tau_i)\, \pi_i = \sum_{i=1}^{n} (1 - \tau_i) \left[\rho_i + \psi_i - \gamma \frac{\psi_i^2}{\rho_i} \right], \tag{5.3}$$

subject to the constraint that

$$\sum_{i=1}^{n} \psi_i = 0. \tag{5.4}$$

The first-order conditions for ψ_i imply

$$\psi_i = \rho_i \left[\frac{1 - \tau_i - \mu}{2\gamma(1 - \tau_i)} \right], \tag{5.5}$$

where μ is the Lagrange multiplier corresponding to the constraint (5.4)[75]. We find, as expected that $\psi_i > 0$ in low-tax countries, where $\tau_i < 1 - \mu$, and conversely.

If firms invest facing an opportunity cost of funds of r, then the true marginal product of capital (denoted f_K) will satisfy:

$$f_K = \frac{r}{\left[(1 - \tau_i) \left(1 + \frac{\gamma \psi_i^2}{\rho_i^2} \right) \right]}. \tag{5.6}$$

Without evasion, we instead would have found that $f_K = r/(1 - \tau_i)$. This is also the investment condition that would be faced by local firms, who cannot make use of foreign operations to reduce taxes. A multinational firm's avoidance opportunities therefore give it a competitive advantage over local firms to the extent that $\psi_i \neq 0$. Equation (5.5) implies that the size of this competitive advantage is larger in countries with more extreme tax rates, both small and large. The investment pattern of multinationals should therefore be a U-shaped function of the local tax rate[76].

Reallocating income into a tax haven avoids current tax liability. However, home country taxes are deferred but not altogether avoided as long as profits must ultimately be repatriated. Some investors may nevertheless be able to avoid repatriation taxes as well. One approach is to locate the parent firm itself in a tax haven. Another approach is to remove profits from the tax haven subsidiary in a way that does not generate tax liabilities for the parent firm. For example, the subsidiary can finance directly the expenditures (either at home or elsewhere abroad) that the parent firm would otherwise finance itself. Alternatively, the firm can simply continue investing abroad in other financial or real assets, earning the going rate of return pretax, thereby postponing any domestic taxes due at repatriation indefinitely. A number of countries have adopted rules trying to restrict deferral to real investments only[77].

---

[75] The value of μ adjusts to ensure that Equation (5.4) holds with equality.

[76] In countries with high tax rates, multinationals have advantages over local firms, because they are able to reallocate taxable profits to reduce the impact of the high local taxes. Their advantage over local firms in tax havens stems from the desirability of tax haven operations as recipients of taxable income reallocated from elsewhere.

[77] For example, the U.S. Subpart F rules impose tax at accrual on any income earned on financial investments abroad. As noted by Weichenrieder (1996), these provisions make real investments abroad more attractive, distorting allocation decisions.

Many but not all aspects of the behavior of multinationals are consistent with this focus on the role of multinationals as tax avoiders. Certainly, income reallocation efforts can explain the low observed pretax profit rates in high-tax countries, and the high profit rates in low-tax countries. However, income reallocation also implies that multinationals will invest more heavily in countries with extreme tax rates, both low and high. While the evidence does indicate substantial investment in tax havens, it is not consistent with the forecast of substantial investment as well in high-tax countries.

The theory also does not easily rationalize observed tax policies. Standard models indicate that the optimal source-based tax rate on capital income is zero. If firms can easily reallocate profits in response to tax rate differences, this only reinforces a country's incentive to reduce its source-based tax rate – and these incentives were sufficient, even without income shifting, to drive tax rates to zero. Given the evidence reported by Gordon and Slemrod (1988) and Kalambokidis (1992) that capital taxes in the United States (between the mid-1970's and the mid-1980's) collected no net revenue, perhaps tax policy in practice is not all that distant from the forecasts of the theory. Actual policy, however, generates a wide range of more detailed distortions, however, that are also inconsistent with the theory.

One further complication is that multinational firms can avoid taxes not only on their capital income but also on the income generated by the ideas and efforts of the entrepreneurs responsible for the firm. In particular, rather than receiving wage payments in return for their efforts, which are then taxable under the personal income tax, entrepreneurs can instead leave their earnings within the firm, so that they are taxed as corporate income [78]. Through adept income reallocation, the earnings might then even be taxed at as low a rate as that available in a tax haven, rather than the domestic corporate tax rate. Under an optimal labor income tax, this return to entrepreneurial effort would be taxed at the same rate as applies to the return to efforts expended elsewhere [79].

Gordon and MacKie-Mason (1995) explore ways in which tax policy can be designed to deal with this threat of tax avoidance on the earnings of entrepreneurs. In a closed economy, the solution would be simply to impose a corporate tax at a rate equal to the top personal tax rate. In an open economy, in which firms can reallocate taxable profits between countries, enforcement is more difficult. If any foreign profits must ultimately be repatriated, then Gordon and MacKie-Mason argue that the same outcome is achieved by including the cash-flow between the parent and the subsidiary in the corporate tax base, e.g., tax all repatriations in full but allow a deduction for all funds sent abroad. If foreign profits cannot be fully taxed at repatriation, however, perhaps due to detection problems, then the corporate tax rate should be set below

---

[78] When earnings are retained, entrepreneurs may then owe taxes on realized capital gains at some point in the future when they sell their shares in the firm.

[79] If entrepreneurial effort generates positive externalities, however, then a reduced tax rate on this form of effort could be justified. See Gordon (1998) for further discussion.

the labor income tax rate but above the corporate tax rates in tax havens, trading off domestic and international income shifting.

5.2.3. Multinationals as owners of intangible capital

Another theoretical modification suggested by the data is that multinational firms possess intangible capital, in the form of unique technologies or products, which they can profitably exploit in foreign countries [80]. As a result, multinationals earn returns on their intangible capital as well as on any physical capital they own. This modification is commonly used outside the tax literature in order to explain the economic role of multinationals [81].

When multinational firms possess such intangible capital, competition need not eliminate all pure profits. Multinationals therefore face even greater pressure to locate any pure profits in countries with low corporate tax rates. For example, if the fixed factor responsible for diminishing returns to scale is a limited number of skilled and trusted managers, these managers along with their subsidiary can in principle be relocated between countries. Consider the case in which the costs of relocating are zero, e.g., all other employees are perfect substitutes across locations. In particular, let the subsidiary earn the same pure profits, π, regardless of the country in which it is located. Due to the scarcity of managers available to oversee the technology, the multinational will invest in only those few countries that yield the highest net-of-tax return. Ignoring the repatriation tax, a subsidiary would earn a net-of-tax income of $[f(K_n) + \pi](1 - \tau_n)$ in country n, leaving it a net profit of $\pi(1 - \tau_n)$ after compensating investors at the going rate of return [82]. Without a repatriation tax, the firm would then want to locate all of its subsidiaries in tax havens.

In contrast, if profits are repatriated every year and subject to tax at repatriation, then the firm's net-of-tax income from its foreign subsidiary becomes

$$\left(\frac{rK}{1 - \tau_n} + \pi \right) [1 - \max(\tau_h, \tau_n)], \tag{5.7}$$

in which τ_h is the corporate tax rate in the home country. Now the firm strictly prefers to establish subsidiaries in countries with corporate tax rates just equal to τ_h – net of tax profits are lower in countries with both lower and higher corporate tax rates. As a result, FDI should be greatest in countries with "average" corporate tax rates.

---

[80] Leasing technology is an alternative to FDI, but encounters many difficulties. The lessee cannot easily be assured that they will gain access to all the information that is valuable in operating the unique technology effectively, while the lessor will fear competition from the lessee both in the product market and in the market for access to the technology.

[81] See, e.g., Dunning (1985).

[82] This is based on the assumption that, in equilibrium, $f(K_n)(1 - \tau_n) = r$.

If instead repatriation is postponed until date T, then the net return to investing in the subsidiary equals

$$[1 + r + \pi (1 - \tau_n)]^T - \left\{ [1 + r + \pi (1 - \tau_n)]^T - 1 \right\} \max \left(\frac{\tau_h - \tau_n}{1 - \tau_n}, 0 \right). \qquad (5.8)$$

In the limit as T becomes large, this expression will again be largest for subsidiaries located in tax havens, and the shift occurs at a lower T for firms earning greater fractions of their returns in the form of pure profits. The observed FDI in tax havens could then represent investments by multinationals that earn high pure profits and that can postpone repatriating these profits for a considerable period of time.

If subsidiaries earning the highest pure profits are pushed into tax havens, whereas those earning closer to a normal rate of return are confined to countries with corporate tax rates above the domestic tax rate, then this model helps explain the higher reported rate of return in tax havens. If many multinationals do earn large pure profits, then it also explains their observed concentration in tax havens.

This argument assumes that subsidiaries are costlessly mobile. The alternative extreme assumption is that the firm can profitably sell its output in a country only by locating a subsidiary there, as might be true when exports from operations elsewhere incur very high transportation costs. The firm then establishes a subsidiary in a country only if local taxes are not too high[83]. Assume, for example, a world of monopolistic competition among multinationals, where each multinational in equilibrium earns just enough profits, aggregated across all its operations, to offset its initial R&D costs[84]. Assume, for example, that a subsidiary in country i earns profits of $\pi_i \equiv f(K_i, R) - rK_i$ before royalty payments, in which K_i is the subsidiary's capital stock, R is the amount of R&D it has undertaken, and $f(\cdot)$ is a concave production function. The multinational could then face a cost function $c(R)$, and choose R to maximize worldwide profits.

This model implies that the government in a small country i would want to impose a 100% cash-flow tax on the subsidiary, i.e., not allow any deductions for royalty payments or R&D expenses[85]. The tax collects revenue yet creates no offsetting

---

[83] Note that the relevant tax rate is then the average tax rate, since the firm faces a zero-one decision. For further discussion, see Devereux and Griffith (1998).

[84] Firms in principle would then report zero profits in each location, after R&D costs are divided appropriately across locations. However, there are no clear rules for dividing these R&D expenses across subsidiaries. The purpose of the analysis is to analyze what effective tax rates host countries would prefer to impose on local subsidiaries. Such taxes (if positive) may then be implemented through restrictions on deductions for royalty payments and R&D expenses, or withholding taxes on royalty payments.

[85] In general, a cash-flow tax falls only on any existing assets of the firm, since new investment is deductible. By the same logic a government may attempt to expropriate such existing assets through a 100% cash flow tax. If anticipated, however, the original investment would not have occurred. R&D is different, since the investment is a public good from the perspective of each country, so should be only modestly affected by any one country's cash-flow tax, even if anticipated.

efficiency costs from the perspective of a small country, since a cash-flow tax does not distort the subsidiary's choice of K_i and a small country can ignore the implications of the tax for R[86]. Taken together, however, these tax policies make R&D unattractive, leading to an inefficient outcome.

While multinational firms can select the locations of their foreign subsidiaries, some countries may prove to be significantly more attractive than the next best alternatives, perhaps due to high costs of producing elsewhere and shipping to local customers. In such countries profits taxes on multinationals can survive in equilibrium. However, the maximum profit tax rate that avoids inducing subsidiaries to relocate varies by firm. As tax rates rise, a larger fraction of potential investment moves elsewhere. This relocation causes local wage rates to fall and local customers to face higher prices. These costs will limit the size of the optimal tax rate on multinationals.

Another issue that arises when multinationals own intangible capital is the difficulty of enforcing intellectual property rights. Multinational firms cannot necessarily rely on host governments to prevent local firms from learning and making use of its subsidiary's proprietary technology. It is not even clear that the rigorous enforcement of intellectual property rights is the most efficient policy, since the incentives for R&D activity need to be balanced against the efficiency gains from having existing technologies employed widely in production[87]. Even if rigorous enforcement were the most efficient policy from a global perspective, however, this does not mean than every country individually would gain from such rigorous enforcement – countries with no technologies to sell would almost surely lose from it. As a result, if a country is in a position to impose some additional cost on local subsidiaries without inducing exit, then it may choose to do so by aiding domestic firms to gain use of the technology owned by the foreign multinational instead of collecting cash payments from the firm. The choice between these alternative "taxes" would largely depend on the size of the gain to local firms from access to the technology compared to the cost to the multinational from the resulting additional competition. If local firms produce noncompeting goods, for example, then the leakage of information imposes little or no cost on the multinational. When the losses to the multinational from leakage of information about its proprietary technology to local firms is large enough to prevent it from entering, yet the gains to these local firms exceed the loss to the multinational, the host government may even want to subsidize multinationals to locate subsidiaries there.

The above arguments assume, however, that financial profits π_i must be reported in the same location as the physical capital K_n responsible for production. To some

---

[86] Huizinga (1992) and Mintz and Tulkens (1990) explore a closely related problem in which the host country is restricted to taxing the return to capital investments at the same rate as applies to pure profits, and also find that the optimal tax rates on foreign-owned subsidiaries are positive.

[87] Because of fixed factors of production, the multinational may not be able to pursue all profitable uses of its technology, yet find it difficult to design a contract to sell or lease the information to other firms that can profitably employ the technology.

degree, the multinational firm can relocate its financial profits independently of its physical operations. For example, if its subsidiary in a tax haven owns the key patents, the firm can then make royalty payments from its operations elsewhere to this tax haven subsidiary in an attempt to have π_i taxed at a low rate while maintaining flexibility over the physical location of the rest of its operations [88]. Firms with excess foreign tax credits are in even simpler situations, since they are effectively untaxed by their home countries on any foreign-source royalty income, and therefore have incentives to locate patent ownership in parent firms.

5.2.4. Testing alternative explanations

There remain two plausible – and nonexclusive – explanations for the dominant role of FDI, particularly in tax havens, and the high reported profit rates of subsidiaries that do locate in tax havens: tax avoidance activity and multinational ownership of intangible capital. Their forecasts differ sharply, however. Multinational ownership of intangible capital implies that tax havens would attract subsidiaries from industries earning the highest rates of pure profits, whereas tax avoidance implies that tax havens would instead attract firms that can most easily reallocate profits without detection. Also, the subsidiaries located in high tax countries would report below normal profit rates if profit reallocation were important, while they would report normal profits if the explanation for the dominant role of FDI were the existence of intangible capital. Another difference between the two explanations is that the gain from adjusting transfer prices is the same whether FDI takes the form of acquiring an existing firm or establishing a new firm (greenfield investment), as long as the ease of profit reallocation is the same. If multinational investment instead occurs because of the important role of intangible capital, then multinationals would again be indifferent between acquisitions and greenfield investment when investing in high-tax countries. They would invest in low-tax countries, however, only if it is possible to earn a high enough profit rate, which rules out acquiring an existing firm [89]. Therefore, FDI in tax havens would be limited to greenfield investment. Finally, predicted FDI is a U-shaped function of the local tax rate with income reallocation, but an L-shaped function of the local tax rate in the presence of intangible capital.

Another source of evidence on the relative merit of competing explanations for the dominant role of FDI and the large multinational presence in tax havens is the response to the U.S. Tax Reform Act of 1986. Following this Act, FDI in the United States increased substantially [Hines (1996a)]. One explanation proposed by Scholes,

---

[88] Host governments, however, may attempt to limit this process, for example by restricting the size of royalty payments or imposing withholding taxes on them.

[89] The existing owner would value a firm earning $[rK + \pi(1 - \tau_L)]$ at $[K + \pi(1 - \tau_L)/r]$. If the multinational acquired the firm, it would end up with lower profits net of tax because of the taxes due at repatriation yet would still face a required rate of return of r. Therefore, it could not afford to pay enough to convince the current owners to sell.

Wolfson, Erickson, Maydew and Shevlin (2002) is that U.S. firms faced an effective tax increase as a result of the tax reform, but that foreign-owned subsidiaries who owe further home-country taxes when they repatriate their profits would not be as much affected by the tax increase, since they receive extra credits against their home-country taxes to compensate for the extra U.S. tax payments. This explanation does not clarify, however, why the foreign subsidiaries are located in the United States. If foreign investors do in fact owe additional taxes at repatriation, then they would not want to locate in the United States if by doing so they earn no more than the going net-of-tax rate of return r. If opportunities for income reallocation were the reason for their presence in the United States, then the reduction in the *statutory* tax rate in 1986 would reduce the gains from transfer pricing, making U.S. investment less attractive. If foreigners invest in the United States in order to earn pure profits by exploiting firm-specific intangible assets, then the drop in the U.S. statutory tax rate could well leave them with a larger share of these pure profits after tax, making further investment in the United States more attractive than before. This explanation most likely predicts an increase in greenfield investments, however, since any firms wishing to make use of a unique technology would normally find it cheaper to build a plant incorporating the technology directly rather than convert an existing plant. Yet the observed increase in FDI primarily took the form of acquisitions [Auerbach and Hassett (1993)]. One factor that does help explain the observed jump in foreign acquisitions of U.S. equity is simply that the fall in U.S. personal income tax rates, and the rise in capital gains taxation, induced American investors to shift their portfolios away from equity towards bonds. In equilibrium, foreign residents facing high personal tax rates would then acquire this equity. The importance of dividend imputation schemes abroad, for example, could then explain why foreigners acquired U.S. equity through FDI rather than portfolio investment. This portfolio reallocation process is very much consistent with a jump in acquisitions but not greenfield investment.

6. Understanding existing international tax provisions

Tax systems in the world today differ substantially from those implied by the simple theories reviewed in Section 2. Source-based corporate income is taxed at high rates by all major capital importing countries, and has been so for years, in spite of any competitive pressures to reduce tax rates to zero. While personal taxes on capital income typically apply to the worldwide dividend and interest income of domestic residents, as forecast by the theory, in practice capital flight significantly reduces the effective taxation of this source of income for residents of many countries. The persistence of capital income taxation therefore also requires an explanation, since the threat of capital flight should exert substantial pressure to reduce or eliminate existing personal taxes on dividend and interest income. This section considers directions in which the theory of international taxation might be modified in order to account for observed international tax practices.

The discussion in Section 5 draws attention to two important considerations that are not addressed by simple theories, the ability of multinational firms to reallocate taxable profits between countries, and the use of FDI to exploit firm-specific intangible assets. Simply adding these complications to the initial models, however, only increases the implied pressure to reduce source-based capital tax rates. The ability of firms to reallocate taxable income and to earn pure profits from intangibles gives countries incentives to select corporate tax rates just below those prevailing elsewhere, since doing so increases the tax base both by attracting firms earning larger pure profits and by encouraging firms to report higher taxable incomes. If countries are symmetric, the only resulting equilibrium is one in which all countries have zero source-based corporate tax rates.

The pressure to reduce tax rates describes a form of tax competition that arises due to fiscal externalities. When a country succeeds in increasing its tax base through a cut in its tax rate, much of this increase in tax base occurs through a reduction in the tax base elsewhere. While in theory foreign individual workers and investors are indifferent at the margin to the resulting changes in investment patterns, foreign governments are not, since their tax bases fall and with them their tax revenues. One government's action therefore imposes a fiscal externality on other governments. In the presence of such externalities, the resulting equilibrium pattern of tax rates will be too low from the perspective of the various governments. In particular, while each government would be indifferent to a marginal increase in its tax rate starting from the equilibrium values, other governments would benefit from the increase, leading to a Pareto improvement[90]. However, observed attempts at policy coordination through bilateral tax treaties uniformly involve reductions rather than increases in tax rates, suggesting that fiscal externalities somehow produce tax rates that are too high rather than too low.

Modifications to the simple theory of international taxation may help to explain the use of source-based taxes on capital income. One modification is to incorporate the fact that capital once invested is commonly sunk. While *ex ante* a country may not want to distort investment incentives through a source-based tax, *ex post* it would want to seize past investments, a classic time consistency problem. This seizure is particularly tempting when the owners are foreign, so that their own welfare is of minimal policy concern. Given the time inconsistency, however, a government would want to commit not to tax capital in the future, if possible, despite actually wanting to seize assets currently. Other governments (of countries in which foreign investors reside) also would want to see such a commitment. Both pressures are consistent with binding bilateral tax treaty agreements to reduce tax rates.

A second modification, as in Huizinga (1992), is to posit that firms with unique technologies or other intangible assets may be able to earn rents in a country only by locating a subsidiary there. The host country then can impose tax obligations as

---

[90] See Razin and Sadka (1991b) for further discussion.

up to the size of these rents without changing the firm's location decision[91]. This tax discourages investment in R&D, but the resulting costs are shared worldwide. Equilibrium tax rates are therefore too high relative to those that would arise if countries could coordinate their policies. When firms have market power, as well as pure profits, additional complications arise in any model of optimal taxes, even in a closed economy[92].

A third modification, explored in Gordon and MacKie-Mason (1995), concerns the implications of possible income shifting between the domestic personal and corporate tax bases. While a source-based corporate tax encourages firms to reallocate taxable profits abroad, it discourages employees from shifting their personal incomes into the corporate tax base. If there were no tax on repatriated profits, then it would be possible to avoid taxes even on labor income. While there is no incentive per se in this model to tax foreign investors in the domestic economy, such taxes may still be needed to deter residents from disguising themselves as foreign investors. This generates an efficiency gain from using information sharing to detect foreign-source income rather than relying on taxes on "foreign" investors, consistent with the provisions of many tax treaties.

A final modification, suggested by the empirical findings of Feldstein and Horioka (1980) and the home bias literature and explored for example in Gordon and Varian (1989) and Gordon and Gaspar (2001), is to posit that capital investments are not so easily mobile across countries, due for example to risk diversification or hedging reasons. If capital investments are less than perfectly mobile, then countries may find some taxation of capital investments to be attractive. Gordon and Gaspar argue, however, that this scenario provides only weak theoretical support for significant capital taxation by optimizing governments.

7. Conclusion

Economies are rapidly becoming more open, not only to trade in goods and services, but also to capital flows and even to labor migration. This paper considers the effect of taxation on international business activity, and the implications of open borders for the taxation of capital income. There is considerable evidence that international taxation influences the volume and location of foreign direct investment, and is responsible for a wide range of tax avoidance. The observed responsiveness of international economic activity to its taxation carries direct implications for the formation of international tax policy and indirect, but no less important, implications for the formation of domestic tax policy. Indeed, given the extent to which international considerations influence

---

[91] Since the country has no incentive to discourage local capital investment, it prefers to impose a cash-flow tax.

[92] See Devereux and Hubbard (2000) for a recent attempt to extend such results to an open economy setting.

domestic tax choices, it is not clear whether countries are any longer able to pursue purely domestic tax policies.

Any analysis of capital taxation in an open economy that seeks to be consistent with observed behavior and actual tax policies must consider the implications of tax avoidance, and should recognize the potential importance of investment driven by firm-specific intangible assets. Even these added complications do not explain certain aspects of individual behavior, such as "home bias" in financial portfolios, and are insufficient to rationalize easily the current tax treatment of capital income. Since international considerations were afterthoughts in the design of most countries' tax systems, it may be that policies around the world have yet to catch up with events. There is a bright future for research on international taxation, not only because there are many unanswered questions and a worldwide laboratory to use in answering them, but also because the formulation of domestic as well as international tax policy turns on the answers.

References

Adler, M., and B. Dumas (1983), "International portfolio choice and corporation finance: a synthesis", Journal of Finance 38:925–984.

Altshuler, R., and H. Grubert (2002), "Repatriation taxes, repatriation strategies and multinational financial policy", Journal of Public Economics, forthcoming.

Altshuler, R., and J.M. Mintz (1995), "U.S. interest-allocation rules: effects and policy", International Tax and Public Finance 2:7–35.

Altshuler, R., and T.S. Newlon (1993), "The effects of U.S. tax policy on the income repatriation patterns of U.S. multinational corporations", in: A. Giovannini, R.G. Hubbard and J. Slemrod, eds., Studies in International Taxation (University of Chicago Press, Chicago) pp. 77–115.

Altshuler, R., T.S. Newlon and W.C. Randolph (1995), "Do repatriation taxes matter? Evidence from the tax returns of U.S. multinationals", in: M. Feldstein, J.R. Hines Jr and R.G. Hubbard, eds., The Effects of Taxation on Multinational Corporations (University of Chicago Press, Chicago) pp. 253–272.

Altshuler, R., H. Grubert and T.S. Newlon (2001), "Has U.S. investment abroad become more sensitive to tax rates?" in: J.R. Hines Jr, ed., International Taxation and Multinational Activity (University of Chicago Press, Chicago) pp. 9–32.

Atkinson, A.B., and N.H. Stern (1974), "Pigou, taxation, and public goods", Review of Economic Studies 41:119–128.

Auerbach, A.J. (1979), "Wealth maximization and the cost of capital", Quarterly Journal of Economics 93:433–446.

Auerbach, A.J. (1991), "Retrospective capital gains taxation", American Economic Review 81:167–178.

Auerbach, A.J. (2002), "Taxation and corporate financial policy", in: A.J. Auerbach and M. Feldstein, eds., Handbook of Public Economics, Vol. 3 (Elsevier, Amsterdam) pp. 1251–1292.

Auerbach, A.J., and K.A. Hassett (1993), "Taxation and foreign direct investment in the United States: a reconsideration of the evidence", in: A. Giovannini, R.G. Hubbard and J. Slemrod, eds., Studies in International Taxation (University of Chicago Press, Chicago) pp. 119–144.

Auerbach, A.J., and J.R. Hines Jr (1988), "Investment tax incentives and frequent tax reforms", American Economic Review 78:211–216.

Auerbach, A.J., and J.R. Hines Jr (2002), "Taxation and economic efficiency", in: A.J. Auerbach and M. Feldstein, eds., Handbook of Public Economics, Vol. 3 (Elsevier, Amsterdam) pp. 1347–1421.

Auerbach, A.J., and L.J. Kotlikoff (1987), Dynamic Fiscal Policy (Cambridge University Press, Cambridge, UK).

Bernheim, B.D. (2002), "Taxation and saving", in: A.J. Auerbach and M. Feldstein, eds., Handbook of Public Economics, Vol. 3 (Elsevier, Amsterdam) pp. 1173–1249.

Boadway, R., and N. Bruce (1992), "Problems with integrating corporate and personal income taxes in an open economy", Journal of Public Economics 48:39–66.

Bond, E.W. (1981), "Tax holidays and industry behavior", Review of Economics and Statistics 63:88–95.

Bond, E.W., and L. Samuelson (1989), "Strategic behavior and the rules for international taxation of capital", Economic Journal 99:1099–1111.

Boskin, M.J., and W.G. Gale (1987), "New results on the effects of tax policy on the international location of investment", in: M. Feldstein, ed., The Effects of Taxation on Capital Accumulation (University of Chicago Press, Chicago) pp. 201–219.

Bottazzi, L., P. Pesenti and E. van Wincoop (1996), "Wages, profits and the international portfolio puzzle", European Economic Review 40:219–254.

Bradford, D.F. (1981), "The incidence and allocation effects of a tax on corporate distributions", Journal of Public Economics 15:1–22.

Bradford, D.F. (1996), "Fixing capital gains: symmetry, consistency, and correctness in the taxation of financial instruments", Working Paper 5754 (National Bureau of Economic Research, Cambridge, MA).

Bucovetsky, S. (1991), "Asymmetric tax competition", Journal of Urban Economics 30:167–181.

Bucovetsky, S., and J.D. Wilson (1991), "Tax competition with two tax instruments", Regional Science and Urban Economics 21:333–350.

Clausing, K.A. (2001), "The impact of transfer pricing on intrafirm trade", in: J.R. Hines Jr, ed., International Taxation and Multinational Activity (University of Chicago Press, Chicago) pp. 173–194.

Cnossen, S., ed. (2000), Taxing Capital Income in the European Union: Issues and Options for Reform (Oxford University Press, New York).

Collins, J.H., and D.A. Shackelford (1992), "Foreign tax credit limitations and preferred stock issuances", Journal of Accounting Research 30:103–124.

Collins, J.H., and D.A. Shackelford (1995), "Corporate domicile and average effective tax rates: the cases of Canada, Japan, the United Kingdom and the United States", International Tax and Public Finance 2:55–83.

Collins, J.H., D. Kemsley and M. Lang (1998), "Cross-jurisdictional income shifting and earnings valuation", Journal of Accounting Research 36:209–229.

Commission of the European Communities (1992), Report of the Committee of Independent Experts on Company Taxation (Office for Official Publications of the European Communities, Luxembourg).

Coughlin, C., J.V. Terza and V. Arromdee (1991), "State characteristics and the location of foreign direct investment within the United States", Review of Economics and Statistics 73:675–683.

Desai, M.A., and J.R. Hines Jr (1999a), "'Basket' cases: tax incentives and international joint venture participation by American multinational firms", Journal of Public Economics 71:379–402.

Desai, M.A., and J.R. Hines Jr (1999b), "Excess capital flows and the burden of inflation in open economies", in: M. Feldstein, ed., The Costs and Benefits of Price Stability (University of Chicago Press, Chicago) pp. 235–268.

Desai, M.A., C.F. Foley and J.R. Hines Jr (2001), "Repatriation taxes and dividend distortions", National Tax Journal 54:829–851.

Devereux, M.P., and H. Freeman (1995), "The impact of tax on foreign direct investment: empirical evidence and the implications for tax integration schemes", International Tax and Public Finance 2:85–106.

Devereux, M.P., and R. Griffith (1998), "The taxation of discrete investment choices", Working Paper W98/16 (Institute for Fiscal Studies, London, UK).

Devereux, M.P., and R.G. Hubbard (2000), "Taxing multinationals", Working Paper 7920 (National Bureau of Economic Research, Cambridge, MA).

Diamond, P.A., and J. Mirrlees (1971a), "Optimal taxation and public production, I: Production efficiency", American Economic Review 61:8–27.

Diamond, P.A., and J. Mirrlees (1971b), "Optimal taxation and public production, II: Tax rules", American Economic Review 61:261–278.

Dixit, A.K. (1985), "Tax policy in open economies", in: M. Feldstein and A.J. Auerbach, eds., Handbook of Public Economics, Vol. 1 (North Holland, Amsterdam) pp. 313–374.

Doyle, C., and S. van Wijnbergen (1994), "Taxation of foreign multinationals: a sequential bargaining approach to tax holidays", International Tax and Public Finance 1:211–225.

Dunning, J.H., ed. (1985), Multinational Enterprises, Economic Structure and International Competitiveness (Wiley, UK).

Eaton, J., and M. Gersovitz (1981), "Debt and potential repudiation: theoretical and empirical analysis", Review of Economic Studies 48:289–309.

Eldor, R., D. Pines and A. Schwartz (1988), "Home asset preference and productivity shocks", Journal of International Economics 25:165–176.

Feldstein, M. (1976), "Inflation, income taxes, and the rate of interest: a theoretical analysis", American Economic Review 66:809–820.

Feldstein, M. (1980), "Inflation, tax rules, and the stock market", Journal of Monetary Economics 6:309–331.

Feldstein, M., and C.Y. Horioka (1980), "Domestic saving and international capital flows", Economic Journal 90:314–329.

French, K.R., and J.M. Poterba (1991), "Investor diversification and international equity markets", American Economic Review 81:222–226.

Froot, K.A., and J.R. Hines Jr (1995), "Interest allocation rules, financing patterns, and the operations of U.S. multinationals", in: M. Feldstein, J.R. Hines Jr and R.G. Hubbard, eds., The Effects of Taxation on Multinational Corporations (University of Chicago Press, Chicago) pp. 277–307.

Froot, K.A., M. Kim and K. Rogoff (1995), "The law of one price over 700 years", Working Paper 5132 (National Bureau of Economic Research, Cambridge, MA).

Fullerton, D., J.B. Shoven and J. Whalley (1978), "General equilibrium analysis of U.S. taxation policy", in: 1978 Compendium of Tax Research, United States Office of Tax Analysis, Department of the Treasury, (Government Printing Office, Washington, DC).

Gammie, M. (1992), "Corporate tax harmonization: an 'ACE' proposal", European Taxation 31:238–242.

Giovannini, A., and J.R. Hines Jr (1991), "Capital flight and tax competition: are there viable solutions to both problems?" in: A. Giovannini and C. Mayer, eds., European Financial Integration (Cambridge University Press, Cambridge, UK) pp. 172–210.

Gordon, R.H. (1982), "Interest rates, inflation, and corporate financial policy", Brookings Papers on Economic Activity 2:461–488.

Gordon, R.H. (1983), "An optimal taxation approach to fiscal federalism", Quarterly Journal of Economics 98:567–586.

Gordon, R.H. (1986), "Taxation of investment and savings in a world economy", American Economic Review 76:1086–1102.

Gordon, R.H. (1988), "Comment on 'Tax policy and international competitiveness.'" in: J.A. Frenkel, ed., International Aspects of Fiscal Policies (University of Chicago Press, Chicago) pp. 380–386.

Gordon, R.H. (1992), "Can capital income taxes survive in open economies?" Journal of Finance 47:1159–1180.

Gordon, R.H. (1998), "Can high personal tax rates encourage entrepreneurial activity?" IMF Staff Papers 45:49–80.

Gordon, R.H., and A.L. Bovenberg (1996), "Why is capital so immobile internationally?

Possible explanations and implications for capital income taxation", American Economic Review 86:1057–1075.

Gordon, R.H., and V. Gaspar (2001), "Home bias in portfolios and taxation of asset income", Advances in Economic Analysis & Policy 1:1–28.

Gordon, R.H., and J. Jun (1993), "Taxes and the form of ownership of foreign corporate equity", in: A. Giovannini, R.G. Hubbard and J. Slemrod, eds., Studies in International Taxation (University of Chicago Press, Chicago) pp. 13–44.

Gordon, R.H., and J. MacKie-Mason (1995), "Why is there corporate taxation in a small open economy? The role of transfer pricing and income shifting", in: M. Feldstein, J.R. Hines Jr and R.G. Hubbard, eds., The Effects of Taxation on Multinational Corporations (University of Chicago Press, Chicago) pp. 67–91.

Gordon, R.H., and J. Slemrod (1988), "Do we collect any revenue from taxing capital income?" in: L.H. Summers, ed., Tax Policy and the Economy, Vol. 2 (MIT Press, Cambridge, MA) pp. 89–130.

Gordon, R.H., and H. Varian (1989), "Taxation of asset income in the presence of a world securities market", Journal of International Economics 26:205–226.

Gros, D. (1990), "Tax evasion and offshore centres", in: H. Siebert, ed., Reforming Capital Income Taxation (Mohr, Tübingen) pp. 113–127.

Grubert, H. (1998), "Taxes and the division of foreign operating income among royalties, interest, dividends and retained earnings", Journal of Public Economics 68:269–290.

Grubert, H., and J. Mutti (1991), "Taxes, tariffs and transfer pricing in multinational corporate decision-making", Review of Economics and Statistics 73:285–293.

Grubert, H., and J. Slemrod (1998), "The effect of taxes on investment and income shifting to Puerto Rico", Review of Economics and Statistics 80:365–373.

Grubert, H., T. Goodspeed and D.L. Swenson (1993), "Explaining the low taxable income of foreign-controlled companies in the United States", in: A. Giovannini, R.G. Hubbard and J. Slemrod, eds., Studies in International Taxation (University of Chicago Press, Chicago) pp. 237–270.

Harris, D., R. Morck, J. Slemrod and B. Yeung (1993), "Income shifting in U.S. multinational corporations", in: A. Giovannini, R.G. Hubbard and J. Slemrod, eds., Studies in International Taxation (University of Chicago Press, Chicago) pp. 277–302.

Harris, D.G. (1993), "The impact of U.S. tax law revision on multinational corporations' capital location and income-shifting decisions", Journal of Accounting Research 31:111–40.

Hartley, P. (1986), "Portfolio theory and foreign investment: the role of non-marketed assets", Economic Record 62:286–295.

Hartman, D.G. (1979), "Taxation and the effects of inflation on the real capital stock in an open economy", International Economic Review 20:417–425.

Hartman, D.G. (1984), "Tax policy and foreign direct investment in the United States", National Tax Journal 37:475–487.

Hartman, D.G. (1985), "Tax policy and foreign direct investment", Journal of Public Economics 26:107–121.

Hassett, K.A., and R.G. Hubbard (2002), "Tax policy and business investment", in: A.J. Auerbach and M. Feldstein, eds., Handbook of Public Economics, Vol. 3 (Elsevier, Amsterdam) pp. 1293–1343.

Hines Jr, J.R. (1988), "Taxation and U.S. multinational investment", in: L.H. Summers, ed., Tax Policy and the Economy, Vol. 2 (MIT Press, Cambridge, MA) pp. 33–61.

Hines Jr, J.R. (1991), "The flight paths of migratory corporations", Journal of Accounting, Auditing and Finance 6:447–479.

Hines Jr, J.R. (1993), "On the sensitivity of R&D to delicate tax changes: the behavior of U.S. multinationals in the 1980s", in: A. Giovannini, R.G. Hubbard and J. Slemrod, eds., Studies in International Taxation (University of Chicago Press, Chicago) pp. 149–187.

Hines Jr, J.R. (1994), "Credit and deferral as international investment incentives", Journal of Public Economics 55:323–347.

Hines Jr, J.R. (1995), "Taxes, technology transfer, and the R&D activities of multinational firms", in: M. Feldstein, J.R. Hines Jr and R.G. Hubbard, eds., The Effects of Taxation on Multinational Corporations (University of Chicago Press, Chicago) pp. 225–248.

Hines Jr, J.R. (1996a), "Altered states: taxes and the location of foreign direct investment in America", American Economic Review 86:1076–1094.

Hines Jr, J.R. (1996b), "Dividends and profits: some unsubtle foreign influences", Journal of Finance 51:661–689.

Hines Jr, J.R. (1997), "Tax policy and the activities of multinational corporations", in: A.J. Auerbach, ed., Fiscal Policy: Lessons from Economic Research (MIT Press, Cambridge, MA) pp. 401–445.

Hines Jr, J.R. (1999a), "Lessons from behavioral responses to international taxation", National Tax Journal 52:305–322.

Hines Jr, J.R. (1999b), "The case against deferral: a deferential reconsideration", National Tax Journal 52:385–404.

Hines Jr, J.R. (2001), "'Tax sparing' and direct investment in developing countries", in: J.R. Hines Jr, ed., International Taxation and Multinational Activity (University of Chicago Press, Chicago) pp. 39–66.

Hines Jr, J.R., and R.G. Hubbard (1990), "Coming home to America: dividend repatriations by U.S. multinationals", in: A. Razin and J. Slemrod, eds., Taxation in the Global Economy (University of Chicago Press, Chicago) pp. 161–200.

Hines Jr, J.R., and A.B. Jaffe (2001), "International taxation and the location of inventive activity", in: J.R. Hines Jr, ed., International Taxation and Multinational Activity (University of Chicago Press, Chicago) pp. 201–226.

Hines Jr, J.R., and E.M. Rice (1994), "Fiscal paradise: foreign tax havens and American business", Quarterly Journal of Economics 109:149–182.

Hines Jr, J.R., and K.L. Willard (1992), "Trick or treaty? Bargains and surprises in international tax agreements" Working Paper (Harvard University, Cambridge, MA).

Horst, T. (1980), "A note on the optimal taxation of international investment income", Quarterly Journal of Economics 94:793–798.

Hoyt, W.H. (1991), "Property taxation, Nash equilibrium, and market power", Journal of Urban Economics 30:123–131.

Huizinga, H. (1992), "The tax treatment of R&D expenditures of multinational enterprises", Journal of Public Economics 47:343–359.

Huizinga, H. (1996), "The incidence of interest withholding taxes: evidence from the LDC loan market", Journal of Public Economics 59:435–451.

Huizinga, H., and S.B. Nielsen (1997), "Capital income and profit taxation with foreign ownership of firms", Journal of International Economics 42:149–165.

Kalambokidis, L.T.J. (1992), "What is being taxed? A test for the existence of excess profit in the corporate income tax base", Ph.D. dissertation (University of Michigan, Ann Arbor, MI).

Kanbur, R., and M. Keen (1993), "Jeux sans frontières: tax competition and tax coordination when countries differ in size", American Economic Review 83:877–892.

Keen, M., and H. Piekkola (1997), "Simple rules for the optimal taxation of international capital income", Scandinavian Journal of Economics 99:447–461.

Klassen, K., M. Lang and M. Wolfson (1993), "Geographic income shifting by multinational corporations in response to tax rate changes", Journal of Accounting Research 31:141–173.

Leechor, C., and J.M. Mintz (1993), "On the taxation of multinational corporate investment when the deferral method is used by the capital exporting country", Journal of Public Economics 51:75–96.

Levi, M.D. (1977), "Taxation and 'abnormal' international capital flows," Journal of Political Economy 85:635–646.

Lovely, M.E. (1989), Taxes, trade, and the pattern of world production", Ph.D. dissertation (University of Michigan, Ann Arbor, MI).

Markusen, J.R. (1995), "The boundaries of multinational enterprises and the theory of international trade", Journal of Economic Perspectives 9:169–189.

Mintz, J.M. (1990), "Corporate tax holidays and investment", World Bank Economic Review 4:81–102.

Mintz, J.M., and H. Tulkens (1986), "Commodity tax competition between member states of a federation: equilibrium and efficiency", Journal of Public Economics 29:133–172.

Mintz, J.M., and H. Tulkens (1990), "Strategic use of tax rates and credits in a model of international corporate income tax competition", Discussion Paper 9073 (CORE, Louvain-la-Neuve, Belgium).

Naito, H. (1999), "Re-examination of uniform commodity taxes under a nonlinear income tax system and its implications for production efficiency", Journal of Public Economics 71:165–188.

Newlon, T.S. (1987), "Tax policy and the multinational firm's financial policy and investment decisions", Ph.D. dissertation (Princeton University, Princeton, NJ).

Olsen, T.E., and P. Osmundsen (2001), Strategic tax competition: implications of national ownership", Journal of Public Economics 81:253–277.

Ondrich, J., and M. Wasylenko (1993), Foreign Direct Investment in the United States: Issues, Magnitudes, and Location Choice of New Manufacturing Plants (W.E. Upjohn Institute for Employment Research, Kalamazoo, MI).

Organisation for Economic Cooperation and Development (2000), Towards Global Tax Cooperation: Progress in Identifying and Eliminating Harmful Tax Practices (OECD, Paris).

Papke, L.E. (2000), "One-way treaty with the world: the U.S. withholding tax and the Netherlands Antilles", International Tax and Public Finance 7:295–313.

Parsley, D.C., and S.-J. Wei (1996), "Convergence to the law of one price without trade barriers or currency fluctuations", Quarterly Journal of Economics 111:1211–1236.

Pesenti, P., and E. van Wincoop (2002), "Can nontradeables generate substantial home bias?" Journal of Money, Credit and Banking 34:25–50.

Razin, A., and E. Sadka (1991a), "Efficient investment incentives in the presence of capital flight", Journal of International Economics 31:171–181.

Razin, A., and E. Sadka (1991b), "International tax competition and gains from tax harmonization", Economics Letters 37:69–76.

Richman, P.B. (1963), Taxation of Foreign Investment Income: An Economic Analysis (Johns Hopkins Press, Baltimore).

Scholes, M.S., M. Wolfson, M. Erickson, E.L. Maydew and T. Shevlin (2002), Taxes and Business Strategy: A Planning Approach (Prentice Hall, Upper Saddle River, NJ).

Shoven, J.B. (1991), "Using the corporate cash flow tax to integrate corporate and personal taxes", Proceedings of the Annual Conference of the National Tax Association 83:19–27.

Sinn, H.-W. (1988), "U.S. tax reform 1981 and 1986: impact on international capital markets and capital flows", National Tax Journal 41:327–340.

Sinn, H.-W. (1993), "Taxation and the birth of foreign subsidiaries", in: H. Herberg and N. Van Long, eds., Trade Welfare, and Economic Policies: Essays in Honor of Murray C. Kemp (University of Michigan Press, Ann Arbor, MI) pp. 325–352.

Slemrod, J. (1988), "Effect of taxation with international capital mobility", in: H.J. Aaron, H. Galper and J.A. Pechman, eds., Uneasy Compromise: Problems of a Hybrid Income-Consumption Tax (Brookings, Washington, D.C.) pp. 115–148.

Slemrod, J. (1990), "Tax effects on foreign direct investment in the United States: evidence from a cross-country comparison", in: A. Razin and J. Slemrod, eds., Taxation in the Global Economy (University of Chicago Press, Chicago) pp. 79–117.

Slemrod, J., C. Hansen and R. Procter (1997), "The seesaw principle in international tax policy", Journal of Public Economics 65:163–176.

Summers, L.H. (1988), "Tax policy and international competitiveness", in: J.A. Frenkel, ed., International Aspects of Fiscal Policies (University of Chicago Press, Chicago) pp. 349–375.

Swenson, D.L. (1994), "The impact of U.S. tax reform on foreign direct investment in the United States", Journal of Public Economics 54:243–266.

Swenson, D.L. (2001), "Transaction type and the effect of taxes on the distribution of foreign direct investment in the United States", in: J.R. Hines Jr, ed., International Taxation and Multinational Activity (University of Chicago Press, Chicago) pp. 89–108.

Tesar, L.L., and I.M. Werner (1994), "International equity transactions and U.S. portfolio choice", in: J.A. Frankel, ed., The Internationalization of Equity Markets (University of Chicago Press, Chicago) pp. 185–216.

Trandel, G.A. (1992), "Evading the use tax on cross-border sales: pricing and welfare effects", Journal of Public Economics 49:313–331.

Wahl, J.B. (1989), "Tax treatment of foreign exchange gains and losses and the Tax Reform Act of 1986", National Tax Journal 42:59–68.

Weichenrieder, A.J. (1996), "Anti-tax avoidance provisions and the size of foreign direct investment", International Tax and Public Finance 3:67–81.

Werner, I.M. (1994), "Capital income taxation and international portfolio choice", Journal of Public Economics 53:205–222.

Wilson, J.D. (1986), "A theory of interregional tax competition", Journal of Urban Economics 19: 296–315.

Wilson, J.D. (1991), "Tax competition with interregional differences in factor endowments", Regional Science and Urban Economics 21:423–451.

Wilson, J.D. (1999), "Theories of tax competition", National Tax Journal 52:269–304.

Yang, Y. (1996), "Tax competition under the threat of capital flight", Economics Letters 53:323–329.

Young, K.H. (1988), "The effects of taxes and rates of return on foreign direct investment in the United States", National Tax Journal 41:109–121.

Zodrow, G.R., and P.M. Mieszkowski (1986), "Tiebout, property taxation and the underprovision of local public goods", Journal of Urban Economics 19:356–370.

Chapter 29

LOCAL PUBLIC GOODS AND CLUBS*

SUZANNE SCOTCHMER

University of California, Berkeley; and National Bureau of Economic Research

Contents

* I thank Alan Auerbach, Jayasri Dutta, Birgit Grodal, Dennis Epple, Oded Hochman, Richard Romano, William Strange, Jacques Thisse, Alain Trannoy, Raquel Fernandez, David Pines, and Shlomo Weber for comments. This work was funded in part by the National Science Foundation.

Handbook of Public Economics, Volume 4, Edited by A.J. Auerbach and M. Feldstein

Abstract

I discuss recent contributions to the theory of group formation and the provision of jointly consumed public goods and services. I highlight the distinction between models of pure group formation, and models where the formation of groups and the sharing of public goods are constrained by a division of geographic space into jurisdictions. Much of the literature concerns the distortions that arise when price systems or tax systems are constrained, for example, to serve the dual roles of redistributing income and funding public services. I also highlight the distortions that can arise from arbitrary divisions of space, and review recent contributions that emphasize the distortions that arise when there are both public and private providers of services. My focus is mainly on equilibrium concepts and policy instruments.

Keywords

clubs, local public goods, capitalization, externalities

JEL classification: H0, H4, H7

1. Introduction

Local public economics is a large subject, which warrants more than one review. In this review, I discuss theories of group formation, financing of local public goods, incentives to provide them efficiently, the role of geography in constraining the formation of groups, and the distortions that arise when shared services are provided by both public and private providers. I try to concentrate on how the subject has developed since reviews in previous *Handbooks*. The expository technique is to illuminate ideas through examples, which will hopefully be useful for introductory courses. Many important topics are left out, such as empirical findings and fiscal federalism.

Theories of group formation have bifurcated into "club theory", which concerns nonspatial group formation, and "local public goods", which blends group formation with geography and sometimes with voting mechanisms. I begin in Section 2 with club theory because it is a simpler economic context, and creates a benchmark against which to measure the complexities introduced by geography and restrictions on pricing created by public policy concerns. In all of what follows, I try to emphasize the complexities introduced by heterogeneity, since previous surveys have mostly assumed that agents are alike.

Section 3 addresses what is perhaps the most studied equilibrium concept for local public goods, namely, free mobility with majority voting on local public goods. Section 4 focuses on funding and the fact that consumption of local public goods is coupled with the consumption of space. In fact, space can be coupled with the consumption of many different local public goods, and also with employment opportunities. This bundling creates enormous complexity.

Section 5 describes some new ideas regarding the interaction of private and public institutions for providing public goods, and Section 6 concludes with some "orphan" ideas that do not fit easily elsewhere.

The later Sections 3–6 are probably the most useful ones in pointing graduate students to open questions.

2. Club economies

Club models are models of group formation. Because clubs are not identified with geographic space or with occupancy of land, they are hard to interpret as "jurisdictions". My own view is that club theory is a branch of general equilibrium theory more than a branch of public finance, although traditionally treated there. Shared goods such as schools and libraries easily fit the club model. The thrust of club theory is that the competitive market will function efficiently to provide club goods, so there is no reason that such goods should be publicly provided at all. I return to this issue below.

The basic notion of club economies is that agents form groups to confer externalities on each other. The main source of these externalities in the original Buchanan (1965) paper are public services. Buchanan assumes that agents band together to share the cost of (excludable) public goods. Optimal sharing groups are bounded in size because of a second externality, crowding. While a large membership reduces the per capita cost of the public services, large membership also increases crowding costs. Tiebout (1956) assumes that optimal sharing groups are bounded in size due to the cost structure of producing the public services. Modern theories incorporate both aspects. The key premise is that for sufficiently large groups, the crowding costs or increased cost of provision dominate the benefits of sharing the costs of public services. Consequently, large groups cannot improve on what is achievable by small groups in providing public services, and this is why the models have been interpreted as models of "local" public goods.

Club models have been analyzed according to various equilibrium concepts, each of which has some resemblance to the "real world". Since equilibrium concepts govern allocative outcomes, I begin by describing some important equilibrium concepts, using the Buchanan model. The Buchanan model assumes "anonymous" crowding, which means that the number of members of a club matters for the externalities they confer, but not the members' characteristics. After discussing the equilibrium concepts, I explain how Buchanan's ideas have been modified to include the notion that agents with different characteristics confer different externalities, and how complementarities between private goods and club goods affect the conclusions about optimal group formation.

2.1. Equilibrium concepts

Following Buchanan (1965), assume that everyone is alike, with utility represented by $U(x, n, \gamma)$, where $x \in \mathfrak{R}_+$ is the amount of a single private good consumed, n is the size of the sharing group, and $\gamma \in \Gamma$ represents the public services in the club. Letting $c(n, \gamma) \in \mathfrak{R}_+$ represent the cost of the public services and w the per-capita endowment of the private good, the per-capita utility available in a club of size n is

$$v(n) \equiv \max_{\gamma \in \Gamma} U\left(w - \frac{c(n, \gamma)}{n}, n, \gamma\right). \tag{1}$$

Let the maximizer on the right-hand side be $\gamma^*(n)$. The basic assumption of club theory is that the maximizer of $v(n)$, say n^*, is finite.

The main equilibrium concepts that have been applied to this model are the core, competitive equilibrium, Nash equilibrium and free mobility equilibrium. The "definitions" given here are very informal, hopefully without causing confusion. For the complete treatments, the reader should consult the original texts.

The core: In this equilibrium notion, which was introduced to the study of club economies by Pauly (1967, 1970a,b), agents act cooperatively to maximize their utility. An allocation is in the "core" of a club economy if no group of agents can make themselves better off using only their own endowments. Provided the economy is larger than n^*, an allocation in the core must have the equal-treatment property: all agents must receive the same utility, namely, $v(n^*)$, since otherwise a low-utility agent could bribe members of a club to let him replace a high-utility agent. Letting N represent the number of agents in the economy, clubs of type $(\hat{\gamma}, \hat{n})$ can only be part of a core allocation if it holds that

$$
U\left(w - \frac{c(n, \gamma)}{n}, n, \gamma\right) \leqslant U\left(w - \frac{c(\hat{n}, \hat{\gamma})}{\hat{n}}, \hat{n}, \hat{\gamma}\right) \equiv v(\hat{n})
\tag{2}
$$

for all (n, γ) such that $\gamma \in \Gamma, n \leqslant N$.

Pauly's main observations were that club allocations in the core are efficient, but that the core is typically empty. Club formation will be unstable in the sense that some group of agents will typically have an incentive to form a new group. In this simple case, the agents who are in a group smaller than n^* can "bribe" some of the other agents to join them, in order to form a group of size n^*.

One might hope that stability would be restored if group formation is slightly costly. At least two notions of "approximate" core have been used to address this question. The weak-ε core, due to Shapley and Shubik (1966), is a notion of stability under which no group of agents has an incentive to defect into a new group if they must pay ε per member to do so. The fat-ε core, due to Anderson (1985), is a similar notion under which a defecting group must pay ε times the number of agents in the economy rather than in the group. Under certain restrictive conditions, the weak-ε core has been shown to be nonempty in large games [e.g., Wooders (1980, 1988)]. A (somewhat incomplete) intuition is as follows. In a large economy, most agents can be accommodated in optimal groups, but there will be a few leftovers. In the example above, then regardless of how large the economy is, there are fewer than n^* agents who cannot be accommodated in optimal groups. The agents in optimal groups can be taxed in order to compensate the leftovers, in order to equalize utilities. If the economy is large, the burden on each member of an optimal group will be small, and the equalized utilities will be close to the maximum that is achievable in optimal groups. Further, if there is a small cost of forming a new group, this situation may be stable. There is only a small benefit to forming a new group, and there is a cost of doing so. It the cost is greater than the benefit, the allocation of agents to groups is stable.

However, the argument depends on restrictive conditions. For one thing, the argument is mainly for economies with "types" of agents. Second, restrictive conditions on preferences are required in order to ensure the compensations can be made. One condition that has been used is that utility is "transferable". Another is Mas-Colell's (1975, 1980) assumption that private goods are "essential", which has been used in many economic contexts with indivisible choices. It is a very strong assumption[1]. For more general economies, such transfers may be impossible, and the weak-ε core can be

---

[1] The assumption has many names. For a discussion of what it means and how it has been named, see Gilles and Scotchmer (1997, p. 365).

empty for small ε, no matter how large the economy; see Example 5.2 of Ellickson, Grodal, Scotchmer and Zame (EGSZ, 2001). In light of the example, EGSZ show nonemptiness of the Anderson fat-ε core instead of the weak-ε core. Their Theorem 4.3 on nonemptiness of approximate cores in large economies gets away from the notion that agents' preferences are drawn from a finite set of "types", and avoids the restrictive assumptions on preferences listed here.

I do not focus on notions of approximate stability because they have not been imported to models where consumption of "local public goods" is tied to geography. They are models of pure group formation, and they are related to a larger literature on nonemptiness of the core in large games and economies, which I do not review here.

Competitive equilibrium: A second strand of inquiry is whether memberships in clubs can be thought of as commodities like any other privately traded commodities, and whether an allocation can be thought of as governed by prices. Unlike, say, Lindahl equilibrium, it is not public goods *per se* that are bought and sold in the market, but rather *memberships in groups*. The groups in which memberships are sold can commit to certain public services, and possibly to a certain profile of other members. The tricky issue is how to define the commodity space and price system. Key features of a price-taking equilibrium are that (i) the commodity space is defined independently of the set of agents, (ii) the price system is complete with respect to the set of commodities, (iii) prices are anonymous, and (iv) agents optimize with respect to the price system, but not by observing other agents' preferences or endowments[2]. Of course, the idea of a price-taking equilibrium is rather far afield from the way local public economies operate, and this is why I consider club theory to be a motivator for the subject of local public economics, but not the subject itself[3].

For the Buchanan economy, the commodity space would be memberships in clubs of all types $(\gamma, n) \in \Gamma \times Z_+$ and the membership prices would be

---

[2] The competitive conjecture has a very long history for club economies, although not initially formulated as here. These features were introduced to club economies by Scotchmer and Wooders (1987a; see also 1987b), and clubs are fully integrated into general equilibrium by Ellickson, Grodal, Scotchmer and Zame (EGSZ) (1999a,b, 2001), e.g., getting away from the restrictive notion that there are "types" of preferences. Previous notions of equilibrium lack at least some of the listed features, and many use notions related to "utility-taking", where decision makers are assumed to observe aspects of agents' indifference maps instead of a price system. Previous contributors to the competitive model include Stiglitz (1977), Boadway (1982), Berglas (1976a,b, 1984), Bewley (1981), Brueckner and Lee (1989, 1991), Wooders (1978, 1981, 1980, 1989), Berglas and Pines (1981), Brueckner (1994), Scotchmer (1997) and Conley and Wooders (1997). As in Scotchmer and Wooders (1987a), some of the later papers emphasize the need for anonymous prices. Ellickson (1979) described a true competitive equilibrium, although not in a model with externalities among club members. There is also a long history of club models with Lindahl prices [recently, Conley and Wooders (1998) and Wooders (1997)], but since I view Lindahl prices as unconvincing, I do not discuss them.

[3] The club model has many other applications. For example, a firm or academic department is a group that is governed by prices. For most such applications, the model below with heterogeneous crowding is apt. See Ellickson, Grodal, Scotchmer and Zame (1999b) for how clubs can be interpreted as firm formation, school formation, etc.

$\{q(\gamma, n) \in \mathfrak{R}: (\gamma, n) \in \Gamma \times Z_+\}$. A formal definition of competitive equilibrium, extending to a much broader class of club economies, can be found in Ellickson, Grodal, Scotchmer and Zame (1999a). The main requirements, in addition to feasibility, are that (i) every potential club makes nonnegative profit, and clubs in equilibrium make zero profit, and (ii) no agent can improve his utility by joining a different combination of clubs.

To illustrate this idea in the Buchanan context, assume for simplicity that all clubs in equilibrium are of the same type, say (γ^*, n^*), as will be true if there are unique maximizers of Equation (1). The equilibrium conditions require that for all $(\gamma, n) \in \Gamma \times Z_+$

$$nq(\gamma, n) - c(\gamma, n) \leqslant 0 \text{ with strict equality for } (\gamma^*, n^*)$$
$$U\left(w - q(\gamma, n), n, \gamma\right) \leqslant U\left(w - q(\gamma^*, n^*), n^*, \gamma^*\right).$$

It follows that Equation (2) holds, so that if an equilibrium allocation exists, it is in the core. In fact something stronger is true: provided the economy is larger than n^*, every allocation in the core is a competitive equilibrium. In this sense, the small-groups assumption that n^* is finite seems to lead to the conclusion of core/competitive equivalence. Cooperative and competitive behavior lead to the same outcome, at least when there is only one private good. (But see Example 4 below.)

Because of core/competitive equivalence, the existence problem that Pauly identified for the core carries over to competitive equilibrium. If the population is not an integer multiple of n^*, competitive equilibrium does not exist, and the core is empty. Ellickson, Grodal, Scotchmer and Zame (1999a) solve this problem by assuming that there is a continuum of agents.

Nash equilibrium: A consequence of the fact that the economy is finite is that clubs will not be perfectly competitive. As in industrial organization, one can study profit-motivated club formation in an oligopoly rather than assuming perfect competition. Suppose, for example, that the firms' strategies are the public services provided by the club and the membership price, namely, (γ, q). In Nash equilibrium, services will be provided efficiently within each club (since that enhances the value of memberships, which can be extracted through price), and the price will determine the number of members. By analogy with Bertrand competition in markets for private goods, one might have thought that price competition would lead to competitive prices. However there is an important difference, namely, that the club's quality is endogenous to the price. Lowering the price degrades quality by attracting more members and adding to congestion. As a consequence, a club does not get the whole market even if it has the lowest price and the most attractive services. In fact, equilibrium prices will typically be higher than the competitive price, although they converge to the competitive price (in a two-stage game of entry) in large populations [Scotchmer (1985a,b)].

The nature of Nash Equilibrium depends on what the strategies are, and also on the objective function. The economic question behind choice of strategies is "What does the jurisdiction manager think the other jurisdictions will hold fixed when his own policy changes?" In club economies it might be natural to take as fixed the prices and services offered in other clubs, as above, and to assume that the manager maximizes profits. But in local public goods economies, both the strategies and objective function are less obvious. For institutional reasons, budgets within local jurisdictions might have to be balanced, so the objective could not be to maximize profit. With a balanced budget, migration to or from a jurisdiction due to another jurisdiction's change in policies will necessitate a change in either taxes or expenditures. In that case, the Nash equilibrium will depend on which of those two variables, taxes or expenditures, is thought to be held constant when a single jurisdiction changes its policies. Such issues are explored by Wildasin (1988)[4].

Free mobility equilibrium: Tiebout (1956) conjectured that if agents can "vote with their feet", they will find the jurisdictions that best satisfy their tastes, and that this should be a strong force toward efficiency. The idea of free mobility lies at the heart of a large literature, and I devote the next section to it. The basic notion is that a partition of agents into jurisdictions is stable if no agent wants to move. Any agent has a right to move to any existing jurisdiction. Freedom to migrate is constitutionally guaranteed in many Western democracies, and that is why the equilibrium concept is of interest.

The free-mobility notion does not permit the kind of coordinated deviations that motivate the "core" concept, and it does not permit an entrepreneur to assemble a new jurisdiction simply by announcing the type of club he will provide (public services and memberships), and then admitting members according to the price system, as the competitive concept does. The options for creating a new type of jurisdiction are correspondingly limited, with consequences that can be seen by applying the free mobility notion to Buchanan clubs[5].

In general, a definition of a free mobility equilibrium must include a rule that establishes how the public services will be decided in each jurisdiction. However, in the simple Buchanan model, all agents are alike, and will agree on the best provision of public services once the jurisdiction is formed. Assume, therefore, that for each n, a group of size n will choose the efficient public services $\gamma(n)$, and will fund them with equal cost shares.

Suppose that the per-capita utility function v is strictly quasiconcave and single peaked, so that there is a unique utility-maximizing size n^*, and suppose that there are more agents than $2n^*$. I argue that jurisdictions will typically be larger than the efficient size n^* even if an unlimited number of jurisdictions are possible, and may be arbitrarily large. This is in contrast to what happens under the other equilibrium concepts discussed above.

---

[4] Other variants on Nash equilibrium have been studied as well. For example, Barham, Boadway, Marchand and Pestieau (1997) show that noncontractual contributions of effort in producing a club good will be suboptimal. To mitigate this problem, club sizes in equilibrium will also be suboptimal relative to the case that effort levels are contractual. See also Cremer, Marchand and Pestieau (1997), Konishi, LeBreton and Weber (1997), and Boadway, Pestieau and Wildasin (1989).

[5] The following discussion follows Jehiel and Scotchmer (1993).

We can characterize the free mobility equilibrium by the numbers of members in different jurisdictions, say $n_1, n_2, \ldots$ By free mobility, it cannot be the case for any two jurisdictions i, j, that $v(n_j) < v(n_i + 1)$, since a member of jurisdiction j would move to i. Thus, no two jurisdictions i, j can satisfy $n_i \leqslant n_j < n^*$. If two jurisdictions are both smaller than the utility-maximizing size, then a migrant from the smaller jurisdiction to the larger one can improve both his own utility and that of the other members. Thus, at most one jurisdiction can be smaller than the utility-maximizing size n^*. Further, if for any $\hat{n} \geqslant n^*$ it is possible to partition the agents so that each group is of size $\hat{n}$ or $\hat{n} + 1$, then the partition is a free-mobility equilibrium. Thus, free mobility often leads to jurisdictions that are larger than efficient. This is in contrast to the core or competitive equilibrium, which have the property that, if equilibrium exists, it is efficient. The difference arises from the fact that, in free mobility equilibrium, only unilateral actions are permitted. There is no opportunity, either explicitly as in the core, or implicitly as in competitive equilibrium, for a group of agents to make a coordinated decision to reassemble in an efficient size group.

Randomized memberships: Cole and Prescott (1997) have proposed an equilibrium concept in which agents are allowed to randomize on club memberships. Since they emphasize heterogeneous crowding, and since it is hard to illustrate the concept in the Buchanan model, the concept is illustrated in the next subsection.

2.2. Heterogeneous crowding

Anonymous crowding means that members of a club care how many other members there are, but do not care about the members' characteristics. However, in most group situations, participants impose different externalities according to characteristics such as productive skills, niceness, whether they smoke, and how educated they are[6]. An important example arises in schools, discussed below, where there may be peer effects. A student's behavior, abilities or resources can all confer externalities on other students.

The competitive theory described above for club economies with anonymous crowding extends to club economies with heterogeneous crowding, but heterogeneity compounds the problems of existence. In the model with anonymous crowding, an

---

[6] Heterogeneous crowding was introduced to the club model by Berglas (1976b). Other contributors include Stiglitz (1983), Scotchmer and Wooders (1987b), Brueckner and Lee (1989), Wooders (1989), McGuire (1991), Brueckner (1994), Epple and Romano (1996a,b,c), Engl and Scotchmer (1996), Gilles and Scotchmer (1997), Oates and Schwab (1991), Scotchmer (1997), Cole and Prescott (1997), Conley and Wooders (1997, 2001) and Ellickson, Grodal, Scotchmer and Zame (1999a,b, 2001). Except for the latter, these models are still restricted to "types" of preferences. Benabou (1993) introduces the idea that agents invest in their external characteristics, which then earn a market return. See also Ellickson, Grodal, Scotchmer and Zame (1999b), who show that clubs can be interpreted as firms and schools, and show how skills acquisition interacts with the set of club (firm) technologies that are available. Helsley and Strange (2000b) introduce the notion that externalities are generated by the agents' actions, which are chosen rather than endowed.

existence problem arises because of scale effects. The population size might not be a multiple of the optimal "small group". Example 1 shows that, when it is efficient to group agents with different external characteristics, the existence problem has another dimension. Even if there are no scale effects defining the optimal size of a group, it might be impossible to match people in groups with the most preferred combinations of characteristics.

Example 1. *The existence problem with heterogeneous crowding*: Suppose the population has equal numbers of two types of agents, type-G and type-B. Suppose that each agent must belong to exactly one club, and preferences are described by $U_B(b,x)$, $U_G(b,x)$, where x is consumption of private good, and b is the ratio of type-B to type-G in the club:

$$U_B(2,x) = x + 1,$$
$$U_B(b,x) = x \qquad \text{if } b \neq 2,$$
$$U_G(\tfrac{1}{2},x) = x + 1,$$
$$U_G(b,x) = x \qquad \text{if } b \neq \tfrac{1}{2}.$$

Thus, type-B agents prefer a club with a preponderance (ratio 2 to 1) of type-B agents, and type-G prefers a preponderance (ratio 2 to 1) of type-G agents.

The example is designed without scale effects. Unlike the existence problem illustrated above for anonymous crowding, utility is not affected by the size of the club, but only by the composition of its membership, the ratio of type-B to type-G. The problem with existence will not arise because of crowding costs and the requirement that each club be a particular optimal size, but because the agents' preferences on composition cannot be accommodated with the relative numbers of people in the population.

Since utilities are quasi-linear, an efficient (or competitive) allocation maximizes total utility. This is accomplished by putting half the people in clubs with composition $b = 2$ (such clubs include 2/3 of the type-B people and 1/3 of the type-G people) and by putting the other half in clubs with composition $b = \tfrac{1}{2}$ (such clubs include 1/3 of the type-B people and 2/3 of the type-G people). Thus, $\tfrac{2}{3}$ of the people are in their most preferred clubs.

Equilibrium will not exist unless it is possible to put all the people in the two optimal types of clubs in these proportions. This is where the existence problem lies. If, for example, there are 5 people of each type, it will not be possible to partition the population into clubs of the two types, since 2/3 of 5 is not an integer. Notice that if the population were a continuum instead of finite, the existence problem is overcome. The total "number" of type-B people in clubs with composition $b = 2$ would be, for example, $\tfrac{10}{3}$. ∎

Because of both the integer problem and the problem of accommodating a finite group of agents consistently in "optimal" clubs, the core will typically be empty in any finite club economy, and competitive equilibrium will not exist.

As mentioned above, the idea that club memberships should be treated like other commodities in general equilibrium has a long history. However, club formation could not be integrated into general equilibrium theory until it was understood how to solve the problem of ensuring that agents' choices as to memberships were "consistent" with each other. That problem was solved by Ellickson, Grodal, Scotchmer and Zame (1999a, 2001). There is a finite set Ω of possible external characteristics (such as helpfulness, intelligence, skills), and an agent a is endowed with characteristics $\omega_a \in \Omega$ as well as private goods. Each possible club type specifies the numbers of members with the different characteristics, which is modeled as a vector π, as well as (possibly) a costly activity or shared facility, which is modeled as a choice γ from an abstract set Γ. The consistency problem is to ensure that, whenever some agent wants to belong to a particular clubtype, there are other agents wanting to fill the other places in that club type. Ellickson, Grodal, Scotchmer and Zame (1999a) solve this problem with a continuum of agents. They show that equilibrium exists, is efficient, and, in fact, coincides with the core.

The existence problem still arises with a finite number of agents, as in the above example. In fact, the problem is much deeper than illustrated in the example. In the example, it is clear at the outset what the optimal or "chosen" club types will be. In general, there will be a large set of possible club types, and the ones that are chosen in equilibrium will depend on endowments of private goods and on agents' preferences, which will typically be different for all agents. Nevertheless, Ellickson, Grodal, Scotchmer and Zame (2001) show that in a large, finite club economy, the fat-ε core is nonempty (see above); and the core can "almost" be decentralized as an equilibrium. Ellickson, Grodal, Scotchmer and Zame (1999b) show how these papers can very simply be extended so that membership characteristics can be chosen instead of endowed, which makes it natural to interpret characteristics as skills, as in Benabou (1993), and to interpret the club model as a model of firm formation or school formation. The Ellickson, Grodal, Scotchmer and Zame (EGSZ) papers are more in the spirit of general equilibrium theory than previous models of clubs, in that they avoid the assumption that agents' preferences are drawn from a finite set of "types". In addition, they permit memberships in several clubs simultaneously[7].

Following the main premise of club theory, the competitive foundation of the EGSZ model is that clubs are small. The expression of this assumption is that there is an exogenously given set of "club types", each one defined by its public services and the external characteristics of its members, all bounded in size[8]. The membership

---

[7] This seemingly small change necessitates a revision of analytical techniques. The decentralization arguments of previous authors, e.g., Gilles and Scotchmer (1997), used a two-part construction of prices. After constructing the private goods prices, membership prices were constructed as willingness-to-pay. This technique does not extend in any obvious way to multiple memberships.

[8] For Buchanan clubs, the efficiency of small groups arises as a consequence of congestion. Club papers with heterogeneous crowding tend to make the assumption more primitive, e.g., Scotchmer and Wooders (1987b) and Conley and Wooders (1997) restrict attention to clubs that are bounded in size.

prices have the form $q(\omega, (\pi, \gamma))$, where ω is the member's external characteristic, and (π, γ) specifies the type of club. Such prices make sure that, in choosing their club memberships, agents account for the externalities they impose. Externalities can be positive or negative, and hence the admissions prices can be positive or negative, although some must be positive if there are resource costs to providing the public services within the club. Nevertheless, agents with very attractive external characteristics might be paid to join clubs. If prices could not depend on the external characteristics, equilibrium might not exist. This is illustrated in the next example.

Example 2. *Necessity of externality pricing*: Consider an economy with equal numbers of (B)ad students and (G)ood students. There is one private good, of which each student has 2 units endowment. A school has two students, and costs 2 units of the private good to run. All schools have two students, so a school can be GG, BG or BB. Preferences are described by

$$u_B(x; BB) = 4 + x \qquad u_B(x; BG) = 7 + x$$
$$u_G(x; GG) = 6 + x \qquad u_G(x; BG) = 4 + x$$

The preferences reflect the fact that students receive positive externalities from good students. The externalities can be thought of as supplements to future income. The efficient allocation is for good students and bad students to share schools, in order to create these externalities. Write $q(\omega, BB)$, $q(\omega, GG)$, $q(\omega, BG)$ for the tuition prices paid by students with external characteristics $\omega = B, G$. A type-B consumer cannot join a type-GG club and vice versa.

At equilibrium, tuition must cover the cost of 2, hence $q(B, BB) = q(G, GG) = 1$. At these prices, bad students can obtain utility $2 - q(B, BB) + 4 = 5$ by choosing a homogeneous school with two bad students, and utility $2 - q(B, BG) + 7$ by choosing a mixed school with a good student. A good student can obtain utility $2 - q(G, GG) + 6 = 7$ by choosing a homogeneous school with two good students, and utility $2 - q(G, BG) + 4$ by choosing a mixed school with a bad student. In order that both students will prefer the mixed school, prices must satisfy $5 < 9 - q(B, BG)$ and $7 < 6 - q(G, BG)$. The price for good students must be negative, $q(G, BG) \leqslant -1$, in order to induce them to share a school with bad students. However, it is in the interest of the bad students to subsidize them, since the positive externalities they receive outweigh the subsidy. The bad students will pay a price $q(B, BG) \leqslant 4$, part of which will cover the resource cost of the school, and part of which will be a payment to good students. If the prices for good and bad students cannot differ, no equilibrium exists. Members of the mixed school would have to pay $q(B, BG) = q(G, BG) = 1$, the same prices as for homogeneous clubs. But then bad students prefer the mixed school BG, while good students prefer a homogeneous school GG. ∎

Brueckner and Lee (1989) assume that only the relative numbers matter, and not the size. Ellickson, Grodal, Scotchmer and Zame assume that there is an exogenously given set of possible clubtypes. Since the set is finite, clubs are automatically bounded in size.

Cole and Prescott (1997) have criticized the above equilibrium concept as being inefficient. They point out that, in general, an equilibrium where agents randomize on memberships can increase expected utility. The following example illustrates their point, but of course it only applies if the utility function can be interpreted as a von Neumann–Morgenstern utility function[9].

Example 3. *Randomized memberships*: Suppose that there are two types of agents, *G* and *B*. There are twice as many *B* agents as *G* agents. There is only one type of club, consisting of one agent of each type. Type-*G* agents only care about private good consumption, but type-*B* agents receive more utility from their private good consumption when in a club. In particular, the utility of type-*B* is $f(x) + 1$ when in a club, where x is the consumption of private good, and $f(x)$ when not in a club. The function f is concave.

Assume that all agents have an endowment w of the private good. An equilibrium of the EGSZ type, with nonrandom memberships, has all the type-*G* agents matched in clubs, and half the type-*B* agents. The price of a type-*B* membership must be the q that solves $f(w - q) + 1 = f(w)$ in order that the excluded type-*B* agents are indifferent between membership and not. Since the club makes zero profit, type-*G* agents receive a subsidy of q from the type-*B* agents. That is, type-*G* agents pay a negative price of q. In this equilibrium type-*G* agents receive utility $w + q$ and type-*B* agents receive utility $f(w)$.

Now suppose instead that each type-*B* agent pays $q/2$ to flip a coin to establish whether he joins a club. Then type-*G* agents are equally well off (they still receive the subsidy of q), and type-*B* agents are better off *ex ante* because they receive expected utility $f(w - q/2) + 1/2$, which (using concavity of f) is greater than $(1/2)f(w) + (1/2)f(w - q) + 1/2 = f(w)$. Thus, randomization increases the expected utility of type-*B* agents *ex ante*, although they receive different utility *ex post*, depending on whether they receive club membership. ■

A limitation of the equilibrium concepts described above is that the externalities created by a club member do not depend on intensity of use. Variable use is discussed in Berglas (1981), Scotchmer (1985b) and Scotchmer and Wooders (1987a) for the case of anonymous crowding. (Also see Example 10 below on p. 2028.)

2.3. Trade in private goods

The sufficiency of small groups for providing utility is the basis for a competitive theory of club formation in both the Buchanan model and its extensions to

---

[9] Randomization does not solve the existence problem in finite club economies, but is purely a tool to increase expected utility. In the full model, the consumer must randomize on the entire consumption bundle, including private goods and club memberships. Cole and Prescott (1997) point out that an equivalent randomization on wealth would work, but the particular randomization depends on the prices of private goods, so the randomization on wealth presupposes the later equilibrium on clubs and private goods.

heterogeneous crowding. However, the competitive theory of clubs has more in common with general equilibrium theory than is apparent from the above discussion. In particular, if private goods are traded by agents in different clubs, the equivalence between the core and competitive outcomes, as exposited above for Buchanan clubs, no longer holds in finite economies. This is because clubs are no longer self-contained, isolated units in the economy. Clubs are linked to other clubs through trade. Such linkage has an interesting implication. If club memberships have an impact on demand for private goods, then club formation can change the terms of trade in the economy. In fact, club membership can create gains to trade that otherwise would not exist, thus improving utility opportunities, and that can be a motivation for club formation.

The latter point is illustrated by Example 4. All agents are assumed to be alike, as in a Buchanan economy, but there are two private goods. If all agents belonged to the same type of club, as in a Buchanan economy, there would be no opportunity for trade. In the example, however, the agents' demands for private goods depend on their club memberships. In order to profit from trade, they form clubs that alter their demands for private goods. Even though the example has the club feature that only small groups are efficient (in fact all clubs are size 1 or 2), the core/competitive equivalence exposited above for the case of a single private good no longer holds.

Example 4. *How trade in private goods matters*: Suppose there are no public goods, that each agent is endowed with one unit of each of two private goods, and club membership affects the demands for private goods as follows.

$$U(x, n) = x_1 + x_2 \qquad \text{if } n = 2,$$
$$U(x, n) = \sqrt{2}x_1 + \tfrac{1}{2}x_2 \text{ if } n = 1,$$
$$U(x, n) = 0 \qquad \text{if } n > 2.$$

If the economy only has two people, then it is optimal to put them in a club of size 2. However, if the economy is replicated so that there are 4 people, then, surprisingly, it is not optimal to replicate the size-2 club. Instead, it is optimal to have one club of size 2 and two singleton clubs, with the private goods shared among the clubs and consumed efficiently. In fact, the maximum per-capita utility is achieved when the proportion of agents in groups of size 2 is $k^* = \frac{1}{1+\sqrt{2}}$. Only members of size-2 groups consume good 2 (since their marginal rate of substitution favors good 2), and only singletons consume good 1. The proportion k^* is chosen to ensure that there is exactly enough endowment of each type of good so that the agents can specialize in consumption while utility is equalized.

But this is the source of the existence problem. Even though the core is nonempty for every finite economy, competitive equilibrium does not exist except at the scale of the economy that maximizes per capita utility. [For the argument, see Gilles and Scotchmer (1997), where this example appears.] Since k^* is an irrational number, there is no finite economy that will permit a proportion k^* to be in groups of size 2, and hence competitive equilibrium does not exist for any finite economy. This shows that core/competitive equivalence fails for every finite economy.

To make the nonexistence of competitive equilibrium more concrete, suppose there are 10 agents. Per-capita utility is maximized with a proportion .4 people in groups of size 2 (2 groups). But .4 is slightly less than k^*, and utility must be equalized by letting the singletons consume some x_2 as well as x_1. The price ratio must be the marginal rate of substitution of singleton agents, namely, $\frac{p_1}{p_2} = \frac{\sqrt{2}}{1/2}$. Such an allocation cannot be a competitive equilibrium, since the agents in singleton clubs are spending more than the value of their endowment. ∎

The fundamental premise of club theory, as described above, is that, if an allocation can be blocked, then it can be blocked by a group that is small[10]. Thus, all economic power is possessed by small groups. According to the above example, this idea is not preserved exactly when private goods are traded among members of different clubs. However, an approximate version of small-group effectiveness has long been known for private goods exchange economies, and could possibly be extended to general club economies. See Schmeidler (1972) and Grodal (1972) for continuum economies and Mas-Colell (1979) for large finite economies.

Following the intuition that club economies and exchange economies are not fundamentally different, Ellickson, Grodal, Scotchmer and Zame (2001) show a type of core/competitive equivalence for large finite club economies. Their interpretation is that large club economies are competitive because agents with the same characteristics are substitutes for each other in forming clubs, and since each agent belongs to a bounded number of clubs, no agent has more than a negligible impact on the economy. This is an application of Ostroy's (1980) requirement for perfect competition, namely, that no agent in the economy has more than a negligible impact on the utilities of others.

3. Free mobility equilibrium

The free-mobility notion is that there are no restrictions on migration, provided the migrant is willing to abide by the rules of the jurisdiction where he lives. Local services within jurisdictions are provided according to some pre-established rule, usually majority voting. Free mobility and voting outcomes are of interest because they seem to mimic social institutions, at least in Western democracies. However, they lead to inefficiencies and problems of existence. In this section I summarize some basic ideas about majority voting and redistribution in free-mobility models. Many of

---

[10] This idea lies at the heart of the papers on clubs in economies with single private goods, in particular, Buchanan (1965), Pauly (1970a,b), Stiglitz (1977), Wooders (1978, 1981, 1980), Boadway (1982), Berglas and Pines (1981), Scotchmer and Wooders (1987a,b) and Conley and Wooders (1997). It has been given many different names, for example, "optimal groups", "bounded groups", "efficient scale", and some that are defined for special cases like games with transferable utility [e.g., "effective small groups", Wooders (1992)].

the interesting applications concern parallel provision of services by public and private entities, which are discussed in Section 5 below.

Most models of free mobility equilibrium differ from the price-taking equilibrium of club economies in several important ways:

- There are implicit restrictions on side payments or "prices", which are given by the cost-sharing rule within the jurisdiction, usually established by majority-voting.
- Immigration to a jurisdiction (and entitlement to its local public services) may require occupancy of land, which might be scarce. The rental price on land is then an implicit price of residency, along with taxes.
- Consumers can only belong to one jurisdiction.
- Instead of choosing within an abstract set of jurisdiction types, which might or might not exist, the agent is restricted to the jurisdictions that actually exist (or to no jurisdiction at all).

The importance of the last point was illustrated by applying the free-mobility idea to Buchanan clubs, where it led to groups of inefficient size. The inefficiency arises because free mobility does not allow coordinated deviations by many agents simultaneously.

In contrast to clubs, jurisdictions are typically defined geographically, so that their number is fixed. Limited geographic space is a natural source of crowding. In contrast to the club model, where crowding externalities occur because of direct interactions among agents, or because a larger membership increases the cost of providing the public good, crowding is caused in a geographic model by the scarcity of land, reflected in its equilibrium price. Regardless of how attractive the jurisdiction's policies are, immigration can be limited by the high price of land.

The coupling of land consumption with the consumption of local public goods is the subject of Section 4. In the models there, agents are also freely mobile, assuming they are willing to pay the taxes imposed by jurisdictions. The focus is on efficiency. I ask what objectives the local jurisdiction should pursue, and how the local public goods should be funded, in order to ensure that local public goods are provided efficiently and residential choices are also efficient. In contrast, most concepts of free mobility equilibrium do not incorporate a local objective for a jurisdiction manager. Instead they assume that local decisions are made by majority vote.

In the papers on free mobility with majority voting, the policy space is generally collapsed to a single dimension, in order to avoid voting cycles. Example 5 follows that technique. Since taxes and expenditures are both modeled by a tax rate (they are linked by budget balance), it is hard to separate taxation for redistribution from taxation to fund local public goods. Income taxes have a redistributive aspect. However, the following example shows that both income taxes and local per-capita taxes will have distortionary effects on location choices.

Example 5. *Free mobility and redistribution*: Suppose that each of two jurisdictions, $i = 1, 2$, has an area equal to 1. Let the agents be indexed by their incomes $y \in [0, 1]$, where y is uniformly distributed on the interval. We shall refer to each jurisdiction as a subset of the agents, $J_1, J_2 \subset [0,1]$, where $J_1 \cup J_2 = [0,1]$. Each resident occupies space in amount $1/N_i$ in jurisdiction i, where N_i is the number of residents. We will assume that agents differ only by their endowment of income, and that their willingness to pay for public services increases with income (or private goods consumption). The utility function of an agent will be U, where $U^y(x,z,s) = x + b(z,y) + f(s)$. The variable x represents private goods consumption, z represents the level of public services, and s represents the land he consumes. Private goods endowment y is in the benefits function b to allow that the benefits for public services z can increase with private goods consumption, or incomes. (I use y instead of x to make the example simpler.)

Instead of using the utility function as given, we will write $y(1 - t_i) + b(t_i Y_i, y) + f(1/N_i)$ for the utility that an agent with income y receives in a jurisdiction with tax rate t_i, and total income $Y_i = \int_{J_i} y \, dy$. Then $t_i Y_i$ represents the public services provided, which is equal to the revenue collected.

First we consider the voting outcome, conditional on residency choices. A type-y resident prefers the tax rate, say $t(y)$, that satisfies (assuming that b is concave in its first argument)

$$-y + b_1 (t_i Y_i, y) \, Y_i = 0, \tag{3}$$

or

$$y/\hat{y}_i - N_i b_1 (t_i Y_i, y) = 0, \tag{4}$$

where b_1 is the partial derivative with respect to the first argument, namely, the marginal willingness to pay for local public services, and $\hat{y}_i$ is mean income in jurisdiction i. If the marginal willingness to pay for public services $b_1(\cdot)$ does not change very much with income y, then the voter's preferred tax rate $t(y)$ will be decreasing with y. The fact that a high-income voter pays a disproportionate share of the cost will dominate the fact that he has higher willingness to pay for public services than low-income voters.

Whether the preferred tax rate is increasing or decreasing with income, the median voter's preferred level of public services could be close to efficient. Because of the uniform distribution of y in this example, the mean income and the median income coincide. If the marginal willingness to pay for public services increases with income at more or less a constant rate, then the average willingness to pay for a marginal increase in public services, $1/(N_i) \int_{y \in J_i} b_1(t_i Y_i, y) \, dy$, will be close to the willingness to pay of the median voter, $b_1(t_i Y_i, \hat{y}_i)$. Thus, the Samuelson condition for efficient provision of public goods, which is $1 = \int_{y \in J_i} b_1(t_i Y_i, y) \, dy$, is "almost" satisfied by Equation (3), evaluated for the median voter, $\hat{y}$.

Interestingly, when taxes are the same for all residents, say τ_1, τ_2, rather than pro rata on income, $t_1 y, t_2 y$, the median voter will still choose public services close to the efficient level. In that case, the utility function for a resident of jurisdiction i is $-\tau_i + b(\tau_i N_i, y) + f(1/N_i)$. The residents' preferred tax rates satisfy

$$-1 + N_i b_1 (\tau_i N_i, y) = 0. \tag{5}$$

The preferred tax rate, say $\tau(y)$, increases with income, provided that the cross-partial of b is positive. In this example, neither the income tax nor the per-capita tax substantially distorts the provision of public services, at least conditional on the allocation of residents to jurisdictions.

But although the two tax systems do not lead to substantial differences in the provision of local services, the two tax systems lead to opposite distortions in how the residents are divided. For purposes of showing this, I shall now assume that, under each tax system, the median voter implements the efficient level of public services in each jurisdiction, conditional on the division of agents between jurisdictions. We shall refer to these efficient expenditures on public services as $e(J_1)$ and $e(J_2)$.

For expository purposes, I shall focus on allocations in which the population is divided such that $J_1 = [0, \bar{y})$ and $J_2 = [\bar{y}, 1]$, so that agents with lower demand for public services are concentrated in jurisdiction 1, and agents with higher demand are concentrated in jurisdiction 2.

I first consider how a social planner would divide the population, and use the efficient division as a benchmark for evaluating the equilibrium. Since utility is quasilinear, the efficient partition would maximize total utility,

$$\int_0^{\bar{y}} (y + b(e(J_1), y) + f(1/N_1)) \, dy - e(J_1) + \int_{\bar{y}}^1 (y + b(e(J_2), y) + f(1/N_2)) \, dy - e(J_2).$$

Then the optimal expenditures $e(J_i)$, $i = 1, 2$, satisfy the Samuelson condition, $\int_{J_i} b_1(e(J_i), y) \, dy = 1$. The optimal dividing point $\bar{y}$ will satisfy

$$[b(e(J_1), \bar{y}) + f(1/N_1)] - [b(e(J_2), \bar{y}) + f(1/N_2)] \\ = [(1/N_1)f'(1/N_1)] - [(1/N_2)f'(1/N_2)]. \tag{6}$$

Equation (6) can be interpreted to say that the direct benefits to the marginal person who moves from jurisdiction 1 to 2 must be balanced by the spatial congestion effects he generates. He liberates space in jurisdiction 1 and squeezes the other residents in jurisdiction 2.

Now consider the free mobility outcome. There could easily be multiple equilibria in how the population is divided, and, depending on details of the functions b and f, equilibrium might not exist at all. The prices of land in the two jurisdictions will be $f'(1/N_i)$, $i = 1, 2$, and the equilibrium lot sizes will be $1/N_i$. Accounting for expenditures on land, the marginal resident's utility in jurisdiction i is thus $\bar{y}(1 - t_i) - (1/N_i)f'(1/N_i) + b(e(J_i), \bar{y}) + f(1/N_i)$. In order that the marginal resident has no incentive to move, he should receive the same utility in both jurisdictions, accounting also for the difference in tax shares paid:

$$(t_2 - t_1)\, y + \left[b\,(e\,(J_1)\,,\bar{y}) + f\,(1/N_1) - (1/N_1)\, f'\,(1/N_1)\right]$$
$$- \left[b\,(e\,(J_2)\,,\bar{y}) + f\,(1/N_2) - (1/N_2)\, f'\,(1/N_2)\right] = 0. \tag{7}$$

Conditions (6) and (7) are the same except for the first term in Equation (7), representing the difference in taxes.

Starting from an efficient allocation, as described by Equation (6), consider whether the marginal person has incentive to move. It is reasonable to think that the tax rate in the high-demand jurisdiction will be lower than in the low-demand jurisdiction, that is, $t_2 < t_1$. Of course, this depends on the income-elasticity of demand for public services, but even with $t_2 < t_1$, the public services could be substantially higher in jurisdiction 2 than in jurisdiction 1, due to the higher mean income. If $t_2 < t_1$, then at the optimal $\bar{y}$, the marginal resident has incentive to move from jurisdiction 1 to jurisdiction 2, essentially to avoid the subsidy that he implicitly makes to lower-income residents.

Now suppose that the taxes are per-capita rather than pro-rata on income. Replace $(t_2 - t_1)y$ with $(\tau_2 - \tau_1)$ in Equation (7). In this case, it is reasonable to assume that $\tau_2 > \tau_1$, at least if the jurisdictions have similar numbers of residents. This is because higher-income residents have higher demand for public services, and therefore the per-capita taxes will be higher. The marginal resident in jurisdiction 2 has relatively low demand for public services (because he has relatively low income), but pays the same fraction of cost as the higher-income residents. He has incentive to move to jurisdiction 1, which has lower public services, in order to escape the onerous taxation. He is avoiding a subsidy to higher-demand residents, whose preference for a high level of public goods determines the level of provision, and is partly subsidized lower-demand residents like himself. ∎

The example suggests that, although voting creates certain distortions from the first best and may cause equilibrium not to exist, much of the distortion arises from the residency choices. The example shows two ways in which local taxes can be distortionary. Residents will locate to avoid paying a disproportionate share of the cost of public services when taxes are linked to income, and may relocate to avoid paying even an equal share, when the provision is greater than they prefer. Fernandez and Rogerson (1996) use such a model to study the effect of fragmentation and stratification on provision of schooling. Residents vote on linear income taxes, as above, and the taxes determine the quality of education provided. Two policy objectives – redistribution and provision of education – are governed by a one-dimensional policy variable. Jurisdictions with high average income vote for good schools. The free mobility equilibrium can be inefficient in the sense that moving some agents could increase the average income (hence the quality of education) in both jurisdictions. Fernandez and Rogerson discuss remedies to this problem, some of which mimic the solution in the clubs literature, namely, to price differentially (e.g., with subsidies) to reflect externalities.

In Example 5, the public services are a "pure public good" in the sense that the cost does not depend on the number of sharers. There is a crowding cost, but it arises entirely from the scarcity of land, which is separately priced. Therefore the arguments of Section 4.1 below apply: the form of taxation that does not distort location decisions is a land tax. With a land tax, there would be no tax term in Equation (7), and the residents' choices of location would coincide with the optimum. On the other hand, with a land tax, landowners instead of residents pay for the public services. Hence the residents might vote for an inefficiently high provision of public services, in order to transfer income from landowners to themselves. This observation highlights the importance of timing in the definition of equilibrium. The incentive to vote for high public services funded by land taxes would be damped if the residents predicted that such a policy would attract migration and push up the rental price of land, so that the benefits of high public services were capitalized. In most definitions of free mobility equilibrium, the voting public is assumed to be myopic in that it does not account for any migration that might be induced by a change in policies. Similarly, there is an issue of whether a migrant views the public services in his destination as fixed, or whether he predicts his own impact on the voting outcome.

Most of the literature on free mobility equilibrium has been focussed on existence. Equilibrium might not exist both because of majority voting and because of the instability that can be caused by a unilateral right to migrate. A good summary of various approaches to existence can be found in Konishi (1996), who presents a general existence theorem and summarizes the contributions of Ellickson (1971, 1973, 1977), Westhoff (1977), Rose-Ackerman (1979), Dunz (1989), Guesnerie and Oddou (1981), Greenberg (1983), Greenberg and Weber (1986), Greenberg and Shitovitz (1988), Epple, Filimon and Romer (1983, 1984, 1993), Epple and Romer (1991). See also Fernandez (1997), Fernandez and Rogerson (1995, 1996, 1998, 1999), Jehiel and Scotchmer (1993, 2001). Most of these papers do not involve crowding externalities within jurisdictions, aside from land. Crowding has been introduced by some of the more game theoretic papers; see Konishi, LeBreton and Weber (1998) and Conley and Konishi (2002). Some of these papers treat the pure voting problem, assuming that residents are not mobile. The definitions of equilibrium differ according to the timing of moves, and also in the cost structure of public services.

So far we have not considered direct externalities among residents. As in the clubs model, if agents cannot be taxed or subsidized to account for the externalities they create, then they will not account for the impact of their location decisions on the utility of other residents. This idea is particularly important when the direct externalities arise from peer effects, as with education. The implications have been explored, for example, by de Bartolome (1990), Benabou (1993) and Epple and Romano (2002). Example 6 gives a flavor of how uncompensated direct externalities among residents can lead to inefficient location choices. In a more complicated model with endogenous labor skills and costly education, Benabou (1993, 1996a,b) shows that free mobility can not only reduce average welfare relative to the first best, but can do so without making any of the citizens better off. These papers emphasize how the distribution of population among jurisdictions affects the incentives to invest in labor skills, which again have a feedback effect on productivity and how the population is segregated (or not) in equilibrium.

The following example was suggested by work in progress of Nicolas Gravel and Alain Trannoy.

Example 6. *Free mobility with externalities among residents*: Suppose that agents are differentiated by their incomes $y \in [0, 1]$, and that each agent's utility of consuming private goods x and space s in a jurisdiction with mean income $\hat{y}$ is given by $x + \log(s) + \hat{y}$. That is, he receives a positive externality from being grouped with high-income agents. Suppose that there are two jurisdictions $i = 1, 2$, each with land area equal to 1. Every resident of each jurisdiction will occupy the same amount of space, $s_i = 1/N_i$, $i = 1, 2$. The price of land will be equal to the marginal utility of space, which is $1/s_i$, so that each agent's expenditure on land in each jurisdiction is 1. An agent's utility can therefore be re-expressed as depending on the number of residents in the jurisdiction he occupies, and the average income, i.e., as $y - 1 - \log(N_i) + \hat{y}$.

Consider equilibria that can be described by a partition into two jurisdictions $J_1 = [0, \bar{y})$, $J_2 = [\bar{y}, 1]$. Since utility is quasi-linear, an allocation that maximizes the sum of utilities is efficient, and thus the dividing point $\bar{y} = (1/2)$ is optimal. However, this will not be a free-mobility equilibrium. At that partition, the jurisdictions are the same size and have the same land prices, but have different mean incomes. The marginal agent will leave jurisdiction 1 for jurisdiction 2, which has higher mean income. By doing so, he lowers the average income in both jurisdictions, a negative externality that he does not account for in deciding to migrate. Since the average incomes in the two jurisdictions are, respectively, $\bar{y}/2$ and $(1/2) + \bar{y}/2$, and since $N_1 = \bar{y}$, $N_2 = 1 - \bar{y}$, the equilibrium $\bar{y}$ satisfies

$$\bar{y} - 1 - \log(\bar{y}) + \bar{y}/2 = \bar{y} - 1 - \log(1 - \bar{y}) + (1/2) + \bar{y}/2,$$

which implies that the equilibrium $\bar{y}$ is less than $(1/2)$. The high-income jurisdiction is too large because agents will migrate there until land prices are high enough to discourage further immigration.

Another efficient partition is $J_1 = [0, 1/4) \cup [3/4, 1]$, $J_2 = [1/4, 3/4)$. This partition is a candidate for a free-mobility equilibrium[11], since, in contrast to the other efficient partition, all agents are indifferent between the two jurisdictions. But since the agents

---

[11] Whether this is a free mobility equilibrium depends on nuances of the definition. Suppose that a high-income agent contemplates migrating to jurisdiction 2. If the migrant accurately predicts that he will raise land prices and the average income in jurisdiction 2, and if, to overcome the artificiality of the continuum, a "small subset" is allowed to migrate, and if the increased average income adds more to his utility than the increase in land price subtracts, then this is not an equilibrium.

have no opportunity for coordinated action or side payments, they could get stuck in an equilibrium of the type previously described. ∎

One of the messages in Section 2 is that externalities must be priced in order to ensure that an equilibrium (which will be efficient) exists. A message of Examples 5 and 6 is that free-mobility equilibrium might exist even without externality pricing, but will not typically be efficient.

The literature's attention to free mobility is presumably because it seems to be how Western economies operate, at least internally. However, this stylization is not entirely accurate. Many jurisdictions impose tests for admission, for example, a demonstration of potential to earn income. Remarkably little attention has been paid to the consequences of imposing such tests. A natural test for allowing a migrant to enter is majority consent, which would presumably capture the residents' fear that an immigrant would be a burden on the state. But the following example shows that, at least in one class of cases, majority consent is no more restrictive than an untested right to migrate.

Example 7. *Admission by majority vote* [12]: Suppose that in a free mobility equilibrium the jurisdictions are indexed $j = 1, \ldots, J$, and the public services provided are $z^1, \ldots, z^J$. The costs of public services are given by a function $c(z)$, shared equally by the residents, and the numbers of residents in the jurisdictions are $n^1, \ldots, n^J$. Agents have willingness to pay parameters $\theta \in [\theta_o, \theta^o]$ and the utility of a type-θ person in jurisdiction j is $U^\theta(z^j, y - \frac{c(z^j)}{n^j})$. We assume that in each jurisdiction, the public services z^j are those preferred by the median θ in that jurisdiction. Suppose that a migrant shifts the median voter and changes the public services by dz^j. (In a continuum model, the shift will be infinitesimal.) In addition, the size of the jurisdiction changes by dn^j. The willingness to pay for this shift of a type-θ member is

$$dU^\theta(\cdot) = \frac{\partial U^\theta(\cdot)}{\partial z^j} dz^j + \frac{\partial U^\theta(\cdot)}{\partial n^j} dn^j.$$

The first term is positive for half the members (the half with high θ if dz^j is positive), zero for the median voter, and negative for half the members. If this were the only effect, they would be evenly split on whether to admit the new member, whether his effect is to increase or decrease the public services. But the second term is positive, since every member's cost share decreases. Thus, at least half the members will approve the immigrant, whether dz^j is positive or negative, and the only test of equilibrium is whether anyone wants to migrate. The criterion of majority approval adds no restriction beyond free mobility. ∎

---

[12] This example follows Jehiel and Scotchmer (2001).

4. Land, location and capitalization

In a certain sense, the club model can be interpreted as a model of endogenous jurisdiction formation in geographic space. Interpret one of the private goods as homogeneous land[13]. Agents sharing a particular jurisdiction (club) purchase land in addition to other private goods, and can be assumed to occupy contiguous lots, so the club could reasonably be interpreted as a "jurisdiction". The price of land in each of these endogenous jurisdictions is the same, which means that there are no capitalized differences among jurisdictions. This may seem curious, but it is a natural consequence of the hypothesis that land is fungible among jurisdictions. A piece of land can be annexed to a jurisdiction and removed from another, simply by transferring title from a member of one jurisdiction to a member of the other.

But, contrary to this re-interpretation of the club model, space is not fungible among jurisdictions. Instead of being decoupled as in the club model, the enjoyment of local public goods is coupled with consumption of land, of which there might be a fixed supply. This seems to be the essence of the local public goods problem.

The coupling of land with local public goods has three effects, which are explored in the following three subsections. First, it creates the possibility of capitalization. "Capitalization" means that the value of local public goods is captured in the price of the land to which the local public goods are attached. Second, the local public goods might be "located" in space, as museums and schools are, so that capitalization differs within jurisdictions as well as between jurisdictions. "Location" creates a problem of optimal siting. Third, consumption of land is bundled with consumption of local public goods, and because of this bundling, local public goods and also wage opportunities are "bundled" in the consumer's choice set.

Capitalization has been used in two ways to guide the efficient provision of public goods. First, capitalization effects have been used to estimate willingness to pay for public goods in cost-benefit analysis [see Rubinfeld (1987)]. Second, the theoretical literature has argued that an appropriate objective function for jurisdictions is to maximize the capitalized value of the land, as discussed below. A third way to use capitalization is suggested by Example 8. Namely, it could guide the efficient drawing of jurisdiction boundaries.

4.1. Diffused local public goods and capitalization

In this subsection I consider the economic environment most often discussed in the literature on local public goods with land, namely, that geographic space is pre-assembled into jurisdictions with exogenously given boundaries, and that the local

---

[13] The model of homogeneous land is itself limited, however. See Berliant and Dunz (1999) for the existence problems that can arise when agents care about the shape or other characteristics of their parcels.

public goods are "diffused", for example, quality of the road system, communications, and (perhaps) densely sited local schools. This is in contrast to the situation studied in the next subsection, where local public facilities are "located".

I focus on two important aspects of efficiency: agents' location choices must be efficient, and the public services within each jurisdiction must be efficient. The literature has addressed the following two questions about efficient allocations: (a) What price and tax systems are required to decentralize an allocation that is efficient in both senses, and (b) what should the objectives of local jurisdictions be, in order that in aggregate they will provide optimal local services, and agents will be allocated efficiently to jurisdictions? I consider these in the next two subsections.

4.1.1. How to pay for local public goods

In this subsection I do not consider how local public goods are chosen, but only how they are paid for, and how the taxes affect location decisions. An optimal scheme to pay for the local public goods is more complicated with geographic space than in the club model because there is a dual price system, consisting of both local taxes and land prices that arise anonymously in general equilibrium. The land prices play two allocative roles:
- Land prices allocate space within jurisdictions;
- Land prices capitalize the value of local externalities and public services, and thus affect residency choices.

Given that land prices play dual roles, it is perhaps surprising that, if the cost of local public services does not depend on the number of residents, and if there are no direct externalities among agents (as in Example 9 below), an efficient allocation should be financed entirely from land taxes. Otherwise residents will not locate efficiently.

Many arguments have been given in defense of this idea, mostly in models with homogeneous agents, e.g., Wildasin (1980) (who also assumes quasilinear utility) and Hochman (1981). See also the survey by Mieszkowski and Zodrow (1989). The intuition is basically that land in each jurisdiction is a private good, and private goods will be allocated efficiently by the market (conditional on the local public goods and fixed boundaries). If we think of the agents as bidding for places in jurisdictions, then the places will be allocated to the highest bidders, as would be efficient. The bid process capitalizes the public services into the land prices in different jurisdictions. If the price is high, agents will want to economize on lot size, which makes room for more residents, as is also efficient. This is how the dual roles of the land prices fit together. (See Fujita (1989) or Scotchmer (1994) for more formal discussions of these two roles.) There is no mention of taxes in this argument. Taxes that would distort the consumers' choices would obstruct the efficient functioning of the land market. And of course the argument assumes that the local public goods have been chosen efficiently in advance, and that the cost does not change when residents change jurisdictions.

In contrast to land taxes, income or local sales taxes affect residency choices. The thrust of the literature, illustrated in Example 8 below, is that such taxes should only be used to fund the local public goods if agents impose externalities on each other. Such externalities could be direct, as when a cat owner moves into a neighborhood of bird watchers, or it could be indirect, such as when the resident has many school-age children who increase the cost of local schools. Example 8 shows that, when there are externalities, land taxes must be supplemented by jurisdiction-specific taxes that internalize marginal costs imposed by the resident. Without such taxes, agents will not be allocated efficiently among jurisdictions.

The examples below show the following points about decentralizing an optimum when jurisdiction boundaries and local public goods are fixed in advance. There is a rich literature from which these principles derive, including Starrett (1980), Pogodzinski and Sjoquist (1993), Strazheim (1987), and Brueckner (1979).

- If the cost of local public goods depends on the number or characteristics or residents, then the local public services in an efficient allocation should not be financed with land taxes alone. Taxes with allocative effects are also necessary.
- Land prices can capitalize differences in local public goods, but consumers could be better off if land could be transferred among jurisdictions so that capitalization vanished.
- If residents' utility depends on the external characteristics of other residents, such as noisiness, criminal propensities or education, then an equilibrium may not exist without imposing different taxes on residents with different external characteristics. And such prices are required for efficiency.

Example 8. *Dual price system*: Suppose that there is a per-resident cost of 1 for providing crime control. There is a continuum of agents with willingnesses to pay θ, uniformly distributed on $[0, 2]$. Consumers have preference $\theta z + x + \log s$ where $z \in \{0, 1\}$ is the level of crime control, x is private good consumption and s is the amount of space occupied. There are two jurisdictions with sizes $A_2 = A_1 = 1$. Suppose for simplicity that there are absentee landlords [14], and that crime control is financed by land taxes which have no affect on the allocation of space or residency. Then the following is an equilibrium: jurisdiction 2 provides crime control, but not jurisdiction 1. Land prices are related to lot sizes by $p_i = 1/s_i$, $i = 1, 2$. Agents $\theta \in [\bar\theta, 2]$ reside in jurisdiction 2 (there are $(2 - \bar\theta)/2$ such agents), and agents $\theta \in [0, \bar\theta]$ reside in jurisdiction 1 (there are $\bar\theta/2$ such agents), where $\bar\theta$ satisfies

$$-\log\left[\left(2 - \bar\theta\right)/2\right] + \bar\theta = \log s_2 + \bar\theta = \log s_1 = -\log\left[\bar\theta/2\right].$$

Hence $0 < \bar\theta < 1$.

---

[14] A land owner cannot escape land taxes by changing his residency, since the land is still taxed. This is why it has no allocative effect. Further, there is no reason to think that each person owns land in the jurisdiction he occupies. Residency choices can be decoupled from land ownership. Thus, the incentive effects of different kinds of taxes can be understood in the simplest kind of model where everyone is a renter.

However this is not efficient. In an efficient allocation, half the agents, $\theta \in [0, 1]$, are in jurisdiction 1 with no crime control, and the other half, $\theta \in (1, 2]$, are in jurisdiction 2 with crime control. All agents consume the same amount of space. In the equilibrium there are too many agents in jurisdiction 2 with crime control because they are not required to pay the marginal cost of providing it. This shows that the efficient allocation cannot be supported only with land taxes. The inefficiency could be corrected by imposing a head tax in jurisdiction 2, equal to the marginal cost of providing the local public good to an additional person.

In this example with linear costs, the revenues from the optimal head tax cover the whole cost of the local public goods. If there were fixed costs as well as marginal costs, the head tax would have to be supplemented with a tax on land. ∎

Krelove (1993) and Wilson (1997) recognize the importance of internalizing cost externalities, and argue that if direct taxes on residents are not allowed, then property taxes (including taxes on structures) are superior to land taxes as an approximation. Nechyba (1997a) considers the possibility of income taxation as well as property taxation, and argues that jurisdictions will always opt for property taxes, since they can make their communities relatively more attractive by switching from income to property taxes. Income taxes, to the extent they are used, are imposed by higher levels of government. Nechyba (1997b) shows existence of an equilibrium in which local public goods are financed through property taxes and national public goods are financed by income taxes. Both are established by the vote of residents, rather than by an objective function such as land value or profit. He does not address the efficiency of such an equilibrium.

I now continue Example 8 to show that the nonfungibility of land creates the capitalization effect, and imposes a social cost on the economy as a whole, by creating an artificial scarcity of the produced local public goods. (I distinguish natural local amenities, such as views and climate, from produced local public goods. Both can be capitalized into the price of land, but the natural amenities cannot be changed, and the capitalization effect cannot be avoided.)

Example 8 (continued). *Capitalization and the nonfungibility of land*: We showed that, since residents impose marginal costs on the provision of the local public good, the cost should be at least partially covered by taxes with allocative effects such as head taxes. Assume then that residents pay the marginal cost 1 so that their net willingness to pay for crime control is $\psi = (\theta - 1) \in [-1, 1]$. Suppose that in an optimum all agents $\psi > \hat{\psi}$ occupy jurisdiction 2, where $\hat{\psi}$ satisfies

$$\hat{\psi} + \log s_2 = \hat{\psi} + \log\left[A_2/(1 - \hat{\psi})\right] = \log\left[A_1/(\hat{\psi} + 1)\right] = \log s_1.$$

If $A_2 < A_1$, this implies that $\hat{\psi} > 0$ and $p_1 < p_2$. That is, the differential value of crime control is capitalized into the land price in jurisdiction 2 when agents are partitioned optimally. Agents in jurisdiction 1 with positive net willingness to pay are deterred from moving to jurisdiction 2 by the high price of land. They would like to annex their land to jurisdiction 2. If this were possible, the price of land would end up equal in both jurisdictions, and the population would be better served, since all agents with $\psi > 0$ would receive crime control. The fact that the geographic space has been divided in advance creates an artificial scarcity of crime control, and creates a capitalization effect. ∎

The next example illustrates the principle, suggested by the club arguments above, that when there are direct externalities among the agents, an allocation must be supported by taxes that include transfers among agents with different external characteristics.

Example 9. *Internalizing externalities*: Suppose there are two types of external characteristics, B and G. For simplicity, assume that agents of each type have the same preferences, and that each agent is endowed with 1 unit of a private good. There is a continuum of each type with measure 1. Let b represent the ratio of type-B agents to type-G agents in a jurisdiction.

Suppose there are no local public goods except externalities among agents. External-ities are experienced only by the type-G agents, who have utility function $(b + \log s + x)$, where s is land consumption and x is private good consumption. Type-B agents have utility function $(\log s + x)$. There are two jurisdictions. It is optimal for one jurisdiction, say jurisdiction 1, to include all the type-G agents and a fraction, say n_B, of type-B agents, and for jurisdiction 2 to include only the remaining $1 - n_B$ type-B agents. For efficiency in the allocation of space, all agents in the same jurisdiction will occupy the same amount of space, s_1 or s_2, but $s_1 < s_2$. The total space in each jurisdiction is 1. The prices of land are $p_i = (1/s_i)$, $i = 1, 2$, so $p_1 > p_2$.

To support this allocation as an equilibrium, type-B agents must be indifferent between the two jurisdictions. They must be "bribed" to live in jurisdiction 1, which has a higher price for land. The bribe can be accomplished with a transfer tax from the type-G agents to the type-B agents living in jurisdiction 1. Since type-B agents confer positive externalities on type-G agents, type-G agents must compensate them for their presence. It would not suffice for the agents to pay different prices for land instead of head taxes, as that would distort the allocation of space. If public goods were provided, then the transfer tax could take the form of assigning a smaller share to type-B. ∎

4.1.2. The local objective function

The previous subsection investigated how the local services should be financed, recognizing that taxes can affect agents' location decisions as well as paying for the local public goods. We now ask the broader question of whether local jurisdictions have incentive to provide local services efficiently, and whether they have incentive to use the tax systems that result in optimal location decisions. Two key questions are:

(1) what is the jurisdiction manager's objective function, and (2) does he wield tax instruments consistent with the prescriptions in the previous subsection? [15]

An old hypothesis is that if jurisdiction managers act on behalf of land owners, they will achieve an allocation that is efficient both in its public goods provisions, and in the allocation of residents to jurisdictions. Pines (1991) refers to this hypothesis as "Tiebout without Politics", and I shall refer to it as the "capitalization hypothesis". Its roots go back at least as far as Hamilton (1975) and Sonstelie and Portney (1978), with ongoing discussion by Wildasin (1979, 1987), Wildasin and Wilson (1991), Epple and Zelenitz (1981), Brueckner (1979, 1983), Henderson (1985), Starrett (1981), Pines (1985) and Scotchmer (1994) (giving an argument where residents have different tastes). By the argument given above, residency choices will be efficient as a consequence of individuals' optimizing choices and endogenous land prices, provided the right tax instruments are used to fund the local public goods. The intuitive argument for efficient provision of the public services is even more straightforward: The way to maximize land values is to cater to residents' preferences, so that they bid up the price of land. If the cost of public services is covered by land taxes, then maximizing land value is like maximizing the residents' aggregate willingness to pay for public goods, net of costs.

However, there are at least two unresolved issues related to the capitalization hypothesis. First, jurisdictions can overlap in geographic space, which means that the local public goods provided at each location are provided by different jurisdictions. An agent cannot unbundle these local public goods in choosing his residency. To my knowledge, the capitalization hypothesis has not been extended to accommodate overlapping jurisdictions. Suppose, for example, that a county-level government has responsibility to provide public transportation, and the cities have responsibility to provide roads. Suppose that both levels of government are motivated to choose the policies that maximize land values. Can they nevertheless get stuck in an inefficient equilibrium where, for example, counties fail to provide bus service because the roads are inadequate, and cities fail to improve the roads because they are not needed for bus service?

Second, when a jurisdiction manager contemplates an improvement to local services, how does he predict the consequences for land value? Such a prediction is an essential part of the theory. Depending on agents to "vote with their feet", as suggested by Tiebout, will not lead to efficiency in public goods provision unless managers are proactive in choosing the public goods that will attract residents. If, for example, all jurisdictions in the economy have a common level of services, e.g., bad schools, there is no reason for agents to choose any jurisdiction over any other. There will be no

---

[15] I assume here that the only possible policy instruments are the level of local public services and the tax instruments. Some authors have assumed that the jurisdiction manager can choose the residents directly. I find this assumption unsatisfying, as there could be a conflict between the desires of the manager and the optimal choices of prospective residents. Another policy instrument is zoning; see Wheaton (1993).

variation in land prices, and no evidence from the cross-section that an improvement would lead to a net-of-tax increase in property value or an increase in aggregate consumer welfare.

In fact, the cross section may be an inadequate guide to predicting capitalization even if there is variation in local public services. Whatever the local provisions of public services are, agents will sort themselves to jurisdictions efficiently. Those with relatively high demand for, say, good schools will reside in jurisdictions with good schools. The land price in a jurisdiction with good schools will reflect the valuations of the people who live there, but not of the people who live elsewhere. Because of this sorting, a jurisdiction that improves its public services so that it is similar to another jurisdiction will not typically end up with the same land prices; in fact, if the number of jurisdictions is finite, land prices in both jurisdictions could fall.

Despite its longevity, the capitalization hypothesis has only been proved in very simple models. Apparently this is due to difficulties in formulating how the jurisdiction manager would evaluate the capitalization effects of a local change. The technique most closely tied to competitive theory would be to hypothesize a price system that is independent of the local manager's policies [16]. As suggested by Example 9, the price system must be dual. It must include the externality taxes required to support an efficient allocation of residents to jurisdictions. And of course it must include land prices to measure the capitalization effect. The land prices would capitalize the taxes as well as the local services in each jurisdiction. As I have mentioned, such a price system could not reliably be found by observing the cross section.

Arguments for the capitalization hypothesis have relied on notions of "perfect competition", most often formulated as "utility-taking". Utility-taking means that the policies of any single jurisdiction do not affect the utility opportunities of residents or potential residents elsewhere. That is why the capitalized value of a change in the local policy will reflect the residents' willingness to pay. If the competitive hypothesis is reformulated as price-taking, as suggested above, then the notion would be that the prices for every type of local jurisdiction would be immune to any change in a single jurisdiction's policy, and that is why utility opportunities elsewhere do not depend on the local policy.

The competitive hypothesis does not hold if each jurisdiction is "large" relative to the rest of the world. The benefits of an improvement in local public services can be exported via pecuniary externalities. For example, if an improvement in local public services will induce immigration, reducing the price of land in other jurisdictions, it makes the residents who remain in the other jurisdictions better off [Scotchmer (1986)]. Capitalization in the improved jurisdiction is thus damped, and underestimates the value of the improved services.

Two alternatives to maximizing land values are majority voting, discussed above, and maximization of residents' welfare. A problem with welfare maximization is how

---

[16] Scotchmer (1994) uses this technique, but not in a model with crowding externalities.

to deal with migration. Migration must be allowed, since residency choices are an important aspect of allocative efficiency. But with migration, whose welfare counts to a jurisdiction manager? Does he take account of the immigrants or emigrants? Boadway (1982) postulated a welfare function that takes account of residents' and nonresidents' utility together, but in a model with one type of agent, so that any increase in local utility is exported equally to residents of other jurisdictions. Maximizing the welfare of all agents, both residents and nonresidents, seems difficult when agents differ, and when they sort themselves according to the jurisdictions they prefer. In addition, an objective function in which each jurisdiction takes account of the welfare of the whole economy seems to contradict the notion of "decentralization".

An issue that has received considerable attention in the literature is "tax-exporting". Can jurisdictions create value for their residents by taxing nonresidents? This idea was explored by Arnott and Grieson (1981), who argued that jurisdictions have an incentive to pay for their local public goods by taxing commodities that are consumed by nonresidents, or possibly by taxing land and housing that are owned by nonresidents. Similar ideas have been discussed more recently by Crane (1990) and Kim (1998).

However, the attempt to export taxes to nonresidents can be foiled by capitalization. Suppose, for example, that landowners are nonresidents, and a jurisdiction imposes a tax of T per parcel, which it then rebates to residents. This looks on the surface like a transfer from nonresidents to residents, but the transfer is at least partly foiled by capitalization. Rental values in the jurisdiction (hence the capitalized value of land) will increase. In fact, if the number of lots in the jurisdiction is fixed, then the rental price increases by T, so that both residents and landowners end up in their initial positions. There are nuances to this line of reasoning, but the basic insight is that capitalization makes it difficult to create benefits for residents at the expense of landowners. Conversely, it is difficult to create benefits for landowners except by creating benefits for residents. This observation lies at the heart of why maximizing land values leads to efficiency, regardless of whether residents are renters or owners.

On the other hand, taxing the *structures* on land is similar to taxing externally owned capital. With a local tax on capital, less housing capital will flow to the jurisdiction, which hurts residents even if their local public services are partly covered by capital owners who live elsewhere. For a more complete discussion of the relationship between capital taxation and property taxation, see Mieszkowski and Zodrow (1989).

The local incentive to export taxes is closely tied to issues of "fiscal federalism", the label under which authors have asked how the authority to tax and spend should be divided among hierarchical governments. For an integrative survey, see Oates (1999). Inman and Rubinfeld (1996), following Gordon (1983) and Arnott and Grieson (1981), argued that tax exporting should be prevented, since it has distortionary effects. It can be prevented by paying for local public goods with federal taxation rather than local taxation. However subsidies from the federal government to local governments also lead to perverse incentives, mostly centered on asymmetries of information.

4.2. Location

The model of the previous section has "land without location". The public goods are diffused throughout the jurisdiction, and residency within the jurisdiction entitles (or obligates) the resident to enjoy them. Such goods might be the transportation system, communications system or crime control. However, local public goods such as schools and museums are "located" within the jurisdiction. Strident politics surround their siting, and land values within the jurisdiction depend on where they are. Users must pay a transportation cost to enjoy them, in addition to any user fees. This leads to several additional questions: what rules should be obeyed in siting facilities optimally? Do local jurisdictions have incentive to obey those rules? How does "location" affect the optimal mix of taxes?

Location is the aspect of local public goods that has probably been discussed least. It is discussed under the name "spatial clubs" by Starrett (1988), and under the name "neighborhood goods" by Fujita (1989). See also Arnott and Stiglitz (1979), Thisse and Wildasin (1992), Thisse and Zoller (1982), Hochman (1981, 1982a,b, 1990) and Hochman, Pines and Thisse (1995). Location blurs the line between private and public goods. The theory of spatial clubs is very close to the theory of firm location, and inherits all the difficulties that arise there. A Hotelling firm sells to all the customers who are willing to bear the transportation cost, and because of its local monopoly, can make profit even if it has high fixed costs and zero marginal costs. If a spatial club has only a fixed cost and no marginal congestion costs due to the number of users, then it is precisely a Hotelling firm selling a private good. The same location theory applies, provided the spatial clubs are provided by profit-maximizing firms rather than by public institutions. The main conclusions of the Hotelling-based theory concern the fact that an equilibrium might not exist, and if it does exist, might be inefficient in both the locations of firms and their pricing policies. See Anderson, De Palma and Thisse (1992, Chapter 8), for a summary of these theories.

However, location theory as it has been applied to public facilities has a different focus than location theory as it has been applied to firms. Instead of focussing on the existence and properties of a noncooperative equilibrium, the focus has been on the social planning problem of where facilities *should* be located, and how their costs *should* be covered. In ordinary nonspatial clubs of the Buchanan type, the optimal size of a club balances congestion costs against the benefits of sharing the costs of a facility. An efficient size has the property that the marginal congestion cost imposed by the marginal member is just equal to the cost of the facility averaged over members. However, Example 10, which follows an idea of Hochman, Pines and Thisse (1995), shows how this conclusion must be modified if clubs are located in space. They conclude that

- Unlike nonspatial clubs, the cost of spatial clubs should not typically be covered entirely from user fees. Spatial clubs should also be subsidized from land rent.
- Each jurisdiction should contain many facilities of each type (schools, hospitals), each serving an optimal area. Since optimal areas differ for different types of facilities, such a jurisdiction might have to be very large.

- Given that jurisdictions have the right size, land-value maximization should lead to the right mix of land-rent subsidies and user fees, as in the previous section.

Example 10. *Spatial clubs*: Let every agent's utility be represented by $U(v) + x$ where v is the number of visits, x is the private good consumed, and U is concave. Let the cost of the facility be given by $C(V)$ where V is the total number of visits to the facility. Assume that C is U-shaped. If the facility were provided optimally in a nonspatial context, the optimal number of visits and members, (v^*, n^*) would satisfy $U'(v^*) = \frac{C(n^*v^*)}{v^*n^*} = C'(n^*v^*)$. Thus, the optimum would be supported if each agent pays a price per visit equal to the marginal cost $C'(n^*v^*)$, and the club is self-supporting [17].

However, when the club is located in space, each visit requires a transportation cost. Suppose that residents have measure one on each unit of an infinite line. Then it is optimal to locate spatial clubs at equal distances, and for residents to travel to the closest facility. The number of residents traveling to each facility is equal to the distance between facilities, but residents will visit with different frequency, depending on their personal distances to a facility. Let $v(t; T)$ represent the frequency of visits by agents who live at distance t from the closest facility when the distance between facilities is T (so that the "market area" of each facility extends a distance $T/2$ on each side). Assume that the cost of travel is \$1 per unit distance per visit.

I will solve the optimal siting problem in two parts. The optimal visit function $v(\cdot; T)$ maximizes

$$2 \int_0^{T/2} [U(v(t; T)) - tv(t; T)] \, dt - C \left(2 \int_0^{T/2} v(t; T) \, dt \right),$$

and satisfies

$$U'(v(t; T)) = t + C' \left(2 \int_0^{T/2} v(t; T) \, dt \right), \quad t \in \left[0, \frac{T}{2}\right]. \tag{8}$$

That is, the marginal utility of a visit from each distance t must equal the travel cost plus the marginal resource cost of the visit. Once the facilities are located, optimal visit rates can be guaranteed by charging a price per visit that is equal to the marginal cost $C'(\cdot)$, as one would expect.

However, since the marginal cost depends on total usage, and since total usage depends on how the facilities are spaced, the question of whether the revenue from optimal visit prices will cover the total cost of the facility is connected to the optimal spacing of the facilities. Letting $v(\cdot; T)$ be the solution satisfying Equation (8), and

---

[17] To see how equilibrium theories described above relate to this version of the club problem, see Scotchmer (1985b) and Scotchmer and Wooders (1987a).

letting $V(T) = 2 \int_0^{T/2} v(t; T) \, dt$ (the total number of visits to a facility when they are spaced at distance T), the optimal distance T maximizes per-capita utility:

$$\frac{1}{T} \left[2 \int_0^{T/2} [U(v(t; T)) - tv(t; T)] \, dt - C(V(T)) \right].$$

The optimum T satisfies

$$
\begin{aligned}
U & \left(v \left(\tfrac{1}{2}T; T \right) \right) - \tfrac{1}{2} Tv \left(\tfrac{1}{2}T; T \right) - v \left(\tfrac{1}{2}T; T \right) C'(V(T)) \\
& = \frac{1}{T} \left[2 \int_0^{T/2} [U(v(t; T) - tv(t; T)] \, dt - C(V(T)) \right] \\
& = \frac{1}{T} \left[V(T) C'(V(T)) - C(V(T)) \right] \\
& + \frac{1}{T/2} \int_0^{T/2} \left[U(v(t; T) - tv(t; T) - C'(V(T)) v(t; T) \right] \, dt.
\end{aligned}
\tag{9}
$$

Using Equation (8) and the concavity of U, and the fact that $v(\cdot, T)$ is decreasing, the integrand of the last term of Equation (9) is decreasing with t. Hence

$$
\begin{aligned}
U & \left(v \left(\tfrac{1}{2}T; T \right) \right) - \tfrac{1}{2} Tv \left(\tfrac{1}{2}T; T \right) - v \left(\tfrac{1}{2}T; T \right) C'(V(T)) \\
& < \frac{1}{T/2} \int_0^{T/2} \left[U(v(t; T) - tv(t; T) - C'(V(T)) v(t; T) \right] \, dt.
\end{aligned}
\tag{10}
$$

Together with Equation (9), (10) implies that $[V(T) C'(V(T)) - C(V(T))] < 0$. Thus, if each visitor is charged the optimal visit price equal to $C'(V(T))$, the costs will exceed the revenue. The deficit can be made up by taxing property.

The intuitive reason that revenues fall short is that spatial clubs should optimally be more plentiful (have smaller membership) than nonspatial clubs, since transportation costs can be reduced by having more clubs. Each club operates on the downward sloping part of its U-shaped average cost curve, which implies that marginal cost pricing will not be sufficient to cover costs.

If there are many different types of facility, then the jurisdiction must be of an appropriate size to accommodate integer numbers of optimal "market areas", say $T_1^*, \dots, T_m^*$. It follows that the jurisdiction might have to be very large.

Further, the example has implications for fiscal federalism. Since many different types of clubs will typically have to be subsidized out of the same land value, presumably under a single taxing authority, that same authority should have competency for providing all the public facilities. ∎

4.3. Bundling

The club model in Section 2 decouples geography from group formation. In my view, the decoupling is what distinguishes clubs from local public goods. When local public goods and other externalities are tied to a geographic location through the consumption of land and housing, then the consumer faces choices among *bundles* of local public goods, and the local public goods are also bundled with production opportunities and land. Each jurisdiction represents a different bundle, and to gain access, the resident must pay for some land.

Perhaps the most underexplored consequence is that many local services are bundled with occupancy of a single plot of land. They are provided by different jurisdictions, including, in the USA, the city, the county, special assessment districts, and the state. There is potentially a problem of coordination, as suggested by the bus and road example above.

The bundling of labor opportunities and provision of local public goods was first explored by Berglas (1976b), who considered the conflict between forming heterogeneous groups in order to exploit their complementarities in production, and forming homogeneous groups in order to exploit their shared tastes for public goods. Notice that if the agents could join "firms" that are different than "consumption communities", then no conflict would arise. They would join different groups for different purposes, as in Ellickson, Grodal, Scotchmer and Zame (1999a,b, 2001).

Bundling of production and local public goods is further explored by Wilson (1986), McGuire (1991) and Brueckner (1994). While Berglas, Brueckner and McGuire focus on production functions with two types of labor, Wilson focuses on a production function with labor and land. He shows that if there are two private goods – one with a labor-intensive production function and another with a land-intensive production function – then the communities should specialize so that workers can mostly live in a community using the labor-intensive production technology, and reaping the benefits of high public services, which are provided to them cheaply due to economies of scale. Even though people are alike, communities should be asymmetric. Asymmetry is the consequence of bundling in all these models.

Much of the focus in these investigations is on whether groups should be "homogeneous" or "heterogeneous". In my view, this is not an instructive question, since, typically, no two agents will be alike, and it is not obvious how to stylize their similarities. It is almost tautological that agents with the same tastes who face the same prices will make the same choices. But if they differ in productive skills or other external characteristics, they will not necessarily face the same prices. A competitive economy should get the grouping right under the right kind of pricing scheme, irrespective of what the optimal grouping happens to be. We should not need to know in advance whether the efficiencies from exploiting complementarities in production outweigh the inefficiencies from grouping people with different tastes for public goods.

5. The public–private interface

It is not obvious what we should mean by "public" and "private" provision of local public goods. The most natural distinction is probably one of objectives. In the clubs model of Section 2, clubs are supplied in response to the profit motive. The geographic model in Section 4 was originally motivated as a model of profit-maximizing land developers, who would furnish their land with infrastructure and services only to the extent that it increased the value of the land. It was a later realization that managers of public jurisdictions could adopt the same objective function as land developers. These are profit objectives, and they lead to efficiency. If local jurisdiction managers choose some other objective, it is presumably because they have values other than efficiency. The profit motive can even cause decision makers to internalize crowding externalities, provided that all such externalities occur within the club or jurisdiction.

I have mentioned two other objectives that public decision makers might plausibly follow, namely, the objective of maximizing local residents' welfare, and the rule of deciding local public goods by majority vote. As I have noted, the objective of maximizing welfare is not easily implemented when changes in local policy lead to migration. In fact, most authors studying the parallel provision of services by public and private entities have assumed that the public provision is decided by majority vote, where the voters do not account for the effect of their policies on migration.

Other differences between public and private providers might arise because public authorities are legally bound not to exclude users, or legally bound not to price differently according to externalities. And, most importantly, they might have a mandate to tax progressively, rather than according to the tax instruments discussed above that support efficient allocations. Thus, many authors assume that the tax instrument must be an income tax.

It should be apparent that the right to migrate can obstruct redistributive policies. There is a body of scholarship, mostly not reviewed in this paper, that focuses precisely on how migration undermines redistribution. See Epple and Romer (1991) and Epple and Platt (1998). Example 5 shows that if agents are paying too much for public services that they do not value, they will decamp to a jurisdiction with fewer services. Policies with a redistributive aspect may cause high-income citizens to go somewhere with lower taxes, or to a location where they will be subsidized instead of subsidizing, thus undermining the attempt to redistribute.

However, in many instances it is difficult or impossible to escape taxation by forming a new jurisdiction or migrating, e.g., when the tax is imposed by the highest level of a federal system. But even if agents cannot escape taxation, they can form private "quasi-governments" in parallel [Helsley and Strange (1991, 1998, 2000a)]. A parallel quasi-government formed by a select group of citizens can have two effects, both of which could benefit the members, but have ambiguous effects on nonmembers. First, the quasi-government can supplement the public services in accordance with the members' preferences. Second, depending on the cost structure, their private provision might crowd out the public supply, thus reducing the subsidy they must make to nonmembers.

The following example, adapted from Helsley and Strange (1998), investigates crowding-out.

Example 11. *Private supplements to public services*: Suppose that the willingness to pay for quality of service is θ, and that θ is uniformly distributed on a domain $[0, 1]$. Let g represent the quality of service, and suppose that preferences are $\theta f(g) - t$, where f is concave and t is the tax paid.

We will consider two cases, first that the cost of providing service is linear on the number of persons served, but depends on quality, and then that the cost of local services has the "pure public goods" feature that the cost is independent of the number of residents.

Suppose first that the cost is cg per person served, and that residents share the costs equally, so each resident's tax is cg. Then preferences are given by $\theta f(g) - cg$. Let $G(\theta)$ represent the preferred quality of type-θ, namely the value which satisfies $\theta f'(G(\theta)) = c$, and notice that the preferred quality increases with θ. For any group say $\Theta \subset [0, 1]$ let $E(\theta \mid \Theta)$ represent the mean value of θ in the group. Then $G(E(\theta \mid \Theta))$ is the level of public service that maximizes the group's total utility, $f(g) \int_{\Theta} (\theta - cg) \, dH(\theta)$.

The best quality for the group as a whole is $G(E(\theta \mid [0, 1]))$. This is a smaller level of public service than any subset of high-demand residents, $\Theta = [\hat{\theta}, 1]$, would prefer. Suppose that such a group decides to provide a supplement to its members, e.g., by funding after-school activities. The total level of public service in the splinter group will be $g + \gamma$, representing the services provided by the two sectors respectively. Whatever the service g provided by the public sector, the splinter group will choose γ to satisfy $\gamma = G(E(\theta \mid \Theta)) - g$. That is, it will make up any difference between the public's provision and its preferred level of public service. It follows that the level of public service enjoyed by the splinter group will be higher than if they did not form a parallel quasi-government. As long as there are no fixed costs associated with formation, they will also be better off than if they did not form the group.

The rest of the population will receive less public service than otherwise. Knowing that γ will be chosen to satisfy $f'(g + \gamma) E(\theta \mid \Theta) = c$, the public sector will provide $G(E(\theta \mid \sim \Theta))$, where $\sim \Theta$ represents the nonmembers of the splinter group. Thus, the nonmembers will receive less service than if the splinter group did not form.

So far this sounds like an unambiguously good arrangement, since both groups end up with a provision of services closer to their optima. However, Helsley and Strange show that, when there are fixed costs associated with forming the parallel quasi-government, the splinter group might be better off if they could commit in advance not to supplement the public offering. There is a kind of strategic downloading: the public sector provides a low level of service, leading high-demand agents to incur the fixed costs of forming a splinter group to supplement the services. But even though forming a splinter group is a best response to a low public offering, the members would be better off with the higher offering that the public administrator would make if no splinter group was allowed to supplement.

Now modify the example so that the public services have the cost structure of "pure public goods", namely, that the cost depends only on the quality of service provided, namely the total cost is cg. The cost does not increase with the number of residents sharing the public good. (Above, the total cost was cg times the number of residents.) Suppose that a splinter group of high-demand residents, $[\bar{\theta}, 1]$, forms in order to supplement the public goods. The total public goods will be $g + \gamma$, where γ is the supplement. Since the splinter group receives the publicly provided goods g as well as the supplement γ, their decision rule is to increase γ until $f'(g + \gamma)(1 - \bar{\theta}) = c$. The public authority's objective is to provide the public goods g efficiently to the whole population, so their decision rule is $\bar{\theta}f'(g) + (1 - \bar{\theta})f(g + \gamma) = c$. If $g > 0$ and $\gamma > 0$, these two decision rules are inconsistent. The timing of moves would matter in defining an equilibrium, but it is reasonable to conclude that there is no real advantage to forming a splinter group, since, if the public authority obeys its own objective, the splinter group would not want to supplement the public goods. ■

This example suggests that if the cost structure of public services is more like private goods than public goods, then splinter groups may form. But if public services have the cost structure of pure public goods, then there is no reason for a splinter group to form, since the public authority always prefers a greater aggregate provision, since it accounts for all residents' willingness to pay, rather than only a splinter group's.

Of course, if the cost structure is more like a private good than a public good, there is the question of why the public is involved at all. Why isn't every resident responsible for his own education and health care? One possible answer is externalities. If there are external benefits to a high level of health care (as, for example, when there are contagious diseases) or a high level of education (when, for example, education prevents crime or reduces public assistance), then the public should force a higher level of consumption than individuals would choose. In that case, the public authority might want to prohibit private supplements by high-demand residents, precisely on grounds that it reduces consumption of the public service by low-demand residents.

Another reason for public involvement is that taxing to provide public services gives an opportunity for redistributing income by imposing different tax shares. Epple and Romano (1996c) investigate a model of a publicly-provided private good such as health care, funded by redistributive income taxes. The tax share is higher for high-income residents even though the resource cost is the same for every resident served. The level of public services and the amount of redistribution are both controlled by a single policy lever, the tax rate. This policy lever is established by vote, rather than by a welfare-maximizing manager as above. Epple and Romano compare regimes where the private good is publicly provided, privately provided, and publicly provided with discretionary private supplements. They show that the latter is preferred by a majority who simultaneously vote on the tax rate and the regime. Their argument uses the fact that, at a given tax rate, everyone prefers allowing discretionary private supplements. This is for much the same reason as in the example above, with the twist that funding through an income tax has a redistributive element. High-income residents want to supplement the public provision because they can increase their services without increasing their subsidies. Low-income residents are indifferent to subsidization, and want at least some government provision, because the income tax system gives them an implicit subsidy from high-income residents.

The above example concerns private *supplements* to publicly provided services. In the case of schools, the private supplement would pay for after-school activities. In the case of health care, the supplement would pay for better specialists. In addition, there are private *alternatives* to public provision. It is possible that an agent will opt out of the public system entirely, and choose a private alternative. See, for example, Ireland (1990), Epple and Romano (1996a) and Glomm and Ravikumar (1998). Of course, opting out of the public offering does not typically allow the resident to escape taxation, so the preferences for public services are again combined with the desire to avoid or exploit redistributive taxes. The dual purposes of the policy lever create difficulties in sorting out preferences. An important consequence of the right to opt out is that preferences over public tax/expenditure packages are not single-peaked. Epple and Romano (1996a) summarize previous work on this subject, and extend it in an interesting way. They show that typically it is the low-income (low-demand) residents, together with the high-income (high-demand) residents who will oppose tax increases, whereas the middle class both uses the publicly provided service, and prefers higher taxes and higher provision.

Models of the private–public interface in the spirit of club theory have been built around the contentious subject of private supplements to public education. As in club theory, it is assumed that students confer externalities on each other in small groups (schools). If students differ in ability, achievement may depend on "peer group" effects, often captured by the mean ability of the student's school. Prices to internalize the externality, as described in Section 2 above, are not allowed in the public system. Consequently equilibrium is inefficient and might not exist. The peer groups idea was introduced by Arnott and Rowse (1987), who modeled the optimal partition into schools as a tradeoff between demand for good schools, which depends on income, and efficient provision of peer-group externalities, which depends on ability. See also Brueckner and Lee (1989). Epple and Romano (1996b) analyze a similar model from an equilibrium perspective, pointing out that public schools with no flexibility in pricing will end up with the low-ability and low-income students, while students with high income, high ability or both will end up in private schools. Private schools will price so that students with high income and low ability, who demand good peers, will cross subsidize students with low income and high ability. Public schooling introduces an inefficiency by not pricing in a way that internalizes peer-group externalities. Poor kids with high ability can be lifted out of poverty by the self-interested tuition policies of private schools trying to create peer-group effects. However Fernandez and Rogerson (1995) give a reason to be skeptical about public subsidies to education when it is only partially subsidized. They point out that because there must be a private supplement, high-income residents are more likely to take advantage of the subsidy, which therefore becomes a transfer from the poor to the rich.

There is another body of literature on education which focuses on the inefficiencies that arise because of second-best pricing policies, but does not concern itself with the public–private interface. In the free-mobility model of Fernandez and Rogerson (1996), the equilibrium level of education is determined by the average income in groups. They show that, due to income taxation, the population will typically end up partitioned such that the average income (hence average achievement) in two jurisdictions could both by increased by moving some people from a wealthy community to a poorer one. They investigate policies to undo that inefficiency.

Benabou (1993) introduces the notion that there are two types of externalities in the education environment. First, an environment with many highly skilled workers makes it cheaper to become skillful. In addition, the productivity of agents with different types of skills depends on their relative numbers. The two types of externalities interact in complex ways, but in particular there is no way to augment the reward for becoming highly skilled to reflect the externality it confers in the education process. Consequently highly skilled agents might want to form homogeneous communities even though, for efficiency, they should mix with less skilled agents in order to create positive externalities. Similar ideas are developed by Benabou (1996a,b).

6. Some new ideas

In this chapter I have tried to focus on ideas that have emerged since the previous handbook articles. Some of the new ideas do not fit easily into the categories above, so I include them separately.

The section above on the local objective function takes a rather normative view. It asks what the local objective function *should* be in order that the economy achieves efficiency in consumers' location choices and provisions of local services. A completely different idea is proposed by Glomm and Lagunoff (1998). Instead of assuming that jurisdictions compete in their provisions of local public goods and taxes, they assume that jurisdictions compete in the *rules* for choosing local public goods and taxes. In particular, they assume that one jurisdiction offers residents the opportunity to make voluntary contributions to the local public goods, and that another lets the residents vote on the level of local public goods, funding it with coercive income taxes. They show circumstances in which either both communities or only one can survive. Although the two proposed rules do not seem particularly realistic, the idea that jurisdictions compete in their institutional arrangements is an interesting one.

It has long been recognized that spillovers between geographic jurisdictions are rampant. Residents of one jurisdiction might visit the local facilities of another jurisdiction, such as museums, and are harmed by pollution spillovers such as acid rain. The local objective functions described in Section 4 would not account for such spillovers. However, Jehiel (1997) introduces the idea that local public goods with spillovers are established by a bargaining process in which jurisdictions can swap externalities and establish their local public goods cooperatively. Nevertheless, because of migration between the jurisdictions, he finds that the local public goods will not be provided efficiently. The result depends on some specific assumptions about bargaining and instruments of reciprocity, but opens a new line of inquiry about whether such bargaining should be restricted or encouraged.

An area where local public economics and political economy overlap is in trying to understand the formation of markets. Group formation can affect trade either because of complementarities between private goods and the public services or other features of the group (see Example 4 above), or because the public services themselves facilitate trade [Casella (1992), Casella and Feinstein (2001)].

None of the above models of local public goods describes the migration features that nations actually employ. The club model is not a good approximation to jurisdiction formation because jurisdictions do not use the kind of externality-based pricing required by Example 2, because there is no free entry, because jurisdictions are not profit maximizers, and because of the bundling discussed in Section 3. The free mobility notion is a good approximation to relationships between sub-jurisdictions such as states in the USA and provinces in Canada, but the theory is very limited. At the level of nations themselves, migration is severely restricted. None of the models above explains why this should be so. Is there an efficiency reason that the intra-country rules for migration should be different from the inter-country rules for migration? This question has not been addressed, but a related question is what should be the rules of migration among states if they could be set constitutionally within a nation. Jehiel and Scotchmer (2001) introduce three new migration rules, and compare them with free mobility. These are (i) admission by majority vote, (ii) admission by unanimous consent, and (iii) admission with public good demands above a threshold.

Neither the club model nor free mobility adequately describes secession. Alesina and Spolaore (1997) and LeBreton and Weber (2000) explore a hybrid type of model which permits coordinated deviations, but possibly with restrictions on side payments. Instead of voting on the level at which a public service will be provided, the residents vote on the location of a "capital city". Each agent's preferred location is near his residence, in order to minimize transportation costs, and the median voter will get his preferred location. If a group of unfavored agents secedes (those who are distant from the capital city), they can locate a new capital city closer to their own residences. The objective of these papers is to explain when a country will be immune to secession, and also to explain the distribution schemes that will create stability. LeBreton and Weber show that side payments can be used to create stability, and stability will require side payments such that agents' utility declines with distance from the capital city. That is, the distant agents are somewhat "bribed" not to secede, but not so much that wellbeing is entirely equalized. Those located close to the capital city are still better off than those located far away.

References

Alesina, A., and E. Spolaore (1997), "On the number and size of nations", Quarterly Journal of Economics 112:1027–1056.

Anderson, R.M. (1985), "Strong core theorems with nonconvex preferences," Econometrica 53:1283–1293.

Anderson, S.P., A. de Palma and J.-F. Thisse (1992), Discrete Choice Theory of Product Differentiation (MIT Press, Cambridge, MA).

Arnott, R., and R.E. Grieson (1981), "Optimal fiscal policy for a state and local government", Journal of Urban Economics 9:23–48.

Arnott, R., and J. Rowse (1987), "Peer group effects and educational attainment", Journal of Public Economics 32:287–305.

Arnott, R., and J.E. Stiglitz (1979), "Aggregate land rents, expenditure on public goods, and optimal city size", Quarterly Journal of Economics 93:471–500.

Barham, V., R. Boadway, M. Marchand and P. Pestieau (1997), "Volunteer work and club size", Journal of Public Economics 65:9–22.

Benabou, R. (1993), "Workings of a city: location, education and production", Quarterly Journal of Economics 108:619–652.

Benabou, R. (1996a), "Equity and efficiency in human capital investment: the local connection", Review of Economic Studies 63:237–64.

Benabou, R. (1996b), "Heterogeneity, stratification and growth: macroeconomic implications of community structure and school finance", American Economic Review 86:584–609.

Berglas, E. (1976a), "On the theory of clubs", Papers and Proceedings of the American Economic Association 66:116–121.

Berglas, E. (1976b), "Distribution of tastes and skills and the provision of local public goods", Journal of Public Economics 6:409–423.

Berglas, E. (1981), "The market provision of club goods once again", Journal of Public Economics 15:389–393.

Berglas, E. (1984), "Quantities, qualities, and multiple public services in the Tiebout model", Journal of Public Economics 25:299–322.

Berglas, E., and D. Pines (1981), "Clubs, local public goods, and transportation models: a synthesis", Journal of Public Economics 15:141–162.

Berliant, M., and K. Dunz (1999), "A foundation of location theory: existence of equilibrium, the welfare theorems and the core", Mimeograph (Washington University, St. Louis).

Bewley, T.F. (1981), "A critique of Tiebout's theory of local public expenditures", Econometrica 49: 713–740.

Boadway, R. (1982), "On the method of taxation and the provision of local public goods: comment", American Economic Review 72:846–851.

Boadway, R., P. Pestieau and D.E. Wildasin (1989), "Noncooperative behavior and efficient provision of public goods", Public Finance – Finances Publiques 44:1–7.

Brueckner, J.K. (1979), "Property values, local public expenditures and economic efficiency", Journal of Public Economics 11:223–245.

Brueckner, J.K. (1983), "Property value maximization and public sector efficiency", Journal of Urban Economics 14:1–16.

Brueckner, J.K. (1994), "Tastes, skills and local public goods", Journal of Urban Economics 35:201–220.

Brueckner, J.K., and K. Lee (1989), "Club theory with a peer group effect", Regional Science and Urban Economics 19:399–420.

Brueckner, J.K., and K. Lee (1991), "Economies of scope and multiproduct clubs", Public Finance Quarterly 19:193–208.

Buchanan, J.M. (1965), "An economic theory of clubs", Economica 33:1–14.

Casella, A. (1992), "On markets and clubs: economic and political integration of regions with unequal productivity", American Economic Review Papers and Proceedings, May 1992.

Casella, A., and J. Feinstein (2001), "The role of market size on the formation of jurisdictions", Review of Economic Studies 68:83–108.

Cole, H.L., and E.C. Prescott (1997), "Valuation equilibrium with clubs", Journal of Economic Theory 74(1):19–39.

Conley, J., and H. Konishi (2002), "The Tiebout theorem: on the existence of asymptotically efficient migration-proof equilibria", Journal of Public Economics, forthcoming.

Conley, J., and M.H. Wooders (1997), "Equivalence of the core and competitive equilibrium in a Tiebout economy with crowding types", Journal of Urban Economics 41:421–440.

Conley, J., and M.H. Wooders (1998), "Anonymous Lindahl pricing in a Tiebout economy with crowding types", Canadian Journal of Economics 31:952–974.

Conley, J., and M.H. Wooders (2001), "Tiebout economies with different genetic types and endogenously chosen crowding characteristics", Journal of Economic Theory 98:261–294.

Crane, R. (1990), "Price specification and the demand for public goods", Journal of Public Economics 43:93–106.

Cremer, H., M. Marchand and P. Pestieau (1997), "Investment in local public services: Nash equilibrium and social optimum", Journal of Public Economics 65:23–35.

de Bartolome, C.A.M. (1990), "Equilibrium and inefficiency in a community model with peer group effects", Journal of Political Economy 98:110–133.

Dunz, K. (1989), "Some comments on majority rule equilibria in local public good economies", Journal of Economic Theory 19:228–234.

Ellickson, B. (1971), "Jurisdictional fragmentation and residential choice", American Economic Review 61:334–339.

Ellickson, B. (1973), "A generalization of the pure theory of public goods," American Economic Review 63:417–432.

Ellickson, B. (1977), "The politics and economics of decentralization", Journal of Urban Economics 4:135–149.

Ellickson, B. (1979), "Competitive equilibrium with local public goods", Journal of Economic Theory 21:46–61.

Ellickson, B., B. Grodal, S. Scotchmer and W. Zame (1999a), "Clubs and the market", Econometrica 67:1185–1218.

Ellickson, B., B. Grodal, S. Scotchmer and W. Zame (1999b), "A model of firm formation and skills acquisition", Conference paper for the 2000 World Congress of the Econometric Society.

Ellickson, B., B. Grodal, S. Scotchmer and W. Zame (2001), "Clubs and the market: large finite economies", Journal of Economic Theory 101:40–77.

Engl, G., and S. Scotchmer (1996), "The core and the hedonic core: equivalence and comparative statics", Journal of Mathematical Economics 26:209–248.

Epple, D., and G.J. Platt (1998), "Equilibrium and local redistribution in an urban economy when households differ in both preferences and incomes", Journal of Urban Economics 43:23–51.

Epple, D., and R.E. Romano (1996a), "Ends against the middle: determining public service provision when there are private alternatives", Journal of Public Economics 62:297–325.

Epple, D., and R.E. Romano (1996b), "Competition between private and public schools, vouchers and peer group effects", American Economic Review 88:33–66.

Epple, D., and R.E. Romano (1996c), "Public provision of private goods", Journal of Political Economy 104:57–84.

Epple, D., and R.E. Romano (2002), "Neighborhood schools, choice and the distribution of educational benefits", in: Caroline Hoxby, ed., The Economic Analysis of School Choice (National Bureau of Economic Research, Cambridge, MA) forthcoming.

Epple, D., and T. Romer (1991), "Mobility and redistribution", Journal of Political Economy 99:828–858.

Epple, D., and A. Zelenitz (1981), "The implications of competition among jurisdictions: does Tiebout need politics?", Journal of Political Economy 89:1197–1217.

Epple, D., R. Filimon and T. Romer (1983), "Housing, voting, and moving: equilibrium in a model of local public goods with multiple jurisdictions," Research in Urban Economics 3:59–90.

Epple, D., R. Filimon and T. Romer (1984), "Equilibrium among local jurisdictions: toward an integrated approach of voting and residential choice", Journal of Public Economics 24:281–308.

Epple, D., R. Filimon and T. Romer (1993), "Existence of voting and housing equilibrium in a system of communities with property taxes", Regional Science and Urban Economics 23:585–610.

Fernandez, R. (1997), "Odd versus even: comparative statics in multicommunity models", Journal of Public Economics 65:177–192.

Fernandez, R., and R. Rogerson (1995), "On the political economy of education subsidies", Review of Economic Studies 62:249–262.

Fernandez, R., and R. Rogerson (1996), "Income distribution, communities and the quality of public education", Quarterly Journal of Economics 111:135–164.

Fernandez, R., and R. Rogerson (1998), "Education-finance reform and the distribution of education resources", American Economic Review 88:789–812.

Fernandez, R., and R. Rogerson (1999), "Equity and resources: an analysis of education finance systems", Mimeograph (New York University).

Fujita, M. (1989), Urban Economic Theory (Cambridge University Press, Cambridge, UK).

Gilles, R., and S. Scotchmer (1997), "On decentralization in replicated club economies with multiple private goods", Journal of Economic Theory 72:363–387.

Glomm, G., and R. Lagunoff (1998), "A Tiebout theory of public vs private provision of collective goods", Journal of Public Economics 68:91–112.

Glomm, G., and B. Ravikumar (1998), "Opting out of publicly provided services: a majority voting result", Social Choice and Welfare 15:187–199.

Gordon, R.H. (1983), "An optimal tax approach to fiscal federalism", Quarterly Journal of Economics 8:567–586.

Greenberg, J. (1983), "Local public goods with mobility: existence and optimality of a general equilibrium", Journal of Economic Theory 30:17–33.

Greenberg, J., and B. Shitovitz (1988), "Consistent voting rules for competitive local public goods economies", Journal of Economic Theory 46:223–236.

Greenberg, J., and S. Weber (1986), "Strong Tiebout equilibrium under restricted preference domain", Journal of Economic Theory 38:101–117.

Grodal, B. (1972), "A second remark on the core of an atomless economy", Econometrica 40(3): 581–583.

Guesnerie, R., and C. Oddou (1981), "Second best taxation as a game", Journal of Economic Theory 25:67–91.

Hamilton, B.W. (1975), "Zoning and property taxation in a system of local governments", Urban Studies 12:205–211.

Helsley, R.W., and W.C. Strange (1991), "Exclusion and the theory of clubs", Canadian Journal of Economics 24:889–899.

Helsley, R.W., and W.C. Strange (1998), "Private government", Journal of Public Economics 69:281–304.

Helsley, R.W., and W.C. Strange (2000a), "Potential competition and public sector performance", Regional Science and Urban Economics 30:405–428.

Helsley, R.W., and W.C. Strange (2000b), "Social interactions and the institutions of local government", American Economic Review 90:1477–1490.

Henderson, J.V. (1985), "The Tiebout hypothesis: bring back the entrepreneurs", Journal of Political Economy 93:248–264.

Hochman, O. (1981), "Land rents, optimal taxation and local fiscal independence in an economy with local public goods", Journal of Public Economics 15:59–85.

Hochman, O. (1982a), "Congestable local public goods in an urban setting", Journal of Urban Economics 11:290–310.

Hochman, O. (1982b), "Clubs in an urban setting", Journal of Urban Economics 12:85–101.

Hochman, O. (1990), "Cities, scale economies, local goods and local governments", Urban Studies 27:45–66.

Hochman, O., D. Pines and J.-F. Thisse (1995), "On the optimal structure of local governments", American Economic Review 85:1224–1240.

Inman, R.P., and D.L. Rubinfeld (1996), "Designing tax policy in federalist economies: an overview", Journal of Public Economics 60:307–334.

Ireland, N.J. (1990), "The mix of social and private provision of goods and services", Journal of Public Economics 43:201–219.

Jehiel, P. (1997), "Bargaining between benevolent jurisdictions or when delegation induces inefficiencies", Journal of Public Economics 65(1):61–74.

Jehiel, P., and S. Scotchmer (1993), "On the right of exclusion in jurisdiction formation", Working Paper 96-05 (CERAS, École Nationale des Ponts et Chaussées, Paris).

Jehiel, P., and S. Scotchmer (2001), "Constitutional rules of exclusion in jurisdiction formation", Review of Economic Studies 68:393–413.

Kim, J. (1998), "Local property taxation with external land ownership", Journal of Public Economics 48:113–135.

Konishi, H. (1996), "Voting with ballots and feet: existence of equilibrium in a local public good economy", Journal of Economic Theory 68:480–509.

Konishi, H., M. LeBreton and S. Weber (1997), "Pure strategy Nash equilibrium in a group formation game with positive externalities", Games and Economic Behavior 21:161–182.

Konishi, H., M. LeBreton and S. Weber (1998), "Equilibrium in a finite local public goods economy", Journal of Economic Theory 79:224–244.

Krelove, R. (1993), "The persistence and inefficiency of property tax finance of local public expenditures", Journal of Public Economics 51:415–35.

LeBreton, M., and S. Weber (2000), "The art of making everybody happy: how to prevent a secession", Mimeograph (CORE, Catholic University of Louvain-la-Neuve, Belgium).

Mas-Colell, A. (1975), "A model of equilibrium with differentiated commodities", Journal of Mathematical Economics 2:263–296.

Mas-Colell, A. (1979), "A refinement of the core equivalence theorem", Economics Letters 3:307–310.

Mas-Colell, A. (1980), "Efficiency and decentralization in the pure theory of public goods", Quarterly Journal of Economics 94:625–641.

McGuire, M. (1991), "Group composition, collective consumption and collaborative production", American Economic Review 81:1391–1408.

Mieszkowski, P.M., and G.R. Zodrow (1989), "Taxation and the Tiebout model", Journal of Economic Literature 27:1098–1146.

Nechyba, T.J. (1997a), "Existence of equilibrium and stratification in local and hierarchical tiebout economies with property taxes and voting", Economic Theory 10:277–304.

Nechyba, T.J. (1997b), "Local property and state income taxes: the role of interjurisdictional competition and collusion", Journal of Political Economy 105:351–384.

Oates, W.E. (1999), "An essay on fiscal federalism", Journal of Economic Literature 37:1120–1149.

Oates, W.E., and R.M. Schwab (1991), "Community composition and the provision of local public goods: a normative analysis", Journal of Public Economics 44:217–238.

Ostroy, J. (1980), "The no-surplus condition as a characterization of perfectly competitive equilibrium", Journal of Economic Theory 22:183–207.

Pauly, M.V. (1967), "Clubs, commonality and the core: an integration of game theory and the theory of public goods", Economica 34:314–324.

Pauly, M.V. (1970a), "Optimality, 'public' goods, and local governments: a general theoretical analysis", Journal of Political Economy 78:572–585.

Pauly, M.V. (1970b), "Cores and clubs", Public Choice 9:53–65.

Pines, D. (1985), "Profit maximizing developers and the optimal provision of local public goods in a closed system of a few cities", Revue Economique 36:45–62.

Pines, D. (1991), "Tiebout without politics", Regional Science and Urban Economics 21:469–489.

Pogodzinski, J.M., and D.L. Sjoquist (1993), "Alternative tax regimes in a local public good economy", Journal of Public Economics 50:115–141.

Rose-Ackerman, S. (1979), "Market models of local government: exit, voting and the land market", Journal of Urban Economics 6:319–337.

Rubinfeld, D.L. (1987), "The economics of the local public sector", in: A.J. Auerbach and M. Feldstein, eds., Handbook of Public Economics, Vol. 2 (North Holland, Amsterdam) pp. 571–646.

Schmeidler, D. (1972), "A remark on the core of an atomless economy", Econometrica 40:579–580.

Scotchmer, S. (1985a), "Profit maximizing clubs", Journal of Public Economics 27:25–45.

Scotchmer, S. (1985b), "Two-tier pricing of shared facilities in a free-entry equilibrium", The RAND Journal of Economics 16(4):456–472.

Scotchmer, S. (1986), "Local public goods in an equilibrium: how pecuniary externalities matter", Regional Science and Urban Economics 16:463–481.

Scotchmer, S. (1994), "Public goods and the invisible hand", in: J. Quigley and E. Smolensky, eds., Modern Public Finance (Harvard University Press, Cambridge, MA).

Scotchmer, S. (1997), "On price-taking equilibria in club economies with nonanonymous crowding", Journal of Public Economics 65:75–87.

Scotchmer, S., and M.H. Wooders (1987a), "Competitive equilibrium and the core in club economies with anonymous crowding", Journal of Public Economics 34:159–173.

Scotchmer, S., and M.H. Wooders (1987b), "Competitive equilibrium and the core in club economies with nonanonymous crowding", Mimeo (University of California, Berkeley).

Shapley, L.S., and M. Shubik (1966), "Quasi-cores in a monetary economy with non-convex preferences", Econometrica 34:805–827.

Sonstelie, J.C., and P.R. Portney (1978), "Profit maximizing communities and the theory of local public expenditure", Journal of Urban Economics 5:263–277.

Starrett, D.A. (1980), "On the method of taxation and the provision of local public goods," American Economic Review 70:380–392.

Starrett, D.A. (1981), "Land value capitalization in local public finance", Journal of Political Economy 89:306–327.

Starrett, D.A. (1988), Foundations of Public Economics (Cambridge University Press, Cambridge, UK).

Stiglitz, J.E. (1977), "The Theory of Local Public Goods", in: M.S. Feldstein and R.P. Inman, eds., The Economics of Public Services (Macmilllan, New York).

Stiglitz, J.E. (1983), "Public goods in open economies with heterogeneous individuals", in: J.-F. Thisse and H.G. Zoller, eds., Locational Analysis of Public Facilities (North-Holland, Amsterdam).

Strazheim, M. (1987), "The theory of urban residential location", in: E.S. Mills, ed., Handbook of Regional and Urban Economics, Vol. 2, Urban Economics (Elsevier, New York) pp. 717–758.

Thisse, J.-F., and D.E. Wildasin (1992), "Public facility location and urban spatial structure – equilibrium and welfare analysis", Journal of Public Economics 48:83–118.

Thisse, J.-F., and H.G. Zoller, eds (1982), Locational Analysis of Public Facilities (Elsevier, Amsterdam).

Tiebout, C.M. (1956), "A pure theory of local expenditures", Journal of Political Economy 64:416–424.

Westhoff, F. (1977), "Existence of equilibrium in economies with a local public good", Journal of Economic Theory 14:84–112.

Wheaton, W.C. (1993), "Land capitalization, Tiebout mobility, and the role of zoning regulations", Journal of Urban Economics 34:102–117.

Wildasin, D.E. (1979), "Local public goods, property values, and local public choice", Journal of Urban Economics 6:521–534.

Wildasin, D.E. (1980), "Locational efficiency in a federal system", Regional Science and Urban Economics 10:453–471.

Wildasin, D.E. (1987), "Theoretical Analysis of Local Public Economics", in: E.S. Mills, ed., Handbook of Regional and Urban Economics, Vol. 2 (North-Holland, Amsterdam) pp. 1130–1178.

Wildasin, D.E. (1988), "Nash equilibria in models of fiscal competititon", Journal of Public Economics 35:229–240.

Wildasin, D.E., and J.D. Wilson (1991), "Theoretical issues in local public economics – an overview", Regional Science and Urban Economics 21:317–331.

Wilson, J.D. (1986), "A theory of inter-regional tax competition", Journal of Urban Economics 19: 296–315.

Wilson, J.D. (1997), "Property taxation, congestion, and local public goods", Journal of Public Economics 64:207–217.

Wooders, M.H. (1978), "Equilibria, the core, and jurisdiction structures in economies with a local public good", Journal of Economic Theory 18:328–348; and (1981) "Correction", Journal of Economic Theory 25:144–151.

Wooders, M.H. (1980), "The Tiebout hypothesis: near optimality in local public goods economies", Econometrica 48(6):1467–1485.

Wooders, M.H. (1988), "Stability of jurisdiction structures in economies with a local public good", Mathematical Social Sciences 15:24–29.

Wooders, M.H. (1989), "A Tiebout theorem", Mathematical Social Sciences 18:33–55.

Wooders, M.H. (1992), "Large games and economies with effective small groups", Sonderforschungs-bereich 303 (University of Bonn, Germany) March, revised June.

Wooders, M.H. (1997), "Equivalence of Lindahl equilibrium with participation prices and the core", Economic Theory 9:115–127.

Part 6

PUBLIC EXPENDITURE PROGRAMS

Chapter 30

PUBLICLY PROVIDED EDUCATION *

ERIC A. HANUSHEK

Stanford University; and NBER

Contents

* Helpful comments and suggestions were provided by Alan Auerbach, John Kain, Susanna Loeb, Derek Neal, Tom Nechyba, and Steve Rivkin.

Handbook of Public Economics, Volume 4, Edited by A.J. Auerbach and M. Feldstein

Abstract

Historically, most attention in public programs has been given to the resources devoted to the activity, and resources have been used to index both commitment and quality. Education differs from other areas of public expenditure because direct measures of outcomes are available, making it is possible to consider results and, by implication, to consider the efficiency of provision. Early interpretations of the evidence, emanating from popular interpretations of the Coleman Report that "schools do not make a difference", are incorrect, but the basic evidence behind the statement suggests serious performance problems of government supply, because purchased inputs to schools are not closely related to outcomes. This paper reviews that evidence along with providing an evaluation of the various controversial aspects including issues of causality, consumer behavior, and estimation approaches. Two detailed policy areas are discussed in terms of the evidence on performance: public versus private provision and the financing of schools.

Keywords

public education, school finance, efficiency, school quality, school achievement, peers, local public finance, international achievement, private schools, school choice

JEL classification: H4, I2

Introduction

The provision of education is a major public sector activity around the world, and both developed and developing nations frequently act as if ensuring an appropriate education ranks close in priority to providing for the safety and security of their citizens. And, much like these other fundamental areas, governments not only provide a majority of the funding for schools but also typically operate the schools. The objectives of this chapter include not only a consideration of the purposes and rationale for governmental involvement in schooling but also an evaluation of performance in addressing the underlying goals.

Even though government's presence in education is commonly accepted without much question, the degree and form of involvement warrants attention. The amount and quality of education is known to contribute to the income and well-being of individuals. Recent analyses also suggest that education has a powerful effect on the strength and growth of national economies. These factors do not, however, necessarily justify the extent or manner of governmental involvement.

Regardless of one's opinion about the involvement of government, it is valuable to assess how well government does at providing education. Historically, most attention in public programs has been given to the resources devoted to the activity, and resources have been used to index both commitment and quality. Such a perspective, while forced on many areas of governmental activity by lack of good measures of outcomes, is obviously quite limited. Importantly, education increasingly differs from other areas of public expenditure because direct measures of outcomes are becoming more readily available. Thus, instead of measuring governmental human capital investments just by expenditure, it is possible to consider results and, by implication, to consider the efficiency of provision. Such consideration reveals a complicated picture of expenditure patterns that are not matched by performance, although the conclusions and policy implications to be derived from this general finding are not straightforward. Because of the ability to consider performance directly, the study of publicly provided educational services also provides a possible window on one of the critical policy questions that continuously arises in mixed economies: how well does government do in directing society's resources to meet its public goals? Nonetheless, given our current state of knowledge, considerable uncertainty necessarily remains about whether or not any inefficiencies of the educational system are typical of governmentally provided services.

The distribution of educational outcomes is also an element of any evaluation of educational performance. Education is not a pure public good, available without diminution to all. Instead, it is a complicated intermediate good that is partially produced by government through provision that varies across local jurisdictions and that interacts with the endowments and actions of students and families. Substantial portions of the rewards of more schooling accrue directly to the individual. Thus, education has more of the character of a publicly provided private good. As such, the distribution of outcomes is not only an important concern in judging the performance of government provision but also an object of policy.

Education clearly encompasses a wider variety of things than can be readily covered here. The central issues analyzed are the organization, financing, and production of educational services. This discussion is placed within the context of the role of government in intervening in the market for education. The following section more fully delineates the scope of this investigation and provides a roadmap through the subsequent discussions.

1. Scope and roadmap for discussion

This essay comes in the midst of a rapidly expanding analytical base on the economics of education. The importance attached to human capital in many areas of economic research plus the intense policy concerns about schooling have heightened interest in scholarly exploration of the education sector per se. A primary purpose of this overall discussion is to highlight the most promising lines of research and to project future areas of productive research. In doing this, some limits on the scope of this endeavor are necessary.

Much of the discussion centers on experiences in the USA with the provision of primary and secondary education. This focus permits a clear development of the issues of service delivery that can be based on a very extensive analytical base. It is, nonetheless, a somewhat arbitrary delineation of the overall set of potential topics. Although the provision of formal schooling by government includes extensive interventions in tertiary education, higher education involves quite different institutional structures. More importantly, little progress has been made in the measurement of outcomes of higher education, thus precluding direct analysis of the financing and production issues that are central to this analysis[1].

The restriction to formal schooling situations excludes important aspects of human capital investment. Most countries have governmental involvement in various aspects of job training, including both formal vocational training and work with private employers. This involvement ranges from governmentally provided training programs to interventions in apprentice programs arranged directly with firms. The institutional

---

[1] As developed below, the largest issues in primary and secondary education are whether or not various structures and financing schemes lead to qualitative differences in the performance of schools. For primary and secondary education, a variety of readily available measures of student outcomes, including test scores and differential labor market performance, permits direct analysis. But, no similar measures of higher education outcomes – beyond pure quantity differences – are available and accepted. A few attempts to look at labor market outcomes of higher educational quality are available [e.g., Solmon (1973), Sewell and Hauser (1975), James and Alsalam (1993), Behrman, Rosenzweig and Taubman (1996), Behrman, Kletzer, McPherson and Schapiro (1998), Eide, Brewer and Ehrenberg (1998), Dale and Krueger (1999)], but the field remains largely undeveloped.

structure of such programs differs widely across countries, but it is frequently more closely linked to the labor ministries of government than to the education ministries. This separation of function, while perhaps unfortunate from an overall policy perspective, implies that the issues and analyses of training programs have developed very differently from those related to formal schooling[2]. This analysis also generally follows the American custom of separating preschool programs from formal schooling. Again, however, a full treatment of human capital investment policies should span this period, because there is some indication that investments early have high pay-offs, and some discussion is provided below[3].

The restriction generally to US experience is an unfortunate limitation forced by the availability of comparable studies from other countries and other institutional experiences. The wide international variation in governmental institutions should be and is an advantage for some analyses. While the limitation is rapidly disappearing with significant data development and analytic efforts around the world, the more limited range of analyses that are currently available makes consideration of the international similarities and differences impossible to develop in depth. To the extent possible, comparisons with both developed and developing countries are made throughout this discussion, but they generally cannot be summarized and organized as clearly as the US experiences.

The discussion begins with an overview of stylized facts about schooling and with a discussion of how human capital enters into overall economic output and performance. A consideration of the conceptual basis for governmental involvement in education follows this.

The performance of government in providing education is a central element to the entire interpretation of both research and policy in this area. Beginning with a general conceptual model of the educational production process, detailed attention is given to what research has said about the effectiveness of inputs to education. This summary of analytical studies leads naturally to discussion of potential analytical issues that arise in the area and to how one might interpret the range of results.

The study of school performance is related to a variety of organizational issues that are key elements of governmental intervention and participation in education. Two of the most significant organizational aspects are the relationship between public schools and private schools and the form and means of financing education. The substantial literatures on each provide insights into these significant policy choices.

Finally, even though there is rapid expansion of research in this area, a number of areas remain underexplored. The last section identifies a series of issues that appear to be productive areas for the continual development of the area.

---

[2] A review of materials on job training can be found in Heckman, LaLonde and Smith (1999). For a general consideration of optimal human capital investment across the life cycle, see Heckman, Lochner and Taber (2000).

[3] See, for example, Gramlich (1986), Barnett (1992), Heckman (2000), Currie and Thomas (1995, 1999), U.S. General Accounting Office (1997), Currie (2001).

2. Overview of schooling issues

Economists generally view schooling as an investment both by students and by the society at large. Each incurs costs, and each reaps rewards. For a student, the costs of education include the direct costs of tuition, books, and other school-related expenditures as well as the income that the student forgoes when attending school instead of taking a paying job. Similarly society incurs direct costs in subsidizing a school system that provides free or heavily subsidized education to its citizens. It also forgoes the opportunity to devote the skills, people and resources that are engaged in education to other projects. This viewpoint – regarding education as an investment – dates back to the 17th century with the writings of Sir William Petty and includes work by Adam Smith and other influential economists [see Kiker (1968)]. It was brought into mainstream economics, however, by Schultz (1961, 1963), Becker (1993) and Mincer (1970, 1974) and has become the basis of a steady stream of subsequent theoretical and empirical analyses.

2.1. Quantity of schooling

A look at the history of the twentieth century suggests that schooling has generally been a good investment, buoyed by steady increases in the demand for skilled workers. Individuals have dramatically increased their own investments in education.

In the USA, at the beginning of the twentieth century, only six percent of the adult population had finished high school. After the first world war, high school graduation rates began to increase rapidly. But changes in education work their way only slowly through the overall population. By 1940, only half of Americans aged 25 or older had completed more than eight years of school, that is, had had any high-school education at all. Not until 1967 did attainment of the median adult aged 25 or over exceed high school[4]. Since 1967, however, the increase in the number of years of schooling completed by Americans has slowed. The young adult population, aged 25 to 29, has had stable completion rates for almost two decades. At the turn of the 21st century, over 80% of Americans over 25 had completed high school or more.

The changes in other nations have been even more dramatic. Table 1 shows the percentages of different age groups completing upper secondary schools for a sample of more developed countries[5]. The different age groups effectively trace the normal schooling in different decades in the past, so that the changes with age show the rate of increase in schooling. While the USA has been stable since the 1960s, most of the other countries have undergone massive increases in high school completion – mirroring the historical developments in the USA before and immediately after World War II [Goldin (1998)].

---

[4] See U.S. Bureau of the Census (1975, 2000) and Goldin (1998).
[5] A comprehensive comparison of schooling across nations can be found in Barro and Lee (2001).

Table 1
Percentage of population attaining upper secondary education or more, by country: 1999[a]

Country	Ages 25–64	Ages 25–34	Ages 35–44	Ages 45–54	Ages 55–64
OECD countries					
Australia	57	65	59	55	44
Austria[b]	74	83	78	69	59
Belgium	57	73	61	50	36
Canada	79	87	83	78	62
Czech Republic	86	93	89	85	75
Denmark	80	87	80	79	70
Finland	72	86	82	67	46
France[b]	62	76	65	57	42
Germany	81	85	85	81	73
Greece	50	71	58	42	24
Hungary	67	80	76	70	36
Iceland	56	64	59	53	40
Ireland[b]	51	67	56	41	31
Italy	42	55	50	37	21
Japan	81	93	92	79	60
Korea	66	93	72	47	28
Luxembourg	56	61	57	52	41
Mexico	20	25	22	16	9
New Zealand	74	79	77	71	60
Norway[b]	85	94	89	79	68
Poland[b]	54	62	59	53	37
Portugal	21	30	21	15	11
Spain	35	55	41	25	13
Sweden	77	87	81	74	61
Switzerland	82	89	84	79	72
Turkey	22	26	23	18	12
UK[b]	62	66	63	60	53
USA	87	88	88	88	81
OECD mean	62	72	66	58	45

continued on next page

Table 1, *continued*

Country	Ages 25–64	Ages 25–34	Ages 35–44	Ages 45–54	Ages 55–64
World Education Indicators participants					
Brazil[b]	24	29	27	21	12
Chile[b]	43	55	45	35	24
Indonesia	22	33	21	15	9
Jordan	51	55	55	43	25
Malaysia[b]	35	50	35	20	10
Peru[b]	46	58	48	35	24
Philippines	44	55	45	34	24
Sri Lanka[b]	36	46	36	31	21
Thailand[b]	16	23	17	9	6
Tunisia	8	11	9	6	3
Uruguay[b]	32	39	34	28	20
Zimbabwe	29	51	19	11	7

[a] Source: Organisation for Economic Cooperation and Development (2001).
[b] Year of reference is 1998.

The benefits of education to individuals are also clear. The average incomes of workers with a high school education remain significantly above those of the less educated, and the average income of workers with a college education now dwarf those of the high-school educated. In the USA, the rapidly increasing earnings of college-educated workers during the past two decades currently provides them with a premium of more than 70% higher earnings than a high school graduate with similar job experience[6].

The earnings patterns elsewhere in the world appear quantitatively more varied, but there is a strong similarity in the earnings effects associated with more schooling. Table 2 shows earnings distributions by level of schooling and by gender across the adult labor force, again for a sample of developed countries. While the earning distribution is more compressed in some countries than others – probably reflecting characteristics of labor markets – invariably there are obvious gains in earnings to more

---

[6] More detail on the patterns of earnings can be found in Murphy and Welch (1989, 1992), Kosters (1991), Pierce and Welch (1996) and Deere (2001). McMahon (1991) reports slightly lower private rates of return for high school completion than for college completion, although they remain substantial. These calculations all rely on just salary differentials, and greater equality in the provision of fringe benefits may act to compress the differences for total compensation. However, no analysis of schooling returns in terms of total compensation is available.

Table 2

Relative earnings of the population with income from employment, by level of educational attainment for the population 25 to 64 years of age (*upper secondary education = 100*)[a,b]

Country	Year	Male			Female		
		Lower secondary and below	Higher education (nonuni-versity)	Higher education (university)	Lower secondary and below	Higher education (nonuni-versity)	Higher education (university)
Australia	1997	87	120	144	85	113	154
Canada	1997	84	109	148	76	116	164
Czech Republic	1999	75	177	178	72	127	172
Denmark	1998	87	122	148	89	118	144
Finland	1997	94	128	186	100	122	176
France	1999	88	128	178	79	131	158
Germany	1998	77	105	149	85	104	160
Hungary	1999	72	240	218	67	138	159
Ireland*	1997	72	100	149	57	129	171
Italy	1998	54	n.a.	n.a.	61	n.a.	n.a.
Korea	1998	88	105	143	69	118	160
Netherlands	1997	86	142	138	71	128	145
New Zealand	1999	76	n.a.	n.a.	74	n.a.	n.a.
Norway	1998	85	125	133	84	142	136
Portugal	1998	61	149	188	62	131	190
Spain	1996	75	96	178	68	82	155
Sweden	1998	87	n.a.	n.a.	89	n.a.	n.a.
Switzerland	1999	81	122	144	73	131	154
UK	1999	73	126	159	68	139	193
USA	1999	65	119	183	63	120	170
Country mean		78	130	163	75	123	162

[a] Source: Organisation for Economic Cooperation and Development (2001).
[b] n.a., not available.

schooling. Not only are wages higher for the better educated, but they also tend to enjoy greater job opportunities and suffer less unemployment [U.S. Department of Education (1996a), Organisation for Economic Cooperation and Development (2001)].

For individuals the increased relative incomes of more educated people have been sufficient to offset the costs. An individual can expect significant financial benefit from extended schooling, even after appropriately considering costs[7]. Individuals also gain non-financial benefits from education. For example, there is evidence that more educated people make better choices concerning health, so they tend to live longer and to have healthier lives. There is also evidence that the children of more educated parents get more out of school. They attend longer and learn more. Such benefits of schooling simply reinforce those from the labor market[8].

The common interpretation of the overall returns is that high technology economies produce large demands for skilled workers, workers who can adapt to new technologies and manage complicated production processes effectively. Formal models with this character are developed in Nelson and Phelps (1966) and Welch (1970) and summarized in the ideas of dealing with disequilibrium in Schultz (1975).

Society as a whole also benefits from education. National income rises directly with earnings from workers with more and better skills. The more educated are more prone to be civically involved, to vote in local and national elections, and to be a better informed and more responsible electorate[9]. Increases in the level of education are associated with reductions in crime [e.g., Ehrlich (1975), Lochner and Moretti (2001)].

Recent economic studies argue that education may provide economic benefits to society greater than the sum of its benefits to individuals – by providing a rich environment for innovation, scientific discovery, education can accelerate the growth

---

[7] While most economists think of schooling as involving the production of human capital in individuals, the screening or signaling perspective is a clear alternative [e.g., Spence (1973), Wolpin (1977), Weiss (1995)]. The screening model in the extreme suggests that individuals begin schooling with differing abilities and that schooling merely allows employers to identify those with more ability. From the individual's viewpoint, it does not matter what the source of earnings enhancement is, be it production by schools or screening. The individual will be equally induced to make schooling investments based on the comparison of returns and costs. The two may, however, yield quite different incentives to governments to invest, because signaling may lead to different social and private returns to schooling. As a general matter, these models are not identified with just labor market outcome data. A variety of specialized tests under different maintained assumptions about individual motivations and firm behavior have been conducted but have not provided clear support for screening. These tests include looking for "sheepskin effects", particularly high returns to completing given institutional levels, as in Layard and Psacharopoulos (1974). Some support of screening does come from analysis of incentives to complete high school when there are fewer college graduates [Bedard (2001)]. See Riley (2001) for a review of general theoretical and empirical work. The key difficulty with these tests, however, remains that they focus on labor market outcomes, where the private returns to schooling are generally expected to exist independent of the underlying causal mechanism. The analysis below concentrates importantly on outcomes that relate directly to the schooling process (the point where the two models are hypothesized to differ significantly).

[8] See, for example, Michael (1982), Haveman and Wolfe (1984), Wolfe and Zuvekas (1995) and Leibowitz (1974). Many factors are unclear, however, because of questions of causality; see, for example, Farrell and Fuchs (1982).

[9] The pattern of US voting over time can be found in Stanley and Niemi (2000). An analysis of the partial effects of educational attainment (which are positive in the face of overall declines in voter turnout over time) is presented in Teixeira (1992).

rate of the economy; see, for example, the analyses of growth by Lucas (1988), Romer (1990a), Barro (1991), Jorgenson and Fraumeni (1992) and Barro and Sala-I-Martin (1995). The growth effects depending on the aggregate level of education in the economy enter as an externality to the individual. (Estimation by Acemoglu and Angrist (2000), however, questions this effect, at least at the state level).

Education appears also to have helped to achieve both greater social equality and greater equity in the distribution of economic resources. Schooling was a centerpiece of the US War on Poverty in the 1960s, and the benefits of improved schooling are demonstrated in comparisons of the earnings of different social and ethnic groups. Earnings by blacks and whites have converged noticeably since the Second World War, and much of this convergence is attributable to improved educational opportunities for African-Americans [see Smith and Welch (1989), Jaynes and Williams (1989)]. However, as discussed below, that convergence slowed down noticeably in the 1980s with skill differences being cited as a prime determinant [Juhn, Murphy and Pierce (1993)].

Nonetheless, while there are many well-documented associations between amount of schooling – either individually or in the aggregate – and desirable economic outcomes, significant questions remain about the magnitude and interpretation of these relationships. First, the association may misstate the causal impact of changes in schooling for individuals and the aggregate [10]. Second, the average effects may not correspond to the marginal effects. Third, in general externalities have been notoriously elusive and difficult to estimate convincingly, and education proves to be no exception. Finally, the measurement issues, as highlighted in the next section, are significant. Each of these topics (with the possible exception of the last) has received surprisingly limited research and is a fertile area for future work. In many contexts, they are key to both analytical and policy concerns.

2.2. Quality considerations

For most of the 20th century, the US debate over the economic consequences of schooling concentrated on the amount of school attained or, simply, the quantity of schooling of the population. Policy deliberations focused on school completion rates, on the proportion of the population attending postsecondary schooling, and the like. And analyses of the benefits of schooling were most concerned with the effects of quantity of schooling whether benefits are seen in terms of individual incomes or social benefits like improved voting behavior of citizens.

---

[10] For example, Bils and Klenow (2000) question the importance of education as a cause of growth, as opposed to the relationship going the other way around. See also the perspectives in Mankiw, Romer and Weil (1992) and Benhabib and Spiegel (1994). At the individual level, see Card (1999).

Most policy and analytical attention has now switched to quality dimensions of schooling. In the USA, with the slowing of individual income growth [11] and of income convergence by race [12], improving the quality of schooling, or how much is learned for each year, has been seen as the natural policy focus. Similar concerns, albeit generally with a lag, have diffused to other developed and developing countries.

The economic effects of differences in the quality of graduates of our elementary and secondary schools are much less understood than the effects of quantity, particularly with regard to the performance of the aggregate economy. The incomplete understanding of the effects of educational quality clearly reflects difficulties in measurement. Although quality of education is hard to define precisely, it is natural to use the term quality to refer to the knowledge base and analytical skills that are the focal point of schools. Moreover, to add concreteness to this discussion, much of the discussion will rely on information provided by standardized tests of academic achievement and ability.

Relying on standardized tests to provide measures of quality is controversial – in part because of gaps in available evidence and in part because of the conclusions that tend to follow (as discussed below). The contrasting view emphasizes measuring "quality" by the resources (i.e., inputs) going into schooling. Early investigations include Wachtel (1975), Akin and Garfinkel (1977) and Rizzuto and Wachtel (1980). Most recent along this line is Card and Krueger (1992a); see also the reviews of the discussion in Burtless (1996b) and Betts (1996). In the context of developing countries, where these issues might be more important, see Behrman and Birdsall (1983). A substantial part of the controversy relates to the adequacy or effectiveness of expenditure or resource measures as a proxy for worker skills (as discussed below). In the end, cognitive skill measures appear to be the best available indicators of quality and do relate to outcomes that we care about, where resource measures are quite inadequate.

A variety of studies of the labor market have been concerned about how individual differences in cognitive ability affect earnings and specifically modify the estimated returns to quantity. The early work was subsumed under the general topic of "ability bias" in the returns to schooling. In that, the simple question was whether the tendency of more able individuals to continue in school led to an upward bias in the estimated returns to school (because of a straightforward omitted variables problem) [13]. These studies have focused on the estimated returns to years of schooling, although that

---

[11] See, for example, Levy and Murnane (1992) for a review of US earnings patterns. See also Welch (1999) for an update and interpretation of distributional patterns.

[12] Discussion of distributional issues including earnings differences by race can be found in Smith and Welch (1989), O'Neill (1990), Card and Krueger (1992b), Levy and Murnane (1992), Bound and Freeman (1992), Boozer, Krueger and Wolkon (1992), Juhn, Murphy and Pierce (1993), Hauser (1993), Kane (1994), Grogger (1996), Welch (1999) and Deere (2001).

[13] See, for example, Griliches (1974). More recently, see Taber (2001). Discussions of alternative approaches to dealing with ability bias can be found in Card (1999). That discussion in general does not consider school quality, although some of the formulations could be recast in that way.

seems to be a badly formulated question. The correction most commonly employed was the inclusion of a cognitive ability or cognitive achievement measure in the earnings function estimates. In interpreting that work, one must believe that quantity of schooling is uncorrelated with quality as measured by tests of cognitive ability and achievement.

These studies, nonetheless, provide insight into quality measurement issues through their common control for cognitive effects on earnings. The results of the early work generally indicated relatively modest impacts of variations in cognitive ability after holding constant quantity of schooling[14]. In this work, there was no real discussion of what led to any observed cognitive differences, although much of the work implicitly treated it as innate, and not very related to variations in schooling[15]. Further, all of the early work relied on generally small and nonrepresentative samples of the population.

The most recent direct investigations of cognitive achievement, however, have generally suggested larger labor market returns to measured differences in cognitive achievement. For example, Bishop (1989, 1991), O'Neill (1990), Grogger and Eide (1993), Murnane, Willett and Levy (1995), Neal and Johnson (1996), Currie and Thomas (2000), Murnane, Willett, Duhaldeborde and Tyler (2000) and Murnane, Willett, Braatz and Duhaldeborde (2001) each find that the earnings advantages to higher achievement on standardized tests are quite substantial[16]. These results are derived from quite different approaches. Bishop (1989) considers the measurement errors that are inherent in most testing situation and demonstrates that careful treatment of that problem has a dramatic effect on the estimated importance of test differences. O'Neill (1990), Bishop (1991), Grogger and Eide (1993) and Neal and Johnson (1996) on the other hand, simply rely upon more recent labor market data along with more representative sampling and suggest that the earnings advantage to measured skill differences is larger than that found in earlier time periods and in earlier studies (even without correcting for test reliability). Currie and Thomas (2000) provide evidence for a sample of British youth and rely on a long panel of

---

[14] This limited impact of cognitive achievement was also central to a variety of direct analyses of schooling that reformulated the earnings determination process such as Jencks, Smith, Acland, Bane, Cohen, Gintis, Heyns and Michelson (1972), Bowles and Gintis (1976) and Bowles, Gintis and Osborne (2001).

[15] Manski (1993a) presents more recent work with this same general thrust. He recasts the issue as a selection problem and considers how ability or quality interacts with earnings expectations to determine continuation in schooling. Currently, however, no empirical work along these lines identifies the quantitative importance of selection or the interaction of school quality and earnings in such models.

[16] Outside of the USA, few studies are available. One exception for developing countries that finds significant effects of cognitive skills on income is Boissiere, Knight and Sabot (1985). The NAS/NRC study on employment tests Hartigan and Wigdor (1989) also supports the view of a significant relationship of tests and employment outcomes, although the strength of the relationship appears somewhat less strong than that in the direct earnings investigations. Nonetheless, it seems likely that, for the purposes here, the GATB may not be a good measure of the cognitive outcomes of schools and may not correspond well to standard measures of cognitive achievement.

representative data. Murnane, Willett, Braatz and Duhaldeborde (2001), considering a comparison over time, demonstrate that the results of increased returns to measured skills hold regardless of the methodology (i.e., whether simple analysis or error-corrected estimation). Murnane, Willett, Duhaldeborde and Tyler (2000) and Murnane, Willett, Braatz and Duhaldeborde (2001) provide further evidence of the effects of cognitive skills (although offering some caution in the interpretation of strength of cognitive effects versus other traits). Ultimately, the difficulty of separating cognitive skills from pure schooling has made this estimation very difficult [Cawley, Heckman, Lochner and Vytlacil (2000), Heckman and Vytlacil (2001)] and leaves ambiguity about the exact magnitude of effects.

An additional part of the return to school quality comes through continuation in school. There is substantial evidence that students who do better in school, either through grades or scores on standardized achievement tests, tend to go farther in school [see, for example, Dugan (1976), Manski and Wise (1983)]. Rivkin (1995) finds that variations in test scores capture a considerable proportion of the systematic variation in high school completion and in college continuation. Indeed, Rivkin (1995) finds that test score differences fully explain black–white differences in schooling. Bishop (1991) and Hanushek, Rivkin and Taylor (1996) find that individual achievement scores are highly correlated with school attendance. Behrman, Kletzer, McPherson and Schapiro (1998) find strong achievement effects on both continuation into college and quality of college; moreover, the effects are larger when proper account is taken of the endogeneity of achievement. Hanushek and Pace (1995), using the High School and Beyond data, find that college completion is significantly related to higher test scores at the end of high school.

This work, while less complete than might be desired, leads to a conclusion that variations in cognitive ability, as measured by standardized tests, are important in career success. Variation in measured cognitive ability is far from everything that is important, but it is significant in a statistical and quantitative sense.

The linkage of individual cognitive skills to aggregate productivity growth is more difficult to establish. There is no clear consensus on the underlying causes of improvements in the overall productivity of the US economy, nor on how the quality of workers interacts with economic growth [17]. The analysis of the impact of schooling

---

[17] One observation is useful, however. When looking at the history of productivity increase in the US economy, several distinct time periods stand out. Productivity growth continued at some two percent per year through the 1960s, but fell off subsequently – first to one percent in the 1970s and then to virtually zero in the 1980s. It subsequently rebounded in the 1990s. Noting that productivity changes in these time periods through the 1980s mirror the aggregate pattern of the Scholastic Aptitude Test (SAT) scores, which fell dramatically from 1964 through 1980 before partially recovering, some have gone on to presume that the test scores are driving the productivity changes. Such could not, however, be the case – since, as Bishop (1989) makes clear, the test takers with lower scores remained a small proportion of the total labor force through the 1980s. Lower test scores in the 1980s may signal later problems, but they cannot be an explanation for past changes in the economy.

quality on cross-country differences in growth by Hanushek and Kimko (2000), however, suggests that quality may be very important and could even dominate effects of the quantity of schooling differences across countries. They develop measures of labor force quality based on several different international mathematics and science tests and then find these to be highly correlated with international differences in growth rates. The concern in such work is the direction of causality. While a series of specification tests in Hanushek and Kimko (2000) indicates that there is a causal relationship between quality and growth, the exact magnitude of the effect is open to question.

Parallel to the work on individual wage determination, a number of studies have also pursued how school resource differences correlate with economic growth. These differences, however, have not shown a close relationship with international growth [see Barro and Sala-I-Martin (1995), Hanushek and Kimko (2000) and Barro and Lee (2001)].

2.3. Aggregate resources and school outcomes

School policy in the USA and elsewhere has focused attention on quality issues and desires to improve student outcomes. It is useful in this light then to consider briefly how this policy attention has shown up and what the results have been. The simplest picture comes from the aggregate data.

The concern in the USA about the quality of schooling has undoubtedly contributed to the growth in spending on schools. The USA has increased the resources devoted to students dramatically over the entire 20th century, with per pupil spending rising at $3\frac{1}{2}\%$ per year in real terms for a 100-year period [Hanushek and Rivkin (1997)]. Importantly, between 1960 and 1995 when performance measures become available, real spending per pupil tripled [18]. Clearly some of this recent expenditure was required simply to compete with other sectors for highly educated women and does not represent

---

[18] The measurement of real increases in resources has been the subject of some controversy and is difficult to do with precision. The preceding calculations deflate nominal spending by the Consumer Price Index (CPI). This is an output price index and is likely to diverge from appropriate input price indices. Education is a labor intensive industry, which historically has shown little productivity improvement. The consumer price, or alternatively the GDP deflator, indicates how much of society's resources are being devoted to schooling. But, because of real wage increases in the economy, input costs in the education sector are likely to rise more rapidly than the CPI, so that the CPI-adjusted increases will overstate the increases in real inputs to education [e.g., Scitovsky and Scitovsky (1959) or Baumol (1967)]. Rothstein and Miles (1995) suggest an alternative approach of using a modified service-sector CPI. This approach, based on a different measure of output prices emphasizing the service sector, cannot, however, solve the problem of obtaining more accurate measures of input prices, although it can provide a means of developing comparisons of productivity change across labor-intensive sectors [Hanushek (1997b)]. While development of accurate input price indices is difficult because of issues of quality measurement for teachers, the difference between CPI-adjusted and input-adjusted measures is important to keep in mind. Use of a simple wage index or of a measure of increases in salaries for college graduates nonetheless still shows large real resource increases to schools.

an expansion of school activities, but, even allowing for this, expenditure shows a strong trend[19].

While US spending on education has increased significantly during the last quarter of century, quality of student performance measured by test performance has remained roughly constant. Beginning in 1970, the USA embarked on an extensive testing program for students, the National Assessment of Educational Progress (NAEP), that was designed to track performance over time. It appears that the performance of US 17-year-olds has remained roughly constant over the thirty-year period of observation. The simple comparison of NAEP scores from the early 1970s through the 1990s, shows lower science scores, roughly the same reading scores, and higher math scores[20]. Obviously, a variety of factors could influence the aggregate pattern of performance and costs, including for example changes in the student population or the structure of schools–topics discussed below. Nonetheless, the aggregate comparison of resources and performance creates a *prima facie* case that performance of public schools warrants careful consideration.

While the USA remains near the top of all nations in terms of spending per pupil, a number of other countries now spend similar amounts or even greater amounts. Table 3 displays estimates of both the absolute levels of spending and the proportion of GDP per capita devoted to primary and secondary schooling[21]. The comparison of spending patterns across countries shows considerable variation, part of which might be accounted for by higher proportions of private spending for schooling[22].

Interestingly, the amount of spending internationally does not have a very close relationship to the performance of students. Table 4 displays national scores of eighth graders and twelfth graders on the Third International Mathematics and Science Study (TIMSS), conducted in 1995. Countries are rank ordered from highest to lowest in

---

[19] See Flyer and Rosen (1997) for a discussion of the competing forces on teacher labor markets.

[20] The earliest testing date for NAEP differs by subject area with the first science test in 1969, first reading test in 1971, and first math test in 1973. Tests have been given approximately every four years and also involve earlier ages. Each of the subject areas has exhibited some change over the entire time period, and, while only endpoints are reported, it is also true that each of the tests has been roughly flat during the 1990s. See U.S. Department of Education (2000).

[21] Such comparisons across countries are clearly difficult to do with any precision. The absolute spending patterns require an international exchange rate, but even then are prone to inaccuracies because of differences in teacher labor markets. Further, countries differ in what is included in statistics for spending on schools. The GDP comparisons get around the exchange rate issues but suffer from lack of any models of how spending should change with national income. See U.S. Department of Education (1996b) and Organisation for Economic Cooperation and Development (2001).

[22] Data on private expenditures are difficult to find on a consistent and complete basis. The Organisation for Economic Cooperation and Development (2001) tabulations for developed countries display private spending in the form of tuition and other expenditures on private schools. But they leave out private tutoring which appears to represent a significant investment in a variety of countries – mostly notably the East Asian countries. Moreover, countries use different definitions of what is included in school expenditures, of the age period for schooling, and the like. The OECD analysis attempts to standardize data collection, but this is obviously difficult to do completely.

Table 3
Expenditure per student and spending relative to GDP (1998)[a,b]

Country	Expenditure[c] (US$)		Expenditure relative to GDP[d] (%)
	Primary	Secondary	
OECD countries			
Australia	3981	5830	3.8
Austria[e]	6065	8163	4.2
Belgium[f]	3743	5970	3.5
Belgium (Flemish)[g]	3799	6238	3.6
Canada	n.a.	n.a.	4.1
Czech Republic	1645	3182	3.1
Denmark	6713	7200	4.3
Finland	4641	5111	3.7
France	3752	6605	4.4
Germany	3531	6209	3.7
Greece[f]	2368	3287	3.5
Hungary	2028	2140	3.1
Ireland	2745	3934	3.3
Italy[e]	5653	6458	3.5
Japan	5075	5890	3.0
Korea	2838	3544	4.0
Mexico	863	1586	3.5
Netherlands	3795	5304	3.1
Norway[e]	5761	7343	4.4
Poland	1496	1438	n.a.
Portugal	3121	4636	4.2
Spain	3267	4274	3.7
Sweden	5579	5648	4.5
Switzerland[e]	6470	9348	4.5
Turkey[e]	n.a.	n.a.	2.3
UK[f]	3329	5230	n.a.
USA	6043	7764	3.7
Country mean	3940	5294	3.7
OECD total	3915	5625	3.6

continued on next page

Table 3, *continued*

Country	Expenditure[c] (US$)		Expenditure relative to GDP[d] (%)
	Primary	Secondary	
World Education Indicators participants			
Argentina[e]	1389	1860	3.1
Brazil[e,f]	837	1076	n.a.
Chile	1500	1713	3.9
Indonesia[e]	116	497	1.4
Israel	4135	5115	5.5
Malaysia[e]	919	1469	n.a.
Paraguay[e]	572	948	n.a.
Peru	479	671	3.3
Philippines[e]	689	726	4.9
Thailand	1048	1177	3.8
Tunisia[e]	891	1633	n.a.
Uruguay[e]	971	1246	n.a.
Zimbabwe	768	1179	n.a.

[a] Source: Organisation for Economic Cooperation and Development (2001)
[b] n.a., not available.
[c] Expenditure per student in US dollars converted using PPPs on public and private institutions, by level of education, based on full-time equivalents.
[d] Direct and indirect expenditure on educational institutions from public and private sources, by level of education, source of fund and year.
[e] Expenditure amounts for public institutions only.
[f] Expenditure amounts for public and government-dependent private institutions only.
[g] Year of reference for expenditure amounts is 1997.
[h] Year of reference for expenditure amounts is 1999.

each and compared to performance in the USA. (Bold indicates significantly above the USA, and italics indicates significantly below the USA). Clearly, national scores are not closely related to the spending rankings in the previous table. More systematic investigation reveals the same results: performance on the international tests is not closely related to resources of the school systems in these countries[23].

The overview of education attainment, spending, and performance demonstrates the importance of schooling to individuals along with the commitments of governments to the provision of schooling. This provides a backdrop for consideration of government's involvement.

---

[23] See Hanushek and Kimko (2000) for analysis of results on international mathematics and science tests through 1990; see Woessman (2000, 2001) for consideration of the TIMSS scores across nations.

Table 4
Country ranking of performance on Third International Mathematics and Science Study (TIMSS), 1995 [a]

8th grade performance [b]		12th grade performance [b]	
Mathematics	Science	Mathematics	Science
Singapore	**Singapore**	**Netherlands**	**Sweden**
Korea	**Czech Republic**	**Sweden**	**Netherlands**
Japan	**Japan**	**Denmark**	**Iceland**
Hong Kong	**Korea**	**Switzerland**	**Norway**
Belgium – Flemish	**Bulgaria**	**Iceland**	**Canada**
Czech Republic	**Netherlands**	**Norway**	**New Zealand**
Slovak Republic	**Slovenia**	**France**	**Australia**
Switzerland	**Austria**	**New Zealand**	**Switzerland**
Netherlands	**Hungary**	**Australia**	**Austria**
Slovenia	England	**Canada**	**Slovenia**
Bulgaria	Belgium – Flemish	**Austria**	**Denmark**
Austria	Australia	**Slovenia**	Germany
France	Slovak Republic	**Germany**	France
Hungary	Russian Federation	**Hungary**	Czech Republic
Russian Federation	Ireland	Italy	Russian Federation
Australia	Sweden	Russian Federation	*USA*
Ireland	*USA*	Lithuania	Italy
Canada	Germany	Czech Republic	Hungary
Belgium – French	Canada	*USA*	Lithuania
Sweden	Norway	*Cyprus*	*Cyprus*
Thailand	New Zealand	*South Africa*	*South Africa*
Israel	Thailand		
Germany	Israel		
New Zealand	Hong Kong		
England	Switzerland		
Norway	Scotland		
Denmark	*Spain*		
USA	*France*		
Scotland	*Greece*		
Latvia	*Iceland*		
Spain	*Romania*		
Iceland	*Latvia*		
Greece	*Portugal*		

continued on next page

Table 4, *continued*

8th grade performance[b]		12th grade performance[b]	
Mathematics	Science	Mathematics	Science
Romania	*Denmark*		
Lithuania	*Lithuania*		
Cyprus	*Belgium – French*		
Portugal	*Iran*		
Iran	*Cyprus*		
Kuwait	*Kuwait*		
Columbia	*Columbia*		
South Africa	*South Africa*		

[a] Source: U.S. Department of Education (1999)
[b] Note: **bold**, significantly above USA; *italics,* significantly below USA.

3. Role of government

As is well-known, the existence of large returns to quantity or quality of schooling does not by itself warrant large scale governmental involvement. Large returns imply that individuals have strong incentives to obtain schooling, without the intervention of government. There are several primary justifications generally given for the level of governmental involvement in education: externalities, economies of scale, market failures in general, and redistributive motives. In the presence of these, purely private decisions are unlikely to lead to optimal social decisions.

Externalities are frequently proposed as central to government's interest in education. In general, activities that are perceived to have significant externalities are prime candidates for increased governmental support. With positive externalities, Pigouvian subsidies can be used so that individuals make decisions in line with the appropriate social calculus. Or other governmental interventions might be used to move toward a social optimum. But, as is also well recognized, externalities are noticeably elusive, and, while optimal tax and subsidy policies in the face of externalities are well understood conceptually, few estimates of the magnitude of externalities exist anywhere. Nevertheless, economists and citizens, if polled on externalities in education, would probably support the view that education involves extensive externalities [Cohn and Geske (1990)].

Leading candidates for areas of external benefits involve citizen involvement in the community and government, crime reduction, family decision making and child upbringing, and economic growth. There is evidence that more schooling does have a positive impact in each of these areas.

In each area, a significant portion of the beneficial effect of education appears to come from comparing very low levels of school attainment with significantly higher levels. Thus, extensive discussions of the social benefits of schooling in developing countries would seem both warranted and correct[24]. It is difficult to have, for example, a well-informed citizenry when most of the population is illiterate. It may also be difficult to introduce advanced production technologies, at least in a timely manner, if workers cannot be expected to read the accompanying technical manuals.

On the other hand, even if accepting the importance of externalities at minimal levels of schooling, there is little reason to believe that there are constant marginal externalities when expanded on both the extensive and intensive margins[25]. Specifically, arguments about the social benefits of expanded education seem much stronger in the case of developing countries of Africa than in the case of the USA during the 21st century. Where half of the population has attended some postsecondary schooling, another year of average schooling seems unlikely to change dramatically the political awareness of the US population. Similarly, if the average high school student scores somewhat higher on the National Assessment of Educational progress, it is doubtful that many would expect noticeable changes in the identified extra social benefits of education.

Although education may be associated with a variety of social outcomes, a particularly relevant question is whether there is a causal relationship or not. With very little done on even assessing the magnitude of effects – largely because of poor measurement, progress on understanding the underlying causal structure has been even more limited. For example, one of the few direct investigations of causation indeed opens serious questions about common interpretations. Behrman and Rosenzweig (2002) present evidence on the role of mother's education in the intergenerational transmission of skills. In this, they pay particular attention to identifying the causal impact of mother's education through use of identical twins and conclude that it is not only much smaller than believed but possibly negative[26].

A leading candidate for potential externalities of education in the USA and other developed countries, however, would revolve around economic growth. If a highly skilled workforce permits entirely different kinds of technologies to be introduced, or to be introduced earlier in a development cycle, expanded education of an individual may indeed affect other workers in the economy. Or, if improved abilities of the best students lead to more rapid invention and development of new technologies,

---

[24] Interestingly, policy discussions of education in developing countries tend to concentrate most on private rates of return and the market outcomes of added schooling, even if they make some reference to other social benefits such as political participation and lower fertility. See, for example, Heyneman and White (1986), Psacharopoulos, Tan and Jimenez (1986) and Lockheed and Verspoor (1991).

[25] This issue is raised by Friedman (1962) and remains for the most part in the discussions of college education in Hartman (1973) and Mundel (1973). None of these, however, provides empirical evidence on the existence or magnitude of any externalities. The early primer on externalities in education [Weisbrod (1964)] concentrates chiefly on geographic spillovers and fiscal effects and downplays the issues raised here. A discussion of the magnitude of externalities that is similar to the one here is found in Poterba (1996).

[26] For an early study of family effects, see Leibowitz (1974).

spillovers of educational investments may result. Nevertheless, little evidence exists that distinguishes externalities in economic growth from simply the impact of better workers and more human capital [27].

Beyond externalities, government also has a natural role when there are other market failures. The most obvious possibility comes through capital market imperfections. If individuals cannot borrow against their human capital – because human capital is embodied in the individual – there may be underinvestment in education [cf. Becker (1993)]. This possibility, only observable in postsecondary education when government freely provides lower education, has not received strong empirical support [Cameron and Heckman (1999)], but the current interventions in the market make it difficult to assess completely the importance of this. Further, if there are economies of scale, say, from some fixed components of school operations, governmental intervention may provide for efficient operations. Nonetheless, while the empirical analysis is thin, little support for pervasive economies of scale exists.

An additional imperfection that deserves mention, and that enters into the discussion later, involves information. Student achievement involves a complex mixture of educational inputs including the student's own abilities, the influence of parents and friends, and the impact of schools. These factors are not easily separated, so that individuals themselves may have trouble assessing the independent influence of schools. If such is the case, informational problems may impede the decision making of individuals in terms of human capital investments. It may be that government can produce superior information about the quality of school inputs than the individual – although, if this is the rationale for governmental involvement, the form of intervention is important. In particular, government would not need to operate schools in order to provide information about their performance [28].

The second major category of justification for governmental intervention is a redistributive motive. If society has certain goals for the distribution of income and well-being in society, normal market operations are unlikely to achieve those goals. The precise form of societal goals and the relationship to schooling has not been given

---

[27] A recent consideration employs cross-sectional wage information to look at productivity spillovers and finds little evidence after considering endogeneity of schooling [Acemoglu and Angrist (2000)]. These issues can also be found in discussions of endogenous growth models such as Nelson and Phelps (1966), Romer (1990b), Mankiw, Romer and Weil (1992), Benhabib and Spiegel (1994) and Hanushek and Kimko (2000).

[28] As mentioned before, a different aspect of information failures would relate to signaling and screening models. A common interpretation of these models is that schooling does not increase productivity, it only identifies more able people through their use of school attendance to convey their ability. In such a case, the social returns to schooling may be considerably less than the private returns – indicating that government should work to lessen the amount of costly schooling. Or, government may also not want to pursue programs designed to reduce school dropouts if it lessens the information on individuals that is available.

much attention [29]. (Note also that redistributive goals may also interact with concerns about capital market constraints, where the desire is to break any linkages of poverty that exist because parents cannot provide appropriate schooling opportunities to their children).

An alternative redistributive motive actually appears to guide much policy and to interact with a range of policy initiatives discussed below [30]. Because housing in the USA and in many other places tends to lead to concentrations of poor people, minorities, and others who traditionally have not faired as well in schools, schools tend also to reinforce these concentrations [31]. To the extent that concentrations of poverty have added effects on schooling over and above individual poverty per se, there is an externality that interacts with any redistribution objectives, and government may again have a clear role for correcting a market failure.

Without pursuing the details of any mandate for public action, however, two conclusions are important. First, while various market interventions are frequently employed to justify governmental intervention into education, very little explicit research or consideration has been given to the exact nature of these. For example, are the externalities related to the quality of schooling or just the minimal quantity? Second, as underscored by Poterba (1996), even less attention has been given to the appropriate mechanism for any governmental intervention. For example, if government wished to deal with capital market imperfections, should it provide free or reduced priced schools, make loans to students, operate the schools directly, or give grants to students to attend schools? A simple comparison is useful. The organization of the educational sector has moved toward government financing *and* government provision, while similar issues in the health sector have led to very different institutional structures (at least in the USA). With few exceptions, little policy attention is given to any underlying consideration of the scope and form of governmental intervention.

---

[29] Fair (1971) considers optimal policies for income distribution when it is an explicit component of the social welfare function. Becker and Tomes (1976, 1979) concentrate on intergenerational aspects of income transmission and distribution. Behrman, Taubman and Pollak (1982) pursue intergenerational distribution issues from an alternative model of parental behavior. Hanushek, Leung and Yilmaz (2001) evaluate using education as a redistributive device compared to the other mechanisms of negative income taxes and wage subsidies.

[30] These issues arise most significantly when talking about policies that affect peer groups (e.g., desegregation policies) and policies that affect the financing of schools across local educational districts or agencies.

[31] Much of the past work on concentrations of poverty has involved crime, health, and welfare outcomes. As discussed below, the analytical complications of this work are serious. As Brock and Durlauf (2001), Manski (1993b) and Moffitt (2001) point out, the empirical analysis of peer influences has been inhibited by both conceptual and data problems – problems that raise serious questions about interpretation of many existing studies. These critiques, in part precipitated by analyses of neighborhood poverty [e.g., Mayer and Jencks (1989), O'Regan and Quigley (1999), Rosenbaum and Popkin (1991)], point to a number of potentially severe empirical problems that are at least partially present in the recent set of randomized housing experiments aimed at understanding neighborhood effects [e.g., Rosenbaum (1995), Katz, Kling and Liebman (2001), Ludwig, Duncan and Hirschfield (2001)].

The summary from considering the role of government is that the arguments for the currently large intervention – one quite generally including both financing and provision of services – remain not well analyzed. Thus, the remainder of this essay addresses a more limited issue: how well does government do at what it is trying to do.

4. Efficiency of production

Because of the heavy involvement of the public sector in the actual provision of schooling, understanding the efficiency of production becomes an important issue. With competitive, private provision, little attention is given to economic or technical efficiency. Barring obvious market imperfections, there is general faith that market forces will push firms toward efficient use of resources. Even with market imperfections, there is generally little attention given to issues of technical efficiency, because firms are presumed to produce the highest possible levels of output given the chosen inputs–even if the firms are producing at the wrong level or not using the economically best set of inputs. But, the involvement of government in production, frequently in near-monopoly situations, alters the focus considerably. The possibility of inefficient production becomes a much more serious concern.

The attention to performance and efficiency in education began chiefly with *Equality of Educational Opportunity* (the "Coleman Report"), a US government publication that appeared in 1966 [Coleman, Campbell, Hobson, McPartland, Mood, Weinfeld and York (1966)]. The specific focus of the Coleman Report, mandated by the Civil Rights Act of 1964, was the extent of racial discrimination in US public schools. Two aspects led to the broad attention given to it and contributed to the controversy that has followed. First, it took the position that the central issue was not so much governmental inputs to schooling as it was student outcomes. Second, it is widely interpreted to imply that "schools are not important"[32].

Public programs are frequently measured by the magnitude of public spending on them or the array of specific real resources (personnel of various types, capital in buildings or laboratories, etc.) going into a program. An extension of this is that variations in spending or resources indicate varying amounts of public involvement. The presumption behind employing spending measures is that funds are used effectively, implying spending is a simple index of the outcomes. The presumption behind the use of real resource measures is that the specific resources are important components indicating differences in quality, even if input prices vary across schools.

---

[32] The Coleman Report was heavily criticized on methodological grounds [Bowles and Levin (1968), Cain and Watts (1970), Hanushek and Kain (1972)]. The most serious issue was the use of an analysis of variance procedure that biased the findings against any school factors being important and toward family factors. As discussed below, this study also confused measurability of inputs with the importance of teachers and schools.

The Coleman Report, which was required to look at the extent of racial discrimination in the public provision of schooling, needed a measure of the importance of various inputs to the schooling process. This requirement led the researchers to turn to measuring student outcomes and to relating various inputs directly to outcomes. This focus, which had not been applied very broadly in education or in other areas of government-provided services, dramatically changed the basic form of analysis.

Much discussion of schools tends to use the terms "quality" and "resources" interchangeably, but this usage presumes efficient operations of schools. A central part of the analysis discussed here looks directly at aspects of how effectively public schools use resources – and concludes that considerable inefficiency in resource usage exists. At a minimum, school quality should not be simply measured by expenditure patterns or by specific resources. More importantly, policy should logically reflect this reality.

The attention to the Coleman Report reflected the popular interpretation of the analysis that "schools do not make a difference". That interpretation, as discussed below, is incorrect, but the basic evidence behind the statement suggests serious performance problems of government, because purchased inputs to schools are not closely related to outcomes. Evaluation of the alternative interpretations, nonetheless, requires more general treatment of the educational production process and the empirical results that are available.

4.1. General structure

The framework of analysis of educational performance considers a general production function such as

$$O_{it} = f\left(F_i^{(t)}, P_i^{(t)}, S_i^{(t)}, A_i\right) + v_{it},$$ (1)

where O_{it} is the performance of student i at time t, $F_i^{(t)}$ represents family inputs cumulative to time t, $P_i^{(t)}$ the cumulative peer inputs, $S_i^{(t)}$ the cumulative school inputs, A_i is innate ability, and a stochastic term v_{it}.

This general structure has motivated an extensive series of empirical studies. The typical empirical study collects information about student performance and about the various educational inputs and then attempts to estimate the characteristics of the production function using econometric techniques.

Two aspects of this formulation are important to point out. First, a variety of influences outside of schools enter into the production of achievement. Second, the production process for achievement is cumulative, building on a series of inputs over time. Both of these are important in the specification and interpretation of educational production functions.

The relevance of many factors outside schools highlights the necessity of going beyond simple comparisons of student performance across schools. Most of the attention in analytical studies has focused on the measurement of school attributes. This focus seems natural from a policy point of view. It also reflects the common use of administrative data in estimating production functions, because administrative data are frequently short of many measures of family background. Nonetheless, this lack of attention is unfortunate. First, increasing attention has been given to potential policies related to families – such as preschool and daycare programs, after school programs, parent education and the like. Second, because families frequently exert preferences for the schools that their children will attend, incomplete measurement of external influences on performance raise intense issues of selection bias and preclude simple statements about causal influences of schools. Such an observation of course does not seem very profound, but, as discussed below, many empirical studies give little attention to nonschool influences in addressing the impact of school factors. Moreover, public policy debates surprisingly frequently rely on simple accounting of performance across schools. For example, much of the current movement toward increased school accountability often relies on just aggregate student scores for a school[33]. Just the level of student performance is not a reliable indicator of the quality of schools students are attending.

The cumulative nature of achievement, where the learning in any time period builds on prior learning, implies that any analysis must take into account the time path of inputs. This places heavy demands on measurement and data collection, because historical information is frequently difficult to obtain.

The cumulative nature of the production process has been a prime motivation for considering a value-added formulation. At least in a linear version of Equation (1), it is possible to look at the growth in contemporaneous performance over some period of time, instead of the level of performance, and relate that to the flow of specific inputs. The general value-added formulation can be written as:

$$O_{it} - O_{it^*} = f^* \left(F_i^{(t-t^*)}, P_i^{(t-t^*)}, S_i^{(t-t^*)} \right) + \upsilon_{it} - \upsilon_{it^*}, \tag{2}$$

where outcome changes over the period $(t-t^*)$ are related to inputs over the same period. Note that this formulation dramatically lessens the data requirements and eliminates anything that appears as a fixed effect in the level of achievement (Equation 1)[34].

---

[33] With the increasing popularity of publishing average performance of students in different schools, the interpretation of scores becomes more important. In fact, without consideration of the various inputs that go beyond just schools, alternative accountability systems can have perverse effects [cf. Hanushek and Raymond (2001)]. The integration of the underlying theoretical and empirical analysis of the determination of achievement with accountability and incentive systems is an important but underdeveloped area of investigation.

[34] This formulation presumes that innate abilities are constant and thus fall out of achievement growth. With more information on variations over time, it is also possible to allow for ability differences in growth [Rivkin, Hanushek and Kain (2001)]. Alternative formulations have prior achievement, O_{it^*}, on the right hand side, allowing for coefficient different than one [Hanushek (1979)]. This latter approach has the advantages of allowing for different scales of measurement in achievement during different

A final key issue is how student performance is measured. A prime justification for the attention to education, as described previously, is its hypothesized effects on labor market outcomes. The question remains about how best to measure educational output for understanding production relationships and policy options. With few exceptions [e.g., Betts (1995), Grogger (1996)], accurate measures of school inputs have not been related to subsequent earnings, making direct analysis impossible[35]. Thus, most analyses have conceptualized this as a two-stage problem: school resources and other things are related to test scores, school completion, or other intermediate outcomes, and these outcomes are related to subsequent success[36].

4.2. Effects of teacher and schools

The most obvious complication of estimating models such as Equation (1) is the necessity to specify precisely the various inputs into the production of student achievement. A logical starting place is estimation of the magnitude of differences across teachers and schools.

Consider

$$O_{it} - O_{it^*} = f^* \left(F_i^{(t-t^*)}, P_i^{(t-t^*)} \right) + \sum t_j T_{ij} + (v_{it} - v_{it^*}), \qquad (3)$$

where T_{ij} is an indicator variable if student i has teacher j during the period $t - t^*$. This general covariance, or fixed-effect, formulation identifies teacher and school effects by systematic differences in achievement gains by students. In this formulation, teacher quality is measured implicitly by the average gain in achievement for the students of each teacher (adjusted for other factors influencing achievement).

Such analyses consistently show large and significant differences among teachers [e.g., Hanushek (1971, 1992), Murnane (1975), Murnane and Phillips (1981), Armor, Conry-Oseguera, Cox, King, McDonnell, Pascal, Pauly and Zellman (1976), Rivkin, Hanushek and Kain (2001)]. In the general formulation of Equation (3), however, identification and interpretation of teacher and school effects is nonetheless complicated, since any factors that are constant across the period $t - t^*$ and across the students with teacher j are incorporated in the estimated effect, t_j. Thus, for example, teacher effects, school effects and classroom peer effects are not separately identified if

years and introducing the possibility that growth in performance differs by starting point. It has the disadvantages of introducing measurement error on the right hand side and of complicating the error structure, particularly in models relying on more than a single year of an individual's achievement growth.

[35] Another class of studies, those aggregated to high levels such as the state level, have also considered labor market outcomes [e.g., Akin and Garfinkel (1977), Card and Krueger (1992a)]. These studies, which introduce a wider set of analytical concerns, are discussed below.

[36] In more pragmatic terms, if interested in understanding policy influences on student outcomes, one would not want to wait decades until the ultimate impact in the labor market is observed.

the estimates come from a single cross section of teachers. Hanushek (1992), however, demonstrates the consistency of teacher effects across grades and school years, thus indicating that the estimated differences relate directly to teacher quality and not the specific mix of students and the interaction of teacher and students. Rivkin, Hanushek and Kain (2001) remove separate school and grade fixed effects and observe the consistency of teacher effects across different cohorts – thus isolating the impact of teachers as opposed to just some combined teacher and classroom effects[37].

The magnitude of differences in teacher quality is noteworthy. The estimated difference between a "good" and a "bad" teacher in poverty schools of Gary, Indiana, was approximately one grade level per academic year; i.e., a student with a good teacher might progress at 1.5 grade equivalents in a school year, while those with a bad teacher might progress at 0.5 grade equivalents [Hanushek (1992)]. Alternatively, Rivkin, Hanushek and Kain (2001) produce lower bounds on estimates of the variance in teacher quality entirely from heterogeneity of teachers within Texas schools. The estimates indicate that one standard deviation in teacher quality is equal to one-fifth of the average gap in performance between low income and higher income students. In other words, contrary to some conclusions emanating from Coleman, Campbell, Hobson, McPartland, Mood, Weinfeld and York (1966), schools have the ability to compensate for educational differences arising from family backgrounds. A string of five above average teachers can, by the previous estimates, entirely close the average achievement gap by income level within Texas schools.

The identification of teacher and school effects also relies on the linearity of effects. If teachers, for example, have different effects on certain subgroups of students, the estimates of Equation (3) do not separate out pure teacher effects. This problem, which also exists for estimation that relies upon specific measures of teacher characteristics, can be investigated through straightforward extensions of the model to allow t_j to vary across groups or according to other characteristics.

While estimation of this general fixed effect model demonstrates the significant impact of variations in teacher and school quality, it does not pinpoint the underlying characteristics or causes of these differences. Estimation by Murnane (1975) and by Armor, Conry-Oseguera, Cox, King, McDonnell, Pascal, Pauly and Zellman (1976) demonstrates that school principals are able to identify variations in teacher quality in the value-added sense of t_j. Thus, evidence suggests that quality variations are observable – an important issue in light of the next section that demonstrates that quality is not captured by measures of common characteristics such as degrees and experience of teachers.

---

[37] The approach in Rivkin, Hanushek and Kain (2001), however, relies on just variations within schools (having removed any fixed school and grade effects on achievement). Therefore, it cannot identify either the magnitude of between school differences in teacher quality or the importance of overall school differences such as that reflecting school leadership, quality of facilities, or the like. Even though for many purposes understanding the magnitude of between school quality differences is also important, an important objective of this paper is eliminating any possibility of selection effects.

4.3. Components of school inputs

The vast majority of analyses of educational production have pursued a different approach: the specification and estimation of hypothesized components of the teacher and school effects. This work returns to the specifications in Equations (1) or (2) and attempts to incorporate specific measures of the components of S_{it}, the relevant inputs from the school. High on the list of characteristics has been a variety of measures of the resources going into schools, since budgeting for added expenditures of various sorts presents a series of obvious hypotheses about which factors influence achievement. This approach has not been very productive from the viewpoint of empirical description of the educational progress. But that in itself is significant because, as discussed below, these measured inputs are frequently the object of governmental decision making and policy.

Studies of educational performance include a variety of different measures of resources devoted to schools. Commonly employed measures include 1) the real resources of the classroom (teacher education, teacher experience, and class size or teacher-pupil ratios); 2) financial aggregates of resources (expenditure per student and teacher salary); and 3) measures of other resources in schools (specific teacher characteristics, administrative inputs, and facilities).

The real resource category receives the bulk of analytical attention. First, these best summarize variations in resources at the classroom level. Teacher education and teacher experience are the primary determinants of teacher salaries. When combined with teachers per pupil, these variables describe the most significant variations in the instructional resources across classrooms. Second, these measures are readily available and well-measured[38]. Third, they relate to the largest changes in schools over the past three decades. Table 5 displays the dramatic increases in these school inputs for the USA, with pupil–teacher ratios falling steadily, teacher experience increasing, and the percent of teachers with a masters' degree actually doubling between 1960 and 1990. Similar increases in resources have been well documented in other countries around the world [Organisation for Economic Cooperation and Development (2001)]. Fourth, studies of growth in performance at the classroom level like Equation (2), commonly thought to be the superior analytical design, frequently have these resource measures available but not the others.

The analytical design of studies of real resources stands in contrast with that for the other resource measures. The financial aggregates, particularly expenditure per pupil, are typically not even calculated for the classroom or the school, but instead are only available for the school district or for entire states or nations. As a result, studies employing these are typically the most aggregated studies, a source of analytical

---

[38] A majority of existing analyses of student performance has relied upon administrative data from schools. The real resource variables are commonly collected and reported within such data, and, because they are frequently the basis of payments or regulations across levels of government, they tend to be reported accurately.

Table 5
Public school resources in the USA, 1960–1995

Year	Resource			
	Pupil–teacher ratio	% Teachers with master's degree or more	Median years teacher experience	Current expenditure/ADA (1996–97 $'s)
1960	25.8	23.5	11	2122
1970	22.3	27.5	8	3645
1980	18.7	49.6	12	4589
1990	17.2	53.1	15	6239
1995	17.3	56.2	15	6434

[a] Source: U.S. Department of Education (1997).

problems discussed below. Moreover, studies focusing on spending are not amenable to value-added specifications, causing the set of specification problems described previously. The study of spending is directly relevant for many policy discussions[39], but these expenditure studies are noticeably lower quality than the best, and the typical, study investigating real classroom resources. The measures of other school resources typically are measured poorly and tend to be available only at the district level[40]. Since resources such as facilities tend to be relatively smaller in terms of overall spending, one would also expect these factors to be less important in determining student achievement.

4.4. Results of production function estimation for the USA

Existing estimation of educational production functions provides considerable information about governmentally provided schooling. The intellectual heritage of this is the Coleman Report [Coleman, Campbell, Hobson, McPartland, Mood, Weinfeld and York

---

[39] Some studies include expenditure per pupil along with measures of the real classroom resources. In such a case, since variations in classroom instructional expenditure are held constant, expenditure per student is interpreted as spending outside of the classroom. If only some of the classroom resources are included, the interpretation is more ambiguous and depends on the specific specification.

[40] For example, policy deliberations often consider the relative proportion of resources going to administration versus instruction. In the USA, the proportion of expenditures at the classroom level has fallen dramatically over time [Hanushek and Rivkin (1997)], leading some to view this as a measure of waste. However, without accounting for the uses of these resources and their effects on achievement, it is difficult to make such efficiency statements. Unfortunately, little work has concentrated on expenditures outside of the classroom. Data are imprecise, because even the definition of what are administrative expenditures is not settled. When available, administrative and other expenditure categories are generally not disaggregated at the school level. Similarly, measures of resources like laboratories or libraries are noted by their existence, as opposed to any idea extent or quality.

(1966)]. This governmentally sponsored study spawned a large body of subsequent analyses, in large part because of its conclusions that cast doubts on the productivity on public schools. Perhaps more important, it set a standard of studying outcomes of schooling. Because of the common approach to studies conducted since the Coleman Report, it is possible to provide a consistent summary of the results of how resources and other inputs affect student performance.

Providing a consistent summary is especially important in this area, because the large number of existing studies, taken individually, appear to support a number of disparate conclusions which do not hold when put in the context of the entire body of evidence. A tendency to focus selectively on a few studies and findings is exacerbated by the relationship between the research and serious policy discussions. The results of this research have been entered into legislative debates, judicial proceedings, and executive proposals – frequently placing heavy weight on the subset of studies that supports a particular position.

This discussion begins with tabulation of all studies meeting rudimentary quality standards (published in a refereed journal or book, including some measure of family background, and presenting information about the statistical properties of estimates). By including the universe of US studies (available through 1994), the initial analysis provides an overview that is not affected by selectivity of results.

Estimates of key production function parameters come from 376 separate published estimates, found in 89 separate articles or books[41]. The estimated relationships vary in a variety of substantive ways (by measure of student performance, by grade, by included measures of resources). These studies also vary widely in quality, as generally captured by methodology and adequacy of data. Subsequent discussion considers how any results might be affected by key dimensions of focus and quality. In particular, the following sections delve into both analytical issues (methodology and data) and substantive specification issues (behavior and organization).

4.4.1. Basic results

Table 6 presents the overall summary of results of estimates of the effects of key resources for US public schools. The tabulations note the numbers of separate estimates for each parameter along with their estimated direction of effect and with their statistical significance (5% level).

---

[41] A more complete description of the studies can be found in Hanushek (1997a), which updates the analysis in Hanushek (1986). The tabulations here correct some of the original coding of effects in that publication. They also omit the estimates from Card and Krueger (1992b). In reviewing all of the studies and estimates, it was discovered that these estimates were based on models that did not include any measures of family background differences. This specification requirement is a minimal quality criterion, since omission will almost certainly lead to biased resource estimates. Family backgrounds have been shown to be quite generally correlated with school resources and have been shown to have strong effects on student outcomes.

Table 6
Percentage distribution of estimated effect of key resources on student performance, based on 376 studies[a]

Resources	Number of estimates	Statistically significant		Statistically insignificant
		Positive	Negative	
Real classroom resources				
Teacher–pupil ratio	276	14%	14%	72%
Teacher education	170	9	5	86
Teacher experience	206	29	5	66
Financial aggregates				
Teacher salary	118	20	7	73%
Expenditure per pupil	163	27	7	66
Other				
Facilities	91	9	5	86
Administration	75	12	5	83
Teacher test scores	41	37	10	53

[a] Source: Hanushek (1997a), revised.

In terms of real classroom resources, only 9% of the estimates for the level of teachers education and 14% of the estimates for teacher–pupil ratios show positive and statistically significant effects on student performance[42]. These relatively small numbers of statistically significant positive results are balanced by another set finding statistically significant negative results reaching 14% in the case of teacher–pupil ratios or the same percentage as finding the expected positive effect. Most estimates (72% of the teacher–pupil ratio estimates and 86% of the teacher education estimates) are statistically insignificant and those reporting the sign of insignificant estimated coefficients are split fairly evenly between positive and negative. A higher proportion of estimated effects of teacher experience are positive and statistically significant: 29%. Importantly, however, 71% still indicate worsening performance with experience or less confidence in any positive effect. And, because more experienced teachers can

---

[42] The individual studies tend to measure each of these inputs in different ways. For example, while many studies include an indicator variable for whether or not the teacher has a master's degree, some will include measures of the graduate credits. With teacher–pupil ratio, some measure actual class size, while the majority measure teacher–pupil ratio. A variety of functional forms has been used, ranging from simple linear relationships to different nonlinear forms with thresholds, quadratics, and the like. In all cases, estimated signs are reversed if the measure involves pupil–teacher ratios or class size instead of teacher–pupil ratio. Further, where nonlinearities indicate positive effects over some range but not others, say with ranges of teacher experience, the most favorable for the hypothesis of positive effects is recorded.

frequently choose their school and/or students, a portion of the positive effects could actually reflect reverse causation [Greenberg and McCall (1974), Murnane (1981), Hanushek, Kain and Rivkin (2001c)]. In sum, the vast number of estimated real resource effects gives little confidence that just adding more of any of the specific resources to schools will lead to a boost in student achievement. Moreover, this statement does not even get into whether or not any effects are 'large'. Given the small confidence in just getting noticeable improvements, it seems somewhat unimportant to investigate the size of any estimated effects, at least for the aggregation of studies.

The financial aggregates provide a similar picture. There is very weak support for the notion that simply providing higher teacher salaries or greater overall spending will lead to improved student performance. Per pupil expenditure has received the most attention, but only 27% of the estimated coefficients are positive and statistically significant. In fact, seven percent even suggest some confidence in the fact that adding resources would harm student achievement. In reality, as discussed below, studies involving per pupil expenditure tend to be the lowest quality studies, and there is substantial reason to believe that even these weak results overstate the true effect of added expenditure.

Outside of the basic resource factors, a vast number of specific measures of teachers and schools have been included at one time or another, but few measures have been repeated frequently enough to permit any sort of tabulation. One set of exceptions involves either administrative inputs or facilities. While these categories include a wide range of specific measures, the results of such investigation as tabulated in Table 6 show little consistent effect on student performance [43]. An additional exception is teacher test score, where teachers have been given some sort of achievement or IQ test and their score on that has been related to their students' performance. Table 6 displays the results of the 41 studies that include teacher test scores. Of all of the explicit measures that lend themselves to tabulation, stronger teacher test scores are most consistently related to higher student achievement, even though only 37% provide positive and statistically significant effects.

4.4.2. Components of results

The forgoing tabulations combine the available evidence in a variety of ways – across grade levels, across measures of outcomes, and across studies of varying quality. While study quality is considered in the next section, the other issues do not have a strong influence on the overall findings. Real resources tend to show the same inconsistent pattern with achievement at both elementary and secondary school levels (not shown). Similarly, the results of real or financial resources are not very different

---

[43] Administrative inputs are measured with such things as overall spending, the salaries of administrators, or the qualifications of administrators. Facilities include expenditures and specific measures such as availability of laboratories, the size and presence of a library, and the property of the school. In all cases, results are tabulated such that more of the measured characteristic means greater resources.

for studies focusing on test scores as the measure of performance and those focusing on other outcome measures. One specific issue has received extra attention. Do high resource schools encourage students to stay in school longer (which has obvious impacts on earnings)? Answering this question is, perhaps, more difficult than the straight achievement question, because labor market opportunities will affect the school completion decision as will net tuition and parental financial support when contemplating college. That question is a focal point of Hanushek, Rivkin and Taylor (1996). In that study of school completion, school resources have no significant impact on student behavior once individual achievement and school costs are considered[44]. The issue of performance measurement has arisen specifically within the context of results for achievement tests and results for labor market outcomes (see controversies, below). Nonetheless, except for the differences in aggregation of the underlying estimation, no significant differences in results are found.

4.4.3. The role of peers

Schools are made up of teachers and other personnel but also include other students – peers. In fact, early sociological discussion of schools emphasized peers, and the Coleman Report [Coleman, Campbell, Hobson, McPartland, Mood, Weinfeld and York (1966)] is commonly interpreted as arguing that peers played a more significant role in student achievement than did the resources and other formal structure of the schools. The interest in peers and integration of this with Tiebout choices of families are set out in an interesting set of papers emphasizing the general equilibrium outcomes including de Bartolome (1990), Manski (1992), Benabou (1993, 1996), Epple and Romano (1998, 2003), Nechyba (2000, 2003a), and Caucutt (2002). A central element running through these papers is how financing mechanisms, particularly vouchers, interact with demands of families for different peers. While the structure of the vouchers and the mechanisms for individual behavior affect the solutions, these papers suggest that important peer influences can have direct ramifications for overall welfare and for the distribution of outcomes. These papers consider the outcomes of sorting, assuming that peer groups are important. Unfortunately, the development of empirical work has not kept pace with the theoretical investigations.

---

[44] Resource effects on college continuation are emphasized in Card and Krueger (1996). The estimation of resource impacts on school continuation is, however, particularly prone to specification problems. One might expect state effects to be particularly important in determining school continuation, since the availability and expense of public colleges and universities and the opportunity costs implied by different local labor markets vary significantly across states. The studies of college attendance in general do not control for interstate differences, leading to serious specification errors. (State policies and their impacts on production function estimates are discussed below). Betts (1996) reviews a number of these studies of educational attainment and does suggest some positive effects of resources. For the studies tabulated here (which differ from those considered by Betts), there tend to be positive effects of expenditure on school attainment, but there are only 25 total studies and only five estimated from within individual states. Thus, the small samples make it difficult to resolve this issue conclusively.

The empirical analysis of peers is very difficult to conduct and the results have been hard to interpret because they become confused with issues of the underlying estimation. Manski (1993b, 2000), Moffitt (2001) and Brock and Durlauf (2001) describe a variety of econometric issues surrounding the topic.

Perhaps the most significant issue in estimating peer effects is the presence of omitted or mismeasured variables for schools and peers. Mismeasured individual factors or neglected influences that are common to the peers lead naturally to further identification issues, because mismeasured individual factors may be proxied by aggregate measures for the peers. Importantly, omitted variables bias will under very general circumstances lead to overstating peer influences, so peer effects can appear significant even in the case where they have no true effect [Hanushek, Kain, Markman and Rivkin (2003)]. As the previous analysis of measured school factors indicates, characterizing school quality has been difficult, and thus it is highly likely that standard estimation of educational production functions with peers will overstate peer influences.

The theoretical econometric literature has concentrated more on the endogeneity of peer influences. Peer effects can be thought of as a simultaneous equation system where each student affects the others in the class and is in turn affected by the others, implying that standard issues of identification arise. These issues are very difficult to deal with, particularly if the main effect of peers is through contemporaneous interactions. Specifically, if my behavior affects peer behavior and peer behavior affects me, estimation is problematic. Normal exclusion conditions, or even random assignment of students to classrooms, offer little hope in this case. If instead it is the characteristics of peers, such as how prepared they are for the curriculum or their general motivation and outlook, the development of both econometric estimators and the use of sample randomization becomes more feasible. In this case, nonetheless, the pure measurement issues still impinge on the ability to separate individual effects from peer effects.

Early empirical investigations provide mixed results about the importance of peers [Hanushek (1972, 1992), Henderson, Mieszkowski and Sauvageau (1976) and Summers and Wolfe (1977)]. More recent analysis has taken alternative approaches to identification of peer effects. Hanushek, Kain, Markman and Rivkin (2003) consider changes in the peer composition that arise from small changes across grades and cohorts in demographics and prior achievement. They are able to eliminate any time invariant effects of schools and grades in schools through a fixed effect strategy and then to identify the effects of peers. They find small but significant differences of having smarter peers, and they find some effects of racial composition.

A separate strand of research, which has generally not been too careful about the structure of peer estimation, has looked at questions of ability tracking, or streaming, in schools. Conventional wisdom has suggested that heterogeneous grouping is good because the higher achievers help the lower achievers but are not affected by having low achieving classmates [Oakes (1985, 1992)]. A careful review of this literature along with new estimation of tracking effects is found in Argys, Rees and Brewer (1996).

Nonetheless, this important policy issue deserves more attention, particularly in terms of the underlying methodological difficulties.

Peer effects have been considered in an international context by Zimmer and Toma (2000). Their analysis, using data from the second international mathematics and science tests given in 1981, estimated achievement models across five countries (Belgium, France, New Zealand, Canada, and the USA) and incorporated public and private schools. They find that peer ability appears important, especially for low achieving students, and that peer effects may be more important in public than in private schools.

Because peer effects enter into a wide variety of other economic analyses and because they are the subject of intense policy deliberation, it remains surprising that there has not been more empirical research into the topic.

4.4.4. Racial integration

Racial integration of schools has been one of the most significant factors in US public schools over the past fifty years. Yet, while there has been an enormous amount of legislative and judicial attention to racial desegregation of schools, the analysis of its effects is quite limited.

The US Supreme Court ruling in *Brown v. Board of Education* (1954) held that separate but equal was unconstitutional because separate could not be equal[45]. This ruling led to dramatic changes in schools throughout the country. While school integration started slowly, the decade of the 1970s witnessed a substantial reduction in segregation brought about largely through legal pressure on local school districts [Welch and Light (1987)].

Many of the early (post-Brown) analyses, which focused on short run effects of purposefully moving students to less segregated schools, consider a variety of student outcomes and yield mixed effects of desegregation [Crain and Mahard (1978), Cook (1984), Armor (1995)]. These studies are, however, plagued by methodological problems – largely related to sample selection issues but also including the heterogeneity of desegregation circumstances – making it difficult to assess the general impact of desegregation efforts.

Another segment of this literature focused not so much on student outcomes but on the impact of desegregation efforts on the subsequent racial composition of schools. The large-scale exodus of whites from many cities and towns clearly dampened the impact of school desegregation on interracial contact, and beginning with analysis of "white flight" in the face of court-ordered desegregation by Coleman, Kelley and Moore (1975), much of the analytical focus shifted to outcomes defined in terms of racial contact [Welch and Light (1987), Clotfelter (2001)][46].

---

[45] *Brown v. Board of Education*, 347 U.S. 483 (1954).

[46] A related line of inquiry investigates racial composition and private schools [e.g., Clotfelter (1976) or Fairlie and Resch (2002)]. Whether or not private schools tend to be more segregated than public

Finally, a related but distinct strand of research focuses on whether peer racial composition, as opposed to desegregation actions, affects achievement for blacks as well as for other demographic groups. Coleman, Campbell, Hobson, McPartland, Mood, Weinfeld and York (1966) and its offshoots [U.S. Commission on Civil Rights (1967)] provided empirical evidence that racial isolation harms academic achievement[47]. Subsequent work by Crain (1970), Boozer, Krueger and Wolkon (1992), Grogger (1996) and Hoxby (2000c) finds that school racial composition affected academic, social, or economic outcomes. Hanushek (1972) finds that higher concentrations of blacks hurts both whites and blacks, but is concerned that the racial composition of the school may simply be a proxy for heterogeneity in school quality and other omitted factors. Rivkin (2000) finds no evidence that exposure to whites increases academic attainment or earnings for Black men or women in the high school class of 1982, and Cook and Evans (2000) indicate that little of the black–white difference in National Assessment of Educational Progress scores can be attributed to racial concentration. On the other hand, Hanushek, Kain and Rivkin (2001b) find that the racial composition of the school has a significant effect on black students, but not whites or Hispanics. Moreover, the negative effect of being in a school with higher concentrations of blacks is highly concentrated on blacks in the upper ability groups. The use of stacked panel data that permits controlling for other inputs in a very general manner suggests that unmeasured school quality can be ruled out as the primary cause of these findings and that specialized peer effects are the most likely explanation.

Most existing estimates have not paid close attention to the methodological issues surrounding identification of peer effects[48]. Moreover, the research has often failed to even separate out the most rudimentary differences in school quality[49]. Further research into aspects of the racial composition of schools, similar to peer research, appears to be a challenging but high value line of inquiry.

---

schools has also been the subject of considerable policy debate since Coleman, Hoffer and Kilgore (1982). These issues are, however, beyond the scope of this analysis.

[47] The Coleman Report data, collected in 1965, largely reflect the legal and behavioral equilibrium before court-ordered desegregation efforts, because most desegregation plans were instituted in subsequent periods [Welch and Light (1987)].

[48] A recent comprehensive review finds the evidence on achievement and psychological differences is very mixed [Schofield (1995)] and attributes the inconclusiveness largely to methodological shortcomings.

[49] See for example the U.S. Commission on Civil Rights (1967), which neglects any consideration of school factors [Hanushek (1972)]. Of course, an alternative argument for policy purposes might be that only the reduced form relationship is needed, because the correlates of racial composition may adjust with desegregation. Moreover, much of the discussion about school segregation goes far beyond the simple discussions of student achievement.

4.4.5. Family inputs

The emphasis of the original Coleman Report on the role of families in education has generated little subsequent disagreement. Most empirical studies of school performance include some measure of family background[50]. In fact, having some controls for family differences was a requirement for the previous tabulation of resource results, because ignoring these differences will undoubtedly bias resource coefficients through the correlation of family background and resources. Nonetheless, this research for the most part has not considered the details of what aspects of families are most important or of the causal structure of family effects.

The general argument has been that changing the important underlying characteristics of the family would be extraordinarily expensive even if policy makers wished to consider such an approach. Thus, for example, if mother's education were known to be important in a child's achievement, the best short-run policy probably is not to send all mothers back to school. For this reason, researchers have not paid close attention to the precise measurement and specification of family effects.

On the other hand, long run policies may nonetheless reasonably relate to family factors. For example, arguments for improving women's education in developing countries may reflect the potential impacts on children's achievement more than the normal arguments about the return to the mother of human capital investment, particularly in countries where women do not work much in the formal market[51].

But, if long-run policies are directed at family factors, it is important to know the exact nature and causal impact of families. Is it the education of mothers that is important? Or is it the education of fathers (which often is not given the same analytical attention)? Or is it some other aspect of the family – wealth, attitudes, expectations, or other things – that is truly important and that shows up through its correlation with parental education?

The little work that has been explicitly related to family factors has opened serious question about the underlying causal structure. For example, Behrman and Rosenzweig (2002) suggest that mother's education may not be as important in children's schooling as commonly believed, once proper attention is paid to the possibility of omitted factors[52]. Similarly, Mayer (1997) questions whether income per se affects the kinds of family outcomes that are normally subsumed under the topic of poverty and income.

---

[50] One large exception to this rule is that many studies of labor market effects or other performance measures that are collected after completion of schooling often neglect background information. See the review and discussion in Betts (1996).

[51] These arguments also interrelate with a variety of economic models of fertility that consider trade-offs between child quantity and quality, although most do not directly consider child achievement [see Becker and Lewis (1973), Willis (1973) and Hanushek (1992)].

[52] Their analysis relies on a sample of identical twins to separate the effects of mothers from other possible influences. While their cross-sectional estimates reproduce the common positive effects of mother's education, their refinements alter the sign.

Part of the issue in understanding families effects may arise from heterogeneous incentives within and across families [cf., Becker and Tomes (1976), Weinberg (2001)].

As policy debates venture into policies that are designed to change families, it is important to understand better the underlying structure. For example, as described previously, a variety of policies for developing countries point to family factors. But, in developed countries similar policy initiatives such as those designed to strength the family role or to ameliorate adverse family influences are increasingly discussed. The general problem has been that existing studies lack a convincing identification strategy that distinguishes true structural aspects of families from a variety of correlated proxies.

4.5. The importance of study quality

The conclusions that should be drawn from the prior tabulations of results have been questioned because no weighting is used to distinguish among the quality of the studies. While the previous discussion presents the universe of available evidence, the studies of educational performance clearly differ in quality and the potential for yielding biased results.

Two elements of quality, both related to model specification and estimation, are particularly important[53]. First, education policy in the USA is made by the 50 separate states, and the variations in spending, regulations, graduation requirements, testing, labor laws, and teacher certification and hiring policies are large. These potentially important differences – which are also the locus of most policy debates in the states – imply that any studies of student performance across states must include descriptions of the policy environment of schools or else they will be subject to standard omitted variables bias. The misspecification of models that ignore variations in state education policy (and other potential state differences) interacts with the estimation approach. As Hanushek, Rivkin and Taylor (1996) demonstrate, any bias in the estimated parameters will be exacerbated by aggregation of the estimation sample[54]. Nonetheless, the direction of any bias is an empirical issue, because it depends on the correlation of the omitted state regulatory and finance factors and the included school measures such as class size or spending.

---

[53] Krueger (2000) introduces a different measure of study quality. His proposed measure is the number of separate parameter estimates in a given published analysis. So, for example, a publication that included estimates from a production function for eighth grade reading and one for high school graduation would necessarily be lower quality than a publication that only reported on third grade mathematics. Because this criterion is not related to conventional statistical arguments about model misspecification, estimation bias, or the quality of the underlying data base, it is not pursued here.

[54] Loeb and Page (2000) argue that in some circumstances, such as their analysis of compensating differentials in teacher wages, state aggregate data will be superior because it averages over choices across districts within states. To deal with state policy variations they concentrate on within state differences with a state specific time trend employing a panel of salaries and school attainment.

Table 7

Percentage distribution of estimated effect of teacher–pupil ratio and expenditure per pupil by state sampling scheme and aggregation[a]

Level of aggregation of resources	Number of estimates	Statistically significant		Statistically insignificant
		Positive	Negative	
A. Teacher–pupil ratio				
Total	276	14%	14%	72%
Single-state samples[b]	157	11	18	71
Multiple-state samples[c]	119	18	8	74
Disaggregated within states[d]	109	14	8	78
State level aggregation[e]	10	60	0	40
B. Expenditure per pupil				
Total	163	27%	7%	66%
Single-state samples[b]	89	20	11	69
Multiple-state samples[c]	74	35	1	64
Disaggregated within states[d]	46	17	0	83
State level aggregation[e]	28	64	4	32

[a] Source: Hanushek (1997a), revised.
[b] Estimates from samples drawn within single states.
[c] Estimates from samples drawn across multiple states.
[d] Resource measures at level of classroom, school, district, or county, allowing for variation within each state.
[e] Resource measures aggregated to state level with no variation within each state.

Second, as noted, education is a cumulative process, but a majority of studies are purely cross-sectional with only contemporaneous measures of inputs. In other words, when looking at performance at the end of secondary schooling, many studies measure just the current teachers and school resources and ignore the dozen or more prior years of inputs. Obviously, current school inputs will tend to be a very imperfect measure of the resources that went into producing ending achievement. This mismeasurement is strongest for any children who changed schools over their career (a sizable majority in the USA) but, because of the heterogeneity of teachers within schools, also holds for students who do not move [see Hanushek, Kain and Rivkin (2001a)]. Even if contemporaneous measures were reasonable proxies for the stream of cumulative inputs, uncertainty about the interpretation and policy implications would remain. The coefficients would bear an ambiguous relationship to the underlying structure parameters of interest, making policy calculations difficult. But there is little reason to believe that they are good proxies.

While judgments about study quality have a subjective element, it is possible to make a crude cut based on violations of these two central problems. Table 7 provides insight into the pattern and importance of the specific omitted variables bias resulting from lack of information about key educational policy differences across states. This table considers two input measures: teacher–pupil ratio and expenditure per pupil. These inputs, on top of being important for policy, are included in a sufficient number of analyses at various levels of aggregation that they can provide direct information of potential misspecification biases. As discussed previously, the percentage of all estimates of the impact of teacher pupil ratios with significant positive estimates is evenly balanced by those with significant negative estimates. But this is not true for estimates relying upon samples drawn entirely within a single state, where the overall policy environment is constant and thus where any bias from omitting overall state policies is eliminated. For single state studies, the statistically significant effects are disproportionately negative. Yet, as the samples are drawn across states, the relative proportion positive and statistically significant rises. For those aggregated to the state level, almost 60% of the estimates are positive and statistically significant. The pattern of results also holds for estimates of the effects of expenditure differences, which are more likely to come from highly aggregate studies involving multiple states. (Expenditure studies virtually never provide direct analysis of performance across different classrooms or schools, since expenditure data are typically available only at the district level. Thus, they begin at a more aggregated level than many studies of real resources.)

This pattern of results is consistent with expectations from considering specification biases when favorable, but omitted, state policies tend to be positively correlated with resource usage. As noted, while the direction of any bias depends on the degree of correlation, under quite general circumstances any bias will tend to be more severe if estimation is conducted at the state level than if conducted at the classroom level [Hanushek, Rivkin and Taylor (1996)] [55]. The initial assessment of effects from Table 6 indicated little reason to be confident about overall resource policies. The refinement on quality in Table 7 indicates that a number of the significant effects may primarily be artifacts of the sampling and methodology.

The second problem is a different variant of model specification. Because education is a cumulative process, relating the level of performance at any point in time just to the current resources is likely to be misleading. The standard approach for dealing with this is the estimation of value-added models such as Equation (2) where attention is restricted to the growth of achievement over a limited period of time (when the flow of resources is also observed).

Table 8 displays the results of studies that consider value-added models for individual students. The top panel shows all such results, while the bottom panel follows the earlier approach of concentrating just on studies within a state. With the most refined investigation of quality, the number of studies gets quite small and

---

[55] The discussion of aggregation is part of a broader debate trying to reconcile the findings of Card and Krueger (1992a) with those presented here. See discussion below.

Table 8

Percentage distribution of estimated influences on student performance, based on value-added models of individual student performance[a]

Resources	Number of estimates	Statistically significant		Statistically insignificant
		Positive	Negative	
A. All studies				
Teacher–pupil ratio	78	12%	8%	80%
Teacher education	40	0	10	90
Teacher experience	61	36	2	62
B. Studies within a single state				
Teacher–pupil ratio	23	4%	13%	83%
Teacher education	33	0	9	91
Teacher experience	36	39	3	58

[a] Source: Hanushek (1997a), revised.

selective. In these, however, there is no support for systematic improvements through increasing teacher–pupil ratios and hiring teachers with more graduate education[56]. The effects of teacher experience are largely unaffected from those for the universe of studies. Again, because of the small and selective nature of these value-added studies within a single state, uncertainty about the precise effect of ignoring history remains. They do, however, make a *prima facie* case that the prior results about the effects of specific resources were not simply an artifact of study quality.

4.6. International evidence

Analysis of how schools affect student performance has been conducted considerably more in the USA than in other countries. Nonetheless, similar investigations have been conducted in other parts of the world, even though data limitations have tended to be more severe.

The evidence for countries other than the USA is potentially important for a variety of reasons. Other countries have varying institutional structures, so different findings could help to identify the importance of organization and overall incentives. Moreover, other countries frequently have much different levels and exhibit larger variance in resource usage, offering the prospect of understanding better the importance of pure

---

[56] Other possible explanations of the results also exist. For example, as discussed in more detail below, Rivkin, Hanushek and Kain (2001) are able to find statistically significant but small effects of class size differences, and these effects differ by socioeconomic status of the family. This analysis, based on very large samples, suggests the possibility that other analyses lack sufficient statistical power to detect the small and varying effects of some of the school factors.

Table 9
Percentage distribution of estimated expenditure parameter coefficients from 96 studies of educational production functions: developing countries[a]

| Input | Number of estimates | Statistically significant | | Statistically insignificant |
		Positive	Negative	
Teacher–pupil ratio	30	27%	27%	46%
Teacher education	63	56	3	41
Teacher experience	46	35	4	61
Teacher salary	13	31	15	54
Expenditure/pupil	12	50	0	50
Facilities	34	65	9	26

[a] Source: Hanushek (1995).

resource differences. For example, one explanation of the lack of relationship between resources and performance in the USA is its schools may be generally operating in an area of severe diminishing marginal productivity where marginal resource effects are small. By observing schools at very different levels of resources, however, it would be possible to distinguish between technological aspects of the production relationship and other possible interpretations of the evidence such as imprecise incentives for students and teachers.

Analysis in less developed countries has shown a similar inconsistency of estimated resource effects across studies. While these estimates typically come from special purpose analyses and are frequently not published in refereed journals, they do provide insights into resource use at very different levels of support. Table 9 provides evidence on resource effects from studies completed by 1990[57]. Two facets of these data compared to the previous US data stand out: 1) in general, a minority of the available studies suggests much confidence that the identified resources systematically and positively influence student performance; and 2) there is generally somewhat stronger support for these resource policies than that existing in US studies. Thus, the data hint that the importance of resources may vary with the level of resources, a natural presumption. Nonetheless, the evidence still does not suggest that pure resource policies can be expected to have a significant effect on student outcomes.

Similar evidence to that in the USA shows that very significant differences exist among teachers [Harbison and Hanushek (1992)]. Their analysis in the very poor region of northeast Brazil finds very large differences in total teacher effects. Surprisingly these differences are not related to simple measures such as the amount

---

[57] This compilation of results from Hanushek (1995) incorporates information from Fuller (1985), Harbison and Hanushek (1992), and a variety of studies during the 1980s.

of teacher education or experience, even though, for example, teacher education can be as little as four years.

The evidence on developed countries outside of the USA is more difficult to compile. The review by Vignoles, Levacic, Walker, Machin and Reynolds (2000) points to a small number of studies outside of the USA and shows some variation in them similar to that already reported among estimates elsewhere.

A set of consistent estimates for recent periods using the data from the Third International Mathematics and Science Study (TIMSS) is presented in Hanushek and Luque (2003). They employ the data on variations in scores within countries. The 36 countries with complete data are weighted toward more developed countries but do include poor countries. They find little evidence that any of the standard resource measures for schools are related to differences in mathematics and science scores within countries[58]. Moreover, there is no evidence in this consistent work that there are different effects of resources by income level of the country or by level of the resources. Thus, contrary to the conclusions of Heyneman and Loxley (1983), school resources do not appear relatively more important for poorer countries.

Woessman (2000, 2001) looks at cross national differences in TIMSS math and science scores and concludes that the institutional structure matters importantly for achievement. By pooling the student test scores across countries and estimating models that include both school and national characteristics, he finds suggestive evidence that the amount of competition from private schools and the amount of decentralization of decision making to schools have significant beneficial impacts, while union strength is detrimental and standard differences in resources across countries are not clearly related to student performance. The limited number of national observations for institutions nevertheless leaves some uncertainty about the estimates and calls for replication in other samples that permit, say, variations within countries in the key institutional features.

While the international evidence has been more limited, this situation is likely to be reversed profitably in the future. A key problem historically has been less available performance data for different countries, but this lack of information is being corrected. As student outcome data become more plentiful – allowing investigation of value added by teachers in schools in different environments, international evidence can be expected to grow in importance.

5. Interpretation of evidence on school performance

The previous work on educational production has provided substantial evidence that there are vast differences among teachers and schools. At the same time, these

---

[58] Estimation considered 9-year-old and 13-year-old students with the most countries available for the older populations (36) and fewer for the younger populations (21). Some countries were omitted because they failed to provide data on student backgrounds. The set of countries potentially offering data is shown in Table 4.

differences are not easily described by the resources employed or by any simple set of programmatic or behavioral descriptions. More importantly, since policy is often directed at the resource levels, questions about the effectiveness of the public provision of schooling naturally arise.

The evidence does not say that money and resources never matter. Nor does it say that money and resources could not matter. It simply describes the central patterns of results given the current organization and incentives in schools. Indeed, a plausible interpretation of the evidence is that some schools in fact use resources effectively but that these schools are counterbalanced by others that do not. At the same time, the expansion of resource usage unaccompanied by performance gains implies a high level of inefficiency in the current operations of schools.

The implications of these results, however, depend fundamentally on how the policy and decision making process is conceived. At one level, these conclusions clearly imply that educational policy making is more difficult than many would like. If resources had a consistent and predictable effect on student performance, policy making would be straightforward. State and national governments could decide how much money to invest in schools and could trust local districts to apply funds in a productive manner. But, the fact that local districts do not use funds effectively complicates this picture. The clearest message of existing research is that uniform resource policies are unlikely to work as intended.

The considerations of overall spending levels, either in legislatures or the courts, largely rest on the premise that local districts are best situated and motivated to use funds wisely and productively. The evidence currently does not support the effectiveness of local decision making in the current environment. There is ample evidence, moreover, that policy makers do not fully believe that local decision makers will do a good job. The extensive bodies of rules and regulations at the federal and state level are mainly designed to ensure that local districts do not do undesirable things in operating their schools and indicate a considerable distrust of the motivations and/or abilities of local districts. This, of course, runs into similar information problems. To set regulations appropriately, one would need to know how resources or process considerations affect student performance – which we do not know in any way sufficient for designing most regulatory approaches to good schooling.

An alternative perspective is simply that current incentives, within the public provision of schooling, do not motivate schools toward improving student performance [Hanushek (1994)]. The simple premise is that the unresponsiveness of performance to resources is largely a reflection that very little rests on student performance. Good and bad teachers or good and bad administrators can expect about the same career progressions, pay, and other outcomes making the choice of programs, organization, and behaviors less dependent on student outcomes than on other things that directly affect the actors in schools. Such a description is, however, itself much too simple, because we have limited experience with alternative incentive schemes [Hanushek (1994)]. The alternative incentive structures include a variety of conceptual approaches to providing rewards for improved student performance and range from merit pay for teachers to privatization and vouchers. Performance incentives recognize that there might be varying approaches by teachers and schools that are productive. Thus, they avoid the centralized "command and control" perspective of much current policy. At the same time, they recognize that simply decentralizing decision making is unlikely to work effectively unless there exist clear objectives and unless there is direct accountability[59]. Nonetheless, while some evidence is provided below, limited information is available about the design and impact of alternative incentive schemes in schools.

The existing work does not suggest resources never matter, but it also cannot describe circumstances where resources are used well. It does clearly indicate that the current organization and incentives of schools do little to ensure that any added resources will be used effectively.

5.1. Controversies

The preceding interpretations of the general ineffectiveness of school resource policies have been challenged on several grounds. The challenges generally suggest that the evidence and its interpretation may be biased.

5.1.1. Causality

A key issue in considering the results of the educational production function studies is whether they identify causal relationships. Resource allocations are determined by a complicated series of political and behavioral choices by schools and parents. The character of these choices could influence the estimates of the effectiveness of resources. Consider, for example, the result of systematically assigning school resources in a compensatory manner. If low achieving kids are given extra resources – say smaller classes, special remedial instruction, improved technology, and the like – there is an obvious identification problem. Low class size could simply mean kids need more help. Issues of this kind suggest both care in interpretation of results and the possible necessity of alternative approaches.

At the individual student level, correlations with aggregate district resources through either formula allocations or community decisions are not a major cause of concern. The classroom allocations may, however, be a concern. For example, within a school, low achievers may be placed in smaller classes, suggesting the possibility of simultaneity bias. Any such problems should be largely ameliorated by value-added models, which consider the student's prior achievement directly. The only concern then becomes allocations made on the basis of unmeasured achievement influences that are unrelated to prior achievement.

---

[59] While the decentralization considered here really refers to pure resource policies and general funding, the evidence supports this conclusion even at the level of school-based management; see Summers and Johnson (1996).

Lazear (2001) develops an optimizing model that provides motivation for the decisions of schools in setting class size. His theoretical model, based on profit maximizing schools, emphasizes the externality related to disruptive students. One key issue in the context of the previous empirical results is whether variations in disruption probabilities should be thought of as exogenous or whether alternatively they represent components of the teacher's classroom management ability, i.e., elements of teacher skill. Such a distinction is obviously very important in interpreting the model and the implications of it. While his model underscores the ambiguities of estimating reduced form models, the appropriate approach for testing the overall model or for estimating the behavioral equations is not developed.

Particularly in the area of class size analysis, a variety of approaches do go further in attempting to identify causal effects, and the results are quite varied. Hoxby (2000b) used de-trended variations in the size of birth cohorts to identify exogenous changes in class size in small Connecticut towns. Changes in cohort sizes, coupled with the lumpiness of classes in small school districts, can provide variations in class size that are unrelated to other factors. After pursuing her instrument strategy, she finds no significant impact of class size on achievement. Other studies have used aggregation approaches (by school or state) to construct instrumental variables estimators for the effects of class size [Akerhielm (1995), Boozer and Rouse (1995)] and have found more positive effects.

Several international studies have also pursued instrumental variables strategies that rely upon specific institutional structure. Angrist and Lavy (1999) note that Maimonides' Rule requires that Israeli classes cannot exceed forty students, so that, like in Hoxby's analysis, the lumpiness of classrooms may lead to large changes in class size when the numbers of students in a school approaches multiples of forty (and the preferred class size is greater than forty). They formulate a regression discontinuity approach to identify the effects of class size, but many of their estimates also use class size variation other than that generated by the discontinuities. The results provide generally positive but varying support for the effects of class size in different grades and circumstances. Case and Deaton (1999) rely upon the distinct policy regime of apartheid in South Africa to identify the effects of changes in resources and class size for black citizens. They argue that mobility restrictions and white decision making break the possible correlation of resources and individual errors, allowing them to identify the causal impact of resources. They find a significant positive relationship between pupil-teacher ratios (interpreted more generally as overall resources) and both attainment and achievement. Hanushek and Luque (2003), using the TIMSS data, perform a cross-country analysis restricted just to rural schools where mobility is restricted and schools frequently have a single classroom in the relevant grade, eliminating the normal concern about compensatory decision making. They not only find little evidence of consistent benefits from class size reduction but instead tend to find class size is positively related to achievement[60]. A final alternative is Lindahl (2000), who hypothesizes that differential summer learning across students could mask the importance of differences in school resources. Employing achievement data on a sample of Swedish students, the effects of resources are identified by assuming that parental inputs are the same in the summer and in the school year, while school inputs operate only during the school year. He estimates significant effects of class size differences[61].

Unfortunately, identification of truly exogenous determinants of class size, or resource allocations more generally, is sufficiently rare that other compromises in the data and modeling are frequently required. These coincidental compromises jeopardize the ability to obtain unbiased estimates of resource effects and may limit the generalizability of any findings. Rivkin, Hanushek and Kain (2001), employing better data of multiple cohort panels, make use of exogenous variations in class sizes within Texas schools across grades and cohorts to identify the impact of class size. The very large samples in that analysis provide estimates of small but statistically significant effects of class size on performance for earlier grades but not later grades and that the effects vary with student background[62].

In sum, these alternative approaches yield inconsistent results both in terms of class size effects and in terms of the effects of alternative methodologies. The results in each of these studies tend to be quite sensitive to estimation procedures and to model specification. As a group, nonetheless, the results are more likely to be statistically significant with the expected sign than those presented previously for all studies, but the typical estimate (for statistically significant estimates) tends to be very small in magnitude. At the same time, the results of these approaches are inconsistent in terms of statistical significance, grade pattern, and magnitude of any effects, making it difficult to understand to what circumstances any results might generalize.

Consideration of the determination of school inputs has not been undertaken systematically, although anecdotal evidence suggests that it should be given more attention. For example, many teacher contracts in the USA allow more experienced teachers to choose the schools where they teach, leading to the previous concerns about the underlying behavior behind estimated achievement and experience relationships [Greenberg and McCall (1974), Murnane (1981), Hanushek, Kain and Rivkin (2001c)].

---

[60] A second approach removes a common achievement difference if the student's classroom is below the average for the grade, thus removing an average compensatory effect (if it exists) for each country. This approach similarly leads to little difference from the basic estimation.

[61] This analysis follows prior work on summer learning differentials [e.g., Heyns (1978), Entwisle and Alexander (1992)], but he also suggests implications for the analysis of school differences. He concludes that the previous value-added specifications may be tainted by differential summer learning.

[62] The large samples in that analysis, approaching one million students, permit very precise estimates of the small effects. Krueger (1999) suggests that one reason many estimates are statistically insignificant is that the underlying parameter is very small and the typical estimation sample is insufficiently large to discriminate between small and zero. Of course, the small size of the parameter is relevant for any policy deliberations, because small effects must be compared to the costly nature of the interventions.

At the same time, little has been done on overall expenditure determination and its possible effects[63]. Similarly, while various policies and incentives drive much of the education of teachers, the effects of this have not generally been integrated into the achievement analysis.

While these topics are reconsidered below, it is clear that further work into the determination of resource patterns and the relationship to production function analysis is an important area for additional research. The difficulty of course is finding ways to identify the separate relationships in a convincing manner.

5.1.2. Labor market outcomes

Taken as a group, the production function studies give little indication that variations of resources have anything to do with present variations in student performance. The overall findings related, for example, to teacher–pupil ratios are dominated by estimates for test score measures of outcomes (217 out of 276). Test scores are nonetheless not generally the ultimate object of educational policy, but their use instead reflects growing evidence suggesting variations in test scores have important effects in the labor market. However, the widely-publicized findings of Card and Krueger (1992a) are taken as contrary evidence to the general picture given previously by indicating that variations in school resources are related to earnings differences among workers[64]. Some discussion has suggested that the most important difference between this latter study and the bulk of those reported previously comes from the measurement of outcomes, i.e., labor market experiences versus (typically) test scores [see Burtless (1996a)].

On the other hand, the test score–earnings linkage previously discussed provides a *prima facie* case that outcome measurement is not the source of difference. Moreover, specific reviews of the larger set of estimates in the resource-earnings literature suggest no significant differences from the overall results presented above [Betts (1996), Hanushek (1997a)]. Yet, because of frequent citations of the different findings by Card and Krueger, it is useful to investigate the possible sources of the differences.

The divergent findings may simply be explained by variations in the level and environment of schooling across different eras. The Card and Krueger (1992a) analysis begins with samples of adult workers from the 1970 and 1980 Censuses of Population and fills in information about the schooling circumstances of individuals from information about their year and state of birth. The workers in their sample

---

[63] Some work has considered specific expenditures, such as special education [see, for example, Lankford and Wyckoff (1996), Cullen (2002)]. General expenditure determination and its effects on production function estimation has not, however, received much attention.

[64] The Card and Krueger (1992a) analysis of school resources and earnings is the most discussed, but it follows a larger line of research. See, for example, Welch (1966), Johnson and Stafford (1973) and Wachtel (1976). An insightful review of past studies that considers underlying characteristics of the studies is Betts (1996).

attended schools between the 1920s and the 1970s, implying variations in the level of resources going far beyond what is found today. If added resources have diminishing effects on student achievement, current school operations may be largely "on the flat" of the production function, while Card and Krueger observe ranges from the past where resources had stronger effects[65].

A related possibility might be that the political economy of schools has changed over time. For example, with the rise of teachers unions and the resulting change in bargaining positions, resources might be used in different ways and have different student achievement implications now than in the past [e.g., Borland and Howsen (1992), Peltzman (1993), Hoxby (1996b)]. In other words, it is quite possible that the enormous changes in educational resources did have an effect on outcomes in the first half of the 20th century, but that more recent studies are also correct in finding no effect for the sorts of resource changes discussed in current schools.

Nonetheless, the most important set of reasons for the different conclusions likely involves specification issues. To begin with, many of the direct analyses of earnings include just the level of school resources, but none of the other factors that might influence student achievement and skill development. For example, it is plausible that students attending schools with a high level of resources also have parents who contribute more time, energy, and money to their education. If parental inputs are left out of the calculation, any estimated effects of school resources would tend to overstate the true independent effect of resources[66]. Further, as pointed out above, aggregation of school inputs is also likely to exacerbate any biases due to specification issues [Hanushek, Rivkin and Taylor (1996)]. Most of the earnings analyses observe school resources measured only at the aggregate state level. The Card–Krueger estimate comes from resource data aggregated to the state level, but no measures of state policy differences are included, so their estimates are subject to this bias[67].

As critiques by Speakman and Welch (1995) and Heckman, Layne-Farrar and Todd (1996a,b) show, the Card and Krueger (1992a) estimates are very sensitive to

[65] The key element is that at high levels of resources the marginal productivity of added resources may be significantly less than at low levels of resources. While not a direct test of this on-the-flat thesis, the lack of significantly stronger resource effects in developing countries introduces some question about this hypothesis; see Hanushek (1995), or, in a growth context, Hanushek and Kimko (2000).

[66] For example, Card and Krueger (1992b) do not include any family background factors, so – in addition to the general aggregations issues of missing state policies – the effects of pupil–teacher ratios will be confounded with any family factors that are correlated at the state level. They stratify by race but include no measures of family background variations that might permit identification of a pure effect of pupil–teacher ratios.

[67] If, on the other hand, there are important measurement errors in the school resources, aggregation could be beneficial because this would tend to average out any measurement problems. A central concern of Hanushek, Rivkin and Taylor (1996) is distinguishing between the harmful effects of aggregation and model misspecification and the beneficial effects of aggregation and measurement error. That analysis rejects the hypothesis that measurement error is a primary element in the apparent importance of resources in the more aggregated studies.

the specific estimation procedure. Moreover, the state earnings differences cannot be interpreted in terms of school quality differences in the way that Card and Krueger interpret them. In order to identify their estimates of school quality, Card and Krueger (1992a) must assume that the migration of people across states is random and not based on differential earnings opportunities. Heckman, Layne-Farrar and Todd (1996a,b) show that there is selective migration and that this fundamental requirement for their interpretation is untrue[68].

Thus, while some of the discrepancy in results could be attributed to different changes in schools over time, much of it appears to arise simply from the analytical problems in Card and Krueger (1992a). In more general consideration going beyond this specific paper, there appears to be little difference in results.

5.1.3. Meta-analysis and the summary of results

Alternative procedures exist for summarizing the results of studies. These approaches, more common to other fields of study, sometimes go under the general title of "meta-analysis". A preferred approach to assessing disparate results would involve combining the underlying data of the studies directly to develop statistical inferences and tests of hypotheses across the studies. Unfortunately the original data are seldom available for reanalysis and even when they are, combining data from different sources can be difficult which forces a variety of compromises in the aggregation of results. The previous data on studies in Tables 6–8 represent one approach to the aggregation of results, an approach which relies on the minimal set of factors standardly reported. But, instead of simply reporting the distribution of results, others have attempted to do formal statistical tests[69]. An attempt to apply formal statistical tests to education production function data is found in Hedges, Laine and Greenwald (1994) and Greenwald, Hedges and Laine (1996). They wish to do formal hypothesis testing using the available data from essentially the same set of published studies employed here[70]. The most basic problem with their statistical analysis is that it

---

[68] They also show that the results differ significantly across time and that they are very sensitive to the precise specification of the models. Speakman and Welch (1995) further show that virtually all of the effects of state school resources work through earnings of college attendees, even though the resource measures relate only to elementary and secondary schools.

[69] The primary argument against the simple tabulations, or vote-counting, employed here derives from the stylized analysis of combining a series of small experiments employing tests with low power, where more studies can actually lead to false conclusions. These examples have little relevance to the statistical tests developed in a regression framework with the very large samples frequently available.

[70] Some of the problems with doing this are immediately evident. Combining testing information is best motivated from thinking about variations in estimates of a single common parameter, something that is hard to define given the variations in underlying model specifications. More importantly, published articles frequently do not (and cannot) provide sufficient information. For example, if parameter estimates are correlated across studies, say because they reflect performance in different grades of one school district, estimation of the combined variance of the estimator would require knowledge of the

fails to address the fundamental problem of whether resources are consistently related to performance. Instead, the question they pose is whether there is any evidence that resources or expenditure differences *ever* appear to affect student performance. They explicitly test the null hypothesis that all parameters indicating the effect of a specific resource on student performance are simultaneously equal to zero; i.e., H_0: $\beta_1 = \beta_2 = \cdots = \beta_n = 0$, where the β_i are the underlying parameters relating a specific resource to student performance in one of the n available estimates. If any single underlying parameter (i.e., one β_i) for the combined sample of studies across varied schooling circumstances is not zero, the null hypothesis is false (that is, someplace there is an effect on student performance). Their statistical procedures are designed in such a case to reject the null hypothesis, leading to acceptance of the alternative that at least one study indicated the resource was related to performance[71]. They reject the null, but it does not change the overall interpretation of the econometric results.

5.1.4. Experimental evidence (STAR experiment)

In attempting to understand the effects of specific resources on student performance, an appealing alternative to econometric estimation is the use of random-assignment experiments. Such an approach can overcome a variety of concerns raised above about selection, causation, and the like. In the mid-1980s, because of ambiguity about the effects of class size on student performance, the State of Tennessee launched a random-assignment experiment in reducing class sizes. The design was heavily influenced by an early summary of research by Glass and Smith (1979) that suggested student achievement was roughly constant across class sizes until the class size got down to approximately 15 to 1. After 15 to 1, reductions in class size appeared to yield gains in student performance. Based on this, a group of kindergarten through third graders in Tennessee was randomly assigned to either large classes (22–24 students) or small classes (14–16 students)[72]. Students were followed over time as they progressed from kindergarten through third grade.

The student testing shows that children in smaller classes did better at the end of kindergarten and that this better performance was maintained through the third grade.

---

covariances – something that is never provided. Problems on nonindependence enter into the tabulations previously presented, but they are clearly less central to the interpretation of the results than in the case of combined significance testing.

[71] In discussing precisely the issue of how to interpret rejection of this null hypothesis, Hedges and Olkin (1985, p. 45) state: "It is doubtful if a researcher would regard such a situation as persuasive evidence of the efficacy of a treatment".

[72] The design was actually more complicated. The large classes were broken into two groups, one with teacher aides and one without aides. To be eligible for participating in the experiment, a school also had to be large enough so as to ensure that there was at least one small and large class. For a description the experiment and the basic results, see Word, Johnston, Bain, Fulton, Zaharies, Lintz, Achilles, Folger and Breda (1990).

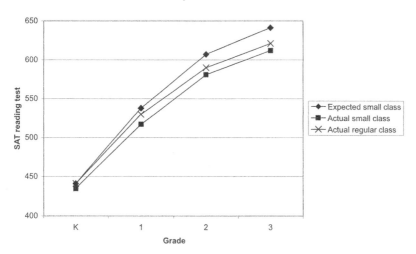

Fig. 1. Actual and expected student performance in reading in project STAR, by grade.

This evidence is sometimes taken as refuting the econometric evidence on teacher–pupil ratios that was presented earlier, but two aspects are important to consider. First, while the use of experimentation is an important research approach [Hanushek (1994), Mosteller (1995)], the actual implementation of this experiment is open to question. Second, the findings, which pertain to a very large policy change in very specific circumstances, yielded small and difficult to interpret results.

A number of questions arise about the quality of the randomization in the STAR experiment. Specifically, because of lack of data, it is difficult to assess the randomization of students or teachers into the experiment. There was substantial nonrandom attrition from the experiment; 51% of students initially in the experiment left before the end of the experiment. Substantial numbers (up to 12% by test) did not take annual tests; significant proportions of students changed experimental group (with the largest numbers going from large to small classes) during the experiment. It is difficult to assess the impact of any of these with the existing data [see Hanushek (1999), Krueger (1999)].

The second issue is interpretation of the results. The initial achievement differences found in the year students entered a small class were maintained but did not become wider through the grades [Word, Johnston, Bain, Fulton, Zaharies, Lintz, Achilles, Folger and Breda (1990), Krueger (1999)]. Because they continue to get more resources (smaller classes), these resources should, according to the general hypothesis, keep producing a growing advantage. Figure 1 shows the difference in reading performance in small classes that was observed across grades in Project STAR. (The results for math performance are virtually identical in size and pattern). It also shows how the observed outcomes diverge from what would be expected if the impact in kindergarten were also obtained in later grades.

Even if taken at face value, however, a significant issue remains: to what circumstances should the results be generalized?[73] The Tennessee experiment identified performance differences related to very large changes in class size at the entry into school. No similar experimental evidence looks at schools outside of Tennessee, at later grades, at smaller reductions, or at different absolute levels of class size. The previous econometric evidence found that some introductions of lower class appeared effective, even if across the board results were unlikely. But, like the Tennessee results, there is no indication from the econometric studies of when class size reduction is likely to work.

In sum, the potential application of random assignment experiments to schools is a very important innovation. Indeed, it offers an attractive alternative to the more common event, moving directly to major public funding of full-scale programs[74]. The existing results from the one major experiment that exists, however, do not offer any substantial contradiction to the previous econometric findings.

5.1.5. Consumer behavior

The concept of increased consumer choice with respect to schools has been high on a variety of reform agendas. At the same time there is considerable choice of schools that comes through residential choice that is frequently tied to specific schools. While moving residence is clearly costly and clearly provides a blunt instrument for school choice, it nonetheless operates on the margin. Each year one-fifth of American households change location, allowing considerable room for exercising consumer choice of schools. An issue here is whether this choice by consumers affects the results observed about the operations of schools[75].

A general conceptual argument against the inefficiency in school provision revolves around consumers and keys on notions of Tiebout moving behavior [Tiebout (1956)].

---

[73] A second significant issue, discussed below, is whether the resulting effects are large enough to justify further policy initiatives. The magnitude of the difference in performance is very small: a 1/3 reduction in class size over four years produced an average gain of about 0.2 standard deviations of student achievement.

[74] In 1996, the State of California moved to a statewide program of providing significant additional funds to all schools that lowered class sizes in primary grades to state-prescribed levels. This program appears to have been the policy implementation of perceived results from the STAR experiment. Having done this on a statewide basis, there is also no effective way to evaluate the results of such an initiative, so that neither California nor other states can learn from this program. The existing evidence provides little reason to be optimistic about the future achievement effects of this policy Stecher and Bohrnstedt (1999).

[75] A different perspective on Tiebout effects comes from consideration of estimation of expenditure demand functions, where choice of communities by families will generally lead to overstating the income elasticity of demand [Goldstein and Pauly (1981), Bergstrom, Rubinfeld and Shapiro (1982), Gramlich and Rubinfeld (1982) and Rubinfeld, Shapiro and Roberts (1987)].

Consumers appear to desire higher spending for schools; if wasted, one would expect lessened demand and/or moving of consumers to districts where there was more efficient production. This in turn would put pressure on districts to become more efficient.

The evidence suggests that there is consumer pressure, but that it is insufficient to overcome the existing variations in efficiency. The one direct investigation of jurisdictional competition is Hoxby (2000a) that considers how the numbers of districts in a metropolitan area – a measure of the potential for Tiebout competition – affects performance of the public schools[76]. She finds that more competition increases outcomes measured by test scores, attainment, and early career earnings. She also suggests that districts are more efficient when there is more competition among districts.

Most work has not focused directly on the relationship between school efficiency and consumer behavior but instead has investigated pieces of consumer choices. First, consumers have been shown to be willing to pay for schools with higher test performance. In particular, estimation of hedonic price indices for housing, beginning with Kain and Quigley (1975) and Rosen and Fullerton (1977), demonstrate positive effects of school achievement levels on housing demand. More recently, Black (1999) refines this approach by considering houses very close to school district boundaries – where contamination of unmeasured neighborhood quality is likely to be small – and finds that test scores of local schools have a strong effect on house prices. Similarly, Weimer and Wolkoff (2001) confirm such within district capitalization of school performance. Second, consideration of the political economy of school budgeting suggests that budget maximizing bureaucrats may act to push expenditure above the optimum [Romer and Rosenthal (1979), Filimon, Romer and Rosenthal (1982), Romer, Rosenthal and Munley (1992), Inman (1987), Rothstein (1992)]. By gaming voters in the face of budget reversion levels, bureaucrats are able to push the median voter above her optimum spending level. Third, investigations of demand for spending – which typically assumes that expenditure is the same as quantity demanded – have paid no attention to quality of governmental services [e.g., Borcherding and Deacon (1972), Bergstrom and Goodman (1973), Poterba (1997)]. In short, most existing analyses do not consider either consumer awareness of inefficiencies or consumer reactions to any inefficiencies.

An alternative view of the forces behind the inefficiency of schools relates to self-interest of school personnel. Pritchett and Filmer (1999) consider how the interests of school personnel align with the decisions that are made and conclude that such self-interest appears important. Because of the special role of school personnel in setting policy, these forces could distort the preferences and choices of consumers.

---

[76] The underlying analysis uses instrumental variables (based on local geography) to circumvent endogeneity problems with district choice. The estimates of Tiebout choice effects disappear when endogeneity is not considered. An alternative set of estimates of public school choice on outcomes is found in Hanushek and Rivkin (2003).

A basic problem with all of these indirect approaches is the failure to distinguish school quality, or the value-added by schools, from the level of achievement in a school. Indeed, this is almost certainly the problem facing consumers and offers an explanation for remaining inefficiency. Without information about the contributions of families and of schools, consumers face a critical information problem. This information problem, which by all accounts appears to be serious, will in turn lead consumers to make nonoptimal decisions about location, school spending, and the degree of inefficiency that exists in local schools.

The analysis of school changing by Hanushek, Kain and Rivkin (2001a) does suggest that parents obtain reasonable (value-added) information about school quality, even though such information is not directly provided by standard accountability systems. A difficulty in analyzing choice through mobility is that families move for a wide variety of reasons including changes in jobs and family circumstances. Some of these underlying causes will directly affect student performance, and the analysis of school choice must take this into account. The analysis in Hanushek, Kain and Rivkin (2001a) concentrates on long run achievement effects of a move, under the presumption that the effects of other factors die out after a move, and finds that families moving to and within suburban areas tend to increase their children's achievement.

Clearly, the role of consumers within the determination of school policies and outcomes is an area for research, because the role of consumer demand is central to many perspectives on schools. We return to part of this issue below.

5.1.6. Inefficiency and estimation approach

Another approach to estimating production frontiers involves variants of mathematical programming models or imposition of assumptions about the errors in an econometric formulation to capture the frontier notion. The underlying production theory calls for estimating the maximum feasible output from a set of inputs. If inefficiency exists in some schools, estimation should conceptually take it into account. The approaches follow a variety of estimation strategies with data envelope analysis (DEA) being one of the more common (see, for example, the early work in Charnes, Cooper and Rhodes (1978) or Ruggiero (1996) and the references therein). Related work along more conventional econometric lines concentrates on the specialized nature of the error term that would be generated in the context of a production frontier [e.g., Aigner and Chu (1968), Aigner, Lovell and Schmidt (1977)]. An extension combining some features of both can be found in Grosskopf, Hayes, Taylor and Weber (1997).

The programming model has been used chiefly to consider both the trade-off between alternative outcomes (e.g., math and reading or test scores and graduation rates) and to uncover the most efficient way to produce these outcomes. The basic idea is that an efficient school is one producing the maximum output for its inputs. The estimation then constrains schools to lie on or below the production frontier. As is typical of these approaches, the number of "efficient" schools will be the same as the number of separate inputs, and all other schools will be compared to the efficient ones. Since this approach provides a direct measure of efficiency, it is conceptually possible to investigate how consumers behave when faced with varying efficiency. These approaches, however, suffer from the presumption that the small number of inputs fully captures the relevant production factors and that no measurement error exists[77]. For computational reasons, only a small number of inputs are considered, and these often do not take into account the influence of family background or other nonschool factors. But to fit the underlying theory, it must be the case that other firms can reproduce the output of the efficient firm – which would not be really possible if performance relied on other unmeasured inputs such as managerial skill or missing dimensions of teacher quality.

The stochastic versions relax these assumptions by explicitly including a one-sided error for efficiency (constrained to be less than zero) along with a symmetric error. That is, consider modifying the error in Equation (1) such that:

$$v_{it} = \epsilon_{it} + \eta_{jt},$$

where individual i attends school j during year t and school j has a stochastic efficiency term with $\eta_{jt} \leqslant 0$. If η is uncorrelated with the family and school inputs, then ordinary least squares estimation provides consistent estimation and, with specification of the distributions of ϵ and η, maximum likelihood provides efficient estimates. But, of course, the key assumption is that inefficiency is uncorrelated with any of the observed inputs – an unlikely event unless there is truly nothing systematic about the efficiency of schools. A variety of approaches expand on these models to incorporate both the notions of production frontiers involving multiple outputs and stochastic elements [see, for example, Grosskopf, Hayes, Taylor and Weber (1997)], but these will be subject to the same underlying issues.

The investigation of inefficiency by schools is clearly a worthwhile pursuit, especially in light of the previous evidence about performance of schools. Nevertheless, the current limitations of programming solutions and other econometric approaches appear overwhelming.

5.1.7. Multiple outputs

Much of the analysis of school performance treats the production of achievement in a given area as independent of that in other areas. Thus, for example, the determination of mathematics performance is separate from that of reading performance. If, however, schools are actively deciding among outcomes and they compete for resources (generally denominated in terms of time), differences in performance among schools when measured in a single dimension may simply reflect different motivation to

---

[77] Because they do not begin with a stochastic formulation, the programming approaches typically do not yield information about the statistical significance of any parameter estimates.

produce a given array of outputs. That is, a school emphasizing reading may look inefficient in the production of mathematics if the performance in mathematics is compared to the total set of inputs to the school. A number of studies have directly investigated varying student performance in a multiple outcome fashion through traditional simultaneous equations estimation [e.g., Levin 1970, Boardman, Davis and Sanday (1977)]. The problem in this estimation is the difficulty in identifying the separate equations for each outcome – because it is generally difficult to find factors that affect one outcome but not the others. One novel approach, however, is Brown and Saks (1975). In their formulation, school districts are portrayed as maximizing a welfare function defined over both the level and the variance in achievement. They then estimate reduced form equations for each. They demonstrate that, while school resources are not systematically related to the level of achievement in a majority of the estimates, their apparent strength is increased by also considering the variance in performance. One difficulty with this approach is that it rests upon a presumed common objective function that is not observable. Thus, much like the problems of basing estimates of consumer demand functions on the researcher's presumption of the utility function, this analysis gets it power from specifying the elements of the common preferences of school districts. But, again, the largest problem is that identification of the underlying structural parameters is not possible, making the application of this less useful for any policy purposes.

The common solution for maximizing multiproduct production functions requires some source of the relative weights for each output – making prices particularly attractive in the analysis of general firm behavior. Such prices are not readily available for school outputs.

The previously discussed data envelope analysis (DEA) lists as one of its virtues the ability to handle multiple outputs. Contrary to the normal production theory optimization, outputs are not aggregated according to any simple value maximization process. A discussion of the criteria employed can be found in Grosskopf, Hayes, Taylor and Weber (1997). A key element in this aggregation is that any inefficiency is found in the transformation of inputs into aggregate output, as opposed to finding the output combination that maximizes any social welfare function[78].

Finally, by going to the dual of the production problem it is possible to frame the estimation in terms of cost functions [e.g., Downes and Pogue (1994) or Duncombe, Ruggiero and Yinger (1996)][79]. With maximization, this approach provides an

---

[78] An alternative statistical approach to dealing with multiple outputs is the estimation of canonical correlation models [e.g., Gyimah-Brempong and Byapong (1991)]. These methods use statistical criteria to maximize the correlation of aggregate outputs and inputs, but the criteria in general is not clearly related to underlying structural models or optimization on the part of schools.

[79] These dual approaches also yield qualitatively the same results as the direct expenditure studies except that the impacts are inverted. An expenditure parameter in a production function estimate that is close to zero translates into a very large cost of obtaining any given student outcome. Thus, for example, Duncombe, Ruggiero and Yinger (1996) suggest implausibly that it costs two and half times as much to

alternative estimation approach that can characterize directly the relationships among various outputs. But the estimation relies not only on maximization of outcomes but also on having accurate measures of input prices. Input prices are particularly problematic with respect to the primary input – teachers. As discussed below, the supply function for teachers of varying quality is unknown, making it difficult to integrate into the production analysis.

Many policy discussions relate directly to consideration of varying outcomes of the educational process, yet little is known either about the trade-offs that are present or about differential consumer demand for outcomes. As data on multiple outcomes increasingly become available, the possibilities of inferring consumer demand from behavior and choices expand.

5.2. Cost considerations

One remarkable aspect of most considerations of educational performance and school decisions is a general lack of attention to the costs of alternatives. Perhaps because the evidence about systematic effects of different programs, of different attributes of schools, or of various other inputs has been so inconsistent, most attention has focused on whether or not a particular input has a positive and statistically significant effect on achievement. But knowing that something might be expected to improve student performance is insufficient to make it the object of public policy. One would clearly want to know whether there were alternative uses of funds that produced higher achievement, or even higher value outside of schools.

The policy problem is easy to see in the case of discussions of policies to reduce class size. Most of the debate has centered on whether one can expect any achievement gain from a simple policy of reducing class sizes. But even if one takes the results of the Tennessee STAR experiment as accurate, they suggest a very small magnitude of effect on performance: a 1/3 reduction in class size over four years produced an average gain of about 0.2 standard deviations of student achievement [Krueger (1999)][80]. Any consideration of class size reductions should clearly be put in terms of the cost of the program and alternative uses of funds.

An important part of the problem, however, is that the cost of alternative inputs is not well understood. In order to assess the relative benefits of employing alternative inputs, it would be appropriate to weight by the cost of each input. Yet, particularly when the inputs reflect different attributes of teachers (e.g., experience) or inputs (e.g., science laboratory quality), little information is available about costs of the inputs[81].

---

achieve a gain in achievement in some downstate New York districts as compared to the average school district in New York State.

[80] These estimates are roughly similar to those for disadvantaged fourth grade students found in Rivkin, Hanushek and Kain (2001), but considerably larger than those for more advantaged students. Putting these results into cost terms reinforces the small magnitude of the estimates.

[81] Levin and McEwan (2001) describe cost analysis based on adding the average cost of components of programs. This approach moves in the right direction of introducing costs into educational decisions,

Teachers are perhaps the best example. It is possible to identify how effective different salaries are in attracting a pool of teachers without regard to their characteristics [Murnane, Singer, Willett, Kemple and Olsen (1991)]. It is also possible to make some assessment about the relationship between salaries and specific characteristics of teachers [e.g., Hanushek and Pace (1995), Ballou (1996), Ballou and Podgursky (1997)] or labor markets [Toder (1972), Antos and Rosen (1975), Chambers (1977), Levinson (1988)]. More generally, compensating differentials for teachers may lead to nominal salary differentials that are misleading in terms of individual decision making [e.g., Loeb and Page (2000)]. Finally, by looking across time, one can see how teacher salaries cut the distribution of all college graduates, as a possible indication of the overall quality of teachers [Hanushek and Rivkin (1997), Flyer and Rosen (1997)]. However, even suspending concerns about the value of separate teacher attributes, the existing studies do not give sufficient information to integrate any potential benefits with costs. Little progress has been made on characterizing the supply function for quality.

The analysis of teachers has been more detailed than analyses of other school inputs. Even such apparently straightforward calculations as the costs of altering class size have been generally neglected. When attempted, the difficulties become apparent, because the specification of precisely how the policy is implemented along with other complementary changes that would be required has received little attention [see, for example, Stecher and Bohrnstedt (1999)].

In many ways it is surprising that the discussion of costs is so short. Programmatic costs do not seem to enter systematically in much educational decision making, suggesting a clear reason for observed inefficiencies in resource use. It also suggests that investigation of costs, particularly for quality aspects of school inputs, is a fertile area of study.

5.3. Institutional structure and incentives

The existing evidence is conditioned by the organization and structure of existing schools. Specifically, the prevailing incentives in schools may not create very strong pressures for improving student performance [Hanushek (1994)]. Altered incentives, on the other hand, could potentially lead to very different outcomes.

At the outset, however, it is important to note that a variety of incentives currently exist and that school personnel respond to them. Traditionally few incentives have existed with respect to improved student performance, but instead have pointed in other directions. For example, financial incentives from state payments to schools for children in special education have distorted classification rates into special education [Cullen (2002)]. Or, unionization has influenced the efficiency of school and the

---

but it cannot deal with quality concerns and other reasons why the average and marginal cost might differ.

patterns of their resource usage [Hoxby (1996b)]. Public schools also appear to react to consumer choices, perhaps because of the relationship to property values discussed previously. In any event, schools facing wider competition from other districts show improved performance and efficiency [Hoxby (2000a), Hanushek and Rivkin (2003)]. The issue is not the existence of incentives but the direction, force, and focus of incentives. While consideration of incentives derived from competition with public schools is considered next, some altered incentives have been attempted within the public schools, and they are the focus of this section.

Perhaps the most discussed incentive topic is merit pay – providing differential pay for teachers based on judgments of performance. Most people think this is a natural kind of policy, mimicking pay systems found in other industries. The common evaluation of those policies attempted is that they fail [Cohen and Murnane (1986), Hatry, Greiner and Ashford (1994)]. The generalizations are that these systems tend to evolve into systems of relatively uniform pay and that they often tend to end up being extra pay for extra work instead of extra pay for good performance. The lessons from existing attempts at merit pay, however, remain unclear. Because performance contracts exist broadly outside of schools, it seems necessary to describe why education is different from other sectors. For example, other areas, similar to education, have difficulty in measuring the contributions of each individual in the firm and need cooperation among workers – yet they maintain differentiated pay. Indeed, even closely related activities like business schools use substantial merit systems and find considerable success [Brickley and Zimmerman (2001)]. Private nonsectarian schools appear to use merit pay more extensively than public schools [Ballou (2001)] and also to rely more frequent judgments about teachers and to let go teachers who are not performing well [Ballou and Podgursky (1997)].

Part of the issue in assessing merit pay plans revolves around expectations for the incentives. Most merit pay plans have been evaluated in terms of the performance of the existing teachers. This assessment assumes that the most significant issue is whether or not teachers are trying hard to do well. If they are not, merit pay may induce more and better efforts, leading to improved student performance. An alternative view is that the most significant aspect of merit pay proposals revolves around changes in the stock of teachers, or the selection issue. Merit pay schemes might provide incentives for better teachers to stay and for poorer teachers to leave and thus may have little to do with variations in effort. Existing evaluations have not focused on the employment aspects.

Schools have not made much use of personnel incentive systems developed in other industries. Nor have they considered the theoretical literature developed for other organizations. A key element of parts of this has to do with partial measurement performance and the potential incentives set up by this within organizations [e.g., Baker (1992, 2002)].

A key element in any individual-specific accountability system is accurate and reliable measurement of performance. On this score, a variety of approaches have related student performance directly to teachers. Most notable is the Tennessee Value-

Added Assessment System (TVAAS) that is mandated by state law but does not include rewards or sanctions for individual teachers [Sanders and Horn (1994, 1995)]. Alternative approaches have been developed in Dallas, Texas [Mendro, Jordan, Gomez, Anderson and Bembry (1998)] and would include the previously discussed statistical models for estimating teacher effects. A variety of concerns have been raised about relying specifically on student test performance, including undue focus on tests that partially measure performance, but importantly there is evidence that principal ratings are highly correlated with estimates of value-added by teachers [Murnane (1975), Armor, Conry-Oseguera, Cox, King, McDonnell, Pascal, Pauly and Zellman (1976)]. Nonetheless, analysis of methodology for evaluating teachers on the basis of performance and of incentive systems that utilize such information remains limited.

States have, however, moved away from developing teacher-specific incentive systems and toward group ratings and accountability. A currently popular reform approach – standards-based reform and school accountability – can be thought of as providing different incentives, although some incentives in these reform efforts are quite confused [Hanushek and Raymond (2001)][82]. The clearest expression of this is the development of accountability systems that report the scores of students in a school and that may condition rewards on student performance. The approach highlights student performance, often calling for explicit measurement of outcomes along with mechanisms for aiding schools to perform better. For example, a number of states have moved to substantial rewards to schools that perform highly on the state standards[83]. On the other hand, little existing evaluation has been conducted[84]. Much of the discussion has concentrated on the explicit evaluation of outcomes [e.g., Koretz (1996)].

Some innovative theoretical modeling has begun to describe some of the competing forces generated by many of the common accountability systems that have emerged with standards-based reform [Betts and Costrell (2001)]. They demonstrate some surprising outcomes when accountability systems have multiple roles.

---

[82] The evaluation of behavior under different accountability systems is currently limited, although it is likely to expand rapidly as increased testing and use of varying accountability systems expands. For example, Deere and Strayer (2001) suggest that individuals react to public accountability systems but that some of the reaction may not be desirable. An initial evaluation of the Florida program for using vouchers to deal with failing schools has led to considerable controversy over the interpretation of the incentives; see Greene (2001a,b) and Carnoy (2001).

[83] The idea of rewarding schools instead of teachers relates to arguments used against merit pay. Because teachers must work with each other in a variety of ways, an incentive system that led to "hoarding" of information by teachers or general lack of cooperation would be unfortunate. There has been little analysis of such approaches.

[84] Conducting evaluations of existing state plans for accountability is very difficult. Because many plans cover entire states, it is necessary to do comparative studies across states. But, many other state policies are simultaneously affecting schools in each state. As discussed previously, problems of misspecification and aggregation to state levels can severely distort any such analysis.

The movement of policy toward accountability system and standards-based reform has some important antecedents in the work of John Bishop. In a series of papers he hypothesizes that centralized testing systems have powerful incentive effects on students [for example, Bishop (1996), Bishop, Mane, Bishop and Moriarty (2001)]. He argues that the strength of incentives for students differ dramatically when there is a consequential central examination as compared with, say, relative grading by classroom teachers. While evaluating this proposition is difficult since testing regimes tend to coincide with state or national jurisdictions that make isolation of test effects difficult, the line of research highlights the importance of students in the educational process. Most of the other analyses of achievement have stressed the role of schools and have brought in students largely assuming that they have fixed impact, but this line of inquiry emphasizes the role of student behavior in affecting achievement and therefore brings in the necessity of incentives for students as well as school personnel.

The general consideration of incentives provides the contrast between the traditional regulatory approach to running schools and the value of concentrating on outcomes without detailing the approaches to achieving them. The incentive approach has the advantage of not requiring detailed knowledge about the production process in various local situations. Incentives, however, are not without their own complications. Specifically, little experience indicates how to devise the best incentive structures, and the details within the complex organization of schools are almost certainly very important. Some early experimental work into incentive contracts provides a simple example. The US Office of Economic Opportunity, as part of the War on Poverty in the late 1960s and early 1970s, experimented with performance contracting, i.e., providing firms direct payments based on the achievement of students to whom they offered remedial instruction. In the end, virtually nothing was learned from the experiment because the flawed contract led firms to react in ways that limited what could be learned about basic approaches to remedial instruction [Gramlich and Koshel (1975)]. The conclusion from this experiment and other incentive designs is that considerably more research is necessary to understand the best approach to designing incentives. The possibility of such research is likely to increase noticeably as education policy increasingly recognizes the importance of incentives.

6. Public versus private provision

If one distinguishes between the financing and the provision of education, it is possible to consider whether private schools, which perhaps have different incentive structures, perform better than public schools. The importance of competition for public schools was emphasized early by Friedman (1962) and has been discussed and implemented in a wide variety of forms. The investigation of this has nonetheless proved to be difficult and controversial.

Since 1970, about 11% of the US student population has attended private schools. The private schools are overwhelmingly schools with a religious affiliation, but the religious affiliation has changed dramatically over time. In 1997, 50% are Catholic, 35% were other religious schools, and the remaining 15% are nonsectarian, but in 1970 three-quarters were Catholic [see Sander (2001)]. Private schools are restricted from receiving public funding, so those students attending private schools pay tuition. Additionally, since the taxes to support the public schools – most of which are property taxes at the local level – are paid regardless of attendance, students attending private schools in essence pay for both public and private schooling.

The fundamental analytical question that has dominated the literature is whether or not performance in private schools exceeds that in public schools *ceteris paribus*. In particular, if private school performance exceeds that in the public schools, is it good schools or good kids?

6.1. Unsubsidized choice

Uncovering the relative advantage of public and private provision of education is confounded by the underlying choice of schools. Consider the following stylized choice problem where attention is concentrated just on public and Catholic schools for now.

$$O^p = f^p(F, P, S, A) + v^p, \qquad (4)$$

$$O^c = f^c(F, P, S, A) + v^c, \qquad (5)$$

$$\text{Prob}(c) = g(F, P, S, A, X) + \epsilon. \qquad (6)$$

Equations (4) and (5) (which follow directly from Equation 1) describe production in the public (p) sector and Catholic (c) sector. Equation (6) describes the selection equation governing choice of Catholic schools based on the production characteristics and other factors, X, such as religious preferences.

The fundamental difficulty in uncovering the differences between public and private provision comes from the selection equation. It is clear from the beginning that families that send their children to private schools are different, because they could have attended the public schools but instead paid tuition to attend the private school. Specifically, if parents with the largest interest in schooling tend simultaneously to pick Catholic schooling and to provide more motivation or a better learning environment for their children, v and ϵ will be correlated. As is well known, the estimated effect of schools will be biased if the production functions are estimated without taking into account the selection of parents.

The estimation of these relationships takes a variety of forms. The simplest forms of estimation pursue two similar strategies. First, assuming the impact of families, peers, and school factors is the same except for a level difference in performance, a pooled production function combining Equations (4) and (5) is estimated with the addition of an indicator variable for attendance at a Catholic school [Neal (1997)]. Second, separate production functions are estimated within the public and Catholic school populations and then the difference in performance is calculated by evaluating the production functions at common levels of all of the inputs and comparing the predicted performance [e.g., Coleman, Hoffer and Kilgore (1982)]. Both of these approaches, however, require attention to selection [85].

Perhaps the most common approach to selection correction is to consider how own religious preference affects choice of public or Catholic schools. The argument is that a Catholic background will increase the chance that a student attends Catholic schools but will not affect the school outcome. But this instrument would not be valid if, for example, Catholics on average had higher or lower abilities or were more supportive of their children than non-Catholics. A better choice, however, is the density of Catholic households or schools in an area [e.g., Neal (1997)]. In any event, some variant of religious affiliation is commonly employed, though the validity and usefulness of these instruments remains a matter of concern. The stringent requirements for a valid instrument are generally difficult to meet. An alternative approach is to consider value-added models where variations in early achievement are considered. This approach, found in Coleman and Hoffer (1987), implicitly controls for selection if the outside factors entering into achievement are summarized in the initial levels of achievement. Again, while this estimation strategy has appeal, assessing whether any further selection effects remain is difficult.

The common result from estimation is that Catholic schools tend to achieve higher graduation rates after making selection corrections and holding other input factors constant [see Evans and Schwab (1995), Neal (1997), Grogger and Neal (2000)]. At the same time, the estimation of effects on measured test scores is not as clear. Estimation yields varying views of the effects of Catholic schools, and the results are frequently not statistically different from zero [see the summary in Neal (1998)].

A key element of evaluation of relative performance is defining the relevant comparison. As Neal (1997) demonstrates, comparisons of public and private schools differ significantly by the group considered. While suburban public and private schools appear roughly comparable, urban Catholic schools, especially those serving minority populations, appear noticeably superior on average to urban public schools. The reasons for this difference in results have not been fully analyzed, but it is consistent with differential abilities to move and to select schools. If poor and minority populations have limited ability to change residences, and thus to select school districts, opening up choice through Catholic schools offers more potential gain. It is also consistent with the possibility that urban schools are on average inferior to suburban

---

[85] The investigation of relative performance of Catholic schools started intensively with Coleman, Hoffer and Kilgore (1982). That analysis estimated separate public and Catholic school production functions and then standardized for differing levels of inputs (F, P, and S) in deriving the differences in performance of the two types of schools. This analysis started a heated controversy [see, for example, Noell (1982), Murnane, Newstead and Olsen (1985)] over the importance of selection in Catholic schools. Selection could also be dealt with through estimation of the choice Equation (6), although it is difficult to do this in a way that also can realistically identify achievement relationships. See, on choice, Lankford and Wyckoff (1992).

schools [cf. Hanushek, Kain and Rivkin (2001a)]. Sander (1996), however, suggests that heterogeneity of the population attending Catholic schools is important, with positive effects isolated in the non-Catholic school population and no gains for Catholic students.

The variation in results by the measure of outcomes, if not a statistical artifact in the small number of available studies, is difficult to interpret. Student achievement and graduation are closely related according to past estimation, so it seems surprising that the influence of Catholic quality shows up in one dimension but not the other. Yet, the differences in school completion continue through college graduation, suggesting that these are significant differences. One possibility is that the statistical problems with the achievement estimation are greater, but more attention is needed to the variations in performance across the different outcomes[86].

A larger problem with this line of research is that it provides no information on the distribution of results. As discussed above, the bulk of research about educational production is aimed at understanding the wide variation in performance of public schools. It seems natural to believe that Catholic schools also exhibit wide variation in performance, although none of the existing analyses document either the magnitude of differences or the potential causes of such differences. For example, assume that there is a difference in the mean performance of Catholic schools compared to public schools. It is important to understand whether this comes from a simple shifting of the entire quality distribution or from a truncation in the bottom of the quality distribution or from a narrowing of the entire distribution with a loss at both the top and bottom of the quality distribution. With the character of underlying changes in quality for Catholic schools being unknown, there is an ambiguity about the exact lessons to be drawn for any policy purposes.

The comparison of Catholic and public schools is based entirely on performance, but a more complete analysis would also incorporate the costs of production. Many observe that Catholic schools appear to be run with significantly lower expenditure levels, but accurate cost accounting is not readily available.

One final area deserves attention. The focus on Catholic schools, or private schools more generally, is motivated by the idea that more choice will lead to competition among schools that will then lead to improvement either in overall performance or in the effectiveness of resource usage. The competition for students argument is the commonly held explanation for any difference in public-Catholic performance. But, if that competition affects the Catholic schools, it should also affect the public schools. This effect on public schools is in fact the primary interest in private school competition, because even a general widening in the availability and access

---

[86] The High School and Beyond survey, which is used in the Coleman work and others, employed a short test that is likely to be noisy. Further, the sampling design behind the National Educational Longitudinal Survey (NELS) employed in Grogger and Neal (2000) makes selection on test taking important but difficult to deal with.

to private schools would leave a large public sector. Pursuing this theme, Hoxby (1994) suggests that public schools located in areas where there is more competition from Catholic schools perform better than comparable public schools facing less competition. This competition is estimated to affect the level of output measured by educational attainment and graduate rates. Sander (1999), on the other hand, does not find such spillovers, leaving the question of competitive impacts open.

Note, however, that if public schools react to the existence of private schools, the evaluation problem becomes difficult. Any estimate of the performance difference of Catholic schools would understate the true impact.

6.2. Subsidized choice

Much of the attention to choice and its impact on results emanates from early arguments by Friedman (1962) about governmental provision of schools. He argued that, even if government had a role in the financing of schools, it did not have to provide the service. Instead, by providing vouchers given to parents, citizens would be able to choose among potential schools – both securing an education that suited them and opening up competitive forces to improve the provision of schooling.

In the USA, with a few exceptions there has historically been limited general, publicly supported choice. A number of states and districts have supported some kind of choice among public schools. Part of this reflects efforts both to accommodate and to subvert the racial desegregation of US schools [Armor (1995)]. Another part reflects efforts to provide more options and, implicitly, to broaden competition. The latter efforts have included intradistrict and interdistrict school choice [Nathan (1989), Hanushek (1994)] along with new efforts to free individual "charter" schools [Nathan (1996)]. In recent years, charter schools have dramatically expanded[87]. Subsidized choice plans are to date considerably more limited: publicly provided vouchers in Milwaukee and Cleveland and privately subsidized vouchers in Dayton, New York City, and Washington[88].

The wide variety of choice options implies that the incentives under each can be quite different. For example, the impact of a plan permitting students to choose any public school in the district would have very different incentives depending on

---

[87] Charter schools provide provisions for individual schools to opt out of district regulations and to provide an alternative program. The rules governing these schools vary widely by state, but the common element is that they are supported by public funds and remain officially part of the public school system. These schools must attract students who choose them over the regular public schools. While most states have less than one percent of their students in charter schools in 2000, some such as Arizona (3.7%) and Michigan (2.8%) have developed a substantial competitive public sector. The District of Columbia has over 8% in charters. The start of this expansion along with a description of the kinds of schools in the charter sector is described in Finn, Manno and Vanourek (2000)).

[88] Note that privately provided scholarship plans for attending private schools are actually much more extensive, but the individual plans generally have been small and have not been evaluated.

how any excess demand for a school is dealt with, what happens to teachers and administrators in schools with a large number of vacancies, how transportation of students is handled, and the like. Similarly, when students are permitted to attend public schools outside of the district, issues about fiscal transfers, the handling of excess demand, and transportation become critical. For voucher plans, the size of the voucher, the eligibility of potential schools, the treatment of excess demand, the range of programs that are permissible, the legitimate grounds that schools can use to select students, and more will determine the character and results of the program. A variety of underlying theoretical models have identified specific elements of importance. For example, Manski (1992) concentrates on the role of peers under different choice plans, while Chubb and Moe (1990) emphasize school decision making. Little empirical work has been done on identifying or assessing the key elements of choice plans.

The existing public school choice plans have not received thorough analysis in terms of student outcomes. A primary deterrent to analysis is disentangling selection from program effects. The issues are identical to those sketch for understanding the impact of Catholic schools, but the development of suitable instruments for the selection equation is much more problematic. One exception is an analysis of open enrollment plans in Chicago public schools that suggests most observed better performance by choice students comes from selection [Cullen, Jacob and Levitt (2000)].

The voucher programs are different. The most thorough analysis of the voucher programs has occurred in Milwaukee. This publicly supported voucher, while not an experiment but instead an on-going program, had an evaluation plan set up at the outset [Witte (1999)]. Subsequently, a number of studies, taking different approaches and reaching somewhat different conclusions, have looked at the same impact of vouchers in Milwaukee [Peterson, Greene and Noyes (1996), Greene, Peterson and Du (1998), Rouse (1998), Witte (1999)].

Three issues are important in the analysis: how to define outcomes, how long to wait to observe results, and what the comparison group of students should be. In terms of the outcomes of choice, the available analyses from the Milwaukee program suggest that parents choosing voucher schools are happier with them than with the public schools and that the choice schools generally spend noticeably less than the public schools. Thus, from a simple consumer viewpoint, the vouchers seem useful. Nonetheless, the majority of attention has focused on measured student achievement. The analyses of student achievement show no real gains in vouchers schools during the first years, but by the fourth year of operation voucher schools are doing as well as or better than the Milwaukee public schools, depending upon the precise performance measure. The findings on achievement also depend upon the precise comparison groups. Comparisons to people applying but not enrolling in the voucher program or to the low income eligible population show the voucher schools on the whole as doing better, while comparisons to the entire public student population in Milwaukee show less gain.

The Milwaukee program is one specific set of rules and institutions. It is not a general test of vouchers versus public schools. At its inception in 1990, participating schools had to be already existing nonsectarian schools that also served a substantial unsubsidized population [Witte (1999)]. Participating students had to come from low income families[89]. The number of participants was initially restricted to less than 1% of the public school population but grew to 15% by 1995. Therefore, this experiment does not represent a general test of vouchers, but instead a very specific kind of application of the ideas. For example, an important element of the original Friedman (1962) proposals is the induced supply response which engages markets in innovating in ways that appeal to consumers – something that is really not a part of the Milwaukee experience.

The voluntary, privately-funded voucher programs offer a separate view of the impact of vouchers. While these have only been operating for short periods of time, some preliminary results are available. Peterson, Howell, Wolf and Campbell (2003) and Howell and Peterson (2002) suggest that these programs have had positive effects for some minority students but not for others. The variations in effectiveness thus leave open many questions that are central to many of the policy discussions.

The short run evaluations of performance in voucher programs, while interesting and useful, necessarily provide a limited picture. The primary arguments for introducing competition involve incentives for new private schools to develop and incentives for the public schools to improve. These are, however, long run effects, making the evaluation problems and perspectives on these programs analogous to evaluating merit pay plans for teachers[90].

Throughout most of the discussion, very little mention is made of costs. As operated, the existing voucher programs, including that in Milwaukee, appear to be running at noticeably lower expenditure than the comparable Milwaukee public school system. Part of this is easily explicable by the public schools' responsibility for taking all students, including high needs students such as those with handicapping conditions. But part also seems to be simple differences in cost structures. It is important to know if the voucher programs are truly operating at lower costs while producing the same (or better) results.

6.3. International evidence

Other countries have of course operated much broader choice systems than found in the USA. While it is possible to find descriptive information and information about the flows of students, little is available about the relative performance of private schools under different institutional structures [see, for example, James (1987, 1993), Glenn (1989), West (1996), Cohn (1997) and the case studies therein, Fiske and Ladd (2000)

---

[89] Family incomes had to be less than 175% of the federal poverty level. The official poverty line for a family of four was approximately $17 500 in 1990.

[90] Note, however, that Hoxby (2003) provides early results that suggest public schools respond quickly when they face direct competitive pressures.

and Jimenez and Sawada (2001)]. Again, as with the analysis of production functions, developing information about the performance has been hindered by measures of student outcomes. Nonetheless, evidence on choice is beginning to develop, including McEwan and Carnoy (2000) and McEwan (2001) on the Chilean experience, and Angrist, Bettinger, Bloom, King and Kremer (2001) on the Colombian experience.

International evidence currently offers the best chances for understanding the impacts of voucher systems, particularly the longer run implications. Not only is choice better established in many countries than in the USA but also the institutional structure for choice shows much more variation.

7. Financing of schools

State governments in the USA have had the primary responsibility of the provision of schooling. The federal government has provided between 5–7% of the total funding for schools, and this funding has been focused on special populations – with economically disadvantaged and handicapped students receiving the bulk of the funding[91]. The federal government has also promulgated laws with major effect on schools. The most important are Constitutional prohibitions against segregation of schools and federal legislation about service requirements and standards for handicapped students (so called "special education"). Because of the limited role of the federal government, however, this discussion will concentrate on state and local spending.

State constitutions invariably identify the role of the state government in establishing and running a public school system that is free to all students. While the exact arrangements differ, state governments have historically set the general operating structure for schools in terms of regulations and laws governing the schools and then given local jurisdictions the responsibility for running the schools. Although there is wide variation across states, local governments typically share funding responsibilities with the states. The determination of funding levels is the complicated outcome of local decisions, voter and political outcomes, and state rules and regulations.

Perhaps the principal policy lever of the states has been the funding level for local education. States have provided grants to local school districts to cover special purpose, or categorical, items, but most spending goes for general operating expenditure. The decisions facing state legislatures concern both the level and the distribution of spending. All states use their funding mechanisms to offset different abilities of school districts to raise funds locally. Particularly as the value of high quality education has become more apparent, states have turned their funding toward the goal of improving student achievement. The problem facing the legislatures has been an inability to turn

---

[91] Funding for primary and secondary schooling (and higher education) comes through the US Department of Education. Funding for Head Start, another large education-related program for disadvantaged 4–5 year olds, has come through the Department of Health and Human Services and generally is not included in the usual accounting of total spending for education.

funding into student achievement with any assurance – the general issue discussed earlier. One result has been an increasing tendency to add further regulations on activities along with further funding. This discussion, however, concentrates on the funding aspect and the implications of state fiscal federalism.

The discussion of state funding is heavily influenced by legal cases. School finance in the USA was relatively stable through much of the 20th century. Early developments emphasized the role of states in ameliorating the largest differences in local wealth [Strayer and Haig (1923)]. In the late 1960s, the case of *Serrano v. Priest* was entered into California state courts and changed the stability in financing[92]. This case alleged that the state funding of schools violated the 14th amendment of the US constitution that requires equal treatment of individuals under the law. State funding provided a portion of the funds needed by local districts, and districts were expected to raise the remainder. California, like a majority of other states, permitted local jurisdictions to use the property tax as its major revenue source. The *Serrano* suit argued that, because local property tax bases differ, this funding arrangement discriminated against students in poor districts by making the funding dependent upon the wealth of others in the community [Coons, Clune and Sugarman (1970)]. While the US Supreme Court ultimately ruled in 1973 that the state funding formula did not violate the federal constitution[93], the *Serrano* case and similar subsequent ones in a majority of the states were argued on the grounds that the method of funding violated the individual state constitutions. While court cases in states continue, few general conclusions can be drawn from the legal decisions that have variously upheld and struck down existing state funding formulae.

Similar policy dilemmas face the courts in school finance cases as face the state legislatures that are formally charged with funding decisions. The courts have entered into education decision making in deciding on suits brought by people who argue that their districts are receiving insufficient state funding. While frequently motivated by concerns about student achievement, in reality both the judicial statement of the issue and the proposed remedies invariably revolve around the level and distribution of resources.

An important issue in these discussions is the effect of financing on student outcomes. While explicitly considered below, the prior discussions on the limited evidence about any consistent relationship between resources and student performance should provide an early note of caution about the potential results of resource based policy decisions.

7.1. *Alternative funding schemes*

With a few exceptions, states and local school districts share the financing of local schools. This sharing, however, varies in several important dimensions. State financing

---

[92] *Serrano v. Priest*, 5 Cal. 3d 584,589, 487 P.2d 1241, 1244, 96 Cal. Rptr. 601, 604 (1971).
[93] *San Antonio Independent School District v. Rodriguez*, 411 U.S. 1 (1973).

is frequently characterized in terms of a formula of identifying state funding per pupil in relationship to local capacity, local effort, and characteristics of the local student body. The details, the methods of describing the allocation mechanisms, and even the nomenclature differ across states. Nonetheless, three basic funding mechanisms characterize the options – and most states use a combination of them. Categorical aid funds districts based upon specific identified needs; foundation aid compensates for different tax capacity of the local district; and variable matching aid adjusts state support for both different tax capacity and the taxing decisions of the local district.

To understand the funds available to a district, it is easiest to ignore federal subsidies and to concentrate on the state and local funding. For simplicity the funding formulae are written in terms of a property tax base, reflecting the fact that tax on real property is the most frequently employed local revenue raising instrument. With number of students N_j, tax base per student B_j, and local tax rate r, school district j can raise L_j in local funds:

$$L_j = N_j \times rB_j. \tag{7}$$

Districts with larger tax bases clearly can raise funds more easily if they choose to increase revenues. Note, however, that the tax base is actually endogenous. Because the tax base includes not only residential property but also commercial and industrial property, local residents in districts with a smaller proportion of the tax base from residential property pay less of the total local tax bill. In other words, the "tax price" of raising an extra dollar of local revenue is less than one dollar for the residents [Ladd (1975)]. Other things being equal, then, districts with a low tax price are more attractive, and demand for housing in them will be high – leading to housing prices being bid up and to the tax base being larger [Oates (1969)]. This endogeneity obviously also enters into policy actions. For example, if the state prohibited local districts from taxing certain kinds of commercial property, some districts would lose two ways: B, the tax base, would fall with the loss of the commercial property from its tax base and the district would likely become relatively less attractive so that housing values fell, bringing B down further.

State governments routinely act to ameliorate the largest disparities in revenue abilities of districts and to even out cost differences across districts. The simplest kinds of state subsidy formulae provide fixed payments for categorical purposes such as

$$C_j = c \times N_j. \tag{8}$$

Where the subsidy from the central authority (state) to district j is a flat amount, c, times the number of eligible students (N). Thus, for example, the state might provide a flat amount for each student classified as gifted or talented. Categorical aid is identified with specific purposes and often requires specific expenditures[94]. Categorical

---

[94] Of course, as is generally true, funds are fungible – implying that requirements to spend categorical funds would not be binding unless the local education authority wished to spend less than c per eligible

aid flows for a variety of purposes including student transportation, books and supplies, special education, and bilingual education programs. Districts, however, cannot be assumed to be impervious of incentives. As described below, there is evidence that the number of "categorical" students is endogenous, related to the fiscal incentives that are presented [95].

Most attention, however, has focused on alternative ways of providing general revenue – revenue with few specific use restrictions. By far the most common aid formula is foundation aid where the state subsidy varies inversely with the local property tax base per student such as

$$C_j = N_j \times (F - r_o B_j). \tag{9}$$

F is the "foundation," or the amount the district would get per student if it had no ability to tax itself, r_o is the fixed tax rate used to calculate what the local district might be expected to raise itself. Because local revenue capacity rises with the taxable base (Equation 7), states typically reduce their subsidy for districts with higher B.

Several aspects of foundation aid are important, although to varying degrees across different states. First, the foundation aid formula can clearly lead to negative subsidies for districts with large tax bases, i.e., when $r_o B_j > F$. States have generally had mixed reactions to whether or not they should recapture any excess funds that a district may be able to raise. Without recapture, districts with large amounts of property wealth continue to have more revenue raising opportunities than those with lower tax bases.

Second, if a district chooses a tax rate, r_j, that is greater than r_o, state subsidies are unaffected and jurisdictions with larger tax bases can capture the full benefit of their tax base [96]. Total education spending (E_j) under a foundation plan combines local and state funding as in

$$E_j = L_j + C_j = N_j \times \left[(F) + (r_j - r_o) B_j \right]. \tag{10}$$

The incentive to raise the local tax rate of course depends on the desired spending of the community. Thus, as the foundation level – that "guaranteed" by the state formula –

student. Some evidence, however, suggests that this is not the case. Evidence of the "flypaper effect" suggests that funds tend to stick where they are provided [e.g., see Gramlich (1977), and the discussion in Oates (1994)].

[95] Another element of categorical programs is identifying and adjusting for program costs. For example, special education funding is frequently adjusted for different handicapping conditions of students. Existing estimates of costs that are built into many funding formula begin with the expenditure choices of schools, making them somewhat problematic. See Chaikind, Danielson and Brauen (1993) and Lankford and Wyckoff (1996). Other attempts to deal with local cost differences involve both choices of what costs are important and estimation of the their magnitude – but this again is difficult when based largely on the choices of districts which also involve varying preferences about teacher quality [Ballou and Podgursky (1997)].

[96] Many states require that the district levy some minimum tax rate, often r_o, as a way of ensuring that districts bear a minimum portion of the total taxes for schools. Some states also cap the tax rate that local jurisdictions can apply (r_j) in an effort to limit variations in local spending.

increases, local communities have less incentive to spend more than F per student and tend to choose tax rates closer to the nominal rate of the state, r_0.

Third, the number of students is frequently adjusted to take into account special factors. For example, special education students, instead of being paid simple categorical funds as in Equation (8), may be credited as if they are additional effective students. Therefore, for example, a disabled student who has an identified learning disability may count as, say, 1.6 students. In such a case, the state subsidy for categorical aid depends upon the local tax capacity. But, of course, this also raises the possibility that N_j is really endogenous to the extent that districts can vary populations. For example, Cullen (2002) shows that school districts adjust the numbers identified as requiring special education according to their fiscal incentive[97]; Cullen and Rivkin (2003) also show that further reactions to the provision of special education services by family choices of residence are possible.

Finally, a variable matching grant by states takes into account the actual tax choices of the district. While this formulation comes under many different names (and equivalent ways of writing the formula), perhaps the simplest is to think of this as a "guaranteed tax base" as in

$$C_j = N_j \times r_j \left(B_0 - B_j \right), \tag{11}$$

where B_0 is the tax base that is guaranteed to the district. (Other common descriptions include wealth neutralizing, power equalizing, and percentage equalizing). For any district with an actual tax base less than the guaranteed base, the state supplements the local tax revenue. Again, a key element is what happens when $B_j > B_0$. If recapture is required, the local district sends the excess revenues to the state. In such a case, the effective revenue schedule for all districts (combining Equations 7 and 11) is simply:

$$E_j = N_j \times r_j B_0, \tag{12}$$

and districts differ in spending just to the extent that they choose varying local tax rates. A variant of this formulation was first popularized by Coons, Clune and Sugarman (1970) and is the intellectual backdrop to the original school finance law suits from *Serrano v. Priest* through recent suits. Again, however, recapture provisions have generally proved unpopular and are generally only imposed in response to court orders.

An important aspect of the fiscal consideration is that the formulae provide an indication of the *opportunities* that face a district. They do not necessarily foretell the distribution of spending outcomes that will occur, because these require knowing more about the behavioral responses of individuals. Behavioral responses occur in two

---

[97] An important feature of the analysis is separating out the causal impact. In this, Cullen develops a series of plausible instruments that permit identification of the impact on classification.

primary ways: the choice of districts by individuals and the expression of preferences within each district.

7.2. Fiscal effects of alternative plans

While courts and legislatures have significantly changed the fiscal responsibilities for schools since the early 1970s, surprisingly little is known about the effects of these alterations. Some efforts have been made to track the spending patterns of these changes, but less attention has gone to consideration of the overall level.

Wyckoff (1992) traces the within-state variations in spending over a substantial period of change. By calculating alternative measures of spending variations, he concludes that state court action has tended to lead to some narrowing in spending variations, but this is not uniform[98]. In a comprehensive study of existing court and legislative actions, Murray, Evans and Schwab (1998) estimate models of spending variation which incorporate information about the timing of court actions. They also conclude that court action has led to significant narrowing of the spending distribution. However, the state court actions directly consider just variations within states, while Murray, Evans and Schwab (1998) find that the most significant narrowing of the spending distribution has been between states.

The exact nature of the changes in the distribution has been the focus of a number of different analyses. In an early analysis, Stern (1973) focuses on how changes in the financing formula would affect equalization of funding within Massachusetts. His simulations indicate that a variable matching subsidy would reduce disparities due to fiscal capacity differences of states but not those due to socioeconomic differences. The key element, understanding the underlying preferences of individuals, was extended by Feldstein (1975). He specifically considered how wealth neutrality approaches might lead to unexpected spending outcomes where spending was inversely related to local wealth. Craig and Inman (1982, 1986) consider spending patterns in light of reforms that involve moving spending responsibilities to lower levels of government. Their work builds upon an explicit model of decision making at different levels of government and highlights the importance of the fiscal federal system. They find surprisingly strong reactions to changes in funding patterns[99].

Court rules may have effects on the level of spending in addition to any effects on the distribution. Most court rulings do not specify how the state should distribute funds, only that an existing funding system does not meet constitutional requirements. This typically requires that the state legislature alter its approach to funding. A variety of political economy models could describe the resultant changes. The simplest

---

[98] An early predecessor to the systematic consideration of state funding variations along with discussion of alternative measures of the distribution of spending is Berne and Stiefel (1984).

[99] While not emphasized here, they also demonstrate the importance of institutional structure including how grants often have surprising effects. For example, because of the "flypaper effect", tax reductions exhibit different effects on spending than unconditional grants [cf. Oates (1994)].

model recognizes that pure distributional changes dictate a large number of losing districts that find their state funding being decreased. To offset these changes, political incentives push toward increasing the overall level of spending at the same time that there is a redistribution of spending. Downes and Shah (1996) provide some evidence for this effect, although it is relatively small.

One natural interpretation of the results is that there are simply too many different circumstances and court rulings to imply uniform effects on spending. In fact, Hoxby (2001) pursues exactly the characterization of alternative plans. By separating the key parameters and assessing how these differ by states, she is able to estimate the effects of legislative and court actions on overall spending levels. Following the earlier analyses of behavioral responses to altered incentives, she shows convincingly that the naïve, no-behavioral-response analysis that accompanies many plan changes is very misleading.

7.3. Effect of equalization on equity

If resource availability is not a good index of educational outcomes or if providing for overall resource levels does not ensure a desired level of performance, the courts face the same dilemma as legislatures. Simply providing more funding or a different distribution of funding is unlikely to improve student achievement (even though it does affect the distribution of tax burdens for school financing across the citizens of a state).

A related issue – one highlighted in some recent school finance court cases – centers on whether funding for schools is "adequate" [cf. Clune (1994)]. The idea of adequacy has been to provide sufficient funds to ensure some chosen level of achievement for all students in a state[100]. Such concepts may have popular appeal, but they have no policy superiority to traditional district equity arguments when translated into resource requirements. First, what is adequate is a purely political and economic issue that it likely to change both with the demands of the economy and with political views on appropriate levels of government support of programs. Second, and more important, the previous conclusion that resources are not a good index of student performance holds no matter what goals are placed for student achievement or how these goals are arrived at. Thus, there is no objective method of indicating what resources are required for an 'adequate' level of student performance[101].

A variation of this general adequacy theme is to argue that, while resources alone may not be sufficient to guarantee achievement, adequate resources are surely necessary. Undoubtedly, this is an accurate statement at some level, because a school with no funds would not be expected to add anything to student achievement.

---

[100] An important aspect of the legal and legislative discussions of adequacy is translation into expenditure. The situation might be very different if equity and adequacy were truly defined in terms of student outcomes, but in such a situation there would be little way of ensuring any given distribution of performance – making judicial or legislative mandates generally impossible.

[101] See, for example, the difficulty in defining adequacy in Ladd and Hansen (1999).

Nonetheless, as shown in Table 5 for the USA, real spending per student rose dramatically between 1960 and 1995, even though US student performance appears to have been essentially unchanged. Further, nothing in the previous analytical results about the effects of resources suggests that there is a level below which resources have clear and powerful effects on achievement which would be a demonstration that some schools are below the threshold of 'necessity.' Just asserting that there is some level of necessary expenditure does not make the case for pure resource policies in today's schooling environment.

Analyses considering spending variations do not, for the reasons previously described, give direct information about any effects on student performance. Perhaps surprisingly given the extent of legal actions during the 1970s, 1980s, and 1990s, there has been little direct analysis of performance differences related to funding equalization. Downes (1992) investigates whether the early alterations in California arising from the *Serrano v. Priest* case had any impact on variations in student test performance. He finds no significant impact on performance when he looked at variations before and after equalization of local spending. Hanushek and Somers (2001) pursue a different tack. They consider whether variations in spending within a state are ultimately reflected in earnings variations when the students progress into the labor market. This analysis, a generalization of that in Card and Krueger (1992a), finds little evidence that earnings variations correspond to earlier spending variations [102]. These findings are consistent with the earlier evidence that suggested little or no systematic improvement in student performance from changes in funding.

One of the impacts of court cases has been increased centralization of funding. Particularly during the 1970s, the average share of funding coming from the state level rose and surpassed the share at the local level. Centralization of funding itself could have implications for both funding levels and performance. As funding responsibility moves from the locality to higher levels of government, individuals are more detached from the taxing and spending decisions and standard free rider problems increase. The arguments for this position are largely conceptual [e.g., Hoxby (1996a)]. The direct empirical analysis typically must confront the concerns about aggregation bias raised previously when they rely on evidence across states [e.g., Walberg and Walberg III (1994), Peltzman (1993)]. Indirect evidence on reactions to changes over time, however, provides additional support. Specifically, movements toward more centralization of state finance have been related to efforts to control overall levels of spending by Fischel (1989), Silva and Sonstelie (1995) and Courant and Loeb (1997). The argument is that, in reaction to state court decisions to equalize spending, California voters supported Proposition 13 that placed strict limits on levels of taxes

---

[102] The Hanushek and Somers analysis concentrates on the within state variance in funding and the subsequent variations in earnings of people educated in a given state. Thus, it avoids the largest problems associated with differences in state policy environments, as discussed previously.

and spending[103]. A similar analysis by Loeb (2001), simulating the effects different financing systems, shows that the amount of local control of supplementation can have dramatic impacts on the level and distribution of spending across districts and that these effects are very dependent on the distribution of local preferences[104].

7.4. Mobility, distribution, and equilibrium

One very significant problem in considering state financing of schools is that the analysis generally assumes that districts and their residents are fixed. Additionally, it is often assumed that property wealth – the common basis for local taxation – is an acceptable index of the economic well-being of a jurisdiction's population. These assumptions prove to be very problematic and difficult to deal with in any complete fashion [Hanushek (1991)].

If the property tax base just incorporated residential property, the tax base would be a reasonable measure of the economic well-being of the population, but the inclusion of commercial and industrial property in the tax base breaks this relationship. Thus, for example, some cities have large proportions of their students in poverty even though they have large tax bases (e.g., New York City) while other cities have large poverty populations and small tax bases (e.g., Newark, New Jersey). Most of the funding formulae emphasize the local ability of districts to raise funds, but often incorrectly suggest that this is synonymous with poverty. Moreover, the tax advantage of having large amounts of commercial and industrial property in a city will, to the extent that potential tax revenues exceed the costs of providing public services to these properties, be capitalized into the value of residential properties. Thus, two identical properties located in jurisdictions with different tax capacities will sell for different amounts.

Additionally, as discussed previously, communities that have good schools will generally be more desirable than communities with bad schools, and housing prices will be bid up in places with good schools [Kain and Quigley (1975), Rosen and Fullerton (1977), Black (1999), Weimer and Wolkoff (2001)][105]. In other words, residents in school districts with larger capitalization of school quality are actually paying more for their schools than is apparent by a simple comparison of tax rates to support schools. This variation in capitalization also has apparent feedbacks to the quality of schools, since schools in more competitive areas tend to be more effective [Hoxby (2000a), Hanushek and Rivkin (2003)]. The overall endogeneity of the tax

---

[103] Related work on the causes and consequences of tax limitation initiatives have also had a component of looking at student performance in addition to the more common study of the effects on spending and its composition. See Figlio (1997) and the discussion there.

[104] An innovation in this work is relaxing a common assumption that there is perfect sorting by income, which allows her to base simulations on the observed wealth distributions of school districts.

[105] The capitalization relationships are complicated by variations in the efficiency of schools in producing any quality of outcomes; see Somers (1998).

base is ignored in most considerations of school finance policy – both legislatively and judicially.

Behind the capitalization of aspects of tax base and schools into housing prices is the choice of communities and mobility of residents. The high level of mobility in school age population underscores the levels of potential adjustment to school cost and quality that occurs regularly[106]. If thought of in terms of the different possible margins of adjustment, as in the exit and voice of Hirschman (1970), it also highlights the equilibrium nature of school finance policy and changes in such policy. Thus, for example, a change in school funding by a state would set in motion a pattern of changed housing values, altered residential and school choices, and adjusted spending and performance patterns of schools. The resulting equilibrium outcomes in terms of the distribution of expenditure and performance patterns across the population are not easy to project.

Several research programs have addressed various aspects of this general equilibrium problem and have provided insights into the effects of different fiscal policies. An early and interesting line of work, although following a different path than here, involves understanding the effects of financing mechanisms on economic growth [Glomm and Ravikumar (1992, 1998)]. This work concentrates on how public and private schooling interact with economic growth. Their analysis of endogenous growth models suggests a trade-off between higher per capita incomes with private schools and more equality with public schools. By explicitly considers voting and public choice mechanisms, they also suggest that voters are likely to choose public schools.

Fernandez and Rogerson (1996, 1997, 1998) develop calibrated models of schooling and labor market outcomes that incorporate different jurisdictions. This apparatus allows investigation of different financing schemes, and the complete characterization of individuals in the economy permits welfare comparisons derived from different financing schemes. While the exact welfare comparisons appear dependent upon the key parameters of their economy, they develop a structure that identifies how individual behavior responds to changing in financing schemes. A key insight from their work is that it is difficult to predict the impact of different financing schemes on the level of educational spending from a partial equilibrium setting. In their models, however, the schooling sector itself is very simple (efficient provision of public education depending just on spending), making it impossible to trace out implications of policy for the schooling sector.

Epple and Romano (1996, 1998, 2003) develop more detailed models of household location that interact consumer choices and schooling outcomes. A central element of their analyses is variations in school quality that depend on peers in the school, leading

---

[106] Hanushek, Kain and Rivkin (2001a) describe school mobility and its effects on achievement. Interestingly, the detailed consideration of moving causes in the Current Population Survey does not attempt to investigate whether moving behavior is related to public services or schools; see Schacter (2001a,b). For within county movers, 26% move for family-related reasons, 6% for work-related reasons, and 65% for housing-related reasons.

to an externality from high ability students. Households of different incomes with children of different abilities seek out communities that maximize utility. The presence of a private sector supported by vouchers permits the private schools to internalize the externality of high ability students, but the exact solution depends on the size of the voucher. Epple and Romano (1998) sets out the basic properties of equilibrium including the key predictions that private schools will trade off income and ability, private tuitions declining in ability, and a strict hierarchy of schools. Epple and Romano (2003) turn to the alternative of public school choice and traces out equilibrium models of neighborhood choice, showing that residential stratification is a likely result that interacts with tax and expenditure policies.

In a series of papers, Nechyba (1999, 2000, 2001, 2003a,b) develops rich models of the interplay of residential location, school policies, and segregation. Much of the discussion of private schools, for example, suggests that segregation of schools is a likely result, but these discussions ignore the current incentives to segregate in communities. Nechyba (2000) shows that vouchers work in part to sever the link between residential location and schools. As a result, the pressures to segregate in residential communities are lessened, and vouchers produce less segregation than a pure public school system. Nechyba (2003a) introduces private schools in the absence of vouchers, mirroring the observed US equilibrium, and – even in the absence of vouchers – a private school alternative is shown to reduce segregation more than a completely centralized (and equalized) system. Nechyba (2003b) further explores the interaction of public school efficiency, private schools, and schooling choice, again showing that the general equilibrium responses differ markedly from simple partial equilibrium predictions.

Each of these approaches necessarily concentrates on some specific issues, while highly simplifying others. At the same time, each demonstrates vividly that the general equilibrium can differ quite dramatically from the partial equilibrium results. As more experience is gained in these models, they can enrich their descriptions of behavior and can provide important insights about central issues in the financing of schools.

8. Some underexplored topics

While much has been learned about publicly provided education, a variety of important issues remain underresearched. Most of these are apparent from replaying the prior discussions of what is currently known. Therefore, this discussion is designed to highlight a few areas rather than to develop the areas in any depth.

Perhaps at the top of the list is the behavior of consumers in the face of public provision of schools. If schools are inefficient in their use of public funds, why is consumer and voter behavior so ineffective? Attention to consumer behavior and to underlying issues of political economy has focused almost exclusively on issues of the level of spending, ignoring questions of the results of spending [107]. Understanding the elements of citizen behavior is important for both positive theories of spending and for consideration of the feasibility of alternative policy regimes.

The incentive structure of schools is the keystone to educational policy, but little headway has been made in understanding this more generally. Many reform proposals – from expanded consumer choice to heightened accountability systems – involve direct attempts to change incentives. Nonetheless, existing research, which has generally relied upon the few natural experiments with different incentives, remains very rudimentary. The empirical analyses typically relate to very specific programs whose generalizability is not well understood. The conceptual work is even farther behind, failing in general to develop much of a vocabulary or taxonomy for incentive schemes and thus leaving open a wide range of important measurement issues. In a larger political view, current participants clearly have preferences over a variety of the potential incentive schemes and exert influence on both their adoption and their evolution – and understanding the political aspects of program development is important. Pressures for changes in incentives currently being contemplated or implemented, however, open large new areas for research.

As discussed throughout, the analysis has been heavily weighted toward studies of the US experience. This slant to research is particularly unfortunate, because international schooling offers a very wide range of experiences. The variations in organization, funding, and institutions that are found internationally offer promise for resolving some of the questions that have not been fully addressed within the more limited US experience.

The analysis of schooling policies generally pays little attention to the array of policies and influences outside of school: daycare, preschool, after school programs, extracurricular activities, and the like. These facets of children's development are typically treated independent of schools in both analytical and policy discussions, even though they undoubtedly interact with schools and should be considered in a larger optimizing framework for governmental programs.

References

Acemoglu, D., and J. Angrist (2000), "How large are the social returns to education? Evidence from compulsory schooling laws", In: B.S. Bernanke and K. Rogoff, eds., NBER Macroeconomics Annual 2000 (MIT Press, Cambridge, MA) pp. 9–59.

Aigner, D.J., and S.F. Chu (1968), "On estimating the industry production function", American Economic Review 58(4):826–839.

Aigner, D.J., A.K. Lovell and P. Schmidt (1977), "Formulation and estimation of stochastic frontier production function models", Journal of Econometrics 6:21–38.

---

[107] Exceptions include Somers (1998) and Pritchett and Filmer (1999). Somers considers how school efficiency and consumer demands interact in determining spending levels and patterns of districts. Pritchett and Filmer consider how self-interest of school decision makers affects patterns of inefficiency.

Akerhielm, K. (1995), "Does class size matter?" Economics of Education Review 14(3):229–241.

Akin, J.S., and I. Garfinkel (1977), "School expenditures and the economic returns to schooling", Journal of Human Resources 12(4):460–481.

Angrist, J.D., and V. Lavy (1999), "Using Maimondides' rule to estimate the effect of class size on scholastic achievement", Quarterly Journal of Economics 114(2):533–575.

Angrist, J.D., E. Bettinger, E. Bloom, E.N. King and M. Kremer (2001), "Vouchers for private schooling in Columbia: evidence from a randomized natural experiment", Working Paper 8343 (National Bureau of Economic Research, Cambridge, MA).

Antos, J.R., and S. Rosen (1975), "Discrimination in the market for teachers", Journal of Econometrics 2:123–150.

Argys, L.M., D.I. Rees and D.J. Brewer (1996), "Detracking America's schools: equity at zero cost?" Journal of Policy Analysis and Management 15(4):623–645.

Armor, D.J. (1995), Forced Justice: School Desegregation and the Law (Oxford University Press, New York).

Armor, D.J., P. Conry-Oseguera, M. Cox, N. King, L. McDonnell, A. Pascal, E. Pauly and G. Zellman (1976), Analysis of the School Preferred Reading Program in Selected Los Angeles Minority Schools (Rand Corp., Santa Monica, CA).

Baker, G.P. (1992), "Incentive contracts and performance measurement", Journal of Political Economy 100(3):598–614.

Baker, G.P. (2002), "Distortion and risk in optimal incentive contracts", Journal of Human Resources 37(4).

Ballou, D. (1996), "Do public schools hire the best applicants?" Quarterly Journal of Economics 111(1):97–133.

Ballou, D. (2001), "Pay for performance in public and private schools", Economics of Education Review 20(1):51–61.

Ballou, D., and M. Podgursky (1997), Teacher Pay and Teacher Quality (W.E. Upjohn Institute for Employment Research, Kalamazoo, MI).

Barnett, W.S. (1992), "Benefits of compensatory preschool education", Journal of Human Resources 27(2):279–312.

Barro, R.J. (1991), "Economic growth in a cross section of countries", Quarterly Journal of Economics 106(2):407–443.

Barro, R.J., and J.-W. Lee (2001), "International data on educational attainment: updates and implications", Oxford Economic Papers 53(3):541–563.

Barro, R.J., and X. Sala-I-Martin (1995), Economic Growth (McGraw-Hill, New York).

Baumol, W.J. (1967), "Macroeconomics of unbalanced growth: the anatomy of urban crisis", American Economic Review 57(3):415–426.

Becker, G.S. (1993), Human Capital: A Theoretical and Empirical Analysis, with Special Reference to Education, 3rd Edition (University of Chicago Press, Chicago); 1st Edition published in 1964.

Becker, G.S., and H.G. Lewis (1973), "On the interaction between the quantity and quality of children", Journal of Political Economy 81:S279-S288.

Becker, G.S., and N. Tomes (1976), "Child endowments and the quantity and quality of children", Journal of Political Economy 84:S143-S162.

Becker, G.S., and N. Tomes (1979), "An equilibrium theory of the distribution of income and intergenerational mobility", Journal of Political Economy 87(6):1153–1189.

Bedard, K. (2001), "Human capital versus signaling models: university access and high school dropouts", Journal of Political Economy 109(4):749–775.

Behrman, J.R., and N. Birdsall (1983), "The quality of schooling: quantity alone is misleading", American Economic Review 73(5):928–946.

Behrman, J.R., and M.R. Rosenzweig (2002), "Does increasing women's schooling raise the schooling of the next generation?" American Economic Review 92(1):323–334.

Behrman, J.R., P. Taubman and R.A. Pollak (1982), "Parental preferences and provision for progeny", Journal of Political Economy 90(1):52–73.

Behrman, J.R., M.R. Rosenzweig and P. Taubman (1996), "College choice and wages: estimates using data on female twins", Review of Economics and Statistics 78(4):672–685.

Behrman, J.R., L.G. Kletzer, M.S. McPherson and M.O. Schapiro (1998), "The microeconomics of college choice, careers, and wages: measuring the impact of higher education", Annals of the American Academy of Political and Social Science 559:12–23.

Benabou, R. (1993), "Workings of a city: location, education, and production", Quarterly Journal of Economics 434(3):619–652.

Benabou, R. (1996), "Heterogeneity, stratification, and growth: macroeconomic implications of community structure and school finance", American Economic Review 86(3):584–609.

Benhabib, J., and M.M. Spiegel (1994), "The role of human capital in economic development: evidence from aggregate cross-country data", Journal of Monetary Economics 34(2):143–174.

Bergstrom, T.C., and R.P. Goodman (1973), "Private demands for public goods", American Economic Review 63(3):280–296.

Bergstrom, T.C., D.L. Rubinfeld and P. Shapiro (1982), "Micro-based estimates of demand functions for local schools expenditure", Econometrica 50(5):1183–1206.

Berne, R., and L. Stiefel (1984), The Measurement of Equity in School Finance: Conceptual, Methodological, and Empirical Dimensions (Johns Hopkins University Press, Baltimore, MD).

Betts, J.R. (1995), "Does school quality matter? Evidence from the National Longitudinal Survey of Youth", Review of Economics and Statistics 77(2):231–247.

Betts, J.R. (1996), "Is there a link between school inputs and earnings? Fresh scrutiny of an old literature", In: G. Burtless, ed., Does Money Matter? The Effect of School Resources on Student Achievement and Adult Success (Brookings, Washington, DC) pp. 141–191.

Betts, J.R., and R.M. Costrell (2001), "Incentives and equity under standards-based reform", In: D. Ravitch, ed., Brookings Papers on Education Policy: 2001 (Brookings Press, Washington, DC) pp. 9–74.

Bils, M., and P.J. Klenow (2000), "Does schooling cause growth?" American Economic Review 90(5): 1160–1183.

Bishop, J. (1989), "Is the test score decline responsible for the productivity growth decline?" American Economic Review 79(1):178–197.

Bishop, J. (1991), "Achievement, test scores, and relative wages", In: M.H. Kosters, ed., Workers and Their Wages (AEI Press, Washington, DC) pp. 146–186.

Bishop, J. (1996), "Signaling, incentives, and school organization in France, the Netherlands, Britain, and United States", In: E.A. Hanushek and D.W. Jorgenson, eds., Improving America's Schools: The Role of Incentives (National Academy Press, Washington, DC) pp. 111–145.

Bishop, J.H., F. Mane, M. Bishop and J. Moriarty (2001), "The role of end-of-course exams and minimal competency exams in standards-based reforms", In: D. Ravitch, ed., Brookings Papers in Education Policy 2001 (Brookings, Washington, DC) pp. 267–345.

Black, S.E. (1999), "Do better schools matter? Parental valuation of elementary education", Quarterly Journal of Economics 114(2):577–599.

Boardman, A.E., O. Davis and P. Sanday (1977), "A simultaneous equations model of the educational process", Journal of Public Economics 7(1):23–49.

Boissiere, M.X., J.B. Knight and R.H. Sabot (1985), "Earnings, schooling, ability, and cognitive skills", American Economic Review 75(5):1016–1030.

Boozer, M.A., and C.E. Rouse (1995), "Intraschool variation in class size: patterns and implications", Working Paper 5144 (National Bureau of Economic Research, Cambridge, MA).

Boozer, M.A., A.B. Krueger and S. Wolkon (1992), "Race and school quality since Brown v. Board of Education", In: M.N. Bailey and C. Winston, eds., Brooking Papers (Brookings, Washington, DC) pp. 269–338.

Borcherding, T.E., and R.T. Deacon (1972), "The demand for the services of non-federal governments", American Economic Review 62(5):891–901.

Borland, M.V., and R.M. Howsen (1992), "Student academic achievement and the degree of market concentration in education", Economics of Education Review 11(1):31–39.

Bound, J., and R.B. Freeman (1992), "What went wrong? The erosion of relative earnings and employment among young black men in the 1980s", Quarterly Journal of Economics 107(1):201–232.

Bowles, S., and H. Gintis (1976), Schooling in Capitalist America: Educational Reform and the Contradictions of Economic Life (Basic Books, New York).

Bowles, S., and H.M. Levin (1968), "The determinants of scholastic achievement – an appraisal of some recent evidence", Journal of Human Resources 3(1):3–24.

Bowles, S., H. Gintis and M. Osborne (2001), "The determinants of earnings: a behavioral approach", Journal of Economic Literature 39(4):1137–1176.

Brickley, J.A., and J.L. Zimmerman (2001), "Changing incentives in a multitask environment: evidence from a top-tier business school", Journal of Corporate Finance 7:367–396.

Brock, W.A., and S.N. Durlauf (2001), "Interactions-based models", In: J.J. Heckman and E. Leamer, eds., Handbook of Econometrics, Vol. 5 (Elsevier, Amsterdam) pp. 3297–3380.

Brown, B.W., and D.H. Saks (1975), "The production and distribution of cognitive skills within schools", Journal of Political Economy 83(3):571–593.

Burtless, G. (1996a), Does Money Matter? The Effect of School Resources on Student Achievement and Adult Success (Brookings, Washington, DC).

Burtless, G. (1996b), "Introduction and summary", In: G. Burtless, ed., Does Money Matter? The Effect of School Resources on Student Achievement and Adult Success (Brookings, Washington, DC) pp.1–42.

Cain, G.G., and H.W. Watts (1970), "Problems in making policy inferences from the Coleman Report", American Sociological Review 35(2):328–352.

Cameron, S.V., and J.J. Heckman (1999), "Can tuition policy combat rising wage inequality?" In: M.H. Kosters, ed., Financing College Tuition: Government Policies and Educational Priorities (AEI Press, Washington, DC).

Card, D. (1999), "Causal effect of education on earnings", In: O.C. Ashenfelter and D. Card, eds., Handbook of Labor Economics, Vol. 3A (Elsevier, Amsterdam) pp. 1801–1863.

Card, D., and A.B. Krueger (1992a), "Does school quality matter? Returns to education and the characteristics of public schools in the United States", Journal of Political Economy 100(1):1–40.

Card, D., and A.B. Krueger (1992b), "School quality and black–white relative earnings: a direct assessment", Quarterly Journal of Economics 107(1):151–200.

Card, D., and A.B. Krueger (1996), "School resources and student outcomes: an overview of the literature and new evidence from North and South Carolina", Journal of Economic Perspectives 10(4):31–50.

Carnoy, M. (2001), School Vouchers: Examining the Evidence (Economic Policy Institute, Washington, DC).

Case, A., and A. Deaton (1999), "School inputs and educational outcomes in South Africa", Quarterly Journal of Economics 114(3):1047–1084.

Caucutt, E.M. (2002), "Educational policy when there are peer group effects – size matters", International Economic Review 43(1):195–222.

Cawley, J., J.J. Heckman, L. Lochner and E. Vytlacil (2000), "Understanding the role of cognitive ability in accounting for the recent rise in the economic return to education", In: K. Arrow, S. Bowles and S. Durlauf, eds., Meritocracy and Economic Inequality (Princeton University Press, Princeton, NJ) pp. 230–265.

Chaikind, S., L.C. Danielson and M.L. Brauen (1993), "What do we know about the costs of special education? A selected review", Journal of Special Education 26(4):344–370.

Chambers, J.G. (1977), "The impact of collective bargaining for teachers on resource allocation in public school districts", Journal of Urban Economics 4(3):324–339.

Charnes, A., W.W. Cooper and E. Rhodes (1978), "Measuring the efficiency of decision making units", European Journal of Operational Research 2:429–444.

Chubb, J.E., and T.M. Moe (1990), Politics, Markets and America's Schools (The Brookings Institution, Washington, DC).

Clotfelter, C.T. (1976), "School desegregation, "tipping", and private school enrollment", Journal of Human Resources 22(1):29–50.

Clotfelter, C.T. (2001), "Are whites still fleeing? Racial patterns and enrollment shifts in urban public schools", Journal of Policy Analysis and Management 20(2):199–221.

Clune, W.H. (1994), "The shift from equity to adequacy in school finance", Educational Policy 8(4): 376–394.

Cohen, D.K., and R.J. Murnane (1986), "Merit pay and the evaluation problem: understanding why most merit pay plans fail and a few survive", Harvard Educational Review 56(1):1–17.

Cohn, E. (1997), Market Approaches to Education: Vouchers and School Choice (Pergamon, Oxford, UK).

Cohn, E., and T.G. Geske (1990), The Economics of Education, 3rd Edition (Pergamon Press, Oxford, UK).

Coleman, J.S., and T. Hoffer (1987), Public, Catholic, and Private Schools: The Importance of Community (Basic Books, New York).

Coleman, J.S., E.Q. Campbell, C.J. Hobson, J. McPartland, A.M. Mood, F.D. Weinfeld and R.L. York (1966), Equality of Educational Opportunity (U.S. Government Printing Office, Washington, DC).

Coleman, J.S., S.D. Kelley and J.A. Moore (1975), "Trends in school integration, 1968–73", Paper 722-03-01 (Urban Institute, Washington, DC).

Coleman, J.S., T. Hoffer and S. Kilgore (1982), High School Achievement: Public, Catholic and Private Schools Compared (Basic Books, New York).

Cook, M.D., and W.N. Evans (2000), "Families or schools? Explaining the convergence in white and black academic performance", Journal of Labor Economics 18(4):729–754.

Cook, T.D. (1984), "What have black children gained academically from school desegregation? A review of the metaanalytic evidence", In: School Desegregation (National Institute of Education, Washington, DC).

Coons, J.E., W.H. Clune and S.D. Sugarman (1970), Private Wealth and Public Education (The Belknap Press of Harvard University Press, Cambridge, MA).

Courant, P.N., and S. Loeb (1997), "Centralization of school finance in Michigan", Journal of Policy Analysis and Management 16(1):114–136.

Craig, S.G., and R.P. Inman (1982), "Federal aid and public education: an empirical look at the new fiscal federalism", Review of Economics and Statistics 64(4):541–552.

Craig, S.G., and R.P. Inman (1986), "Education, welfare, and the "new" federalism: state budgeting in a federalist public economy", In: H.S. Rosen, ed., Studies in State and Local Public Finance (University of Chicago Press, Chicago) pp. 187–222.

Crain, R.L. (1970), "School integration and occupational achievement of Negroes", American Journal of Sociology 75(4):593–606; part II.

Crain, R.L., and R.E. Mahard (1978), "Desegregation and black achievement: a review of the research", Law and Contemporary Problems 42(3):17–53.

Cullen, J.B. (2002), "The impact of fiscal incentives on student disability rates", Journal of Public Economics, forthcoming.

Cullen, J.B., and S.G. Rivkin (2003), "The role of special education in school choice", In: C.M. Hoxby, ed., The Economics of School Choice (University of Chicago Press, Chicago, IL) forthcoming.

Cullen, J.B., B. Jacob and S. Levitt (2000), "The impact of school choice on student outcomes: an analysis of the Chicago public schools", Working Paper 7888 (National Bureau of Economic Research, Cambridge, MA).

Currie, J. (2001), "Early childhood education programs", Journal of Economic Perspectives 15(2): 213–238.

Currie, J., and D. Thomas (1995), "Does head start make a difference?" American Economic Review 85(3):341–364.

Currie, J., and D. Thomas (1999), "Does head start help Hispanic children?" Journal of Public Economics 74:235–262.

Currie, J., and D. Thomas (2000), "Early test scores, socioeconomic status, school quality, and future outcomes", Mimeo (Department of Economics, UCLA).

Dale, S.B., and A.B. Krueger (1999), "Estimating the payoff to attending a more selective college: an application of selection on observables and unobservables", Working Paper 7322 (National Bureau of Economic Research, Cambridge, MA).

de Bartolome, C.A.M. (1990), "Equilibrium and inefficiency in a community model with peer group effects", Journal of Political Economy 98(1):110–133.

Deere, D. (2001), "Trends in wage inequality in the United States", In: F. Welch, ed., The Causes and Consequences of Increasing Inequality (University of Chicago Press, Chicago) pp. 9–35.

Deere, D., and W. Strayer (2001), "Putting schools to the test: school accountability, incentives, and behavior", Department of Economics, Texas A&M University (March 2001).

Downes, T.A. (1992), "Evaluating the impact of school finance reform on the provision of public education: the California case", National Tax Journal 45(4):405–419.

Downes, T.A., and T.F. Pogue (1994), "Adjusting school aid formulas for the higher cost of educating disadvantaged students", National Tax Journal 47(1):89–110.

Downes, T.A., and M.P. Shah (1996), "The effect of school finance reforms on the level and growth of per pupil expenditures", Working Paper 95-4 (Tufts University, Medford, MA).

Dugan, D.J. (1976), "Scholastic achievement: its determinants and effects in the education industry", In: J.T. Froomkin, D.T. Jamison and R. Radner, eds., Education as an Industry (Ballinger, Cambridge, MA) pp. 53–83.

Duncombe, W., J. Ruggiero and J. Yinger (1996), "Alternative approaches to measuring the cost of education", In: H.F. Ladd, ed., Holding Schools Accountable: Performance-Based Reform in Education (Brookings, Washington, DC) pp. 327–356.

Ehrlich, I. (1975), "On the relation between education and crime", In: F.T. Juster, ed., Education, Income, and Human Behavior (McGraw-Hill, New York).

Eide, E., D.J. Brewer and R.G. Ehrenberg (1998), "Does it pay to attend an elite private college? Evidence on the effects of undergraduate college quality on graduate school attendance", Economics of Education Review 17(4):371–376.

Entwisle, D.R., and K.L. Alexander (1992), "Summer setback: race, poverty, school composition, and mathematics achievement in the first two years of school", American Sociological Review 57(1): 72–84.

Epple, D., and R.E. Romano (1996), "Ends against the middle: determinating public service provision when there are private alternatives", Journal of Public Economics 62(3):297–325.

Epple, D., and R.E. Romano (1998), "Competition between private and public schools, vouchers, and peer-group effects", American Economic Review 88(1):33–62.

Epple, D., and R.E. Romano (2003), "Neighborhood schools, choice and the distribution of educational benefits", In: C.M. Hoxby, ed., The Economics of School Choice (University of Chicago Press, Chicago, IL) forthcoming.

Evans, W.N., and R.M. Schwab (1995), "Finishing high school and starting college: do Catholic schools make a difference?" Quarterly Journal of Economics 110(4):941–974.

Fair, R.C. (1971), "The optimal distribution of income", Quarterly Journal of Economics 85(4):551–579.

Fairlie, R.W., and A.M. Resch (2002), "Is there "white flight" into private schools? Evidence from the National Educational Longitudinal Survey", Review of Economics and Statistics 84(1):21–33.

Farrell, P., and V.R. Fuchs (1982), "Schooling and health: the Cigarette Connection", Journal of Health Economics 1(3):217–230.

Feldstein, M. (1975), "Wealth neutrality and local choice in public education", American Economic Review 65(1):75–89.

Fernandez, R., and R. Rogerson (1996), "Income distribution, communities, and the quality of public education", Quarterly Journal of Economics 111(1):135–164.

Fernandez, R., and R. Rogerson (1997), "Education finance reform: a dynamic perspective", Journal of Policy Analysis and Management 16(1):67–84.

Fernandez, R., and R. Rogerson (1998), "Public education and income distribution: a dynamic quantitative evaluation of education-finance reform", American Economic Review 88(4):813–833.

Figlio, D.N. (1997), "Did the "tax revolt" reduce school performance?" Journal of Public Economics 65:245–269.

Filimon, R., T. Romer and H. Rosenthal (1982), "Asymmetric information and agenda control: the bases of monopoly power in public spending", Journal of Public Economics 17:51–70.

Finn, C.E.J., B.V. Manno and G. Vanourek (2000), Charter Schools in Action (Princeton University Press, Princeton, NJ).

Fischel, W.A. (1989), "Did Serrano cause Proposition 13?" National Tax Journal 42:465–474.

Fiske, E.B., and H.F. Ladd (2000), When Schools Compete: A Cautionary Tale (Brookings Institution Press, Washington, DC).

Flyer, F., and S. Rosen (1997), "The new economics of teachers and education", Journal of Labor Economics 15(1):104–139; part 2.

Friedman, M. (1962), Capitalism and Freedom (University of Chicago Press, Chicago).

Fuller, B. (1985), Raising School Quality in Developing Countries: What Investments Boost Learning? (The World Bank, Washington, DC).

Glass, G.V., and M.L. Smith (1979), "Meta-analysis of research on class size and achievement", Educational Evaluation and Policy Analysis 1(1):2–16.

Glenn, C.L. (1989), Choice in Schools in Six Nations (U.S. Government Printing Office, Washington, DC).

Glomm, G., and B. Ravikumar (1992), "Public vs. private investment in human capital: endogenous growth and income inequality", Journal of Political Economy 100(4):818–834.

Glomm, G., and B. Ravikumar (1998), "Opting out of publicly provided services: a majority voting result", Social Choice and Welfare 15:187–199.

Goldin, C. (1998), "America's graduation from high school: the evolution and spread of secondary schooling in the twentieth century", Journal of Economic History 58:345–374.

Goldstein, G.S., and M.V. Pauly (1981), "Tiebout bias on the demand for local public goods", Journal of Public Economics 16:131–144.

Gramlich, E.M. (1977), "Intergovernmental grants: a review of the empirical literature", In: W.E. Oates, ed., The Political Economy of Fiscal Federalism (Heath-Lexington, Lexington, MA).

Gramlich, E.M. (1986), "Evaluation of education projects: the case of the Perry preschool program", Economics of Education Review 5(1):17–24.

Gramlich, E.M., and P.P. Koshel (1975), Educational Performance Contracting (The Brookings Institution, Washington, DC).

Gramlich, E.M., and D.L. Rubinfeld (1982), "Micro estimates of public spending demand functions and tests of the Tiebout and median voter hypotheses", Journal of Political Economy 90(3):536–560.

Greenberg, D., and J. McCall (1974), "Teacher mobility and allocation", Journal of Human Resources 9(4):480–502.

Greene, J.P. (2001a), An Evaluation of the Florida A-Plus Accountability and School Choice Program (Center for Civic Innovation, Manhattan Institute, New York).

Greene, J.P. (2001b), "The looming shadow: Florida gets its 'F' schools to shape up", Education Next 1(4):76–82.

Greene, J.P., P.E. Peterson and J. Du (1998), "School choice in Milwaukee: a randomized experiment", In: P.E. Peterson and B.C. Hassel, eds., Learning from School Choice (Brookings Institution, Washington, DC) pp. 335–356.

Greenwald, R., L.V. Hedges and R.D. Laine (1996), "The effect of school resources on student achievement", Review of Educational Research 66(3):361–396.

Griliches, Z. (1974), "Errors in variables and other unobservables", Econometrica 42(6):971–998.

Grogger, J.T. (1996), "Does school quality explain the recent black/white wage trend?" Journal of Labor Economics 14(2):231–253.

Grogger, J.T., and E. Eide (1993), "Changes in college skills and the rise in the college wage premium", Journal of Human Resources 30(2):280–310.

Grogger, J.T., and D. Neal (2000), "Further evidence on the effects of Catholic secondary schooling", In: W.G. Gale and J.R. Pack, eds., Brookings-Wharton Papers on Urban Affairs, 2000 (Brookings Institution Press, Washington, DC).

Grosskopf, S., K.J. Hayes, L.L. Taylor and W.L. Weber (1997), "Budget-constrained frontier measures of fiscal equality and efficiency in schooling", Review of Economics and Statistics 74(1):116–124.

Gyimah-Brempong, K., and A.O. Byapong (1991), "Characteristics of education production functions: an application of canonical regression analysis", Economics of Education Review 10(1):7–17.

Hanushek, E.A. (1971), "Teacher characteristics and gains in student achievement: estimation using micro data", American Economic Review 60(2):280–288.

Hanushek, E.A. (1972), Education and Race: An Analysis of the Educational Production Process (Health-Lexington, Cambridge, MA).

Hanushek, E.A. (1979), "Conceptual and empirical issues in the estimation of educational production functions", Journal of Human Resources 14(3):351–388.

Hanushek, E.A. (1986), "The economics of schooling: production and efficiency in public schools", Journal of Economic Literature 24(3):1141–1177.

Hanushek, E.A. (1991), "When school finance 'reform' may not be good policy", Harvard Journal on Legislation 28(2):423–456.

Hanushek, E.A. (1992), "The trade-off between child quantity and quality", Journal of Political Economy 100(1):84–117.

Hanushek, E.A. (1994), Making Schools Work: Improving Performance and Controlling Costs (Brookings Institution, Washington, DC). In collaboration with C.S. Benson, R.B. Freeman, D.T. Jamison, H.M. Levin, R.A. Maynard, R.J. Murnane, S.G. Rivkin, R.H. Sabot, L.C. Solmon, A.A. Summers, F. Welch and B.L. Wolfe.

Hanushek, E.A. (1995), "Interpreting recent research on schooling in developing countries", World Bank Research Observer 10(2):227–246.

Hanushek, E.A. (1997a), "Assessing the effects of school resources on student performance: an update", Educational Evaluation and Policy Analysis 19(2):141–164.

Hanushek, E.A. (1997b), "The productivity collapse in schools", In: W.J. Fowler Jr., ed., Developments in School Finance, 1996 (National Center for Education Statistics, Washington, DC) pp. 185–195.

Hanushek, E.A. (1999), "Some findings from an independent investigation of the Tennessee STAR experiment and from other investigations of class size effects", Educational Evaluation and Policy Analysis 21(2):143–163.

Hanushek, E.A., and J.F. Kain (1972), "On the value of 'equality of educational opportunity' as a guide to public policy", In: F. Mosteller and D.P. Moynihan, eds., On Equality of Educational Opportunity (Random House, New York) pp. 116–145.

Hanushek, E.A., and D.D. Kimko (2000), "Schooling, labor force quality, and the growth of nations", American Economic Review 90(5):1184–1208.

Hanushek, E.A., and J.A. Luque (2003), "Efficiency and equity in schools around the world", Economics of Education Review 22(4), forthcoming.

Hanushek, E.A., and R.R. Pace (1995), "Who chooses to teach (and why)?" Economics of Education Review 14(2):101–117.

Hanushek, E.A., and M.E. Raymond (2001), "The confusing world of educational accountability", National Tax Journal 54(2):365–384.

Hanushek, E.A., and S.G. Rivkin (1997), "Understanding the twentieth-century growth in U.S. school spending", Journal of Human Resources 32(1):35–68.

Hanushek, E.A., and S.G. Rivkin (2003), "Does public school competition affect teacher quality?" In: C.M. Hoxby, ed., The Economics of School Choice (University of Chicago Press, Chicago, IL) forthcoming.

Hanushek, E.A., and J.A. Somers (2001), "Schooling, inequality, and the impact of government", In: F. Welch, ed., The Causes and Consequences of Increasing Inequality (University of Chicago Press, Chicago) pp. 169–199.

Hanushek, E.A., S.G. Rivkin and L.L. Taylor (1996), "Aggregation and the estimated effects of school resources", Review of Economics and Statistics 78(4):611–627.

Hanushek, E.A., C.K.Y. Leung and K. Yilmaz (2001), "Redistribution through education and other transfer mechanisms", Working Paper 8588 (National Bureau of Economic Research, Cambridge, MA).

Hanushek, E.A., J.F. Kain and S.G. Rivkin (2001a), "Disruption versus Tiebout improvement: the costs and benefits of switching schools", Working Paper 8479 (National Bureau of Economic Research, Cambridge, MA).

Hanushek, E.A., J.F. Kain and S.G. Rivkin (2001b), "New evidence about Brown v. Board of Education: the complex effects of school racial composition on achievement", Working Paper 8741 (National Bureau of Economic Research, Cambridge, MA).

Hanushek, E.A., J.F. Kain and S.G. Rivkin (2001c), "Why public schools lose teachers", Working Paper 8599 (National Bureau of Economic Research, Cambridge, MA).

Hanushek, E.A., J.F. Kain, J.M. Markman and S.G. Rivkin (2003), "Does peer ability affect student achievement?" Journal of Applied Econometrics, forthcoming.

Harbison, R.W., and E.A. Hanushek (1992), Educational Performance of the Poor: Lessons from Rural Northeast Brazil (Oxford University Press, New York).

Hartigan, J.A., and A.K. Wigdor (1989), Fairness in Employment Testing: Validity Generalization, Minority Issues, and the General Aptitude Test Battery (National Academy Press, Washington, DC).

Hartman, R.W. (1973), "The rationale for federal support for higher education", In: L.C. Solmon and P.J. Taubman, eds., Does College Matter? Some Evidence on the Impacts of Higher Education (Academic Press, New York) pp. 271–292.

Hatry, H.P., J.M. Greiner and B.G. Ashford (1994), Issues and Case Studies in Teacher Incentive Plans, 2nd Edition (Urban Institute, Washington, DC).

Hauser, R.M. (1993), "The decline in college entry among African Americans: findings in search of explanations", In: P.M. Sniderman, P.E. Tetlock and E.G. Carmines, eds., Prejudice, Politics, and the American Dilemma (Stanford University Press, Stanford, CA) pp. 271–306.

Haveman, R.H., and B.L. Wolfe (1984), "Schooling and economic well-being: the role of nonmarket effects", Journal of Human Resources 19(3):377–407.

Heckman, J.J. (2000), "Policies to foster human capital", Research in Economics 54:3–56.

Heckman, J.J., and E. Vytlacil (2001), "Identifying the role of cognitive ability in explaining the level of and change in the return to schooling", Review of Economics and Statistics 83(1):1–12.

Heckman, J.J., A. Layne-Farrar and P. Todd (1996a), "Does measured school quality really matter? An examination of the earnings–quality relationship", In: G. Burtless, ed., Does Money Matter? The Effect of School Resources on Student Achievement and Adult Success (Brookings, Washington, DC) pp. 192–289.

Heckman, J.J., A. Layne-Farrar and P. Todd (1996b), "Human capital pricing equations with an application to estimating the effect of schooling quality on earnings", Review of Economics and Statistics 78(4):562–610.

Heckman, J.J., R. LaLonde and J. Smith (1999), "The economics and econometrics of active labor market programs", In: O. Ashenfelter and D. Card, eds., Handbook of Labor Economics, Vol. 3A (Elsevier, Amsterdam) pp. 1865–2097.

Heckman, J.J., L. Lochner and C. Taber (2000), "General equilibrium cost benefit analysis of education and tax policies", In: G. Ranis and L.K. Raut, eds., Trade, Growth and Development: Essays in Honor of T.N. Srinivasan (Elsevier, Amsterdam) pp. 291–393.

Hedges, L.V., and I. Olkin (1985), Statistical Methods for Meta-Analysis (Academic Press, San Diego, CA).

Hedges, L.V., R.D. Laine and R. Greenwald (1994), "Does money matter? A meta-analysis of studies of the effects of differential school inputs on student outcomes", Educational Researcher 23(3):5–14.

Henderson, J.V., P.M. Mieszkowski and Y. Sauvageau (1976), Peer Group Effects and Educational Production Functions (Economic Council of Canada, Ottawa, Canada).

Heyneman, S.P., and W. Loxley (1983), "The effect of primary school quality on academic achievement across twenty-nine high and low income countries", American Journal of Sociology 88:1162–1194.

Heyneman, S.P., and D.S. White (1986), The Quality of Education and Economic Development (World Bank, Washington, DC).

Heyns, B. (1978), Summer Learning and the Effects of Schooling (Academic Press, New York).

Hirschman, A.O. (1970), Exit, Voice, and Loyalty: Responses to Decline in Firms, Organizations, and States (Harvard University Press, Cambridge, MA).

Howell, W.G., and P.E. Peterson (2002), The Education Gap: Vouchers and Urban Schools (Brookings Institution, Washington, DC).

Hoxby, C.M. (1994), "Do private schools provide competition for public schools?" Working Paper 4978 (National Bureau of Economic Research, Cambridge, MA).

Hoxby, C.M. (1996a), "Are efficiency and equity in school finance substitutes or complements?" Journal of Economic Perspectives 10(4):51–72.

Hoxby, C.M. (1996b), "How teachers' unions affect education production", Quarterly Journal of Economics 111(3):671–718.

Hoxby, C.M. (2000a), "Does competition among public schools benefit students and taxpayers?" American Economic Review 90(5):1209–1238.

Hoxby, C.M. (2000b), "The effects of class size on student achievement: new evidence from population variation", Quarterly Journal of Economics 115(3):1239–1285.

Hoxby, C.M. (2000c), "Peer Effects in the Classroom: Learning from Gender and Race Variation", Working Paper 7867 (National Bureau of Economic Research, Cambridge, MA).

Hoxby, C.M. (2001), "All school finance equalizations are not created equal", Quarterly Journal of Economics 116(4):1189–1231.

Hoxby, C.M. (2003), "School choice and school productivity (or could school choice be a tide that lifts all boats?)", In: C.M. Hoxby, ed., The Economics of School Choice (University of Chicago Press, Chicago) forthcoming.

Inman, R.P. (1987), "Markets, governments, and the "new" political economy", In: A.J. Auerbach and M. Feldstein, eds., Handbook of Public Economics, Vol. 2 (Elsevier, Amsterdam) pp. 647–777.

James, E. (1987), "The public/private division of responsibility for education: an international comparison", Economics of Education Review 6(1):1–14.

James, E. (1993), "Why do different countries choose a different public-private mix of educational services?" Journal of Human Resources 28(3):571–592.

James, E., and N. Alsalam (1993), "College choice, academic achievement and future earnings", In: E.P. Hoffman, ed., Essays on the Economics of Education (W.E. Upjohn Institute for Employment Research, Kalamazoo, MI) pp. 111–137.

Jaynes, G.D., and R.M.J. Williams (1989), A Common Destiny: Blacks and American Society (National Academy Press, Washington, DC).

Jencks, C., M. Smith, H. Acland, M.J. Bane, D. Cohen, H. Gintis, B. Heyns and S. Michelson (1972), Inequality: A Re-assessment of the Effects of Family and Schooling in America (Basic Books, New York).

Jimenez, E., and Y. Sawada (2001), "Public for private: the relationship between public and private school enrollment in the Philippines", Economics of Education Review 20(4):389–399.

Johnson, G.E., and F.P. Stafford (1973), "Social returns to quantity and quality of schooling", Journal of Human Resources 8(2):139–155.

Jorgenson, D.W., and B.M. Fraumeni (1992), "Investment in education and U.S. economic growth", Scandinavian Journal of Economics 94:51–70.

Juhn, C., K.M. Murphy and B. Pierce (1993), "Wage inequality and the rise in returns to skill", Journal of Political Economy 101(3):410–442.

Kain, J.F., and J.M. Quigley (1975), Housing Markets and Racial Discrimination (National Bureau of Economic Research, Cambridge, MA).

Kane, T. (1994), "College enrollments by blacks since 1970: the role of college costs, family background, and the returns to education", Journal of Political Economy 102(5):878–911.

Katz, L.F., J.R. Kling and J. Liebman (2001), "Moving to opportunity in Boston: early results of a randomized mobility experiment", Quarterly Journal of Economics 116(2):607–654.

Kiker, B.F. (1968), Human Capital: In Retrospect (University of South Carolina, Columbia, SC).

Koretz, D. (1996), "Using student assessments for educational accountability", In: E.A. Hanushek and D.W. Jorgenson, eds., Improving America's Schools: The Role of Incentives (National Academy Press, Washington, DC) pp. 171–195.

Kosters, M.H. (1991), "Wages and demographics", In: M.H. Kosters, ed., Workers and their Wages (AEI Press, Washington, DC) pp. 1–32.

Krueger, A.B. (1999), "Experimental estimates of education production functions", Quarterly Journal of Economics 114(2):497–532.

Krueger, A.B. (2000), "An economist's view of class size research; the class size debate", Working Paper (Economic Policy Institute, Washington, DC).

Ladd, H.F. (1975), "Local educational expenditures, fiscal capacity, and the composition of the property tax base", National Tax Journal 28:145–158.

Ladd, H.F., and J.S. Hansen (1999), Making Money Matter: Financing America's Schools (National Academy Press, Washington, DC).

Lankford, H., and J. Wyckoff (1992), "Primary and secondary school choice among public and religious alternatives", Economics of Education Review 11(4):317–337.

Lankford, H., and J. Wyckoff (1996), "The allocation of resources to special education and regular instruction", In: H.F. Ladd, ed., Holding Schools Accountable: Performance-Based Reform in Education (Brookings, Washington, DC) pp. 221–257.

Layard, R., and G. Psacharopoulos (1974), "The screening hypothesis and the returns to education", Journal of Political Economy 82(5):985–998.

Lazear, E.P. (2001), "Educational production", Quarterly Journal of Economics 116(3):777–803.

Leibowitz, A. (1974), "Home investments in children", Journal of Political Economy 82(2):S111-S131.

Levin, H.M. (1970), "A new model of school effectiveness", in: U.S. Office of Education, eds., Do Teachers Make a Difference? (U.S. Government Printing Office, Washington, DC).

Levin, H.M., and P.J. McEwan (2001), Cost-Effectiveness Analysis: Methods and Applications, 2nd Edition (Sage Publications, Inc., Thousand Oaks, CA).

Levinson, A.M. (1988), "Reexamining teacher preferences and compensating wages", Economics of Education Review 7(3):357–364.

Levy, F., and R.J. Murnane (1992), "U.S. earnings levels and earnings inequality: a review of recent trends and proposed explanations", Journal of Economic Literature 30(3):1333–1381.

Lindahl, M. (2000), "Home versus school learning: a new approach to estimating the effect of class size on achievement", Mimeo (Swedish Institute for Social Research, Stockholm University, Sweden).

Lochner, L., and E. Moretti (2001), "The effect of education on crime: evidence from prison inmates, arrests, and self-reports", Working Paper 8605 (National Bureau of Economic Research, Cambridge, MA).

Lockheed, M.E., and A. Verspoor (1991), Improving Primary Education in Developing Countries (Oxford University Press, New York).

Loeb, S. (2001), "Estimating the effects of school finance reform: a framework for a federalist system", Journal of Public Economics 80(2):225–247.

Loeb, S., and M.E. Page (2000), "Examining the link between teacher wages and student outcomes: the importance of alternative labor market opportunities and non-pecunieary variation", Review of Economics and Statistics 82(3):393–408.

Lucas, R.E. (1988), "On the mechanics of economic development", Journal of Monetary Economics 22:3–42.

Ludwig, J., G.J. Duncan and P. Hirschfield (2001), "Urban poverty and juvenile crime: evidence from a randomized housing-mobility experiment", Quarterly Journal of Economics 116(2):655–679.

Mankiw, N.G., D. Romer and D. Weil (1992), "A contribution to the empirics of economic growth", Quarterly Journal of Economics 107(2):407–437.

Manski, C.F. (1992), "Educational choice (vouchers) and social mobility", Economics of Education Review 11(4):351–369.

Manski, C.F. (1993a), "Adolescent econometricians: how do youth infer the returns to schooling?" In: C.T. Clotfelter and M. Rothschild, eds., Studies in Supply and Demand in Higher Education (University of Chicago Press, Chicago) pp. 43–57.

Manski, C.F. (1993b), "Identification of endogenous social effects: the reflection problem", Review of Economic Studies 60:531–542.

Manski, C.F. (2000), "Economic analysis of social interactions", Journal of Economic Perspectives 14(3):115–136.

Manski, C.F., and D.A. Wise (1983), College Choice in America (Harvard University Press, Cambridge, MA).

Mayer, S.E. (1997), What Money Can't Buy: Family Income and Children's Life Chances (Harvard University Press, Cambridge, MA).

Mayer, S.E., and C. Jencks (1989), "Growing up in poor neighborhoods: how much does it matter?" Science 243:1441–1445.

McEwan, P.J. (2001), "The effectiveness of public, Catholic, and non-religious private schools in Chile's voucher system", Education Economics 9(2):103–128.

McEwan, P.J., and M. Carnoy (2000), "The effectiveness and efficiency of private schools in Chile's voucher system", Educational Evaluation and Policy Analysis 22(3):213–240.

McMahon, W.W. (1991), "Relative returns to human and physical capital in the U.S. and efficient investment strategies", Economics of Education Review 10(4):283–296.

Mendro, R.L., H.R. Jordan, E. Gomez, M.C. Anderson and K.L. Bembry (1998), "An application of multiple linear regression in determining longitudinal teacher effectiveness", Paper presented at 1998 Annual Meeting of the American Educational Research Association, April 1998, San Diego, CA.

Michael, R.T. (1982), "Measuring non-monetary benefits of education: a survey", In: W.W. McMahon and T.G. Geske, eds., Financing Education: Overcoming Inefficiency and Inequity (University of Illinois Press, Urbana, IL) pp. 119–149.

Mincer, J. (1970), "The distribution of labor incomes: a survey with special reference to the human capital approach", Journal of Economic Literature 8(1):1–26.

Mincer, J. (1974), Schooling Experience and Earnings (National Bureau of Economic Research, New York).

Moffitt, R. (2001), "Policy interventions, low-level equilibria, and social interactions", In: S. Durlauf and H.P. Young, eds., Social Dynamics (MIT Press, Cambridge, MA) pp. 45–82.

Mosteller, F. (1995), "The Tennessee study of class size in the early school grades", The Future of Children 5(2):113–127.

Mundel, D.S. (1973), "Whose education should society support?" In: L.C. Solmon and P.J. Taubman, eds., Does College Matter? Some Evidence on the Impacts of Higher Education (Academic Press, New York) pp. 293–315.

Murnane, R.J. (1975), Impact of School Resources on the Learning of Inner City Children (Ballinger, Cambridge, MA).

Murnane, R.J. (1981), "Teacher mobility revisited", Journal of Human Resources 16(1):3–19.

Murnane, R.J., and B. Phillips (1981), "What do effective teachers of inner-city children have in common?" Social Science Research 10(1):83–100.

Murnane, R.J., S. Newstead and R.J. Olsen (1985), "Comparing public and private schools: the puzzling role of selectivity bias", Journal of Business and Economic Statistics 3(1):23–35.

Murnane, R.J., J.D. Singer, J.B. Willett, J.J. Kemple and R.J. Olsen (1991), Who Will Teach? (Harvard University Press, Cambridge, MA).

Murnane, R.J., J.B. Willett and F. Levy (1995), "The growing importance of cognitive skills in wage determination", Review of Economics and Statistics 77(2):251–266.

Murnane, R.J., J.B. Willett, Y. Duhaldeborde and J.H. Tyler (2000), "How important are the cognitive skills of teenagers in predicting subsequent earnings?" Journal of Policy Analysis and Management 19(4):547–568.

Murnane, R.J., J.B. Willett, M.J. Braatz and Y. Duhaldeborde (2001), "Do different dimensions of male high school students' skills predict labor market success a decade later? Evidence from the NLSY", Economics of Education Review 20(4):311–320.

Murphy, K.M., and F. Welch (1989), "Wage premiums for college graduates: recent growth and possible explanations", Educational Researcher 18(4):17–26.

Murphy, K.M., and F. Welch (1992), "The structure of wages", Quarterly Journal of Economics 107(1): 285–326.

Murray, S.E., W.N. Evans and R.M. Schwab (1998), "Education-finance reform and the distribution of education resources", American Economic Review 88(4):789–812.

Nathan, J. (1989), "Progress, problems, and prospects with state choice plans", In: J. Nathan, ed., Public Schools by Choice: Expanding Opportunities for Parents, Students, and Teachers (Institute for Learning and Teaching, St. Paul, MN) pp. 203–224.

Nathan, J. (1996), Charter Schools: Creating Hope and Opportunity for American Education (Jossey-Bass Publishers, San Francisco).

Neal, D. (1997), "The effect of Catholic secondary schooling on educational attainment", Journal of Labor Economics 15(1):98–123.

Neal, D. (1998), "What have we learned about the benefits of private schooling?" FRBNY Economic Policy Review 4:79–86.

Neal, D., and W.R. Johnson (1996), "The role of pre-market factors in black–white differences", Journal of Political Economy 104(5):869–895.

Nechyba, T.J. (1999), "School finance induced migration patterns: the impact of private school vouchers", Journal of Public Economic Theory 1(1):5–50.

Nechyba, T.J. (2000), "Mobility, targeting, and private-school vouchers", American Economic Review 90(1):130–146.

Nechyba, T.J. (2001), "Centralization, segregation, and the nature of communities", Working paper (Department of Economics, Duke University, Durham, NC).

Nechyba, T.J. (2003a), "Introducing school choice into multi-district public school systems", In: C.M. Hoxby, ed., The Economics of School Choice (University of Chicago Press, Chicago, IL) forthcoming.

Nechyba, T.J. (2003b), "Centralization, fiscal federalism and private school attendance", International Economic Review, forthcoming.

Nelson, R.R., and E. Phelps (1966), "Investment in humans, technology diffusion and economic growth", American Economic Review 56(2):69–75.

Noell, J. (1982), "Public and Catholic schools: a reanalysis of public and private schools", Sociology of Education 55:123–132.

Oakes, J. (1985), Keeping track: how schools structure inequality (Yale University Press, New Haven, CT).

Oakes, J. (1992), "Can tracking research inform practice? Technical, normative, and political considerations", Educational Researcher 21(4):12–21.

Oates, W.E. (1969), "The effects of property taxes and local public spending on property values: an empirical study of tax capitalization and the Tiebout hypothesis", Journal of Political Economy 77(6):957–971.

Oates, W.E. (1994), "Federalism and government finance", In: J.M. Quigley and E. Smolensky, eds., Modern Public Finance (Harvard University Press, Cambridge, MA) pp. 126–151.

O'Neill, J. (1990), "The role of human capital in earnings differences between black and white men", Journal of Economic Perspectives 4(4):25–46.

O'Regan, K.M., and J.M. Quigley (1999), "Accessibility and economic opportunity", In: C. Winston, J.A. Gomez-Ibanez and W. Tye, eds., Essays in Transportation Economics (Brookings Institution, Washington, DC) pp. 436–468.

Organisation for Economic Cooperation and Development (2001), Education at a Glance (OECD, Paris).

Peltzman, S. (1993), "The political economy of the decline of American public education", Journal of Law and Economics 36:331–370.

Peterson, P.E., J.P. Greene and C. Noyes (1996), "School choice in Milwaukee", Public Interest 125: 38–56.

Peterson, P.E., W.G. Howell, P.J. Wolf and D.E. Campbell (2003), "School vouchers: results from randomized experiments", In: C.M. Hoxby, ed., The Economics of School Choice (University of Chicago Press, Chicago, IL) forthcoming.

Pierce, B., and F. Welch (1996), "Changes in the structure of wages", In: E.A. Hanushek and D.W. Jorgenson, eds., Improving America's Schools: The Role of Incentives (National Academy Press, Washington, DC) pp. 53–73.

Poterba, J.M. (1996), "Government intervention in the markets for education and health care: how and why?" In: V.R. Fuchs, ed., Individual and Social Responsibility: Child Care, Education, Medical Care, and Long-Term Care in America (University of Chicago, Chicago; National Bureau of Economic Research, Cambridge, MA) pp. 277–304.

Poterba, J.M. (1997), "Demographic structure and the political economy of public education", Journal of Policy Analysis and Management 16(1):48–66.

Pritchett, L., and D. Filmer (1999), "What education production functions really show: a positive theory of education expenditures", Economics of Education Review 18(2):223–239.

Psacharopoulos, G., J.-P. Tan and E. Jimenez (1986), Financing Education in Developing Countries: An Exploration of Policy Options (World Bank, Washington, DC).

Riley, J.G. (2001), "Silver signals: twenty-five years of screening and signaling", Journal of Economic Literature 39(2):432–478.

Rivkin, S.G. (1995), "Black/white differences in schooling and employment", Journal of Human Resources 30(4):826–852.

Rivkin, S.G. (2000), "School desegregation, academic attainment, and earnings", Journal of Human Resources 35(2):333–346.

Rivkin, S.G., E.A. Hanushek and J.F. Kain (2001), "Teachers, schools, and academic achievement", Working Paper 6691, revised (National Bureau of Economic Research, Cambridge, MA).

Rizzuto, R., and P. Wachtel (1980), "Further evidence on the returns to school quality", Journal of Human Resources 15(2):240–254.

Romer, P. (1990a), "Endogenous technological change", Journal of Political Economy 99(5):S71-S102.

Romer, P. (1990b), "Human capital and growth: theory and evidence", Carnegie-Rochester Conference Series on Public Policy 32:251–286.

Romer, T., and H. Rosenthal (1979), "Bureaucrats vs. voters: on the political economy of resource allocation by direct democracy", Quarterly Journal of Economics 93(4):563–587.

Romer, T., H. Rosenthal and V.G. Munley (1992), "Economic incentives and political institutions: spending and voting in school budget referenda", Journal of Public Economics 49:1–33.

Rosen, H.S., and D.J. Fullerton (1977), "A note on local tax rates, public benefit levels and property values", Journal of Political Economy 85(2):433–440.

Rosenbaum, J.E. (1995), "Changing the geography of opportunity by expanding residential choice: lessons from the Gautreaux Program", Housing Policy Debate 6(1):231–269.

Rosenbaum, J.E., and S.J. Popkin (1991), "Employment and earnings of low-income Blacks who move to middle-class suburbs", In: C. Jencks and P.E. Peterson, eds., The Urban Underclass (Brookings Institution, Washington, DC) pp. 342–356.

Rothstein, P. (1992), "The demand for education with 'power equalizing' aid: estimation and simulation", Journal of Public Economics 49:135–162.

Rothstein, R., and K.H. Miles (1995), Where's the Money Gone? Changes in the Level and Composition of Education Spending (Economic Policy Institute, Washington, DC).

Rouse, C.E. (1998), "Private school vouchers and student achievement: an evaluation of the Milwaukee Parental Choice Program", Quarterly Journal of Economics 113(2):553–602.

Rubinfeld, D.L., P. Shapiro and J. Roberts (1987), "Tiebout bias and the demand for local public schooling", Review of Economics and Statistics 69(3):426–437.

Ruggiero, J. (1996), "Efficiency of educational production: an analysis of New York school districts", Review of Economics and Statistics 78(3):499–509.

Sander, W. (1996), "Catholic grade schools and academic achievement", Journal of Human Resources 31(3):540–548.

Sander, W. (1999), "Private schools and public school achievement", Journal of Human Resources 34(4):697–709.

Sander, W. (2001), Catholic Schools: Private and Social Effects (Kluwer Academic Publishers, Boston).

Sanders, W.L., and S.P. Horn (1994), "The Tennessee value-added assessment system (TVAAS): mixed-model methodology in educational assessment", Journal of Personnel Evaluation in Education 8: 299–311.

Sanders, W.L., and S.P. Horn (1995), "The Tennessee Value-Added Assessment System (TVAA): mixed model methodology in educational assessment", In: A.J. Shinkfield and D.L. Stufflebeam, eds., Teacher Evaluation: Guide to Effective Practice (Kluwer Academic Publishers, Boston) pp. 337–376.

Schacter, J. (2001a), "Geographic mobility: March 1999 to March 2000", In: Current Population Reports (U.S. Census Bureau, Washington, DC).

Schacter, J. (2001b), "Why people move: exploring the March 2000 Current Population Series", In: Current Population Reports (U.S. Census Bureau, Washington, DC).

Schofield, J.W. (1995), "Review of research on school desegregation's impact on elementary and secondary school students", In: J.A. Banks and C.A.M. Banks, eds., Handbook of Research on Multicultural Education (Macmillan, New York) pp. 597–616.

Schultz, T.W. (1961), "Investment in human capital", American Economic Review 51(1):1–17.

Schultz, T.W. (1963), The Economic Value of Education (Columbia University Press, New York).

Schultz, T.W. (1975), "The value of the ability to deal with disequilibria", Journal of Economic Literature 13:827–846.

Scitovsky, T., and A. Scitovsky (1959), "What price economic progress?" Yale Law Review 49:95–110.

Sewell, W.H., and R.M. Hauser (1975), Education, Occupation, and Earnings: Achievement in the Early Career (Academic Press, New York).

Silva, F., and J.C. Sonstelie (1995), "Did Serrano cause a decline in school spending?" National Tax Journal 48(2):199–215.

Smith, J.P., and F. Welch (1989), "Black economic progress after Myrdal", Journal of Economic Literature 27(2):519–564.

Solmon, L.C. (1973), "The definition and impact of college quality", In: L.C. Solmon and P.J. Taubman, eds., Does College Matter? (Academic Press, New York) pp. 77–102.

Somers, J.A. (1998), "The connection between educational spending and educational outcomes", Dissertation (University of Rochester, NY).

Speakman, R., and F. Welch (1995), "Does school quality matter? – A reassessment", Mimeo (Texas A&M University).

Spence, A.M. (1973), "Job market signalling", Quarterly Journal of Economics 87(3):355–374.

Stanley, H.W., and R.G. Niemi (2000), Vital Statistics on American Politics (CQ Press, Washington, DC).

Stecher, B.M., and G.W. Bohrnstedt (1999), Class Size Reduction in California: Early Evaluation Findings, 1996–98 (American Institutes for Research, Palo Alto, CA).

Stern, D. (1973), "Effects of alternative state aid formulas on the distribution of public school expenditures in Massachusetts", Review of Economics and Statistics 55(1):91–97.

Strayer, G.D., and R.M. Haig (1923), The Financing of Education in the State of New York (Macmillan, New York).

Summers, A.A., and A.W. Johnson (1996), "The effects of school-based management plans", In: E.A. Hanushek and D.W. Jorgenson, eds., Improving America's Schools: The Role of Incentives (National Academy Press, Washington, DC) pp. 75–96.

Summers, A.A., and B.L. Wolfe (1977), "Do schools make a difference?" American Economic Review 67(4):639–652.

Taber, C.R. (2001), "The rising college premium in the eighties: return to college or return to unobserved ability?" Review of Economic Studies 68(3):665–691.

Teixeira, R.A. (1992), The Disappearing American Voter (Brookings, Washington, DC).

Tiebout, C.M. (1956), "A pure theory of local expenditures", Journal of Political Economy 64:416–424.

Toder, E. (1972), "The supply of public school teachers to an urban metropolitan area: a possible source of discrimination in education", Review of Economics and Statistics 54(4):439–443.

U.S. Bureau of the Census (1975), Historical Statistics of the United States, Colonial Times to 1970 (U.S. Government Printing Office, Washington, DC); bicentennial edition, Vols. 1 and 2.

U.S. Bureau of the Census (2000), Statistical Abstract of the United States: 2000 (U.S. Government Printing Office, Washington, DC).

U.S. Commission on Civil Rights (1967), Racial Isolation in the Public Schools (Government Printing Office, Washington, DC).

U.S. Department of Education (1996a), Education Indicators: An International Perspective (National Center for Education Statistics, Washington, DC).

U.S. Department of Education (1996b), Pursuing Excellence: A Study of U.S. Eighth-Grade Mathematics and Science Teaching, Learning, Curriculum, and Achievement in International Context (National Center for Education Statistics, Washington, DC).

U.S. Department of Education (1997), Digest of Education Statistics (National Center for Education Statistics, Washington, DC) 1997 edition.

U.S. Department of Education (1999), Highlights from TIMSS: The Third International Mathematics and Science Study (National Center for Education Statistics, Washington, DC).

U.S. Department of Education (2000), Trends in Academic Progress: Three Decades of Student Performance (National Center for Education Statistics, Washington, DC).

U.S. General Accounting Office (1997), "Headstart: Research Provides Little Information on Impact of Current Program (U.S. General Accounting Office, Washington, DC).

Vignoles, A., R. Levacic, J. Walker, S. Machin and D. Reynolds (2000), "The relationship between resource allocation and pupil attainment: a review", DPOZ (Centre for the Economics of Education, London School of Economics and Political Science, London).

Wachtel, P. (1975), "The effect of school quality on achievement, attainment levels, and lifetime income", Explorations in Economic Research 2(4):502–536.

Wachtel, P. (1976), "The effect on earnings of school and college investment expenditures", Review of Economics and Statistics 58(3):326–331.

Walberg, H.J., and H.J. Walberg III (1994), "Losing local control", Educational Researcher 22(5):19–26.

Weimer, D.L., and M.J. Wolkoff (2001), "School performance and housing values: using non-contiguous district and incorporation boundaries to identify school effects", National Tax Journal 54(2):231–253.

Weinberg, B.A. (2001), "An incentive model of the effect of parental income on children", Journal of Political Economy 109(2):266–280.

Weisbrod, B. (1964), External Benefits of Public Education: An Economic Analysis (Princeton University, Princeton, NJ).

Weiss, A. (1995), "Human capital vs. signalling explanations of wages", Journal of Economic Perspectives 9(4):133–154.

Welch, F. (1966), "Measurement of the quality of schooling", American Economic Review 56(2): 379–392.

Welch, F. (1970), "Education in production", Journal of Political Economy 78(1):35–59.

Welch, F. (1999), "In defense of inequality", American Economic Review 89(2):1–17.

Welch, F., and A. Light (1987), New Evidence on School Desegregation (U.S. Commission on Civil Rights, Washington, DC).

West, E.G. (1996), "Education vouchers in practice and principle: a world survey", HCO Working Paper (World Bank, Washington, DC).

Willis, R.J. (1973), "A new approach to the economic theory of fertility behavior", Journal of Political Economy 81:S14-S64.

Witte Jr, J.F. (1999), The Market Approach to Education (Princeton University Press, Princeton, NJ).

Woessman, L. (2000), "Schooling resources, educational institutions, and student performance: the international evidence", Working Paper 983 (Kiel Institute of World Economics, Kiel, Germany).

Woessman, L. (2001), "Why students in some countries do better", Education Matters 1(2):67–74.

Wolfe, B.L., and S. Zuvekas (1995), "Nonmarket outcomes of schooling", Discussion Paper 1065-95 (Institute for Research on Poverty, University of Wisconsin, Madison, WI).

Wolpin, K.I. (1977), "Education and screening", American Economic Review 67(5):949–958.

Word, E., J. Johnston, H.P. Bain, B.D. Fulton, J.B. Zaharies, M.N. Lintz, C.M. Achilles, J. Folger and C. Breda (1990), Student/Teacher Achievement Ratio (STAR), Tennessee's K-3 Class Size Study: Final Summary Report, 1985–1990 (Tennessee State Department of Education, Nashville, TN).

Wyckoff, J. (1992), "The intrastate equality of public primary and secondary education resources in the U.S., 1980–1987", Economics of Education Review 11(1):19–30.

Zimmer, R.W., and E.F. Toma (2000), "Peer effects in private and public schools across countries", Journal of Policy Analysis and Management 19(1):75–92.

Chapter 31

HEALTH CARE AND THE PUBLIC SECTOR *

DAVID M. CUTLER

Harvard University; NBER

Contents

* I am extremely grateful to Dan Altman and Sarah Reber for research assistance, to Alan Auerbach and Richard Zeckhauser for helpful comments, and to the National Institutes on Aging for research support.

Handbook of Public Economics, Volume 4, Edited by A.J. Auerbach and M. Feldstein

Abstract

This chapter summarizes the many aspects of public policy for health care. I first consider government policy affecting individual behaviors. Government intervention to change individual actions such as smoking and drinking is frequently justified on externality grounds. External costs of smoking in particular are not very high relative to current taxes, however. More important quantitatively are the internal costs of smoking to the smoker. A recent literature has debated whether such internalities justify government action.

I then turn to markets for medical care and health insurance. Virtually all governments provide health insurance for some part of the population. Governments face several fundamental choices in this provision. The first choice is between operating the medical system publicly or contracting for care from private providers. The make-or-buy decision is difficult in medical care because medical quality is not fully observable. Thus, private sector efficiency may come at the expense of quality. A second choice is in the degree of cost sharing. More generous insurance reduces the utility cost of illness but also leads to overconsumption of care when sick. Optimal insurance balances the marginal costs of risk bearing and moral hazard. In the USA, government policy has historically tilted towards more generous insurance, by excluding employer payments for health insurance from income taxation. The welfare loss from this subsidy has been a theme of much research. Finally, governments face issues of competition and selection. Sick people prefer more generous insurance than do healthy people. If insurers know who is sick and who is healthy, they will charge the sick more than the healthy. This differential pricing is a welfare loss, since it denies sick people the benefits of *ex ante* pooling of risk type. Even if insurers cannot separate sick from healthy, there are still losses: high costs of generous plans discourage people from enrolling in those plans. Generous plans also have incentives to reduce their generosity, to induce sick people to enroll elsewhere. Adverse selection is empirically very important. To date, public policies have not been able to offset it.

Finally, I turn to the distributional aspects of medical care. Longstanding norms support at least basic medical care for everyone in society. But the generosity of health programs for the poor runs up against the possibility of crowding out private insurance coverage. Analysis from Medicaid program expansions shows that crowd-out does occur. Still, coverage expansions are worth the cost, given the health benefits they bring.

Keywords

moral hazard, adverse selection, managed care, HMO, indemnity insurance, pooling equilibrium, separating equilibrium, coinsurance, deductible, stop-loss, externality, internality, crowd-out

JEL classification: H11, H21, H51, I11, I18

Introduction

Governments are involved in the medical sector in many ways. The most noticeable role of government is as a health insurer. In most developed countries, governments guarantee health insurance to the entire population. The United States is an outlier; governments insure some, but not all, of the population. Some governments also provide medical services. Medical care delivery is entirely public in some countries and even in the privately-dominated US, governments run 15% of the hospitals. The tax side of the ledger is also important. In the United States, the Federal government subsidizes employer-provided health insurance by excluding contributions for this insurance from taxable income. The amount of revenue foregone by this exclusion is nearly $60 billion in income taxes alone per year, or about 15% of direct government payments for medical care. In addition, governments tax goods with adverse health consequences, such as smoking and drinking, with the idea of improving health. Finally, governments regulate health care. Governments restrict insurance companies (what can be offered and to whom), license medical care providers, and approve new drugs and devices before they can be sold.

What role should the government have in health care? What is the empirical evidence about the efficacy of government interventions? Since health care is so central to the public sector, addressing these questions is a prime concern of public economics. I pursue these questions in stages.

Figure 1 shows a conceptual diagram underlying the public sector role in health care. Individual utility depends on health and other goods. Health, in turn, depends on many factors. Individual behaviors are important; behaviors influence health and also utility directly. The environment affects health, more so in the past when water and sanitation were serious health hazards than today, but even today environmental issues are important. Medical care is a third factor influencing health. Medical care cannot be understood without analyzing the health insurance market, its subsidiary. Other factors noted in the figure might also influence health but are farther removed from the public sector, including genetics and socioeconomic status[1]. I thus focus on behavioral, environmental, and medical influences on health.

The simplest situation to analyze is the health-related behaviors that people engage in. The canonical individual cases here are smoking and drinking; both have benefits to the individual (direct consumption value), but adverse health consequences for the individual using them and possibly others. At the firm level, pollution has similar characteristics; it helps to produce goods and services that individuals want, but has byproducts that are harmful to health.

The classic economic rationale for government involvement in such activities is on externality grounds; people who smoke, drink, or pollute cause harm to others, and

---

[1] There is some literature claiming that in societies with more inequality in income, average health is lower [Wilkinson (1996)]. Such claims are controversial, though [Deaton (2001)].

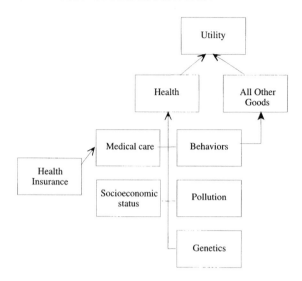

Fig. 1. Health and utility.

these costs should be internalized when people make their behavioral decisions. As we shall see, however, the situation is not so clear. Estimating the external costs of smoking and drinking is not so straightforward in part because smoking, and to a lesser extent drinking, is associated with some external benefits, as people pay taxes over their working life but die at a younger age. There is a spirited debate about whether these activities are on net costly or beneficial to society, and thus whether the optimal tax is high or low.

In addition to concerns about externalities, governments may also want to intervene to prevent people from worsening their own health. Rational people will take personal health harms into account when making behavioral decisions. But if consumption decisions are not rational, driven by impulse, fashion, or fad, taxes might be needed for 'internality' reasons. While it is difficult to know how much of these costs are accounted for in the individual consumption decision, the total internal costs of smoking and drinking dwarf the external costs, making this issue particularly salient. Economic research on the external and internal costs of health-related individual behaviors is summarized in Section 2.

By far the largest government involvement in the health sector is in the market for medical care, and its derivative health insurance. Medical care markets are plagued by a host of potential problems, presented in Section 3: incomplete information on the part of patients; asymmetric information between consumers and producers about what patients really need; inability to tell whether services are justified, even *ex post*; externalities from consumption; moral hazard from insurance; adverse selection in insurance; and redistributive goals not met by the market. With such a litany of problems, it is no surprise that free markets for medical care function poorly.

These market failures sometimes lead governments to provide medical care directly. The choice between government and private provision of services is an important one, and countries differ on this decision. The central issue in this debate is whether public and private incentives are properly aligned. Government provision is generally believed to be less technically efficient than private provision, and medical care is no exception. But lack of a profit motive may be a virtue in some cases. When private providers would not act in the public interest, as for example a for-profit hospital that skimps on medical care because skimping is hard to detect, government provision may be superior to private sector provision. The empirical import of this argument is unknown. But such an analysis offers a lens through which to view institutional norms in the medical care field (the Hippocratic Oath; not-for-profit firms) that have traditionally worked to keep medical care quality high. These issues are explored in Section 4.

While governments are only sometimes involved in medical service provision, they are universally involved in health insurance provision. No developed country has an entirely private system of health insurance, even though many countries have (essentially) private medical care delivery systems.

In the case of one individual purchasing insurance, there is a classic economic tradeoff that governments must respect. Insurance smooths the financial risk associated with medical costs[2]. Optimal insurance from a risk-bearing perspective involves no out-of-pocket spending. But insurance also creates moral hazard; people spend more when they have insurance than they would otherwise because the price of medical services is lower. As insurance increases in generosity, the marginal gain from risk bearing falls while the marginal loss from moral hazard rises. The optimal level of insurance is the point at which the marginal gain in reduced risk bearing from additional insurance just equals the marginal loss from additional moral hazard. For a government running a health insurance system, this is the rule it needs to know.

Even in a private health insurance system, this rule has significant import. In the United States, the tax treatment of health insurance distorts the tradeoff between risk sharing and moral hazard. Where out-of-pocket spending on medical care must be purchased with after-tax dollars, employer payments for health insurance are not counted as income for personal tax purposes and thus receive an implicit subsidy. This subsidy encourages the provision of overly generous insurance. This has been alleged to lead to too much moral hazard, with empirical estimates suggesting a welfare loss of up to 10% of medical spending. There is substantial uncertainty about the true welfare loss, however, because the relevant elasticities are not all known, because this calculation does not account for the dynamics of technological innovation, and because the tax subsidy may offset other market failures such as adverse selection and crowding

---

[2] As discussed below, this is not technically right. The goal of insurance is to equalize the marginal utility of income in different states of nature. In many cases, this can be achieved by smoothing the financial costs of medical care, but not always.

out of private insurance by other public programs. Section 5 examines this host of issues.

Traditional analysis of optimal insurance, including the welfare loss from the tax subsidy, has concentrated on the demand side of the medical care market, controlling utilization by making patients pay more for the services they receive. Insurance might also affect the supply side of the market, by changing what physicians and hospitals provide. Managed care in the United States, along with virtually all medical care systems in other countries, uses supply side measures to limit overall spending. Theoretical analysis suggests, and empirical evidence confirms that supply-side measures are a complement to demand-side measures, since physicians respond to payment incentives along with price. The optimal use of supply and demand side restrictions, and the implications of supply side measures for other government policies such as the tax exclusion of employment-based health insurance is explored in Section 6.

If individuals are heterogeneous with respect to their underlying medical risk, even more problems arise. Individuals who are greater risk for medical care spending like more generous health insurance than those who are lower risk. If insurers know who is high risk and who is low risk, they can price policies accordingly. Individuals will be fully insured, but higher risk people will pay higher premiums. While this is efficient *ex post* (after risk types are known), it is a welfare loss *ex ante*. People would like to insure their risk type but do not get to do so.

In other settings, knowledge of individuals' risk type is limited or insurers are not allowed to use such information in pricing. This situation might appear better than the previous one, since insurers cannot segment risks on their own. But problems arise here as well. As people sort themselves across plans, the sick will drive up the price of more generous plans, while the less generous plans remain much cheaper. This process, termed adverse selection, leads to three sources of welfare loss. First, the sick once again pay more for insurance than the healthy, leading to the same risk segmentation loss noted above. Second, marginal people are induced to enroll in less generous insurance plans, so that they can benefit from the lower insurance premiums that being with healthy people allows. Third, plans are encouraged to reduce the generosity of their benefits, to attract the healthy and repel the sick. Empirical evidence shows large distortions from adverse selection. In nearly every setting without a mandatory, universal insurance plan, the sick wind up paying more for insurance than the healthy.

A variety of public sector activities may address problems of risk segmentation and adverse selection, ranging from mandatory pooling in one plan (as is done in many countries), to restrictions on what private insurers can offer to individuals. To date, public policies to combat adverse selection short of having a single national insurance plan have been only marginally successful. Problems arising from heterogeneity and the impact of public policies in these situations are discussed in Section 7.

The analysis of heterogeneity brings up a related topic: whether people should be allowed to supplement public insurance with private insurance. Were everyone homogeneous, a single public (or private) plan would be appropriate. When individuals are heterogeneous, however, supplementation may be a valuable option. The most controversial form of supplementation is allowing the wealthy to buy better care than the public system provides the rest of society. Some countries forbid this on egalitarian grounds; others allow it. Theoretically, this type of supplementation need not harm, and could help the poor, if the government saves enough off of the rich opting out to afford more care for the poor. I discuss this issue in Section 8.

Finally, Sections 9 and 10 turn to intragenerational and intergenerational distributional aspects of health and medical care policy. The goal of many governments is to ensure adequate quality of medical care to the poor. In universal health insurance systems, such goals are relatively easily met. When health insurance is not universal, special programs must be designed for the poor. The United States has a patchwork of such programs: Medicaid provides health insurance for the poor; public hospitals provide significant uncompensated care; and even private hospitals provide 'free care' to the uninsured. The design of health programs for the poor poses a classic economic tradeoff: more generous public coverage promotes health but may also induce people who would have bought private coverage to drop that coverage.

The health and insurance consequences of programs for the poor can be evaluated using a unique natural experiment: in the 1980s and 1990s, Medicaid eligibility was expanded to people with somewhat higher incomes and different family circumstances. I review the literature on whether the Medicaid expansions crowded out private insurance coverage, and whether they led to health improvements for the poor. Crowding out is a significant empirical issue. Estimates suggest that up to one-half of the increase in public coverage from Medicaid eligibility expansions is offset by reductions in private coverage. Even with this crowding out, however, some evidence suggests that the Medicaid spending is worth the cost. Because health is worth so much, even small improvements in health from additional insurance can justify its high cost.

Before starting the analysis it is important to note several background points. I focus on public sector health issues exclusively. This chapter is not a synthesis of health economics writ large. Readers interested in learning more about health economics as a whole should consult the recent two volume Handbook series on the topic [Culyer and Newhouse (2000a,b)].

I also focus to a large extent on the United States. This is in many ways inevitable; the data with which to analyze medical care systems are better in the United States than in other countries. Conceptually, the United States also presents many interesting economic issues, since the range of institutions and observed outcomes is much greater.

Finally, I note the crucial distinction between *health* and *medical care.* Good health is what people want; medical care is a means to that end. I shall use the terms health and medical care precisely, with one exception: I shall write about health insurance and not medical care insurance. While the latter is technically more appropriate, the former is too ingrained in the literature for me to do otherwise.

Before turning to the analytic issues about the public sector role in health care, I start in the next section by providing more background on medical systems generally and the role of the public sector in those systems.

1. Medical care and the public sector

The medical sector is a large part of most developed countries. The average country in the OECD[3] spent 8% of national income on medical care in 1995. The high was 14% (the United States); the low was 6% (Greece). Further, the medical sector is growing rapidly. Since 1929, the earliest year for which we have data, medical care in the United States has increased at a rate of 3.8% in real, per person terms. GDP growth, in comparison, has been only 1.7%, more than 2 percentage points lower. This differential is large in other countries as well. Medical spending in the average OECD country increased over 2 percentage points more rapidly than GDP growth between 1960 and 1995.

Governments pay for a significant share of medical expenses, as Figure 2 shows. In the United States, governments pay for nearly 50% of medical spending. This is the lowest in the OECD. The average share is 76%, and ranges as high as 93% (Luxembourg). Government wasn't always so important. In 1929, governments in the United States accounted for 14% of medical spending. As late as 1965, the government's share was only one-quarter.

By another metric, nearly 20% of Federal government spending in the United States is devoted to medical care, with a similar share for state and local governments.

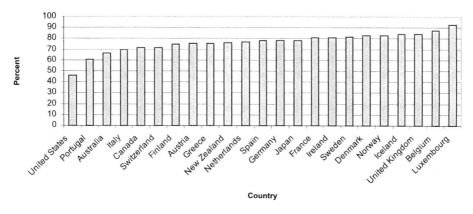

Fig. 2. Public sector share of medical spending, 1995.

---

[3] Throughout this section, I consider the 23 most developed countries in the OECD, omitting Turkey and newer members such as the Czech Republic, Hungary, Korea, Mexico, and Poland.

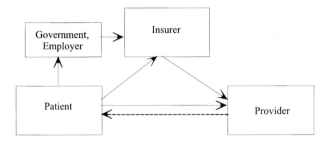

Fig. 3. The medical care triad. The solid lines represent money flows; the dashed line represents service flows.

Table 1
Examples of different medical care systems[a]

Private insurance, private provision	Public insurance, private provision	Public insurance, public provision
United States	Canada Germany Japan France	United Kingdom Sweden Italy

[a] Source: OECD.

Understanding what government does in the medical sector requires more detail about that sector. Figure 3 depicts the medical sector in a fundamental fashion, via the medical care triad. There are three actors in the medical care system, shown as the points on the triad: patients, providers, and insurers. Patients pay money to insurers, and sometimes directly to providers. Insurers pay for the bulk of medical services, and also set rules on when and where patients can seek care. Providers diagnose medical problems, recommend appropriate treatment, and provide those treatments.

Governments can be involved in the medical care system at several levels [Besley and Gouveia (1994)]. Some countries have a largely private system of insurance and medical care delivery, with government having a predominantly regulatory role. The United States is an example of such a system, as Table 1 shows. It is the only developed country without universal insurance coverage. Other countries, including Canada and Germany, have public insurance with predominantly private providers. Finally, some countries have public insurance and public ownership of medical care delivery. The United Kingdom is a leading example of this type of country.

The history of the public sector in medical care is a movement towards increasing government involvement [Cutler and Johnson (2001)]. The first government health insurance system was enacted by Bismarck in the 1880s; health insurance was created with Old Age Insurance to give people a stake in the survival of the state. The United Kingdom introduced a health insurance program for the poor early in the 20th century. But such programs were small because medical care could not do a lot. In the late 19th and early 20th centuries, effective medical treatments were rare and medical costs were not highly variable. Medical insurance became more valuable for reasons other than redistribution as spending became more variable.

It wasn't until after World War II that medical care insurance became a priority. The efficacy of penicillin was demonstrated around that time, and advances in surgery were made. With technological change came variability in medical spending; having access to the medical sector became more important. The post-World War II period saw a flowering of health insurance and provision systems [Cutler (2002)]. The British set up the first truly national medical care system in 1946. The NHS provided insurance and delivered medical services. This was followed in subsequent decades by other European countries and Canada. Generally, the later the country established national insurance, the less the government became involved in medical care delivery and the more it took an insurance role.

The United States was relatively late to enact public insurance. Private insurance coverage grew steadily during and after World War II, but there was no significant public insurance until Medicare and Medicaid were created in the mid-1960s. And while the United States has tinkered with these systems continuously since then, there have been no major expansions in public insurance since that point[4].

Because so much research on health economics is conducted using US data, it is instructive to describe that system in more detail. Table 2 shows the sources of insurance coverage in the United States. There are two significant public programs for medical care. Medicare is the larger program, spending about $200 billion annually, or one-fifth of total medical care spending. Essentially everyone over age 65 is eligible for Medicare, along with the blind and disabled and people with end-stage kidney failure[5]. Medicare insures 14% of the population.

Most Medicare beneficiaries (about 85%) are in the traditional fee-for-service insurance plan. Beneficiaries in that plan have complete choice about which providers to see. But covered services are limited. Unlike essentially all private insurance policies, the traditional Medicare program does not cover outpatient prescription drugs. It also does not cover chronic need for long-term care services such as a nursing home or home health aid, although this is generally absent from private policies as well. In total, Medicare beneficiaries account for 37% of medical costs. This share is greater

---

[4] The Medicaid expansions of the late 1980s and early 1990s, discussed in Section 9, were the most significant insurance expansions since then.

[5] Formally, eligibility is for workers or dependents of workers with 40 quarters of Social Security covered earnings. Only a few percent of the elderly are not eligible for Medicare. The disabled are on Medicaid until they qualify for Medicare.

Table 2
Insurance coverage and spending in the USA[a]

Program	Eligibility	Share of people (%)	Share of dollars[b]	
			For those people (%)	From that policy (%)
Public				
Medicare	Age 65+; Blind/disabled; people with kidney failure	14	37	21
Medicaid	Non-elderly poor; Blind and disabled; Medicare cost sharing for poor elderly; Nursing home costs for chronically impaired	10	8	9
Other	Veterans; Native Americans; Defense employees	1	1	5
Private				
Employer	Workers and dependents; Retirees	60	49	44
Non-group	Families	3	2	
Uninsured		12	4	21[c]

[a] Source: 1996 Medical Expenditure Panel Study (MEPS).
[b] The fourth column is total spending for people with each type of insurance. The fifth column is total medical care spending accounted for by that plan.
[c] Total out-of-pocket medical spending.

than Medicare's share of spending (about 20% of total costs), reflecting the relatively limited scope of Medicare covered services.

About 15% of Medicare beneficiaries are in managed care arrangements. Medicare pays managed care plans a fixed amount for each person they enroll. Because the payments traditionally did not account for adverse selection adequately, these payments were believed to exceed the cost of caring for Medicare beneficiaries. Medicare lost money when people enrolled in managed care [Sing, Brown and Hill (1998)]. Medicare is now implementing a system to more accurately account for adverse selection in plan payments, as discussed in Section 7.

Medicaid is the other major public insurance program. Medicaid eligibility is more heterogeneous. Two-thirds of program enrollees are poor, non-elderly women and children. These beneficiaries were traditionally in fee-for-service policies but increasingly have been enrolled in managed care plans. The blind and disabled are another recipiency group, prior to Medicare eligibility. Medicare eligibles can receive Medicaid if they have low incomes, or if their medical spending makes them have low disposable income. For these "dual eligibles", Medicaid will pay for cost sharing required by Medicare and uncovered services such as prescription drugs and long-term care. Because the elderly and disabled are more expensive than women and children, program spending is distributed relatively equally between the non-elderly poor, the blind and disabled, and the elderly. Ten percent of people have Medicaid as their primary insurance policy; these people in total account for 8% of medical spending[6].

Finally, there are other, small public programs, including services for veterans, Native Americans, and dependents of active duty military personnel. These insure 1% of people and account for 5% of total medical spending.

The vast bulk of the non-elderly population (90% of those with insurance) has insurance through employment; only 10% of private insurance is purchased individually. The reason for this predominance of employment-based insurance is the tax subsidy to employer-provided health insurance, discussed below. Private insurance spending accounts for nearly half of total medical spending.

Finally, about 12% of the population is uninsured[7]. Such people still receive care and account for about 4% of medical spending[8]. But uninsured people do not pay for all of their utilization. The average uninsured person pays for only 44% of the medical services he uses. Part of the rest is financed by other government programs (for example, the Veterans Administration system), while another part is financed indirectly, by providers marking up the bills to other payers and using the additional revenues to offset the losses of the uninsured.

2. Public policy for health-related behaviors

Individual and firm behaviors are a clear factor affecting health, both positively and negatively. Smoking and drinking reduce health, while exercise and vitamin consumption improve health. At the firm level, pollution and the work setting also affect health. I start the analytic analysis of government policy for health care by considering health-related behaviors. At first glance, the analysis of health-related goods is no different than the analysis of any other good. If people value consumption of cigarettes and are willing to pay the monetary and health consequences of their actions, public policy need not intervene in this decision. This analysis is incomplete for two reasons, however. First it ignores external effects – the harms these behaviors bring to others that the individual smoker or drinker does not take into account. Governments may want to tax or subsidize these activities to get people to account for these effects. Second, people may not make the right decisions about health-related activities on their own. This is particularly true for goods with an addictive component. I consider these two rationales for government intervention in turn.

---

[6] People with both Medicare and Medicaid coverage are included in the Medicare row, since Medicare is their primary insurance policy.

[7] Different surveys give somewhat different estimates of the uninsured population. The most commonly used number is about 15%, from the Current Population Survey. The MEPS data in Table 2 show slightly lower shares, but the difference is not important in this context.

[8] Out-of-pocket payments in total account for one-fifth of medical spending.

2.1. External consequences of individual actions

The simplest case to analyze is one where individuals make appropriate decisions for themselves but where there are external consequences to consumption of particular goods. I start with this analysis. For simplicity, I consider a good that individuals consume that has adverse health consequences, such as smoking. Firm decisions about production of goods that pollute are dealt with in Chapter 23 in Volume 3 of this Handbook [Bovenberg and Goulder (2002)], so I do not consider the issue further here[9].

Suppose there are two goods: X, the consumption of which affects only the individual involved; and S, a good with external consequences. Utility for any individual i depends on goods consumption (X_i and S_i) and health. Health is a function of both own consumption of S and consumption of S by everyone else, denoted S_{-i}:$H[S_i, S_{-i}]$. The dependence of person i's health on consumption of S by others is the first external effect. For simplicity, I assume that all consumption of S by other individuals has the same impact on health, although this needn't be the case (only nearby second-hand smoke is bothersome). Combining terms, utility can be represented as

$$U_i = U(X_i, S_i, H[S_i, S_{-i}]). \tag{1}$$

For simplicity, I assume everyone has the same income, Y. Disposable income is income net of medical care costs. I denote insurance costs for each individual as $T(\sum_i S_i)/N$, where N is the total population size. T is alternatively taxes used to finance public health care, or private insurance premiums. These common costs are the second external effect of consumption of S. Normalizing the price of X at 1 and denoting P_s as the price of good S, the budget constraint is

$$Y - \frac{T\left(\sum_i S_i\right)}{N} = X_i + P_s S_i. \tag{2}$$

An optimizing individual will maximize Equation (1) subject to Equation (2), taking as given the consumption decisions of others and the tax burden. The solution to this problem is given by (omitting the i subscript):

$$\frac{U_S + U_H H_S}{U_X} = P_S. \tag{3}$$

The left-hand side is the marginal rate of substitution between X and S. The numerator of Equation (3) is the marginal benefit of additional consumption of S – the utility

---

[9] The analysis is conceptually very similar, although the firm does not suffer health consequences, so only the financial externalities are relevant.

benefits of S plus the health (dis)utility. Scaling by the marginal utility of good X turns this into a monetary value. Individuals will trade off consumption of X and S until the marginal rate of substitution is equal to the ratio of prices.

A utilitarian social planner, in contrast, will maximize the sum of social welfare $(\sum_i U_i)$, subject to the constraint that aggregate consumption must equal aggregate income. The solution to this equation is given by

$$\frac{U_S + U_H H_S + \sum_{-i} U_H H_{S_{-i}}}{U_X} = P_S + \frac{T'}{N}. \tag{4}$$

Equation (4) differs from Equation (3) in two respects. First, the social planner takes account of the effects of S_i on other people's health in determining the social value of additional consumption of S by i. The term $\sum_{-i} U_H H_{S_{-i}} / U_X$ is the dollar value of marginal (dis)utility to others associated with S_i. For a good with adverse external health effects, this term is negative, and the social value of S_i is lower. The reverse is true if consumption of S_i increases the health of others. The second difference is the financial consequences of S_i. The full monetary cost of S_i is the sum of the out-of-pocket price (P_S) plus the additional increase in taxes required as a result of good-S consumption (T'/N). The utilitarian social planner will take this social cost into account.

For individuals to make the right decisions about S_i they must face the right prices. The free-market price, P_S, may be too high or too low, depending on whether good S has beneficial or adverse effects on the health and financial circumstances of others. The optimal tax rate on good S, termed the Pigouvian tax rate, is the rate that makes individuals internalize all of the external consequences of their actions. The optimal Pigouvian tax rate τ is given by

$$\tau = \frac{T'}{N} - \frac{\sum_{-i} U_H H_{S_{-i}}}{U_X}. \tag{5}$$

Goods with adverse health consequences ($H_{S_{-i}} < 0$) or adverse financial consequences ($T' > 0$) will face positive taxes. Some goods may be subsidized.

Taxation is not the only possible solution to the externality problem. Governments could limit or ban entirely consumption of goods with adverse external effects, and mandate consumption of goods with positive external effects. The relative virtues of taxation versus regulation depend in large part on the specifics of the good being considered. Taxation is most appropriate for goods where consumption decisions are made by numerous heterogeneous individuals; smoking is a prime example. But not all goods with these characteristics are taxed. Substances such as cocaine and heroin are banned, even though their demand characteristics are similar. When consumers are homogeneous, or production externalities result from a limited number of producers, regulation may be more appropriate [10].

---

[10] Taxation and regulation also differ in situations of uncertainty. Taxes allow quantities to vary in situations where demand shocks change the marginal value of the good, while regulation does not. Such

Historically, government action was much more important than taxation or subsidies in promoting health-improving behavior. Early in the 20th century, for example, the government cleaned the water supply and built sewers to improve population health, when it could alternatively have taxed dirty water or poor sanitation. In the case of these public health improvements, the gains were so large [Preston (1996)] that government action may have been the efficient solution.

2.2. Estimating external consequences of smoking and drinking

There has been a spirited economic debate about the optimal Pigouvian taxes on smoking and to a lesser extent drinking[11]. The issue is particularly difficult because it is not even clear whether these goods have negative external costs. Although smokers use more medical services for smoking-related illnesses than non-smokers, they also die at younger ages. As a result, smokers pay into social programs such as Social Security and Medicare throughout their working lives, but collect much less in old age. This death benefit offsets some or all of the fiscal costs of smoking.

Table 3 summarizes the literature on the external costs of smoking and drinking. The start of any such analysis is defining internal and external costs. Damages that the smoker suffers as a result of smoking are clearly internal. But are damages to other household members from second-hand smoke? What about damages to an unborn fetus from a pregnant woman smoking? There is no obvious answer here. The most common assumption is that the family is the unit of decision-making, so that consequences of smoking and drinking for other family members are internalized[12].

One must then specify the external costs to consider. The most important financial costs are medical care payments financed by insurance (either public or private), and Social Security payments net of taxes paid in. Other more minor costs include life and disability insurance premia, and the costs of fires from smoking. Possible health consequences from second-hand smoke are more controversial. While the literature is clear that there are adverse health consequences for some conditions such as childhood respiratory illnesses, there is more uncertainty about more costly illnesses such as cancer and cardiovascular disease in adults.

The first complete analysis of the external costs of smoking and drinking was presented in Manning, Keeler, Newhouse, Sloss and Wasserman (1989, 1991)[13].

---

variability may or may not be valuable, depending on the sensitivity of social damages to changes in consumption [Weitzman (1974)].

[11] See Chaloupka and Warner (2000) and Cook and Moore (2000) for discussions of the economics of smoking and drinking, respectively.

[12] One could assert that some effects outside of the family are internalized. If a person chooses to ride in a car with a friend who drives drunk and kills them both, the death of the passenger is counted as an external cost but is conceptually similar to a fully-informed decision to live with a smoker.

[13] The relation between smoking and Social Security payments was first noted by Shoven, Sundberg and Bunker (1989).

Table 3
External costs of smoking and drinking and optimal sin taxes

Reference	Methodology	Costs included	Results
Smoking			
Manning, Keeler, Newhouse, Sloss and Wasserman (1989, 1991)	Construct group of "non-smoking" smokers who are similar to smokers in terms of age, sex, education, drinking habits, etc. but have never smoked. Estimate and compare spending profiles for hypothetical profiles of men and women with and without smoking.	Medical care, sick leave, group life insurance, nursing home, retirement pension, fires, taxes to finance above programs	Estimate of external costs is sensitive to discount rate; range from −$0.91 per pack (0% discount rate) to $0.24 per pack (10% discount rate), in 1986 dollars.
Viscusi (1995)	Similar to Manning et al.; updates many of the estimates using more recent data; accounts for falling tar content of cigarettes.	Medical care, sick leave, group life insurance, nursing home care, retirement pensions, fires, taxes on earnings, environmental tobacco smoke (ETS) related lung cancer and heart disease	Net external costs to society excluding the effects of ETS are −$0.32 to −$0.23; including effect of ETS, estimates rise to as much as $0.41.
Evans, Ringel and Stech (1999)	Similar to Manning et al.; expand analysis to include additional costs.	ETS-related low birthweight, SIDS deaths, infant mortality and fetal loss; do not do additional analysis but include costs from Manning et al. and Viscusi	The external costs of smoking range from $0.42 to $0.72 per pack in 1994.
Summary			Estimates depend critically on the discount rate assumed and especially on whether the costs of ETS-related deaths due to heart disease, lunch cancer and maternal smoking are considered.

continued on next page

Table 3, *continued*

Reference	Methodology	Costs included	Results
Drinking			
Pogue and Sgontz (1989)	Develop theoretical model of optimal alcohol taxes; tax depends on relative elasticity of demand for abusers and non-abusers, fraction of alcohol consumed by abusers, and external costs associated with drinking	Use existing estimates of elasticities and external costs to estimate optimal tax	Depending on assumptions about relative elasticities, alcohol tax (in 1983) ranges from about right to half the optimal level. "Best guess" is that optimal tax is twice actual tax.
Manning, Keeler, Newhouse, Sloss and Wasserman (1989, 1991)	Same as for cigarettes (described above)	Medical care, sick leave, group life insurance, nursing home, retirement pension, taxes on earning, motor vehicle accidents, costs associate with the criminal justice system	External costs less sensitive to discount rate than for cigarettes; range from 1.08 to 1.56 per excess ounce of alcohol. Forty percent of consumption is excess ounces, implying an external cost per ounce of about $0.48.
Kenkel (1996)	Estimates elasticities for moderate and heavy drinkers using cross-sectional variation (at state level) in prices. Uses 1985 Health Interview Survey.	Uses estimates from Manning et al. (1989) plus external costs of the risks drunk drivers create for others.	Current alcohol taxes are too low (about half) the optimal tax; stricter drunk driving laws and information provisions would reduce optimal tax.
Summary			Current alcohol tax is well below optimal tax on externality grounds.

Consistent with the literature at the time, Manning et al. assumed no external costs from second-hand smoke. Thus, the only external costs they consider are financial. Manning et al. conclude that the external costs of smoking are modest, ranging from −$0.91 to $0.24 per pack with different discount rates. The high estimates of external costs are associated with high discount rates; at those rates, the external benefits of smokers dying young are minimized. With no or low discounting, the external costs of cigarette usage are negative.

Current cigarette taxes are substantially greater than this amount[14]. Formal cigarette taxes at the Federal and state level average about $0.75 per pack in the United States. The recent Master Settlement Agreement between the states and tobacco companies resulted in price increases of about $0.45 per pack, effectively a further increase in taxes [Cutler, Epstein, Frank, Hartman, King, Newhouse, Rosenthal and Vigdor (2000), Cutler, Gruber, Hartman, Landrum, Newhouse and Rosenthal (2002)][15]. Thus, by these estimates cigarette taxes are well above the optimal tax based on externalities alone. This conclusion has been refined by Viscusi (1995), with similar findings.

The conclusion that cigarettes are overtaxed has drawn several critiques. One critique is the omission of damages from second-hand smoke. Although the scientific evidence on the effect of second-hand smoke on illness is still sketchy, some estimates indicate very large effects on health [U.S. Environmental Protection Agency (1992), Glantz and Parmley (1995)]. Related to this issue is the assumption that the family is the unit of decision-making and not the individual. If the individual were the unit of analysis, external effects such as damages from second-hand smoke within the family and the increased probability of pregnant women having low birthweight infants would also enter into the analysis. Such effects can be very large. Viscusi (1995), for example, estimates that the external costs of second-hand smoke including lung cancer and heart disease may be $0.10 or more per pack. Evans, Ringel and Stech (1999) conclude that the external costs of smoking including maternal behavior are extremely high, ranging from $0.42 to $0.72 per pack. Current cigarette taxes are not unreasonable given these estimates.

The third, and more fundamental critique, has to do with the exclusion of internal costs. This analysis implicitly assumes that individuals know about and adequately incorporate all adverse health consequences to themselves. I return to this assumption below.

Estimates of the external costs of drinking are complicated by the fact that not all drinking is associated with adverse consequences. Most of the external costs of drinking result from substantial drinking at one time – generally defined as alcohol

---

[14] Taxation is not the only government involvement in smoking. There is a long history of cigarette regulations, including bans on radio and television advertisements, minimum purchase and consumption ages, and restrictions on smoking in public places. On the other side are subsidies to tobacco farmers. Generally, the literature finds that non-price policies do affect consumption, although the effects are relatively modest [Chaloupka and Warner (2000)].

[15] And in some other countries, cigarette taxes are even greater.

above 2 ounces per sitting. About 40% of alcohol consumed is believed to be above this level. If taxes change the share of heavy drinkers in comparison to light drinkers, it will also change the Pigouvian tax rate.

The bottom panel of Table 3 shows the estimates of the external costs of drinking. Manning et al. estimated the external costs of alcohol at $1.19 per excess ounce of alcohol (in 1986 dollars). The most important external costs are from with motor vehicle fatalities resulting from drunk driving. Since these occur shortly after the drinking episode, the estimates of external costs are not very sensitive to the discount rate chosen.

Current alcohol taxes in the United States are below the optimal tax rates shown in Table 3. Federal, state and local taxes are about $0.27 cents per ounce for spirits, $0.13 cents per ounce for beer, and $0.12 per ounce for wine. Thus, the Manning et al. estimates suggest that alcohol tax rates should be substantially increased if they are designed to offset Pigouvian externalities.

Other studies have refined, but not substantially changed, this analysis. Pogue and Sgontz (1989) note that alcohol taxes involve a deadweight loss for light and moderate drinkers, who currently face higher taxes than is optimal (since the costs of light and moderate drinking are low). Pogue and Sgontz (1989) and Kenkel (1996) both conclude that even taking this into account, current taxes are well below the optimal tax.

There are a range of other goods that could be analyzed in a similar fashion, but have not been. Gun ownership, for example, imposes substantial external costs, but there are no estimates of external costs in the literature. Extending this analysis to other goods is a clear research priority.

2.3. Internal costs and rational addiction

Perhaps the most important economic issue in the analysis of individuals behaviors is the question of whether individuals correctly account for the adverse effects of such behavior on their own health. If individuals do not, the case for corrective government action is even stronger. Consider just the case of smoking. Smokers on average die about 6 years younger than non-smokers, a loss of roughly 2 hours per pack of cigarettes. Consensus estimates in the literature value a year of life at about $100 000 per year [Viscusi (1993), Tolley, Kenkel and Fabian (1994), Cutler and Richardson (1997)][16]. Thus, the cost to a smoker from early mortality alone (ignoring morbidity or out-of-pocket medical expenses and not discounting) is about $22 per pack. Such costs dwarf the external costs presented above.

For most goods, economists are willing to assume that individuals correctly internalize these costs. After all, if a person were buying a good he did not value,

---

[16] This estimate may not apply to specific years at older ages. In general, not much work has examined how willingness to pay estimates differ by age, although Krupnick, Alberini, Cropper, Simon, O'Brien, Goeree and Heintzelman (2000) generally find similar willingness to pay estimates for the old.

he could simply stop buying the good. In the case of smoking and drinking, however, the situation is more complicated. Such goods are addictive, and it is not as easy to end consumption of an addictive good as it is for non-addictive goods.

Addictiveness by itself does not mean that consumption is inefficient. Becker and Murphy (1988) and Becker, Grossman and Murphy (1994) present a theoretical model of rational addiction, showing that individuals may rationally decide to consume goods that are bad for them, if the current and future consumption benefits are sufficiently high. The idea is straightforward: rational smokers know that utility in the future depends on smoking decisions today, and factor in future utility costs and benefits when they decide how much to smoke today. People who do this correctly will not be helped by government intervention, other than providing information about true health risks. This is in contrast to the pure myopic model of addiction, where individuals make consumption decisions today without thinking about their future consequences. Government policy can help such myopic individuals to account for the future consequences of their current actions.

Testing the rational addiction model empirically is not easy, since the interesting alternative hypothesis is not the myopic model, but instead a model of addiction in which consumption is forward-looking but less than perfectly so. Most empirical analysis has focused on a test of forward looking behavior itself: does higher anticipated price lower current consumption? In a rational model, it would; if people know that future prices will be higher, they will value current consumption less, since part of the benefit of current consumption is that it increases the marginal utility of consumption in the future. When future prices are higher, the value of that future consumption is lower. In a myopic model, future prices are not associated with current consumption [17].

Becker, Grossman and Murphy (1994) were the first to test this prediction empirically. Their test involves regressing current cigarette consumption on past consumption, current prices of cigarettes, and future cigarette consumption. They instrument for past and future consumption with past and future prices. The key test is whether future prices influence current consumption, via the effect on future consumption, controlling for current prices. The data are at the state-level from 1955 to 1985. Becker, Grossman, and Murphy find evidence for the rational model: higher future prices are associated with lower current consumption, controlling for current prices and past consumption. These results have been extended and applied to other addictive behaviors by Chaloupka (1991), Sung, Hu and Keeler (1994), Waters and Sloan (1995), Olekalns and Bardsley (1996) and Grossman, Chaloupka and Sirtalan (1998) [18].

---

[17] A different type of test is whether smokers accurately perceive the health costs of their smoking decision. Viscusi (1994) argues that smokers, if anything, overstate the health consequences of smoking. Schoenbaum (1997) suggests this is not true for heavy smokers.

[18] The robustness of this methodology has been called into question, but an alternative methodology distinguishing anticipated from unanticipated price changes reaches similar conclusions [Gruber and Koszegi (2001)].

But such results do not rule out all other models. Showalter (1999) argues that the relation between future prices and current consumption may be a function of rational firm behavior, not rational individual behavior. Rational firms will recognize that current smoking affects the future value of smoking and thus price accordingly.

More fundamentally, the Becker, Grossman, and Murphy results show only that the pure myopic model is wrong, not that smokers are fully rational. Several papers have argued that smoking is only incompletely rational. Laux (2000) argues that the discount rate implied by the Becker, Grossman, and Murphy analysis is too high; individuals appear to discount the future more at rates substantially higher than current interest rates. Gruber and Koszegi (2001) show that this result is consistent with a model where individuals are forward looking but have preferences that are not time consistent, as in Laibson (1997): people use high discount rates between periods in the near future and lower discount rates between periods in the more distant future. For example, if a rational consumer has a utility function given by $U - \sum_{t=0}^{T} \delta^t U_t$, a hyperbolic discounter would have utility $U = U_0 + \beta \sum_{t=1}^{T} \delta^t U_t$. The parameter β reflects the overall discounting of the future compared to the present; for near future versus far future events, discounting is as in the standard model.

With hyperbolic discounting, individuals are forward looking in their smoking decisions but outcomes are still inefficient. People would prefer, on the basis of lifetime utility, not to smoke, but in each year they are not able to refrain from smoking. The desire to quit is a distinguishing feature of cigarette consumption.

In addition, most of the empirical analysis has focused on whether people rationally decide to continue or discontinue smoking given that they are already smoking. But if people do not rationally make the initial smoking decision, these later decisions begin from an inefficient outcome. Since most people start smoking as youths (42% of smokers start before age 16 and 75% begin before age 19), it is not obvious that initial smoking decisions are made with full information. Indeed, most smokers begin smoking below conventional ages of full maturity.

While non-smokers do not necessarily know if they will become addicted, this by itself does not imply that such decisions are inefficient. Orphanides and Zervos (1998) present a model where adolescents sample cigarettes but are uncertain about whether they will become addicted. If adolescents have unbiased knowledge about the true share of people who will become addicted, the adolescent decision is still rational. In practice, there is evidence that youths are overly optimistic about their ability to subsequently quit cigarettes. In a study of high school seniors, 56% said they would not be smoking in five years, but only 31% had quit by that time [U.S. Department of Health and Human Services (1994)].

Individuals may in some cases take account of their self control problems. If individuals know they have hyperbolic preferences, for example, they will look for ways to bind their future actions in a favorable way. For example, people might commit to give away a certain amount of money if they do not stop smoking or commit to enter smoking treatment centers in the future. If such commitment devices are effective, they can solve the time consistency problem.

In the absence of such pre-commitment devices, however, government intervention will be appropriate, including taxation or regulation. The goals of government intervention are not so obvious, however. If one's current self wants to smoke but one's future self would prefer that one not, which self should the government favor in making policy decisions?

Overall, the optimal role of government for health-related goods with internal costs is unknown. In light of the potentially large welfare consequences associated with this issue, however, (internal costs up to 100 times greater than external costs considering mortality effects alone) further theoretical and empirical work on understanding these issues is extremely important.

3. The market for medical care services

Once sick, an individual's health depends to a significant extent on the medical care he receives. Public intervention in medical care is pervasive, for good reason. I lay out in this section why that is the case, and analyze particular aspects of public intervention in subsequent sections[19].

Information problems. A first problem with medical care is the nature of information. People do not know the complexities of medical care diagnosis or treatment. This is common of many goods[20]. But in the medical care case, people often do not have enough time to learn this information before consumption decisions must be made. In other settings, there is usually more time.

This information asymmetry gives physicians market power. Physicians recommend to people what services are appropriate and often provide those services after they are recommended. Physicians also have leeway in pricing, at a time when consumers have little ability to price shop. Unless physicians have objective functions looking out for patient welfare, inefficient outcomes will result.

Further, determining the quality of services is difficult, even *ex post*. Medical care is a credence good – a good where the quality of the service is often not learned even after it has been provided [Tirole (1988), Darby and Karni (1973)]. If a patient had a bypass surgery operation, was it truly necessary? Not all doctors would agree. If there were post-operative complications, were they the fault of the surgeon, or simply a result of the patient's underlying sickness? Again, there is room for disagreement.

Since quality is so hard to measure, competitive markets will not necessarily work to improve quality. A surgeon wishing to improve his bypass surgery mortality rate could

---

[19] Arrow (1963) was the first to highlight the conglomeration of difficulties in the medical care marketplace and much of the subsequent literature draws from that analysis.

[20] Perhaps the closest analogy is automobile repair. See Triplett (2001).

work on his surgical technique or could simply avoid performing surgery on patients with a high mortality risk. The latter step is easier and may have a larger impact on observed death rates. It will also be inefficient, if the patients at high mortality risk are those who need surgery the most. Perceptions that medical care may be provided inefficiently have been a factor contributing to public involvement in medical care systems.

Externalities. Some medical care has external effects. A person who is not vaccinated for a communicable disease is at risk of infecting others. Similarly, a person who uses antibiotics but stops in mid-course contributes to the development of antibiotic-resistant bacteria. These types of externalities are conceptually identical to the externalities associated with smoking and drinking. Thus, they are not considered further.

Insurance and moral hazard. Medical care demand is unpredictable. Healthy people do not need much medical care; sick people need substantial amounts. This large uncertainty about demand is the central rationale for health insurance. Full insurance eliminates the risk associated with uncertain medical expenses by having the insurer pay for the full cost of all treatments. But such insurance creates its own problems, the most important of which is *moral hazard* [21] – the phenomenon where an individual uses more services because he is insured than he would choose to do if he could contract for services before he knew what diseases he would have [Arrow (1965), Pauly (1968, 1974), Zeckhauser (1970), Spence and Zeckhauser (1971), Kotowitz (1987). Insurance must balance this moral hazard against the gains from improved risk sharing.

Heterogeneity, risk segmentation, and adverse selection. In a population of individuals whose underlying health risks are heterogeneous, more and less healthy people will demand different insurance policies. Sicker people generally want more extensive health insurance than healthier people. This differential demand creates problems for the efficient provision of health insurance. If insurers can segment sick from healthy, all people will be insured but at different prices. If they cannot, people will have incentives to pretend they are healthier than they truly are, a factor termed *adverse selection*. In either case, there are problems with market equilibria: people pay different amounts for insurance when they would have chosen to pool together *ex ante*; the allocation of people across plans may be inefficient; and plans may skimp on quality to attract the healthy and repel the sick. For all of these reasons, the government may want to be involved.

Equity. Access to medical care is commonly viewed as a right, not a good in the sense of luxury cars or expensive houses. People are unhappy when poor people are not able to get necessary medical care. One might justify this concern for the poor on a public health argument; if one person has a communicable disease and does not get

---

[21] There are other problems as well, but these work in the same direction. For example, administrative cost considerations argue for excluding small bills from coverage but paying for larger bills. This is similar to the optimal insurance policy with moral hazard.

treated, others are at risk as well. But this characterizes only a small share of disease in a developed country. There is a fiscal externality argument as well; when people are healthy, they earn more and pay more in taxes. But the argument for redistribution is really much more basic. Medical care, along with food and shelter, is a good that society feels everyone should have access to.

This fact has enormous implications for public policy. Because medical care is so expensive, the poor cannot be made to pay for it on their own. Thus, government intervention is necessary to pay for the medical care of the poor. Designing such an income transfer system is a central public economics question. In part, this is an optimal income tax problem of the type considered in the chapter by Auerbach and Hines (2002). But there is a twist: some of the poor will have insurance prior to the public subsidy. Thus, in addition to labor supply and savings issues that result from redistribution, there is also the problem of 'crowding out', where an increased government subsidy encourages more people to join the public program. Crowding out makes the value of public insurance expansions difficult to determine *ex ante*.

4. Government versus private provision

Given the information problems noted above, it is not obvious that doctor–patient interactions in an unregulated market will lead to efficient outcomes. Profit-maximizing physicians may skimp on care when such skimping cannot be detected. They may provide more care than is appropriate if they are paid more for doing so and patients do not know such care is unnecessary. And prices may be above marginal cost because patients cannot easily shop for providers.

Governments thus face a fundamental decision in the medical sector; should medical services be provided privately, or should the government provide medical services itself? Countries have made very different decisions about this issue. In the United Kingdom, hospitals at least historically were run by governments. Governments set staffing levels, determined technology allocation, and decided on appropriate investments. In the United States, in contrast, providers are mostly private. Most hospitals are not-for-profit organizations, and physicians are independent practitioners working (at least historically) on a fee-for-service basis. The government has a large say in how providers are paid and what technology investments are made, but it does not control day-to-day resource decisions. Other countries are in the middle.

Countries also change systems over time. The United Kingdom has introduced some market forces into the medical sector. General practitioners 'fundholders' can now bargain for rates among different hospitals and send patients to the hospital of their choosing. Many hospitals are not-for-profit trusts. In the United States, there have been substantial conversions of hospitals between government, private not-for-profit, and for-profit organizational form over time [Cutler and Horwitz (1999)].

The make or buy decision in health care has been a subject of debate for decades [see Propper and Green (2002), for discussion of health care, and Shleifer (1998) and Poterba (1996), for a more general discussion]. The traditional debate pitted arguments of monopoly and monopsony on the one side, and innovation on the other. Government intervention was justified because of monopoly power of physicians and the information problems noted above. By controlling medical provision, it was believed that the government could use its monopsony power to purchase such services at a low price. The counter-argument focused on incentives for efficiency. Without market incentives, it was feared that government production would be technologically inefficient and innovation would be stifled.

Empirically countries where the public sector runs the medical system spend less on medical care than countries with private providers. In OECD countries, for example, the correlation between the public sector share of financing and the share of GDP devoted to medical care is −0.41. More formal analysis controlling for additional variables also finds this conclusion [Globerman and Vining (1998)]. There is also evidence for the inefficiency view. People in many European countries are disenchanted with the quality of medical care, and these countries have struggled to increase the efficiency of the medical care system in recent years [Cutler (2002)].

A recent literature emphasizing the role of public sector contracting has expanded the dimension of this analysis, considering issues of allocational as well as technical efficiency [Hart, Shleifer and Vishny (1997), Shleifer (1998)]. Consider the question of whether a government should provide hospital services itself or contract with a for-profit hospital company to provide the services. For-profit companies will respond to financial incentives more rapidly than government-run companies, since for-profit managers receive more of the payoff from responding to these incentives. Thus, contracting to a for-profit provider will be preferred if the incentives that the firm faces are the correct ones. If the incentives are not correct, however, having more responsive for-profit firms may lead to poor outcomes, and providing the service in house might be preferred.

Suppose, for example, that hospitals can skimp on quality without being detected. For-profit hospitals will skimp more than government-run hospitals, since the for-profit firm benefits financially from such skimping. If skimping results in substantial welfare loss, government provision would be preferable to contracting out, even though the for-profit firm may be more technically efficient. In contrast, if the government can write a contract that appropriately incentivizes the for-profit firm or penalizes the firm for skimping on quality, contracting out would be superior to in-house provision. Neither in-house production nor contracting out is necessarily preferred. It depends on the contracts the government can write, and the regulatory and monitoring ability of the government.

Taking this analysis further, one can think about social institutions in the medical care field as a form of quasi-government institution designed to counteract the adverse incentives that pure profit-maximization would lead to[22]. Two such institutions are

---

[22] Arrow (1963) was the first to make this argument.

important. First, doctors have an ethic to earn the trust of their patients. This is codified in the Hippocratic Oath of promoting the best medical outcomes for patients. Second, not-for-profit firms dominate the medical sector. Two-thirds of hospitals in the United States are private not-for-profits, many of them associated with religious institutions. By renouncing the ability to turn profits into personal gain, not-for-profit hospitals commit themselves to less strict incentives for profit-maximization [Glaeser and Shleifer (2001), Hubbard and Hassett (1999)]. Each of these institutions may help to counteract the adverse results that profit maximization with poor information and distorted incentives might produce.

The relative performance of different organizational forms within a system, or different levels of public and private ownership across systems, is ultimately an empirical question. Substantial recent literature has explored this question. In the United States, comparisons of the quality of medical care between for-profit, private not-for-profit, and government hospitals generally suggest that quality is about the same in different organizational forms [see Sloan (2000), for a review][23]. But there is substantial heterogeneity in quality within each organizational type, the source of which is not readily apparent.

Quality of care comparisons at the level of particular institutions are of limited value, however, because different organizational forms will influence each other in the marketplace. Hansmann (1980) argued that quality at for-profit hospitals was kept high because their not-for-profit competitors provided high quality, making deviations from quality by for-profit hospitals more readily detectable. On the other hand, Cutler and Horwitz (1999) and Silverman and Skinner (2000) argue for an 'inverse-Hansmann effect', where for-profit hospitals lead not-for-profit hospitals to change their behavior in socially-adverse ways.

Thus, a more relevant question may be whether quality differs across markets with different overall levels of organizational form: predominantly public, predominantly private not-for-profit, or predominantly private for-profit. Such analyses might be conducted in the United States, or across countries. Research along these lines has not progressed as rapidly as research at the institutional level. It is clear that medical care quality differs substantially across areas; what is less clear is why [Fisher, Skinner and Wennberg (1998)]. Examining how quality relates to overall organizational form is an important research priority.

5. Moral hazard and the tax subsidy to insurance

Medical spending is extremely variable, as Table 4 shows. In any year, the top 1% of medical care users consume about 30% of all medical care services, and the top 10%

---

[23] The organizations may differ along other lines, though. Duggan (2000) shows that for-profit and private not-for-profit hospitals respond similarly to incentives to cream-skim the healthiest patients, while government hospitals are less responsive.

Table 4
The variability of medical care spending[a]

Distribution	Share of dollars (%)	Average spending ($)
99+%	27.5	56459
95–99%	27.7	14271
90–95%	14.0	5778
70–90%	21.2	2186
<70%	9.6	281
Average		2060

[a] Source: Data are from the 1996 Medical Expenditure Panel Study (MEPS).

use about 70% of resources. Much of this differential use is uncertain; people may know they are at risk of a serious disease, but rarely do they know the exact amount of their future spending.

This uncertainty about medical care needs drives the demand for health insurance. Health insurance redistributes money from when people are healthy to when they are sick, alleviating the financial cost associated with illness and allowing people to afford medical services they would otherwise not be able to afford. But health insurance creates problems of its own. In particular, by making it easier for people to get medical care when sick, it encourages people to use too much care. The use of excessive medical services because people are insured is termed moral hazard. In this section, I discuss the tradeoff between risk bearing and moral hazard.

5.1. Optimal insurance with fixed spending

To see the value of insurance most clearly, consider a one-period model where initially identical individuals are either healthy or sick. People are sick with probability p; if they get sick, they need a fixed amount of medical care, m, after which they are restored to perfect health[24]. People are healthy with probability $1 - p$, in which case they require no medical care.

---

[24] I assume m is affordable given y, and that the person will always want to pay for the medical care if sick. If medical care does not restore a person to perfect health, the situation is a bit more complicated. The individual will want to redistribute income to the point where marginal utility is the same in sick and healthy states. If marginal utility is higher when sick than when healthy (for example, because of the need to pay for help around the home or other assistive devices), then optimal insurance will transfer more than m when sick. If the reverse is true (for example, if people value vacations more when healthy than when sick), insurance will transfer less than m when sick. See Cutler and Zeckhauser (2000) for more discussion.

Individual utility, U, depends on non-medical consumption. If individuals have income Y[25], consumption in the absence of insurance is Y if the person is healthy and $Y - m$ if the person is sick. Expected utility is therefore:

$$V_N = (1 - p) U(Y) + pU(Y - m),$$ (6)

where the subscript N denotes being uninsured. I assume that $U(\cdot)$ has the standard concavity properties: $U' > 0$ and $U'' < 0$.

Actuarially fair insurance will pay for the individual's medical care when sick, financed by a constant premium. The fair premium, π, is equal to expected spending, or pm. People who are insured will always have consumption $Y - \pi$, so utility will be:

$$V_1 = U(Y - \pi).$$ (7)

Using a Taylor series expansion of Equation (6)[26], we can approximate that equation as:

$$V_N \approx U(y - \pi) + U'(U''/2U')\pi(m - \pi).$$ (8)

Therefore, the value of insurance is

$$\text{Value of Insurance} = \frac{V_1 - V_N}{U'} \approx \tfrac{1}{2}(-U''/U')\pi(m - \pi).$$ (9)

The left-hand side of Equation (9) is the difference in utility from being insured relative to being uninsured, scaled by marginal utility to turn it into a dollar value. The right-hand side is the benefit of risk removal. Here, $(-U''/U')$ is the *coefficient of absolute risk aversion*; it is the degree to which uncertainty about marginal utility makes a person worse off. Because utility is concave, this term is positive. The term $\pi(m - \pi)$ represents the extent to which after-medical expenditure income varies because the person does not have insurance. It too is positive. The product of terms on the right-hand side of Equation (9), therefore, is necessarily positive, implying that actuarially fair insurance is preferred to being uninsured. The dollar value of risk spreading increases with risk aversion and with the variability of medical spending.

---

[25] Assume, for simplicity, that this income endowment is fixed, and that individuals can neither borrow or lend.

[26] The Taylor series is taken about the level of income net of insurance premiums. From Equation (6), $V_N \approx (1 - p)[U(y - \pi) + U'B + \tfrac{1}{2}U''\pi^2] + p[U(y - \pi) - U'(m - \pi) + \tfrac{1}{2}U''(m - \pi)^2]$. Collecting terms, this simplifies to $V_N \approx U(y - \pi) + U'\{(1 - p)\pi - p(m - \pi)\} + \tfrac{1}{2}U''\{(1 - p)\pi^2 + p(m - \pi)^2\}$. The term $(1 - p)\pi - p(m - \pi)$ is zero. The term $(1 - p)\pi^2 + p(m - \pi)^2$ can be expanded as $(1 - p)\pi^2 + pm^2 - 2pm\pi + p\pi^2$. Since $pm = \pi$, this simplifies to $pm^2 - \pi^2 = \pi(m - \pi)$.

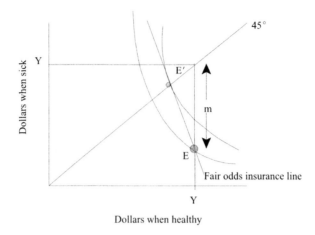

Fig. 4. The welfare gains from health insurance.

This point is shown graphically in Figure 4. Consumption when healthy and sick are shown on the horizontal and vertical axes. The endowment point is E. Fair insurance takes money from people when they are healthy and gives them money when they are sick. The downward sloping line reflects this fair insurance[27]. If insurers break even, individuals can trade off income in the two states at actuarially fair rates.

The first-best equilibrium is full insurance. The intuition supporting this result is that risk averse individuals would like to smooth the marginal utility of income – to transfer income from states of the world where their marginal utility is low (healthy state) to states of the world when their marginal utility is high (sick state). In the absence of insurance, a person's marginal utility of income when healthy is $U'(Y)$ is below that when sick, $U'(Y - m)$. Transferring income from healthy states to sick states until marginal utility is equalized maximizes total expected utility. Health insurance carries out this transfer.

The form of insurance imagined by this policy is indemnity insurance. Indemnity insurance is a fixed payment made to an individual or provider depending on the diagnosis of the individual. The simplest indemnity policy, first offered by private insurers, reimbursed people a fixed amount per day they were in the hospital (for example, $5 per day). Such policies were common in the United States as recently as the 1960s. More sophisticated indemnity insurance policies might condition payment on the diagnosis of the individual, for example $5000 payment if a person has pneumonia and $15 000 if the person has cancer.

Indemnity policies are closely related to their precursor, a pre-payment policy. In this policy, a person pays a doctor a fixed amount of money each year, with the doctor

---

[27] With fair insurance, premiums when healthy equal payments when sick. A $1 premium when healthy can therefore pay the individual s when sick, where $-(1 - p) = ps$. The slope of the fair odds line is therefore $s = -(1 - p)/p$.

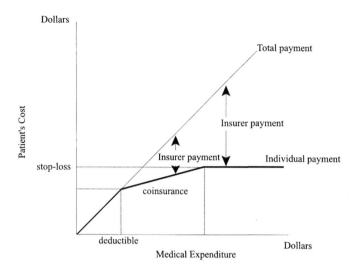

Fig. 5. Cost sharing under insurance.

agreeing to care for the person whenever he is sick. The first Blue Cross/Blue Shield policies were like this. Blue Cross, and later Blue Shield, plans were sponsored by providers. In exchange for fixed monthly payments, people were guaranteed a certain number of days in the hospital if they were needed (Blue Cross) and physician services (Blue Shield).

Indemnity insurance is optimal if medical costs conditional on a disease are known [Zeckhauser (1970)]. Prepayment is optimal if the providers one wants to use are all part of the plan and the providers can bear the payment risk that is required of them. But neither of these conditions is necessarily true. If there is variability in disease severity within indemnity groups which cannot be contracted on – for example variation in the particular intervention needed or in recovery time – a fixed indemnity payment still exposes the individual to substantial risk. Exposure to this risk involves a welfare loss. As medical technology has become more complex and optimal treatments have become more differentiated, the ability to adequately design such policies has declined.

Thus, in practice health insurance has moved to a third model, a service benefit policy[28]. Such a policy pays for a percentage of the actual costs of treatment. Service benefit policies are characterized by three features, shown in Figure 5: a deductible (the first amount that a patient pays before receiving any reimbursement); a coinsurance rate (the share of costs the patient pays above the deductible); and a stop-loss (the maximum amount the patient can pay). In the United States, private service benefit policies

---

[28] Unfortunately, the service benefit policy is typically called indemnity insurance (and contrasted with managed care insurance) in the literature. I retain the terminology of service benefit to contrast it with true indemnity insurance.

generally have a family deductible of about $500 (roughly $200 for an individual), a coinsurance rate of 20%, and a stop-loss of $1500 to $2000 [Kaiser Family Foundation and Health Research and Educational Trust (2000)]. The Medicare program has much higher cost sharing. Inpatient care has an $800 deductible per episode. Outpatient care has a $100 annual deductible and 20% coinsurance rate, with no stop loss.

Service benefit policies insure a greater share of risk than do indemnity policies. The central problem created by service benefit insurance is moral hazard. By lowering the cost of medical care at the time of use, the service benefit policy encourages excessive use of services. This limits the optimal degree of insurance coverage, as I now show.

5.2. Optimal insurance with moral hazard

To illustrate the impact of moral hazard, I modify the model presented above. Suppose that rather than being healthy or sick, the individual has a range of potential illness severities, s, with s distributed with density function $f(s)$. Health is given by $H = H[s, m]$. The patient's s will determine the optimal treatment. A simple way to depict uncertainty about optimal care is to assume that the insurer does not know the patient's s, and hence cannot make an optimal indemnity payment.

Before deriving the optimal policy in this situation, it is useful to consider the optimal policy with full information, and thus no moral hazard. With full information, the coinsurance rate can be conditioned directly on s. The individual will therefore choose $m(s)$ to maximize feasible utility:

$$\max_{m(s)} \int U(y - \pi - c(s), H[s, m]) f(s) \, ds, \tag{10}$$

where the first term is non-medical consumption and the second term is health. π is the insurance premium and is equal to

$$\pi = \int (m(s) - c(s)) f(s) \, ds. \tag{11}$$

An atomistic consumer takes the insurance premium as fixed when making medical care consumption decisions. The solution to this problem therefore sets: [29]

$$H_m U_H = E[U_x], \tag{12}$$

where $x = Y - \pi - c(s)$. The left-hand side of Equation (12) is the marginal gain in utility from spending another dollar on medical care, the product of the marginal effect

---

[29] This assumes that these functions are well behaved, hence that local optima are global optima. Some medical expenditures may offer increasing returns over a relevant range. For example, it may cost $200 000 to do a heart transplant, with $100 000 accomplishing much less than half as much. Efficiency then requires the insurance program spend at least to the minimum average cost of benefits point, or not at all.

of medical care on health and the marginal effect of health on utility. This marginal gain will be the same in each state of nature. This is equated with weighted average expectation of the marginal utility of consumption in different illness states, namely

$$E[U_x] = \int U_x(y - \pi - c(s), H[s, m]) f(s) \, ds. \tag{13}$$

Equation (12) says that with the optimal first-best policy, the expected marginal utility gained from an additional dollar of medical care in each state of the world equals the utility cost of that dollar.

In the case where the marginal utility of income does not depend on the health state [30], imposing a coinsurance payment in any health state – e.g., a variable $c(s)$ – increases the variability of income and thus reduces expected utility. The optimal policy for this commonly studied case is thus no coinsurance, and an indemnity payment $m^*(s)$ that fully reimburses optimal spending in each state.

Now consider the case where the insurer cannot observe s, only m. Therefore, the insurer must implement a cost-sharing rule depending on m, $c(m)$.

The sick consumer will choose medical care utilization $m^{\#}(s)$ to maximize utility given this cost sharing requirement and his knowledge of s. The consumer's problem is formally

$$\max_{m(s)} U(Y - \pi - c(m), H[s, m]) \quad \forall \, s. \tag{14}$$

The solution to this problem, for each s, is given by the first-order condition

$$H_m U_H = c'(m) U_x \quad \forall \, s. \tag{15}$$

The left-hand side once again represents the gain in utility from spending another dollar on medical care, which is equated to the utility cost to the individual from spending that dollar.

Taking expectations of Equations (12) and (15) shows the welfare loss from moral hazard. There are two losses. First, the expected marginal gain from foregoing medical spending in the situation with moral hazard, $E[c'(m) U_x]$ is below the equivalent expectation in the situation without moral hazard, $E[U_x]$. Because people face a lower price for medical care, they will consume more resources in every state of nature where the coinsurance rate is below 1.

Moral hazard can take two forms. *Ex ante* moral hazard refers to the possibility that people may not take as good care of themselves if they are insured, since they know that health insurance will pay for their care if they do get sick. *Ex post* moral hazard refers to people using more services when they are sick than they would have used if

---

[30] This would be the case if utility were separable in income and health.

they could perfectly commit to service use before they become sick. *Ex post* moral hazard is likely more important in the medical care context than *ex ante* moral hazard, since the uncompensated losses of not taking care of oneself in the first place (possible death and disability) are so large. But *ex ante* moral hazard is present to some extent; cigarette consumption, for example, would certainly fall if people faced the full cost of smoking in higher out-of-pocket medical payments.

In addition, there are losses from the variability in the marginal utility of income across states of nature. If the coinsurance rate varies with medical spending, the marginal rate of substitution between health and other goods will vary as well. When coinsurance rates are lower, even more is spent on medical care and the marginal rate of substitution between health and other goods falls. Smoothing the marginal rate of substitution across states of nature would improve welfare.

Not all of the demand response to having insurance is moral hazard. The thought experiment is whether the individual would pay for the medical expenditure in expectation, before he knew his condition, not *ex post*, given his income while sick. Suppose that bypass surgery optimally costs $50 000. Before a person knows if he will have a heart attack, he might agree to pool economy-wide the $50 000 cost for people who have a heart attack. Now suppose that *ex post* two people have a heart attack: one with insurance and one without. The person without insurance finds the bypass surgery too expensive and does not receive it. The person with insurance has the operation, and because he is insured uses $60 000 of medical care. The moral hazard here is the $10 000 of use above the optimal amount, not the $60 000 of total spending difference between the insured and uninsured person. In other words, moral hazard is the *substitution effect* of people spending more on medical care when its price is low, not the *income effect* of people spending more on medical care because income has been transferred to when they are sick [de Meza (1983), Nyman (1999)].

An insurer recognizing moral hazard will design a policy with that in mind. Denoting $m^{\#}$ as the optimal amount of medical care for the consumer to receive, the solution to Equation (15), the insurer's problem is to find the cost sharing rule $c^*(m^{\#})$, to maximize expected utility:

$$E[U^*] = \max_{c(m^{\#})} \int U(Y - \pi - c^*(m^{\#}), H[s, m^{\#}]) f(s) \, ds. \tag{16}$$

Insurers maximize this subject to the zero profit constraint.

The optimal insurance policy can be formally written as a problem in dynamic optimization [Blomqvist (1997)][31]. The analytic solution balances two factors. The first is the reduced overconsumption from making people pay more out of pocket for medical care. If the coinsurance rate is increased in some range, people in that range pay more for medical care, as do people at all higher levels of spending (because

---

[31] The problem is formally analogous to the optimal tax problem in public finance when ability is unobservable [Mirrlees (1971)].

their coinsurance rates have been increased). This increases the efficiency of provision. Countering this, however, is a loss in risk spreading benefits. As people are made to pay more out of pocket, they are exposed to more risk, and this reduces their welfare. The optimal coinsurance rate balances these two effects.

The optimal health insurance policy in practice may be a combination of disease-based and spending-based payments [Chernew and Frick (1999)]. Contrast a disease like cancer where minimum treatment involves thousands of dollars with treatment of a common infection. In the former case, it is optimal to have no cost sharing over the range of the minimum acceptable treatment. In the latter case, cost sharing should be highest at low levels of spending. Combining disease and spending based payments is an example of tagging, which I discuss later.

5.3. Taxation and health insurance design

A government running a health insurance system could implement the optimal second-best policy. Government policy may not be necessary for efficiency, however. In the absence of external influences on insurance policies and with all individuals having the same risk distribution[32], individuals and insurers would agree to these policies as well. Thus, government policy should treat insurance and out-of-pocket expenses symmetrically.

In the United States, public policy is not neutral towards insurance choices. The most important policy influence on health insurance design is the tax code. Three aspects of the tax code affect health insurance choices (see Gruber and Poterba (1996), for discussion). First, employer spending on health insurance is excluded from income for personal income taxation purposes, while wage and salary payments are taxed as personal income at the individual level. The price of employer spending on health insurance is thus $(1 - \tau_F - \tau_S - \tau_{SI})/(1 + \tau_{SI})$, where F, S, and SI are the marginal Federal income tax rate, the marginal State income tax rate, and the marginal Social Insurance tax rate (Social Security, Disability, and Medicare). The numerator of this expression is the personal income tax saved by paying for health insurance instead of giving the money as wages. The denominator grosses this up by the employer's share of social security payments, which is assumed to be born by individuals.

In addition, employee payments for health insurance are excluded from income if they are part of qualified benefit plans[33]. Not all employee payments meet this criterion; in 1993, about one-quarter of employee payments were made on a pre-tax basis. Denoting E as employer payments for health insurance, G as employee payments, and δ as the share of employee payments that are eligible for favorable tax treatment,

---

[32] If there is heterogeneity of risk, issues of adverse selection arise and may encourage insurers to adopt inferior policies, as discussed below.

[33] For discussion of the criteria for a qualified plan, see U.S. Joint Committee on Taxation (1999).

a share $(E + \delta G)/(E + G)$ of total employment-based insurance payments are eligible for favorable tax treatment. The share $(1 - \delta) G/(E + G)$ of payments are not and face a relative price of 1.

The employer and partial employee exclusions of health insurance payments are quantitatively important. It is estimated that in 1999 the Federal income tax revenue loss from this exclusion was $60 billion, over 10% of total Federal spending on medical care. There were additional losses to Social Security, although these are offset by lower payments in the future, so the present value loss is much smaller (if even positive).

Potentially offsetting these first two factors is a provision allowing individuals to deduct out-of-pocket medical spending from income if such spending is in excess of 7.5% of adjusted gross income and if they itemize their deductions. The effective price of out-of-pocket spending is therefore $(1 - \alpha\tau_F)$, where $\alpha = 1$ if the individual has large medical expenses and is an itemizer. Because not many people meet this criterion, the total revenue cost of this provision is much lower, about $4 billion.

Combining these three terms, the relative price of employer-provided insurance compared to out-of-pocket spending is given by

$$\frac{P_{HI}}{P_{OOP}} = \frac{\left[\left(\frac{1 - \tau_F - \tau_S - \tau_{SI}}{1 + \tau_{SI}}\right) \cdot \left(\frac{E + \delta G}{E + G}\right) + \frac{(1 - \delta) G}{E + G}\right]}{1 - \alpha\tau_F}. \tag{17}$$

Gruber and Poterba (1996) estimate this expression for a representative sample of individuals in 1994. The average person with employer-provided insurance faced a relative price of insurance of 0.66, a 34% subsidy to insurance payments relative to out-of-pocket spending. The tax subsidy varies over time with changes in tax rates; as marginal tax rates have declined in the 1980s and 1990s, the tax subsidy has fallen.

This tax subsidy to insurance encourages employees and employers to offer generous health insurance: lower deductibles, coinsurance rates, and stop-loss limits [Feldstein (1971, 1973), Pauly (1986)]. When paid for by insurance, these bills cost less in total than when paid for out-of-pocket. Indeed, one might particularly want to buy insurance for *predictable* expenditures, since the tax benefits of this transaction are most readily realized. Excessively generous insurance, in turn, leads to more moral hazard than is optimal.

The magnitude of the resulting welfare loss depends on the elasticity of insurance coverage with respect to price, and the price elasticity of demand for medical care. A substantial economic literature has examined these two issues. Table 5 presents estimates of the response of health insurance design to price.

Four aspects of the health insurance demand have been estimated. One strand of literature examines the response of firms offering insurance to prices. The most convincing studies examine how variation in tax rates across states or over time

Table 5
The elasticity of demand for insurance

Reference	Data (Years)	Empirical strategy	Results
Price elasticity of demand for firm insurance offering			
Helms, Gauthier and Campion (1992)	Pilot programs	Analyzes firm responses to pilot program providing subsidies to firms to offer insurance	Finds wide range of responses across sites; elasticities of −0.4 to −1.1.
Thorpe, Hendricks, Garnick, Donelan and Newhouse (1992)	Pilot program in New York	Analyzes firm response to 50% subsidy to the price of insurance for small firms	Actual elasticity of −0.07; estimate elasticity would have been −0.33 if all firms were aware of the program.
Leibowitz and Chernew (1992)	Health Insurance Association of America survey of firms (1989)	Models offering decision as a function of premiums (variation across areas) and tax subsidy for small firms. Average marginal tax rates for firms are imputed based on CPS.	Elasticity of −0.8 for premiums and −2.9 for tax subsidies.
Gentry and Peress (1994)	Occupation Compensation Survey (1988–1992)	Models cross-city differences in the average share of workers offered insurance as a function of the state after-tax price of insurance	The percentage of workers offered insurance declines by 1.8% for a 1 percentage point increase in the price of insurance.
Morrisey, Jensen and Morlock (1994)	Survey of small firms (1993)	Use small firms' answers to hypothetical questions about whether they would offer insurance at different prices	Elasticity of offering of −0.92.
Feldman, Dowd, Leitz and Blewett (1997)	Sample of Minnesota firms (1993)	Imputes premiums to firms not offering coverage. Models offering as a function of premiums in cross-section.	Price elasticities of −3.9 for single coverage and −5.8 for family coverage.

continued on next page

Table 5, continued

Reference	Data (Years)	Empirical strategy	Results
Royalty (2000)	CPS of Employee Benefits (1988, 1993)	Models offering as a function of tax subsidy. Uses cross-state variation in marginal tax rates to identify elasticity	Elasticity of −0.68 across all employers.
Marquis and Long (2001)	Robert Wood Johnson Foundation Employer Health Insurance Survey (firms in 10 states) (1993)	Imputes premiums to firms not offering coverage. Models offering as a function of premiums in cross-section	40% reduction in premiums would increase offering by 2 to 3 percentage points.
Finkelstein (2002)	Canadian Social Survey (1991, 1994)	Models (supplemental medical) insurance offering as a function of after-tax price. DD comparing change in offering of insurance before and after repeal of tax subsidy in Quebec to change in rest of Canada	Elasticity of about −0.50.
Summary			−0.14 to −5.8
Price elasticity of demand for insurance spending			
Long and Scott (1982)	Current Population Reports and Employment and Earnings (1947–1979)	Time series analysis of fringe benefit share of income as a function of marginal tax rates.	A 10% increase in marginal tax rates increases the share of compensation devoted to health insurance by 4.1%.
Taylor and Wilensky (1983)	National Medical Care Expenditure Survey (1977)	Individual-level analysis of premiums as a function of price (measured as 1 minus the marginal tax rate), income, and demographic controls	Price elasticity is −0.21; income elasticity is 0.02.

continued on next page

Table 5, *continued*

Reference	Data (Years)	Empirical strategy	Results
Woodbury (1983)	Employee Compensation in the Private Nonfarm Economy (biennial, 1966–1974), Census of Governments (1977)	Estimates demand for non-wage compensation as a function of imputed marginal tax rates; unit of observation is a employee group-establishment-size cell (4 employee groups and 3 establishment sizes). Also estimates similar equations with school district as unit of observation.	Elasticity of demand for fringe benefits ranging from −1.2 to −3.0.
Holmer (1984)	Health insurance choices of Federal employees selecting family coverage (1982)	Estimates discrete choice model of health insurance demand as a function of income and marginal tax rate	Average price elasticity of demand for more generous health insurance of −0.16; income elasticity of 0.01.
Vroman and Anderson (1984)	National Medical Care Expenditure Survey – Employer Health Insurance Cost Survey (1977)	Cross-sectional analysis of health insurance spending per eligible employee; firm is unit of observation. Independent variables are the average effective marginal tax rate, loading factors (based on firm size), wages, and region dummies	Loading factors are consistently significant and negative. Mixed results for effects of tax rates. In full sample, 10% increase in effective tax rate is associated with 7.4% increase in employer-based insurance coverage; effects of tax rates are insignificant when sample is split by wages.
Sloan and Adamache (1986)	Survey of Employer Expenditures for Employee Compensation (1968, 1972, 1977); March CPS	Analyzes employer contributions to life–health insurance and private pension plans (per worker and as a fraction of compensation); imputes average marginal tax rate for firm from March CPS	Tax elasticity of 1.7 for life–health insurance per worker-hour and 0.6 for payments as a fraction of total compensation.

continued on next page

Table 5, *continued*

Reference	Data (Years)	Empirical strategy	Results
Turner (1987)	NIPA, Statistics of Income (1954–1979)	Time series analysis of share of labor income going to benefits, including health insurance, as a function of average marginal tax rate, controlling for demographics	Changes in tax rates can explain less than 5% of the growth in the share of income going to fringe benefits.
Woodbury and Hamermesh (1992)	Panel of compensation and benefits for faculty at 1477 institutions (1984–85, 1988–89)	Estimate demand for fringe benefits among faculty as a function of average imputed marginal tax rate (with controls); also use instrument capturing variation due to year-state-specific tax rules; also estimate models with school fixed effects	Significant negative effect of relative price of fringe benefits (due to differential tax treatment) on fringes' share of compensation; estimates are twice as large in absolute value for IV and fixed-effects specifications, compared to OLS.
Summary			−0.2 to −1.0
Price elasticity of demand for insurance coverage by individuals			
Marquis and Phelps (1987)	Rand Health Insurance Experiment individual questionnaire	Uses individuals responses to questions about willingness to pay for supplementary coverage.	Elasticity of demand for supplementary insurance of −0.6.
Gruber and Poterba (1994)	Current Population Survey (1985–96, 1988–89)	Uses change in tax treatment of insurance for the self-employed to identify elasticity. DD comparing change in coverage among self-employed and employed before and after TRA86	Elasticity of up to −1.8.
Marquis and Long (1995)	SIPP (1987) and May and March CPS (1988)	Uses cross-area variation in insurance premiums to identify responsiveness of demand for individual policies to price	Elasticity of −0.3 to −0.4.

continued on next page

Table 5, *continued*

Reference	Data (Years)	Empirical strategy	Results
Chernew, Frick and McLaughlin (1997)	Small Business Benefits Survey (1992, 1993)	Estimates probit regressions of demand for health insurance among low-income workers in small firms; price is employee contribution to premium	Elasticity of demand for employer-provided coverage for those offered coverage (take-up) with respect to employee share of −0.09.
Summary			−0.6 to −1.8
Price elasticity of demand for plan switching			
Welch (1986)	BLS Level of Benefits Study (1981–82)	Models HMO market share at employer as a function of out-of-pocket premium in cross-section	Elasticity of demand for HMO (relative to conventional insurance) −0.6 with respect to out-of-pocket premiums.
Feldman, Finch, Dowd and Cassou (1989)	Survey of employees in 20 Minneapolis firms (1984)	Models individual plan choice as a function of out-of-pocket premiums, plan characteristics, and individual characteristics	Plan choice is very sensitive to out-of-pocket premiums. A $5 (1984$) increase in out-of-pocket premium can causes a plan to lose 40% of its market share.
Dowd and Feldman (1994)	Panel data on employees' health plan choices in 5 Twin Cities employers (1988–1993)	Models plans' market share at an employer as a function of relative out-of-pocket premium. Includes firm, plan, type of coverage, and year fixed effects	Elasticity of demand for more generous plan with respect to out-of-pocket premium of −7.9 for single coverage.
Buchmueller and Feldstein (1997)	Panel data on UC Berkeley employees' health plan choices (1993–1994)	Compare plan switching among employees experienced increases in out-of-pocket premiums due to employer pricing reform to those whose premiums were unchanged	Employees facing $10 increase in out-of-pocket premiums were 5 times as likely to switch plans as those with constant premiums.

continued on next page

Table 5, continued

Reference	Data (Years)	Empirical strategy	Results
Cutler and Reber (1998)	Panel data on Harvard employees' health plan choices (1994–1996)	Compare plan switching behavior of employees affected by changes in out-of-pocket premiums to those not affected	Elasticity of demand for generous plan of −0.6 with respect to out-of-pocket premium (elasticity of −2 with respect to total premium).
Royalty and Solomon (1999)	Panel data on Stanford employees' health plan choices supplemented with employee survey (1993–1995)	Multinomial logit model of plan choice as a function of out-of-pocket premium and individual characteristics.	Own-price elasticity of −0.2 to −0.5 (elasticity of −1 to −1.8 with respect to total premium).
Summary			Wide variability, generally greater than elasticity of offering

influence firm decisions to offer coverage[34]. Elasticity estimates in these studies range from relatively small (−0.4) to quite large (−2.9). A related set of studies examines the effect of taxation on overall firm spending for insurance. This includes the offer decision and other decisions such as the generosity of benefits and the share of premiums that employers pay for. These studies also find a significant response of insurance spending to price, with a general range of −0.2 to −1.0. The fact that this is less than the offering response in some studies may indicate that the lower values of elasticity of offering is correct, or may simply reflect the difficulty of estimating the overall firm response to taxation.

A third set of studies examines the responsiveness of individual purchase decisions to price. Again, the studies using taxes as the source of price variation are most convincing. The responses are of comparable magnitude and variability to the firm estimates, ranging from −0.6 to −1.8.

A final set of studies examines the responsiveness of individual choices of insurance policies when offered multiple plans. One would expect the choice of a particular plan to be more responsive than the decision to purchase insurance at all, and this is indeed the case. While the studies do not all present elasticities, those that do generally report elasticities greater in magnitude than −2 and sometimes as high as −8.

Thus, it is clear that insurance coverage decisions are responsive to price, although the exact magnitude is not so clear. And the literature has not addressed perhaps the most important question for the welfare loss – the response of specific cost sharing provisions to price. It is the cost sharing provisions, after all, that lead individuals to overconsume medical care. Still, one suspects that this dimension of insurance is responsive to price.

The second empirical question is the effect of insurance generosity on medical care spending. A comprehensive review of the literature on the elasticity of demand for medical care is contained in Cutler and Zeckhauser (2000). Table 6 shows a summary of that literature. A substantial literature in the 1970s estimated the elasticity of demand for medical care using cross-sectional data, or cross-sectional time series data. Pre-eminent among these papers are Feldstein (1971), Phelps and Newhouse (1972a), Rosett and Huang (1973) and Newhouse and Phelps (1976). Feldstein (1971) was the first statistically robust estimate of price elasticities using time-series micro

---

[34] Other study designs are more problematic. One alternative strategy is to examine whether employers offered higher premiums are less likely to offer insurance [Feldman, Dowd, Leitz and Blewett (1997), Marquis and Long (2001)]. The difficulty with this strategy is that insurance premiums are not observed for firms not offering insurance. Thus, some imputation method must be devised, and the results depend critically on that method. In practice, the studies give very different elasticity estimates. A second strategy is to analyze the response of firms to pilot programs that subsidized insurance [Helms, Gauthier and Campion (1992), Thorpe, Hendricks, Garnick, Donelan and Newhouse (1992)], or to hypothetical questions about insurance coverage [Morrisey, Jensen and Morlock (1994)]. The difficulty with these studies is the permanence of the tax change and the relevance of the hypothetical question. These studies also give quite variable answers.

Table 6
Estimates of the elasticity of demand for medical care[a]

Reference	Data	Restrictions	Estimation method	Total price elasticity	Visits price elasticity
P.J. Feldstein (1964)	1953, 1958 Health Information Foundation and NORC surveys	General care	Cross-section estimates of physician visits	−0.19 (physician visits)	
M. Feldstein (1970)	BLS survey; NCHS 1963–64 survey; physician interviews	Aggregated physician service data	Time-series regression	1.67 (physician services)	
Rosenthal (1970)	1962 sample of New England hospitals	68 of 218 general, short-term hospitals	Univariate estimates for short-term care categories	0.19 to −0.70	
M. Feldstein (1971)	AHA survey of hospitals, 1958–1967, NCHS 1963–64 survey	All hospitals, aggregated by state	Time-series regression	−0.49 for total bed days	−0.63 for visits to hospital
Davis and Russell (1972)	1970 guide issue of "Hospitals"	Aggregated hospital outpatient care; 48 states' not-for-profit hospitals	Cross-sectional estimates	−0.32	
Fuchs and Kramer (1972)	1966 Internal Revenue Service tabulations	Physician services, aggregated into 33 states	TSLS: IV's are number of medical schools, ratio of premiums to benefits, and union members per 100 population	−0.10 to −0.36	

continued on next page

Table 6, *continued*

Reference	Data	Restrictions	Estimation method	Total price elasticity	Visits price elasticity
Phelps and Newhouse (1972a)	Palo Alto Group Health Plan, 1966–68	Physician and outpatient ancillary services	Natural experiment: introduction of coinsurance	−0.14[b] OLS, −0.118 Tobit (physician visits)	
Scitovsky and Snyder (1972)	Palo Alto Group Health Plan, 1966–68	Physician and outpatient ancillary services	Natural experiment: introduction of coinsurance	−0.060[b] (ancillary)	−0.14[b] (physician visits)
Phelps (1973)	Verified data from 1963 CHAS (University of Chicago) survey	Hospitalization and physicians' services	Cross-sectional Tobit estimates	Not significantly different from zero	
Rosett and Huang (1973)	1960 Survey of Consumer Expenditure	Hospitalization and physicians' services	Cross-sectional Tobit estimates	−0.35 to −1.5	
Beck (1974)	Random sample of poor population of Saskatchewan	Physicians' services	Natural experiment; introduction of copayments	−0.065[b]	
Newhouse and Phelps (1974)	1963 CHAS survey	Employeds' hospital stays within coverage	Cross-sectional OLS (TSLS estimates insignificant)	−0.10 (length of stay)	−0.06 (physician visits)
Phelps and Newhouse (1974)	Insurance plans in USA, Canada, and UK	General care, dental care, and prescriptions	Arc elasticities across coinsurance ranges	−0.10	

continued on next page

Table 6, *continued*

Reference	Data	Restrictions	Estimation method	Total price elasticity	Visits price elasticity
Newhouse and Phelps (1976)	1963 CHAS survey (larger sample than in previous work)	Employeds and non-employeds	Cross-sectional OLS (TSLS estimates insignificant)	−0.24 (hospital), −0.42 (physician)	
Scitovsky and McCall (1977)	Palo Alto Group Health Plan, 1968–72	physician, outpatient ancillary services	Natural experiment: coinsurance increases	−2.56[b] (ancillary)	−0.29[b] (physician visits)
Colle and Grossman (1978)	1971 NORC/CHAS health survey	Pediatric care	Cross-sectional estimates	−0.11	−0.039
Goldman and Grossman (1978)[c]	1965–66 Mindlin–Densen longitudinal study	Pediatric care	Hedonic model		−0.060 (compensated −0.032)
McAvinchey and Yannopoulos (1993)	Waiting lists from UK's National Health Service	Acute hospital care	Dynamic intertemporal model	−1.2	
Newhouse and the Insurance Experiment Group (1993)	RAND Health Insurance Experiment	General care	Randomized experiment	−0.17 to −0.31 (hospital); −0.17 to −0.22 (outpatient)	
Bhattacharya, Vogt, Yoshikawa and Nakahara (1996)	1990 Japanese Ministry of Health and Welfare survey	Outpatient visits	Cox proportional hazards model	−0.22	

continued on next page

Table 6, *continued*

Reference	Data	Restrictions	Estimation method	Total price elasticity	Visits price elasticity
Cherkin, Grothaus and Wagner (1989)	Group Health Cooperative of Puget Sound	Non-Medicare HMO patients	Natural experiment: introduction of copayments	−0.035 [b] (all visits); −0.15 [b] to −0.075 [b] (preventive)	
Eichner (1998)	1990–92 insurance claims from employees and dependents of a Fortune 500 firm	Employees aged 25 to 55	One- and two-stage Tobit regressions of out-of-pocket costs	−0.32	
Summary				−0.20	−0.05 to −0.15

[a] See Cutler and Zeckhauser (2000) for details.
[b] Elasticities computed according to appendix of Phelps and Newhouse (1972b).
[c] Quality price elasticity: −0.088 (compensated −0.085).

data, in this case on hospitals. Feldstein identified the effect of coinsurance rates on demand using cross-state variation in insurance coverage and generosity, estimating a demand elasticity of about −0.5. The subsequent papers use patient-level data and more sophisticated study designs. The elasticities that emerged from these papers ranged from as low as −0.14 [Phelps and Newhouse (1972a)] to as high as −1.5 [Rosett and Huang (1973)]. The implication of this range of elasticity estimates was that moral hazard was likely a significant force.

To identify this key parameter more precisely, the Rand Health Insurance Experiment was designed [Newhouse and the Insurance Experiment Group (1993)]. That experiment randomized people into insurance plans with different levels of cost sharing and estimated demand elasticities for medical spending. The ultimate elasticity that emerged was −0.2, at the low end of the previous literature. This estimate is generally taken as the gold standard in current research and policy work.

The fact that insurance provision is responsive to price and medical spending is responsive to insurance implies that there is a welfare loss from the tax subsidy to health insurance. The magnitude of the loss has been estimated by several papers. Feldstein and Friedman (1977) was the first estimate of the magnitude of the loss. Using estimates of insurance and medical care demand from Feldstein's earlier work, Feldstein and Friedman estimate the welfare loss at about 10% of medical care spending.

As the elasticities of medical care demand were refined, the estimated welfare loss from the tax subsidy fell. Chernick, Holmer and Weinberg (1987) used a similar methodology and more recent data to estimate the loss from the tax exclusion at about 5%.

Other analyses have not examined the tax exclusion per se but have simulated optimal insurance policies and compared them to actual policies. Some of these studies find that optimal insurance is less generous than current insurance policies, consistent with the tax loss hypothesis [Feldstein (1973), Blomqvist (1997)]. Other studies, however, find that current policies are roughly optimal [Buchanan, Keeler, Rolph and Holmer (1991), Newhouse and the Insurance Experiment Group (1993), Manning and Marquis (1996)][35]. The difference between these studies has not been fully reconciled. In light of the empirical evidence above, one suspects that there must be some welfare loss from the tax exclusion. The magnitude is unlikely to be as high as 10%, however.

5.4. Qualifications

Several factors are omitted in this analysis. The first is dynamics – insurance can influence the development and diffusion of new technology. As noted above, cost

---

[35] Feldman and Dowd (1991) compared welfare under a free care plan and a plan with moderate cost sharing (a $1000 deductible) and found the latter to be preferred.

growth in medical care has been persistently above that in the economy as a whole for many decades. A majority of this cost growth is a result of technological change in medical practice [Newhouse (1992)]. The introduction of new procedures and devices, and their application to more patients, have been prominent in medical care. At least some of this technological change likely results from the generosity of health insurance [Weisbrod (1991)]. Generous health insurance encourages the diffusion of innovations once they are available, and in turn the development of new innovations.

To the extent that tax policy has led to more generous medical insurance, it has also encouraged additional innovation in medical care. This will have significant welfare consequences, but the direction of these effects is unknown. If medical innovation would have been at the efficient level in the absence of the tax subsidy, the static estimates of welfare loss of the tax subsidy underestimate the true welfare loss. But free markets are not guaranteed to produce the right amount of innovation. Some of the return to medical innovations cannot be appropriated privately, for example general knowledge about physiological and biochemical functioning. The public good nature of this innovation suggests that private market innovation would be too low. In this case, the tax subsidy would be a welfare improvement.

Other arguments suggest that free market innovation might be too high. The patent race literature shows how the prospect of a patent can encourage excessive research, as potential innovators race to become the first discoverer of the good. By further exacerbating this trend, the tax subsidy would result in additional welfare loss.

There has been some empirical work on the value of technological change in medicine. Studies of medical outcomes typically find that the average product of changes in medical technology over time is high [Cutler and McClellan (2001)]. Thus, technological change may not have been too rapid, and the tax subsidy may be efficiency enhancing.

A related point is that the tax subsidy may influence the direction of technological change. For example, it might be the case that without the tax subsidy there would be more innovation in cost-reducing but quality-neutral innovation, while with the tax subsidy innovations are biased towards those that increase quality and cost. The welfare implications of such a bias depend on the same factors that were highlighted in the previous paragraphs.

The second qualification about the welfare loss from the tax exclusion is that it ignores the value of the subsidy in promoting overall rates of insurance coverage. By subsidizing insurance through employment, the tax subsidy encourages more people to be insured than would otherwise be the case. This is important because there are other public subsidies, discussed below, that encourage people to be uninsured. Counteracting these incentives could therefore improve welfare.

This effect may be substantial. Recall that the tax subsidy to insurance is, on average, about 34%. If the demand elasticity for insurance is −0.5, well within the range indicated above, the reduction in insurance coverage from eliminating the tax exclusion is about 17%[36]. If all these people became uninsured, the uninsurance rate would double. For this reason, many policy proposals have suggested capping, but not eliminating, the tax subsidy to health insurance. If the subsidy were capped at a level roughly equal to relatively inexpensive plans, people would still receive an inframarginal subsidy to purchase insurance, but face no marginal subsidy to choose more generous insurance. The reduction in coverage would be smaller.

Finally, the tax subsidy encourages the provision of insurance through employment. Without the tax subsidy, there would be relatively little reason for employers to provide health insurance rather than just giving employees cash. The link between insurance and employment has both good and bad consequences. Since employment groups are formed relatively independently of sickness, encouraging insurance through employment minimizes some of the problems of adverse selection that occur when individuals buy insurance on their own. On the other hand, employment-based insurance leads to a host of labor market problems associated with people being 'locked' into jobs because their health insurance would have to change if they changed employers. Some estimates suggest that this job lock plays a significant role in reducing overall rates of turnover in the labor market, although the issue is not settled [Gruber (2000), Krueger and Meyer (2002)].

6. The supply side

This analysis of optimal insurance has focused entirely on the demand side of the market – designing incentives to get individuals to reduce their demand for medical care while still reducing risk. Implicitly, providers were being paid at cost, and thus acted as perfect agents for their patients. Insurers and providers did not interact, other than for billing purposes. This was a moderately accurate picture of the market for medical care in the United States up to the early 1980s[37], but it is no longer a good description of how health insurance operates today. Nor is it relevant for other countries.

In the United States, the dominant trend in the medical care marketplace over the past two decades has been the growth of 'managed care'. Managed care is a collection of insurance arrangements in which utilization and prices are limited on the supply, not the demand-side of the market. Patients usually face little if any cost sharing at the time of service use. Instead, providers face a variety of incentives to control utilization. There are many forms of supply-side restrictions, including forming

---

[36] Using individual data and a similar elasticity of -0.5, Gruber and Poterba (1996) estimate that employer spending would decline by about 25% if the subsidy were eliminated.

[37] There is some debate about whether providers were paid at or above cost. Most economists believed that providers were paid above marginal cost and thus 'induced demand' for their services [Fuchs (1996)].

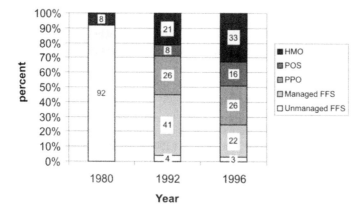

Fig. 6. Changes in health plan enrollments. The sample is people with private (employer or individual) insurance. Data source: Lewin-VHI.

networks of providers that agree to lower fees, monitoring and prescribing what doctors can and cannot do, and giving physicians financial incentives to reduce utilization.

Figure 6 shows the transformation of the private insurance industry in the United States. In 1980, 92% of the population was in unmanaged fee-for-service insurance. Today, the share is below 5%. In its place are a variety of managed care plans, including Health Maintenance Organizations (HMOs), Preferred Provider Organizations (PPOs) and Point of Service Plans (POSs)[38]. Even traditional fee-for-service plans are generally managed, with the insurer monitoring for excessive utilization and requiring pre-authorization for some services.

Public programs in the United States also use supply side techniques in varying degrees. In most states, a significant part of the Medicaid population is enrolled in managed care plans. Managed care enrollment is much lower in Medicare (only about 15%), but the fee-for-service program does make some use of supply side measures. For example, hospitals are paid on a per admission basis for Medicare enrollees. Additional days in the hospital or minor tests and procedures are not reimbursed at the margin.

In most countries with universal insurance systems, medical care utilization is limited by supply-side measures more than demand-side measures. For example, Canada and the United Kingdom both limit the capacity of hospitals to provide care (for example, by constraining the number of open heart surgery units). As a result,

---

[38] PPOs are groups of physicians who accept lower fees for access to a network. Patients face less cost sharing when using preferred providers than in using providers outside the network. HMOs include group or staff model plans, where doctors work only for that plan and patients can see doctors only in the plan, and looser network or independent practice arrangement plans, where doctors in the community sign up with one or more plans and may see patients with multiple plans. Point of service plans are HMOs that provide some reimbursement if the enrollee chooses to use providers out of the network.

fewer procedures are done, and overall spending is lower. Indeed, the greater ability to use supply-side constraints is almost certainly the reason why countries that operate the medical system spend less than those that provide universal coverage but use private providers.

The availability of supply side techniques opens up a host of issues for the public sector. One central question concerns design of optimal insurance for a country providing such insurance publicly. If one has appropriate supply-side cost sharing, is demand-side cost sharing useful? There is a lengthy literature on this question. A rough summary [Cutler and Zeckhauser (2000)] is that demand-side and supply-side constraints are not perfect substitutes. Both methods limit utilization, but do so on somewhat different margins. Demand-side cost sharing has a relatively greater impact on whether a person visits a provider at all, while supply-side cost sharing has a relatively greater impact on what is done once someone gets into the system. Thus, the optimal public system probably includes a combination of demand and supply side constraints.

A related question concerns the impact of supply-side controls on the welfare loss from the tax exclusion. If managed care eliminates excessive medical care utilization, has the welfare loss from the tax exclusion declined? There is no empirical information on this question. The fact that demand and supply side cost sharing are not perfect substitutes means that there is likely still to be some welfare loss from excessive moral hazard in managed care plans, but it is almost certainly smaller.

Other issues are important as well. For supply-side or demand-side rationing to be efficient, one needs to know that the people not receiving care are the ones who value the care the least. This is not guaranteed to be the case. In the case of demand-side rationing, the evidence generally suggests few adverse health effects from cost sharing, consistent with the efficient-rationing view [Newhouse and the Insurance Experiment Group (1993)]. Most estimates of the impact of managed care on health outcomes in the United States reach a similar view; it is hard to find evidence that health is worse under managed care plans [Glied (2000), Miller and Luft (1997)]. In other countries, however, outcomes do appear to suffer because of supply side constraints [Cutler (2002)].

These issues are too complex to be addressed in detail in this chapter, however. For additional discussion, interested readers should consult Glied (2000) or Cutler and Zeckhauser (2000).

7. Heterogeneous risks and selection

I now turn from the analysis of a single individual purchasing insurance to a market setting with multiple individuals. The central complication introduced by this is the heterogeneity of risk: some people are at high risk of being sick, while others are at low risk. On average, people at higher risk for disease want more generous insurance than those at lower risk. This fact creates enormous difficulties for insurance markets, as I now demonstrate.

7.1. Risk segmentation

To illustrate the problems that result from individual heterogeneity in insurance demand, consider a simple model with two risk types. Low risks have a small probability of being sick, while high risks have a greater probability. Both groups would like to purchase insurance, because for each group there is uncertainty about whether they will be sick. To keep matters simple, I suppose there is no moral hazard or other insurance market imperfection. I further assume that insurers know as well as individuals their expected risk; with genetic tests and medical histories, such knowledge is becoming increasingly common.

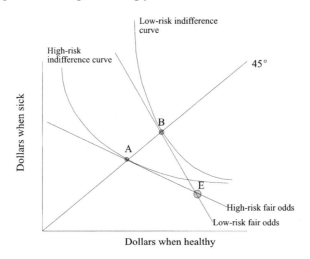

Fig. 7. Equilibrium with risk segmentation.

The analysis of this situation is shown in Figure 7. Rather than one line with fair insurance, as presented in Figure 4, there are now separate fair odds lines for high and low risks. The fair odds line for high risks lies inside that of low risks, since a greater premium is required to get a given payment when sick.

Offered the option of purchasing insurance at actuarially fair prices, both high and low risks will choose to buy full insurance; in the absence of moral hazard there is no reason not to do so. The equilibrium will therefore be at A and B. Both groups are fully insured, but high risks pay more for insurance than low risks.

In practice, if high risks are sufficiently risky or expensive, the insurer may simply choose not to offer these very high risk groups coverage rather than charge the required price and face public relations difficulties. High risks might then be "medically uninsurable". This is a more of a political than an economic term, however.

The equilibrium in Figure 7 is efficient *given risk types*. But from an *ex ante* perspective, before people know their risk type, it is not. Consider asking people before they know if they are high or low risk – potentially before birth – whether they would like to buy insurance against the probability that they will be high risk and thus face higher insurance premiums. Individuals would be willing to purchase this insurance were it sold at an actuarially fair price; they get a reduction in financial uncertainty at no expected cost. The fact that people wind up paying different prices for insurance reflects the failure of this insurance market.

This loss seems counterintuitive: everyone has full information and gets full insurance every year. What is the source of the loss? The welfare loss derives from a missing market for insurance against one's risk type. Risk averse individuals would like to insure against the possibility of being discovered to be high risk. There is no market where they can do so. Given that a market is missing, there is no guarantee that efficient pricing on the basis of known information as opposed to level pricing (as if ignorant) will enhance welfare. This is a classic illustration of the theory of the second best.

The market failure might also be thought of as stemming from a contracting failure. Contracts for health insurance are renegotiated after medical information is known. Such periodic recontracting allows new information to enter into the contractual arrangement over time, which individuals *ex ante* would choose to keep out.

It is possible to imagine private contracts that solve this problem [Cochrane (1995), Pauly, Kunreuther and Hirth (1995)]. Suppose that people purchase two insurance policies each year; one to cover their medical costs that year, and a second "premium insurance" policy to cover any increase in premiums they may face in the future as a result of information learned that year. Full premium insurance would give people an amount of money equivalent to the discounted expected increase in their future medical spending from events that year.

Such premium insurance does not exist; the question is why. Several factors have been identified. Regulatory barriers have been suggested as the culprit [Cochrane (1995)]. Moral hazard (people with premium insurance would take insufficient care of their health) and adverse selection (people expecting declines in health would more likely take up the insurance) are possibilities. The aggregate risk phenomenon provides a fourth explanation [Cutler (1996)]. Implementing such contracts requires a lot of information about how changes in health status today affect the entire future course of expected medical spending. There is substantial uncertainty in this forecast which full premium insurance would have to insure against. But future medical cost changes will be common to everyone with the contract. As a result, insurers will be unable to diversify this risk [39]. For all but the first explanation, private markets will be imperfect, and government intervention is warranted.

---

[39] Insurers might get around this the way that they do with term life insurance: guaranteeing the right to renew at then prevailing prices. But then the value of the insurance product is limited, as people are locked into one policy.

7.2. Adverse selection and market failure

The government might respond to the risk segmentation problem by requiring insurers to offer everyone the same price for each contract. Many employers who run health systems for their employees do this. Indeed, information systems were historically not well enough developed for insurers to differentiate who was high and low risk; they could only set one price for each group.

This pooling at first glance seems to solve the risk segmentation problem, since everyone can enroll in each plan at the same terms. But the solution is illusory. It moves from a system of full information to one of asymmetric information: individuals know more than insurers about their risk types. In such a situation, market outcomes will again be inefficient. This analysis was first demonstrated by Rothschild and Stiglitz (1976) and Wilson (1977).

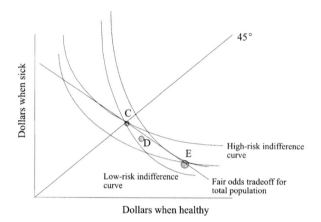

Fig. 8. Lack of a pooling equilibrium. The dotted lines are indifference curves with no insurance.

This inefficiency can be demonstrated using Figure 8. Constrained to charge only one price per plan, suppose that insurers offer plan C, full insurance at the group average price (assuming equal numbers of high and low risks). Plan C is a pooling equilibrium; it fully insures *ex ante* risk, thus solving the risk segmentation problem. But plan C is not stable. Consider an insurer that came along and offered a policy that was a bit less generous than plan C but cost less, such as plan D. Low risk people would choose plan D over plan C; since they are overpaying for insurance, low risks prefer less generous insurance if they can get it at existing prices. High risks prefer C to D; given the implicit subsidy they receive, high risks want full insurance. As a result, introducing plan D would break the pooling equilibrium. Rothschild and Stiglitz and Wilson show that in a competitive insurance market with two risk types, pooling is not an equilibrium; low risks will never voluntarily pool with high risks.

There is only one possible equilibrium, shown in Figure 9. That equilibrium involves high risks in plan A and low risks in plan F. Plan A provides full insurance at actuarially

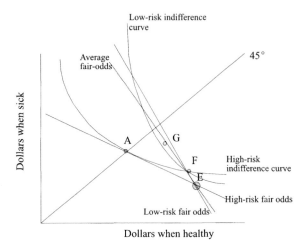

Fig. 9. The separating equilibrium.

fair rates for high risks. Plan F is the most generous actuarially fair plan for low risks that is not preferred by the high risks to plan A. High risks are tempted to join plan F by the low premium, but are discouraged by the incomplete coverage. Plan F is just stingy enough to make switching unattractive for high risks. Low risks would prefer more generous coverage at their risk-specific cost, but this cannot be obtained without also pooling with the high risks[40].

There are two inefficiencies in this equilibrium. First, high risks have to pay more for their coverage simply because they are high risk, the risk segmentation problem noted above. Second, low risks do not obtain full insurance coverage, even though full insurance is optimal. Plans distort themselves to attract low risks, in the process reducing the value of their insurance.

In this model, the generosity of insurance coverage is measured by the amount paid in the sick state; but in practice other dimensions of the plan may be used as screening devices. For example, having good cancer care is likely to appeal to the sick more than the healthy; thus, plans for low risks will avoid such specialists. Well baby care or complementary health club memberships, which appeal to the low risks, would be better. Even advertizing and location can be used to select good and bad risks.

Rothschild and Stiglitz go further and show that even the separating equilibrium may not be stable. Figure 9 also shows this situation. Suppose that instead of an equal mix of low and high risks, the economy consists almost entirely of low risks. Thus, the fair odds line for the two risks together is the dotted line. Relative to utility at point F,

---

[40] This discussion has been presented in a case where individuals are paying for the cost of insurance and thus pay less when they join plans with low risk people. A related situation is present if all people are given a uniform voucher for insurance. Then, low risks do not benefit by having plans for low risks only, but insurers do. As a result, insurers will design the same sort of policies.

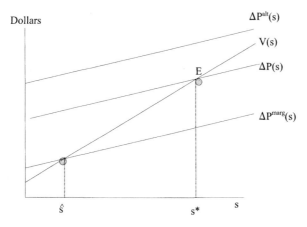

Fig. 10. Equilibrium with multiple risk types.

the low risks would prefer a pooled policy such as G. The high risks would prefer G as well, since they get a much lower premium and only somewhat less coverage. Point G would thus undermine the separating equilibrium. But the analysis above still holds; the pooling equilibrium is not stable either. Thus, with no stable pooling equilibrium and no stable separating equilibrium, the market will not reach an equilibrium[41].

The simple two-risk example of adverse selection suggests that if an equilibrium exists, high risks will receive full coverage, while low risks will receive only partial coverage. Very different, but still inefficient, equilibria can be achieved with multiple risk types [Feldman and Dowd (1991), Cutler and Reber (1998) and Cutler and Zeckhauser (1998)]. Suppose there are two health plans, a generous plan and a moderate one. It is easiest, although not necessary, to think of the generous plan as a traditional service benefit policy and the moderate plan as a managed care policy. There is a continuous distribution of risks in the population, denoted by s. For simplicity, I take s to be the person's expected spending in the generous policy. The value of more generous insurance to an individual is $V(s)$, where $V' > 0$ (the sick value generous policies more than the healthy)[42]. Figure 10 shows $V(s)$. At any additional cost for choosing the more generous policy, people will divide into plans by risk. If s^* is the sickness level of the person indifferent between the two policies, people with $s > s^*$ will choose the generous policy, and people with $s < s^*$ will choose the moderate

---

[41] Many papers have analyzed equilibrium in such markets. Some equilibrium concepts do yield an equilibrium, but in no case is the equilibrium first best efficient. Wilson (1977) and Riley (1979) proposed equilibria where insurers do not offer plans if those plans would become unprofitable if other plans left the market (Wilson) or if other plans entered the market (Riley). Grossman (1979) proposes a model where insurers can screen applicants before selling them insurance, thus limiting losses from high risks.

[42] It is not needed that V depends only on s. All that is needed is that V is correlated with s in some fashion.

policy. Average sickness in the generous and moderate policies are $s_G = E[s \mid s > s^*]$ and $s_M = E[s \mid s < s^*]$.

Suppose that the moderate policy costs a fraction α ($\alpha < 1$) of what the generous policy would spend for the same person[43]. In a competitive insurance market, premiums will equal costs: $P_G = s_G$, and $P_M = \alpha s_M$. The premium difference between the two plans is therefore:

$$\Delta P(s) = P_G - P_M = (1 - \alpha) s_M + [s_G - s_M]. \tag{18}$$

The first term in this expression is the cost savings the moderate plan offers to its average enrollee. The second term is the difference in the average sickness level in the two plans, a consequence of adverse selection.

As marginal people move from the generous to the moderate plan, the average sickness in each of the plans will rise. Depending on the distribution of s, the price difference between plans may widen or narrow. Because medical spending in practice is significantly right-skewed (Table 4), it is natural to conjecture that the premium in the generous plan will rise by more than the premium in the moderate plan. Figure 10 reflects this expectation as an upward-sloping $\Delta P(s)$ curve.

Equilibrium is where the price difference and enrollments are consistent, at point E. Point E is unlikely to be efficient, however[44]. The efficient price is where the marginal person pays exactly his additional utilization to join the generous plan. Defining $\hat{s}$ as the efficient marginal person:

$$\Delta P^{\mathrm{marg}}(\hat{s}) = (1 - \alpha)\hat{s}, \tag{19}$$

the difference between equilibrium and efficient prices is two-fold. The first term in Equation (18) is generally below the efficient differential in Equation (19); it represents the savings from the moderate plan for the *average* person in the moderate plan, not the *marginal* person in the plan, for whom the savings would be greater. Working in the opposite direction, adverse selection [the second term in Equation (18)] will raise the premium in the generous plan relative to the premium in the moderate plan. Depending on the distribution of medical expenditures, the market differential could be above or below the efficient level. The right skewness of medical spending suggests that the adverse selection effect will tend to predominate. This is shown in Figure 10 by virtue of the fact that the $\Delta P(s)$ line is above the $\Delta P^{\mathrm{marg}}(s)$ line. The premium differential for the generous plan is above the efficient differential, and too few people enroll in that plan.

---

[43] For example, empirical evidence suggests that HMOs spend about 10% than traditional service benefit policies for the same individuals [Glied (2000)].

[44] To be precise, efficient given risk types. There is still the case for full pooling of risks to insure one's s.

Indeed, it is possible that because of adverse selection, the generous plan itself may disappear. If $\Delta P^{\text{alt}}(s)$ described the cost differential rather than $\Delta P(s)$, then $V(s)$ would not intersect that line and the equilibrium would have no enrollment in the generous plan. The generous plan would disappear because at every price difference, the marginal person always finds the cost savings from the moderate plan sufficiently large to prompt switching[45]. The disappearance of generous plans as a result of dynamic processes of adverse selection is termed a "death spiral". Thus, in this example too few people will have generous insurance coverage.

Considering the various equilibria, there are no guarantees about what an equilibrium with adverse selection will involve, if in fact there is an equilibrium. But the final equilibrium will involve potential welfare losses from three sources. First, people may be in the wrong plans. Adverse selection prompts people at the margin to enroll in less generous policies, when on the basis of their own preferences and costs more people would choose generous plans. Second, plans have incentives to distort their coverage to attract the low risks and repel the high risks. This incentive is present for *all* plans. Every plan gains by being less generous, because at the margin it changes the risk balance towards a lower risk population. This is true even if every person would be willing to pay for it at his actuarially fair rate[46]. Third, people pay more for insurance when they are sick than when they are healthy. This denies people the *ex ante* pooling of risk types that people would want at a fair price.

7.3. Evidence on the importance of biased enrollment

A substantial literature has looked for biased enrollment in insurance markets, the key to adverse selection. This literature is summarized in Cutler and Zeckhauser (2000). Table 7, taken from that paper, shows evidence of enrollment differences along three dimensions: traditional insurance versus managed care; overall levels of insurance coverage; and high versus low option coverage.

---

[45] A numerical example illustrates this possibility. Suppose that the highest-cost person has expected spending of $50 000 and that average costs of the population as a whole in the moderate policy (with or without this person, if he comprises a small part of the total risk) is $3000. Suppose further that the high-cost person values the generous policy at $20 000 more than the moderate policy, and that he spends only $5000 less in the moderate policy than with the generous policy (a 10% savings). Efficiency demands that he should be in the generous policy; the additional value of that policy ($20 000) is greater than the additional cost he imposes there ($5000). If the high-cost person were the only person in the generous policy, however, the cost of that policy would be $47 000 more than the cost of the moderate policy ($50 000 versus $3000), which would lead him to opt for the moderate policy.

[46] There is an apocryphal story about such a situation. A firm was providing benefits to its employees and noticed that all plans put a 90 day limit on inpatient care for mental health benefits. The employer went to the various insurers and asked about the cost of removing the cap. The insurers all replied that they didn't have such a cap in practice, they just said they did to discourage people with severe mental health problems from enrolling in their plan!

Table 7
Evidence on biased enrollment in health insurance[a]

Reference	Data	Empirical methods	Highlights of results	Selection
Selection Between Managed Care and Indemnity Plans				
Bice (1975)	East Baltimore public housing residents (random sample)	Tests of means of health status variables by Medicaid enrollment	Poor health and high expected use of medical services is positively correlated with enrollment in prepaid plans; expected costs are reduced	Favorable
Scitovsky, McCall and Benham (1978)	Stanford University employees' enrollment and survey data	Least-squares regression of plan choice (note dependent variable is binary)	Fee-for-service patients are older and more likely to be single or without children	Adverse
Eggers (1980)	Group Health Cooperative (GHC) of Puget Sound's Medicare Risk Contract, 1974–76	Comparison of usage statistics with control sample from Medicare 20% (Part A) and 5% (Part B) Research Discharge Files	Length of stay 25% higher for non-GHC patients; inpatient reimbursements per person are 2.11 times higher outside GHC	Adverse
Juba, Lave and Shaddy (1980)	Carnegie-Mellon University employees' health insurance enrollment and survey, 1976	Maximum likelihood logit estimates of determinants of plan choice	Lower family self-reported health status results in significantly less chance of selecting HMO enrollment	Adverse
McGuire (1981)	Yale University employees' health plan enrollment statistics (random sample)	Logistic regression of health plan choice given some plan is chosen	Women are less likely to join the prepaid health plan than men, but no significant effect is associated with age	Adverse
Jackson-Beeck and Kleinman (1983)	11 employee groups from Minneapolis–St. Paul Blue Cross and Blue Shield, 1978–81	Comparison of costs and utilization for HMO enrollees and non-enrollees in period before HMO availability	HMO joiners averaged 53% fewer inpatient days before joining than those who chose to stay in FFS	Adverse
Griffith, Baloff and Spitznagel (1984)	Physician visits in the Medical Care Group of St. Louis	nonlinear regression of frequency of visits	high usage rates at managed care plan's initiation eventually fall to lower steady-state levels	Ambiguous

continued on next page

Table 7, *continued*

Reference	Data	Empirical methods	Highlights of results	Selection
Merrill, Jackson and Reuter (1985)	State employees' enrollment and utilization data from Salt Lake City and Tallahassee	Tests of means in plan populations and logit regression of health plan choice	HMO joiners are younger, more often male, less likely to use psychiatric services, but have more chronic conditions in their family units	Ambiguous
Langwell and Hadley (1989)	1980–81 Medicare Capitation Demonstrations	Comparison of HMO enrollees and non-enrollees using two-tailed tests of means; comparison of enrollees and disenrollees using surveys	Non-enrollees' reimbursements are 44% higher than enrollees in two years before capitation; disenrollees have worse past health	Adverse
Brown, Bergeron, Clement, Hill and Retchin (1993)	Medicare spending for enrollees who stayed in traditional system versus those who moved into managed care	Comparison of spending in the two years prior to HMO enrollment	Enrollees who switch to managed care had 10% lower spending than enrollees who stayed in traditional system	Adverse
Rodgers and Smith (1996)	Summary of 1992 Mathematica Policy Research study of Medicare enrollees	Measure cost differences between elderly customers covered by standard Medicare FFS and capitated HMO care	HMO patients are 5.7% costlier	Favorable
Altman, Cutler and Zeckhauser (1998)	Claims and enrollment data from the Massachusetts Group Insurance Commission (GIC)	Age- and sex-adjusted analysis of costs among individuals with different plan choice histories	Adverse selection accounts for approximately 2% of differences between indemnity and HMO plan costs	Adverse
Summary				Adverse

continued on next page

Table 7, *continued*

Reference	Data	Empirical methods	Highlights of results	Selection
Selection of Reenrollment versus Disenrollment/Uninsurance				
Farley and Monheit (1985)	1977 National Medical Care Expenditure Survey	OLS and 2SLS estimation of health insurance purchases	Ambulatory care expenditures have an insignificant impact on health insurance purchases	Ambiguous
Wrightson, Genuardi and Stephens (1987)	Disenrollees from seven plans offering different types of managed care	Comparison of costs and disenrollment rates for insurees	Disenrollees have lower inpatient costs and occupy less risky demographic groups than continuing enrollees	Adverse
Long, Settle and Wrightson (1988)	Enrollment patterns of subscribers to three Minneapolis–St. Paul HMOs	Probit estimation for chance of insuree disenrolling from each of three HMOs	Likelihood of disenrollment rises significantly with increases in relative premium of own plan	Adverse
Cardon and Hendel (2001)	National Medical Expenditure Survey	Tobit-style model of insurance choice	individuals who are younger, male, or in "excellent" self-reported health are significantly less likely to become insured	Adverse
Summary				adverse
Selection of High-Option Plan within Type of Plan				
Conrad, Grembowski and Milgrom (1985)	1980 random sample of claims and eligibility data for dental health insurance by Pennsylvania Blue Shield	2SLS and 3SLS estimation of demand models for premiums and total expenditures	Worse self-perceived dental health corresponds to higher valuation of insurance; experience rating does not always lower premiums	Adverse
Ellis (1985)	1982–83 employee health plan enrollment and expense records of a large firm	Logit estimates of health plan choice	Age and worse previous year's health expenses are associated with choice of more generous health coverage for the next year	Adverse

continued on next page

Table 7, continued

Reference	Data	Empirical methods	Highlights of results	Selection
Dowd and Feldman (1985)	Survey data from 20 Minneapolis–St. Paul firms	Tests of means of characteristics of health plan populations	Fee-for-service patients are older and more likely have serious medical conditions or relatives with such conditions	Adverse
Luft, Trauner and Maerki (1985)	California state employees' enrollment and utilization data	Comparisons of risk indices across plans and years	Patient risk in high option indemnity and fee-for-service plans increases faster than risk in managed care	Adverse
Price and Mays (1985)	Federal Employees Health Benefits Program proprietary data	Comparison of costs and premiums across plan choices	High option Blue Cross plan undergoes a premium spiral with enrollment cut in half over only three years	Adverse
Marquis and Phelps (1987)	Rand Health Insurance Experiment	Probit estimation for take-up of supplementary insurance	Families in highest expenditure quartile were 42% more likely to obtain supplementary insurance than those in lowest quartile	Adverse
Ellis (1989)	Claims and enrollment data from a large financial services firm	Analysis of different plans' member characteristics and expenses	Employees in high option plan are 1.8 years older, 20.1% more likely to be female, and have 8.6 times the costs of the default plan	Adverse
Feldman, Finch, Dowd and Cassou (1989)	Survey of employee health insurance programs at 7 Minneapolis firms	Nested logit for plan selection	Age varies positively with selection of a (relatively generous) IPA or FFS single-coverage health plan	Adverse
Welch (1989)	Towers, Perrin, Forster, and Crosby Inc. study of Federal Employees Health Benefits program	Comparison of premiums between high and low option Blue Cross plans for government workers	High-option premium is 79% higher than low option	Adverse

continued on next page

Table 7, *continued*

Reference	Data	Empirical methods	Highlights of results	Selection
Marquis (1992)	Plan selection of families in Rand Health Insurance Experiment	Comparison of plan choices with age/sex adjustments under various group-rating regimes	73% more individuals in high risk quartile choose most generous plan than those in low risk quartile, even with age/sex/experience rating	Adverse
van de Ven and van Vliet (1995)	Survey and claims data from 20 000 families insured by largest Dutch insurer, Zilveren Kruis	Regression of risk factors on prediction error of difference in costs between members of high- and low-cost plans	Age- and sex-composition of plans explain 40% of error in predicted cost differential between plans	Adverse
Buchmueller and Feldstein (1997)	University of California Health Benefits Program enrollment figures	Historical analysis of enrollment changes and premium increases	Two high-option plans suffered fatal premium spirals in a six-year period; a third was transformed from FFS into POS to prevent a spiral	Adverse
Cutler and Reber (1998)	Claims and enrollment data from Harvard University	Calculation of welfare loss and simulation of long-run effects of changes in health plan prices	Adverse selection creates a welfare loss equal to 2% of baseline health spending; price responses in long run are triple those in short-run	Adverse
Cutler and Zeckhauser (1998)	Claims and enrollment data from Harvard University and the Massachusetts Group Insurance Commission (GIC)	Analysis of different plans' member characteristics and expenses	Employees in GIC's FFS plan spend 28% more, are older, and have significantly more births and heart attacks than HMO members	Adverse
Summary				Adverse

[a] See Cutler and Zeckhauser (2000) for details.

Most empirical work on adverse selection involves data from employers who allow choices of different health insurance plans of varying generosity; some of the studies look at the Medicare market, where choices are also given. In essentially all of these cases, the data show strong evidence of adverse selection[47]. Adverse selection is present in the choice between fee-for-service and managed care plans (8 out of 12 studies, with 2 findings of favorable selection and 2 studies ambiguous), in the choice between being insured and being uninsured (3 out of 4 studies, with 1 ambiguous finding), and in the choice between high-option and low-option plans within a given type (14 out of 14 studies).

7.4. Evidence on the importance of plan manipulation

There are substantially fewer empirical studies on whether plans manipulate their benefits to attract a healthier mix of enrollees than on biased enrollment. Plans, of course, differ greatly in their generosity. But it is difficult to know how much of this variation reflects manipulation by the plans to attract healthy risks as opposed to differential estimates of the most efficient care arrangements.

Though evidence on plan structures is ambiguous, the marketing of managed care plans shows clear efforts to promote favorable selection. Newman, Maibach, Dusenbury, Kitchman and Zupp (1998) document the marketing practices managed care plans use to attract healthy Medicare enrollees, including television ads that show seniors engaged in physical and social activities and marketing seminars held in buildings that are not wheelchair accessible.

7.5. Public policy with heterogeneous risks

Risk segmentation and adverse selection create a clear case for government intervention. This is unlike moral hazard, where private markets have as much ability to combat the problem as the government. Here, the government's ability to compel certain actions is important. The most obvious public solution is to mandate that everyone have insurance, and that they belong to the same plan. Mandatory coverage is required to prevent the healthy from declining coverage. A single plan is required to prevent sorting by risk. This solution is termed single payer insurance. It is the foundation

---

[47] The metric to measure adverse selection is not the same in all studies, ranging from the difference in premiums or claims generated by adverse selection after controlling for other relevant factors [for example, Price and Mays (1985), Brown et al. (1993)] to the likelihood of enrollment in a generous plan conditional on expected health status [for example, Cutler and Reber (1998)] to the predominance of known risk factors among enrollees of more generous health plans compared to those in less generous plans [for example, Ellis (1989)].

of many health care systems around the world[48]. Adverse selection was an explicit concern in the foundation of many public insurance systems.

Single payer systems have other drawbacks, however. Universal systems require substantial income transfers to the poor. In addition to the political economy difficulty of taxing the rich to give to the poor, there are efficiency considerations from raising the taxes used to finance the transfers. Further, issues of government efficiency, noted in Section 4 in the case of government versus private provision, are raised here as well. For these reasons, governments have pursued other options as well.

A second solution is to regulate some degree of pooling more than private markets alone would provide. In the early to mid-1990s, state governments in the United States passed a number of pieces of legislation to limit risk segmentation. This was followed by Federal legislation in 1996. Problems of premium variability are much more acute for small firms than for large firms, since large firms have an internal risk pool that can be used to smooth spending. Thus, this legislation generally applies only to small firms, for example those with fewer than 50 employees. This insurance legislation consisted of some or all of the following: limitations on the rates that could be charged high and low risk purchasers, for example that such rates be no more than 15% above or below average; requirements that insurers guarantee enrollment to new or existing purchasers seeking to renew; and requirements that people moving from one policy to another policy not face pre-existing conditions exclusions or length of service requirements before enrollment.

The impact of this legislation has been the subject of some research. One would expect such legislation in the first instance to compress premium variability. This, in turn, might then affect rates of insurance coverage. The predicted change in coverage is unclear, however. On the one hand, some high risk people whom insurers had previously refused to underwrite or who decided to be uninsured because of high premiums might now purchase coverage. On the other hand, some healthy people could choose not to purchase insurance as their rates increased. The overall implications for rates of insurance coverage are not known *a priori*.

Premium data are much less available than coverage data. Thus, most of the research on the impact of this legislation has focused on overall rates of insurance coverage. Some studies also examine other outcomes, such as who has access to insurance (sick or healthy) and whether small firms offer insurance to their workers. These studies are summarized in Table 8. The studies use a variety of approaches; some use a difference-in-differences approach, comparing changes in insurance coverage in states that adopted reforms at different times; some also compare changes for small and large firms in states that passed such legislation versus states that did not pass such legislation. Other studies do more detailed case studies of reforms in particular states.

---

[48] In Canada, for example, everyone receives health insurance from their provincial government; there is no choice about the policy and no option to be uninsured. In the UK, a base insurance plan is required for everyone, although people can supplement that plan with private insurance.

Table 8
Effects of small-group and individual market regulation

Reference	Data (years)	Empirical strategy	Reforms examined	Results
Buchmueller and Jensen (1997)	Survey of CA employers, 1993 and 1995; compared to national surveys in same years	Difference-in-difference of insurance coverage between small firms in California versus the rest of the nation	Effect of California law requiring guaranteed issue, rate bands, and pre-existing condition limitations	13 percentage point increase in share of California firms offering insurance
Marsteller, Nichols, Badawi, Kessler, Rajan and Zuckerman (1998)	March CPS (1989–1995)	State-level analysis of rates of uninsurance, private insurance, and Medicaid coverage. Model includes state and year fixed effects, controls for economic conditions and demographics	Small group and individual market regulations on issue and rating	Significant positive effect of small group issue reforms on coverage rates (strongest effects for guaranteed issue); negative effect of rating reforms; these effects are offsetting in states with both reforms. Reforms in individual market were associated with statistically significant decreases in coverage
Sloan and Conover (1998)	CPS (1989–1994)	Cross-state changes in insurance coverage, public–private mix of coverage, and group–non group coverage for employees in small firms compared to large firms	Mandates; low cost plans; high risk pools; open enrollment; rate bands	Mandates lower coverage by 4%. No other policies affect overall insurance coverage. Community rating leads to less private and more public coverage, and more coverage for the old in comparison to the young.

continued on next page

Table 8, *continued*

Reference	Data (years)	Empirical strategy	Reforms examined	Results
Hing and Jensen (1999)	National Employer Health Insurance Survey (1993)	Cross-sectional analysis of small firms' decision to offer insurance as a function of small group regulations by state	Rating restrictions, guaranteed renewal, portability, guaranteed issue, pre-existing condition waiting period	Small positive relationship between regulations and percent of firms offering coverage (3–4 percentage points). Small, negative effect for more recent reforms.
Jensen and Morrisey (1999)	Health Insurance Association of America's Annual Employer Health Insurance Survey (1989, 1991) and survey conducted by authors (1993, 1995)	Estimates probability of small firms's offering of health insurance as logit. Cross-sectional analysis using 4 years of data; includes region dummies and other controls. Variation in policy variables is at the state level	Guaranteed issue, guaranteed renewal, portability of coverage, pre-existing conditions, rating restrictions (rating restriction dummies are not included in model due to collinearity)	No significant effect of regulations on probability of offering.
Zuckerman and Rajan (1999)	March CPS (1989–1995)	DD at state level; analyzes "packages" of reforms that tended to adopted together. Dependent variables are uninsurance rate and rate of private coverage	Separate analyses of regulation of group market (guaranteed issue, guaranteed renewal, rating restrictions, pre-existing condition restrictions, portability) and individual market (same except portability)	No statistically significant effect of reforms on coverage in small group market. Individual market reforms have positive, statistically significant effect on uninsurance and negative, statistically significant effect on private insurance rate.
Hall (2000)	Case studies of reforms in a number of states	Case studies	Variety of reforms in small group and individual markets	Reforms have improved access for high-risks at high cost; little effect of small-group reforms on insurance offering; negative effect of individual reforms (guaranteed issue, pure community rating) on coverage

continued on next page

Table 8, *continued*

Reference	Data (years)	Empirical strategy	Reforms examined	Results
Simon (2000a)	CPS (1992–1997)	Cross-state changes in insurance coverage for small firms versus large firms	Full reform (guaranteed issue and rate bands); Partial reform (rate bands only); Barebones (requirement to offer basic plan to uninsured)	Full reforms reduced coverage by 1.9 percentage points; Decline of 6.4 percentage points for low risk workers (young, never married men); Statistically insignificant increase for high risk workers (married women whith children); No effect of partial reforms or barebones package on coverage.
Simon (2000b)	Medical Expenditure Panel Survey Insurance Component List Sample (1994) and National Employer Health Insurance Survey (1997)	Cross-state changes in premiums, employee contributions, small firm offering, coverage, and medical underwriting for small versus large firms	Full reform (guaranteed issue and rate bands); Partial reform (rate bands only); Barebones (requirement to offer basic plan to uninsured)	Full reform increased single premiums by 4% (marginally significant), increase in employee contribution is 65% of total premium increase. No significant effect of full or partial reform on offering. Full reform has statistically significant negative effect on coverage; negative (insignificant) effect on take-up.
Kapur (2000a)	CPS (1991–1999)	Difference-in-differences across states comparing who is hired in small firms with health insurance by measures of expected medical spending	Strong reform (guaranteed issue, rate bands, portability); Moderate reform (only some of these factors); and no reform	Portability and rating reforms have offsetting effects on employment, with no net change in who is hired in small firms.

continued on next page

Table 8, *continued*

Reference	Data (years)	Empirical strategy	Reforms examined	Results
Kapur (2000b)	NMES (1987) and MEPS (1996)	Examines employment changes by firm size conditional on being offered health insurance	Regulations making it hard for insurers to deny coverage or exclude pre-existing conditions	Conditions that were a cause for denial in 1987 did not lead to employment distortions but did in 1996, consistent with such conditions being harder to deny.
Swartz and Garnick (2000)	State data on enrollment through IHCP	Trends in enrollment in Blue Cross and IHCP	Establishment of Individual Health Coverage Program in New Jersey	IHCP may have prevented a continued decline in individual coverage.
Buchmueller and DiNardo (2002)	CPS (1987–1996) for NY, PA, and CT	Difference-in-difference comparing small and large firms in New York versus the other states	Implementation of community rating in New York	Large shift to managed care in New York; no change in insurance coverage overall.
Summary				No or small effect of regulations on insurance coverage.

A consensus from the studies in Table 8 is that there is no effect or very small effects of insurance regulation on overall rates of coverage; negative impact on coverage are more commonly found in studies of individual market regulations, although these effects tend to be small. Additionally, where the authors attempt to look at the effects of regulations on insurance coverage by risk type, they often find that rates among the sicker rise, while rates among the healthy fall somewhat.

There are several possible explanations for a lack of large findings. One problem has to do with the scope of the legislation. States are allowed to regulate purchased insurance but not rates for firms that self-insure. A small firm that formally purchased insurance can choose, after the legislation, to self-insure and purchase stop-loss coverage for individual claims exceeding certain levels. This alternative insurance arrangement, often through the same insurer, involves little or no change in risk born by the firm but gets the firm out of the legislative mandate. A trend towards self-insurance occurred after these regulations were put in place.

A second explanation is that the legislation was undone by the presence of multiple plans. While legislation sometimes required insurers to offer all groups the same price for each policy, groups of healthy employees can still choose less generous policies as a whole and maintain their lower rates, provided that less healthy groups choose not to enroll in those plans. In some cases, insurers were not required to make all plans available to all firms, thus allowing healthy firms an option separate from less healthy firms. In other cases, adverse selection appears to be the source of the failure. Buchmueller and DiNardo (2002) show that many firms moved into managed care plans after such legislation was passed, presumably for adverse selection reasons. In light of all the evidence, it thus seems clear that regulation by itself cannot offset the problems resulting from biased enrollment. Some other solution is also needed.

Since the problems of risk segmentation and adverse selection ultimately result from plans not receiving enough money for high-risk people compared to low risk people, one can think about subsidizing plans that enroll high risk people as a way to combat this situation. Figure 11 shows how a system of subsidies would work. Starting from the initial separating equilibrium at plans A and F, consider increasing required payments by the low risks and using the money to lower required payments by the high risks. High risks still receive full insurance but have more income available when sick and healthy; their equilibrium point moves out along the 45° line. As low risks are made to pay more without receiving additional benefits, their budget constraint rotates inward. If the subsidy equalized rates, the equilibrium would be the pooling equilibrium in Figure 8.

Some amount of subsidy is valued by low risks [Miyazawa (1977), Spence (1978)]. Although low risks pay above expected cost to finance the transfer to the sick, the fact that the high risks can afford insurance at lower cost makes them less likely to opt out of their plan for the low risk plan. Thus, the healthy can increase the generosity of the policy they choose. But not all subsidies are so valued. For complete equality to be achieved (plan C), the healthy must be mandated to participate in the system.

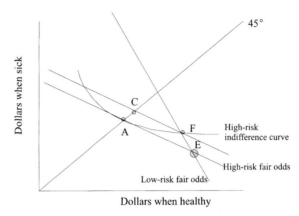

Fig. 11. Equilibrium with subsidies.

This form of differential payment by health status is termed "risk adjustment" [van de Ven and Ellis (2000)]. Risk adjustment must be carried out by a government, or a private agency acting like a government[49], since given the choice, low risks would not voluntarily enter a risk adjustment system.

One way to implement risk adjustment is as a voucher system with differential vouchers for high and low risks. A sufficiently high voucher for the high risks would be enough to offset their higher expected costs. Alternatively, risk adjustment can also be implemented at the plan level. The voucher amounts would be equal, but plans would receive subsidies or pay penalties based on the risk distribution of their enrollees. Plans with low risks would pay money to plans with high risks.

If governments can risk adjust perfectly, adverse selection can be solved and the first best achieved. This is not surprising; it is tantamount to assuming away the information problem that led to adverse selection in the first place. Designing such a system in practice is more difficult, however, because of moral hazard. Typically, the way that one measures risk status is by looking at medical care utilization. People with greater medical claims or more adverse diagnoses are deemed less healthy. But such attributes are under the control of the individual and insurer. If the government pays more for diabetics, for example, the plan can screen carefully for the disease. If the government pays more for very expensive people in general, the incentives to hold down costs are muted. This type of moral hazard limits the desired risk adjustment, just as moral hazard limits optimal risk sharing in the standard case of insurance plan design.

To date, few governments or other organizations have used formal risk adjustment systems [Keenan, Beeuwkes-Buntin, McGuire and Newhouse (2001). The Medicare program in the United States has just moved to such a system, however, and more

---

[49] For example, an employer running an insurance plan in the interests of all of his employees.

information will be available in coming years. Evaluating the impact of these systems will help guide future policies.

Returning to the discussion of Section 5, one can view the tax subsidy to health insurance as an implicit risk adjustment system. By lowering the price of insurance through employment, the subsidy bribes healthy people to pool with less healthy people at their workplace. Since employment is not perfectly correlated with health, this mutes the impact of poor health status on insurance premiums[50].

8. Combining public and private insurance

The previous section examined the problems inherent when heterogeneous people wish to choose different health plans. Without adequate risk adjustment, it was shown that plans might be insufficiently generous, to avoid attracting high risk people. To get around this problem, some countries have mandated that everyone be enrolled in a basic plan that covers services up to a minimally acceptable level, and then allow people to supplement that package with more generous insurance if they wish. This solution seems reasonable on first blush, but it too suffers substantial problems.

Private supplemental insurance might take one of three forms. One type of insurance is for services that the basic plan does not cover. For example, Medicare in the United States does not cover outpatient prescription drugs[51], or most long-term care expenses. Supplemental insurance to cover uncovered services is allowed in most countries, including the United States. About half of the elderly in the United States have private insurance to cover prescription drugs, largely through Medicaid or a former employer.

As one might imagine, adverse selection is a substantial problem for such markets. In the individual market for insurance coverage to supplement Medicare, for example, very few people buy packages with pharmaceutical coverage, and those that do pay dearly for the care [Ettner (1997)]. Supplemental insurance for uncovered services also has cost implications for the public sector. People with coverage for a supplemental service will use more of that service than they would in the absence of insurance. This additional service use might increase or decrease use of services covered under the basic plan, depending on whether covered and uncovered services are complements or substitutes. Coverage for prescription drugs in the United States seems to have relatively little effect on use of physician and hospital services, but the impact of covering other services such as long-term care could be larger [Cutler (2000)].

A second type of insurance is to pay for cost sharing required under the basic plan. The cost sharing required under the Medicare program is high: nearly $800 for inpatient care and 20% coinsurance with no stop-loss for outpatient care. At their

---

[50] The extent to which costs are fully pooled depends on the degree to which individual wages reflect individual health insurance costs. There is strong evidence that employees as a whole bear health insurance costs, but little evidence about whether this occurs on a worker-by-worker basis.

[51] The same is true in Canada for the non-elderly population.

discretion, Medicare beneficiaries can obtain supplemental insurance to pay for these out-of-pocket costs.

This form of supplemental insurance has even clearer cost implications for the government. People who insure required cost sharing use more services than those who do not. Some of this additional utilization is paid for by the public sector. For example, consider a person who has pneumonia and has the choice of staying in a hospital for observation or staying at home. Suppose that the hospital stay will cost $2000. If the person faces an $800 deductible, he might choose not to enter the hospital. With a supplemental insurance policy covering the deductible, however, the person enters the hospital. Only $800 of the additional utilization is paid for by the supplemental insurer; the remaining $1200 is paid for by the primary policy. The supplemental insurance policy is in effect subsidized by the primary plan. This subsidy encourages essentially all elderly without employer-based supplemental insurance or Medicaid to purchase this coverage. Between Medicaid, employer-based supplemental insurance, and individually-purchased supplemental insurance, nearly 90% of Medicare beneficiaries have eliminated the cost-sharing in the Medicare policy. The cost implications of this insurance are large[52]. Christensen and Shinogle (1997) and U.S. Physician Payment Review Commission (1996) estimate that people with supplemental insurance use 20 to 30% more Medicare services than those without such coverage.

The third form of supplemental insurance, and the most controversial[53], is insurance to pay for services already covered under the basic package. The supply-side restrictions on medical service use imposed in many countries have led to waiting lists for care. In some cases, people might have to wait a year or longer for access to non-emergency services. In the face of these waiting lines, some people would choose to pay for private insurance (or pay physicians privately) which would allow them to jump to the front of the queue.

This type of insurance can increase total service utilization at low out-of-pocket cost. Consider a person with a broken hip. On the public system, the person may face a year wait to visit an orthopedist, who then schedules surgery several months later. Supplemental insurance might pay for an orthopedist visit right away. The person can then join the smaller waiting list for the surgery (perhaps moving up in that line, with additional payments to the surgeon), and have the public sector pay for that care. For the cost of one orthopedist visit, the person cuts the length of the wait by a year or more.

The belief that supplemental insurance enables rich people to jump the queue at the expense of poor people has led to this type of insurance being banned in

---

[52] Estimating these additional costs is not straightforward. The additional utilization of people with supplemental coverage over those without it is a product of both moral hazard and adverse selection (since sicker people value supplemental insurance more than healthy people). To estimate the importance of moral hazard, one must first back out the share due to adverse selection or find an instrument for insurance coverage separate from health status.

[53] See Propper and Green (2002) for discussion.

many countries, such as Canada[54]. In other countries such as the UK, supplementary insurance is allowed and is held by nearly 20% of the population. Still others pay out-of-pocket to jump the queue.

While those with supplemental insurance certainly benefit from such a system, it is not obvious that those left behind lose out. In the orthopedist example, when the person pays the orthopedist privately, resources are saved by the public plan. If these resources are used to expand the supply of medical services, the remaining enrollees in the queue will benefit as well, albeit not as much as those with private insurance. In practice, it is not obvious that payments for salaried physicians adjust in an appropriate manner, and some countries have notorious examples where physicians abuse the system to collect multiple salaries. In that case, allowing supplemental insurance could harm those not sufficiently wealthy to afford it[55].

9. Equity concerns and policy for the poor

Equity concerns dominate many public considerations about health care. They were a driving force behind national health insurance in many countries and are a perennial issue in countries like the USA without a national system. I start off by characterizing the medical care utilization of the poor and then turn to the public policy issues.

9.1. Medical care for the poor in the USA

The main health insurance program for the poor is Medicaid. Medicaid eligibility is complex; only a brief summary is presented here [see Gruber (2002) for a detailed discussion of Medicaid and evidence on its effects]. Traditionally, Medicaid eligibility was tied to receipt of cash welfare assistance, formerly known as Aid to Families with Dependent Children (AFDC) and currently known as Temporary Assistance to Needy Families (TANF). AFDC eligibility was restricted to low-income single women with children. Income cutoffs were generally about 50% of the poverty line.

---

[54] Canadians can come to the USA for care. Such events are relatively rare, however, and they pay the full cost for the care.

[55] The political economy of this type of supplemental insurance has also drawn attention. If the rich can opt out of the public system at will, their demand for a high-quality public sector may decline, potentially leading to an unraveling of support for public insurance [Gouveia (1997)]. But the opposite result may also occur. The waiting lines the rich face in the absence of supplemental insurance may diminish their support for public insurance entirely. Scattered empirical evidence suggests that the political economy consequences of opting out have been small [Burchardt, Hills and Propper (1999), Globerman and Vining (1998)].

A further concern is whether having a private sector erodes the monopsony position of governments. If being a monopoly purchaser is a key part of how governments hold down prices, allowing other purchasers will result in increased government costs. In the short run, this would be an efficiency loss, as suppliers are paid more for the same product. Over the long-term, the welfare consequences depend on the supply elasticity of service provision.

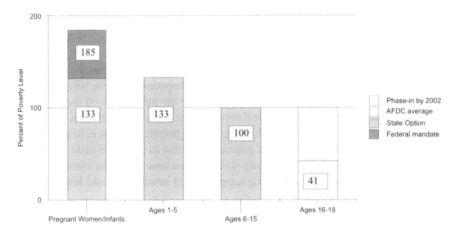

Fig. 12. Eligibility for Medicaid, 1999.

In practice, this left out a lot of needy people. Many pregnant women and young children were not eligible for Medicaid because of family circumstances (the woman was married or living with someone) or because they had income slightly above the AFDC eligibility line. Providing health insurance for these groups was thought to be particularly valuable, and perhaps even cost saving, since keeping pregnant women healthy might reduce the occurrence of costly care for premature birth [Institute of Medicine (1985)].

As a result, in the late 1980s and early 1990s, there was a dramatic expansion of the Medicaid program. Figure 12 shows eligibility rules in 1999. All pregnant women and infants with incomes below 133% of the poverty line are eligible for Medicaid, independent of whether they live in a single or dual parent family. At state option, this can be extended to 185% of the poverty line. Children aged 1 to 5 are eligible for Medicaid up to 133% of poverty, and children aged 6 to 15 are eligible up to the poverty line. Children aged 16 and older are eligible only up to lower incomes, about 41% of the poverty line, but this is being extended to the poverty line as the youngest of these children age. These expansions doubled the share of women eligible for Medicaid if pregnant and increased the share of children eligible by a third.

More recently, there was a further expansion of health insurance eligibility for children. The Child Health Insurance Program (CHIP) was enacted in 1997, with the goal of increasing coverage to even higher levels of income. Under the CHIP, states can cover children in families with incomes below 200% of poverty. The new coverage can be through Medicaid or other systems. CHIP enrollment has been relatively slow (less than 2 million children covered within the first two years, compared to Medicaid coverage of 12 million), however, so there has not been a lot of analysis of this program to date.

The net impact of these changes is shown in Table 9. I report health care coverage for the non-elderly population by income in 1986, prior to most of the expansions, and

Table 9
Insurance coverage by income in the non-elderly US population[a]

Income	1986 coverage (%)			1998 coverage (%)		
	Private	Public	Uninsured	Private	Public	Uninsured
<Poverty	12	42	45	24	40	36
Poverty – 2× Poverty	50	12	38	52	17	31
>2× Poverty	80	3	17	85	3	12

[a] Source: Data are from the March 1987 and 1999 Current Population Surveys.

1998[56]. The table groups people into three income categories: the poor (income below the poverty line); the near poor (income between poverty and twice poverty); and the non poor (income above twice poverty). The impetus behind the Medicaid expansions is readily apparent; nearly as many people between poverty and twice the poverty line were uninsured in 1986 as compared with those with lower incomes.

Medicaid coverage has increased significantly among the near poor – the major expansion group – from 12% to 17% of that group. Medicaid coverage fell among the lowest income group, as welfare reform and a strong economy moved people off the welfare rolls[57]. Medicaid coverage has historically been low among the non-poor.

Being uninsured does not mean that one goes without medical care. Partly by law and partly by tradition, hospitals provide care for all people with medical emergencies, whether or not they can pay. This 'uncompensated care' has been estimated at about 5% of total hospital costs. Physicians provide some care to the uninsured as well, but the amounts are lower. Of course, no care can be truly uncompensated[58]. Hospitals finance unreimbursed care by charging more to those with insurance and using those revenues to pay for the uninsured.

9.2. Optimal policy for the poor

The central question facing governments is how to design a medical care system for the poor. Universal insurance coverage is one option: the government could raise taxes (income, payroll, or consumption) to finance universal coverage. The tax and insurance issues involved in this were discussed above; I do not repeat that discussion here. A second option is a partial public program. This is what the United States has pursued through the Medicaid program: some people are eligible for public insurance but others

[56] There have been some minor changes in the CPS wording about health insurance over this time period, but they are not sufficiently large to explain the trends shown.

[57] The magnitude of this change is large, and it is not completely clear why it all occurred.

[58] Hospitals do receive donations, but donations have fallen over time relative to the costs of medical care.

are not. Overall coverage is a mix between public insurance, private insurance, and uninsurance.

The choice between universal and targeted programs is a classic tradeoff in public finance [Akerlof (1978)][59]. Because universal programs involve more public spending, the deadweight loss from taxation is greater. But partial programs lead to other distortions that universal programs avoid: people will change their behavior to qualify for a partial program, where they would not need to do so under the universal system. Behavioral change might take several forms. People with income above the eligibility line might work less than otherwise would, so they qualify for public insurance. They might change their family circumstances as well, for example not being married. Finally, they might drop their private insurance coverage if they are eligible for the public program. In addition, partial programs have the problem that people may not know about them, and thus may not use the services at the right time.

The Medicaid expansions of the late 1980s and 1990s provide an ideal window to examine these issues. By extending eligibility to higher income groups and dual parent families, the expansions encouraged more Medicaid beneficiaries to work and provided incentives for families to stay together. On the negative side, they also encouraged higher income people to drop their private coverage and enroll in Medicaid[60]. This 'crowding out' of private coverage has become a central concern of the literature because it increases the cost of the Medicaid program without substantial health benefits.

9.3. Crowding out: theory and empirical evidence

Figure 13, taken from Cutler and Gruber (1996a), shows the economics of crowding out. Health insurance purchase is shown on the vertical axis; spending on other goods and services is on the horizontal axis. Indifference curves I_1, I_2 and I_3 show three people with the same income but different valuations of health insurance. Person I_1 is uninsured, I_2 chooses moderate insurance, and I_3 chooses very generous insurance.

Now suppose the government introduces a free[61] health insurance program offering medical care at quality m. The program is designed for people without insurance. But the program can only be offered on the basis of income. Thus, all three people are eligible. This program is more appealing than the status quo for both I_1 and I_2. The

---

[59] Akerlof compared a program focused on income alone to one also conditioning on another factor. The income-only program is effectively a universal one.

[60] The incidence of employer payments for insurance has been a subject of much debate. Theoretical and empirical work generally agree that employees pay for health insurance costs in the form of lower wages. But whether this incidence is on a worker-by-worker basis or a more aggregated level is not clear. See Gruber (2000) and Krueger and Meyer (2002) for discussion.

[61] For simplicity, I ignore the impact of the taxes needed to finance the program. They would not alter the conclusions of the analysis.

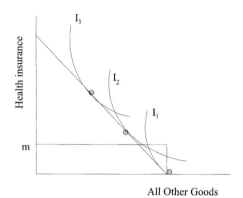

All Other Goods   Fig. 13. Public insurance and crowding out.

increased insurance coverage of I_1 is intended; I_2 has been crowded out of private coverage.

Crowding out increases the cost to the government of public programs relative to the benefits. The coverage expansion may have a positive benefit–cost analysis for I_1 but a negative benefit–cost difference when I_2 joins the program.

Table 9 provides some evidence on the potential magnitude of crowding out. In 1986, before the Medicaid expansions, half the near poor population had private insurance. Roughly one-third were uninsured. Thus, unless the Medicaid expansions were carefully designed to discourage those with private insurance from enrolling, there could be significant crowd-out.

A central empirical issue is how extensive this crowding out has been. Significant research has been directed to this question, which is summarized in Table 10. The first study to examine this question was Cutler and Gruber (1996a)[62]. They analyzed the magnitude of crowding out using data from the 1988–1993 Current Population Surveys (CPS). Different states raised their Medicaid eligibility criteria at different times, and started from different initial levels of coverage. Thus, there is significant geographic variation in the size and timing of the Medicaid expansions. Cutler and Gruber used this variation to identify crowding out. They estimated that crowd-out was about 50%: for every two people taking up Medicaid, one person left private coverage.

The surprising magnitude of this finding has sparked a number of additional studies using different sources of data and methodologies. All of the studies find evidence of crowd-out, although the magnitude of the crowd-out varies. Studies using CPS data, based on repeated cross-sections of the population and examining cross-state as well as time series variation, tend to give similar findings to Cutler and Gruber [Shore-Sheppard (1996)]. Studies using the Survey of Income and Program Participation or the National Longitudinal Survey of Youths, generally following particular individuals over

---

[62] See also Cutler and Gruber (1996b,c).

Table 10

Effect of public health insurance programs on private coverage

Reference	Data (years)	Empirical strategy	Results
Dubay, Norton and Moon (1995)	American Hospital Association Annual Survey (1987–90); March CPS (1988, 1991); HCFA Area Resource File	Estimate effects of Medicaid expansions on uncompensated care provided by hospitals. (Need to get full article)	Overall, Medicaid expansions reduced uncompensated care by 5.4%; reduced uncompensated care by 28.5% for hospitals with a significant commitment to maternity and infant care
Cutler and Gruber (1996a)	CPS (1988–1993)	Identifies effects of expanding Medicaid eligibility on private and Medicaid coverage of women and children using within-state variation due to differential timing of Medicaid expansions. Includes state and year fixed effects	Fifty percent of increase in Medicaid coverage (women and children) was offset by reduction in private insurance. Does not appear that employers reduced offering of insurance in response to expansions.
Dubay and Kenney (1996)	CPS (1989, 1993)	Estimates effect of Medicaid expansions on private coverage for children. Medicaid eligibility is estimated using TRIM2. Compares trends in employer-sponsored private coverage for poor children to trends for men ages 18 to 44	Crowd out of employer-sponsored coverage is estimated to be 17–26% of the increase in Medicaid coverage
Dubay and Kenney (1997)	CPS (1989, 1993)	Estimates effect of Medicaid expansions on private coverage for pregnant women. Insurance coverage, Medicaid eligibility, and pregnancy are simulated using Urban Institute TRIM2. Compares trends in employer-sponsored coverage rates for near-poor pregnant women to those for near-poor men	Crowd-out is about 45% for near-poor women. Crowd-out of private insurance is smaller for poorer women; overall 30% of increased Medicaid enrollment was offset by declines in private coverage.

continued on next page

Table 10, *continued*

Reference	Data (years)	Empirical strategy	Results
Shore-Sheppard (1996)	March CPS (1988–1996)	Compares changes in state–age–income cells with small and large changes in Medicaid eligibility.	Estimates crowd-out between 31 and 57% when data through 1996 are included, 15 to 33% for 1988–1993.
Yazici and Kaestner (1998)	NLSY (1988, 1992)	Compares take-up of Medicaid and dropping of private insurance among children made eligible for Medicaid between 1988 and 1992 to trends for the always eligible and never eligible in panel data	Estimates that 14.5% of new Medicaid enrollment due to expansions came from private insurance.
Blumberg, Dubay and Norton (2000)	SIPP (1990)	Compares transitions from private coverage and uninsurance to Medicaid between 1989 and 1990 for children likely to have been affected by expansions to a comparison group (older children with similar income) in panel data	Estimate that 23% of movement from private coverage to Medicaid was due to displacement. No evidence that those moving from uninsurance to Medicaid would have otherwise taken up private insurance. Overall estimate of displacement of private insurance is 4% of new Medicaid enrollment.
Rask and Rask (2000)	NMES (1987) and NHIS (1989, 1992)	Uses multinomial logit model of insurance choice (Medicaid, private, uninsured) for different income groups in cross-section to estimate relationship between availability of public hospitals, uncompensated care funds, and Medicaid on insurance choices.	Large negative significant relationship between the presence of a public hospital in the county and private coverage. Also significant negative relationship between Medicaid generosity and uninsured care funds on private coverage rates.

continued on next page

Table 10, *continued*

Reference	Data (years)	Empirical strategy	Results
Shore-Sheppard (2000)	March CPS (1988, 1989, 1994, 1995)	Uses variation in impact of Medicaid expansions by region and income decile to identify changes in private coverage, Medicaid coverage and uninsurance. Also uses single men as additional control group. Uses those estimates to form counterfactual distributions of health insurance coverage for children	Estimates of crowd-out between 7.6% and 45.3%. Concludes that expansions had an equalizing effect on coverage over the income distribution.
Shore-Sheppard, Buchmueller and Jensen (2000)	CPS and sample of firms (1989, 1990, 1991, 1993, 1995)	Examines effect of imputed fraction of employees eligible for Medicaid on employer offering of employee and family coverage and employee take-up. Uses CPS to impute fraction of workers in firm who are Medicaid eligible according to states' rules. Includes state and year fixed effects	No evidence Medicaid expansions effected offering of insurance to employees. Statistically significant negative effect of expansions on offering family coverage. Weak evidence of negative effect of Medicaid expansions on take-up of employer-provided insurance.
Summary			Crowd-out ranges from 10 to 50% of Medicaid increase.

time, find smaller estimates of crowd-out, in the 10 to 20% range [Dubay and Kenney (1996, 1997), Blumberg, Dubay and Norton (2000), Yazici and Kaestner (1998)]. One would not expect panel data to yield the same estimate of crowd-out as repeated cross sections, since it examines only whether people drop private coverage when made eligible for Medicaid. Other effects could lead to crowd-out, since as people not taking up coverage as their income changes. Whether the differences in results are due to the different methodologies or different data sets is not generally known.

While most of the studies look at the impact of Medicaid on private insurance, one study examined whether areas with greater uncompensated care provision had less private insurance coverage [Rask and Rask (2000)]. Rask and Rask found significant crowd-out from these programs.

Crowding out might result from individual decisions to drop coverage or employer decisions to increase cost sharing or perhaps drop coverage entirely. Two studies [Cutler and Gruber (1996a) and Shore-Sheppard, Buchmueller and Jensen (2000)] have considered this question. Although the effects of Medicaid generosity on cost-sharing and offering care are imprecisely estimated (it is hard to learn about firm behavior with existing data), both studies suggest that crowding out is a function of employee decisions to drop coverage more than employer decisions to limit or cancel their insurance.

The magnitude of crowding out bears directly on welfare loss from the tax exclusion of employer-provided health insurance. The analysis above highlighted the welfare loss from excessive moral hazard. The crowd-out evidence suggests a countervailing benefit of the subsidy: it offsets other incentives to switch to public insurance. No studies have estimated how the welfare gain from minimizing crowd-out compares to the welfare loss from excessive moral hazard.

9.4. Medicaid expansions and other behaviors

Crowd-out is not the only behavior that may be affected by the Medicaid expansions. The expansions increased the ability of women to work and still retain health benefits, and allowed women to be married and still collect benefits. It also reduced the need for precautionary savings in the event a person became sick. A smaller body of research has examined the empirical import of these effects. In the interests of space, I do not review this literature at length; Gruber (2000) and Krueger and Meyer (2002) provide detailed summaries.

By allowing women to collect health benefits at higher levels of income, the Medicaid expansions increased incentives for women to work. This should result in increased employment and lower welfare participation among this group of the population. Several studies have addressed this issue empirically. Yelowitz (1995), using the cross-state time series methodology described above, found significant evidence that labor supply increased with the expansions. He estimated that increasing the income cutoff for eligibility by 25% of the poverty level increased labor force participation among low income women by 3 percentage points. Meyer and Rosenbaum

(2000) find counter evidence, however. Using the same methodology but a slightly different measure of eligibility, they find no evidence that labor supply increased after the expansions. Ham and Shore-Sheppard (1999) find evidence that Medicaid expansions led some women to leave welfare for work. Thus, the overall evidence on welfare and work decisions is mixed.

Less evidence has been directed at how Medicaid expansions affect marriage, fertility, and savings. Yelowitz (1998) finds that the Medicaid expansions increased the share of women who got married, consistent with the expansion of coverage to dual-parent families. Joyce, Kaestner and Kwan (1998) find that Medicaid increases fertility rates, presumably by making the cost of birth and subsequent medical care cheaper. The increase in fertility comes about largely as a result of reduced abortions [Joyce and Kaestner (1996)]. Finally, Gruber and Yelowitz (1999) present evidence that savings fall by 16% in families made eligible for Medicaid, consistent with reduced need for precautionary savings. The research on all of these issue is just beginning, however.

9.5. Medicaid expansions and health outcomes

The primary goal of the Medicaid expansions was to improve the health of the poor. Thus, they ultimately need to be evaluated along that margin. Several studies, shown in Table 11, have estimated the health impacts of Medicaid expansions.

The evidence suggests the health benefits are relatively modest. Piper, Ray and Griffin (1990), Haas, Udvarhelyi and Epstein (1993), and Joyce (1999) look at the effect of Medicaid expansions on health in particular states or cities – Tennessee, Massachusetts, and New York City respectively. The first two studies find no impact of the expansions on health; Joyce finds a modest positive impact. Other studies have taken a national approach. Currie and Gruber (1996a,b) and Kaestner, Joyce and Racine (2001) use the cross-state and time series methodology described above to evaluate the health impacts of the Medicaid expansions. Currie and Gruber find small but statistically significant improvements in health following the Medicaid expansions. Kaestner, Joyce and Racine (2001) find weak, if any, support for the hypothesis of improved health.

Even relatively modest health benefits might be worth it if the value of life is high. Only one study has explicitly done a cost-effectiveness analysis for the Medicaid expansions [Currie and Gruber (1996a)]. Currie and Gruber estimate that the Medicaid expansions had a cost-effectiveness ratio of roughly $1 million per life, considering only the mortality impact. While this is relatively high, in comparison to the Viscusi (1993) summary of the value of a life ($3 million to $7 million for a middle-aged person), the Medicaid expansions seem to be worth it. Thus, at least some studies find that the Medicaid expansions did have a positive benefit in mortality impacts alone, although the rate of return is not enormously high.

Some explanation for why the health benefits are not larger is provided by Piper, Ray and Griffin (1990). They show that many women did not enroll in Medicaid for prenatal

Table 11
Effects of public programs on health

Reference	Data (years)	Empirical strategy/Program evaluated	Results
Piper, Ray and Griffin (1990)	Vital statistics linked to Medicaid enrollment files for Tennessee (1985–87)	Compare prenatal utilization and birth outcomes for births before and after Medicaid expansion for pregnant women; some specifications focus on groups most likely to be affected by expansion	No effect of Medicaid expansion for pregnant women on birth outcomes or initiation of prenatal care for any group. Increase in fraction of Medicaid covered births where enrollment initiated in last 30 days of pregnancy. Both before and after expansion, more than two-thirds enrolled in last 30 days of pregnancy.
Haas, Udvarhelyi and Epstein (1993)	Massachusetts hospital discharge data for all in-hospital births (1984, 1987)	Compare changes in outcomes of uninsured pregnant women before and after implementation of statewide program for uninsured pregnant women to changes for privately insured and Medicaid patients	No statistically significant differences in changes in adverse outcomes for uninsured patients, compared to Medicaid and privately insured. The probability of cesarean section rose for uninsured relative to other groups.
Currie and Gruber (1996a)	National Health Interview Survey (1984–1992)	Identifies effects of Medicaid eligibility for children on medical care utilization (e.g., doctor visit) and child mortality using within-state variation in eligibility due to differential timing of Medicaid expansions ("simulated instrument")	Medicaid eligibility reduces probability of no doctor's visit in last year by 12.8%, increases probability of hospitalization by 14%. Ten percentage point increase in fraction eligible for Medicaid reduces child mortality by 0.128 percentage points (3.4% of baseline).
Currie and Gruber (1996b)	Vital Statistics (1979–1992), National Longitudinal Survey of Youth (1979–1990)	Identifies effects of Medicaid expansions for pregnant women on utilization and outcomes	Thirty percentage point increase in eligibility is associated with 8.5% reduction in infant mortality. Early, targeted expansions were more cost-effective than later, broad expansions.

continued on next page

Table 11, *continued*

Reference	Data (years)	Empirical strategy/Program evaluated	Results
Joyce (1999)	Medicaid administrative data linked to birth certificates for birth in New York City (1989, 1991)	Cross-sectional analysis of relationship between birth outcomes and Prenatal Care Assistance Program (PCAP) participation, controlling for demographics. Some specifications stratify month of pregnancy prenatal care was initiated. IV estimates using number of PCAP providers in area as instrument for participation	PCAP is associated with 20% increase in WIC participation and 1.3 percentage point decrease in rate of low birth-weight. Financial savings are insufficient to offset the cost of the program.
Currie and Gruber (2001)	Vital Statistics (1979–1992)	Same as above. Examines effects of Medicaid eligibility on medical utilization and outcomes for births	Medicaid eligibility was associated with more intensive treatment and marginal improvements in neonatal mortality. Larger effect on neonatal mortality for mothers living near a hospital with a Neonatal Intensive Care Unit.
Kaestner, Joyce and Racine (2001)	National Health Interview Survey (1989, 1992), Nationwide Inpatient Sample of ambulatory care sensitive discharges (ACS) (1988–1992)	Examines effect of eligibility on maternal reports of child's health and chronic conditions and bed days (NHIS). Uses state–year–income and age–year interactions to instrument Medicaid eligibility for children aged 2–9. DD: children assigned to treatment and control based on median income of zip code (NIS ACS)	Weak, if any, support for the hypothesis that Medicaid improves health.

continued on next page

Table 11, continued

Reference	Data (years)	Empirical strategy/Program evaluated	Results
Dafny and Gruber (2002)	National Hospital Discharge Survey (1983–1996)	Identifies effects of Medicaid eligibility for children on avoidable hospitalizations using within-state variation in eligibility due to differential timing of Medicaid expansions ("simulated instrument")	Estimates 22% decline in avoidable hospitalizations due to expansions. Increase access to hospitalization on newly eligible resulted in net increase of 10% in hospitalizations.
Summary			Small improvements in health.

care until very late in the pregnancy – often at the time of delivery. Thus, they were missing much of the prenatal care that may have the highest cost-effectiveness ratio [Institute of Medicine (1985)]. This may be a result of the incremental nature of the program: information about program eligibility may only diffuse over time, and eligibility rules are complex. A universal system might increase utilization of services more.

The finding of very late use of services, in turn, suggests an important reason why the estimated cost-effectiveness analysis presented above may be understated. The Medicaid expansions provided hospitals with additional revenue they would not otherwise have had – the reimbursement for a delivery that used to be uncompensated. To the extent that these revenue increases led hospitals to provide high quality care more generally, the benefits of this additional care for health should be accounted for as a benefit fo the expansions. Only one study has traced how the Medicaid funds were used. Duggan (2000) shows that hospitals receiving a large amount of money from the Disproportionate Share Hospital Program (DSH) of Medicaid generally saved those funds in the short-term, adding them to balance sheet assets. It will be important to trace through the effects of these funds over time. If used well, it may be that public programs have a more favorable benefit–cost analysis than the individual calculations suggest.

10. Intergenerational aspects of medical care

While most analysis has focused on the intragenerational aspects of medical care programs, there are intergenerational consequences to these programs as well. Public medical care systems are almost always financed on a pay-as-you-go basis. Medicare in the United States, for example, is predominantly pay as you go, with a small surplus currently but the prospect of large deficits looming.

Pay as you go systems involve substantial intergenerational transfers. Generations alive when these systems were created or when the benefits expanded rapidly receive large benefits, while future generations bear the cost. A few studies in the literature have attempted to estimate the magnitude of these intergenerational transfers [Steuerle and Bakija (1997), U.S. Congressional Budget Office (1997), Gokhale and Kotlikoff (1999), Cutler and Sheiner (2000)]. Most of this research has focused on the intergenerational aspects of the Medicare program in the United States.

Figure 14, taken from Cutler and Sheiner (2000) presents the most recent set of estimates. Cohorts born around 1920, and thus reaching Medicare eligibility around 1985, are expected to receive net benefits of over $60 000 from Medicare. Cohorts born today are expected to pay more into the system than they receive out. The rates of return are also high for older cohorts. The 1910 cohort is expected to receive a rate of return of over 25%, compared to 2.2% for cohorts born in 1980[63].

---

[63] Rates of return are extremely high for the very oldest cohorts because they paid so little into the system but get a lot out. For this reason, we do not report rates of return for cohorts prior to those born in 1910.

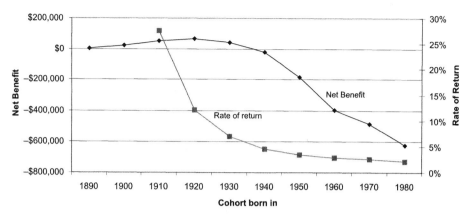

Fig. 14. Intergenerational aspects of Medicare. Source: Cutler and Sheiner (2000).

These estimates use the assumptions of the Medicare actuaries, which project that medical cost increases will slow down in the next 25 years to the growth rate of the economy as a whole. Young cohorts today therefore pay for the rapid cost growth experienced by older cohorts but do not receive benefits from rapid growth themselves. An alternative projection allowing medical cost growth to continue avoids the very large losses for current young populations. But these groups still fare worse than the cohorts that were elderly or near elderly when the program was implemented.

Appropriate government policy towards this intergenerational distribution is a broader question than just Medicare policy, involving issues of savings and labor market behavior, among other behaviors. I do not pursue these issues at length here.

11. Conclusions

As this brief (!) tour through the health sector indicates, the public policy issues raised by health care are vast. I conclude by highlighting what has been learned and providing some direction for future research.

At the most basic level, governments are involved in what people do to themselves – smoking and drinking on the bad side, exercise and eating well on the good. One concern about such behaviors is the externalities they impose; financial and health consequences need to be considered. 'Internalities' may be important as well; there are many reasons to think smokers themselves would be better off if induced not to smoke. The literature has made substantial progress on the externality question, but much less progress has been made on the internality question. Since the potential magnitude of internal damages dwarfs the magnitude of external damages, more research on this question is a clear priority.

Once an individual becomes sick, the medical system takes over. Governments face a first choice about how to provide medical services: through the public or private sector. The answer is complex. Private firms respond to incentives more rapidly than public firms, but the incentives need to be the right ones for the system to be efficient. The wealth of different delivery systems in the United States and abroad creates a host of experimental situations to help judge the appropriate delivery system for medical care. Empirical research on this question is a clear need.

In every country, the government is involved in influencing the health insurance that people receive. In designing such policies, the second-best is the goal. More generous insurance increases the gains from risk sharing but also the losses from moral hazard. The optimal policy balances the marginal insurance gains against the marginal moral hazard losses. An individual in isolation designing such a policy for himself would get the tradeoff right. But government may be involved where it is not warranted. By subsidizing employer-provided insurance at the expense of out-of-pocket spending, the Federal government in the United States encourages more generous insurance, and perhaps too much moral hazard. The 'perhaps' is key, however; the tax benefits of insurance may encourage valuable innovation, may offset other public subsidies encouraging people to be uninsured, or may encourage risk pooling at the expense of adverse selection. Understanding the total impact of the tax subsidy through all of these channels is still to be done.

Putting health insurance in a market creates even more problems. People with different health risks want different insurance plans; low risks will not voluntarily subsidize high risks. As a result, the market will attempt to segregate the two groups, either explicitly (by charging high risks more than low risks) or implicitly (by encouraging low risks to move to less generous plans to avoid the high risks). The problems from such attempts are three-fold: the less healthy will pay more for insurance than the healthy, denying people the *ex ante* risk pooling that they would want; people are encouraged to join plans that are less generous than they would prefer if they faced actuarially fair prices, because such switching saves them from subsidizing the high risks; and plans will have incentives to make their policies less generous, so as to discourage high risks from enrolling.

At the extreme, governments may respond to these problems by mandating insurance in a common plan at a common price. Short of this, the government might enact regulatory barriers to segregation or put in place financial incentives for the sick and healthy to remain together. Empirical evidence on the effects of these policies is not entirely clear; policy action is now awaiting such knowledge.

Finally, governments are involved in distributional issues for the poor, as they always are. Equity in health care is valued more than equity in most other markets; as the saying goes, health care is a right and not a good. Equity is a bigger problem in countries without universal coverage than in those with universal coverage; the United States struggles with equity more than most other developed countries. In recent years, the United States has had incremental expansions of coverage for the poor. These programs have been effective, but marginally so. The costs are high and the benefits only modest. Learning how to design such programs is a key question facing the public sector. This question is particularly pressing because medical care markets are changing so rapidly. The rise of managed care and cutbacks in government payments are squeezing profits from medical care providers. The impact these policies will have on the implicit subsidy system for the poor is worrisome.

Some evidence of the sheer diversity of opinion about public policy for health care is provided by the recent debate about Medicare in the United States. Some look at Medicare and see an inefficient, government-provided insurance system. Thus, one contingent supports a voucher system in the hopes that plan competition will eliminate wasteful spending from the program [Aaron and Reischauer (1995)]. A second group considers the lack of adequate benefits the major problem with Medicare. The poor elderly are faced with high cost sharing, and those without employer-provided supplemental insurance or Medicaid are often uninsured for prescription drugs. Thus, this group favors expanding the Medicare package and promoting increased service use [Moon (1996)]. Finally, some see the high and rising cost of Medicare as the central problem. Increased Medicare spending worsens the Federal budget and reduces national saving. Thus, a third group favors shifting the costs of the current system to the elderly, or forcing middle aged people to save more for medical care needs when they are retired [Gokhale and Kotlikoff (1999), Feldstein (1999)]. Each of these positions is credible in its own right, but the solutions are diametrically opposed. In perhaps no other area of public finance is the range of differing policy prescriptions so great.

This broad range of questions demands serious research attention. Which direction should policy go? What are the next steps? This chapter provides an outline, but only that.

References

Aaron, H.J., and R.D. Reischauer (1995), "The medicare reform debate: what is the next step?" Health Affairs 14:8–30.

Akerlof, G. (1978), "The economics of tagging as applied to the optimal income tax," American Economic Review 68:8–19.

Altman, D., D.M. Cutler and R.J. Zeckhauser (1998), "Adverse selection and adverse retention", American Economic Review 88(2):122–126.

Arrow, K. (1963), "Uncertainty and the welfare economics of medical care", American Economic Review 53(5):941–973.

Arrow, K. (1965), Aspects of the Theory of Risk Bearing (Yrjo Jahnssonin Saatio, Helsinki).

Auerbach, A.J., and J.R. Hines Jr (2002), "Taxation and economic efficiency", in: A.J. Auerbach and M. Feldstein, eds., Handbook of Public Economics, Vol. 3 (Elsevier, Amsterdam) pp. 1347–1421.

Beck, R.G. (1974), "The effects of co-payment on the poor", Journal of Human Resources 9(1):129–142.

Becker, G.S., and K.M. Murphy (1988), "A theory of rational addiction", Journal of Political Economy 96:675–700.

Becker, G.S., M. Grossman and K.M. Murphy (1994), "An empirical analysis of cigarette addiction", American Economic Review 84:396–418.

Besley, T.J., and M. Gouveia (1994), "Alternative systems of health care provision", Economic Policy: A European Forum 9:199–249.

Bhattacharya, J., W.B. Vogt, A. Yoshikawa and T. Nakahara (1996), "The utilization of outpatient medical services in Japan", Journal of Human Resources 31(2):450–476.

Bice, T.W. (1975), "Risk vulnerability and enrollment in a prepaid group practice", Medical Care 13(8):698–703.

Blomqvist, A.G. (1997), "Optimal non-linear health insurance", Journal of Health Economics 16: 303–321.

Blumberg, L.J., L. Dubay and S.A. Norton (2000), "Did the Medicaid expansions for children displace private insurance? An analysis using the SIPP", Journal of Health Economics 19:33–60.

Bovenberg, A.L., and L. Goulder (2002), "Environmental taxation and regulation", in: A.J. Auerbach and M. Feldstein, eds., Handbook of Public Economics, Vol. 3 (Elsevier, Amsterdam) pp. 1471–1545.

Brown, R.S., J.W. Bergeron, D.G. Clement, J.W. Hill and S. Retchin (1993), The Medicare Risk Program for HMOs – Final Summary Report on Findings from the Evaluation, Final Report under HCFA Contract Number 500-88-0006 (Mathematica Policy Research, Inc., Princeton, NJ).

Buchanan, J.L., E.B. Keeler, J.E. Rolph and M.R. Holmer (1991), "Simulating health expenditures under alternative insurance plans", Management Science 37(9):1067–1089.

Buchmueller, T.C., and J. DiNardo (2002), "Did community rating induce an adverse selection death spiral? Evidence from New York, Pennsylvania and Connecticut", American Economic Review 92(1): 280–294.

Buchmueller, T.C., and P.J. Feldstein (1997), "The effect of price on switching among health plans", Journal of Health Economics 16:231–247.

Buchmueller, T.C., and G.A. Jensen (1997), "Small group reform in a competitive managed care market: the case of California, 1993 to 1995", Inquiry 34:249–263.

Burchardt, T., J. Hills and C. Propper (1999), Private Welfare and Public Policy (Joseph Rountree Foundation, York, UK).

Cardon, J., and I. Hendel (2001), "Asymmetric information in health care and health insurance markets: evidence from the National Medical Expenditure Survey", Rand Journal of Economics 32:408–427.

Chaloupka, F. (1991), "Rational addictive behavior and cigarette smoking", Journal of Political Economy 99:722–742.

Chaloupka, F., and K.E. Warner (2000), "The economics of smoking", in: A. Culyer and J. Newhouse, eds., Handbook of Health Economics, Vol. 1B (Elsevier, Amsterdam) pp. 1539–1627.

Cherkin, D.C., L. Grothaus and E.H. Wagner (1989), "The effect of office visit copayments on utilization in a health maintenance organization", Medical Care 27(7):669–679.

Chernew, M., and K. Frick (1999), "The impact of managed care on the existence of equilibrium in health insurance markets", Journal of Health Economics 18:573–592.

Chernew, M., K. Frick and C.G. McLaughlin (1997), "The demand for health insurance coverage by low-income workers: can reduced premiums achieve full coverage?" Health Services Research 32:453–470.

Chernick, H.A., M.R. Holmer and D.H. Weinberg (1987), "Tax policy toward health insurance and the demand for medical services", Journal of Health Economics 6:1–25.

Christensen, S., and J. Shinogle (1997), "Effects of supplemental coverage on use of services by Medicare enrollees", Health Care Financing Review 19(1):5–17.

Cochrane, J. (1995), "Time consistent health insurance", Journal of Political Economy 103(3):445–473.

Colle, A.D., and M. Grossman (1978), "Determinants of pediatric care utilization", Journal of Human Resources 13:115–153.

Conrad, D.A., D. Grembowski and P. Milgrom (1985), "Adverse selection within dental insurance markets", in: R.M. Scheffler and L.F. Rossiter, eds., Advances in Health Economics and Health Services Research, Vol. 6 (JAI Press, Greenwich, CT) pp. 171–190.

Cook, P.J., and M. Moore (2000), "Alcohol", in: A. Culyer and J. Newhouse, eds., Handbook of Health Economics, Vol. 1B (Elsevier, Amsterdam) pp. 1629–1673.

Culyer, A., and J.P. Newhouse, eds (2000a), Handbook of Health Economics, Vol. 1A (Elsevier, Amsterdam).

Culyer, A., and J.P. Newhouse, eds (2000b), Handbook of Health Economics, Vol. 1B (Elsevier, Amsterdam).

Currie, J., and J. Gruber (1996a), "Saving babies: the efficacy and cost of recent changes in the Medicaid eligibility of pregnant women", Journal of Political Economy 104:1263–1296.

Currie, J., and J. Gruber (1996b), "Health insurance eligibility, utilization of medical care, and child health", Quarterly Journal of Economics 111:431–466.

Currie, J., and J. Gruber (2001), "Public health insurance and medical treatment: the equalizing effect of the Medicaid expansions", Journal of Public Economics 82(1):63–89.

Cutler, D.M. (1996), "Why don't markets insure long-term risk", Mimeo (Harvard University, Cambridge, MA).

Cutler, D.M. (2000), "Supplementing public insurance coverage with private insurance coverage: implications for medical care systems", Mimeo (Harvard University, Cambridge, MA).

Cutler, D.M. (2002), "Equality, efficiency, and market fundamentals: the dynamics of international medical care reform", Journal of Economic Literature, forthcoming.

Cutler, D.M., and J. Gruber (1996a), "Does public insurance crowd out private insurance?" Quarterly Journal of Economics 111:391–430.

Cutler, D.M., and J. Gruber (1996b), "Medicaid crowd out and the inverse bind: response to editorial", Inquiry 33:9.

Cutler, D.M., and J. Gruber (1996c), "The effect of Medicaid expansions on public insurance, private insurance, and redistribution" American Economic Review 86:378–383.

Cutler, D.M., and J. Horwitz (1999), "Converting hospitals from not-for-profit to for-profit form: why and what effects?" in: D. Cutler, ed., The Changing Hospital Industry: Comparing Not-for-Profit and For-Profit Institutions (University of Chicago Press, Chicago) pp. 45–79.

Cutler, D.M., and R. Johnson (2001), "The birth of the social insurance state", Mimeo (Harvard University, Cambridge, MA).

Cutler, D.M., and M. McClellan (2001), "Is technological change in medicine worth it?" Health Affairs 20:11–29.

Cutler, D.M., and S.J. Reber (1998), "Paying for health insurance: the trade-off between competition and adverse selection", Quarterly Journal of Economics 113:433–466.

Cutler, D.M., and E. Richardson (1997), "Measuring the health of the U.S. population", Brookings Papers on Economic Activity, Microeconomics, pp. 217–271.

Cutler, D.M., and L.M. Sheiner (2000), "Generational aspects of Medicare", American Economic Review, Papers and Proceedings 90:303–307.

Cutler, D.M., and R.J. Zeckhauser (1998), "Adverse selection in health insurance", in: A. Garber, ed., Frontiers in Health Policy Research, Vol. 1 (MIT Press, Cambridge, MA) pp. 1–31.

Cutler, D.M., and R.J. Zeckhauser (2000), "The anatomy of health insurance" in: A. Culyer and J. Newhouse, eds., Handbook of Health Economics, Vol. 1A (Elsevier, Amsterdam) pp. 563–643.

Cutler, D.M., A.M. Epstein, R.G. Frank, R. Hartman, C. King III, J.P. Newhouse, M.B. Rosenthal and E.R. Vigdor (2000), "How good a deal was the Tobacco Settlement: assessing payments to Massachusetts", Journal of Risk and Uncertainty 21:235–261.

Cutler, D.M., J. Gruber, R. Hartman, M.B. Landrum, J.P. Newhouse and M.B. Rosenthal (2002), "The economic impacts of the Tobacco Settlement", Journal of Policy Analysis and Management 21:1–19.

Dafny, L., and J. Gruber (2002), "Does public insurance improve the efficiency of medical care? Medicaid expansions and avoidable hospitalizations", Journal of Public Economics, forthcoming.

Darby, M.R., and E. Karni (1973), "Free competition and the optimal amount of fraud", Journal of Law & Economics 16:67–88.

Davis, K., and L.B. Russell (1972), "The substitution of hospital outpatient care for inpatient care", Review of Economics and Statistics 54(2):109–120.

de Meza, D. (1983), "Health insurance and the demand for medical care", Journal of Health Economics 2(1):47–54.

Deaton, A. (2001), "Relative deprivation, inequality, and mortality", Working Paper 8099 (National Bureau of Economic Research, Cambridge, MA).

Dowd, B., and R. Feldman (1985), "Biased selection in Twin Cities health plans", in: R.M. Scheffler and L.F. Rossiter, eds., Advances in Health Economics and Health Services Research, Vol. 6 (JAI Press, Greenwich, CT) pp. 253-271.

Dowd, B., and R. Feldman (1994), "Premium elasticities of health plan choice", Inquiry 31:438–444.

Dubay, L., and G.M. Kenney (1996), "The effects of Medicaid expansions on insurance coverage of children", The Future of Children 6:152–161.

Dubay, L., and G.M. Kenney (1997), "Did Medicaid expansions for pregnant women crowd out private coverage?" Health Affairs 16:185–193.

Dubay, L., S.A. Norton and M. Moon (1995), "Medicaid expansions for pregnant women and infants: easing hospitals' uncompensated care burdens?" Inquiry 32:332–344.

Duggan, M. (2000), "Hospital ownership and public medical spending", The Quarterly Journal of Economics 115:1343–1373.

Eggers, P.W. (1980), "Risk differential between Medicare beneficiaries enrolled and not enrolled in an HMO", Health Care Financing Review 1:91–99.

Eichner, M.J. (1998), "Incentives, price expectations and medical expenditures: an analysis of claims under employer-provided health insurance", Mimeo (Securities and Exchange Commision).

Ellis, R.P. (1985), "The effect of prior-year health expenditures on health coverage plan choice", in: R.M. Scheffler and L.F. Rossiter, eds., Advances in Health Economics and Health Services Research, Vol. 6 (JAI Press, Greenwich, CT) pp. 127–147.

Ellis, R.P. (1989), "Employee choice of health insurance", Review of Economics and Statistics 71(2): 215–223.

Ettner, S. (1997), "Adverse selection and the purchase of Medigap insurance by the elderly", Journal of Health Economics 16:543–562.

Evans, W.N., J.S. Ringel and D. Stech (1999), "Tobacco taxes and public policy to discourage smoking," in: J. Poterba, ed., Tax Policy and the Economy, Vol. 13 (MIT Press, Cambridge, MA) pp. 1–55.

Farley, P.J., and A.C. Monheit (1985), "Selectivity in the demand for health insurance and health care", in: R.M. Scheffler and L.F. Rossiter, eds., Advances in Health Economics and Health Services Research, Vol. 6 (JAI Press, Greenwich, CT) pp. 231-252.

Feldman, R., and B. Dowd (1991), "Must adverse selection cause premium spirals", Journal of Health Economics 10:350–357.

Feldman, R., M. Finch, B. Dowd and S. Cassou (1989), "The demand for employment-based health insurance plans", Journal of Human Resources 24:115–142.

Feldman, R., B. Dowd, S. Leitz and L.A. Blewett (1997), "The effect of premiums on the small firm's decision to offer health insurance", Journal of Human Resources 32:635–658.

Feldstein, M. (1970), "The rising price of physicians' services", Review of Economics and Statistics 52(2):121–133.

Feldstein, M. (1971), "Hospital cost inflation: a study of nonprofit price dynamics", American Economic Review 60:853–872.

Feldstein, M. (1973), "The welfare loss of excess health insurance", Journal of Political Economy 81:251–280.

Feldstein, M. (1999), "Prefunding Medicare", American Economic Review, Papers and Proceeding 89:222–227.

Feldstein, M., and B. Friedman (1977), "Tax subsidies, the rational demand for insurance and the health care crisis", Journal of Public Economics 7(2):155–178.

Feldstein, P.J. (1964), "General report", Report of the Commission on the Cost of Medical Care, Part 1 (American Medical Association, Chicago).

Finkelstein, A. (2002), "The effect of tax subsidies to employer-provided supplementary health insurance: evidence from Canada", Journal of Public Economics, forthcoming.

Fisher, E., J. Skinner and J. Wennberg (1998), "The efficiency of Medicare", Mimeo (Dartmouth College, Hanover, NH).

Fuchs, V.R. (1996), "Economics, values, and health care reform", American Economic Review 86:1–24.

Fuchs, V.R., and M.J. Kramer (1972), "Determinants of expenditures for physicians' services in the United States, 1948–68", National Bureau of Economic Research Occasional Paper Series 117.

Gentry, W.M., and E. Peress (1994), "Taxes and fringe benefits offered by employers", Working Paper 4764 (National Bureau of Economic Research, Cambridge, MA).

Glaeser, E., and A. Shleifer (2001), "Not-for-profit entrepreneurs", Journal of Public Economics 81: 99–115.

Glantz, S., and W.W. Parmley (1995), "Passive smoking and heart disease: mechanisms and risk", Journal of the American Medical Association 273:1047–1053.

Glied, S. (2000), "Managed care", in: A. Culyer and J. Newhouse, eds., Handbook of Health Economics, Vol. 1A, Chapter 13 (Elsevier, Amsterdam) pp. 708–745.

Globerman, S., and A. Vining (1998), "A policy perspective on 'mixed' health care financial systems of business and economics", Journal of Risk and Insurance 65:57–80.

Gokhale, J., and L.J. Kotlikoff (1999), "Medicare from the perspective of generational accounting", in: A. Redelmeyer and T. Saving, eds., Medicare Reform: Issues and Answers (University of Chicago Press, Chicago) pp. 153–174.

Goldman, F., and M. Grossman (1978), "The demand for pediatric care: an hedonic approach", Journal of Political Economy 86(2):259–280.

Gouveia, M. (1997), "Majority rule and the public provision of a private good", Public Choice 93: 221–244.

Griffith, M., N. Baloff and E.L. Spitznagel (1984), "Utilization patterns of health maintenance organization disenrollees", Medical Care 22(9):827–834.

Grossman, H. (1979), "Adverse selection, dissembling, and competitive equilibrium", The Bell Journal of Economics 10:336–343.

Grossman, M., F.J. Chaloupka and I. Sirtalan (1998), "An empirical analysis of alcohol addiction: results from monitoring the future panels", Economic Inquiry 36:39–48.

Gruber, J. (2000), "Health insurance and the labor market", in: A. Culyer and J. Newhouse, eds., Handbook of Health Economics, Vol, 1A (Elsevier, Amsterdam) pp. 645–706.

Gruber, J. (2002), "Medicaid", in: R. Moffitt, ed., Means Tested Transfer Programs in the United States (University of Chicago Press, Chicago) forthcoming.

Gruber, J., and B. Koszegi (2001), "Is addiction 'rational': theory and evidence", Quarterly Journal of Economics 116:1261–1304.

Gruber, J., and J.M. Poterba (1994), "Tax incentives and the decision to purchase health insurance: evidence from the self-employed", Quarterly Journal of Economics 109:701–733.

Gruber, J., and J.M. Poterba (1996), "Tax subsidies to employer-provided health insurance", in: M. Feldstein and J.M. Poterba, eds., Empirical Foundation of Household Taxation (University of Chicago Press, Chicago) pp. 135–164.

Gruber, J., and A. Yelowitz (1999), "Public health insurance and private savings", Journal of Political Economy 107:1249–1274.

Haas, J.S., S. Udvarhelyi and A.M. Epstein (1993), "The effect of health coverage for uninsured pregnant women on maternal health and the use of cesarean section", Journal of the American Medical Association 270:61–64.

Hall, M. (2000), "The impact of health insurance market reforms on market competition", American Journal of Managed Care 6:57.

Ham, J.C., and L.D. Shore-Sheppard (1999), "The effect of Medicaid expansions for low income children on Medicaid participation and insurance coverage: estimates from the SIPP", Mimeo (Williams College, MA).

Hansmann, H. (1980), "The role of nonprofit enterprise", Yale Law Journal 89:835–901.

Hart, O., A. Shleifer and R. Vishny (1997), "The proper scope of government: theory and an application to prisons", The Quarterly Journal of Economics 112:1127–1161.

Helms, W.D., A.K. Gauthier and D.M. Campion (1992), "Mending the flaws in the small-group market", Health Affairs 11:7–27.

Hing, E., and G.A. Jensen (1999), "Health insurance portability and Accountability Act of 1996: lessons from the States", Medical Care 37:692–705.

Holmer, M.R. (1984), "Tax policy and the demand for health insurance", Journal of Health Economics 3:203–221.

Hubbard, R.G., and K.A. Hassett (1999), "Noncontractible quality and organizational form in the US hospital industry", Mimeo (Columbia University, New York).

Institute of Medicine (1985), Preventing Low Birthweight (Institute of Medicine, Washington, DC).

Jackson-Beeck, M., and J.H. Kleinman (1983), "Evidence for self-selection among health maintenance organization enrollees", Journal of the American Medical Association 250(20):2826–2829.

Jensen, G.A., and M.A. Morrisey (1999), "Small group reform and insurance provision by small firms, 1989–1995", Inquiry 36:176–187.

Joyce, T. (1999), "Impact of augmented prenatal care on birth outcomes of Medicaid recipients in New York City", Journal of Health Economics 18:31–67.

Joyce, T., and R. Kaestner (1996), "The effect of Medicaid income eligibility expansions on abortion", Demography 30:181–192.

Joyce, T., R. Kaestner and F. Kwan (1998), "Is Medicaid pronatalist? Effects of the Medicaid eligibility expansions on abortions and births", Family Planning Perspectives 30:108–113.

Juba, D.A., J.R. Lave and J. Shaddy (1980), "An analysis of the choice of health benefits plans", Inquiry 17:62–71.

Kaestner, R., T. Joyce and A. Racine (2001), "Medicaid eligibility and the incidence of ambulatory care sensitive hospitalizations for children", Social Science and Medicine 52:305–313.

Kaiser Family Foundation, and Health Research and Educational Trust (2000), Employer Health Benefits (Henry J. Kaiser Family Foundation, Washington, DC).

Kapur, K. (2000a), "Labor market implications of state small group health insurance reform", Mimeo (Rand Corporation).

Kapur, K. (2000b), "The impact of the health insurance market on small firm employment", Mimeo (Rand Corporation).

Keenan, P., M. Beeuwkes-Buntin, T. McGuire and J.P. Newhouse (2001), "The prevalence of formal risk adjustment in health plan purchasing", Inquiry 38:245–259.

Kenkel, D.S. (1996), "New estimates of the optimal tax on alcohol", Economic Inquiry 34:296–319.

Kotowitz, Y. (1987), "Moral hazard", in: J. Eatwell, M. Milgate and P. Newman, eds., Allocation, Information, and Markets. The New Palgrave (W.W. Norton, New York) pp. 207–213.

Krueger, A.B., and B.D. Meyer (2002), "Social insurance and labor supply", in: A.J. Auerbach and M. Feldstein, eds., Handbook of Public Economics, Vol. 4, (Elsevier, Amsterdam) Chapter 33, this volume.

Krupnick, A., A. Alberini, M. Cropper, N. Simon, B. O'Brien, R. Goeree and M. Heintzelman (2000), "Age, health, and the willingness to pay for mortality risk reductions: a contingent valuation survey of Ontario residents", Mimeo (Resources for the Future, Washington, DC).

Laibson, D. (1997), "Golden eggs and hyperbolic discounting", Quarterly Journal of Economics 112: 443–477.

Langwell, K.M., and J.P. Hadley (1989), "Evaluation of the Medicare competition demonstrations", Health Care Financing Review 11(2):65–80.

Laux, F.L. (2000), "Addiction as a market failure: using rational addiction results to justify tobacco regulation", Journal of Health Economics 19:421–437.

Leibowitz, A., and M. Chernew (1992), "The firm's demand for health insurance", in: Health Benefits and the Workforce (U.S. Department of Labor, Washington, DC) pp. 77–83.

Long, J.E., and F.A. Scott (1982), "The income tax and nonwage compensation", Review of Economics and Statistics 64(2):211–219.

Long, S.H., R.F. Settle and C.W. Wrightson (1988), "Employee premiums, availability of alternative plans, and HMO disenrollment", Medical Care 26(10):927–938.

Luft, H.S., J.B. Trauner and S.C. Maerki (1985), "Adverse selection in a large, multiple-option health benefits program: a case study of the California public employees' retirement system", in: R.M. Scheffler and L.F. Rossiter, eds., Advances in Health Economics and Health Services Research, Vol. 6 (JAI Press, Greenwich, CT) pp. 197–229.

Manning, W.G., and M.S. Marquis (1996), "Health insurance: the tradeoff between risk pooling and moral hazard", Journal of Health Economics 15(5):609–639.

Manning, W.G., E.B. Keeler, J.P. Newhouse, E.M. Sloss and J. Wasserman (1989), "The taxes of sin. Do smokers and drinkers pay their way?" Journal of the American Medical Association 261:1604–1609.

Manning, W.G., E.B. Keeler, J.P. Newhouse, E.M. Sloss and J. Wasserman (1991), The Costs of Poor Health Habits (Harvard University Press, Cambridge, MA).

Marquis, M.S. (1992), "Adverse selection with a multiple choice among health insurance plans: a simulation analysis", Journal of Health Economics 11(2):129–151.

Marquis, M.S., and S.H. Long (1995), "Worker demand for health insurance in the non-group market", Journal of Health Economics 14:47–63.

Marquis, M.S., and S.H. Long (2001), "To offer or not to offer: the role of price in employers' health insurance decisions", Health Services Research 36.

Marquis, M.S., and C.E. Phelps (1987), "Price elasticity and adverse selection in the demand for supplementary health insurance", Economic Inquiry 25:299–313.

Marsteller, J.A., L.M. Nichols, A. Badawi, B. Kessler, S. Rajan and S. Zuckerman (1998), "Variations in the uninsured: state and county results", Mimeo (Urban Institute, Washington, DC).

McAvinchey, I.D., and A. Yannopoulos (1993), "Elasticity estimates from a dynamic model of interrelated demands for private and public acute health care", Journal of Health Economics 12:171–186.

McGuire, T.G. (1981), "Price and membership in a prepaid group medical practice", Medical Care 19(2):172–183.

Merrill, J., C. Jackson and J. Reuter (1985), "Factors that affect the HMO enrollment decision: a tale of two cities", Inquiry 22:388–395.

Meyer, B.D., and D.T. Rosenbaum (2000), "Medicaid, private health insurance, and the labor supply of single mothers", Mimeo (Northwestern University, Evanston, IL).

Miller, R.H., and H.S. Luft (1997), "Does managed care lead to better or worse quality of care", Health Affairs 16(5):7–25.

Mirrlees, J. (1971), "An exploration in the theory of optimum income taxation", The Review of Economic Studies 38:175–208.

Miyazawa, H. (1977), "The rat race and internal labor markets", Bell Journal of Economics 8:394–418.

Moon, M. (1996), Medicare Now and In The Future (The Urban Institute, Washington, DC).

Morrisey, M.A., G.A. Jensen and R.J. Morlock (1994), "Small employers and the health insurance market", Health Affairs 13:149–161.

Newhouse, J.P. (1992), "Medical care costs: how much welfare loss?" Journal of Economic Perspectives 6:13–29.

Newhouse, J.P., and C.E. Phelps (1974), "Price and income elasticities for medical care services", in: M. Perlman, ed., The Economics of Health and Medical Care, Chapter 9 (Wiley, New York) pp. 140–161.

Newhouse, J.P., and C.E. Phelps (1976), "New estimates of price and income elasticities of medical care services", in: R.N. Rosett, ed., The Role of Health Insurance in the Health Services Sector, Chapter 7 (National Bureau of Economic Research, New York) pp. 261–313.

Newhouse, J.P., and the Insurance Experiment Group (1993), Free for All? Lessons from the RAND Health Insurance Experiment (Harvard University Press, Cambridge, MA).

Newman, P., E. Maibach, K. Dusenbury, M. Kitchman and P. Zupp (1998), "Marketing HMOs to Medicare beneficiaries: do Medicare HMOs target healthy seniors?" Health Affairs 17(4):132–139.

Nyman, J. (1999), "The value of health insurance: the access motive", Journal of Health Economics 18:141–152.

Olekalns, N., and P. Bardsley (1996), "Rational addiction to caffeine: an analysis of coffee consumption", Journal of Political Economy 104:1100–1104.

Orphanides, A., and D. Zervos (1998), "Myopia and addictive behaviour", Economic Journal 108:75–91.

Pauly, M.V. (1968), "The economics of moral hazard: comment", American Economic Review 58: 531–536.

Pauly, M.V. (1974), "Overinsurance and public provision of insurance: the roles of moral hazard and adverse selection", Quarterly Journal of Economics 88:44–54.

Pauly, M.V. (1986), "Taxation, health insurance, and market failure in the medical economy", Journal of Economic Literature 24:629–675.

Pauly, M.V., H. Kunreuther and R. Hirth (1995), "Guaranteed renewability in insurance", Journal of Risk & Uncertainty 10(2):143–156.

Phelps, C.E. (1973), "The demand for health insurance: a theoretical and empirical investigation", RAND Research Paper Series, No. R-1054-OEO.

Phelps, C.E., and J.P. Newhouse (1972a), "Effect of coinsurance: a multivariate analysis", Social Security Bulletin, pp. 20–28.

Phelps, C.E., and J.P. Newhouse (1972b), "Effects of coinsurance on demand for physician services", RAND Research Paper Series No. R-979-OED.

Phelps, C.E., and J.P. Newhouse (1974), "Coinsurance, the price of time, and the demand for medical services", Review of Economics and Statistics 56:334–342.

Piper, J.M., W.A. Ray and M. Griffin (1990), "Effects of Medicaid eligibility expansion on prenatal care and pregnancy outcome in Tennessee", Journal of the American Medical Association 264:2219–2223.

Pogue, T.F., and L.G. Sgontz (1989), "Taxing to control social costs: the case of alcohol", American Economic Review 79:235–243.

Poterba, J.M. (1996), "Government intervention in markets for education and health care: how and why", in: V.R. Fuchs, ed., Individual and Social Responsibility (University of Chicago Press, Chicago) pp. 277–304.

Preston, S. (1996), "American longevity: past, present, and future", Syracuse University Policy Brief No. 7/1996. Distinguished Lecturer in Aging Series, Center for Economic Policy Research Policy Brief (Syracuse University, NY).

Price, J.R., and J.W. Mays (1985), "Biased selection in the Federal Employees Health Benefits Program", Inquiry 22:67–77.

Propper, C., and K. Green (2002), "A larger role for the private sector in health care? A review of the arguments", Journal of Social Policy, forthcoming.

Rask, K.N., and K.J. Rask (2000), "Public insurance substituting for private insurance: new evidence regarding public hospitals, uncompensated care funds, and Medicaid", Journal of Health Economics 19:1–31.

Riley, J.G. (1979), "Informational equilibrium", Econometrica 47:331–359.

Rodgers, J., and K.E. Smith (1996), "Is there biased selection in Medicare HMOs?" Health Policy Economics Group Report (Price Waterhouse LLP, Washington, DC).

Rosenthal, G. (1970), "Price elasticity of demand for short-term general hospital services", in: H.E. Klarman, ed., Empirical Studies in Health Economics (Johns Hopkins Press, Baltimore, MD) pp. 101–117.

Rosett, R.N., and L. Huang (1973), "The effect of health insurance on the demand for medical care", Journal of Political Economy 81:281–305.

Rothschild, M., and J.E. Stiglitz (1976), "Equilibrium in competitive insurance markets: an essay on the economics of imperfect information", Quarterly Journal of Economics 90:629–650.

Royalty, A.B. (2000), "Tax preferences for fringe benefits and workers' eligibility for employer health insurance", Journal of Public Economics 75:209–228.

Royalty, A.B., and N. Solomon (1999), "Health plan choice: price elasticities in a managed competition setting", Journal of Human Resources 34:1–41.

Schoenbaum, M. (1997), "Do smokers understand the mortality effects of smoking? Evidence from the Health and Retirement Survey", American Journal of Public Health 87:755–759.

Scitovsky, A., and N. McCall (1977), "Coinsurance and the demand for physician services: four years later", Social Security Bulletin, pp. 19–27.

Scitovsky, A., and N.M. Snyder (1972), "Effect of coinsurance on use of physician services", Social Security Bulletin, pp. 3–19.

Scitovsky, A., N. McCall and L. Benham (1978), "Factors affecting the choice between two prepaid plans", Medical Care 16(8):660–675.

Shleifer, A. (1998), "State versus private ownership", Journal of Economic Perspectives 12:133–150.

Shore-Sheppard, L.D. (1996), "Stemming the tide? The effect of expanding Medicaid eligibility on health insurance coverage", Mimeo (Princeton University).

Shore-Sheppard, L.D. (2000), "The effect of expanding Medicaid eligibility on the distribution of children's health insurance coverage", Industrial and Labor Relations Review 54:59–77.

Shore-Sheppard, L.D., T.C. Buchmueller and G.A. Jensen (2000), "Medicaid and crowding out of private insurance: a re-examination using firm level data", Journal of Health Economics 19:61–91.

Shoven, J.B., J.O. Sundberg and J.P. Bunker (1989), "The social security cost of smoking", in: D.A. Wise, ed., The Economics of Aging (University of Chicago Press, Chicago) pp. 231–250.

Showalter, M.H. (1999), "Firm behavior in a market with addiction: the case of cigarettes", Journal of Health Economics 18:409–427.

Silverman, E., and J. Skinner (2000), "Are for-profit hospitals really different? Medicare upcoding and market structure", Mimeo (Dartmouth College, Hanover, NH).

Simon, K.I. (2000a), "Adverse selection in health insurance markets: evidence from state small-group health insurance markets", Mimeo (Cornell University, NY).

Simon, K.I. (2000b), "The effect of state insurance regulations on the price and availability of health benefits in small firms", Mimeo (Cornell University, NY).

Sing, M., R. Brown and S.C. Hill (1998), "The consequences of paying Medicare managed care plans their costs", Inquiry 35:210–222.

Sloan, F.A. (2000), "Not-for-profit ownership and hospital behavior", in: A. Culyer and J. Newhouse, eds., Handbook of Health Economics, Vol. 1B (Elsevier, Amsterdam).

Sloan, F.A., and K.W. Adamache (1986), "Taxation and the growth of nonwage compensation", Public Finance Quarterly 14:115–137.

Sloan, F.A., and C.J. Conover (1998), "Effects of state reforms on health insurance coverage of adults", Inquiry 35:280–293.

Spence, A.M. (1978), "Product differentiation and performance in insurance markets", Journal of Public Economics 10:427–447.

Spence, A.M., and R.J. Zeckhauser (1971), "Insurance, information, and individual action", American Economic Review, Papers and Proceedings 61(2):380–387.

Steuerle, C.E., and J.M. Bakija (1997), Retooling Social Security for the 21st Century (Urban Institute Press, Washington, DC).

Sung, H.-Y., T.-W. Hu and T.-E. Keeler (1994), "Cigarette taxation and demand: an empirical model", Contemporary Economic Policy 12:91–100.

Swartz, K., and D.W. Garnick (2000), "Adverse selection and price sensitivity when low-income people have subsidies to purchase health insurance in the private market", Inquiry 37:45–60.

Taylor, A.K., and G.R. Wilensky (1983), "The effect of tax policies on expenditures for private health insurance", in: J. Meyer, ed., Market Reforms in Health Care (American Enterprise Institute, Washington, DC) pp. 15–94.

Thorpe, K.E., A. Hendricks, D. Garnick, K. Donelan and J.P. Newhouse (1992), "Reducing the number of uninsured by subsidizing employment-based health insurance", Journal of the American Medical Association 19:945–948.

Tirole, J. (1988), The Theory of Industrial Organization (MIT Press, Cambridge, MA).

Tolley, G., D.S. Kenkel and R.G. Fabian (1994), Valuing Health for Policy: An Economic Approach (University of Chicago Press, Chicago).

Triplett, J.E. (2001), "What's different about health? Human repair and car repair in national accounts and in national health accounts", in: D. Cutler and E. Berndt, eds., Medical Care Output and Productivity (University of Chicago Press, Chicago) pp. 15–94.

Turner, R.W. (1987), "Are taxes responsible for the growth in fringe benefits?" National Tax Journal 40:205–220.

U.S. Congressional Budget Office (1997), Long-term Budgetary Pressures and Policy Options (Government Printing Office, Washington, DC).

U.S. Department of Health and Human Services (1994), Preventing Tobacco Use Among Young People: A Report of the Surgeon General (Government Printing Office, Washington, DC).

U.S. Environmental Protection Agency (1992), Respiratory Health Effects of Passive Smoking: Lung Cancer and Other Disorders (Government Printing Office, Washington, DC).

U.S. Joint Committee on Taxation (1999), Estimates of Federal Tax Expenditures for the Years 2000–2004 (Government Printing Office, Washington, DC).

U.S. Physician Payment Review Commission (1996), Annual Report to Congress (Government Printing Office, Washington, DC).

van de Ven, W., and R.P. Ellis (2000), "Risk adjustment in competitive health plan markets", in: A. Culyer and J. Newhouse, eds., Handbook of Health Economics, Vol. 1B (Elsevier, Amsterdam) pp. 755–845.

van de Ven, W., and R.C.J.A. van Vliet (1995), "Consumer surplus and adverse selection in competitive health insurance markets: an empirical study", Journal of Health Economics 14(2):149–169.

Viscusi, W.K. (1993), "The value of risks to life and health", Journal of Economic Literature 31: 1912–1946.

Viscusi, W.K. (1994), Smoking: Making the Risky Decision (Oxford University Press, New York).

Viscusi, W.K. (1995), "Cigarette taxation and the social consequences of smoking", in: J. Poterba, ed., Tax Policy and the Economy (MIT Press, Cambridge, MA) pp. 51–101.

Vroman, S., and G. Anderson (1984), "The effect of income taxation on the demand for employer-provided health insurance", Applied Economics 16:33–43.

Waters, T.M., and F.A. Sloan (1995), "Why do people drink? Tests of the rational addiction model", Applied Economics 27:727–736.

Weisbrod, B. (1991), "The health care quadrilemma: an essay on technological change, insurance, quality of care, and cost containment", Journal of Economic Literature 29:523–552.

Weitzman, M.L. (1974), "Prices vs. quantities", Review of Economic Studies 41:477–491.

Welch, W.P. (1986), "The elasticity of demand for health maintenance organizations", Journal of Human Resources 21:252–266.

Welch, W.P. (1989), "Restructuring the Federal Employees Health Benefits Program: the private sector option", Inquiry 26:321–334.

Wilkinson, R. (1996), Unhealthy Societies: The Afflictions of Inequality (Routledge, New York).

Wilson, C. (1977), "A model of insurance markets with incomplete information", Journal of Economic Theory 16:167–207.

Woodbury, S.A. (1983), "Substitution between wage and nonwage benefits", American Economic Review 73:166–182.

Woodbury, S.A., and D.S. Hamermesh (1992), "Taxes, fringe benefits and faculty", Review of Economics and Statistics 74:287–296.

Wrightson, W., J. Genuardi and S. Stephens (1987), "Demographic and utilization characteristics of HMO disenrollees", Group Health Association of America Journal, pp. 23–42.

Yazici, E.Y., and R. Kaestner (1998), "Medicaid expansions and the crowding out of private health insurance", Inquiry 37:23–32.

Yelowitz, A. (1995), "The Medicaid notch, labor supply, and welfare participation: evidence from eligibility expansions", The Quarterly Journal of Economics 110:909–939.

Yelowitz, A. (1998), "Will extending Medicaid to two-parent families encourage marriage?" Journal of Human Resources 33:833–865.

Zeckhauser, R.J. (1970), "Medical insurance: a case study of the tradeoff between risk spreading and appropriate incentives", Journal of Economic Theory 2:10–26.

Zuckerman, S., and S. Rajan (1999), "An alternative approach to measuring the effects of insurance market reforms", Inquiry 36:44–56.

Chapter 32

SOCIAL SECURITY *

MARTIN FELDSTEIN

Harvard University, and NBER

JEFFREY B. LIEBMAN

Harvard University, and NBER

Contents

* The authors are grateful for comments on a previous draft from the participants in a December 2000 conference of authors of other Handbook chapters and from Tony Atkinson, Alan Auerbach, Jeffrey Brown, Raj Chetty, Peter Diamond, Georges de Menil, Douglas Elmendorf, Estelle James, Lawrence Kotlikoff, Jeffrey Miron, Olivia Mitchell, Alicia Munnell, Peter Orszag, David Pattison, Antonio Rangel, Andrew Samwick, Kent Smetters, and Mark Warsharsky. The authors thank Miriam Rittenberg for her cooperation with this project.

Handbook of Public Economics, Volume 4, Edited by A.J. Auerbach and M. Feldstein

Abstract

This chapter reviews the theoretical and empirical issues dealing with Social Security pensions. The first part of the chapter discusses pure pay-as-you-go plans. It considers the effects of introducing such a plan on the present value of consumption, the optimal level of benefits in such plans, and the empirical research on the effects of pay-as-you-go pension systems on labor supply and saving. The second part of the chapter discusses the transition to investment-based systems, analyzing the effect on the present value of consumption of such a transition and considering such issues as the distributional effects and risk associated with such systems.

Keywords

Social Security, pensions, retirement

JEL classification: H55

1. Introduction

As with all social insurance programs, the provision of old age pensions involves a trade-off between protection and distortion. Social Security benefits protect the aged from poverty and, more generally, from a sharp decline in the standard of living that could occur when regular earnings cease. But the provision of benefits that are conditioned on income or employment and the collection of the taxes needed to finance those benefits also create deadweight losses that result from changing the behavior of both the aged and the younger population. The optimal size and character of the Social Security program, therefore, involves a balancing of this protection and distortion just as the level and structure of the income tax system involves a balancing of distortion and distributional considerations.

Although these issues have in principle been around since the first Social Security programs, it is the rapid increase in current and projected budget costs associated with the aging of the population that has generated government interest in Social Security reform around the world. The imminent retirement of a large baby boom generation will cause these costs to accelerate rapidly during the next several decades. The ratio of retirement costs to GDP will then remain high because of the permanent increase in the relative number of retirees in the population. In the United States, the Social Security actuaries estimate that the cost of the Social Security program will rise from about 10% of covered earnings now to 15% of earnings by 2030 and to more than 18% of earnings in 2050 and beyond. This corresponds to an increase from about 4% of GDP now to about 8% of GDP after 2050, an increase that is equivalent to a 20% increase in total current federal government spending and to a 40% increase in the federal personal income tax[1]. The OECD estimates that the costs of maintaining the existing Social Security retirement programs will increase substantially more in most other countries because of differences in program design and projected demographic changes: by 2040 to 14% of GDP in France, 18% of GDP in Germany, and 21% of GDP in Italy [OECD (1998)]. Because of these fiscal pressures, governments around the world are implementing or considering major reforms in the existing Social Security programs, raising important and interesting analytic and policy questions for economists[2].

The taxes needed to support these programs are, of course, in addition to the basic income tax and to other payroll taxes used to finance health care and other

---

[1] The Congressional Budget Office estimates that the combination of Social Security and Medicare will increase from 6.3% of GDP in 1999 to 9.3% of GDP in 2020 and 13.0% of GDP in 2040. See U.S. Congressional Budget Office (2000a,b). More detailed data on Social Security outlays and receipts are presented in the annual reports of the Social Security Trustees. These are also available online at http://www.ssa.gov.

[2] While this chapter touches on the experience in other countries, most of our examples and research findings relate to the United States. For a discussion of some of these issues in the European context, see the articles in the special issue of the *Scandinavian Journal of Economics* on Social Security in the 21st Century that was published in 2000 and the article by Banks and Emmerson (2000). For analysis related to emerging market countries, see James (1998a,b).

government activities and transfers. The political sensitivity to the prospect of a large tax increase has led to discussions in a wide range of countries of ways to slow the growth of future benefits as well as of ways to reduce the future burden of financing benefits by shifting from existing pure pay-as-you-go systems to ones that incorporate prefunding through investment-based components as well. For economists, the fact that the deadweight loss of a tax system increases with the square of the marginal tax rate makes the demographically-driven increases in projected tax rates a reason for more urgent examination of reform possibilities.

In this essay we focus on the cash benefit pension programs for the aged and disabled that are referred to in the United States as the Social Security program or, more technically, as the Old Age, Survivor and Disability Insurance (OASDI) program[3]. There are many parallel issues in the financing of medical care for the aged (the US Medicare program) and of the long-term institutional care provided in nursing homes [Feldstein (1999a)].

We begin with a discussion of the rationale for government provision of old age retirement benefits, provide a brief comment on the historical evolution of current Social Security systems, and then discuss alternative theories of the political economy of Social Security provision in light of the theoretical considerations and historical evidence. The essay is then divided into two parts. The first part deals with the economics of unfunded (i.e., pay-as-you-go) defined-benefit programs of the type that now exist in the United States and most other industrial countries. The second part of the essay deals with the implications of shifting in whole or in part to a prefunded defined-contribution (i.e., investment-based) system as many countries around the world are now doing or contemplating.

2. Government provision of retirement pensions: rationale and evolution

This section considers the rationale for government provision of the type of retirement pensions that are provided by the US Social Security program and comments briefly on the historical evolution of the program and on the theories of political economy that might explain the observed program and its evolution.

2.1. Alternative forms of retirement pensions

There are in principle many ways that a society can provide for the consumption of the older population. In the atomistic life-cycle model, individuals save during their working years and dissave during retirement. This may be institutionalized through

---

[3] The theoretical models that we discuss refer to the more limited program of pension benefits but the numerical values, tax rate projections, and simulations of alternative policies all include survivor and disability benefits as well as the pension benefits.

corporate pension systems that reduce cash wages during working years and provide retirement benefits. Many societies, including the United States before the introduction of Social Security, assume that individuals will work until they are no longer able to do so and will then finance their consumption by a combination of their own saving and payments from their children, often in the form of living with their adult children.

If the government takes a more active role, it can do so by either mandating or subsidizing private accumulation of saving for retirement or it can provide benefits to individuals who are retired or who exceed some threshold age. The United States subsidizes but does not mandate such private saving through tax policies that encourage a combination of corporate pension plans and Individual Retirement Accounts [see Chapter 18 in Volume 3 of this Handbook by Bernheim (2002)]. Other countries mandate that individuals or their employers must contribute to defined-contribution retirement accounts for their old age (e.g., Argentina, Australia, Chile, and Mexico)[4]. In addition, the United States, like most other OECD countries, directly provides retirement benefits through a Social Security program.

Government Social Security can be either means-tested, with benefits depending on the income or assets of the recipient, or it can be a universal program in which benefits do not depend on the recipients' retirement income or assets[5]. In the USA and other OECD countries, the Social Security program is a universal one. Eligibility for benefits depends on the individual's age but not on the individual's financial status[6]. Until recently, benefits in the USA were not paid to individuals who earned more than a threshold amount, a feature that is now restricted to those under age 65 who want to claim early retirement benefits[7].

A useful four-way classification of pension programs divides them by two criteria: defined-contribution vs. defined-benefit and funded (i.e., based on accumulated assets) vs. unfunded (i.e., pay-as-you-go)[8]. All four possibilities exist in practice, with some countries having more than one type of plan for the same individuals at the same

---

[4] See the separate discussions of these countries by Cottani and Demarco (1998), Edey and Simon (1998), Edwards (1998), Budd (1998) and Sales-Sarrapy, Solis-Soberon and Villagomez-Amezua (1998).

[5] "Universal" programs are sometimes defined in a different way to mean that benefits are paid based on residency rather than previous contributions.

[6] The situation in practice is a bit more complicated by the fact that benefits are subject to the income tax and are sometimes supplemented by a means-tested benefit in the Supplemental Security Income Program.

[7] This loss of benefits was partially offset by an increase in benefits when the workers eventually retired.

[8] See Diamond (1998a) and Geanakoplos, Mitchell and Zeldes (1998) for wideranging discussions of distinctions among and alternative combinations of defined-benefit and defined-contribution programs and of the combinations of funded and unfunded programs. Lindbeck (2002) discusses a richer classification of pension programs based on the response of benefits and of taxes to uncertain events (like demographic changes and changes in wage growth). Lindbeck and Persson (2000) emphasize a four way classification based on funded vs. unfunded and on actuarial vs. non-actuarial that is closer to the four way classification used in the current chapter.

time. Several countries are moving from unfunded defined-benefit plans to unfunded defined-contribution plans or to a mixture of the unfunded defined-benefit plans and funded defined-contribution plans.

In characterizing these four possibilities, it is useful to begin with *funded defined-contribution plans*. In the United States, most *private* pension plans are of this type. In such plans, employees have individual investment accounts to which they and/or their employer make periodic deposits. The rules of the plan define the maximum amount of contribution and the extent of employer matching. When these individuals reach retirement age, they make withdrawals or receive annuity payments based upon the value of the assets in their accounts, which reflect both the original contributions and the accumulated investment return. Several countries, including Argentina, Australia, Chile, and Mexico have adopted this framework for their public Social Security program, requiring employees and/or employers to deposit funds that are invested in a range of private and public securities.

Many older US corporate pension plans are *funded defined-benefit plans*. In such plans, companies accumulate funds in pension accounts (that are legally separated from the companies' other assets) and pay benefits to retirees that reflect the number of years that an employee has been with the company and the level of the employee's earnings in his or her pre-retirement years. These are defined-benefit plans in the sense that the rules of the plan define the benefits that an employee will receive in a way that is independent of the actual investment performance of the assets that have been set aside for this purpose. The company is responsible for providing the funds to meet these benefits and must do so in a way that causes the pension accounts to have assets approximately equal to the actuarial present value of the company's pension liabilities. Most state government pension plans in the United States are of this form.

Although the US Social Security program has accumulated some surpluses in an accounting trust fund, the US plan is more accurately described as an *unfunded defined-benefit program*. This was not always so. When the US Social Security system was created, it was designed to be a funded system to protect future retirees from possible changes in political support. Weaver (1982) quotes then Treasury Secretary Morgenthau's testimony to the Ways and Means Committee of the Congress in 1935:

> There are some who believe that we can meet this problem as we go by borrowing from the future to pay the costs. .... They would place all confidence in the taxing power of the future to meet the needs as they arise. We do not share this view. We cannot safely expect future generations to continue to divert such large sums to the support of the aged unless we lighten the burden upon the future in other directions. .... We desire to establish this system on such firm foundations that it can be continued indefinitely in the future.

However, opponents of funding, most notably Senator Arthur Vandenberg, argued that a government-controlled funded system would (1) lead the fund to be invested in inefficient social investments, (2) eliminate the public debt thereby weakening financial markets, (3) encourage the government to spend more money, and (4) lead to increases in Social Security benefits[9]. In 1939 Secretary Morgenthau dropped his support for a fully-funded system, arguing instead that the system should maintain sufficient funding to pay roughly three years worth of benefits. In the early 1940s, Congress passed a series of bills postponing scheduled increases in the payroll tax, effectively turning the system into a pay-as-you-go system. According to Schieber and Shoven (1999), President Roosevelt continued to favor a fully-funded system. The payroll tax postponement in the Revenue Act of 1943 passed over a rare Roosevelt veto, and the postponement in the Revenue Act of 1945 passed after Roosevelt's death[10].

Thus, the system became a pay-as-you-go program with assets substantially less than its actuarial liabilities. The Social Security (OASDI) Trust Funds at the end of fiscal year 1999 had assets of $855 billion while the present value of the promised benefits is an estimated $9 trillion [Goss (1999)][11].

Finally, Sweden and Italy have recently switched from unfunded defined-benefit programs to unfunded defined-contribution programs. These programs, also known as "notional defined-contribution plans", credit individuals' accounts with the taxes that they and their employers pay and then accumulate these sums with an implicit rate of interest. Since there are no real investments, the implicit rate of interest is just a "notional" amount. When individuals reach retirement age, they can draw an annuity based on this accumulation, again reflecting the notional rate of interest. The effects of and rationale for such notional defined-contribution plans are discussed below.

In the United States and other countries with unfunded defined-benefit plans, individuals' benefits are positively related to the past earnings of those individuals. In the US, benefits rise less than proportionately with the past level of earnings; additional benefits are paid for current and surviving spouses and for dependent children. Many countries combine a flat or means-tested benefit that is independent of past earnings with an earnings related portion that is proportional to past earnings and years of contribution.

2.2. The rationale for government provision

What then is the rationale for a government pension program in general and, in particular, for a pay-as-you-go Social Security program that provides universal benefits that increase with past earnings and with the number of dependents? Why is there

---

[9] The material in this paragraph is drawn from Schieber and Shoven (1999).

[10] One other aspect of the early history of the US Social Security system presaged current debates. Because benefits are determined by lifetime earnings, the US Social Security system requires the Social Security Administration to keep track of lifetime earnings histories for each worker. According to Rodgers (1998, p. 445), "The editors of the London *Economist* thought the idea of individually tracked lifetime accounts so extraordinarily expensive and administratively top heavy that it could not conceivably survive ..."

[11] The economic significance of the trust fund is discussed in Section 3.3.

any government program and why does it take this form instead of one of the other possibilities described above? [12]

The traditional rationale for government intervention in private markets is the existence of significant externalities or other market imperfections. Although it is difficult to identify any externalities that would justify a government role, the historic absence of a market for real annuities does imply a potential role for the government. The absence of such a market reflects not only the typical asymmetric information problem of any insurance market [Rothschild and Stiglitz (1970, 1971, 1976)] but also the difficulty of the private market to provide a real (i.e., inflation adjusted) annuity in the absence of a real security in which to invest. The relatively recent creation of US Treasury Inflation-Indexed Securities (i.e., US government bonds with maturities of up to 30 years with both principal and interest payments fully adjusted for changes in the price level) now provides the opportunity to create such real annuities and at least one US company (TIAA–CREF) has introduced a product based exclusively on investment in such securities. Although the asymmetry of information between the annuity buyer and the insurance company continues to be a problem in creating actuarially fair products for those interested in buying annuities, Brown, Mitchell and Poterba (2000) show that, for the average annuity purchaser today, the expected annuity payments are between 90 and 95% of his premium. A government rule requiring all individuals to annuitize the accumulated assets in a personal retirement account would eliminate the self-selection problem and allow all individuals to purchase annuities with payout rates similar to these [13].

The three most common rationales for the existing Social Security program are: (1) paternalism to counter individual life-cycle myopia; (2) the avoidance of counterproductive "gaming" of the welfare system by the aged; and (3) a desire to redistribute income among individuals based on lifetime earnings rather than a single year's income [14].

Although most American families accumulate only very small amounts of financial assets [15], it is not clear whether this is a reflection of inadequate life-cycle planning or

---

[12] See Diamond (1977) for a general discussion of the rationale for Social Security.

[13] Brown, Mitchell and Poterba (2000) also show that for the average person (i.e., not the average annuity buyer) the annuity load factor would now be between 15% and 20%. Comparing this with the experience of actual buyers shows that adverse selection is responsible for about two-thirds of this gap between premiums and expected payments. Mandatory annuitization on the same terms for everyone would still redistribute based on differences in life expectancy.

[14] A common reason for government intervention in other markets is to foster the consumption of some particular kind of good or service like education, food, or health care. But since Social Security pensions are simple cash payments, the program cannot be justified as a politically expressed desire to encourage a particular form of consumption.

[15] The median financial assets of households with heads age 51 to 61 in 1992 was only $14 500 (authors' calculations from the Health and Retirement Survey). These financial assets include individual retirement accounts, but exclude Social Security wealth and private pensions (whether defined-benefit or defined-contribution).

of the displacement of personal financial asset accumulation by the anticipated benefits of Social Security and private pensions. Nevertheless, common observation suggests that there are many individuals who would not plan adequately for their old age and who would, in the absence of some form of government program, find themselves in poverty or at least with a substantially reduced consumption relative to their pre-retirement years. But even if the existence of such myopia is accepted as the reason for government action, why should it take the form of the government provision of benefits that are both universally provided and positively related to past earnings? The government might instead provide a universal common benefit (rather than one that is greater for individuals with higher preretirement incomes) or a uniform means-tested benefit.

The case for a benefit that increases with preretirement income can be made in terms of the greater personal distress that would result from a larger fall in income, or, equivalently, of a utility function structure that makes the marginal utility of retirement benefits higher for individuals with higher preretirement income[16]. The case against a means-tested benefit is that it might encourage some lower-income individuals to intentionally undersave during their working years so that, by gaming the system in this way, they will qualify for the means-tested benefit[17]. Neither of these first two reasons is necessarily compelling but they are sufficient to indicate why such a program might be appropriate; further analysis of these issues is summarized in Section 4.3 below.

A second rationale for Social Security is to prevent free-riding in the presence of altruism [Buchanan (1975), Kotlikoff (1987), Lindbeck and Weibull (1988)]. Specifically, if individuals know that other members of the society are altruistic and will provide for them if they reach old age without resources, then there will be an incentive for people to undersave and take advantage of the good will of others. This free-riding leads to an inefficient outcome that can potentially be ameliorated with a compulsory program of old age assistance.

Even if these considerations lead to the conclusion that there should be a universal government pension that is positively related to preretirement earnings, it is not clear why this should be done as a pay-as-you-go program rather than a funded program or, alternatively, by mandating that individuals save for their own old age.

Before looking at the basic economics of the pay-as-you-go program more explicitly, we comment briefly on some of the political economy arguments that have been

---

[16] Consider a 2-period model in which individuals i and j work during the first period and retire in the second and in which each individual has an identical multiplicative utility function of the form $U_i = C_{i,1}^a C_{i,2}^{1-a}$. If (1) the first-period consumption of each individual is already given, (2) the individuals are completely myopic and therefore save nothing, and (3) the policy goal is to maximize $U_i + U_j$ subject to $C_{i,2} + C_{j,2} = B$ (the Social Security budget constraint), then the optimal retirement benefits are proportional to the first-period consumption: $C_{i,2}/C_{j,2} = C_{i,1}/C_{j,1}$.

[17] Whether a means-tested program is preferable to a universal program depends on the number of low-income people who would be hurt relative to a universal program and the number of higher-income people who would receive no benefits under a means-tested program. See Feldstein (1987b) and Section 4.3 below.

advanced to explain the current structure of Social Security programs and review some
of the history of the actual programs.

2.3. Historical evolution [18]

Government administered old-age pensions for private sector employees were introduced by Germany in 1889, concluding a decade that had seen Germany pioneer
sickness and accident insurance for industrial workers as well. The distinctive feature
of the German approach to social insurance was that the programs were compulsory
and contributory. In the case of old-age pensions, both employers and workers were
required to make contributions [19], and benefits were paid out to disabled workers and to
former workers who survived beyond the age of seventy. While the immediate political
impetus for creating these programs was Chancellor Otto von Bismarck's desire to
head off the incipient socialist movement and solidify urban working-class loyalty
to the regime, the idea of insuring the risks faced by workers in industrial society
had been spreading for some time. In particular, the German system had antecedents
in the numerous mutual assistance societies self-organized by workers and guilds,
Napoleon III's state-subsidized banks that provided voluntary disability insurance and
old-age annuities, and compulsory insurance pools in high-risk industries such as
mining and maritime.

   While the German model of social insurance was discussed extensively around the
world (and Germany heavily promoted the concept), its spread was quite gradual.
By 1910, the only country that had fully adopted German-style compulsory and
contributory systems was Austria [20]. Meanwhile, an alternative approach for providing
income for the elderly, general-revenue financed means-tested old age pensions, was
adopted in Denmark in 1891, New Zealand in 1898 and in Australia and Britain
in 1908 [21]. The British system provided benefits to citizens over seventy who were
poor and could pass a character test. Benefits were higher than under the German
system and reached three times as many persons [22].

   Old-age pensions were adopted at a relatively late date in North America. Canada
introduced a non-contributory means-tested system in 1927. In the USA, state
governments enacted means-tested old-age pensions funded out of general revenues
during the 1920s, particularly after the stock market crash of 1929. By 1934, 28 states
had old-age pensions and not one was contributory [Moss (2002)]. The US federal
social insurance system was enacted in a single piece of legislation in the midst of the

---

[18] This section draws heavily on Rodgers (1998), Ritter (1986), and Flora and Alber (1981).

[19] The government made some modest contributions from general revenues as well.

[20] Austria's initial social insurance system did not include old-age benefits.

[21] Britain did adopt the contributory approach for its health insurance system in the 1911 National
Insurance Act. Between World War I and World War II, contributory old-age pension systems were
adopted in Belgium, Italy and France.

[22] Rodgers (1998, p. 230).

Great Depression. The Social Security Act of 1935 created Unemployment Insurance, Aid to Dependent Children, Old Age Insurance (OAI), and Old Age Assistance (OAA). Old Age Insurance, a German-style compulsory contributory system, is what gradually evolved into Old Age Survivors and Disability Insurance, the program that Americans now think of as "Social Security". Old Age Assistance, a UK-style means-tested system (jointly funded by the federal and state governments), was replaced by Supplemental Security Income in the early 1970s[23]. Until the 1950s, benefits under OAA were larger than those from OAI, and it has been argued that it was only because the 1935 Act included OAA (which provided for immediate benefits to retirees in the midst of the depression) that it was possible to enact OAI [Costa (1998)].

While the emergence of old-age pensions in the late 19th century and the first half of the 20th century can be attributed to economic factors such as industrialization, urbanization, and increases in life expectancy, and to political developments such as the formation of nation states and their transformation into mass democracies, researchers have generally been unable to explain the order and extent to which countries adopted social insurance using variation in these economic and political factors. As Flora and Heidenheimer (1981) note, "the most democratic and capitalist of the European societies were not the first to develop the institutions and policies of the modern welfare state". Thus the empirical work in Flora and Alber (1981) finds little relationship between the adoption of social insurance programs and industrialization, urbanization, working class participation in politics, or suffrage rates in Western Europe. However, they do find that constitutional-dualistic monarchies were more likely to introduce social insurance systems than were parliamentary democracies. Cutler and Johnson (2000) estimate hazard models for the introduction of old age insurance and health insurance programs, and tentatively conclude that richer countries are more likely to institute minimum systems designed primarily to alleviate poverty while poorer countries are more likely to introduce universal insurance systems. They also find that autocratic countries are more likely to introduce insurance systems.

While nearly all industrial economies had some sort of old-age pension by the time of World War II, many of these systems were quite limited in both the share of the population they covered and the level of benefits that they provided. The 35-years following the war saw tremendous expansions in coverage and benefits levels in most countries, and a number of countries added contributory systems to their pre-war means-tested systems. In the USA, the original OAI system was amended in 1939, before the first benefits were paid out, to add benefits for dependents of retired workers and surviving dependents of deceased workers. Disability benefits were introduced in 1956 and expanded to dependents of disabled workers in 1958. Automatic cost of living increases in benefits were introduced in 1972, following a series of ad hoc increases in benefit levels. These expansions in benefits resulted in total OASDI payroll tax rates of

---

[23] For histories of the US system see Lubove (1968), Weaver (1982), Miron and Weil (1997), Costa (1998), Schieber and Shoven (1999), and Moss (2002).

12.4% compared to the 6% long-run rates that had been scheduled under the 1935 and 1939 Acts. Over this time period, the share of the workforce that was covered by the system expanded greatly, from 43% in 1935 (the original system excluded agricultural workers, government workers, railroad workers, and the self-employed) to 96% today (some state and local government workers are still not part of the system).

The expansions in old-age pensions and in other social insurance programs accounts for a large share of the rapid growth in government spending as a share of GDP that occurred in most industrial democracies after World War II. For example, between 1953 and 1974 government spending in OECD countries grew from an average of 29% of GDP to an average of 39% of GDP, while transfer spending (of which Social Security is a major part) increased from 12% of GDP to 19% of GDP [Peltzman (1980)].

2.4. Political economy explanations of the existing Social Security programs

The historical evolution of Social Security programs shows that while the economic rationales for government provision can explain in part the emergence of such systems as industrialization took hold, it is clear that political factors have played an important role in the development of these programs. A number of economists have studied the political economy of Social Security with the aim of explaining why Social Security systems take the form that they do. In the process, these researchers have developed some additional efficiency arguments for government provision of Social Security beyond the classic ones discussed in Section 2.2.

One strand of this literature has tried to explain why Social Security expenditures are as large as they are given that the elderly are only a minority of the population. Possible explanations include that Social Security provides concentrated benefits and diffuse costs[24], that the elderly and older workers form a coalition [Browning (1975)], or that the elderly and the poor form a coalition in support of a redistributive Social Security system [Tabellini (1990)][25]. Peltzman (1980) argues that the emergence of a relatively homogenous educated middle class voting block led to the large rise in transfer spending in the second half of the 20th century. He also noted that these demographic trends had crested and accurately predicted the deceleration of the growth in government after 1980. More recently, Mulligan and Sala-i-Martin (1999a) suggest that time and single-mindedness are important political resources and that the elderly's large endowment of these two resources can explain a number of features of Social Security systems. Bohn (1999) shows that for the voter of median age, the US Social Security system has a positive net present value, explaining why the system is politically viable even as rates of return have fallen.

---

[24] As Tabellini (1990) points out, the costs per taxpayer of Social Security are so large that it is hard to see the concentrated-benefit diffuse costs argument as fitting in this case.

[25] Historically, all of the generations alive at the introduction of the US Social Security program were net beneficiaries because they were the "initial generations" in a pay-as-you-go system with subsequent program expansions.

Becker and Murphy (1988) attribute the existence of Social Security to an intergenerational compact between the old and the young. Specifically, parents provide investments in the human capital of their children and then receive a return on this investment in the form of Social Security benefits when the children are working and the parents are retired. Because children cannot be parties to a legally enforceable contract, the government needs to provide a mechanism for these transfers to occur. Rangel (2002) shows that in a majority rule system, the existence of programs like Social Security which transfer resources from the young to the old can give present generations the incentive to make investments that will primarily benefit future generations.

In a series of recent papers, Mulligan and Sala-i-Martin note that most existing Social Security systems create incentives for workers to leave the labor force when they reach the age of eligibility for Social Security benefits. They show that most existing positive theories of Social Security have difficulty explaining this feature of Social Security systems [Mulligan and Sala-i-Martin (1999b,c)]. Sala-i-Martin (1996) suggests one possible explanation for this feature: that there are positive externalities in the average stock of human capital and that therefore buying the elderly out of the labor force increases aggregate output[26].

3. The basic economics of pay-as-you-go Social Security

Although pay-as-you-go Social Security has existed since the days of Bismarck, it was Paul Samuelson's classic 1958 paper that first helped the economics profession to understand the basic economics of the pay-as-you-go system. In particular, it showed how a pay-as-you-go system produces an implicit rate of return equal to the rate of growth of the tax base. Following Samuelson, consider an overlapping generations model in which identical individuals each live for two periods, working a fixed amount in the first period and retiring in the second period. The number of individuals grows at the rate of n per period. There is no capital good in the economy; indeed, all products must be consumed in the period in which they are produced. In such an economy, individuals are not able to save privately for their old age. In a pay-as-you-go Social Security program each working generation transfers a fraction θ of its earnings to the concurrent retirees. Samuelson showed that such an arrangement gives each generation an implicit rate of return equal to the rate of population growth, a rate that Samuelson labeled the biological rate of interest.

To see why this occurs, let the number of workers at time t be L_t and the constant wage rate be w. The number of workers grows according to $L_{t+1} = (1 + n)L_t$. The aggregate tax paid by the working generation at time t is $T_t = \theta w L_t$. The benefit that this working generation will receive when it retires, B_{t+1}, is equal in a pay-as-you-go

---

[26] See Mulligan (2000a,b) for further analyses of this issue.

system to the tax paid by the next generation, $B_{t+1} = T_{t+1} = \theta w L_{t+1}$. Thus, the ratio of the benefits received by the retirees to the taxes that those retirees paid when they were working is $B_{t+1}/T_t = T_{t+1}/T_t = L_{t+1}/L_t = 1 + n$.

Social Security is a desirable policy in this economy because it permits individuals to retire and consume despite the lack of any nonperishable good in the economy[27]. If technological progress causes the wage rate in the economy to rise at a rate of g, i.e., $w_{t+1} = (1 + g)w_t$, the Samuelson logic implies an implicit rate of return of approximately $n + g$ since $B_{t+1}/T_t = T_{t+1}/T_t = \theta w_{t+1}L_{t+1}/\theta w_t L_t = (1 + g)(1 + n)$.

In addition to providing a positive implicit rate of return for each generation of workers on the Social Security taxes that they have paid, the pay-as-you-go system also provides a one-time windfall to the initial generation of retirees that receives the initial benefit without having paid any tax during its own working years. Thus, in the absence of any durable capital asset (or fiat money), the introduction of a pay-as-you-go Social Security system is a pareto improvement.

3.1. The present value consumption loss caused by pay-as-you-go Social Security

The Samuelson-type calculations are also valid in an economy with a capital stock, but the Pareto-improving nature of Social Security no longer holds. The initial generations gain but future generations lose. More specifically, the initial generation of retirees receives a windfall of T_0 and each generation of workers receives an implicit rate of return of $(1 + n)(1 + g) - 1 = \gamma$ on the tax T_t that it pays. However, the existence of a capital stock implies that individuals could instead finance their retirement by saving and investing in actual capital goods where they would earn a real return of ρ[28]. In a dynamically efficient economy, the real rate of return ρ must exceed the rate of growth of the economy, γ [Cass (1965)]. Thus, each working generation incurs a loss because it receives a return γ on its Social Security taxes that is less than the return ρ that it would earn by investing those funds in the capital stock.

In a simple economy that is operating at a first-best equilibrium the present value of the consumption losses of all current and future working generations is just balanced by the windfall consumption that the initial retirees receive [Feldstein (1995a,c, 1998c), Murphy and Welch (1998)]. To see this, note that the initial retirees receive

---

[27] Samuelson (1958) notes that the same ability of retirees to consume would also be achieved by the creation of a fixed stock of fiat money. Workers could exchange a fraction of their output for the money held by retirees. When the working generation retires, it could exchange its money holding for some of the output of the next generation. With a fixed amount of fiat money and a growing population, the money would be exchanged for more output than the retirees had paid when they were working, yielding the same rate of return of $1 + n$ on this money. Stated differently, with a fixed amount of money and a growing output, the price level would decline at a rate of $1 + n$, implying a real rate of return of $1 + n$ on the money balances.

[28] Diamond's justifiably famous 1965 paper extends the earlier Samuelson OLG model to include capital accumulation in this way.

a windfall of $T_0 = \theta w_0 L_0$. Each generation of workers pays Social Security tax of $\theta w_t L_t$ and receives a return of $\gamma \theta w_t L_t$. If those funds had instead been invested in the capital stock, the individual would have received a return of $\rho \theta w_t L_t$. Thus, the workers of generation t incur an income loss of $(\rho - \gamma) \theta w_t L_t$. This loss occurs during the retirement period of the individual's life; its present value as of the initial working period of the generation is $(\rho - \gamma) \theta w_t L_t / (1 + \rho)$. Since wages grow at g per period and the labor force grows at n, this generation's loss is equal to $(\rho - \gamma) \theta (1 + \rho)^{-1} w_0 L_0 (1 + \gamma)^t$. The present value of all of these losses (summed from $t = 0$ to infinity) is

$$\frac{\rho - \gamma}{1 + \rho} \theta w_0 L_0 \sum_{t=0}^{t=\infty} \frac{(1 + \gamma)^t}{(1 + \rho)^t} = \theta w_0 L_0 = T_0,$$

exactly equal to the windfall received by the first generation of retirees whose benefits are financed by the initial tax T_0. This demonstration that the introduction of a pay-as-you-go Social Security program induces no present value loss of consumption depends on very strong implicit assumptions that are generally not made explicit by those who assert the lack of a loss in present value: (1) the rate of return that the individual would receive on savings is equal to the marginal product of capital, i.e., there are no capital income taxes; (2) the marginal product of capital is the appropriate rate for the intergenerational discounting of consumption; and (3) the supply of labor is fixed so that the low rate of return on the Social Security tax paid by all working generations induces no deadweight loss.

To see the importance of these assumptions[29], begin by maintaining the assumption that the supply of labor is fixed. Let the real net rate of return that individuals receive on their saving be $r_n < \rho$, the difference reflecting the wedge that corporate and personal taxes on capital income place between the marginal product of capital and the net return to savers. Let the appropriate rate of discount for aggregating consumption across generations be denoted by δ. It might be argued that this is the same as the net return that individuals face (r_n). Alternatively, it can be argued that this social discount rate for aggregating consumption over generations should not be based on the preferences of existing individuals and the rate r_n at which they discount consumption within their own lives but that it should be equal to the rate at which the marginal utility of consumption declines between generations because of the growth of per capita consumption[30].

Consider now the present value loss to a representative member of the first generation of workers. This individual again pays a Social Security tax of θw_0. Let this

---

[29] Feldstein (1995a, 1995c, 1998c). For an earlier discussion of these issues see Feldstein (1987a).

[30] The social rate of discounting consumption over different generations might also reflect a pure time preference. If consumption grows at rate g and the elasticity of the marginal utility function is ϵ, then $\delta = \epsilon g + \eta$, where η is the pure time preference rate at which utility is discounted.

tax reduce the individual's saving by some fractional amount of this: $s\theta w_0$. Thus, first period consumption falls by $(1 - s)\,\theta w_0$. In the retirement period, the foregone saving would have produced $(1 + \rho)\,s\theta w_0$ [31]. With the unfunded Social Security program, the retirees instead receive the Social Security benefits of $(1 + \gamma)\,\theta w_0$. Thus, the change in the present value of consumption for the first cohort of workers due to the introduction of the pay-as-you-go program is

$$-(1 - s)\,\theta w_0 - \{(1 + \rho)\,s\theta w_0 - (1 + \gamma)\,\theta w_0\}\,(1 + r_n)^{-1}.$$

This simplifies to

$$-\theta w_0\,(1 + r_n)^{-1}\,\{(r_n - \gamma) + (\rho - r_n)\,s\}.$$

Note that in the first best case in which there is no tax wedge on capital income ($\rho = r_n$), this expression simplifies to $-(\rho - \gamma)\theta w_0/(1 + \rho)$. In this case the amount of the pay-as-you-go tax that would otherwise have been saved (s) is irrelevant because that saving would earn a return at rate ρ and that return would be discounted by the same rate. The saving matters when $\rho > r_n$ and implies a loss of present value consumption for a member of the first generation of workers equal to $(\rho - r_n)s\theta w_0(1 + r_n)^{-1}$. The other part of the present value consumption loss for this individual reflects the difference between the net-of-tax return and the implicit Social Security return. This is the present value consumption change for a single individual in the first generation of workers. The aggregate consumption change for that generation is thus

$$-\theta w_0 L_0\,(1 + r_n)^{-1}\,\{(r_n - \gamma) + (\rho - r_n)\,s\}$$

and the corresponding aggregate change for any generation t is

$$-\theta w_0 L_0\,(1 + r_n)^{-1}\,\{(r_n - \gamma) + (\rho - r_n)\,s\}\,(1 + \gamma)^t.$$

Discounting this over all generations with a discount rate δ implies a total present value consumption loss of

$$T_0\,(1 + r_n)^{-1}\,\{(r_n - \gamma) + (\rho - r_n)\,s\}\,(1 + \delta)(\delta - \gamma)^{-1}.$$

In the special case in which there is no tax wedge ($\rho = r_n$), this simplifies to

$$T_0(1 + \rho)^{-1}(\rho - \gamma)(1 + \delta)(\delta - \gamma)^{-1},$$

which exceeds T_0 if $\rho > \delta$, i.e., if the marginal product of capital exceeds the social discount rate. The condition $\rho > \delta$ implies that there is less than the optimal

---

[31] We simplify by assuming that this entire amount would have accrued to the retiree generation; a portion of this would be in the form of the net return on saving $(1 + r_n)s\theta w_0$ and the remainder would be in the form of additional tax receipts of the government $(\rho - r_n)s\theta w_0$ that could be used to reduce other taxes of this retiree generation or to provide explicit benefits to them. Individuals nevertheless discount at r_n because for each individual the return on that individual's incremental saving is just r_n. If individuals are myopic it would be more appropriate to assume that $r_n = \delta$, i.e., to substitute the social rate of discount of consumption for the private rate.

amount of capital in the economy (because of a suboptimal tax system or because Social Security benefits crowd out private saving, as discussed below). Only if the appropriate intergenerational discount rate is taken to be the marginal product of capital ($\delta = \rho = r_n$) does the loss to all working generations collapse to T_0 and therefore is equal to the windfall of the initial generation. More generally, however, with $(\rho - r_n)s > 0$ and/or $(r_n - \gamma) > 0$, there is a net present value loss.

To get a sense of the magnitude of the net loss in the more general case, consider an example in which the social discount rate equals the net-of-tax return to savers ($\delta = r_n$). This simplifies the expression for the loss to $T_0\left\{(r_n - \gamma) + (\rho - r_n)s\right\}(r_n - \gamma)^{-1} = T_0\left\{1 + (\rho - r_n)s(r_n - \gamma)^{-1}\right\}$. It is clear that since personal and corporate taxes make $\rho - r_n > 0$, this loss is greater than the initial windfall benefit of T_0 [32].

To evaluate the loss, assume that the annual marginal product of capital is 8.5% and the capital tax wedge is 50%, implying an annual net of tax return to individuals of 4.25%. Putting specific numerical values on these terms requires recognizing that the time period in this derivation is not a year but a generation. Taking that to be 30 years implies, for example, that $r_n = (1.0425)^{30} - 1 = 2.49$. Similarly $\rho = 10.56$ and, if the annual rate of real growth is 3%, $\gamma = 1.43$. Substituting these values into the expression implies a present value loss to current and all future working generations of $T_0\left\{1 + 7.61s\right\}$. If individuals would have saved even one-seventh of the money that they pay in Social Security taxes (i.e., if $s \geqslant \frac{1}{7}$), the present value loss of consumption is more than double the value of the windfall gain to the initial retiree generation.

Note that in thinking about the application of this to any actual Social Security program, the present value of the consumption losses reflect not only the initial creation of the program but also the subsequent program expansions. Each such expansion involves a windfall gain to those who are then retired or near retirement and losses to all current and future taxpayers. This is important in the United States because the program began with a combined employer–employee tax rate of only 2.0% and then expanded over the years to the current 12.4%.

3.2. The deadweight loss caused by the distortion of labor supply and of taxable labor income

The analysis of Section 3.1 assumed that the supply of labor during preretirement years is arbitrarily fixed and does not respond to the imposition of the payroll tax. A more realistic analysis would recognize that individuals do modify their behavior in response to the marginal tax rate on labor income. This induces a deadweight loss for each generation of taxpayers. Unlike the calculation in Section 3.1, there is no offsetting gain for the initial generation of retirees.

---

[32] Note that $(r_n - \gamma) > 0$ since r_n is equal to the social discount rate in this example. If the discount rate were less than the growth rate γ, the series of consumption losses would not converge to a finite present value.

The relevant behavior includes both labor supply and the form of compensation that individuals receive. Labor supply for this purpose can be broadly defined as any change that alters the amount of taxable labor income, including not only the number of hours worked per year, but such other dimensions of labor supply as effort, training, location, risk taking, etc.. A labor income tax also distorts the form in which individuals are compensated, inducing the substitution of fringe benefits and nicer working conditions for the cash income that individuals would otherwise prefer. Both distortions create deadweight losses. The combined deadweight loss can be measured by the elasticity of taxable labor income with respect to the net-of-tax marginal rate (i.e., one minus the marginal tax rate on labor income); see Feldstein (1999b).

In the simple case in which there are no distorting capital income taxes (i.e., in which $\rho = r_n$) and in which forward-looking individuals correctly perceive the link between their Social Security taxes and benefits, the effective Social Security tax rate on the individual employee depends on both the statutory rate (θ) and the gap between the marginal product of capital and the pay-as-you-go rate of return as discounted to the time that the tax is paid $(\rho - \gamma)(1 + \rho)^{-1}$. If the pay-as-you-go implicit rate of return were equal to the marginal product of capital ($\rho = \gamma$) there would be no deadweight loss of the payroll tax, regardless of the statutory payroll tax rate (θ) because individuals would receive in Social Security benefits the same return that they would have obtained by investing those funds [33,34].

In fact, however, ρ is greater than γ and individuals appropriately regard the payroll contributions as an actual tax, although with an effective tax rate that is generally less than the full statutory rate. More specifically, the effective marginal tax rate that enters into the deadweight loss calculation is $t_1 = \theta(\rho - \gamma)(1 + \rho)^{-1}$. With the annual explicit rate of return of $\rho_a = 0.085$ on capital investment and the annual rate of return of $\gamma_a = 3\%$ on the Social Security contributions, the values of ρ and γ for the 30 year period (as discussed in Section 3.1) are $\rho = 10.56$ and $\gamma = 1.43$, implying an effective tax rate of $\tau_1 = 0.79\theta$. Thus, with the actual marginal statutory tax rate of $\theta = 0.124$, the effective marginal tax rate is $\tau_1 = 0.098$. In the extreme case in which individuals receive nothing back in benefits for incremental tax payments, the marginal return on those taxes is $\gamma = -1$ and the effective tax rate is $t_1 = \theta(\rho - \gamma)(1 + \rho)^{-1} = \theta$.

The actual incremental deadweight loss of the Social Security payroll tax depends also on the total marginal rate of other income taxes (say, τ_2). The incremental deadweight loss of the Social Security payroll tax (τ_1) for generation t can therefore be approximated by $\Delta\mathrm{DWL}_t = 0.5E(\tau_1^2 + 2\tau_1\tau_2)(1 - \tau_2)w_tL_t$ where w_tL_t is the income subject to the payroll tax in generation t, and E is the elasticity of taxable earnings

---

[33] This ignores the fact that individuals cannot borrow against future Social Security benefits. If the Social Security program shifts more consumption to the future than the individual would want, the program could involve an effective tax rate even if $\rho = \gamma$.

[34] During the initial phase in of a pay-as-you-go system, some members of the transition generations receive a return that is higher than the market return. For these individuals, the effective tax rate is negative, reducing the deadweight loss of the combined income and payroll taxes.

with respect to the net of tax share. Since $w_t L_t$ grows at rate γ, the present value of this deadweight loss for all generations (discounting at the social discount rate δ) is

$$\Delta DWL = 0.5E\left(\tau_1^2 + 2\tau_1\tau_2\right)(1-\tau_2)^{-1} w_0 L_0 \frac{1+\delta}{\delta-\gamma}.$$

With the "other marginal tax rate" equal to $t_2 = 0.2$ (approximately the average marginal personal income tax rate in the United States), the incremental deadweight loss is $\Delta DWL = 0.031 E w_0 L_0 (1+\delta)/(\delta-\gamma)$. If the value of the relevant tax elasticity is 0.5 [35], the incremental deadweight loss is (using the values of δ and γ from Section 3.1) $\Delta DWL = 0.051 w_0 L_0$. This is roughly 40% of the tax paid by the first generation $(T_0 = \theta w_0 L_0 = 0.124 w_0 L_0)$.

The existence of capital income taxes reduces the magnitude of this deadweight loss because the gap between the after-tax return on savings and the implicit pay-as-you-go return on the payroll tax is smaller. Thus $\tau_1 = (r_n - \gamma)/(1 + r_n)\,\theta$. With an annual net return of 4.25% and a growth rate of 3%, the 30-year time periods imply $(r_n - \gamma)/(1 + r_n) = 0.3037$ and therefore $\tau_1 = 0.0377$. Thus, a 50% effective capital income tax reduces τ_1 by about 60%. The corresponding incremental deadweight loss is then $\Delta DWL = 0.017 w_0 L_0$, one-third of the incremental deadweight loss when there is no capital income tax.

The present value consumption loss to all working generations was calculated with the same parameter assumptions in Section 3.1 to be $T_0\{1 + 7.61s\}$. Subtracting the windfall gain to the initial generation (T_0) implies a net present value consumption loss to all generations of $7.61 s T_0$. By comparison, $\Delta DWL = 0.017 w_0 L_0 = 0.137 \theta w_0 L_0$ with $\theta = 0.124$; thus $\Delta DWL = 0.137 T_0$. This is smaller than the net present value consumption loss for plausible values of the saving rate (s) but is nevertheless large in absolute size.

The magnitude of the incremental deadweight loss is relevant to the policy of notional defined contributions discussed above in Section 2.1. In a Social Security plan in which individuals see no relation between the taxes that they pay and the benefits that they eventually receive, $\gamma = -1$ and the deadweight loss reflects the entire payroll tax rate: $\tau_1 = \theta$. An argument in favor of the notional defined-contribution method is that each individual sees that the taxes paid are returned in the form of future benefits with an implicit rate of return of γ. If γ is close to the rate of return that individuals would otherwise receive on their saving, much of the deadweight loss associated with distorted labor supply is eliminated. More specifically, the effective marginal tax rate is reduced from θ to $\tau_1 = (r_n - \gamma)/(1 + r_n)\,\theta$. With annual values of the net return equal to 4.25% and the annual value of the implicit return on social

---

[35] For evidence on the elasticity of taxable income with respect to the net-of-tax marginal tax rate, see Feldstein (1995b), Auten and Carroll (1999) and Gruber and Saez (2000). Note that those studies refer to the elasticity of total taxable income and not just of the payroll portion. As the equation makes clear, the change in the deadweight loss is proportional to the value of the elasticity.

security equal to 3%, this implies $\tau_1 = 0.3037\theta$. Note that even with a zero implicit rate of return on Social Security contributions ($\gamma = 0$), the understanding that taxes paid will eventually be returned in the form of benefits reduces the effective payroll tax rate to $\tau_1 = r_n/(1+r_n)\,\theta = 0.71\theta$.

Although the Samuelson (1958) analysis explains why the overall rate of return in a pay-as-you-go program is equal to γ, the rates of return in any actual unfunded defined-benefit program can vary substantially among different individuals. Under US law, each individual's potential retirement benefits are based on that individual's "average indexed monthly earnings", i.e., on that individual's earnings relative to the average earnings in the economy. Only the earnings during the 35 years for which the individual's indexed earnings are highest are taken into account. A retired couple can receive the larger of either the combined amount of benefits based on their separate benefit calculations or a single benefit equal to 150% of the benefit of the higher earner. The surviving member of a couple after one member dies receives the higher of the survivor's own benefit amount or the amount to which the deceased spouse would have been entitled. Feldstein and Samwick (1992) calculate the effective tax rates for a variety of different demographic groups under US Social Security rules and find widely different effective tax rates. For example, young people and women often face the full marginal tax rate ($\tau_1 = \theta$) because young people are not in one of their highest 35 earning years and because women will receive benefits based on their husband's earnings. In contrast, a married man who is getting close to retirement age and who has a spouse who will claim benefits based on his earnings may face a negative marginal tax rate ($\tau_1 < 0$) because the additional dollars of earnings will raise the present value of future benefits by more than the tax that the individual pays. Feldstein and Samwick note that this heterogeneity of marginal tax rates increases the deadweight loss of the overall Social Security payroll tax if, as the evidence suggests, the elasticity of labor supply is greater for married women than it is for married men.

3.3. The trust fund in a pay-as-you-go system

In a pure pay-as-you-go system, the taxes paid in each year would be exactly equal to the benefits paid in that year. In practice, however, annual benefits are not literally equal to the taxes paid. In some years, tax receipts exceed benefits while in other years benefits exceed taxes. These differences may reflect simple cyclical fluctuations or an explicit policy to accumulate accounting and/or economic surpluses.

In the United States, the difference between annual benefits and taxes is reflected in a special government account known as the Social Security (OASI) Trust Fund. When taxes exceed benefits, the excess is credited to the Trust Fund while benefits in excess of tax receipts would reduce the Trust Fund balance. The Trust Fund is technically invested in special government bonds so that interest is added to the Trust Fund. Within the overall framework of the US budget accounts, the Social Security program is regarded as a separate or "off budget" activity. The overall annual budget surplus (or deficit) of the federal government is divided into an "off budget surplus" (the sum of Social Security taxes plus the interest received on the Trust Fund balance minus the benefits paid and administrative costs of the program)[36] and an "on budget surplus" (the sum of all other receipts minus all other expenses, including the interest paid to the Social Security Trust Fund). The combination of the "off budget surplus" and the "on budget surplus" is the "unified budget surplus" and equals the net amount of government debt that the government can repurchase from the public. When these surpluses are negative, the unified budget deficit corresponds to the borrowing requirement of the federal government.

The Social Security Trust Fund is an accounting system that keeps track of the accumulated value of past Social Security surpluses. The corresponding economic reality is that the annual Social Security surpluses contribute to the overall ("unified") government budget surplus and therefore potentially to national saving and capital accumulation. This potential increase in national saving is realized if the existence of the Social Security surplus does not cause political decisions that reduce the on-budget surplus or cause on-budget deficits nor private decisions that change household saving.

It is of course not possible to assess with any precision the causal link between off-budget Social Security surpluses and the size of the on-budget surplus or deficit. It is, however, interesting to note what happened after the US Congress voted in 1983 to raise the Social Security payroll tax and to make other changes in order to accumulate a substantial Social Security surplus after the program had been run on a pay-as-you-go basis for many years. This legislative change was made in anticipation of the long-run aging of the population as a way of avoiding a substantial increase in the future payroll tax rate. The expectation at the time was that the Social Security surpluses would accumulate as a large Trust Fund balance that could be run down after the baby boom generation began to retire in about the year 2010. Selling the assets in the Trust Fund in this way would make it unnecessary to raise future payroll tax rates to pay for the increased volume of benefits.

The economic reality corresponding to this accounting plan was the idea of raising the nation's capital stock by the planned budget surpluses (and the equal increases in national saving). Running down the Trust Fund balances by selling government bonds in the future would decrease national saving at that time, permitting the increased consumption by retirees without requiring a decrease in consumption by the future workers. Although the government borrowing from the public that would result from selling the Social Security bonds to the public[37] would mean a slower growth (and possibly an actual decline) of the capital stock, the capital stock that would have accumulated by then would be so much larger than it would have been without the

---

[36] The off budget surplus also includes the surplus of the Post Office. Although Medicare has a trust fund it is not currently an off-budget category.

[37] The Social Security Trust Fund would not literally sell bonds to the public but would redeem them from the Treasury which would, ceteris paribus, have to sell additional bonds to the public to offset these outlays.

1983 policy shift that the capital stock would remain larger for many years into the future.

In practice, the Social Security surpluses did occur and the Trust Fund did increase substantially, although not by nearly as much as originally planned (because of increases in early retirement, greater longevity, and lower interest rates on Trust Fund balances). But during the same years there were also large and persistent deficits in the "on budget" accounts, causing the unified budget to be in deficit until the year 1998. Although an explicit causal link between the large off-budget surpluses and the concurrent on-budget deficits cannot be established, it is certainly possible that the reduced size of the unified deficit that resulted from the large off-budget surpluses gave politicians a degree of comfort that permitted them to avoid the spending cuts or tax increases that might otherwise have been made.

Looking ahead, much of the political concern about Social Security reform in the United States focuses on the projection that the Social Security Trust Fund will be exhausted by sometime around 2038. More specifically, taxes are expected to exceed benefits until 2016. After that, the combination of taxes and interest on the Trust Fund balance will continue to exceed benefits until 2025. The Trust Fund will then begin to decline until all of the assets on the books of the Trust Fund are exhausted in 2038 [Board of Trustees (2001)]. If that occurs, benefits would have to be cut by about one-third to keep benefits within the amount of tax revenue, or payroll taxes would have to be increased by about 50% to maintain the initial rules linking benefits to past earnings. Alternatively, Congress could change the rules to permit Social Security benefits to be financed by income taxes or by general government borrowing.

Although the Trust Fund plays an important political role in discussions of Social Security, the Trust Fund is a legal and accounting construct without direct economic effect. The economics are that Social Security taxes currently exceed benefits, contributing to national saving. After 2014, taxes will be less than benefits and the Social Security financing will reduce national saving. Note that the transfer of interest payments from the on-budget account to the Social Security off-budget account does not alter national saving because it leave the unified budget deficit unchanged; the year 2025 is therefore not qualitatively different from earlier years. Once again, the overall effect on national saving will depend on how the political process responds to the Social Security deficits [Elmendorf and Liebman (2000)]. The net effect need not be negative if the Social Security deficits induce the government to increase its on-budget surplus or to take other steps to increase national saving by shifting from the existing pay-as-you-go system to one that is investment-based. We return to this below in Section 7.1.1, but first we need to consider the ways in which a pay-as-you-go system can be optimized.

4. Optimizing a pay-as-you-go system

Since the Social Security system in the United States and in most other industrial countries is an unfunded defined-benefit plan, it is worth asking how such a system should be designed if it is constrained to be a pure pay-as-you-go program. Such a theory of optimal program design is similar to the two-level theory of optimal income taxation (see Chapter 21 in Volume 3 of this Handbook). In the current context, the problem is to select the parameters of a Social Security program that maximize a social welfare function subject to the constraint that each individual acts to maximize his own utility subject to the parameters of the program. The purpose of such an analysis is not to derive practical parameters but to understand better how different factors influence the optimal parameter values of a pay-as-you-go defined-benefit program.

A basic result of such an analysis is that the optimal Social Security program involves balancing the protection of individuals who are too myopic to save optimally for themselves against the losses that those who are not myopic incur because they are induced to provide for their retirement in a program with a low implicit rate of return [38]. A loss is incurred to the extent that the pay-as-you-go program crowds out other saving, with the loss an increasing function of the difference between the return on capital and the implicit return of the pay-as-you-go program. More generally, the larger the Social Security program, the more protection it offers to those who are too myopic to save for their old age but also the more it distorts saving, labor supply, retirement, and other behavior.

The following analysis simplifies by focusing only on the distortion to saving. The formal model presented here assumes that individuals' labor supply is fixed both during their working years and at the time of retirement. It also ignores differences in tastes and incomes as well as potential problems of risk.

4.1. A baseline case with complete myopia

To start the analysis and provide a baseline case, consider first the extreme assumption that all individuals are completely myopic, i.e., that they consume all available income during their working years and make no provision for the future. The analysis will then relax this assumption and consider individuals who are "partially myopic", i.e., who give too little weight to future consumption. The analysis follows the basic Samuelson (1958) framework of an overlapping generations life-cycle model. The specific optimization analysis is due to Feldstein (1985). We begin by focusing on the steady-state properties and then extend the analysis to an infinite-period model in which the first period is explicitly recognized.

Individuals work a fixed amount in the first period of their lives and are retired in the second. The size of the labor force grows at rate n per period according to $L_t = (1 + n) L_{t-1}$. At time t, the young generation pays payroll tax of $T_t = \theta w_t L_t$ and these funds are used to finance the benefits of the retirees. Since the number of retirees is L_{t-1}, the pay-as-you-go character of the program implies that total taxes

---

[38] See Feldstein (1976a). Social Security also involves intergenerational transfers from future generations to current generations.

collected at time t is equal to the total benefits paid $T_t = B_t$ where $B_t = b_t L_{t-1}$ defines b_t as the level of benefits per retiree and implies that $b_t = \theta w_t (1 + n)$. In a representative year, the social welfare function can be stated as the sum of the identical utilities of the working population $\{L_t u[(1 - \theta) w_t]\}$ and the corresponding utilities of the retired population $\{L_{t-1} v[b_t]\}$. Because of the complete myopia assumption, the working generation consumes all of its after tax income and the retiree generation consumes only the benefits. Thus, the Social Welfare Function in year t can be written (after substituting the balanced budget condition that defines the benefit per retiree) as

$$W_t = L_t u[(1 - \theta) w_t] + L_{t-1} v[\theta w_t (1 + n)].$$

The first-order condition $dW_t / d\theta = 0$ in this simple case implies $u'_t = v'_t$. That is, it is optimal to divide income available in the economy at time t between the two groups to equalize the marginal utilities of workers and retirees. This full egalitarian prescription reflects the assumption that taxes have no distorting effect on any form of behavior. If the utility functions are the same in youth and older age, $u'_t = v'_t$ implies that the arguments of the two functions must also be equal. Therefore, the first-order condition becomes $(1 - \theta^*) w_t = \theta^* w_t (1 + n)$ or $\theta^* = (2 + n)^{-1}$. This implies that the optimal ratio of benefits to the average wage is given by $\beta^* = b^* / w = (1 + n)/(2 + n)$.

Note that the optimal tax and benefit ratios in this case do not depend on the marginal product of capital or the implicit return on Social Security contributions. The reason for this is that with no distortions to saving or work effort, the Social Security program is essentially just an income redistribution program and is carried to the point where the marginal utility of income is the same to retirees and workers.

The optimal tax rate differs from $\frac{1}{2}$ because of the growing population. If the population were constant, n would equal zero and the optimal tax would take half of each worker's wages $(\theta^* = \frac{1}{2})$ and the optimal benefits would give retirees an amount equal to one-half of the wage of current workers $(\beta^* = \frac{1}{2})$. With a growing population, a tax rate of less than 0.5 leaves the workers with more than half of their wage while delivering a retiree benefit that is as large as the after-tax income of the workers. Since the time period in the model is a generation, the value of n is the rate of growth of the population over a generation; assuming a 30-year generation and an annual population growth rate of 1%, $1 + n = (1.01)^{30} = 1.35$. This implies that the optimal tax rate is $\theta^* = 1/2.35 = 0.43$ and that the optimal benefit–wage ratio is $\beta^* = (1.35)/(2.35) = 0.57$. Thus the workers retain 57% of their wage and the retirees get a benefit equal to 57% of the current wage rate (and therefore an even higher percentage of their own preretirement wage rate) [39].

---

[39] This calculation takes no account of the windfall benefit that would accrue to the first generation of retirees. Doing so would require modifying the problem to include some private funds to support consumption during retirement. We skip this type of example to shift directly to consideration of a model with partial myopia.

4.2. *Balancing protection and distortion with partial myopia*

A more realistic example in which individuals respond to changes in Social Security rules can give a richer understanding of the design of optimal Social Security programs [Feldstein (1985)]. To see this, extend the previous model to allow individuals to save an amount s_t during the first period of their life. First period consumption is therefore $C_{1,t} = (1 - \theta) w_t - s_t$ while second period consumption of the same generation (but experienced at time $t + 1$) is $C_{2,t+1} = s_t(1 + \rho) + b_{t+1}$.

The rationale for Social Security in such a model is that individuals do not give adequate weight to their future consumption. This can be represented by assuming that the individual chooses s_t to maximize $u[C_{1,t}] + \lambda v[C_{2,t+1}^a]$ where the individual's anticipated retirement period consumption $C_{2,t+1}^a = s_t(1 + \rho) + \alpha b_{t+1}$, where α indicates that the individual may anticipate less than the full amount of benefits. Thus, a value of $\lambda < 1$ implies that the individual underweights future utility while a value of $\alpha < 1$ implies that the individual underestimates the amount of Social Security benefit that he will receive.

The government selects the level of Social Security taxes (and therefore of benefits) to maximize the actual ex post well-being of the population:

$$\max_\theta W_t = L_t \left\{ u\left[(1 - \theta) w_t - s_t\right] + (1 + n)^{-1} v\left[s_{t-1}(1 + \rho) + b_t\right]\right\},$$

subject to $b_t = \theta w_t(1 + n)$ and to s_t being chosen by the individual to maximize $u[C_{1,t}] + \lambda v[C_{2,t+1}^a]$ subject to $C_{2,t+1}^a = s_t(1 + \rho) + \alpha b_{t+1}$. Note that in the government's optimization there is no discounting of retirement-period utility and that the argument of the retirement-period utility function is the actual retirement consumption, implicitly making $\alpha = 1$. The factor of $(1 + n)^{-1}$ weighting the retirement utility reflects the fact that there are only $(1 + n)^{-1}$ times as many retirees as there are individuals in the first period generation.

The optimal design of the program in this very stylized problem is to choose the value of θ in a way that balances the protection from myopic saving decisions ($\lambda < 1$) against the losses that occur because of the low implicit return on the pay-as-you-go program. To obtain an explicit closed-form solution, let $u[C_{1,t}] = \ln C_{1,t}$ and $u[C_{2,t}] = \ln C_{2,t}$, and $\alpha = 0$ [40].

With these assumptions, the optimal tax rate is given by

$$\theta^* = \frac{(1 + \lambda)(1 + \gamma) - \lambda(1 + \rho)(2 + n)}{(1 + \lambda)(1 + \gamma)(2 + n) - \lambda(1 + \rho)(2 + n)}.$$

The optimal level of taxes and benefits depends on the degree of myopia (λ), the implicit return on the Social Security contributions (γ), the return on real

---

[40] The assumption that $\alpha = 0$ implies that individuals ignore the future Social Security benefits in making their life-cycle saving decisions. As a result, the Social Security program only reduces saving in this specification by reducing disposable income.

investments (ρ), and the relative numbers of workers and retirees $(1 + n)$. In the special case discussed in the previous section in which the individuals are totally myopic ($\lambda = 0$), $\theta^* = 1/(2 + n)$ as previously derived. More generally, taking the derivative of θ^* with respect to the parameters in this equation shows that $d\theta^*/d\lambda < 0$; an increase in the degree of myopia (a decrease in λ) raises the optimal size of the Social Security program. An increase in the implicit rate of return on Social Security contributions also increases the optimal size of the program: $d\theta^*/d\gamma > 0$. And an increase in the rate of return on regular investments raises the opportunity cost of the Social Security program and therefore reduces the optimal size of the program: $d\theta^*/d\rho < 0$.

Explicit numerical solutions of the more general case show that increasing the value of α from the currently assumed $\alpha = 0$ implies $d\theta^*/d\alpha < 0$. With $\alpha > 0$, a larger Social Security program would depress saving more (because individuals take the future benefits into account in deciding how much to save), imposing a bigger adverse effect if $\rho > \gamma$.

It is optimal to have any pay-as-you-go Social Security program in the context of this model only if $\theta^* > 0$. In the above expression, this is true only if the value of λ is less than the critical value $\lambda^* = (1 + \gamma)[(1 + \rho)(2 + n) - (1 + \gamma)]^{-1}$. At higher values of λ, the loss from substituting the low return Social Security benefits for the higher return real investments outweighs the protection that individuals receive through increased retirement income. Based on *annual* values of $\gamma_a = 0.03$, $\rho_a = 0.085$ and $n_a = 0.01$ and a 30-year time period, $\lambda^* = 0.098$. This implies that, in the current framework, individuals must be very myopic if any pay-as-you-go program is to be optimal[41]. If the promise of future benefits depresses savings ($\alpha > 0$) or if the implicit tax that results from $\rho - \gamma > 0$ distorts labor supply, the critical value of λ^* at which a pay-as-you-go program is optimal would be even lower.

This calculation focuses on the optimal Social Security program in a representative year and ignores the windfall gain that would accrue to the initial generation when a pay-as-you-go program is created. Taking that initial gain into account in determining the optimal value of θ requires maximizing the present value of all annual social welfare values: $S = \sum_{t=0} W_t(1 + \eta)^{-t}$ from $t = 0$ to infinity where η is the rate at which society discounts future welfare increments, i.e., future individual utilities[42]. Since the value of W_t increases more slowly than the size of the population (L_t), the

---

[41] A value of λ as low as 0.098 implies that individuals would do very little retirement saving in the absence of Social Security. With the individual maximizing $\ln C_1 + \lambda \ln C_2$ subject to $C_2 = (w - C_1)(1 + \rho)$, an individual who shows no myopia (i.e., $\lambda = 1$ and therefore no discounting of second period utility) will consume half of his income during the working years $[C_1^* = (1 + \lambda)^{-1}w = 0.5w]$ and save the other half for retirement. In contrast, someone with $\lambda = 0.098$ would consume 91% of his income during his working years $[C_1^* = w/(1.098) = 0.91w]$ and save only 9% for retirement.

[42] Note that this is fundamentally different from the rate δ at which changes in the consumption of future generations is discounted in Section 3.1 above. As we noted in footnote 30, the rate δ at which such future consumption is discounted should reflect the rate at which per capita consumption grows (g), the elasticity of the marginal utility function (ε), and the pure time preference at which utility is discounted (η). If the elasticity of the marginal utility is constant, this implies $\delta = \varepsilon g + \eta$.

discounted sum converges if the rate of growth of population is less than the rate at which utility is discounted. If utility is discounted at a sufficiently lower rate, it is only the representative steady state value of W_t that matters.

The specific expressions for the optimal value θ^* and the critical value λ^* reflect the particular way in which the problem of individual myopia is parameterized. An alternative parameterization in which the population is divided into a fraction (μ) of individuals who make fully rational life-cycle saving decisions (i.e., for whom $\lambda = 1$) and a remaining fraction ($1 - \mu$) that is completely myopic ($\lambda = 0$) would also illustrate the idea that the optimal size of the pay-as-you-go Social Security program is an increasing function of the extent of myopia ($d\theta^*/d\mu < 0$) and a decreasing function of the cost of substituting a pay-as-you-go program for real saving ($d\theta^*/d\rho < 0$ and $d\theta^*/d\gamma > 0$) although with some completely myopic individuals it could not be optimal to have no program at all. The possibility that there is heterogeneity in the ability to make life cycle saving decisions does however suggest that it might be desirable to substitute a means-tested program for the universal program that has been analyzed in the current section.

4.3. Universal versus means-tested Social Security benefits

When we shift from a representative-agent model to one with heterogeneous individuals, it becomes meaningful and potentially optimal to have a means-tested program, i.e., a program that provides benefits at retirement age to those whose income would be below some threshold level [43]. In the context of the overlapping generations life-cycle model, this is equivalent to providing benefits only to individuals whose accumulated assets are below some level [44].

In a simple model with no labor supply distortion and no uncertainty, the desirability of having a means-tested program rather than a universal program is analyzed most simply in a model with three types of individuals: a completely myopic group ($\lambda = 0$), a high income group that has no myopia ($\lambda = 1$ and wage w_H) and a low income grow with no myopia ($\lambda = 1$ and wage w_L). Consider an economy with only a means-tested Social Security program. All working individuals pay the Social Security tax at rate θ. Since only some fraction of individuals (ϕ) receive benefits, the means-tested benefit per beneficiary is given by $\theta w^*(1 + \gamma)\phi^{-1}$ where $w^*(1 + \gamma)$ is the average wage on which the payroll tax is levied, i.e., w^* is the average wage during the earlier working years of the retiree generation (corresponding to w_H and w_L) and $1 + \gamma$ is the growth factor that raises that wage to the level on which the tax is levied to support the retirees.

---

[43] The USA has such a means-tested program in addition to the basic universal program. The Supplemental Security Income program supplements the benefits of individuals over age 65 whose regular Social Security benefits and other sources of income are deemed to be too low. See McGarry (2002).

[44] See Feldstein (1987b) for an analysis of such a model.

For the completely myopic group there is no difference between the means-tested program and a universal program. In both programs, that group would consume all of its labor income and depend completely on the Social Security benefits provided to retirees. In contrast, the individuals with no myopia ($\lambda = 1$) decide whether to save (and thus forego the potential Social Security benefits) or to consume all of their earnings and depend in retirement on the Social Security benefits. They do so by comparing the utility levels achievable under the two alternatives. Assuming logarithmic utility, an individual of type i (where $i = $ H or L) who saves and is thus not eligible for the means-tested Social Security benefits[45] has lifetime utility equal to $Z_{\text{No SS}} = \ln C_1 + \ln C_2 = \ln[0.5(1 - \theta) w_i] + \ln[0.5(1 - \theta) w_i(1 + \rho)]$. In contrast, such an individual who decides not to save in order to qualify for the means tested benefit has lifetime utility equal to $Z_{\text{SS}} = \ln(1 - \theta) w_i + \ln[\theta w^*(1 + \gamma) \phi^{-1}]$ where w^* is the average wage on which Social Security taxes are levied and the parameter ϕ reflects the fraction of all retirees who receive benefits.

An individual chooses not to save in order to qualify for benefits if $Z_{\text{SS}} > Z_{\text{No SS}}$, i.e., if $\ln[\theta w^*(1 + \gamma) \phi^{-1}] > \ln 0.5 + \ln[0.5(1 - \theta) w_i(1 + \rho)]$. The likelihood that an individual will choose not to save increases with the level of benefits (and therefore with θ, w^*, $(1 + \gamma)$, and ϕ^{-1}) and decreases with the level of the individual's own wage relative to the average wage and with the rate of return on saving. If the level of the means-tested benefit is not set very high, the high wage group may choose to save while members of the low wage group will choose to consume all of their earnings and depend in retirement on the means-tested Social Security benefit. If so, the level of retirement consumption for this group may be less under the means-tested plan than it would be under the universal plan.

The public policy choice between a universal plan and a means-tested plan can be stated as a comparison of the total utility levels of the three different population groups under the two alternatives. The key disadvantage of the means-tested plan is that it induces a low-income group to avoid saving in order to qualify for the means-tested benefit and therefore leaves them with lower retirement consumption than they would otherwise have. For this group, the higher the benefit level, the more likely individuals are not to save and therefore the higher the tax rate has to be. In addition, the myopic high-income individuals will be worse off if the optimal level of benefits in the means-tested program is less than they would otherwise have received with a universal program. The advantage for the high-income group of rational savers is that they may be able to pay a lower payroll tax than they would in a universal program (because people like themselves do not get benefits) and save at a higher real rate of return. Which system is preferable depends on the relative numbers of individuals with different degrees of myopia and different income levels.

---

[45] An individual with low enough income might save and still be eligible for the means-tested benefits. It would however never be optimal for such an individual to save for retirement since the means-tested program effectively imposes a 100% tax on all retirement period assets.

A richer class of models would have a bivariate distribution of wage rates and myopia values (λ's), would incorporate the adverse effect of higher taxes on labor supply, and might include the possibility of uncertain returns causing savers to qualify for the means-tested benefit.

4.4. Models with variable retirement

Diamond and Mirrlees (1978, 1986, 2000, 2002) analyze models in which workers face uncertainty about the length of their working lives[46]. In particular, there is a random chance in each period that they will become permanently disabled and therefore unable to work. In these models, the government cannot distinguish between those who are unable to work due to disability and those who simply choose not to work. Therefore, in order to optimize its Social Security system, the government needs to determine how best to provide benefits for those out of work in a way that balances protection for the disabled against work disincentives for the able.

The basic intuition behind these models can be seen by referring to Figure 1 which is based on a similar figure in Diamond and Mirrlees (1986). Consider first the case in which benefits for those who do not work are the same regardless of the age at which a person leaves the labor force. In addition, assume that the utility an individual derives from a given combination of leisure and consumption does not vary with age, and that there is no saving. Specifically, let utility be a function of consumption and leisure $U(C, L)$, where $L = 1$ indicates that the person works and $L = 0$ indicates that the person does not work. Furthermore, let C_1 indicate the consumption level from working and C_2 indicate the consumption level when retired (the level of the government provided retirement benefit). In this case, social welfare is maximized by setting retirement benefits at the highest level that will still have the able bodied remain

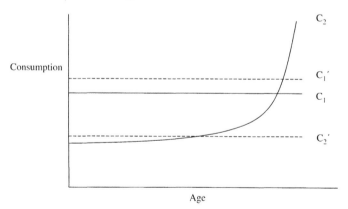

Fig. 1. A model of variable retirement.

---

[46] These models apply to funded systems as well as to pay-as-you-go systems.

in the workforce. Thus, the government sets C_2 so that $U(C_2, 0) = U(C_1, 1)$ [47]. These levels of consumption are illustrated with the dotted lines in Figure 1. The government sets consumption for workers at C_1' and consumption for retirees at C_2'. While the marginal utility of additional consumption for retirees exceeds that of workers, it is not possible to increase social welfare by raising C_2' and lowering C_1' because such a change would cause all workers to retire (i.e., it would result in $U(C_2, 0) > U(C_1, 1)$).

Diamond and Mirrlees show that it is possible to raise social welfare by switching to a benefit path that rises with a worker's date of retirement. In particular, with such a benefit structure it is possible to lower C_1 and provide additional benefits to retirees (who are assumed to have higher marginal utility of consumption than workers at the same level of utility). The basic intuition is that in the case of retirement benefits that rise with age, a worker who decides to leave the labor force will compare the utility from not working against not only the utility from working but also the foregone opportunity to receive higher retirement benefits in the future. This extra consideration makes it possible to pay higher retirement benefits without causing all workers to retire. Moreover, the optimum includes implicit taxation of work as part of providing insurance against a short career (in the presence of asymmetric information).

Diamond and Mirrlees (1978) consider a similar model in which saving is permitted. This model yields an additional result – that the optimal social insurance plan should be supplemented with an interest income tax. This result occurs because allowing people to reach old age with assets narrows the consumption difference between working and retiring and therefore reduces the level of retirement benefits that can be provided without causing able-bodied workers to leave the workforce [48].

4.5. Other aspects of pay-as-you-go program design

The level of benefits in a representative agent model, the choice between means-tested and universal programs, and the relationship between benefits and age are only three of the issues that arise in the design of a pay-as-you-go program. Other issues that could be studied with modifications of the existing model are the relation between benefit levels and pre-retirement earnings (i.e., the extent of redistribution in the benefit formula), the "normal retirement age" at which benefits are paid, and the treatment of married couples.

5. Behavioral effects: theory and evidence

The presence of a pay-as-you-go Social Security system changes the budget constraint faced by individuals and is therefore likely to change their economic behavior,

---

[47] We assume, following Diamond and Mirrlees, that someone who is exactly indifferent between work and leisure will work.
[48] Feldstein (1990) provides an alternative model of the relationship between benefits and age.

particularly their saving, labor supply, and retirement decisions and their portfolio allocations. This section discusses each of these four types of behavioral responses in succession. For each, we consider theoretical models of the responses of individuals, the empirical evidence of the magnitudes of these responses, and, when appropriate, the aggregate impact on the economy.

5.1. Saving

5.1.1. Theory

In a simple life-cycle model, a pay-as-you-go Social Security system that taxes workers when young and provides them with retirement benefits when old will reduce the saving of individuals when young. In the special case of an actuarially fair program, provision of benefits reduces saving by an equal amount. In particular, consider a two-period model in which individuals work in the first period and are retired in the second period. For simplicity, assume that labor supply in the first period is fixed and normalized to equal one and that the lifetime utility function is additively separable:

$$Q = U(C_1) + V(C_2).$$

Consider a Social Security system that imposes a tax at a rate of θ on labor income in the first period and provides a benefit of B in the second period. Then first period consumption is

$$C_1 = (1 - \theta) w - S,$$

where w is the worker's wage and S is savings. With an interest rate on saving of r, second period consumption is

$$C_2 = S(1 + r) + B = [(1 - \theta) w - C_1](1 + r) + B.$$

The individual's first-order condition is

$$dQ\, dS = -U' + V'(1 + r) = 0.$$

Totally differentiating with respect to S, θ, and B yields

$$(wU'')\, d\theta + [U'' + (1 + r)^2 V''] \, dS + (1 + r)\, V''\, dB = 0.$$

To simplify, consider first an actuarially fair Social Security system (i.e., with $r = g$). Then $B = (1 + r)\, \theta w$ and $d\theta = dB/(1 + r)\, w$. Substituting this expression into the line above and rearranging yields $dS = -1/(1 + r)\, dB$. In other words, every dollar of expected discounted Social Security benefits reduces an individual's saving when

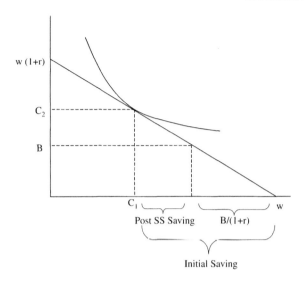

Fig. 2. Impact on saving of an actuarially fair Social Security system.

young by one dollar, allowing the individual to consume at the same combination of C_1 and C_2 as before the system was instituted.

Figure 2 illustrates this case. In the absence of Social Security, the individual consumes C_1 in the first period and C_2 in the second period. Therefore saving is $w - C_1$. This is indicated as "initial saving" on the figure. After the Social Security system is implemented, saving is reduced by the discounted value of future benefits, $B/(1 + r)$ (which equals the amount of payroll tax paid). But because the system is actuarially fair, the individual continues to consume the same amounts as before.

Simple modifications of the basic life-cycle model will lead dS/dB to deviate from $-1/(1 + r)$. For example, if an actuarially fair Social Security system provides benefits that are larger than the level of retirement consumption that is desired by the individual in the absence of Social Security and if it is illegal to borrow against future Social Security benefits, then the individual will reduce saving to zero, but will be unable to reach his pre-Social Security optimum. In this case, saving will fall by less than a dollar per dollar of future Social Security wealth[49]. As a second example, if an individual receives a negative net transfer from Social Security (i.e., the discounted value of the retirement benefit is less than taxes paid), the negative income effect from the transfer can produce changes in saving that are either greater or less than the discounted value of the Social Security benefit: this is illustrated in Figure 3 which is drawn so that consumption falls in both periods, implying that savings falls by less than the amount of the tax. Different preferences could, of course, cause first period consumption to

[49] See Diamond and Hausman (1984b) for empirical evidence suggesting that many US households cannot reduce their wealth in response to increases in Social Security benefits.

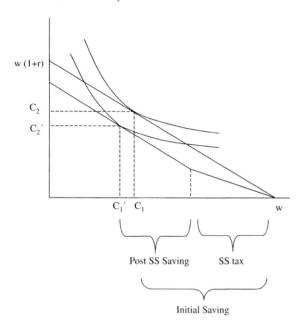

Fig. 3. Impact on saving of a Social Security system with negative transfers.

increase by more or less than this amount. As a third example, many Social Security systems create incentives that encourage workers to retire earlier than they otherwise would have. With additional years of retirement consumption to finance, individuals will desire additional retirement resources. Because this induced retirement effect goes in the opposite direction of the basic wealth replacement effect, the net impact of Social Security on saving is theoretically ambiguous [Feldstein (1974), Munnell (1974)][50]. Thus, even for rational life-cycle savers, economic theory does not provide a simple answer to how saving will respond to a Social Security system. Myopic agents and workers who do not fully trust the government to provide the promised level of benefits will typically respond less than one to one to increases in Social Security benefits. In addition, saving done for reasons other than life-cycle consumption (bequests or precautionary motives for example) need not adjust at all in response to Social Security, though Hubbard, Skinner and Zeldes (1995) show that social insurance programs can significantly reduce precautionary saving as well.

At the aggregate level, determining the impact of Social Security on personal saving in a given year requires adding up the changes induced in the saving behavior of all individuals alive in that year. Even in a model in which individual saving responds dollar for dollar to Social Security wealth, the impact on national wealth will not in general be dollar for dollar.

---

[50] See Feldstein (1977) for a two period model with endogenous retirement. Hu (1979) contains an extension of the endogenous retirement model to a Diamond economy.

To see this, consider first a stationary life-cycle economy in which the number of workers in each generation is constant, as is the wage level. In the absence of a Social Security system, the saving of the young is exactly offset by the dissaving of the old, and there is no net saving in the economy. Therefore, crowding out of saving by the Social Security system has no effect on the steady state equilibrium aggregate national saving rate – the reduced saving by the young is exactly offset by reduced dissaving of the old[51].

In an economy in which both the number of workers and the wage level are rising over time, the saving of the young will exceed the dissaving of the old. Therefore net aggregate saving will be positive, and a reduction in saving by individuals in response to Social Security will reduce aggregate saving.

To be more explicit, assume that each generation with L_t workers and an average wage level of w_t saves a fraction σ of their earnings. Thus, total saving by workers is $\sigma w_t L_t$. Retirees have income of $r\sigma w_{t-1} L_{t-1}$ on the capital $\sigma w_{t-1} L_{t-1}$ that they own. As life-cycle savers, they consume all of their assets and second-period income leading to total consumption by retirees of $(1+r)\sigma w_{t-1} L_{t-1}$. Their saving during retirement (income minus consumption) is therefore negative and net saving in the economy is $\sigma(w_t L_t - w_{t-1} L_{t-1})$. This can be rewritten as $\sigma(g+n+ng) w_{t-1} L_{t-1}$ where $w_t = (1+g)w_{t-1}$ and $L_t = (1+n)L_{t-1}$.

With a pay-as-you-go Social Security system with a tax rate of θ, workers have net of tax earnings of $w_t L_t - \theta w_t L_t$ and with a one-for-one reduction in saving save $\sigma w_t L_t - \theta w_t L_t$. The elderly consume $(1+r)(\sigma - \theta) w_{t-1} L_{t-1} + \theta w_t L_t$, where $\theta w_t L_t$ is the Social Security benefit. Therefore, net saving in the economy is $(\sigma - \theta)(w_t L_t - w_{t-1} L_{t-1}) = (\sigma - \theta)(g+n+ng) w_{t-1} L_{t-1}$, and Social Security reduces saving by $\theta(n+g+ng) w_{t-1} L_{t-1}$, a proportionate reduction of θ/σ.

To assess the empirical magnitude of this reduction, note that a life-cycle saver who expected to work three times as long as he was retired, would save roughly one-fourth of his income in each working year if the real net-of-tax rate is zero and less than that with a positive net-of-tax interest rate. In the USA the Social Security payroll tax is 12.4%. Therefore, such a model suggests a reduction of roughly one-half of aggregate saving due to Social Security (.124/.25) with a zero net-of-tax interest rate and somewhat more with a positive interest rate[52].

5.1.2. Empirical evidence

The ambiguous predictions of the impact of Social Security on saving that come from economic theory and the clear possibility that such impacts could be of an

---

[51] Social Security can nevertheless depress the steady state size of the capital stock. When the pay-as-you-go Social Security system is introduced, the old receive a windfall and increase their consumption by an equivalent amount, reducing the size of the capital stock. The young can save less and the old dissave less in all future periods.

[52] Kotlikoff (1979a) compares partial and general equilibrium impacts on the capital stock in a life-cycle model with retirement effects and suggests that the impact might be somewhat smaller.

economically important magnitude have led to a large empirical literature that has tried to estimate the size of the impact. The papers in this literature can be grouped by the type of variation each uses to identify the impact: time-series, cross-sectional, and cross-country[53].

Feldstein (1974, 1982, 1996b) examined the time-series relationship between saving and Social Security wealth in the USA and consistently found that Social Security crowds out a significant share of overall private saving. In the most recent of these papers, he regressed real per capital consumption (C) on real per capita disposable income (YD), its lagged value (YD_{t-1}), real per capital household wealth (W), and real per capita Social Security wealth from 1930 to 1992 (excluding World War II years). Social Security wealth is defined as the present actuarial value of the future Social Security benefits to which current employees and retirees are entitled. He estimated (standard errors in parentheses):

$$C = 641 + 0.63\,YD + 0.074\,YD_{t-1} + 0.014\,W + 0.028\,\text{SSW}.$$
$$\quad\quad (0.06) \quad\; (0.053) \quad\quad\;\; (0.008) \quad (0.013)$$

Thus every dollar of Social Security wealth leads to 2.8 cents of additional consumption[54]. Since Social Security wealth in 1992 was $14.2 trillion (in 1992 prices)[55], the estimates imply that Social Security wealth raised personal consumption expenditures by $400 billion and therefore that personal saving was reduced by an equal amount. The coefficients on the disposable income variables further imply that saving was reduced by $16 billion by the difference between the Social Security payroll tax and the benefits paid. Since total private saving in 1992 (including both corporate and personal saving) was $333 billion, the $416 billion reduction in saving implied by these estimates is a 56% reduction of private saving from its potential level.

While these results show that there is a strong underlying correlation between the time paths of Social Security wealth and saving in the USA, the limited variation present in a regression of only 56 observations is not sufficient to definitively establish causality. A large literature has examined alternative time-series specifications both in

---

[53] Surveys of this empirical literature are available in Aaron (1982), Atkinson (1987), Danziger, Haveman and Plotnick (1981), and U.S. Congressional Budget Office (1998).

[54] The time series of Social Security wealth in Feldstein (1974) contained a programming error for some of the later years. Leimer and Lesnoy (1982) showed that correcting the programming error reduced the value and statistical significance of the coefficient on Social Security wealth. Revisions of the National Income and Product Account data and extension of the sample in Feldstein (1996b) resulted in a coefficient (shown above) on the Social Security wealth variable just slightly larger and more statistically significant than the estimate in Feldstein (1974).

[55] This "gross" measure of Social Security wealth exceeds the unfunded obligations of the Social Security program because it does not take into account the future Social Security payroll taxes. Such taxes are of course taken into account in the calculation of disposable income. Regressions using a "net" Social Security wealth measure that subtracts the present value of the taxes to be paid by those who are currently in the labor force have coefficients of Social Security wealth that are correspondingly larger.

US data and around the world and has shown that it is possible to find specifications in which the relationship between Social Security wealth and saving is substantially reduced or eliminated. Most notably, Barro (1978) found mixed results from adding a variable measuring the government deficit to the basic Feldstein regression; Leimer and Lesnoy (1982) and Lesnoy and Leimer (1985) point out that workers are unlikely to be capable of calculating their exact future Social Security wealth and show that different plausible models of how individuals approximate their Social Security wealth lead to very different savings results; and Auerbach and Kotlikoff (1983b) conduct simulations with life-cycle consumers and show that estimates from time-series regressions in a Social Security system that has not reached steady state are highly sensitive to the exact time period chosen [56].

Because of the fragility of the time-series results, researchers have attempted to use other sources of variation to estimate the impact of Social Security on saving. In particular there is a large cross-sectional literature that relies on variation in Social Security wealth across individuals for identification. Beginning with Feldstein and Pellechio (1979), researchers have estimated regressions of the form

$$A_i = \alpha_0 + \alpha_1 f(YL_i) + \alpha_2 SSW_i + \alpha_3 X_i,$$

where A_i is the financial wealth of individual i (typically measured around the time of retirement), $f(YL_i)$ is some function of a proxy for lifetime income (often simply a quadratic function of current income), SSW_i is a measure of the present discounted value of future Social Security benefits, and X_i is a vector of demographic variables. The initial estimates by Feldstein and Pellechio using a 1963 Federal Reserve survey of asset holdings were that each dollar of Social Security wealth reduced the accumulation of other financial wealth by about 70 cents. Subsequent studies have typically confirmed the basic result that other financial wealth is reduced in response to Social Security wealth, though the estimated offsets are often lower than the initial estimates [57]. A review of this literature by the U.S. Congressional Budget Office (1998)

---

[56] Other time-series studies include Munnell (1974) and Darby (1979).

[57] Kotlikoff (1979b), using data from the 1966 National Longitudinal Study, finds evidence that Social Security payroll taxes reduce saving, but does not observe the expected impact of future Social Security benefits on saving. Feldstein (1983) presents estimates between −.35 and −.72. Blinder, Gordon and Wise (1983) estimate that Social Security wealth reduces private wealth by −.39. Hubbard (1986) studies the responsiveness of financial wealth to both Social Security and pension wealth and estimates an offset of −.33 for Social Security wealth and −.16 for private pension wealth. Bernheim (1987) argues that the common approach of discounting both for time preference and mortality risk is misguided because such a procedure understates the true value of Social Security in the absence of a private annuity market [see, however, Joustein (2001) who emphasizes that in the presence of sufficiently strong bequest motives the true value of a marginal annuity payout stream is close to the actuarially correct value]. Using a Social Security wealth measure constructed by discounting only for time preference, he estimates an offset of 77 cents per dollar of Social Security wealth. Dicks-Mireaux and King (1984) examine Canadian data and estimate an offset of −0.2. Gullason, Kolluri and Panik (1993) re-run the Feldstein and Pellechio specification on more recent Survey of Consumer Finances data and do not find a statistically significant relationship between Social Security wealth and other wealth.

concludes: "Thus, despite the great variation among the estimates, the cross-section evidence suggests that each dollar of Social Security wealth most likely reduces private wealth by between zero and 50 cents, with the most likely estimate lying near the middle of that range".

There is, however, a fundamental difficulty in interpreting these estimates. Social Security wealth is simply a non-linear function of lifetime income, marital status, and expected mortality. Since all three of these factors are likely to affect wealth accumulation decisions directly, the only thing identifying the coefficient on Social Security wealth is the functional form assumed for the other variables. This is, of course, a common issue in empirical public finance[58], and researchers in the Social Security saving literature since at least Feldstein (1983) have noted the problem and suggested that by using flexible specifications for income and the other variables that enter the Social Security wealth function, regressions would be identified by some of the more idiosyncratic features of the Social Security benefit formula[59]. But it is notable that the quasi-experimental approaches that have been used so successfully to solve similar identification problems in other areas of public finance have not yet been applied to this issue[60].

The final source of variation that has been applied to identify the impact of Social Security on private saving is cross-national variation. The Social Security systems of different countries vary in their generosity, and under the life-cycle model, countries with larger Social Security systems would be expected to have smaller levels of private saving. In practice, all else is not equal and it is quite difficult to construct comparable measures of Social Security wealth across countries. Thus, the estimated signs and magnitudes of the impact of the Social Security displacement effect differ much more widely in these studies than in the US time-series and cross-sectional literatures[61].

[58] See Feenberg (1987) for a discussion of this issue in the context of tax policy.

[59] Bernheim and Levin (1989) implement a particularly ingenious solution to this problem by using a direct measure of individuals' expectations of future Social Security benefits, effectively identifying the impact of Social Security from the idiosyncratic portion of expectations that is not correlated with true benefit levels.

[60] The lack of cross-state variation in Social Security benefits and the complications in specifying the time path on a saving impact from a single federal policy change make it more difficult to apply the quasi-experimental approach to this issue than to many others. One alternative is to examine whether the patterns of savings rates by different cohorts at various ages are consistent with what a life-cycle model would predict in response to expansions in Social Security benefits. Gokhale, Kotlikoff and Sabelhaus (1996) take such an approach and conclude that the postwar decline in US saving can be attributed to two factors: government redistribution to the elderly and an increase in the propensity to consume of older Americans.

[61] Cross-country studies include Barro and MacDonald (1979), Feldstein (1980), Horioka (1980) and Modigliani and Sterling (1983).

5.2. Retirement

There are three main channels through which a pay-as-you-go Social Security system could alter retirement choices. First, for myopic or liquidity-constrained individuals, a mandatory Social Security system will transfer income from working years to retirement years, and the income effect of this transfer would be expected to induce additional consumption of leisure late in life. If the creation or expansion of a Social Security system creates windfalls for people who are old at the time of the policy change, this will accentuate the income effect. Second, many Social Security systems are event-conditioned in the classic social insurance sense, meaning that the benefits are only available once a person is retired. Such systems often alter retirement incentives because the present discounted value of lifetime benefit payments is not independent of the choice of retirement date (even a system such as the US system that adjusts benefits for early retirement in a way that is on average approximately actuarially fair will alter retirement incentives for people whose life expectancy is higher or lower than average). Third, national Social Security systems may change social conventions regarding retirement dates, affecting the design of private pension plans, firm mandatory retirement ages (no longer legal in the USA), and worker tastes[62].

There were dramatic changes in the retirement behavior of men in most OECD countries over the 20th century. Costa (1998) reports that labor force participation rates of men aged 65 and over fell in the USA from 65% in 1900 to 18% in 1990[63]. Over similar time periods, male labor force participation for this age group fell from 61% to 8% in Great Britain, 54% to 4% in France, and 58% to 5% in Germany.

Labor force participation fell at younger ages as well. For example, among US men ages 55–64, labor force participation fell from 91% in 1900 to 67% in 1990 [Costa (1998)]. Similar declines are apparent in the age at which US workers first claim Social Security benefits. Whereas in 1965 (three years after men first became eligible to claim benefits at age 62), 23% of workers claimed Social Security benefits at age 62, 23% claimed benefits at age 65 and 36% claimed benefits at an age above 65, by 1999, 59% were claiming benefits at age 62, only 16% were claiming them at 65, and 7% at ages above 65 [U.S. House of Representatives Committee on Ways and Means (2000)].

---

[62] There are also channels through which Social Security could postpone retirement. For example, by making benefit payments unavailable until age 62, the US system may cause some liquidity constrained individuals to postpone retirement until they are eligible for benefits. Alternatively, by providing an efficient form of annuities, Social Security may raise the value of work for people approaching retirement, lengthening their worklife. See Crawford and Lilien (1981) for a discussion of the ways in which relaxing the assumptions of perfect capital markets, actuarial fairness, and certain lifetimes in standard life-cycle models tend to advance retirement dates. Kahn (1988) shows that liquidity constraints can lead individuals to retire early even in an actuarially fair Social Security system.

[63] Recent research by Quinn (1999) indicates that during the past 10 to 15 years the trend in the USA toward earlier retirement among men has leveled off and possibly reversed itself slightly.

Early retirement is even more common in most other OECD countries. In the USA 26% of men have left the labor force by age 59. However, 58% of men in Belgium, 53% of men in France and Italy, and 47% of men in the Netherlands have left the labor force by that age [Gruber and Wise (1999)] [64]. Much of the reduction in labor force participation by men in their late 50s and early 60s has occurred since 1960. In the early 1960s, labor force participation was over 70% for 60–64 year olds in all 11 OECD countries studied by Gruber and Wise. By the mid-1990s, the rate was below 20% in Belgium, Italy, France, and the Netherlands, was about 35% in Germany, and 40% in Spain. The decline in the USA was relatively modest from 82% to 53%, and in Japan the decline was even smaller, from 83% to 75%. The trends toward earlier retirement are particularly striking in light of the impressive improvements in the health of older workers and in life expectancy, implying that successive cohorts of men are spending smaller percentages of their lives in the work force.

The studies in Gruber and Wise (1999) are the strongest evidence that Social Security systems affect retirement behavior. The individual country studies in that volume show that in country after country, relaxation of early retirement rules and expansions in benefits available at younger ages were followed quickly by trends toward early retirement. While some of the decrease in labor force participation by workers in their late 50s and early 60s likely resulted from the relaxing of liquidity constraints and changing of social norms brought about by these policy changes, there also appears to be a strong cross-country relationship between the level of implicit tax rates on continued work above the early retirement age and the level of labor force participation, with the implicit tax rate explaining more than 80% of the cross-country variation in unused labor capacity of 55 to 65 year olds.

Apart from these recent international studies of early retirement, however, it has been quite difficult for empirical researchers to establish a clear link between Social Security benefit levels and the century-long trend toward earlier retirement in the USA [65]. For example, while Boskin (1977) and Boskin and Hurd (1978) found large impacts of Social Security benefit levels on retirement, Burkhauser and Quinn (1983) found no impact. A series of authors employed quite different strategies in analyzing the Social Security benefit increases in early 1970 mostly with data from the Retirement History Survey. Cross-tabulations in Hurd and Boskin (1984) suggest that much of the decline in labor force participation by elderly men in this time period can be explained by the Social Security benefit increases. In contrast, analysis by Burtless (1986) and Burtless and Moffitt (1984) using non-linear budget set methods and by Hausman and Wise (1985) and Diamond and Hausman (1984a) using hazard models suggest that the Social Security benefit increases in this period did little to accelerate the long-run

---

[64] Of the 11 countries studied by Gruber and Wise, only Japan, with 13%, had a lower share of men out of the labor force at age 59 than the USA.

[65] Surveys of this literature are available in Atkinson (1987), Danziger, Haveman and Plotnick (1981), Burtless (1999) and Coile and Gruber (2000b).

trend toward earlier retirement. Looking at the longer term patterns, Costa (1998) notes that 58% of the total decline in male labor force participation rates between 1880 and 1990 had already occurred by the time that the US Social Security system made its first payments. She notes that similar timing stories apply for other countries as well, suggesting that rising income can explain much of the decline in labor force participation at older ages until the 1960s.

Many of these early cross-section econometric studies of the impact of Social Security on retirement are susceptible to the same critiques as the estimates in the saving literature: the measures of Social Security benefits used are nonlinear functions of other variables that could plausibly effect retirement directly, and therefore the results are highly sensitive to the particular regression specification used. More recent research has tended to emphasize quasi-random identification strategies, careful modeling of the dynamic retirement incentives as suggested by Stock and Wise (1990) and Berkovec and Stern (1991), and greater attention to the particular aspects of the Social Security benefit formula that are producing the identifying variation. For example, Krueger and Pischke (1992) study the Social Security notch generation which received significantly less-generous benefits than those received by the generations that immediately preceded it and found essentially no impact of Social Security benefit levels on retirement. As a second example, Samwick (1998) uses the option value approach to carefully model year to year accrual of private pension and Social Security wealth, and finds that increases in private pensions explain substantially more of the post-war decline in labor force participation at older ages than does Social Security. Finally, Diamond and Gruber (1998) and Coile and Gruber (2000a) model the retirement incentives in the USA and provide measures of both the year to year accrual of retirement wealth from delaying retirement and the gain that would be achieved by postponing retirement to the optimal age. Among their findings are that the Social Security system does not result in a tax or subsidy on work for the median worker at ages 62–64, because increases in benefits from delaying receipt are quite close to actuarially fair. However, at older ages there is a significant tax on work because the current delayed retirement credit is not sufficient to compensate for time preference and mortality risk at those ages[66]. They also show that there is considerable variation in these incentives throughout the population. Coile and Gruber (2000a) show that substantial variation in the Social Security incentive variables remains even after controlling in a flexible way for current and past earnings, marital status, age, and age difference with spouse – suggesting that this residual variation can be used to identify the impact of Social Security on retirement in a credible way. Coile and Gruber (2000b) go on to perform estimation and conclude that forward-looking measures have a significant impact on retirement decisions[67].

---

[66] The credit is being increased between now and 2008, however.

[67] Another important empirical literature has examined the US earnings test [see Gruber and Orszag (2000) and Friedberg (1998, 2000) for recent treatments] and has typically found that the test has relatively small impacts on the labor supply of those affected by it.

On balance, it appears to us that when appropriate specifications are used, Social Security systems do appear to have important impacts on retirement behavior. However, significant uncertainty remains about the particular channels provoking these behavioral responses and the share of the overall decline in male labor force participation that can be explained by Social Security.

5.3. Pre-retirement labor supply

As we briefly discussed earlier, the Social Security payroll tax could increase marginal tax rates by as much as 12.4 percentage points and produce substantial deadweight loss if workers do not perceive a linkage between the taxes they pay and the benefits they receive. Since the payroll tax is larger than the income tax for 62% of US families [Mitrusi and Poterba (2000)], the effective marginal tax rates created by the Social Security system is an important issue. Payroll taxes in most other OECD countries are even larger than in the United States.

What makes the impact of the payroll tax on labor supply more complicated than that of the income tax is the possibility that workers perceive some or all of the linkage between taxes paid and benefits received. Feldstein and Samwick (1992), building on earlier work by Blinder, Gordon and Wise (1980), Gordon (1983), Browning (1985) and Burkhauser and Turner (1985), show that the Social Security benefit rules create net marginal tax rates from the payroll tax that differ substantially across the population depending on a worker's age, sex, marital status, and income. These net marginal tax rates are calculated as the payroll tax rate minus the present actuarial value (discounting for both time preference and mortality risk) of the additional social security benefits per dollar of additional earnings. The present value of the incremental benefits to which an individual becomes entitled by earning an additional dollar depends on the worker's age, sex (since mortality rates vary with sex), beneficiary status (whether the worker will claim benefits as a worker or as a dependent spouse), lifetime income (which determines the replacement rate segment of the benefit schedule that applies to the worker), and income during retirement (which determines the income tax rate that will be applied to Social Security benefits). Young workers who believe that they are not in one of their 35 highest years of earnings, secondary earners (typically wives) who expect to receive retirement benefits based on their spouse's earnings record, and low-income workers who expect to benefit from SSI receive no marginal retirement benefits for additional earnings and face the full payroll tax rate. Married men often face negative marginal tax rates since their additional earnings result in higher benefits for both themselves and their spouse. Older workers generally face lower (and often negative) marginal rates since their incremental benefits are not deferred as far into the future as those for younger workers are.

5.4. Portfolio composition

Social Security is likely to affect the asset holdings of individuals both because it will alter saving and because of its risk properties and covariance with other assets. Hubbard

(1985) estimates a model of portfolio composition using US cross sectional data and finds that the share of wealth represented by Social Security wealth is negatively correlated with holdings of other inflation hedges such as housing and equities as well as with annuities, which guard against longevity risk in a way similar to Social Security. In contrast, Dicks-Mireaux and King (1983) find essentially no impact of Social Security wealth on the composition of portfolios for a sample of Canadian households. Merton (1983) argues that an appropriately designed Social Security system can reduce the economic inefficiencies that result from the nontradability of human capital, allowing younger people to correct the portfolio imbalance in which they hold too much human capital relative to their holdings of physical capital. Merton, Bodie and Marcus (1987) discuss the extent to which private pension plans that are integrated with Social Security help insure against the risk of changes to the Social Security system.

6. Distributional effects of pay-as-you-go Social Security

Pay-as-you-go Social Security systems transfer large sums of money from workers to retirees. In the USA, the Social Security system took in $461 billion in (non-interest) revenue in 1999, mostly from payroll taxation of current workers and paid out $393 billion, mostly in benefit checks to retirees. This large redistribution of resources between individuals of different ages provides for 38% of the total income of households headed by someone of age 65 or older, and measured in a mechanical way causes major shifts in the income distribution by age, geographic region, and race. The true impact of Social Security on the income distribution cannot, however, be measured simply by observing annual flows of taxes and benefits. To the extent that a pay-as-you-go Social Security system is simply substituting for private life-cycle saving, large annual flows may have little impact on consumption patterns. Thus, measuring the impact of Social Security on the annual income distribution requires specifying a counter factual income distribution in the absence of Social Security.

Researchers generally have not taken this approach (which would be quite difficult given the range of possible behavior responses discussed above). Instead, they have focused on measuring ways in which existing pay-as-you-go systems treat different individuals differently over their lifetimes. Most pay-as-you-go systems deviate significantly from the actuarially fair systems described in the simplest models. Substantial intercohort redistribution occurs as systems expand benefit generosity and as demographic patterns change. Moreover, benefit formulas produce significant intracohort redistribution, much of it unrelated to lifetime income.

6.1. The returns to Social Security for different cohorts

The simple models above show that the initial generation in a pay-as-you-go system receives a windfall and that subsequent generations earn a steady-state rate of return

Table 1
Redistribution across cohorts in the US Social Security system (OASI)[a]

Birth cohort	Internal rate of return (%)	Aggregate lifetime net intercohort transfer evaluated in 1989 (billions of 1989 dollars)
1876	36.5	12.1
1900	11.9	112.0
1925	4.8	99.6
1950	2.2	14.0
1975	1.9	−8.0
2000	1.7	−15.2

[a] Source: Leimer (1994). Intercohort transfer calculation uses 2% real discount rate.

equal to the growth of the wage base. In practice, repeated benefit expansions over time have created a series of initial generations all receiving benefits that were many times higher than tax payments. Thus, in the USA, workers who paid payroll tax rates of 2 to 5% during their working years have been beneficiaries of payroll tax rates of 10 to 12% in their retirement years[68]. Table 1 shows internal rates of return and lifetime net transfers from Social Security for successive birth cohorts taken from Leimer (1994). The internal rate of return, i, is the return that equalizes the present discounted value of the total OASI taxes paid and benefits received for the cohort:

$$0 = \sum_{age=0}^{age=max\ age} \frac{benefits_{age} - taxes_{age}}{(1+i)^{age}}.$$

The net transfers received by the cohort are the present discounted value of benefits received minus taxes paid using a real discount rate, in this case 2%. We see that whereas the cohort that was born in 1900 received a rate of return of nearly 12% on its payroll taxes, a person born in 2000 can expect to receive only a 1.7% return on his or her taxes[69]. Similarly, while the accumulated (to 1989) value of the benefits received by members of the cohort born in 1925 was $100 billion more than the taxes the cohort members paid, future cohorts will receive substantially less in benefits than they pay in.

[68] See Burkhauser and Warlick (1981), Moffitt (1984), Duggan, Gillingham and Greenlees (1993), Steuerle and Bakija (1994), and Caldwell et al. (1998).
[69] The numbers shown assume no change in Social Security tax or benefit rules in the future. Leimer (1994) contains additional results under various assumptions for how Social Security's long run deficit is eliminated.

6.2. *Intracohort redistribution in the current US system*

Because the benefit formula in the US Social Security system replaces a greater fraction of the lifetime earnings of lower earners than of higher earners, the program is generally thought to be progressive, providing a "better deal" to low earners in a cohort than to high earners in the same cohort. Recent research [e.g., Liebman (2002), Coronado, Fullerton and Glass (2000), Gustman and Steinmeier (2000)] has shown, however, that much of the intra-cohort redistribution in the US Social Security system is related to factors other than income. Specifically, Social Security transfers income from people with low life expectancies to people with high life expectancies (who receive benefits for a longer period of time), from single workers to the married (particularly one-earner) couples who receive spouse benefits, and from people who work for more than 35 years to those who concentrate their earnings in 35 or fewer years (since taxes are paid on all years of earnings but benefits are based only on the highest 35 years) [70]. These non-income-related factors often result in substantial variation in the amount of redistribution received by families with similar lifetime incomes. Moreover, since high-income households tend to have higher life expectancies and receive larger spouse benefits, some of the progressivity of the basic benefit formula is offset.

Recently four sets of researchers have constructed microsimulation models of the US Social Security system in order to analyze intracohort redistribution. Three of the papers find that Social Security does redistribute income from higher-earners to lower-earners, but not nearly as much as would be expected based on the benefit formula. The fourth paper concludes that by some measures, the current US Social Security is actually regressive. Caldwell et al. (1998) use a microsimulation model based on projections of marriage and earnings patterns for postwar generations. Overall they find that the lifetime net tax rate from Social Security is 5% for the 1950 birth cohort. They find that the lifetime net tax rate averages 2% for individuals with lifetime labor earnings below $200000 (1997 dollars) and around 6% for individuals with lifetime earnings between $200000 and $800000. At life-time earnings levels above $800000, net tax rates fall because the level of earnings subject to the Social Security payroll tax is capped. Liebman (2002) uses a data set that matches the Census Bureau's Survey of Income and Program Participation to the lifetime Social Security earnings histories of sample members. He applies current Social Security rules to data for a cohort that retired in the early 1990s and calculates the within cohort transfer that each individual either receives or pays as the present discounted value of the individual's lifetime Social Security benefits received minus taxes paid, discounted at the rate of return for the cohort as a whole. He finds that the total dollar value of the transfers from individuals receiving less than the cohort's internal rate of return to individuals receiving more than the cohort's internal rate of return is only 13% of total Social

---

[70] See Boskin et al. (1987) and Hurd and Shoven (1985) for early discussions of these issues.

Security benefits received by the cohort. Moreover, much of this redistribution is not related to lifetime income, and lower mortality rates and higher spouse benefits among higher income households offset a substantial share of the progressivity of the Social Security benefit formula, resulting in income-related transfers that are between 5 and 9% of Social Security benefits paid (depending on the measure of lifetime income used), or $19 billion to $34 billion, at 1998 aggregate benefit levels. He emphasizes the wide range of positive and negative transfers from Social Security received by people at the same lifetime income level. Building on earlier work in which they showed that immigrants receive a particularly good deal from the US Social Security system [71], Gustman and Steinmeier (2000) use a microsimulation model based on the Health and Retirement Survey linked to Social Security earnings histories. They emphasize that Social Security looks less progressive after grouping individuals into households and adjusting for variation in earnings by secondary earners than it does looking simply at retired worker benefits. Using a family measure of lifetime income that averages only those years with significant earnings, they find that the redistribution from Social Security increases benefits in the second decile by 7% and reduces them by 7% in the ninth decile. Coronado, Fullerton and Glass (2000) project future earnings and marriage patterns for a PSID-based sample. Ranking households by potential earnings (the lifetime earnings the household would have had if all adults had worked full time in every year) and taking into account the fact that wages above the taxable maximum are not taxed, they conclude that at a sufficiently high discount rate, Social Security is slightly regressive.

   In interpreting these results, it is important to be aware that there are important interactions between the inter and intra cohort rates of return. Because Social Security benefit levels rise with income, higher-income members of cohorts that receive large net transfers will often receive higher dollar transfers than lower-income members of the cohort. Thus, Steuerle and Bakija (1994) emphasize that by this measure, the US Social Security system looked highly regressive in the past, but that this regressivity of Social Security is decreasing as rates of return decline.

6.3. General equilibrium consequences of pay-as-you-go Social Security

A Social Security system that alters saving and labor supply behavior will generally change the total amount of capital and labor supplied in the economy. These changes in factor supplies will alter wages and the returns to capital. Such changes can be important because individual responses to the changing factor prices can offset some of the direct impact of government policies, because these price changes alter the distribution of income between workers and owners of capital, and because the optimal

---

[71] This occurs because pre-immigration years are averaged in as zeros in the Social Security benefit formula, moving immigrants into high replacement rate segments of the Social Security benefit formula [see Gustman and Steinmeier (1998)].

policy response to population aging is sensitive to how the demographic changes alter the relative supplies of capital and labor.

Kotlikoff (1979a) explores steady-state general equilibrium effects in a life-cycle model that generates a one for one saving offset. He finds that incorporating general equilibrium considerations in a growing economy produces additional offsetting income and substitution effects on saving. While the decline in wages induced by the lower capital stock lowers saving when young, the higher interest rate increases saving. In simulations with a Cobb–Douglas production technology calibrated to represent the US economy, the net effect is to dampen by about 50% the reduction in the capital stock caused by the Social Security system. However, the 20% steady state reduction in national saving implied by this model is still substantial.

Hubbard and Judd (1987) consider the general equilibrium impacts of Social Security in an analytic model with capital market imperfections. In particular, they assume market failure in the private provision of annuities and liquidity constraints that make it impossible to borrow against future wages. In the presence of annuity market failures, Social Security can produce significant increases in long-run welfare even while substantially reducing the capital stock. However, with borrowing restrictions, the forced intertemporal transfer of resources from working years to retirement years can substantially offset or eliminate these welfare gains. Hubbard and Judd's life-cycle numerical simulation model shows that the general equilibrium shifts in incomes between labor and capital have significant welfare implications in the presence of capital market imperfections because the fall in wages and rise in interest rates that accompanies the decline in the capital stock exacerbates the welfare losses from the liquidity constraints.

The Kotlikoff and Hubbard and Judd models compare long-run steady states. Auerbach and Kotlikoff (1983a, 1987) develop a dynamic life-cycle general equilibrium simulation model that computes exact transition paths under the assumption that agents act with perfect foresight about future factor prices. In this model, there are no capital market imperfections and retirement dates are fixed. In simulations of the transition to an unfunded Social Security system with a 60% benefit to earnings replacement rate, Auerbach and Kotlikoff (1987) find that in the long run, the capital stock falls by about 24%. In simulations which assume that workers perceive no linkage between Social Security benefits and taxes, labor supply initially falls slightly due to the substitution effect of the Social Security payroll tax. However as capital is crowded out, the income effect comes to outweigh the substitution effect, and long-run labor supply rises a bit compared with the initial steady state. Additional simulations show that welfare gains from making the benefit-tax linkage transparent are significant, suggesting a rationale for the notional account approaches to unfunded Social Security systems and identifying an important source of welfare gains from a switch from a defined-benefit unfunded system to a funded defined-contribution system [see Kotlikoff (1996)].

Cutler, Poterba, Sheiner and Summers (1990) and Elmendorf and Sheiner (2000) have conducted simulations that explore the optimal response of government policy to population aging (caused both by declines in fertility and increases in longevity). They explain that the projected increase in the number of dependents per worker means that per capita consumption will decline in the future, and that this implies that we should increase saving now to finance some additional consumption later. However, there is a second offsetting effect. Because population aging is largely caused by a slow down in fertility and therefore in the growth of the labor force, the amount of additional capital necessary to sustain a given capital to labor ratio will fall over time, suggesting that we reduce saving now. For reasonable policy parameters, Elmendorf and Sheiner find that it is optimal (depending on the rate used to discount the well-being of different generations) to let future generations bear the full burden of population aging. It is important to emphasize that these simulations assume that we are currently at the optimal level of capital accumulation. If, as is likely the case, the current level of the capital stock is too low (because the tax system is not optimal and because Social Security benefits crowd out private saving), then there still may be a strong case for increasing saving now.

6.4. Social Security and the distribution of wealth

Because Social Security wealth is likely to substitute at least in part for other types of wealth (financial, housing, etc.), measures of the wealth distribution that ignore Social Security wealth can present a distorted picture of overall wealth. Feldstein (1976b) shows that conventionally measured wealth distributions look inconsistent with what a life-cycle model would produce, but that after adding back in Social Security wealth, the data are more consistent with life cycle saving behavior. Similar arguments apply for measures of the wealth distribution that ignore private pension wealth.

Gokhale, Kotlikoff, Sefton and Weale (2000) study the relationship between bequests and the distribution of wealth and show that Social Security may greatly increase the inequality in the wealth distribution in the USA by depressing bequests in low and moderate income households. Using a dynamic 88-period OLG model calibrated to study the intergenerational transmission of US wealth inequality via bequests, the authors show that because low-income households rely almost entirely on Social Security to finance their retirement consumption, all of their wealth is in an annuitized form, leaving nothing to bequeath to their heirs. In contrast, higher-income households have substantial bequeathable wealth which is passed along to their children as accidental bequests.

Angus Deaton, Pierre-Olivier Gourinchas and Christina Paxson (2002) study how risk-sharing institutions such as Social Security affect inequality. Their basic insight is that in the absence of such institutions, the inequality of the distribution of wealth will grow over time as the impact of random return and earnings shocks cumulate. Social Security, by substituting pay-as-you-go benefits for individual wealth accumulation, reduces the inequality of wealth and therefore of retirement consumption that would occur if there were greater reliance on individual savings.

7. Investment-based Social Security programs [72]

Many countries around the world are shifting from the traditional pay-as-you-go Social Security programs to programs that are completely or partially investment-based, i.e., in which funds are accumulated to pay future retirement benefits as they would be in a defined-contribution private pension system. The specific design of each program, the reasons for the change, and the mechanism of the transition differ with national economic and political conditions [73].

The primary motivation for making the shift is that the rate of return on incremental national saving permits future benefits to be financed with a lower rate of contribution during working years, eventually permitting a higher standard of living for both workers and retirees. This consideration becomes increasingly important as the prospects of an aging population raises the projected taxes needed to finance existing benefit-wage ratios. The transition to such a program does of course require additional saving (i.e., a reduction in current or near-term consumption) in order to take advantage of the high return.

This section begins by describing how a pure investment-based system would function after the transition to such a system was complete. Although a pure investment-based system is an analytically useful case to study, many of the actual programs involve a combination of an investment-based portion and a traditional pay-as-you-go system. Section 7.1 therefore ends with a discussion of such a mixed system. Section 7.2 discusses how a transition to an investment-based system could work in practice. Sections 7.3 and 7.4 discuss the issues of risk and distribution that arise with investment-based systems.

7.1. The economics of an investment-based system

A typical investment-based system is similar to a private defined-contribution plan with the exception that the government generally mandates the level of contributions that individuals and/or their employers must contribute. Each individual has a personal retirement account into which funds are deposited during working years. Those funds are invested in a portfolio of stocks and bonds and, at retirement age, the accumulated

---

[72] We use the term "investment-based Social Security" to refer to a system in which individuals save and accumulate financial assets in individual accounts. Such a system thus involves what others have referred to as "prefunding", "privatization" and asset "diversification" [e.g., Geanakoplos, Mitchell and Zeldes (1998, 1999) and Orszag and Stiglitz (2001)]. We recognize that much of the economic effect of investment-based reforms could be achieved without *individual* accounts and we return to that issue below. The analysis in this section parallels the discussion in Feldstein (1998b) but draws on substantial new research that has been done since that was written, particularly research done as part of the NBER study of Social Security reform.

[73] See the separate essays in Feldstein (1998a) for discussion of these issues for Argentina, Australia, Britain, Chile and Mexico, and in Feldstein and Siebert (2002) for a discussion of these issues in several western and central European countries.

funds are used to finance an annuity or other periodic payout arrangement. In addition to mandating the level of contributions, the government may also regulate the types of assets in which the funds can be invested and specify the way in which funds can be paid at retirement.

7.1.1. The impact on national saving

The effect on national saving of introducing such an investment-based program depends on how both households and the government respond. If individuals are fully rational life-cycle savers, the introduction of an additional mandatory saving program will have no net effect on national saving because individuals would simply reduce their previous saving by an equal amount [Auerbach and Kotlikoff (1987), Kotlikoff (1996), Mitchell and Zeldes (1996)]. Of course, in a world of such rational life-cycle savers there would be little justification for a Social Security program. If at least some individuals are myopic or do not save for some other reason, introducing a mandatory investment-based Social Security program would raise national saving. Since the evidence indicates that the median financial assets of US households on the verge of retirement is less than six months of income, a program of mandatory saving is likely to raise the national saving rate. Although some critics of investment-based reforms with individual accounts argue that they do not necessarily increase saving [e.g., Orszag and Stiglitz (2001)], even critics generally acknowledge the reforms would be likely to be implemented in ways that have a positive effect on national saving [Diamond (1998a), Geanakoplos, Mitchell and Zeldes (1998, 1999)][74].

   Although households could in principle offset the mandatory saving in investment-based Social Security accounts by reducing other saving, this is particularly unlikely when the investment-based program substitutes for a pay-as-you-go program with the same benefits[75]. If the retirement income provided by the Social Security program is unchanged, even rational life cycle savers would have no reason to reduce their direct discretionary personal saving in response to a mandatory saving program. Moreover, to the extent that the investment-based program reduces the cost to individuals of providing their retirement benefits (i.e., by substituting a smaller amount of mandatory saving for a larger pay-as-you-go tax) individuals have higher disposable income. Although some of that higher income would be used to finance additional current consumption, some of it would also be saved to finance future consumption. The creation of personal retirement accounts may also induce some current non-savers to begin saving because they learn about the mechanics of portfolio investing or simply because they develop a sense of greater responsibility for their own old age.

---

[74] The distinction between privatization (without prefunding) and prefunding is crucial here. Creating private accounts that are only notional would not raise national saving.

[75] That is, introducing an investment-based Social Security program where no Social Security exists might have a much smaller positive effect on saving because individuals could substitute one form of saving for another.

This analysis assumes that the deposits to the investment-based accounts are financed by additional household saving. An alternative that has been proposed is to use a portion of the existing and projected government budget surpluses to finance a relatively small investment-based Social Security program. Since the budget surpluses are already a component of national saving, the effect of this method of financing depends on what would otherwise be done with those budget surpluses. If they otherwise would have been maintained as surpluses and used to reduce the national debt, the shift of those funds to an investment-based Social Security program would have no effect on national saving. If however those projected budget surpluses would otherwise be used to finance additional government spending or tax cuts that lead to increased household spending, shifting those funds into Social Security personal retirement accounts would raise the national saving rate. This is true if the surpluses are in the Social Security program itself ("off-budget surpluses") or are in the non-Social Security part of the budget ("on-budget surpluses"). See Elmendorf and Liebman (2000) and Feldstein and Samwick (2000).

Even a pure debt-financed shift to investment-based accounts can increase national saving in a growing economy under suitable conditions. Section 7.1.3 examines an overlapping generation economy in which a pure pay-as-you-go system is replaced with a pure investment-based system. In the first period, however, the existing obligations to those who have paid into the pay-as-you-go system are compensated by issuing new national debt, so-called recognition bonds. These bonds are never amortized but remain in perpetuity. Nevertheless, as the example shows, the capital stock grows over time if population and wages are increasing.

7.1.2. The rate of return in investment-based accounts

The economically relevant rate of return in an investment-based system is the return that the nation as a whole earns on the additional national saving, i.e., the marginal product of capital for the national economy[76]. The return that portfolio investors earn in the personal retirement accounts is a net return after the federal, state and local governments have collected corporate and property taxes. The full pretax return on incremental capital in the US nonfinancial corporate sector was estimated by Poterba (1998) to have been 8.5% for the period from 1959 to 1996. Of this 8.5%, approximately 3% has been collected in taxes, with two-thirds of those taxes being federal corporate taxes.

Poterba's estimate of an 8.5% real return on nonfinancial corporate capital may overstate the overall marginal return on increased national saving for several reasons: some incremental saving goes into owner-occupied housing which has a low rate of

---

[76] The equity premium over the return on debt is therefore not directly relevant. It is wrong to see the return on Social Security investment as a reflection of the equity premium. We return to the discussion of risk in Section 7.3. See also Feldstein (1996a).

return because of its favorable tax status; some saving goes abroad where foreign governments collect part of the return in the form of their taxes; stock options are being issued to employees as a form of compensation but are not reflected (negatively) in the net company earnings when the options are granted; and some of the apparent return to capital may actually be a return to patents, brands, and other things that create non-constant returns to scale. There are also reasons, however, why the 8.5% figure may understate the real return on incremental saving, including the fact that much of the corporate outlays on research and development, manpower training, etc. are really investments that should not reduce the current measure of profits by as much as they do with conventional accounting.

The real financial rate of return that would be earned in investment-based accounts, although less than the full incremental national rate of return because of the taxes paid by corporations, is a significant consideration because it is the financial return that determines the relation between the individuals' deposits in personal retirement accounts and the annuities that can be paid at retirement. During the 50-year period from 1946 to 1995, a portfolio consisting of 60% stocks (the S and P 500) and 40% corporate bonds had a mean real *level* return of 6.9%[77].

Some part of this financial return would undoubtedly be absorbed in administrative costs, a point emphasized in Diamond (1996, 1997, 1998a, 2000a) and by Murthi, Orszag and Orszag (2001) in their discussions of Chile and the UK. Although opinions differ about the likely magnitude of such costs, our judgement is that they need not be large in the USA and are likely to decline over time. Some US mutual funds offer stock and bond index funds with a fee of only 0.20% of assets or less. TIAA–CREF now offers a variety of options for fund accumulation and variable annuity payments at a cost of less than 40 basis points. Although these accounts have larger balances than most investment-based Social Security personal retirement accounts would have in the early years, they also incur costs of selling and of collecting funds that could be much less in a government-mandated program.

The essays in Shoven (2000) show that the cost of the asset management is small relative to the administrative costs associated with receiving and disbursing funds, providing services to investors, permitting frequent portfolio changes, etc. The cost of administering an investment-based system would, therefore, depend heavily on the range of services offered. Goldberg and Graetz (2000) describe an efficient system

---

[77] Financial research generally refers to *logarithmic* rather than *level* rates of return. The mean real logarithmic return on the 60 : 40 portfolio during the same period was 5.9% with a standard deviation of 12.5%. With log normal returns, $E[\exp(r^*)] - 1 = \exp[Er^* + 0.5\,\mathrm{var}(r^*)] - 1$ where E is the expectations operator, r^* denotes the logarithmic rate of return, and $\mathrm{var}(r^*) = (0.125)^2$. With $Er^* = 0.059$, this implies that the mean level rate of return is $E[\exp(r^*)] - 1 = 0.069$. The sample mean return is somewhat sensitive to the exact period over which it is calculated. Extending the sample period to include more recent years would raise the rate of return. Starting the calculation with a later date would reduce the mean. Excluding the dramatic rise in share prices since 1995 causes a lower mean return than would be obtained for the most recent 50 years. Diamond (2000b) discusses whether similar returns can be expected in the future.

of administration that uses the existing Social Security Administration to collect funds and that limits the frequency of asset substitution. Future technological change would lower administrative costs by permitting more investor activity to be done electronically. The analysis in this essay assumes an administrative cost of 40 basis points, reducing the usable mean real return on a portfolio from 6.9% to 6.5%. The real return before all taxes would be reduced by a similar amount[78].

The substantially higher real return in the investment-based system than in a pay-as-you-go system permits any given level of benefits to be paid with a much smaller "contribution" during working years. A simple example will illustrate the nature and potential magnitude of this difference. Consider an individual who works from age 20 to 60 and then retires from age 60 to 80. He makes deposits to an investment-based plan each year during his working life and then receives an annuity each year during his retirement. The funds earn a real return of 6.5% during both the saving and the pay-out period. To simplify the calculation, assume that the deposit to the investment-based account is made at a single point in time at the mid-point of his working life, age 40. Similarly, replace the twenty year annuity with a single payment at the mid-point of the retirement life at age 70[79]. The funds are thus invested for 30 years. An investment of $1000 at age 40 would grow over 30 years at 6.5% to $6614. In contrast, in a pay-as-you-go program with an implicit rate of return of 2%, a "contribution" of $1000 at age 40 would grow to $1811, only 27% of the amount accumulated with the investment-based return over the same period. Equivalently, it takes $3.70 at age 40 in the pay-as-you-go plan to buy the same amount of retirement income at age 70 as $1.00 could buy in the investment-based plan with a rate of return of 6.5%. This implies that the benefits provided by a pay-as-you-go Social Security program with a 20% tax rate could be provided by an investment-based program with a saving rate of $20/3.70 = 5.4\%$. This of course is a statement about the long-run after a complete transition has occurred. In the transition, it is necessary to finance the pay-as-you-go benefits as well as accumulating the investment-based fund. Before discussing the practical aspects of a transition, we consider in more detail the gain that results from shifting from a pay-as-you-go system to an investment-based system.

The comparison between the 6.5% return on the financial assets and the 2% implicit return in the pay-as-you-go system ignores the issue of risk. An exact comparison is not possible because of the difficulty of quantifying the demographic and political risks in a pay-as-you-go system [see Section 7.3 below and Feldstein (1996a)]. Some have incorrectly argued that there are no gains from shifting from a pay-as-you-

---

[78] In the long run, the extra capital accumulation would cause a decline in the marginal product of capital and therefore in the rate of return to portfolio investors. Calculations by Kotlikoff et al. (2002) indicate that even in the very long run the decline in the pretax real return would be less than 1 percentage point. With Cobb–Douglas technology, even a one-third increase in the capital stock would reduce the marginal product of capital by only about one-fifth, e.g., reducing the net return from 6.5% to 5.2%.

[79] Detailed calculations with annual contributions and withdrawals produce results that are very close to this simplified "center of gravity" inflow and outflow assumption.

go system to a investment-based system once risk is taken into account. However, Geanakoplos, Mitchell and Zeldes (1999, p. 137) calculate that for the population as a whole each dollar shifted from a risk-free government bond (or from an unfunded Social Security program) to an equity investment produces a present value gain equal to 59 cents, or one-fifth of the non risk-adjusted gain[80]. This calculation assumes that some individuals are unable to make equity investments now because of fixed learning costs and therefore have no risk aversion discount on the first dollar. For those individuals and that first dollar, the gain would be the full difference between the return on a risk-free government bond and an equity investment, equivalent in present value to more than two dollars per dollar transferred. The overall average amount is only 59 cents because (1) not all individuals are so constrained to begin and therefore have no gain from the shift, and (2) among those who are initially constrained, the net gain from shifting to equity declines with each additional dollar of risky equity in their portfolio.

7.1.3. The gain from prefunding Social Security[81]

There is substantial controversy about the potential gain from replacing a pay-as-you-go system with an investment-based plan. While the simple example in the previous section suggests a significant long-run potential gain, critics argue correctly that this ignores the inherited obligation to existing retirees and to those current workers who have accumulated claims on future benefits by contributing to the existing pay-as-you-go system [e.g., Geanakoplos, Mitchell and Zeldes (1998, 1999), Orszag and Stiglitz (2001)]. Because of differences in timing, it is not possible to evaluate the potential gain by comparing rates of return. Prefunding reduces the consumption of early generations and increases the consumption of later generations. This implies that the only meaningful comparison is in terms of the present value of the consumption of all generations, and therefore depends on the rate of discount at which society trades off the consumption of different generations.

This section, based on Feldstein (1995c, 1998c), shows that shifting to an investment-based system raises that present value if two conditions are met: the return on capital exceeds the implicit return in the pay-as-you-go program and the capital intensity of the economy is below the welfare maximizing level (i.e., the marginal product of capital exceeds the social discount rate of future consumption.) In some ways of financing the transition, a present value gain only occurs in a growing economy. Since the excess of the return on capital over the implicit pay-as-you-go return is a necessary condition for macroeconomic efficiency and a verifiable fact, and since all economies are experiencing positive economic growth, the present analysis shows that

---

[80] This calculation ignores the political risk in a pay-as-you-go system. Taking such risk into account would increase the gain from shifting to the funded system.

[81] As we noted above, we use the term "prefunding" as a short-hand for the shift from a pay-as-you-go system to an investment-based system with real capital accumulation.

shifting from a pay-as-you-go to an investment-based system would produce a net present value gain if the marginal product of capital exceeds the social discount rate.

Previous analyses that concluded that a shift to a funded system would not increase the present value of consumption have implicitly assumed that the rate at which all future generations' consumption changes should be discounted is the same as the marginal product of capital [e.g., Breyer (1989), Shiller (1999), Sinn (2000)]. This is essentially the same issue that we noted in discussing the change in the present value of consumption that results from introducing a pay-as-you-go Social Security system where none exists (Section 3.1 above).

The key reason for the increase in the present value of consumption is the rise in national saving that results from the shift to an investment-based Social Security system. With the marginal product of capital greater than the consumption discount rate, the increase in saving causes a positive present value change in consumption. This of course implies that the gains in the present value of consumption could also be achieved by other policies that increase national saving. It is difficult, however, to think of other policies that could have as large an impact. Feldstein and Samwick (1998b) show that the accumulated assets in personal retirement accounts financed by saving 2% of earnings would eventually reach about 70% of the future level of GDP. In contrast, even a policy of budget surpluses that paid off the entire US national debt in a way that increased the capital stock by a dollar for every dollar of debt reduction would raise the capital stock by less than half of the current level of GDP. Moreover, the relevant policy issue in the analysis of investment-based Social Security reform is about the effect of Social Security reform and not about the potential effect of other policies.

The formal analysis in this section considers the analytically simplest case of a complete shift from a pure pay-as-you-go program to a completely investment-based one. The transition uses "recognition bonds" to compensate the existing retirees and others who have paid payroll taxes under the pay-as-you-go system. More specifically, the government recognizes its obligation to those who have already paid pay-as-you-go taxes by giving them explicit government bonds of equal value and then servicing that additional national debt in perpetuity[82]. In the overlapping generations framework used here, the initial generation of retirees is therefore completely unaffected by the transition[83]. Each future generation bears the burden of servicing the additional debt

---

[82] This method of creating "recognition bonds" as an explicit part of the national debt has been a common feature of the Social Security reforms in Chile and other Latin American countries. The assumption that the additional national debt is serviced in perpetuity is just one possibility. The debt could of course be paid off more quickly by levying enough additional taxes on future generations. The transition analysis in Feldstein and Samwick (1997, 1998a) does not use explicit recognition bonds but implicitly assumes that the existing obligations are amortized over the period of years corresponding to the life of the employee who is in the youngest age group when the investment-based system begins.

[83] In a two-period overlapping generations framework, there are no current workers who have accrued claims on future benefits. All obligations of the pay-as-you-go system are to the initial retirees. They receive the recognition bonds in place of their benefits.

Table 2
Receipts and payments of overlapping generations

Social Security program and participants	t	$t+1$	$t+2$	$t+3$
Unfunded program				
Retirees (benefits)	$+T_t$	$+T_t(1+\gamma)$	$+T_t(1+\gamma)^2$	$+T_t(1+\gamma)^3$
Employees (taxes)	$-T_t$	$-T_t(1+\gamma)$	$-T_t(1+\gamma)^2$	$-T_t(1+\gamma)^3$
Change in aggregate consumption	0	0	0	0
Investment-based program				
Retirees [a]	$+T_t$	$+T_t(1+\rho)$	$+T_t(1+\gamma)(1+\rho)$	$+T_t(1+\gamma)^2(1+\rho)$
Employees [b]	$-T_t$	$-T_t(1+\gamma)$	$-T_t(1+\gamma)^2$	$-T_t(1+\gamma)^3$
"Debt service"	0	$-\rho T_t$	$-\rho T_t$	$-\rho T_t$
Change in aggregate consumption	0	$-\gamma T_t$	$[(1+\gamma)(\rho-\gamma)-\rho] T_t$	$[(1+\gamma)^2(\rho-\gamma)-\rho] T_t$

[a] Under the funded plan, retirees receive pay-as-you-go benefits at t and then receive the principal and earnings on their savings for all periods after t.
[b] Under the funded plan, employees save these amounts.

but also gains from earning a higher return on its savings than the implicit return that it would have received on the taxes that it would have paid in the pay-as-you-go system. Since the benefits of the initial retirees are unchanged, the net present value depends on the relative magnitude of the future retirement income gains and the future debt service requirements.

Table 2 shows the first four periods of the sequence of income and saving under an existing unfunded plan and the alternative investment-based plan. The process that begins at time t is equivalent to reducing the payroll tax on the then current generation of employees by T_t and issuing national debt in the amount of T_t. If that generation of employees is required to increase saving by making account contributions equal to the amount of the tax reduction, the incremental saving would be just enough to absorb the additional national debt [84]. The debt service during each period in the future is ρT_t [85].

[84] Even if the initial employees are required to save T_t in the mandatory saving fund, they may reduce or increase other saving in response to the income effect of shifting to the investment-based system. As long as there is a positive effect on saving, the conditions under which prefunding an unfunded Social Security program raises the present value of consumption are unchanged, but the magnitude of the gain is altered.

[85] The analysis ignores any potential difference between the interest rate that the government pays on its debt and the marginal product of capital. Although the government may pay a net interest rate that is less than the marginal product of capital, the fact that the increased national debt absorbs T_t of private

With the unfunded system, the taxes and benefits in each period are equal to each other and increase at the rate of growth of aggregate wages (γ); this is shown in the first three lines of Table 2. With the funded system, employees contribute to their personal retirement accounts the same amount that they would otherwise have paid in payroll taxes under the unfunded system[86]. These contributions starts with T_t at time t and then grows at rate γ; this is shown in row 5 of Table 2. Retirees receive benefits funded by a government transfer only in the first period of the transition (at time t)[87]. Future generations of retirees receive the income and principal from their personal retirement account saving. The amount of this retirement income is $T_t(1 + \rho)$ at time $t + 1$ and then grows at rate γ (i.e., in proportion to the earnings of each future generation). This is shown in row 4 of Table 2. Finally, the existence of the government debt reduces real income of each generation by a constant amount ρT_t [88]; this is shown in row 6 of Table 2.

At time t there is therefore no difference between the outlays and receipts of retirees and employees under the existing unfunded plan and under the alternative debt-financed funded plan. At time $t + 1$, the retirees in the funded plan receive $T_t(1 + \rho)$, an increase of $(\rho - \gamma) T_t$ in comparison to the unfunded plan. Since some combination of employees and retirees bears the cost of the increased national debt (ρT_t), the net effect of prefunding on consumption at time $t + 1$ is negative, $-\gamma T_t$. This is shown in the final row of Table 2.

Table 2 shows that, while the negative cost of debt service remains constant at $-\rho T_t$, the retirees' gain from shifting to a funded plan increases in proportion to the growing level of aggregate wages $(\rho - \gamma) T_t(1 + \gamma)^t$. The effect of prefunding therefore eventually shifts from negative (i.e., starting with a negative $-\gamma T_t$ in period $t + 1$ to positive[89].

---

saving (and thereby displaces an equal amount of investment) implies that the lost return is the marginal product of capital times T_t.

[86] This assumption causes the gain from shifting to an investment-based system to take the form of increased benefits rather than reduced taxes. The analysis could alternatively assume that each future generation saves only enough to fund the original level of retirement benefits with the rate of return ρ.

[87] This transfer is financed by issuing "recognition bonds" since the employees at time t are no longer paying the payroll tax.

[88] The debt service involves levying a tax on employees and/or retirees at time t to pay the interest to holders of the debt. The real economic cost arises because the increased national debt absorbs the private saving of the transition generation of employees (and therefore displaces an equal amount of investment). The lost national income is therefore the reduction in the capital stock multiplied by the marginal product of capital, ρT_t.

[89] The decline in consumption in the initial periods is what produces the additional capital and allows for the present value consumption gains. Note that by paying debt service of ρT_t in each period, the debt from the recognition bonds remains constant and therefore declines as a share of the growing economy. If the debt service payments were reduced to $(\rho - \gamma) T_t$, the debt would remain constant as a share of the economy, and there would be no change in aggregate consumption in any period and no welfare gain.

Prefunding raises the present value of consumption if the discounted value of the increased retirement consumption $[\sum_{s=1}^{s=\infty}(\rho - \gamma) T_t(1 + \gamma)^{s-1}(1 + \delta)^{-s}]$ exceeds the present value of the debt service [90] $[\sum_{s=1}^{s=\infty} \rho T_t(1 + \delta)^{-s}]$. The present value of the net gain in consumption from shifting to an investment-based system is therefore $\text{PVG} = \sum_{s=1}^{s=\infty}(\rho - \gamma) T_t(1 + \gamma)^{s-1}(1 + \delta)^{-s} - \sum_{s=1}^{s=\infty} \rho T_t(1 + \delta)^{-s}$, or, equivalently, $\text{PVG} = [(\rho - \gamma)/(\delta - \gamma) - \rho/\delta] T_t$.

In this case, prefunding raises the present value of consumption (i.e., $\text{PVG} > 0$) if three conditions are met: $\rho > \gamma$ (the marginal product of capital exceeds the implicit return in the unfunded program), $\rho > \delta$ (the marginal product of capital exceeds the rate at which future consumption is discounted) [91] and $\gamma > 0$ (the economy is growing).

It is easy to provide an intuitive explanation of each of these conditions. First, an unfunded system has an inferior return to employees in each generation only if $\rho > \gamma$. If $\rho < \gamma$, the economy is dynamically inefficient and consumption can be raised permanently by reducing the initial capital stock [92]. Second, if $\rho < \delta$, additional saving reduces the present value of consumption. Note that both of these conditions are also the conditions that imply that the introduction of an unfunded program reduces the present value of consumption; see Section 3.1 above. If they are not satisfied, an unfunded program raises the present value of consumption and replacing it with a funded program therefore decreases the present value of consumption.

The additional condition that the economy be growing ($\gamma > 0$) is now required to make the gain from increased retirement income exceed the cost of the additional national debt. A positive rate of growth is important in this context because the annual gain to retirees grows with the size of the economy while the cost of the increased national debt remains constant. If the economy does not grow, the annual gain to retirees will remain constant at ρT_t, exactly the same as the cost of debt service.

It is possible to specify other transitions in which the shift to a funded system would increase the present value of consumption even if the economy is not growing. The key requirement is an increase in national saving. With perpetual recognition bonds, the bonds absorb all the new saving if there is no growth. But with other ways of funding the transition, it is possible to have additional saving even if there is no economic growth. The simplest example would be one in which the transition is funded by a lump-sum tax on retirees and initial workers. Since the primary effect of that tax would be a reduction in consumption, the mandated contributions of the workers to the Social Security investment accounts would not be absorbed by government debt or offset by reductions in saving.

---

[90] Recall that the debt service represents the loss of income that results from the initial reduction of the capital stock.

[91] See the discussion of δ in Section 3.1 above. The condition $\rho > \delta$ also means that the capital stock is less than the welfare-maximizing size.

[92] See Aaron (1966), for a discussion of this in the context of Social Security.

The present value consumption gain from shifting to a funded system can be compared in an intuitively useful way with the present value of the consumption loss (PVL) that results from introducing an unfunded program. Section 3.1 showed that in an overlapping generations model this loss is given by:

$$PVL = T_0(1+r_n)^{-1} \{(r_n - \gamma) + (\rho - r_n)\, s\} (1+\delta)(\delta - \gamma)^{-1} - T_0.$$

The assumption that each dollar of Social Security tax reduces private saving by one dollar ($s = 1$) is analogous to the assumption in the current section that the shift to a funded Social Security program adds one dollar to saving for every dollar of Social Security funding. With $s = 1$, the loss becomes

$$PVL = \left[(1+r_n)^{-1} (\rho - \gamma)(1+\delta)(\delta - \gamma)^{-1} - 1 \right] T_0.$$

The calculations of the present value of the gain from prefunding in Table 2 use the same discount rate for combining consumption changes between working years and retirement years for a given cohort and for aggregating over the consumption of different cohorts, implicitly setting $r_n = \delta$. With that same simplification, the PVL becomes

$$PVL = \left[(\rho - \gamma)(\delta - \gamma)^{-1} - 1 \right] T_0.$$

This can be compared with the present value of the gain from shifting to an investment-based program using perpetual recognition bonds:

$$PVG = \left[(\rho - \gamma)(\delta - \gamma)^{-1} - \rho/\delta \right] T_t.$$

The gain here is less than the corresponding loss (per dollar of program at the time of the change) because the unfunded obligation is funded by a perpetual recognition bond that depresses the capital stock permanently by T_t, lowering each future year's income by ρ_t and the present value of the consumption by $\rho T_t / \delta$. If instead the unfunded obligation were financed by a tax on retirees analogous to the windfall that retirees receive when the unfunded program is begun, the present value gain would become

$$PVG = \left[(\rho - \gamma)(\delta - \gamma)^{-1} - 1 \right] T_t,$$

exactly the same as the present value loss of creating an unfunded program. Note that in this case with lump sum financing of the transition there is a gain even if the growth rate is zero since $\rho/\delta > 1$. More generally, any method of financing the unfunded obligation that has a present value cost less than $\rho T_t / \delta$ would permit a present value gain even in an economy with no growth.

The present value consumption gains are in addition to the gain that results from reducing the deadweight loss that results from distorting work and retirement decisions.

In the long-run, the higher return in a funded system allows lower tax rates for all working individuals. The long-run reduction in the deadweight loss of labor distortion is thus not just a reflection of the change, if any, in the extent of intra-cohort redistribution. If the rate of return in the funded system (or in the funded portion of a mixed system) is equal to the net rate of return that individuals would receive in the market, the funded system eliminates the deadweight loss of the payroll tax (except to the extent that it requires individuals to save more for the future than they would otherwise want to do). For individuals for whom the funded Social Security rate of return exceeds the rate of return that they could earn in the market, the effective payroll tax rate is negative and helps to reduce the combined marginal tax rate of the income and payroll taxes. There is, however, a higher tax burden in the earlier years of the transition because individuals are paying both the mandatory saving and the existing payroll tax. The net effect on the present value of the deadweight losses depends on the relative sizes of the short-run losses from increased distortion and the longer-run gains from reduced distortion; see Feldstein and Samwick (1997, 1998a). The present value of these changes in the deadweight loss is a net gain for the same reason that the present value of the consumption is positive, i.e., because the future tax rate reductions are larger than the current tax rate increases. It would of course be possible in theory to get a long-run deadweight loss reduction without any short-run increase in the deadweight loss if the transition is financed by the equivalent of a lump-sum tax, e.g., by cutting the benefits of current retirees and/or the accrued benefit claims of current workers while giving full credit for the savings in individual Social Security accounts (see Kotlikoff (1996) for an example of such a gain).

7.1.4. Government funds or individual accounts

The consumption gains from an investment-based system do not depend on using a defined-contribution system with personal retirement accounts. One alternative that has received substantial attention in the United States and other countries is to place private stocks and bonds in a common account managed by the government or on behalf of the government[93]. Advocates of this approach [e.g., Aaron and Reischauer (1998), Diamond (1998a), Modigliani, Ceprini and Muralidhar (1999)] argue that it would reduce administrative costs relative to a defined-contribution system of individual accounts and would permit an explicitly redistributive defined-benefit system. They note also that a single fund would insulate retirees from the risk of market fluctuations[94].

It is clear that simply shifting the composition of the existing Social Security trust fund from government bonds to private securities without any increase in national

---

[93] This was proposed by President Clinton in his 1999 State of the Union address. Aaron and Reischauer (1998) develop the idea and respond to some criticisms. Canada and Switzerland have created such centrally managed accounts.

[94] See Diamond (1998a) and Aaron and Reischauer (1998) for a discussion of these issues.

saving would raise the rate of return to the Trust Fund, thereby lengthening the period before its balance is exhausted, but would do nothing to increase national income. The extra return earned in the Trust Fund would be balanced by the lower return earned by those who sold the private securities and purchased government bonds[95].

Any gain to national income from increased investment must be the result of increased national saving. Indeed, if national saving is increased, either by requiring individuals to contribute to an enlarged fund or by using a budget surplus that would otherwise be used to finance public or private consumption, it does not matter whether those funds are invested in private stocks and bonds or in government securities. This was the strategy in the 1983 Social Security reforms discussed above. One potential advantage of investing in private securities through individual accounts is that it reduces the political risk that the government accumulation will be used to justify additional government outlays or tax cuts that reduce national saving.

Critics of investing in a common fund of stocks and bonds argue that it will eventually lead to inappropriate political interference in the economy. The government would have a substantial impact on the private economy by the kinds of stocks that it buys or specifically does not buy for the investment account. There could be political pressure to avoid stocks and bonds of tobacco companies, of companies that are foreign owned or that "export jobs" by producing substantial amounts abroad, of nonunion companies, of companies that may have violated anti-trust rules, etc. There would also be problems associated with the government as shareholder during hostile takeovers or as bondholder when there are bankruptcies or debt workouts. With the potential Social Security fund being as large as the entire GDP, these effects could be very substantial [Feldstein (2000)]. Defenders of a common fund argue that such interference could be avoided by a proper administrative structure[96].

Using a single fund would have administrative cost advantages because of economies of scale and avoiding the administrative costs of individual accounts. Balanced against this, a system of private individual accounts may encourage innovation in both products and administration as well as a higher quality of service.

For many people, a major advantage of an individual account investment-based system is apparently that it provides a sense of asset ownership and naturally facilitates making bequests to children or others. Feldstein and Ranguelova (2002) show that permitting the value of the personal retirement account to be bequeathed if the individual dies before age 67 raises the cost of achieving any given benefit level by about one-sixth (for example, from a payroll tax rate of 2.5% to a rate of 3.0%).

---

[95] In a more complete general equilibrium context, the increased demand for riskier assets can either raise GDP [Diamond and Geanakoplos (1999)] or lower it [Abel (2001a)].

[96] Aaron and Reischauer (1998), Diamond (1998b) and Elmendorf, Liebman and Wilcox (2002) discuss these mechanisms.

7.1.5. Mixing pay-as-you-go and investment-based systems

Although completely replacing the pay-as-you-go system with an investment-based system is an analytically convenient way to discuss the general question of funded versus unfunded programs, much of the policy discussion in the United States is about a possible shift from the existing unfunded system to one that combines an unfunded pay-as-you-go program and an investment-based program that uses individual defined-contribution accounts. This is also the approach adopted in other countries including Sweden [Palmer (2002)], the UK [Budd (1998)], and potentially Germany [Rurup (2002)].

Although the net present value gain from shifting to a mixed system would of course be smaller than the gain from shifting to a pure investment-based system, the advocates of a mixed system offer two primary reasons for this alternative. First, a mixed system reduces the extent to which retirement income levels are sensitive to the financial market volatility of a pure investment-based system and to the demographic and political risks of a pay-as-you-go system. Although both types of risks remain, the combination of two different types of risks may present a smaller total risk [Merton (1983)]. Second, the pay-as-you-go portion of a mixed system could be used to achieve any politically desired redistribution among income and demographic groups. We return to both risk and distribution after discussing the issue of how a transition to a pure or mixed investment-based system could be done in practice.

7.2. The transition to an investment-based system

A common objection to an investment-based system is that the transition to such a system involves too much of a burden on the transition generation. Nearly all of the current Social Security tax rate of 12.4% is needed to finance the benefits of existing retirees. The idea of paying the tax to maintain those benefits while accumulating reserves for one's own retirement suggests to some that the tax rate would have to be doubled, an economically and politically impossible prospect. But such a doubling would not be required for two reasons.

First, the cost of maintaining the current benefits in an investment-based system is substantially less than the current payroll tax rate. The example cited in Section 7.1.2 above suggests that with a 6.5% real rate of return the long-run payroll cost of a funded system is only about 27% of the cost of an unfunded system with the same benefits. Even with a more conservative 5.5% real rate of return, the cost of a funded system would be only 36% of the cost of a pay-as-you-go system. Since the Social Security actuaries project a long-run cost of 19% of covered earnings, a funded system could be financed with personal retirement account savings of less than 7% of earnings.

Second, a transition could be done in a way that gradually substitutes personal retirement account annuities for pay-as-you-go benefits. As the investment-based annuities increase, the traditional pay-as-you-go benefits could be reduced without cutting the total retirement benefit from the two sources together. These reductions in the pay-as-you-go benefits permit the corresponding tax to be reduced, permitting the personal retirement account contributions to rise without increasing the sum of the two "contributions"[97].

Feldstein and Samwick (1997, 1998a) develop such a transition for the US Social Security system using detailed economic and demographic assumptions provided by the Social Security Administration in the 1995 Trustees Report on the assumption that the entire marginal product of capital on additional saving could be credited to the personal retirement accounts[98]. More specifically, Feldstein and Samwick (1998a) showed that the transition to a completely investment-based system could be achieved over a long horizon while keeping the combination of the pay-as-you-go tax and the personal retirement account contribution to less than 14%, i.e., an increase of less than 1.6 percentage points on top of the initial 12.4% payroll tax rate. Within 25 years, the combined pay-as-you-go tax and personal retirement account contribution would be below the initial 12.4%. Within the 75 year projection period (for which the Social Security Administration provides demographic and economic projections) the pay-as-you-go tax is fully phased out and the originally projected benefits are financed by the investment-based annuities with a contribution rate of 3.25%[99].

The specific transition path determines how the burden of the transition is spread among different age cohorts and potentially among different generations. An explicit use of recognition bonds that are never amortized but that are serviced in perpetuity causes the burden to be spread over all generations; although at some point the future generations are net beneficiaries, the burden of debt service reduces their net gain. The Feldstein–Samwick method amortizes the cost over a relatively short period.

Who are the net gainers and net losers in any transition depends on what would otherwise have been done. For example, if the alternative to shifting to an investment-based system would be no change in the existing system until the trust fund is exhausted in 2038 and then an increase in the tax rate to maintain benefits, the shift to an investment-based system would impose an extra burden on those who are currently over 30 years old since that generation would otherwise be unaffected. Alternatively, if the pay-as-you-go system would be maintained by raising taxes immediately to a level that would permit benefits to be maintained with no future rise in the tax rate, the shift to an investment-based system would reduce the burden on the currently working

---

[97] Alternatively, the use of "recognition bonds" could allow the obligations to existing retirees and workers to be paid over a wide variety of different longer time paths.

[98] This assumes that the government would credit the incremental corporate tax that results from the additional capital accumulation to the personal retirement accounts. The assumed rate of return on the personal retirement account contributions was thus 9%, the Rippe (1995) estimates before the 1997 revision of the national income and product accounts. Feldstein and Samwick reduce this total return to 8.5% following Poterba's (1998) analysis of the revised NIPA data and focus on the financial market return, which is substantially lower because of corporate taxes.

[99] In an alternative study (done a year later but published earlier) of a shift to a fully funded system, Feldstein and Samwick (1997) assumed that solvency was achieved in 2035 with a temporary tax increase.

generation. Feldstein and Samwick (1997, 1998a) provide explicit analyses of the gains for different age cohorts.

Kotlikoff, Smetters and Walliscr (2001) develop a dynamic general equilibrium life-cycle simulation model that allows them to incorporate macroeconomic feedback effects as they study replacing the existing Social Security system with a privatized system of compulsory saving. In their baseline demographic simulation (which assumes that Social Security's financing gap is eliminated by raising the payroll tax), they find that capital per worker falls in coming decades as the higher payroll tax rates reduce saving by enough to offset the direct capital deepening from the slowdown in labor force growth. However, Social Security privatization provides large welfare gains for future generations, while requiring only small welfare losses for transition generations. Specifically, transition generations experience a 1 to 3% decline in welfare, while the welfare gains for future generations approach 20%. Moreover, the largest gains accrue to the lowest income classes.

In a later study, Feldstein and Samwick (1998b) analyzed the transition to a mixed system that combines the current 12.4% payroll tax rate and an additional 2% of covered earnings contributed to investment-based personal accounts. The analysis uses the economic and demographic assumptions of the 1998 Social Security Trustee's Report and assumes a real rate of return of 5.5% on the assets in the personal retirement accounts. This mixed system is able to maintain the benefits (including retirement, spouse, survivor, dependant and disability benefits) projected in current law[100]. The 2% personal retirement account contribution makes it possible to avoid the increase in the payroll tax to 19% that the Social Security actuaries project would otherwise be needed to maintain projected benefits. Thus, 2% of personal retirement account investments with a 5.5% real rate of return can replace somewhat more than 6% of payroll tax in a pay-as-you-go system[101].

The countries that have made the transition from a pay-as-you-go system to a mixed system or to a pure investment-based system have done so in quite different ways, reflecting national traditions and economic circumstances. Some countries, like England, had well developed financial markets and widespread share ownership. In others, like Chile and Argentina, the capital markets were not well developed and

---

[100] The Social Security Trust Fund decreases but is never exhausted in this adjustment process.

[101] Using only the portfolio return to finance the personal retirement account annuities implies that the federal, state and local governments receive additional tax revenue equal to about 3% of the value of the increased capital stock, with about two-thirds of this going to the Federal government. The Feldstein–Samwick estimates of the accumulated personal retirement account assets implies that by 2030 the incremental Federal income tax is essentially enough to finance the entire 2% contribution to the personal retirement accounts. In effect, the external source of incremental saving can decline from 2% of earnings in the first year to zero after 30 years. Beyond that date, the initial 12.4% could also be reduced while still maintaining the initial projected level of benefits. See also Feldstein and Samwick (2000). These calculations are of course sensitive to the assumptions about the share of incremental saving that flows to domestic corporations rather than to housing and foreign investments; see Elmendorf and Liebman (2000).

relatively few citizens owned financial assets. The experience is a warning against seeking a single formula that is appropriate for all countries and a demonstration that countries with very different preconditions and different stages of financial development can successfully make the transition.

7.3. Risk aspects of investment-based Social Security reform [102]

All Social Security programs involve risks and different programs share these risks in different ways. In a pay-as-you-go system, demographic changes and long-term fluctuations in growth rates alter the tax rate needed to finance any given level of benefits. In an investment-based program, fluctuations in financial markets alter the value of assets and future pensions. In addition, individuals face the "longevity risk" of an unexpectedly long life if their retirement assets are not in the form of an inflation-adjusted life annuity [Brown, Mitchell and Poterba (2000)]. More generally, taxpayers and retirees face unnecessarily large risks in both pay-as-you-go and investment-based systems because there are inadequate opportunities for the international diversification of risk [Shiller (1999), Baxter and King (2001)].

Bohn's (2001) analysis of demographic risks in a neoclassical growth model showed that a pay-as-you-go defined-benefit program may be more efficient in dealing with the risk of birth rate surprises (in a closed economy) than a funded defined-contribution plan because declines in the birth rate that increase the needed tax revenue per worker also raise wage rates (and therefore payroll tax revenues) by reducing the labor–capital ratio.

In practice, the division of the pay-as-you-go risks between retirees and taxpayers is decided by the political process. McHale (2001) shows how key industrial countries, including the United States, have responded to demographic changes by reducing future pension benefits [103]. Rangel and Zeckhauser (2001) consider the risks of the political process in providing intergenerational transfers and conclude that neither the private market nor the voting mechanism can generate an optimal intergenerational allocation of risk.

In an investment-based program, the risk may be borne by retirees, taxpayers, or both. A system of individual defined-contribution accounts places the risk on retirees, although this risk can be reduced or eliminated by government guarantees or by market instruments. In contrast, placing the investments in a Social Security trust fund while promising defined benefits places the risk on future taxpayers, although this risk can be shifted to retirees if benefits are modified when the investment pool does not perform according to expectations. MaCurdy and Shoven (2001) show that substituting

---

[102] This section draws on the papers in Campbell and Feldstein (2001)

[103] In 1983, the United States reduced benefits primarily by delaying the age at which full retirement benefits are available and making a portion of benefits part of taxable income. The US Social Security program was founded as a funded program because of a concern that future generations of voters might not support the benefits provided for in the legislation. See Section 2.1 above.

a stock portfolio for bonds would worsen Social Securities finances roughly 20% of the time, placing extra burdens on taxpayers or retirees. Abel (2001b), Bohn (1997) and Diamond and Geanakoplos (1999) analyze the consequences of such equity investments in a general equilibrium model. Abel's analysis shows that increasing the share of the Social Security trust fund invested in equities causes the economy's capital stock to grow more rapidly and the equilibrium equity premium to decline. Diamond and Geanakoplos (1999) also find that such Trust Fund diversification reduces the equity premium and note that it also raises the utility of workers who hold no equities and of a suitably weighted sum of all household utilities.

An investment-based system of defined-contribution individual accounts without government guarantees places all of the financial market risk of the program on the retirees. Feldstein and Ranguelova (1998, 2001a) examine the magnitude of these risks with a simulation model that assumes that personal retirement accounts accumulate a portfolio that is 60% in stocks (the S&P 500) and 40% in corporate bonds and then convert that portfolio to a variable annuity with the same mix of assets [104]. Using the 1998 demographic and economic assumption of the Social Security actuaries implies that the long-run pay-as-you-go tax rate needed to support the benefits projected in current law (the "benchmark" benefits) would be 18.4%. The simulation model is used to derive long-run risk distributions associated with different account deposit rates. These distributions reflect both the uncertain future mean return and the annual variations in rates of return conditional on that mean return [105]. Higher account deposit rates provide a greater "cushion" against the risks of poor market performance. In a pure investment-based system with a 6% personal retirement account saving rate, the median annuity at age 67 would be 2.12 times the benchmark benefits (implying a ratio of benefits to preretirement earnings of approximately 80%). There is less than one chance in five that the benefits would be less than the benchmark and only a 10% probability that the benefits would be less than 80% of the benchmark. There is however a 5% chance that the benefits would be less than 60% of the benchmark level and a 1% chance in 100 that they would be less than 40% of the benchmark level.

Increasing the personal retirement account saving rate to 9% (just less than half of the 18.4% tax rate that would have to be paid in the pure pay-as-you-go program) raises the median annuity at age 67 to 3.18 times the benchmark benefit and reduces

---

[104] Assuming that the investment portfolio is the same for all individuals and remains the same through the individual's life ignores the important role that a system of investment-based individual account can play in tailoring risks to individual preferences and circumstances, a point emphasized by Campbell et al. (2001).

[105] The portfolio of 60% stocks and 40% bonds had a mean real logarithmic return of 5.5% and a standard deviation of 12.5% for the period from 1946 to 1995. The mean return in the future simulations is taken to be distributed with a mean of 5.5% and a standard deviation of 1.77 percentage points (the 12.5% sample standard deviation divided by the square root of the 50-year sample size.) The annual values during the accumulation and retirement phases are then conditional on this (stochastic) mean with an annual logarithmic return standard deviation of 12.5%.

the probability of getting less than the benchmark amount to under 10%. There is only a 1% chance of getting less than 60% of the benchmark. Explicit expected utility calculations with a constant relative risk aversion utility function show that individuals would prefer the distribution of potential annuity values associated with the 9% saving rate to the sure benchmark benefit if their risk aversion parameter is 3.1 or less [106, 107].

Although many individuals would therefore regard the upside potential as more than adequate compensation for the risk, there are three ways (either singly or in combination) that the risk of a defined-contribution investment-based program can be reduced. One way is to use a mixture of pay-as-you-go and investment-based programs, thus reducing the risk to just that portion of the benefits that are investment-based. Feldstein, Ranguelova and Samwick (2001) analyze such a program that combines a 12.4% payroll tax rate (the current US Social Security tax rate) with personal retirement account savings equal to 2.3% of the same earnings [108]. The analysis assumes that the personal retirement accounts and the subsequent annuities are invested in the stock-bond portfolio with a mean real logarithmic return of 5.5% and a standard deviation of 12.5%. The pay-as-you-go portion would pay benefits equal to somewhat less than two-thirds of the benchmark level of benefits (i.e., than two-thirds of the level of benefits projected in current law). The combination of this pay-as-you-go benefit and the personal retirement account annuity would provide a median retirement annuity equal to 1.27 times the benchmark benefit. There is less than one chance in 10 of receiving less than 80% of the benchmark benefit and less than one chance in 100 of receiving less than two-thirds of the benchmark amount.

A second way of reducing the risk to retirees is by an explicit government guarantee that shifts some or all of the risk of the financial market performance to future taxpayers. Feldstein and Ranguelova (1998) and Feldstein, Ranguelova and Samwick (2001) extend the analysis of the pure investment-based system described earlier in this section by introducing an explicit guarantee: if the personal retirement account annuity that results from saving 6% of earnings and investing it in the stock-bond portfolio described above does not equal or exceed the benchmark level of benefits in any year, the government pays retirees enough to close the gap. As noted above, with a 6% saving rate there is about one chance in five that benefits will be less than the benchmark for retirees at age 67 and one chance in 10 that the group will receive less

---

[106] A relative risk aversion of 3.1 means that doubling the level of income causes the marginal utility of another dollar to fall by a factor of $2^{3.1} = 8.57$. Such an individual who contemplates two possible states of nature – an income of \$20000 in the bad state and \$40000 in the good state – would be indifferent between receiving \$1 in the bad state and \$8.57 in the good state. Someone with lower risk aversion would prefer the \$8.57 option.

[107] The preference for the personal retirement account option is based solely on the comparison between the annuity payment distribution and the benchmark benefit without taking the lower contribution rate (the 9% mandatory saving versus the 18-plus percent tax) into account. Even someone who preferred the benchmark benefit to the riskier distribution might prefer the PRA option because of the lower contribution rate during working years.

[108] This analysis assumes that the pay-as-you-go benefits are riskless.

than 80% of the benchmark. Since each retiree cohort age 67 and older can receive a guarantee payment in any year and there is no offsetting of good years and bad years, the probability that the taxpayers will make a payment in any year is greater than the probability that any single cohort's annuity will fall short of the benchmark benefit. Nevertheless, the Feldstein–Ranguelova analysis shows that the probability that taxpayers will have to provide any guarantee payment (when retirees have saved 6% of their earnings) is less than 50%. There is only a 5% chance that the taxpayers would have to make a transfer as large as 12% of payroll and only a 1% chance that the taxpayers would have to pay as much as 14.8%[109]. Even with the 12% transfer, the combined cost of the transfer plus the 6% saving rate (for their own retirement) would still be less in that year than the 18.4% payroll tax that would be required in the pure pay-as-you-go system.

These calculations of the taxpayer transfer needed to close the gap between the benchmark benefit and 6% personal retirement account annuity ignore the additional corporate tax revenue that results from the increased capital stock. The calculations in Feldstein and Ranguelova (1998) show that incremental corporate tax revenue equal to 2% of the additional capital stock accumulated because of the individual retirement accounts (an amount equivalent to a tax rate of only about two-thirds of the statutory corporate tax rate) would be equal to about 6.3% of GDP and therefore about 15.7% of covered earnings. This extra tax revenue of 15.7% of covered earnings is enough to finance the entire transfer even in the worst 1% of cases[110].

Smetters (2001) warns that government guarantees of this type are effectively grants of put options to future retirees and that the market price of such options could be very large. According to Smetters, calculations based on a simplified model show that, even with a 12% saving rate, shifting to an investment-based system would reduce the unfunded liability of the government by more than one third only if the government guarantee is limited to less than the current benchmark Social Security benefits. Stated differently, because of the implicit price of risk in option pricing models, the value of the put option that the government provides in guaranteeing the benchmark level of benefits can be very high.

Thinking about the benchmark guarantee as a kind of put option suggests a third way that retiree risk could be reduced if there is no government guarantee or only a limited guarantee. Individual employees could buy such put options from the private securities market. An attractive way to finance the purchase of such a put option would be by selling a call option, i.e., by forgoing some of the potential for a very high level of benefits. In the language of financial derivatives, such a contract is a "collar" and can provide "put option" protection at no cash cost by selling a

---

[109] These simulations are based on the average benefits for each cohort. Taking into account the distribution of benefits would increase government payments moderately because the gains of those above the benchmark would not offset the losses of those below the benchmark.

[110] See Elmendorf and Liebman (2000) for reasons why this may overstate the induced increase in tax revenue.

call option of equal value. Bodie (2001) discussed the possibility of such collars and presented examples of the type of collar that could be purchased with a single premium payment. Feldstein and Ranguelova (2001b) developed an explicit method for evaluating a "pension collar", [i.e., a collar associated with a series of asset purchases (the savings deposits to the personal retirement accounts) followed by a series of variable annuity payments[111]] and applied it to a mixed system in which the 12.4% pay-as-you-go tax finances two-thirds of the future benchmark benefits. The price of the put and call options reflect option pricing values that prevail in the current financial market.

The Feldstein–Ranguelova analysis showed that an individual who saves 2.5% of earnings in a personal retirement account invested in the 60 : 40 equity–debt portfolio can buy a collar that guarantees the benchmark level of benefits and provides for gains of up to 116% of the benchmark level (i.e., any gain above the 116% goes to the seller of the collar). Reducing the guarantee level to 90% of the benchmark increases the maximum gain to 150% of the benchmark while raising the saving rate to 3.0% permits guaranteeing the full benchmark while allowing a gain of up to 145% of the benchmark. As these examples show, one of the advantages of the collar approach is that it could, in principle, allow different individuals to obtain the mix of guarantee and upside potential that best reflects their personal taste. The use of the private market to trade risk through time in this way can effectively allow individuals to share risk with individuals of other generations. Unlike the simple overlapping generations model in which individuals work for only one period and then retire, in the actual economy retirees or those near retirement could shift risk via financial markets to younger workers who, because they have relatively little portfolio risk and a larger amount of human capital, would have a greater appetite for risk; as those younger workers age, they can shift the risk to yet younger cohorts.

In addition to the political risks of a pay-as-you-go system and the financial market risks of an investment-based system, there are also the individual longevity risks, i.e., the risk that individuals will live substantially longer than the normal life expectancy, running down their retirement assets if they are not fully annuitized. Brown, Mitchell and Poterba (2001) stress the importance of a life annuity and discuss the limited availability of such annuities in the current market. The existence of a universal investment-based system with mandatory annuitization would change the annuity market fundamentally and eliminate the self-selection problem that currently distorts the pricing of annuities.

---

[111] There is a technical difficulty in evaluating such a collar because the prices of the assets in which personal retirement account deposits must be invested in future years are not known in advance. An evaluation equivalent to the basic Black–Scholes formula can nevertheless be obtained by the risk neutral evaluation method of Cox and Ross (1976).

7.4. Distributional aspects of investment-based reform[112]

Many investment-based Social Security reform proposals would increase the link between a worker's Social Security contributions and retirement income by making deposits in workers' individual saving accounts that are a constant proportion of their earnings. These proposals have led to concern that the amount of redistribution and poverty alleviation accomplished through Social Security would decline if an individual account-based system were established.

While the research discussed in Section 6 above on the redistribution in the current US system suggests that there is less redistribution to lose in moving to a new system than many people believe, it is nonetheless the case that low-income households would potentially be most vulnerable if a new system added significant amounts of market risk and that a reform that required equal percentage benefit cuts for all beneficiaries would likely cause the most distress at the bottom end of the income distribution.

In a mixed system, these concerns can be addressed by making what remains of the traditional defined-benefit program more redistributive, implicitly making the share of income subject to financial market risk rise with income. This is the approach taken in the Personal Saving Account plan of the 1994–1996 Social Security Advisory Council which converted the pay-as-you-go benefit into an equal benefit for all retirees and in legislation introduced by Senators Breaux and Gregg and Congressmen Kolbe and Stenholm who added a new minimum benefit for low-wage workers in order to insulate them from the cuts to the traditional benefit and market risk that are part of their plan.

Feldstein and Liebman (2002a) use the same micro simulation model as Liebman (2002) to explore how workers at different income levels fare under a mixed system. They find that with a 3% of payroll personal savings deposit added on top of the existing 12.4% of payroll pay-as-you-go system, essentially all demographic groups, including those groups that now receive particularly high returns from the current system, end up with higher levels of retirement income. Specifically, they study the long-run steady state after a transition to a mixed system that provides a total benefit equal to 61% of current law Social Security benefits (the amount that can be afforded in the long run without raising the 12.4% payroll tax) plus the proceeds from a 3% of payroll individual account. Some 94% of beneficiaries have higher benefits under the mixed system than under the traditional system, even though this is with a total long run contribution rate of only 15.4% rather than the 19% that would be necessary to maintain the pay-as-you-go system. There are also substantial reductions in the percentage of beneficiaries with benefits below the poverty line. These poverty gains are particularly large for high risk groups. For example, the percentage of widowed, divorced, and never married women with benefits below the poverty line falls from 26% to 9%. Among unmarried black retirees it falls from 53% to 21%.

---

[112] This section draws on the studies presented in Feldstein and Liebman (2002b).

While the gains in the long run from switching to a mixed system extend throughout the population, the percentage gains in retirement income are largest for high income individuals if deposits into the individual accounts are proportional to earnings. Feldstein and Liebman (2002a) show, however, that if the accounts are funded in a redistributive manner, it is possible to have equal percentage gains throughout the income distribution. In particular, if half of total account deposits are equal per capita contributions and half are proportional to earnings, then the accounts essentially match the observed redistribution of the current Social Security system.

In considering the redistributive properties of individual accounts, it is important to note that if annuitization is required and the annuitization occurs at a single price for the entire population, then individual accounts will provide the same sort of redistribution from those with short life expectancies to those with long life expectancies that is found in the current defined-benefit Social Security system. However, if only partial annuitization is required and accounts are therefore partially bequeathable then some of this redistribution based upon life expectancy (which typically flows from low earners to high earners) will be offset.

Feldstein and Ranguelova (2002) examine the potential magnitudes of the bequests that might result in an investment-based plan under different rules about bequests. Permitting employees who die before retirement to bequeath the assets in their Personal Retirement Accounts would reduce the funds available at age 67 by about one-sixth, implying for example that the same level of annuity could be achieved with a 3.6% PRA saving rate and preretirement bequests or a 3.0% PRA with no bequest. Brown (2002) analyzes the financial redistribution that would occur under various annuity and bequest options in an individual accounts program. A key part of his analysis is applying mortality rates differentiated by gender, race, ethnicity and education level to calculate the transfers that would take place between different groups under different assumptions about the structure of the annuity program. Among his findings is that mandating that each individual's retirement benefit be paid as a single life annuity can result in much larger transfers from high mortality groups (such as black males) to low mortality groups (such as white females) than would occur if joint life annuities or bequest options were allowed.

Finally, it is worth emphasizing that the general equilibrium effects of Social Security reform can have important distributional effects. Kotlikoff, Smetters and Walliser (2002) use a computable general equilibrium model to analyze how the shift to an investment-based system would change wages and interest rates. They conclude that an investment-based system would help the poor both because of the higher return on investment-based accounts and because of the increased capital per worker in the economy.

8. Conclusion

The size and social importance of the Social Security program will make this subject a central part of public finance in future years. The evolution of the systems in different countries of the world will provide rich material for students of public finance and an important opportunity to contribute to evolving policy in this important public policy area.

References

Aaron, H.J. (1966), "The social insurance paradox", Canadian Journal of Economics and Political Science 32:371–374.

Aaron, H.J. (1982), Economic Effects of Social Security (Brookings Institution, Washington, DC).

Aaron, H.J., and R.D. Reischauer (1998), Countdown to Reform (Century Foundation Press, New York).

Abel, A. (2001a), "The effects of investing social security funds in the stock market when fixed costs prevent some households from holding stocks", American Economic Review 91:128–148.

Abel, A. (2001b), "The social security trust fund, the riskless interest rate, and capital accumulation", in: J. Campbell and M. Feldstein, eds., Risk Aspects of Investment-Based Social Security Reform (University of Chicago Press, Chicago) pp. 153–202.

Advisory Council on Social Security (1997), Report of the 1994–1996 Advisory Council on Social Security, Vol. I, Findings and Recommendations (Social Security Administration, Washington, DC).

Atkinson, A.B. (1987), "Income maintenance and social insurance", in: A.J. Auerbach and M. Feldstein, eds., Handbook of Public Economics, Vol. 2 (North-Holland, Amsterdam) pp. 779–908.

Auerbach, A.J., and L.J. Kotlikoff (1983a), "National savings, economic welfare, and the structure of taxation", in: M. Feldstein, ed., Behavioral Simulation Models in Tax Policy Analysis (University of Chicago Press, Chicago) pp. 459–498.

Auerbach, A.J., and L.J. Kotlikoff (1983b), "An examination of empirical tests of social security and savings", in: E. Hellman, A. Rabin and E. Saatchi, eds., Social Policy Evaluation: An Economic Perspective (Academic Press, New York) pp. 161–179.

Auerbach, A.J., and L.J. Kotlikoff (1987), Dynamic Fiscal Policy (Cambridge University Press, Cambridge).

Auten, G., and R. Carroll (1999), "The effect of income taxes on household income", Review of Economics and Statistics 81:681–693.

Banks, J., and C. Emmerson (2000), "Public and private pension spending: principles, practice and the need for reform", Fiscal Studies 21:1–63.

Barro, R.J. (1978), The Impact of Social Security on Private Saving (American Enterprise Institute for Public Policy Research, Washington, DC).

Barro, R.J., and G.M. MacDonald (1979), "Social security and consumer spending in an international cross section", Journal of Public Economics 11:275–289.

Baxter, M., and R. King (2001), "The role of international investment in a privatized social security system", in: J. Campbell and M. Feldstein, eds., Risk Aspects of Investment-Based Social Security Reform (University of Chicago Press, Chicago) pp. 371-433.

Becker, G.S., and K.M. Murphy (1988), "The family and the state", Journal of Law and Economics 31:1–18.

Berkovec, J., and S. Stern (1991), "Job exit behavior of older men", Econometrica 59:189–210.

Bernheim, B.D. (1987), "The economic effects of social security: towards a reconciliation of theory and measurement", Journal of Public Economics 33:273–304.

Bernheim, B.D. (2002), "Taxation and saving", in: A.J. Auerbach and M. Feldstein, eds., Handbook of Public Economics, Vol. 3 (Elsevier, Amsterdam) pp. 1173–1249.

Bernheim, B.D., and L. Levin (1989), "Social security and personal savings: an analysis of expectations", American Economic Review 79:97–102.

Blinder, A.S., R.H. Gordon and D.E. Wise (1980), "Reconsidering the work disincentive effects of social security", National Tax Journal 33:431–442.

Blinder, A.S., R.H. Gordon and D.E. Wise (1983), "Social security, bequests, and the life cycle theory of saving: cross-sectional tests", in: F. Modigliani and R. Hemming, eds., The Determinants of National Saving and Wealth (Macmillan, London) pp. 89–122.

Board of Trustees (2001), The 2001 Annual Report of the Board of Trustees of the Federal Old-Age and Survivors Insurance and Disability Insurance Trust Funds (U.S. Government Printing Office, Washington, DC).

Bodie, Z. (2001), "Financial engineering and social security reform", in: J. Campbell and M. Feldstein, eds., Risk Aspects of Investment-Based Social Security Reform (University of Chicago Press, Chicago) pp. 291–320.

Bohn, H. (1997), "Social security reform and financial markets", in: S. Sass and R. Triest, eds., Social Security Reform, Federal Reserve Bank of Boston Conference Series no. 41 (Federal Reserve Bank of Boston, Boston, MA) pp. 228–235.

Bohn, H. (1999), "Will social security and Medicare remain viable as the U.S. population is aging?" Carnegie-Rochester Conference Series on Public Policy 50(June 1999):1–53.

Bohn, H. (2001), "Social security and demographic uncertainty: the risk sharing properties of alternative policies", in: J. Campbell and M. Feldstein, eds., Risk Aspects of Investment-Based Social Security Reform (University of Chicago Press, Chicago) pp. 203–241.

Boskin, M.J. (1977), "Social security and retirement decisions", Economic Inquiry 15:1–25.

Boskin, M.J., and M.D. Hurd (1978), "The effects of social security on early retirement", Journal of Public Economics 10:361–377.

Boskin, M.J., L.J. Kotlikoff, D.J. Puffert and J.B. Shoven (1987), "Social security: a financial appraisal across and within generations", National Tax Journal 40:19–34.

Breyer, F. (1989), "On the intergenerational Pareto efficiency of pay-as-you-go financed pension systems", Journal of Institutional & Theoretical Economics 145:643–658.

Brown, J.R. (2002), "Differential mortality and the value of individual account retirement annuities", in: M. Feldstein and J. Liebman, eds., Distributional Aspects of Social Security and Social Security Reform (University of Chicago Press, Chicago) pp. 401–440.

Brown, J.R., O.S. Mitchell and J.M. Poterba (2000), "Mortality risk, inflation risk, and annuity products", Working paper 7812 (National Bureau of Economic Research, Cambridge, MA).

Brown, J.R., O.S. Mitchell and J.M. Poterba (2001), "The role of real annuities and indexed bonds in a mandatory annuitization system", in: J. Campbell and M. Feldstein, eds., Risk Aspects of Investment-Based Social Security Reform (University of Chicago Press, Chicago) pp. 321–360.

Browning, E.K. (1975), "Why the social insurance budget is too large in a democracy", Economic Inquiry 13:373–388.

Browning, E.K. (1985), "The marginal social security tax on labor", Public Finance Quarterly 13: 227–251.

Buchanan, J.M. (1975), The Samaritan's Dilemma in Altruism, Morality, and Economic Theory, E. Phelps, ed. (Sage Foundation, New York).

Budd, A. (1998), "The pensions system in the United Kingdom", in: M. Feldstein, ed., Privatizing Social Security (The University of Chicago Press, Chicago) pp. 99–127.

Burkhauser, R.V., and J.F. Quinn (1983), "Financial incentives and retirement in the United States", in: L. Soderstrom, ed., Social Insurance (North-Holland, Amsterdam) pp. 207–224.

Burkhauser, R.V., and J. Turner (1985), "Is the social security payroll tax a tax?" Public Finance Quarterly 13:253–267.

Burkhauser, R.V., and J.L. Warlick (1981), "Disentangling the annuity from the redistributive aspects of social security in the United States", Review of Income and Wealth 27:401–421.

Burtless, G. (1986), "Social security, unanticipated benefit increases and the timing of retirement", Review of Economic Studies 53:781–805.

Burtless, G. (1999), "An economic view of retirement", in: H. Aaron, ed., Behavioral Dimensions of Retirement Economics (Brookings Institution, Washington, DC) pp. 7–42.

Burtless, G., and R. Moffitt (1984), "The effects of social security benefits on the labor supply of the aged", in: H. Aaron and G. Burtless, eds., Retirement and Economic Behavior (Brookings Institution, Washington, DC) pp. 135–171.

Caldwell, S., M. Favreault, A. Gantman, J. Gokhale and T. Johnson (1998), "Social security's treatment of postwar Americans", Working paper 6603 (National Bureau of Economic Research, Cambridge, MA).

Campbell, J.Y., and M. Feldstein (2001), Risk Aspects of Investment-Based Social Security Reform (University of Chicago Press, Chicago).

Campbell, J.Y., J.F. Cocco, F.J. Gomes and P.J. Maenhout (2001), "Investing retirement wealth: a life cycle model", in: J. Campbell and M. Feldstein, eds., Risk Aspects of Investment-Based Social Security Reform (The University of Chicago Press, Chicago) pp. 439–482.

Cass, D. (1965), "Optimum growth in an aggregate model of capital accumulation", Review of Economic Studies 32:233–240.

Coile, C., and J. Gruber (2000a), "Social security incentives for retirement", Working paper 7651 (National Bureau of Economic Research, Cambridge, MA).

Coile, C., and J. Gruber (2000b), "Social security and retirement", Working paper 7830 (National Bureau of Economic Research, Cambridge, MA).

Coronado, J.L., D. Fullerton and T. Glass (2000), "The progressivity of social security", Working paper 7520 (National Bureau of Economic Research, Cambridge, MA).

Costa, D. (1998), The Evolution of Retirement: An American Economic History, 1880–1990 (University of Chicago Press, Chicago).

Cottani, J., and G. Demarco (1998), "The shift to a funded social security system: the case of Argentina", in: M. Feldstein, ed., Privatizing Social Security (University of Chicago Press, Chicago) pp. 177–211.

Cox, J.C., and S.A. Ross (1976), "The valuation of options for alternative stochastic processes", Journal of Financial Economics 3:145–166.

Crawford, V., and D. Lilien (1981), "Social security and the retirement decision", Quarterly Journal of Economics 96:505–529.

Cutler, D.M., and R. Johnson (2000), "The birth and growth of the social insurance state: explaining old age and medical insurance across countries", Mimeo (Harvard University).

Cutler, D.M., J.M. Poterba, L.M. Sheiner and L.H. Summers (1990), "An aging society: opportunity or challenge?" Brookings Papers on Economic Activity 1:1–73.

Danziger, S., R. Haveman and R. Plotnick (1981), "How income transfer programs affect work, savings, and the income distribution: a critical review", Journal of Economic Literature 19:975–1028.

Darby, M.R. (1979), The Effects of Social Security on Income and the Capital Stock (American Enterprise Institute, Washington, DC).

Deaton, A., P.-O. Gourinchas and C. Paxson (2002), "Social security and inequality over the life cycle", in: M. Feldstein and J. Liebman, eds., Distributional Aspects of Social Security and Social Security Reform (University of Chicago Press, Chicago) pp. 115–143.

Diamond, P.A. (1965), "National Debt in a neoclassical growth model", American Economic Review 55:1125–1150.

Diamond, P.A. (1977), "A framework for social security analysis", Journal of Public Economics 8: 275–298.

Diamond, P.A. (1996), "Proposals to restructure social security", Journal of Economic Perspectives 10:67–88.

Diamond, P.A. (1997), "Macroeconomic aspects of social security reform", Brookings Papers on Economic Activity 2:1–66.

Diamond, P.A. (1998a), "The economics of social security reform: an overview", in: R.D. Arnold, M. Graetz and A. Munnell, eds., Framing the Social Security Debate: Values, Politics, and Economics (Brookings Institution Press, Washington, DC) pp. 38–64.

Diamond, P.A. (1998b), "Could social security really invest in stocks?" Unpublished manuscript (MIT, MA).

Diamond, P.A. (2000a), "Administrative costs and equilibrium charges with individual accounts", in: J. Shoven, ed., Administrative Aspects of Investment-Based Social Security Reform (The University of Chicago Press, Chicago) pp. 137–162.

Diamond, P.A. (2000b), "What stock market returns to expect for the future?" Social Security Bulletin 63(2):38–52.

Diamond, P.A., and J. Geanakoplos (1999), "Social security investment in equities I: Linear case", Working paper 7103 (National Bureau of Economic Research, Cambridge, MA).

Diamond, P.A., and J. Gruber (1998), "Social security and retirement in the U.S.", in: J. Gruber and D. Wise, eds., Social Security and Retirement Around the World (University of Chicago Press, Chicago) pp. 437–474.

Diamond, P.A., and J.A. Hausman (1984a), "Retirement and unemployment behavior of older men", in: H. Aaron and G. Burtless, eds., Retirement and Economic Behavior (Brookings Institution, Washington, DC) pp. 97–135.

Diamond, P.A., and J.A. Hausman (1984b), "Individual savings and retirement behavior", Journal of Public Economics 23:81–114.

Diamond, P.A., and J. Mirrlees (1978), "A model of social insurance with variable retirement", Journal of Public Economics 10:295–336.

Diamond, P.A., and J. Mirrlees (1986), "Payroll-tax financed social insurance with variable retirement", Scandinavian Journal of Economics 88:25–50.

Diamond, P.A., and J. Mirrlees (2000), Adjusting one's standard of living: two period models", in: P.J. Hammond and G.D. Myles, eds., Incentives, Organization, and Public Economics; Papers in Honour of Sir James Mirrlees (Oxford University Press, Oxford) pp. 107–122.

Diamond, P.A., and J. Mirrlees (2002), "Social insurance with variable retirement and private savings", Journal of Public Economics, forthcoming.

Dicks-Mireaux, L., and M.A. King (1983), "Portfolio composition and pension wealth: an econometric study", in: Z. Bodie and J. Shoven, eds., Financial Aspects of the U.S. Pension System (University of Chicago Press, Chicago) pp. 399–440.

Dicks-Mireaux, L., and M.A. King (1984), "Pension wealth and household saving: tests of robustness", Journal of Public Economics 23:115–139.

Duggan, J.E., R. Gillingham and J.S. Greenlees (1993), "The returns paid to early social security cohorts", Contemporary Policy Issues 11:1–13.

Edey, M., and J. Simon (1998), "Australia's retirement income system", in: M. Feldstein, ed., Privatizing Social Security (University of Chicago Press, Chicago) pp. 63–89.

Edwards, S. (1998), "The Chilean pension reform: a pioneering program", in: M. Feldstein, ed., Privatizing Social Security (University of Chicago Press, Chicago) pp. 33–57.

Elmendorf, D.W., and J. Liebman (2000), "Social security reform and national saving in an era of budget surpluses", in: Brookings Papers on Economic Activity 2 (Brookings Institution, Washington, DC).

Elmendorf, D.W., and L.M. Sheiner (2000), "Should America save for its old age? Fiscal policy, population aging, and national saving", Journal of Economic Perspectives 14:57–74.

Elmendorf, D.W., J. Liebman and D. Wilcox (2002), "Fiscal policy and social security policy during the 1990s", in: J. Frankel and P. Orszag, eds., American Economic Policy in the 1990s (MIT Press, Cambridge, MA) pp. 61–119.

Feenberg, D.R. (1987), "Are tax price models really identified: the case of charitable giving", National Tax Journal 40:629–633.

Feldstein, M. (1974), "Social security, induced retirement and aggregate capital accumulation", Journal of Political Economy 82:905–926.

Feldstein, M. (1976a), "Seven principles of social insurance", Challenge 19:9–11.

Feldstein, M. (1976b), "Social security and the distribution of wealth", Journal of the American Statistical Association 71:800–807.

Feldstein, M. (1977), "Social security and private savings: international evidence in an extended life-cycle model", in: M. Feldstein and R. Inman, eds., The Economics of Public Services (The Macmillan Press, London) pp. 174–205.

Feldstein, M. (1980), "International differences in social security and saving", Journal of Public Economics 14:225–244.

Feldstein, M. (1982), "Social security and private saving: reply", Journal of Political Economy 90: 630–642.

Feldstein, M. (1983), "Social security benefits and the accumulation of pre-retirement wealth", in: F. Modigliani and R. Hemming, eds., The Determinants of National Saving and Wealth (Macmillan, London) pp. 3–23.

Feldstein, M. (1985), "The optimal level of social security benefits", Quarterly Journal of Economics 10:303–320.

Feldstein, M. (1987a), The welfare cost of social security's impact on private saving", in: M. Boskin, ed., Essays in Honor of Arnold Harberger (Basil Maxwell, Oxford) pp. 1–13.

Feldstein, M. (1987b), "Should social security be means tested?" Journal of Political Economy 95: 468–484.

Feldstein, M. (1990), "Imperfect annuity markets, unintended bequests, and the optimal age structure of social security benefits", Journal of Public Economics 41:31–43.

Feldstein, M. (1995a), "Fiscal policies, capital formation and capitalism", The 1994 J. Schumpeter Lecture to the European Economic Association, in: European Economic Review 39:399–420.

Feldstein, M. (1995b), "The effect of marginal tax rates on taxable income: a panel study of the 1986 Tax Reform Act", Journal of Political Economy 103:551–572.

Feldstein, M. (1995c), "Would privatising social security raise economic wellbeing?" Working paper 5281 (National Bureau of Economic Research, Cambridge, MA).

Feldstein, M. (1996a), "The missing piece in policy analysis: social security reform", The R.T. Ely Lecture, in: American Economic Review 86:1–14.

Feldstein, M. (1996b), "Social security and savings: new time series evidence", National Tax Journal 49:151–164.

Feldstein, M., ed. (1998a), Privatizing Social Security (The University of Chicago Press, Chicago).

Feldstein, M. (1998b), "Transition to a fully funded pension system: five economic issues", in: H. Siebert, ed., Redesigning Social Security (Institute of World Economics of the University of Kiel, Germany) pp. 299–315.

Feldstein, M. (1998c), "The effect of privatizing social security on economic welfare; appendix to the Introduction", in: M. Feldstein, ed., Privatizing Social Security (The University of Chicago Press, Chicago) pp. 1–29.

Feldstein, M. (1999a), "Prefunding Medicare", American Economic Review 89:222–227.

Feldstein, M. (1999b), "Tax avoidance and the deadweight loss of the income tax", Review of Economics and Statistics 81:674–680.

Feldstein, M. (2000), "Comment on P. Diamond, Administrative costs and equilibrium charges with individual accounts", in: J. Shoven, ed., Administrative Aspects of Investment-Based Social Security Reform (The University of Chicago Press, Chicago) pp. 162–169.

Feldstein, M., and J. Liebman (2002a), "The distributional effects of an investment-based social security reform", in: M. Feldstein and J. Liebman, eds., Distributional Aspects of Social Security and Social Security Reform (University of Chicago Press, Chicago) pp. 263–322.

Feldstein, M., and J. Liebman, eds (2002b), Distributional Aspects of Social Security and Social Security Reform (University of Chicago Press, Chicago).

Feldstein, M., and A.J. Pellechio (1979), "Social security and household wealth accumulation: new microeconometric evidence", Review of Economics and Statitistics 61:361.

Feldstein, M., and E. Ranguelova (1998), "Individual risk and intergenerational risk sharing in an investment based social security system", Working paper 6839 (National Bureau of Economic Research, Cambridge, MA).

Feldstein, M., and E. Ranguelova (2001a), "Individual risk in an investment based social security system", American Economic Review 91:1116–1135.

Feldstein, M., and E. Ranguelova (2001b), "Accumulated pension collars: a market approach to reducing the risk of investment-based social security reform", Tax Policy and the Economy 15:149–165.

Feldstein, M., and E. Ranguelova (2002), "The economics of bequests in pensions and social security", in: M. Feldstein and J. Liebman, eds., Distributional Aspects of Social Security and Social Security Reform (University of Chicago Press, Chicago) pp. 371–394.

Feldstein, M., and A. Samwick (1992), "Social security rules and marginal tax rates", National Tax Journal 45:1–22.

Feldstein, M., and A. Samwick (1997), "The economics of prefunding social security and Medicare benefits", Working paper 6055 (National Bureau of Economic Research, Cambridge, MA).

Feldstein, M., and A. Samwick (1998a), "The transition path in privatizing social security", in: M. Feldstein, ed., Privatizing Social Security (The University of Chicago Press, Chicago) pp. 215–260.

Feldstein, M., and A. Samwick (1998b), "Potential effects of two percent retirement accounts", Tax Notes 79:615–620.

Feldstein, M., and A. Samwick (2000), "Allocating payroll tax revenue to personal retirement accounts", Tax Notes 87:1645–1652.

Feldstein, M., and H. Siebert (2002), Social Security Pension Reform in Europe (University of Chicago Press, Chicago).

Feldstein, M., E. Ranguelova and A. Samwick (2001), "The transition to investment-based social security when portfolio returns and capital profitability are uncertain", in: J. Campbell and M. Feldstein, eds., Risk Aspects of Investment-Based Social Security Reform (The University of Chicago Press, Chicago) pp. 41-87.

Flora, P., and J. Alber (1981), "Modernization, democratization, and the development of welfare states in Western Europe", in: P. Flora and A.J. Heidenheimer, eds., The Development of Welfare States in Europe and America (Transaction Books, New Brunswick, NJ) pp. 37–80.

Flora, P., and A.J. Heidenheimer (1981), "The historical core and the changing boundaries of the welfare state", in: P. Flora and A.J. Heidenheimer, eds., The Development of Welfare States in Europe and America (Transaction Books, New Brunswick, NJ) pp. 17–34.

Friedberg, L. (1998), "The social security earnings test and labor supply of older men", in: J. Poterba, ed., Tax Policy and the Economy 12 (MIT Press, Cambridge, MA).

Friedberg, L. (2000), "The labor supply effects of the social security earnings test", The Review of Economics and Statistic 82:48–63.

Geanakoplos, J., O.S. Mitchell and S.P. Zeldes (1998), "Would a privatized social security system really pay a higher rate of return?" in: D. Arnold, M. Graetz and A. Munnell, eds., Framing the Social Security Debate (Brookings Institution, Washington, DC) pp. 137–156.

Geanakoplos, J., O.S. Mitchell and S.P. Zeldes (1999), "Social security's money's worth", in: O. Mitchell, R. Myers and H. Young, eds., Prospects for Social Security Reform (University of Pennsylvania Press, Philadelphia) pp. 79–151.

Gokhale, J., L.J. Kotlikoff and J. Sabelhaus (1996), "Understanding the postwar decline in U.S. saving: a cohort analysis", Brookings Papers on Economic Activity 1:315–390.

Gokhale, J., L.J. Kotlikoff, J. Sefton and M. Weale (2000), "Simulating the transmission of wealth inequality via bequests", Journal of Public Economics 79:93–128.

Goldberg, F., and M.J. Graetz (2000), "Reforming social security: a practical and workable system of personal retirement accounts", in: J. Shoven, ed., Aspects of Investment-Based Social Security Reform (The University of Chicago Press, Chicago) pp. 9–37.

Gordon, R.H. (1983), "Social security and labor supply incentives", Contemporary Policy Issues 3: 16–22.

Goss, S. (1999), "Measuring solvency in the social security system", in: O. Mitchell, R. Myers and

H. Young, eds., Prospects for Social Security Reform (University of Pennsylvania Press, Philadelphia, PA) pp. 16–36.

Gruber, J., and P.R. Orszag (2000), "Does the social security earnings test affect labor supply and benefit receipt?" Working paper 7923 (National Bureau of Economic Research, Cambridge, MA).

Gruber, J., and E. Saez (2000), "The elasticity of taxable income: evidence and implications", Working paper 7512 (National Bureau of Economic Research, Cambridge, MA).

Gruber, J., and D.A. Wise (1999), "Introduction and summary", in: J. Gruber and D.A. Wise, eds., Social Security and Retirement Programs Around the World (University of Chicago Press, Chicago) pp. 1–35.

Gullason, E.T., B.R. Kolluri and M.J. Panik (1993), "Social security and household wealth accumulation: refined microeconometric evidence", Review of Economics and Statistics 75:548–551.

Gustman, A.L., and T.L. Steinmeier (1998), "Social security benefits of immigrants and U.S. born", Working paper 6478 (National Bureau of Economic Research, Cambridge, MA).

Gustman, A.L., and T.L. Steinmeier (2000), "How effective is redistribution under the social security benefit formula?" Working paper 7597 (National Bureau of Economic Research, Cambridge, MA).

Hausman, J.A., and D.A. Wise (1985), "Social security, health status and retirement", in: D. Wise, ed., Pensions, Labor and Individual Choice (University of Chicago Press, Chicago) pp. 159–191.

Horioka, C.Y. (1980), "International differences in social security and saving: a comparison of the Barro and Feldstein estimates", Journal of Public Economics 14:238–244.

Hu, S.C. (1979), Social security, the supply of labor, and capital accumulation", American Economic Review 69:274–283.

Hubbard, R.G. (1985), "Personal taxation, pension wealth, and portfolio composition", Review of Economics and Statistics 67:53–60.

Hubbard, R.G. (1986), "Pension wealth and individual saving: some new evidence", Journal of Money, Credit and Banking 18:167–178.

Hubbard, R.G., and K.L. Judd (1987), "Social security and individual welfare: precautionary saving, borrowing constraints, and the Payroll Tax", American Econnomic Review 77:630–646.

Hubbard, R.G., J. Skinner and S.P. Zeldes (1995), "Precautionary saving and social insurance", Journal of Political Economy 103:360–399.

Hurd, M.D., and M.J. Boskin (1984), "The effects of social security on retirement in the early 1970s", Quarterly Journal of Economics 99:767–790.

Hurd, M.D., and J.B. Shoven (1985), "The distributional impact of social security", in: D. Wise, ed., Pensions, Labor and Individual Choice (University of Chicago Press, Chicago) pp. 193–221.

James, E. (1998a), "New models for old age security: experiments, evidence, and unanswered questions", World Bank Research Observer 13(2):271–301.

James, E. (1998b), "The political economy of social security reform: a cross-country review", Annals of Public and Cooperative Economics 69(4):451–482.

Joustein, A. (2001), "Life-cycle modeling of bequests and their impact on annuity valuation", Journal of Public Economics 79:149–177.

Kahn, J.A. (1988), "Social security, liquidity, and early retirement", Journal of Public Economics 35:97–117.

Kotlikoff, L.J. (1979a), "Social security and equilibrium capital intensity", Quarterly Journal of Economics 93:233–253.

Kotlikoff, L.J. (1979b), "Testing the theory of social security and life cycle accumulation", American Economic Review 69:396–410.

Kotlikoff, L.J. (1987), "Justifying public provision of social security", Journal of Policy Analysis and Management, Spring.

Kotlikoff, L.J. (1996), "Privatization of social security: how it works and why it matters", in: J. Poterba, ed., Tax Policy and the Economy 10 (MIT Press, Cambridge) pp. 1–32.

Kotlikoff, L.J., K. Smetters and J. Walliser (2001), "Finding a way out of America's demographic dilemma", Working paper 8258 (National Bureau of Economic Research, Cambridge, MA).

Kotlikoff, L.J., K. Smetters and J. Walliser (2002), "Distributional effects in a general equilibrium analysis of social security", in: M. Feldstein and J. Liebman, eds., The Distributional Effects of Social Security and Social Security Reform (University of Chicago Press, Chicago) pp. 327–361.

Krueger, A.B., and J.-S. Pischke (1992), "The effect of social security on labor supply: a cohort analysis of the notch generation", Journal of Labor Economics 10:412–437.

Leimer, D.R. (1994), "Cohort specific measures of lifetime net social security transfers", Working paper 59 (Office of Research and Statistics, Social Security Administration, Washington, DC).

Leimer, D.R., and S.D. Lesnoy (1982), "Social security and savings: new time series evidence", Journal of Political Economy 90:606–629.

Lesnoy, S.D., and D.R. Leimer (1985), "Social security and private saving: theory and historical evidence", Social Security Bulletin 48:14–30.

Liebman, J. (2002), "Redistribution in the current U.S. social security program", in: M. Feldstein and J. Liebman, eds., Distributional Aspects of Social Security and Social Security Reform (University of Chicago Press, Chicago) pp. 11–41.

Lindbeck, A. (2002), "Pensions and contemporary socio-economic change: balancing market risk and political risk", in: M. Feldstein and H. Siebert, eds., Social Security Pension Reform in Europe (University of Chicago Press, Chicago).

Lindbeck, A., and M. Persson (2000), "What are the gains from pension reform?" Working paper 535 (The Research Institute for Industrial Economics, Stockholm).

Lindbeck, A., and J. Weibull (1988), "Altruism and time consistency: the economics of fait accompli", Journal of Political Economy 96:1165–1182.

Lubove, R. (1968), The Struggle for Social Security: 1900–1935 (Harvard University Press, Cambridge, MA).

MaCurdy, T., and J.B. Shoven (2001), "Asset allocation and risk allocation: can social security improve its future solvency problem by investing in private securities", in: J. Campbell and M. Feldstein, eds., Risk Aspects of Investment-Based Social Security Reform (The University of Chicago Press, Chicago) pp. 11–32.

McGarry, K. (2002), "SSI and the well-being of the elderly poor", in: M. Feldstein and J. Liebman, eds., The Distributional Effects of Social Security and Social Security Reform (University of Chicago Press, Chicago) pp. 49–79.

McHale, J. (2001), "The risk of social security benefit rule changes: some international evidence", in: J. Campbell and M. Feldstein, eds., Risk Aspects of Investment-Based Social Security Reform (University of Chicago Press, Chicago) pp. 247–282.

Merton, R. (1983), "On the role of social security as a means for efficient risk sharing in an economy where human capital is not tradable", in: Z. Bodie and J.B. Shoven, eds., Financial Aspects of the United States Pension System (University of Chicago Press, Chicago) pp. 325–358.

Merton, R., Z. Bodie and A. Marcus (1987), "Pension plan integration as insurance against social security risk", in: Z. Bodie, J. Shoven and D. Wise, eds., Issues in Pension Economics (University of Chicago Press, Chicago) pp. 147–169.

Miron, J., and D. Weil (1997), "The genesis and evolution of social security", Working paper 5949 (National Bureau of Economic Research, Cambridge, MA).

Mitchell, O.S., and S.P. Zeldes (1996), "Social security privatization", American Economic Review 86:363–367.

Mitrusi, A.W., and J.M. Poterba (2000), "The distribution of payroll and income tax burdens, 1979–1999", National Tax Journal 53:765–794.

Modigliani, F., and A. Sterling (1983), "Determinants of private saving with special reference to the role of social security – cross-country tests", in: F. Modigliani and R. Hemming, eds., The Determinants of National Saving and Wealth (MacMillan, London) pp. 24–55.

Modigliani, F., M. Ceprini and A. Muralidhar (1999), "A better solution to the social security crisis: funding with a common portfolio", Working paper 1-01 (World Economy Laboratory, Massachusetts Institute of Technology, Cambridge, MA).

Moffitt, R. (1984), "Trends in social security wealth by cohort, in: M. Moon, ed., Economic Transfers in the U.S. (University of Chicago Press, Chicago) pp. 327–347.

Moss, D. (2002), When All Else Fails – Governments as Ultimate Risk Manager (Harvard University Press, Cambridge, MA).

Mulligan, C.B. (2000a), "Can monopoly unionism explain publically induced retirement?" Working paper 7680 (National Bureau of Economic Research, Cambridge, MA).

Mulligan, C.B. (2000b), "Induced retirement, social security, and the pyramid mirage", Working paper 7679 (National Bureau of Economic Research, Cambridge, MA).

Mulligan, C.B., and X. Sala-i-Martin (1999a), "Gerontocracy, retirement and social security", Working paper 7117 (National Bureau of Economic Research, Cambridge, MA).

Mulligan, C.B., and X. Sala-i-Martin (1999b), "Social security in theory and practice (I): Facts and political theories", Working paper 7118 (National Bureau of Economic Research, Cambridge, MA).

Mulligan, C.B., and X. Sala-i-Martin (1999c), "Social security in theory and practice (II): Efficiency theories, narrative theories, and implications for reform", Working paper 7119 (National Bureau of Economic Research, Cambridge, MA).

Munnell, A.H. (1974), "Impact of social security on personal savings", National Tax Journal 27: 553–567.

Murphy, K.M., and F. Welch (1998), "Perspectives on the social security crisis and proposed solutions", American Economic Review 88:142–150.

Murthi, M., J.M. Orszag and P.R. Orszag (2001), "Administrative costs under a decentralized approach to individual accounts: lessons from the United Kingdom", in: R. Holzmann and J. Stiglitz, eds., New Ideas About Old Age Security (The World Bank, Washington, DC) pp. 308–335.

Organisation for Economic Cooperation and Development (1998), Maintaining Prosperity in an Ageing Society (OECD, Paris).

Orszag, P.R., and J.E. Stiglitz (2001), "Rethinking pension reform: ten myths about social security systems", in: R. Holzmann and J. Stiglitz, eds., New Ideas About Old Age Security (The World Bank, Washington, DC) pp. 17–56.

Palmer, E. (2002), "Swedish pension reform: how did it evolve and what does it mean for the future?" in: M. Feldstein and H. Siebert, eds., Social Security Pension Reform in Europe (University of Chicago Press, Chicago) pp. 171–205.

Peltzman, S. (1980), "The growth of government", Journal of Law and Economics 23:209–287.

Poterba, J.M. (1998), "The rate of return to corporate capital and factor shares: new estimates using revised national income accounts and capital stock data", Carnegie-Rochester Conference Series on Public Policy 48:211–246.

Quinn, J.E. (1999), "Has the early retirement trend reversed?" Paper presented at the first annual joint conference of the Retirement Research Consortia, Washington, DC, May 20–21, 1999.

Rangel, A. (2002), "Forward and backward intergenerational goods: why is social security good for the environment", American Economic Review, forthcoming.

Rangel, A., and R.J. Zeckhauser (2001), "Can market and voting institutions generate optimal intergenerational risk sharing", in: J. Campbell and M. Feldstein, eds., Risk Aspects of Investment-Based Social Security Reform (University of Chicago Press, Chicago) pp. 113–141.

Rippe, R. (1995), "Further gains in corporate profitability", in: Economic Outlook Monthly (Prudential Securities, Inc.) August 1995.

Ritter, G.A. (1986), Social Welfare in Germany and Britain (Berg, New York).

Rodgers, D.T. (1998), Atlantic Crossings: Social Politics in a Progressive Era (Harvard University Press, Cambridge, MA).

Rothschild, M., and J.E. Stiglitz (1970), "Increasing risk I: A definition", Journal of Economic Theory 2:225–243.

Rothschild, M., and J.E. Stiglitz (1971), "Increasing risk II: Its economic consequences", Journal of Economic Theory 3:66–84.

Rothschild, M., and J.E. Stiglitz (1976), "Equilibrium in competitive insurance markets", Quarterly Journal of Economics 90:630–649.

Rurup, B. (2002), "The future of the German pension system: stabilization of contributions by a mandatory saving plan", in: M. Feldstein and H. Siebert, eds., Social Security Pension Reform in Europe (University of Chicago Press, Chicago) pp. 137–163.

Sala-i-Martin, X. (1996), "A positive theory of social security", Journal of Economic Growth 1:277–304.

Sales-Sarrapy, C., F. Solis-Soberon and A. Villagomez-Amezua (1998), "Pension system reform: the Mexican case", in: M. Feldstein, ed., Privatizing Social Security (University of Chicago Press, Chicago) pp. 135–172.

Samuelson, P.A. (1958), "An exact consumption loan model of interest with or without the social contrivance of money", Journal of Political Economy 66:467–482.

Samwick, A. (1998), "New evidence on pensions, social security and the timing of retirement", Working paper 6534 (National Bureau of Economic Research, Cambridge, MA).

Schieber, S., and J.B. Shoven (1999), The Real Deal: The History and Future of Social Security (Yale University Press, New Haven).

Shiller, R. (1999), "Social security and institutions for intergenerational, intragenerational and international risk sharing", Carnegie-Rochester Conference Series on Public Policy 50:165–204.

Shoven, J.B. (2000), Administrative Aspects of Investment-Based Social Security Reform (University of Chicago Press, Chicago).

Sinn, H.-W. (2000), "Why a funded pension system is useful and why it is not useful", Working paper 7592 (National Bureau of Economic Research, Cambridge, MA).

Smetters, K. (2001), "The effect of pay-when-needed benefit guarantees on the impact of social security reform", in: J. Campbell and M. Feldstein, eds., Risk Aspects of Investment-Based Social Security Reform (University of Chicago Press, Chicago) pp. 91–105.

Steuerle, C.E., and J.M. Bakija (1994), Retooling Social Security for the 21st Century (Urban Institute Press, Washington, DC).

Stock, J., and D.A. Wise (1990), "Pensions, the option value of work, and retirement", Econometrica 58:1151–1180.

Tabellini, G. (1990), "A positive theory of social security", Working paper 3272 (National Bureau of Economic Research, Cambridge, MA).

U.S. Congressional Budget Office (1998), Social Security and Private Saving: A Review of the Empirical Evidence (U.S. Government Printing Office, Washington, DC).

U.S. Congressional Budget Office (2000a), The Budget and Economic Outlook: Fiscal Years 2001–2010 (U.S. Government Printing Office, Washington, DC).

U.S. Congressional Budget Office (2000b), The Long-Term Budget Outlook (U.S. Government Printing Office, Washington, DC).

U.S. House of Representatives Committee on Ways and Means (2000), Green Book: Background Material and Data on Programs Within the Jurisdiction of the Committee on Ways and Means (U.S. Government Printing Office, Washington, DC).

Weaver, C.L. (1982), The Crisis in Social Security: Economic and Political Origins (Duke University Press, Durham, NC).

Part 7

LABOR MARKET EFFECTS

Chapter 33

LABOR SUPPLY EFFECTS OF SOCIAL INSURANCE*

ALAN B. KRUEGER

Princeton University; and NBER

BRUCE D. MEYER

Northwestern University; and NBER

Contents

* We thank Melissa Clark, Kenneth Fortson, Jeegar Kakkad and Bradley Heim for helpful research assistance and David Autor, Bertil Holmlund and Peter Orszag for helpful comments. We also thank Alan Auerbach for his patience and persistence in waiting for this chapter, and helpful comments.

Handbook of Public Economics, Volume 4, Edited by A.J. Auerbach and M. Feldstein

Abstract

This chapter examines the labor supply effects of social insurance programs. We argue
that this topic deserves separate treatment from the rest of the labor supply literature
because individuals may be imperfectly informed as to the rules of the programs
and because key parameters are likely to differ for those who are eligible for social
insurance programs, such as the disabled. Furthermore, differences in social insurance
programs often provide natural experiments with exogenous changes in wages or
incomes that can be used to estimate labor supply responses. Finally, social insurance
often affects different margins of labor supply. For example, the labor supply literature
deals mostly with adjustments in the number of hours worked, whereas the incentives
of social insurance programs frequently affect the decision of whether to work at all.

The empirical work on unemployment insurance (UI) and workers' compensation (WC) insurance finds that the programs tend to increase the length of time
employees spend out of work. Most of the estimates of the elasticities of lost work
time that incorporate both the incidence and duration of claims are close to 1.0 for
unemployment insurance and between 0.5 and 1.0 for workers' compensation. These
elasticities are substantially larger than the labor supply elasticities typically found for
men in studies of the effects of wages or taxes on hours of work. The evidence on
disability insurance and (especially) social security retirement suggests much smaller
and less conclusively established labor supply effects. Part of the explanation for this
difference probably lies in the fact that UI and WC lead to short-run variation in wages
with mostly a substitution effect. Our review suggests that it would be misleading
to apply a universal set of labor supply elasticities to these diverse problems and
populations.

Keywords

workers' compensation insurance, unemployment insurance, disability insurance,
social security, labor supply, Natural Experiment

JEL classification: H55, J22, J28, J65

1. Introduction

This chapter summarizes evidence on the labor supply effects of social insurance programs. One may ask, "Why is a separate chapter necessary on the labor supply effects of social insurance? Why can't the labor supply parameters estimated in the voluminous labor economics literature just be plugged into the social insurance formulas"? In our view, a separate consideration of the labor supply effects of social insurance is justified for at least three reasons.

First, the generic labor supply parameters estimated in the public finance and labor economics literatures may not apply to social insurance programs because people are imperfectly informed as to the rules of the programs, or because the parameters may differ for those who are eligible for social insurance programs (i.e., heterogeneous parameters) than for the population at large. For example, a severe disability may change the way an individual perceives the trade off between labor and leisure time. More generally, the people who are on the margin of going on a social insurance program are likely to have different preferences than the wider population.

Second, the labor supply elasticities estimated in the labor economics literature span a huge range. Literature surveys such as Pencavel (1986) and Killingsworth (1983) find wide dispersion in estimates of income and substitution effects. Fuchs, Krueger and Poterba (1998) also find that there is little agreement among economists on the magnitude of labor supply elasticities. A major shortcoming in the broader labor supply literature is that it is difficult to identify exogenous changes in wages or income that can be used to estimate labor supply responses. The variations in social insurance programs may provide natural experiments with which to estimate labor supply parameters and test the relevance of labor supply models.

Third, the design of social insurance raises several theoretical labor supply issues that are not often dealt with in the standard labor supply literature. For example, the prospect of receiving Social Security benefits in the future may induce some young people to enter the work force, while the provision of benefits may induce older workers to leave the work force. Moreover, much of the labor supply literature deals with adjustments in the number of hours worked per week or number of weeks worked per year, whereas the incentives of social insurance programs often affect the decision of whether to participate at all in the labor force. And programs such as Unemployment Insurance (UI) influence job search intensity, which does not figure into standard labor supply models.

To summarize the impact of social insurance on labor supply, it is necessary to have a working definition of what is meant by "social insurance". There is no official definition. For our purposes, social insurance programs are defined as compulsory, contributory government programs that provide benefits to individuals if certain conditions are met. For example, upon turning age 62 eligible individuals may receive Social Security benefits in the United States. In general, social insurance programs are funded by dedicated taxes or premiums, and have compulsory coverage. Benefits are generally restricted to those who contributed to the program's financing.

Under this definition, for example, Medicare is social insurance but Medicaid is not because Medicare receipt is limited to qualified individuals who contributed to the program while Medicaid receipt is available to all individuals with sufficiently low income. Other programs that are considered social insurance include: Social Security retirement benefits, Disability Insurance (DI), Unemployment Insurance, and Workers' Compensation (WC) Insurance. These programs form the basis for this chapter[1]. Although other programs could be classified as social insurance, such as the Railroad Employee Retirement program, these four programs are the four largest social insurance programs in the USA, and illustrate many of the lessons that can be learned of the effect of social insurance on labor supply.

In practice, social insurance programs are the way society typically pools risks for events that have catastrophic consequences (e.g., severe work-related injuries), or events that individuals may not plan for adequately on their own (e.g., retirement). More generous benefits will provide greater protection against risk, but would likely generate larger distortionary effects. For example, generous Unemployment Insurance benefits insure workers against the earnings losses that accompany job loss, but also induce some workers to search less intensively for a new job. A great deal of research has focused on identifying and quantifying the intended and unintended consequences of social insurance. Because the receipt of social insurance is often triggered by withdrawing from work, and because the programs are typically funded by taxes on labor, a major avenue in which social insurance has its intended and unintended consequences is through altering labor supply. Another realm in which social insurance can have an unintended effect is on savings: individuals may not save as much to offset the adverse consequences of negative events if they are insured against those risks by social insurance. See Chapter 32 by Feldstein and Liebman in this Volume for evidence on the impact of Social Security on savings behavior.

Ideally, one would like to balance the intended consequences against the unintended consequences of social insurance to design the optimal benefit level. Determining the optimal balance requires knowledge of the distortionary effects of social insurance as well as the beneficial insurance effect. The labor supply response to benefits is an important input into this calculation. Gruber (1997), for example, provides an exemplary evaluation of the tradeoff between the consumption smoothing benefit of the UI program against the undesired distortion to job search intensity caused by the provision of benefits. Knowledge of the labor supply effects of social insurance is required for governments to optimally design the programs.

The provision of social insurance is a major government function. Figure 1.1 displays the percent of the US federal government budget devoted to social insurance expenditures each year since 1967[2]. In 1967, 15% of government expenditures

---

[1] For the most part, the review focuses on US social insurance programs, but we draw on programs in other countries when the evidence is particularly strong and germane.

[2] Here social insurance includes Old Age Survivors and Disability Insurance, Medicare, Workers' Compensation Insurance and Unemployment Insurance benefits.

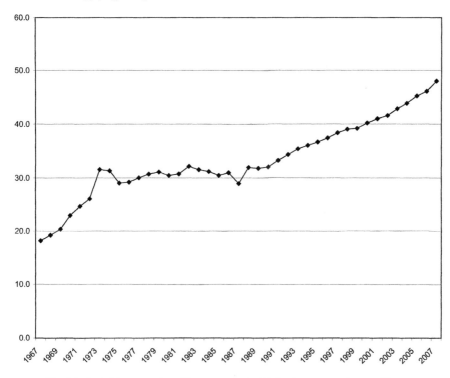

Fig. 1.1. Social insurance benefits as a percent of federal government expenditures.

consisted of social insurance outlays. By 1996, social insurance expenditures rose
to one third of total government spending, and in 2007 social insurance benefits
are predicted to top 44% of government spending. The growth in social insurance
spending is primarily a result of demographic shifts (e.g., an aging population),
increases in program generosity, rising health care costs, and behavioral responses to
program changes. Paul Krugman (2001) did not exaggerate when he observed, "loosely
speaking, the post-cold-war government is a big pension fund that also happens to have
an army".

The USA is not unique in devoting a great deal of the government budget to
social insurance. The first column of Table 1.1 reports the percent of social insurance
spending as a percent of GDP in eight countries, which were selected because they
span a wide range of economic development and had available data. The next two
columns report social insurance expenditures as a percent of the central government's
budget and as a percent of the budget in all levels of government. The social insurance
expenditure data are from the *International Labour Organization,* and cover a broader
range of activities than the measure used in Figure 1.1. In social democratic countries
like Sweden and Germany, social insurance expenditures represent a much greater
share of government and economic activity than they do in the USA. In developing

Table 1.1
Social insurance spending, 1996 [a,b]

Country	Percent of GDP	Percent of central govt expenditures	Percent of total govt expenditures
Sweden	32.47	86.60	49.58
Germany	28.05	82.91	49.44
Mexico	1.36	8.82	6.39
Colombia	6.61	43.33	NA
UK	17.53	43.13	33.77
USA	12.22	59.76	30.02
Japan	2.50	19.44	16.00
Czech Republic	11.89	38.90	25.75

[a] Source: International Labour Organization, *World Labour Report 2000*; International Monetary Fund, *International Financial Statistics*; *UK Statistical Abstract*; and *Japanese Statistical Abstract*.
[b] Social insurance spending includes spending on benefits for old age, survivors, invalidity, employment injury, sickness and health, family, and unemployment. Data from the Czech Republic exclude some health care expenditures. Data for USA pertain to 1995.

countries, social insurance expenditures are a smaller share. Transitioning countries, such as the Czech Republic, appear to be an intermediate case. Social insurance expenditures are surprisingly low in Japan, reflecting in part that country's meager public pension system. Overall, the table gives the impression that social insurance is a normal good, representing a higher share of the government's budget and economic activity in wealthier countries [3]. Not surprisingly, social insurance expenditures have risen over time in many countries as well.

It is natural to question whether the increase in expenditures on social insurance programs has influenced the declining trend in labor force participation. Figure 1.2 illustrates long-term trends in labor force participation of older men in the USA using a series developed by Moen (1987) and Costa (1998) [4]. The figure shows the percent of men age 55–64 or 65 and older who are gainfully employed each Census year. Employment has declined considerably for older men since the beginning of 20th century. Similar – and in some cases sharper – downward trends have occurred in other industrialized countries. The declining employment of older men raises three issues of concern for public economics: first, a smaller proportion of the workforce is

[3] Looking across countries, Rodrik (1998) and Agell (1999) find a positive relationship between the generosity of a variety of social welfare benefits and the openness of the economy, suggesting that social insurance is demanded, in part, to dampen the risk associated with trade shocks.
[4] Quinn (1999) finds that the downward trend in labor force participation of older workers has levelled off or reversed since the mid 1980s. Although this is a very interesting development, our interest here is in the longer term pattern.

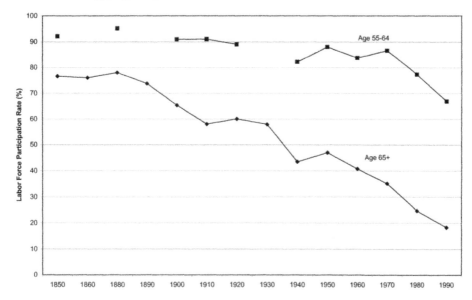

Fig. 1.2. Labor force participation rate.

available to contribute support for social insurance and other government programs; second, more individuals receive Social Security retirement benefits, raising the need for tax revenues; and third, social insurance may distort the economy by inducing some individuals to exit the labor force prematurely[5]. An earlier wave of studies [e.g., Parsons (1980) and Hurd and Boskin (1984)] attempted to explain the fall in aggregate labor force participation by rising social insurance benefits.

As social insurance consumes an even larger share of government budgets, and as the size of the working-age population declines relative to the nonworking-age population, understanding labor supply responses to social insurance will take on even greater importance.

The organization of the remainder of this Chapter is as follows. We first discuss Unemployment Insurance in Section 2, beginning by describing the main program features and how they differ across the states. We also provide some brief information on programs in Canada and other countries. We then discuss the main effects of UI on labor supply, first from a theoretical perspective and then by reviewing the empirical evidence. Section 3 follows the same pattern for Workers' Compensation. We begin by describing the main characteristics of state programs, and then lay out the theoretical predictions and empirical evidence on labor supply responses. In Section 4 we examine Social Security. We describe the theoretical predictions and empirical evidence on labor supply effects. We end this section with a discussion of the timing of retirement and the

---

[5] For a more benign interpretation, see Burtless and Munnell (1991).

effects of the earnings test. In Section 5 we examine Disability Insurance. We describe the operation of the program and then analyze the evidence on its role in explaining trends in labor force participation and self-reported disability rates. Section 6 provides our conclusions.

2. Unemployment insurance

Unemployment insurance (UI) is one of the most extensively studied government programs in the USA and elsewhere. Before describing the main features of UI programs and their labor supply effects, we should note that there are several excellent prior surveys of UI[6]. Though many of the surveys cover a wide range of issues, they generally emphasize the labor supply effects of UI.

2.1. Main features of US unemployment insurance programs

UI programs differ sharply across states due to the provisions of the Social Security Act of 1935 which created the current system and gave states great latitude in designing their programs. State UI programs differ in the earnings required for eligibility, the level of benefits (the replacement rate, the minimum and maximum benefit), the potential duration of benefits, and other parameters. Table 2.1 reports key features of twelve state programs in 2000. It is apparent from this table that there are large differences in program parameters across states. These cross-state differences and their frequent changes over time have been a fundamental source of the identifying variation used to estimate the effects of these programs.

Approximately 97% of all wage and salary workers are in jobs that are covered by unemployment insurance. The main categories of workers not covered are the self-employed, employees of small farms, and household employees whose earnings are below the threshold amount. Despite this near universal coverage, less than forty percent of the unemployed received UI in many recent years[7]. The cause of this low rate of receipt is largely that individuals who are new entrants or reentrants to the labor force, who have irregular work histories, and individuals who quit or are fired from their last job are typically not eligible for benefits. Such individuals are frequently excluded by minimum earnings requirements for eligibility ranging from $130 in Hawaii to $3400 in Florida, with a typical state requiring previous earnings just over $1500[8].

---

[6] See Hamermesh (1977), Welch (1977), Danziger, Haveman and Plotnick (1981), Gustman (1982), Atkinson (1987), Atkinson and Micklewright (1990), Devine and Kiefer (1991), Anderson and Meyer (1993) and Holmlund (1998) for surveys of the UI literature.

[7] See Blank and Card (1991) and Anderson and Meyer (1997a) for studies of the reasons for the low rate of UI receipt.

[8] More precisely, earnings during the first four of the five full calendar quarters prior to the quarter an individual files for benefits. Five states now use alternative time frames that differ from this rule.

Table 2.1
Main characteristics of state unemployment insurance programs in the USA[a]

State	Base period earnings required ($)	Replacement rate[b] (%)	Minimum weekly benefit ($)	Maximum weekly benefit ($)	Quarters of work required for for 26 weeks of benefits
California	1125	39–57	40	230	1.56–2.28
Florida	3400	50	32	275	4
Illinois	1600	49.5[c]	51	296–392	1.38
Massachusetts	2400	50-61.9[c]	24–36	431–646	2.77–3.44
Michigan	3090	67[d]	88	300	2.67
Mississippi	1200	50	30	190	3
Missouri	1500	52	40	220	3.12
Nebraska	1600	52–65	36	214	3–3.9
New Jersey	2060	60[c]	61	429	2.67
New York	2400	50	40	365	1.5
Texas	1776	52	48	294	3.85
Median State	1576	52	39	292	3.12

[a] Source: Highlights of State Unemployment Compensation Laws, January 2000.
[b] Where a range is given, a benefit schedule is used in which the replacement rate is higher for lower paid workers.
[c] Illinois, Massachusetts, and New Jersey have dependent allowances.
[d] Of average after tax weekly wage.

UI benefits are paid on a weekly basis, and except for minimum and maximum benefit amounts, are usually between 50 and 60% of previous earnings[9]. All states have a maximum weekly benefit amount, which varies from a low of $190 in Mississippi to over $600 in Massachusetts if dependents' allowances are included. The median state had a maximum benefit of about $292 in 2000. About 35% of claimants receive the maximum benefit. For these individuals, the fraction of their previous earnings replaced by UI can be much lower than 50%. The minimum weekly benefit is typically very low; the median state has a minimum of about $39.

In almost all states, benefits last up to 26 weeks. However, in all but eight states, total benefits paid are restricted to some fraction of previous earnings or weeks worked. Table 2.1 indicates that a typical state requires just over 3 quarters (39 weeks) of work for a claimant to be eligible for 26 weeks of benefits. This provision causes the potential duration of benefits to be less than 26 weeks for approximately half of

---

[9] A typical benefit schedule would compute the weekly benefit amount as high quarter earnings divided by 23. High quarter earnings are typically the highest calendar quarter of earnings during the first four of the five full calendar quarter prior to the quarter an individual files for benefits.

all recipients [10]. In all but 11 states, there is a waiting period of one week after the beginning of unemployment until one can receive benefits.

In 1970, a permanent Federal-State extended benefits program was established to provide additional weeks of benefits to individuals who exhaust their regular State benefits in periods of high unemployment. When a state's insured unemployment rate is sufficiently high, weeks of benefits are extended 50% beyond that which an individual would be entitled to under State law, with the extension not to exceed 13 weeks. In addition, in times of high unemployment Congress has typically passed ad hoc laws temporarily extending benefits further. Because the unemployment rate has been low in recent years, benefits have only rarely been extended, despite a change that relaxed the threshold for benefit extensions in 1993.

Prior to 1979, UI benefits were not subject to Federal income taxation, but in 1979 they became taxable for high income individuals. In 1982 taxation of UI was extended to most individuals, and in 1987 benefits became taxable for all recipients [11]. UI benefits are not, however, subject to OASDHI (Social Security and Medicare) payroll taxes.

A convenient indicator of the work disincentive of UI is the fraction of previous after-tax earnings replaced by after-tax benefits, the after-tax replacement rate. This replacement rate has fallen dramatically in recent years, particularly due to the taxation of benefits, and is now typically under one-half. As recently as 1986, some people had replacement rates near one (often those lifted by the minimum benefit), implying that they would receive from UI nearly what they would earn if they returned to work [12]. This situation is much less common today. Strong disincentives to work part-time remain, though, as benefits are typically reduced dollar for dollar for earnings greater than a fairly small amount (the earnings disregard).

2.2. Unemployment insurance financing

UI financing in the USA is unique in that a firm's tax rate depends on its layoff history. In other countries benefits are funded through general revenues or payroll taxes that are not determined by a firm's layoffs. The dependence of a firm's tax rate on previous UI use is called experience rating. Federal law levies a 6.2% tax on the first $7000 in wages a year paid to an employee. The law provides for a credit of 5.4% to employers that pay State taxes under an approved UI system, so that all employers pay at least 0.8%.

---

[10] A typical state calculates potential weeks of benefits as the minimum of 26 and base period earnings divided by three times the weekly benefit amount. Base period earnings are usually calculated as earnings during the first four of the five calendar quarters prior to the quarter an individual files for benefits.
[11] In 1979 UI benefits became taxable for married taxpayers filing jointly with income over $25 000, and single filers with income over $20 000. In 1982 the cutoffs changed to $18 000 and $12 000, respectively.
[12] See Feldstein (1974) for an earlier discussion and evidence on high replacement rates.

State experience rating systems take many forms, but the two most common are reserve ratio (30 states and D.C.) and benefit ratio experience rating (17 states)[13]. In reserve-ratio systems, a firm's tax rate depends on the difference between taxes paid and benefits accrued divided by average covered payroll. Taxes paid and benefits accrued are typically summed over all past years and are not discounted, whereas average payroll is typically the average over the last three years. In benefit-ratio systems, a firm's tax rate depends on the ratio of benefits paid to taxable wages, both generally averaged over the last three years.

In reserve-ratio states, a firm's tax rate increases in steps as its reserve ratio decreases (in benefit-ratio states tax rates rise as the benefit ratio rises). However, for most firms in almost all states, the tax rates do not adjust sufficiently when the ratios change to cause firms to pay the full marginal UI costs of laying off a worker. In addition, there are large ranges at the top and bottom, over which a firms layoff history has no effect on its tax payments. This provides an incentive to temporarily lay off workers, and subsidizes industries with seasonal variation in employment. Forty states have a tax base that is higher than the Federal base of $7000. Alaska has the highest at $22 600. Overall, in 1998 UI taxes were a highly regressive 1.9% of taxable wages, and 0.6% of total wages[14].

2.3. Unemployment insurance programs outside of the USA

We should emphasize that there are often very different institutions in other countries to insure the unemployed. Moreover, programs for the unemployed are often combined with other programs, and those eligible for one type of benefit are often eligible for another in certain circumstances. These features often make cross-country comparisons problematic. Subject to these caveats, in Table 2.2 we report UI expenditures as a share of GDP and in absolute terms in 7 countries[15]. Analogous expenditures on compensation for work injuries are reported for comparison. There are pronounced differences across countries. Among these countries, the UK has the lowest share of GDP devoted to UI expenditures at 0.25%, while four other countries have shares at least ten times as big. Part of the explanation for the low GDP share in the UK is that they provide a benefit that does not vary with previous earnings and is set at a fairly low level. For example, a single individual over age 25 was entitled to a weekly benefit of £52.2 ($77) in 2000. This amount is about one-fourth of the typical maximum benefit in the USA.

---

[13] See National Foundation for Unemployment Compensation and Workers' Compensation (2000). Michigan and Pennsylvania are counted as benefit ratio states even though they have hybrids of reserve ratio and benefit ratio systems.

[14] See Anderson and Meyer (2001) for an analysis of the distributional effects of UI taxes and benefits.

[15] For summary measures of the replacement rate and benefit duration in OECD countries, Nickell (1998) provides a nice overview.

Table 2.2
International comparisons of expenditures on unemployment insurance and workers compensation[a,b]

Country	Unemployment insurance		Employment injuries (workers' compensation)	
	% of GDP	$US millions	% of GDP	$US millions
Canada	2.52	13 776	0.85	4624
Denmark	4.54	6113	0.24	325
Germany	3.40	65 049	0.60	11 427
Japan	0.46	19 788	0.25	10 744
Sweden	2.95	5460	0.81	1502
UK	0.25	2445	–	–
USA	0.50	28 334	0.74	41 654

[a] Sources: International Labour Organization, Cost of Social Security 1990–96.
[b] Expenditures include cash and in-kind benefits, and administrative and other expenditures. All figures are in nominal dollars and pertain to 1993 (1991 for the USA).

One of the countries with a GDP share over 2.5% is Canada. The Canadian UI program provides an interesting comparison as Canada is a close neighbor of the USA and has a similar per capita income and industry base. Surprisingly, Canadian expenditures are almost one-half of those in the USA despite Canada having a population less than 11% as large. While Canadian weekly benefits are slightly higher and last slightly longer on average than US benefits, the major difference between the countries is in the ratio of UI recipients to the number of unemployed. An unemployed individual is approximately three and one-half times more likely to receive benefits in Canada than in the USA. This difference is hard to explain on the basis of the composition of unemployment in the two countries or current statutory qualification rules, though Canadian benefits were certainly more generous in the 1970s and 1980s than those in the USA. The amount of earnings in the past needed to qualify for benefits is only slightly higher in Canada. Those who have left their previous job are usually not eligible in the USA, but are often eligible in Canada. It is also true that without experience rating, Canadian employers have less incentive to enforce eligibility rules. However, these features appear to only explain a small part of the difference. Furthermore, the timing of when UI became more generous in Canada than in the USA does not fit particularly well with when the two countries' unemployment rates diverged [16].

---

[16] See Card and Riddell (1993, 1997), Riddell and Sharpe (1998) and Riddell (1999) for detailed comparisons of the US and Canadian UI systems and discussions of the role of UI in explaining unemployment rate differences between the two countries.

2.4. Theoretical responses of labor supply to unemployment insurance

UI affects at least five dimensions of labor supply. First, UI can increase the probability of unemployment by affecting worker and firm actions to avoid job loss. Second, program characteristics affect the likelihood that workers will file a claim for benefits once a worker is laid off. Once a claim has been made, we expect that labor supply will be affected by the adverse incentives of the UI program. Third, once on the program, UI can extend the time a person is out of work. Most research on the labor supply effects of UI has focused on this issue. Fourth, the availability of compensation for unemployment can shift labor supply by changing the value of work to a potential employee. Finally, there are additional effects such as the work responses of spouses of unemployed workers. We discuss these five effects in turn [17].

First, we discuss the effect of UI on the incidence of unemployment. UI can induce eligible workers to search less hard for a different job or work less hard on the current job, both of which can lead to a layoff. There has been some modeling of this issue; for example, Mortensen (1990) examines the effect of UI on search while employed. However, these effects have not been extensively studied. There is a substantial theoretical literature on how the availability of UI may make layoffs more common when firms face variable demand for their product. The presence of UI, particularly UI that is not fully experience rated, may make firms more likely to lay off workers and employees more willing to work in layoff-prone firms [see Baily (1977), Feldstein (1976)]. While this response to UI is partly a labor demand effect, it is also partly a labor supply response as workers are induced to take jobs with higher layoff risk because of UI [18].

Second, the generosity of UI benefits may affect the probability that a person claims benefits conditional on a layoff. As the generosity of benefits rises, it is more likely that the stigma and transaction costs of applying for UI will be outweighed by the benefits. Furthermore, whether someone initially receives UI is partly related to how long they are out of work. A UI claimant in nearly all states must be out of work over a week to be eligible for benefits [19]. It is more likely that a person will remain out of work for the waiting week if benefits are high. In addition to affecting program costs, the increased claim rate in turn affects weeks worked, because once a person is on the UI rolls, they become subject to the implicit taxes on work and the consequent work disincentives.

Third, conditional on beginning an unemployment spell, the duration of time out of work is affected by UI. This issue has received the most attention in the UI literature. Both labor supply and search models suggest that higher and longer duration

---

[17] This classification of the labor supply effects of UI leaves out some effects that can be considered labor supply such as possible improvements in the matching of workers to jobs.

[18] This effect of UI occurs through an outward shift in the labor supply curve to high layoff jobs, so it partly falls under the fourth effect of UI below.

[19] This waiting week can be thought of as the deductible in the UI policy.

UI benefits will cause unemployed workers who receive UI to take longer to find a new job. An elegant, yet fairly realistic search model is provided by Mortensen (1977), though there are many search models incorporating unemployment insurance[20]. Mortensen models workers as choosing a search intensity and a reservation wage while facing a stationary known wage offer distribution and a constant arrival rate of job offers (for a given search intensity). If the worker is offered a job at a wage that exceeds the reservation wage, he or she accepts it. Mortensen incorporates two key features of the UI system in the United States into the model: benefits are assumed to be paid only for a specified duration rather than in every period of an unemployment spell, and new entrants or workers who quit jobs are not qualified for benefits[21].

In this framework, the main labor supply effect of UI is to lengthen unemployment spells. This effect can be seen in the model as increases in either the level or potential duration of benefits raise the value of being unemployed, reducing search intensity and increasing the reservation wage. Thus, the exit rate from unemployment,

$$\lambda(s)[1 - F(w)],$$

falls, as both s and $[1 - F(w)]$ fall, where $\lambda(\cdot)$ converts search effort s into job offers, w is the reservation wage and F is the cumulative distribution function of wage offers.

Mortensen's model also implies our fourth labor supply effect of UI, known as the "entitlement" effect. This effect of UI raises the escape rate from unemployment for workers who currently do not qualify for benefits and for qualified workers close to when benefits are exhausted. That is, because the potential for receiving benefits on a future job makes work more attractive, workers who are ineligible for UI search harder to find a job. Higher benefits reduce the escape rate for recipients when time until exhaustion is high and increase the escape rate around the time of exhaustion. This pattern of UI effects on the hazard of leaving unemployment is illustrated in Figure 2.1. Since the entitlement effect is likely to be small relative to the standard search subsidy effect in many countries, the average duration of unemployment is likely to rise with increases in both the level and potential duration of benefits. The effect of UI on unemployment durations has also been modeled using the standard static labor supply model. In a version of this model, Moffitt and Nicholson (1982) assume people to have preferences over two goods, income and leisure. Unemployment in this model raises utility because of its leisure value. The wage on a new job is fixed and a job can be found at any time. At the time of job loss, an individual chooses income and weeks of unemployment subject to a budget constraint that can be seen in Figure 2.2. The budget constraint becomes flatter as the level of UI benefits increases and is extended outward as the potential duration of benefits increases. Both effects make unemployment more attractive, thus making it more likely that an individual will choose to be unemployed longer.

---

[20] See Mortensen (1986), for example.
[21] See Burdett (1979) for an analysis of a similar model.

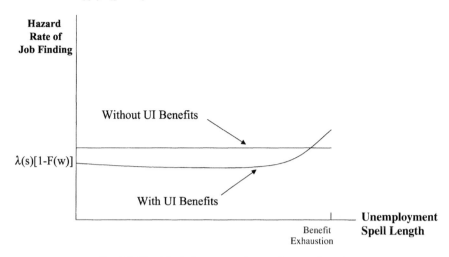

Fig. 2.1. The job-finding rate and unemployment benefits.

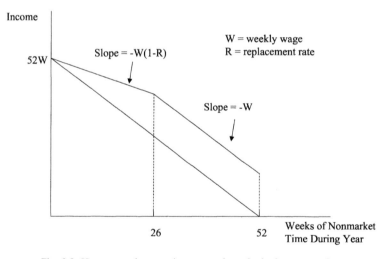

Fig. 2.2. How unemployment insurance alters the budget constraint.

The two models make very different assumptions but have similar predictions. In the Mortensen model the individual is uncertain when a job will be found and what the wage will be. One remains unemployed until a sufficiently high paying job is found. In the Moffitt and Nicholson model one can find a job anytime at a fixed wage. Their model emphasizes the leisure value that a period of unemployment may have if one optimizes over a long period of time such as a year. This explanation has its greatest plausibility when there is a significant demand for home production or it is difficult to take a vacation once a new job has begun[22].

One should note that unemployment benefits affect the labor supply of employed and unemployed workers in other ways. We already mentioned the Mortensen entitlement effect where unemployed workers who are currently not eligible for benefits search harder because a job with UI is more valuable. In a standard labor supply framework, a similar mechanism would shift out the labor supply curve of the unemployed. This type of affect should also apply to the employed. Because UI makes employment more attractive if individuals realize that they may be laid off sometime in the future, the labor supply curve shifts outward (ignoring financing). Anderson and Meyer (1997b), following Summers (1989) and Gruber and Krueger (1991), describe how labor supply may shift in this way in response to the provision of benefits.

UI may also reduce work by spouses and limit part-time work. One of the responses to unemployment in the absence of UI may be an increase in hours worked by the spouse of an unemployed worker. This spousal labor supply is likely to be "crowded out" at least in part by unemployment benefits that reduce the loss in family income when one spouse is unemployed.

As for part-time work, the incentives mentioned earlier discourage part-time work. In particular, one would expect that when there is a decrease in the allowable earnings before an individual's benefits are reduced (the disregard), there will be a decrease in part-time work and a smaller increase in full-time work [McCall (1996)]. In addition, those seeking part-time work are ineligible for benefits in most states. These workers' earnings are taxed to finance the program, yet they are disqualified from receiving benefits. This issue has aroused controversy in recent years.

Finally, we should emphasize that the above results are based on partial equilibrium analyses, i.e., they do not include the effect of the behavior of UI recipients on those that do not receive UI. This issue is discussed briefly below.

2.5. Labor supply effects of unemployment insurance: empirical evidence

There are excellent earlier surveys that include summaries of the labor supply effects of UI, as was mentioned above. Atkinson (1987) in particular, provides concise summaries of the literature up through the mid-1980s. In this survey we will not replow that ground, but rather focus on mostly newer studies, though we will discuss the results in relation to some of the earlier summaries of the literature.

2.5.1. Identification of unemployment insurance and workers' compensation effects

Before discussing estimates of UI program effects, it is useful to make some general comments that apply to both the UI and WC literatures. While good evidence on

---

[22] Implicit in this discussion is the assumption that the search requirement for UI receipt can be satisfied at low cost.

UI and WC effects from outside the English-speaking countries is becoming more common (especially for UI), there are reasons to believe that the best evidence on the effects of UI and WC – especially for programs with features similar to those in the states – is likely to come from the USA. With 50 states and the District of Columbia having essentially the same systems but with often sharply different benefit levels and other characteristics, one has transparent variation in incentives that is arguably exogenous and can be used to estimate the effects of UI and WC. Moreover, there are often differing incentives across groups within a state, and sharp changes in program characteristics for one group, but not another, providing additional levers to identify the effects of the programs.

That states differ in many respects, and that their policies are often driven by these differences, does not invalidate many of the approaches that can be taken with US data. There certainly is work showing that state UI and WC benefits are affected by underlying state attributes[23]. Nevertheless, the best work using data from the States relies on sharp changes in policies (and uses comparison groups), while the underlying determinants of policies tend to move slowly. For example, studies using data immediately before and after benefits have been increased sharply are likely to be immune from a political economy critique, especially when the forces that lead to these policy changes are understood. Other sensible approaches include, for example, the examination of policies that affect one group but not another or have sharply different effects on different groups. For example, US benefit schedules generally do not provide high benefits for all of those in a particular state. Rather, they provide very different benefit replacement rates depending on one's earnings, and these schedules differ sharply across states and over time.

This is not to say that US evidence is applicable to all countries or that non-US studies cannot be convincing. Only a narrow range of policies can be directly evaluated using US data because state differences in UI programs are all within the confines of the parameters of a federal system and because state WC programs are similar (due in part to influential commissions, the efforts of national insurance organizations, unions, and multi-state employers). Furthermore, the economic, cultural and institutional background in other countries may render the US experience not directly transferable. Nevertheless, in the vast majority of non-US studies (and many US studies) it is difficult to see the identifying variation in UI or WC program characteristics across units that allows researchers to estimate program effects. Atkinson and Micklewright (1985, p. 241) in their review of UI research, argue that micro-data studies that do not describe their sample and other basic facts are "likely to be meaningless". We would stress that the same is true of studies that do not make clear the source of differences in program incentives across individuals and why those sources are likely to be exogenous. Other problems arise in cross-country studies that have difficulty holding constant the many country specific features that affect unemployment.

---

[23] For example, see Adams (1986) for UI, and Besley and Case (1994) for WC.

Before describing the central tendencies of the empirical work on UI and WC labor supply effects, we describe an empirical approach that has been used successfully in a number of recent studies. Specifically, a number of recent studies have examined changes in state laws that affected some individuals, but not others, or reforms that provided plausible comparison groups through another means [see Meyer (1995a) for a review of these methods].

A useful place to start is the numerous papers that examine the effects of unemployment insurance (UI) on the length of unemployment spells. In a typical study that does not use exogenous variation from policy changes, the length of unemployment is regressed on the benefit level or the replacement rate, the past wage or earnings, and demographic characteristics. Welch (1977) criticizes this conventional methodology by pointing out that within a given state at a point in time, the weekly UI (or WC) benefit is a constant fraction of previous earnings except when an individual receives the minimum or maximum weekly benefit. Thus, regressions of spell length on weekly benefits and previous earnings consequently cannot distinguish between the effect of UI or WC and the highly correlated influence of previous earnings. This result is especially true if we are uncertain about exactly how previous earnings affect spell length. As we discuss below, this identification problem, which is created by the dependence of program generosity on an individual's previous earnings, is common to many social insurance programs besides UI and WC, including social security and disability insurance. Other sources of differences in benefits, such as family composition and earnings, are also likely to have independent effects on spell length making their use in identification suspect. In many studies of UI outside the USA, eligibility for UI or benefit generosity are often taken as exogenous even though they depend on an individual's work history and place of employment. This problem also arises when other outcomes are examined, such as savings.

Several papers exploit potentially exogenous variation in UI benefit levels from increases in state maximum weekly benefit amounts. These natural experiments are used to estimate the effects of UI on the length of unemployment, reemployment earnings, and the incidence of UI claims. Early work in the spirit of this approach can be found in Classen (1979) and more closely Solon (1985). Classen examines benefit changes, but relies mostly on departures from a linear effect of earnings on outcomes as a measure of benefit effects. Solon examines the length of UI receipt in Georgia just before and after the introduction of federal income taxation of UI for high income individuals in 1979. In the typical study of spell lengths, the variation in UI benefits comes from some combination of different replacement rates in different states, different minima and maxima, and maybe some variation in these parameters over time. Many of the natural experiment type papers are able to isolate one component of this variation which can separately be used to identify the effects of UI.

The main idea for one of the natural experiment papers that we use as a prototype can be seen by examining Figure 2.3, which displays a typical state schedule relating the weekly UI (or WC) benefit amount to previous earnings. The solid line is the schedule prior to a change in a state law which raises the minimum and maximum weekly benefit

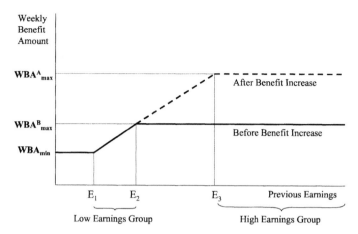

Fig. 2.3. UI or WC benefit schedule in a common natural experiment study approach.

amount (WBA). The dashed line is the schedule after the benefit increase. Between the minimum and the maximum, the weekly benefit amount is a constant fraction of previous earnings (in the case of UI in most states, the highest quarter of earnings during the first four of the last five calendar quarters prior to the quarter of filing for benefits).

For people with previous earnings of at least E_3 (the high-earnings group), one can compare the mean weeks of UI received and reemployment earnings of people who filed for UI benefits just prior to and just after the change in the benefit schedule[24]. Those who file before the increase receive WBA^B_{max} while those filing afterwards receive WBA^A_{max}. An individual's filing date generally determines his UI benefit amount for his entire benefit year (the one year period following date of claim). Thus, two individuals with quarterly earnings greater than E_3 will receive different weekly benefits for their entire period of receipt if one filed a few days before and the other a few days after the effective date of the benefit increase. This is the main idea of this approach. Most of the remaining methodological issues in the approach involve correcting for possible differences between the individuals filing just before and just after the benefit increase. One may also need to account for the dependence between observations from a given earnings group for a given year. In this example, one can use as a comparison group those with earnings between E_1 and E_2 (the low-earnings group) who file just before and just after the benefit increase. The benefits these individuals receive are unaffected by the increase in the maximum benefit amount. The so-called difference-in-differences estimator would then be used. In studies of this type, an additional comparison group may come from states that did not experience a benefit increase.

---

[24] In principle, one could also examine the effects of increases in the minimum weekly benefit amount. However, in many cases few people receive the minimum benefit and it is raised infrequently.

One should not construe this argument as saying that all studies that use this type of approach are convincing, and studies that do not are not convincing. Rather, this example shows that one can make clear the sources of variation that allow the estimation of program effects, and that one can then make a case for their exogeneity (or lack thereof).

2.5.2. Unemployment insurance and unemployment or claim incidence

There is a substantial literature that finds a large effect of UI on the incidence of unemployment or the incidence of UI claims. Table 2.3 summarizes some of these studies. These studies are mostly concerned with labor demand, but we include them for completeness. Feldstein (1978) examines the effect of benefits on layoffs, finding a large effect. The subsequent studies focus on how incomplete experience rating interacts with benefit generosity to affect layoffs. In these studies a key variable is the marginal tax cost of a layoff, denoted by e, which is the fraction of the UI cost of an additional layoff (in present value) that a firm can expect to pay in future taxes. The extent to which e is below one, then, is a measure of the degree to which experience rating is incomplete. The three studies, Topel (1983), Card and Levine (1994), Anderson and Meyer (1994), all find large effects of incomplete experience rating on layoffs. The first two studies find substantially larger effects using state by industry proxies for the tax cost than is found by the third study which employs firm level tax costs. A recent study [Anderson and Meyer (2000)] finds substantial effects of experience rating in Washington State in the 1980s. It is hard to translate these results into effects of the level of benefits, but it should be clear that incomplete experience rating could not have an effect on layoffs unless there were substantial UI benefits. In a paper that is explicitly about labor demand, Anderson (1993) finds that UI-induced adjustment costs have a substantial effect on the seasonality of employment.

A second group of studies, summarized in Table 2.4, examines how UI benefits and other variables affect the frequency of claims for UI conditional on unemployment or a job separation. Corson and Nicholson (1988) and Blank and Card (1991) both examine aggregate data and Panel Study of Income Dynamics (PSID) microdata. They both find substantial effects of the level of benefits in aggregate data, but come to conflicting results using the microdata. Anderson and Meyer (1997a) find substantial effects in administrative microdata. Overall, an elasticity of unemployment or claims with respect to benefits in the neighborhood of .5 is a reasonable summary of these studies.

2.5.3. Unemployment insurance and unemployment durations

The results of many of the more recent studies of unemployment durations as well as some older studies that rely on changes in benefits for identification are reported in Table 2.5. Several of the studies, including Classen (1979), Solon (1985), and Meyer (1990, 1992a), find elasticities of duration with respect to the level of benefits over 0.5.

Table 2.3
Studies of unemployment insurance and the incidence of layoffs

Empirical specification	Data and identification	Findings
Feldstein (1978). Linear regression of temporary layoff probability on the after-tax UI replacement rate, controlling for age, union status, race, marital status, gender, a linear effect of the wage, and industry and occupation (in some specifications).	US March 1971 Current Population Survey (CPS) data for experienced labor force members who were not labor force re-entrants and not selfemployed. Identified by differences in benefits across states and individuals within state.	Elasticity of temporary layoff unemployment rate with respect to the replacement rate ranging from 0.74 to 0.91. "The average UI benefit replacement rate implied by the current law can account for about half of temporary layoff unemployment."
Topel (1983). Estimation of time constant layoff and reemployment hazard rate using cross-section data on labor force status and unemployment. Key UI variable is subsidy rate $b[1/(1-t)-e]$, where b is the benefit, t is the income tax rate and e is fraction of the cost of a marginal layoff that the firm pays through experience rating.	US March 1975 CPS data on full-time, full-year labor force participants. Identified by differences in benefit and experience rating schedules across states interacted with industry unemployment rates.	"... the layoff unemployment rate would have been about 30 percent lower if the subsidy to unemployment caused by the current UI system had been eliminated." Argues that most of the effect is through incomplete experience rating increasing layoffs.
Card and Levine (1994). Estimation of annual and seasonal temporary layoff, permanent layoff and other unemployment rates. Linear models for the probability of unemployment with e (see above for definition) as the main regressor are used, with state, state*year and industry*year controls in some specifications.	US CPS outgoing-rotation-group data for 5 industries in 36 states from 1978 to 1985. Identified by differences in experience rating schedules across states interacted with industry unemployment rates.	"We estimate that a move to complete experience-rating would reduce the temporary layoff unemployment rate by about 1.0 percentage point (or roughly 50 percent) in the trough of a recession, and by about the same amount in the lowest demand months of the year."
Anderson and Meyer (1994). Linear probability models of temporary job separations and all job separations with firm specific measure of e (see above for definition) and controls for past firm layoffs. Some specifications difference the data to remove firm and individual fixed effects.	US Continuous Wage and Benefit History (CWBH) administrative data on both workers and firms from 6 states during 1978–1984. Identified by the differential effects of changes in state tax schedules on different firms.	"Our preferred estimates imply that incomplete experience rating is responsible for over twenty percent of temporary layoffs."

Table 2.4
Studies of unemployment insurance and benefit takeup

Empirical specification	Data and identification	Findings
Corson and Nicholson (1988). Aggregate claims ratio regressed on replacement rate = average weekly benefit of recipients divided by average weekly wage of employed.	US state by year aggregate data on the fraction of unemployed that receive UI.	Elasticity over 0.5.
Micro claims data regressed on variable for income taxation of UI, but replacement rate not used.	Panel Study of Income Dynamics (PSID) individual data on UI claims.	Large effect of benefit taxation variable.
Blank and Card (1991). Aggregate claims ratio adjusted for estimated eligibility regressed on replacement rate = average weekly benefit of recipients divided by average weekly wage of employed.	US state by year aggregate data on the fraction of unemployed that receive UI.	Replacement rate elasticities of 0.32 to 0.58.
Micro claims data regressed on state average replacement rate. No variable for income taxation of UI included.	Panel Study of Income Dynamics (PSID) individual data on UI claims.	Insignificant effect of replacement rate. Coefficient usually of "wrong" sign.
Meyer (1992b). Difference in difference analysis of claim incidence by earnings group, industry and region.	New York administrative data on UI claims from 1988 and 1989. Identification comes from a 36 percent increase in the maximum benefit.	"The numbers are consistent with large effects of the higher benefits on the relative incidence of claims."
Anderson and Meyer (1997b). Linear and logit models of UI receipt conditional on separation. Explanatory variables include logarithms of: weekly benefit, 1-tax on benefits, 1-tax on earnings, and potential duration of benefits. Some specifications with flexible controls for past earnings, state, and state*time.	US CWBH data on both workers and firms from 6 states during 1978–1984. Identified by differences in benefit schedules across states, changes in these schedules, changes in income taxation of benefits.	Elasticity of benefit takeup with respect to benefits of 0.33 to 0.60. Slightly smaller elasticities with respect to (1-tax on benefits). Elasticities of takeup with respect to potential duration about half as large as those with respect to the benefit level.

Table 2.5

Studies of unemployment insurance and the duration of unemployment in the USA

Empirical specification	Data and identification	Findings
Classen (1979). Linear and log-linear regression of unemployment duration on benefits using deviations of relationship from linearity at benefit maximum as an estimate of benefit effects. Tobit models were also estimated.	US Continuous Wage and Benefit History (CWBH) administrative data from Arizona from the year before and year after a 1968 benefit increase.	Benefit elasticity of 0.6 in levels and 1.0 in logarithms.
Solon (1985). Hazard model for exit from unemployment with key variable $b(1-\rho t)$ to capture taxation of benefits.	US CWBH data for Georgia before and after the introduction of income taxation of UI benefits for high income families.	After-tax benefit elasticity of duration equal to 1.0.
Moffitt (1985). Flexible discrete hazard model of exit from unemployment with explanatory variables for benefit level, potential duration at start of spell, past wages, and state unemployment rate.	US CWBH data for 13 states 1978–1983. Identification from differences in benefit schedules across states and changes in benefits and potential duration over time.	"The results indicate that a 10-percent increase in the UI benefit increases spells by about half a week and that a 1-week increase in potential duration increases spells by about 0.15 weeks." These numbers suggest a benefit elasticity of about 0.4 and a potential duration elasticity of 0.34.
Meyer (1990) and Katz and Meyer (1990). Hazard model for exit from unemployment with nonparametric baseline hazard and variables for benefit level, and measures of time until benefits run out. Includes controls for state unemployment and past wages, and state indicator variables.	Subset of Moffitt (1985) data with some recoding. Same as Moffitt, but the inclusion of state indicators weights identification toward changes in schedules and differential treatment across states of those with different levels of earnings.	Elasticity of duration with respect to the weekly benefit of 0.8, and with respect to potential duration of 0.5.
Meyer (1992a). Comparisons of durations of those filing 3 months before and after 17 benefit increases. Most of increases due to automatic cost-of-living adjustments. Estimates with and without controls for demographics.	US CWBH data for six states. Identification of benefit effects comes from changes in benefits due to cost-of-living adjustments in period of high inflation.	A range of estimates, but central tendency of elasticity of duration with respect to the benefit amount of 0.6.

continued on next page

Table 2.5, *continued*

Empirical specification	Data and identification	Findings
Meyer (1992b). Difference in difference analysis of claim duration with extensive controls.	See Table 2.4.	Duration elasticities of 0.24 to 0.42, though several estimates are smaller.
Card and Levine (2000). Hazard models of exit from unemployment receipt.	US administrative data for New Jersey. Examines program that offered 13 weeks of 'extended benefits' for 6 months in 1996. The program was part of a political compromise over funding care for indigent hospital patients.	Elasticity of duration with respect to potential duration of 0.1.

The elasticity estimates with respect to the potential duration (length) of benefits tend to be much lower.

The non-American results reported in Table 2.6 are more varied. Very large effects of potential duration in Canada but no benefit level effect is found by Ham and Rea (1987), while Hunt (1995) finds very large effects of the level and potential duration of benefits in Germany. The studies of Sweden [Carling, Edin, Harkman and Holmlund (1996)] and Norway [Roed and Zhang (2000)] find much smaller effects, though the sources of identification in the former study are far from clearly exogenous. A very thoughtful recent study by Carling, Holmlund and Vejsiu (2001) examines data before and after a benefit cut in Sweden and finds an elasticity over 1.0. The authors discuss a paper written in Swedish that analyzes an earlier cut and also finds large effects. Other work by Abbring, van den Berg and van Ours (2000) suggests large effects of benefit cuts on unemployment duration in the Netherlands, but it is difficult to separate out benefit cuts from other policies in their work. An elasticity of unemployment duration with respect to benefits of 0.5 is not an unreasonable rough summary, though there is a wide range of estimates in the literature. Such an elasticity is not very different from the central tendency of the duration elasticities reported in the Atkinson (1987) survey.

One should note that the elasticity of unemployment with respect to benefits is the sum of the layoff/claim elasticity and the duration elasticity. To see this result, let weeks unemployed, W, be the product of incidence, I, and duration, D. Then, letting the UI benefit be B, we have $W = I \cdot D$, and

$$\frac{\mathrm{d}W}{\mathrm{d}B}\frac{B}{W} = \frac{B}{W}\left(D\frac{\mathrm{d}I}{\mathrm{d}B} + I\frac{\mathrm{d}D}{\mathrm{d}B}\right) = \frac{B}{I}\frac{\mathrm{d}I}{\mathrm{d}B} + \frac{B}{D}\frac{\mathrm{d}D}{\mathrm{d}B}.$$

Overall, the combined effect of benefits on unemployment through incidence and duration is suggested to be near one by these studies. This result is consistent with the aggregate analysis of twenty OECD countries by Nickell (1998) who finds an elasticity of unemployment with respect to the replacement rate of close to one.

Besides cross-sectional regression analyses of benefit effects on duration, we also have evidence from a recent series of randomized social experiments in the USA that are surveyed in Meyer (1995b). Four cash bonus experiments made payments to UI recipients who found jobs quickly and kept them for a specified period of time. Six job search experiments evaluated combinations of services including additional information on job openings, more job placements, and more extensive checks of UI eligibility. The bonus experiments show that economic incentives do affect the speed with which people leave the unemployment insurance rolls. As a result, UI is not a completely benign transfer, but rather it affects claimants' behavior as shown by the declines in weeks of UI receipt found for all of the bonus treatments. The job search experiments found that various combinations of services to improve job search and increase enforcement of work search rules reduce UI receipt. It is hard to extrapolate from these experimental results to elasticities since the treatments were very different

Table 2.6

Studies of unemployment insurance and the duration of unemployment outside the USA

Empirical specification	Data and identification	Findings
Ham and Rea (1987). Models the hazard from unemployment as a function of a polynomial of the duration of unemployment, initial entitlement and its square, weekly benefits and wages, and the provincial and industrial unemployment rates. Estimation is by maximum likelihood.	Canadian Employment and Immigration Longitudinal Labour Force Files with weekly data on men aged 18–64, for 1975–1980. Identification comes from legislative changes in the benefit rate, individuals with weekly wages above the maximum earnings, and changes in weeks of entitlement.	Benefit effect of wrong sign or insignificant. The potential benefit duration coefficients were both significant in all specifications. An increase in the initial potential duration of one week was estimated to increase expected unemployment duration by 0.26 to 0.33 weeks (an elasticity of 1.02–1.33).
Hunt (1995). Models exit from unemployment in a competing risks hazard framework, combined with a difference in differences approach. Control variables are an individual's age group, the time period, the interaction of time and age (treatment groups), and various demographic variables. Identification comes from the differential effect of the policy changes on the treatment and control groups.	German Socioeconomic Panel public use file, for the years 1983–1988. 2236 individuals under age 57. One policy change reduced benefits to the childless unemployed, and three policy changes extended the duration of benefits to unemployed individuals that were of a certain age (aged 49+ for the first, aged 44+ for the second, and aged 42+ for the third). The control group consisted of unemployed individuals that were 41 years old or less.	The extension of benefits lowered by 46% the hazard from unemployment for those aged 44–48, but the other benefit extensions had insignificant effects. For those 44–48 the implied elasticity of mean duration with respect to the maximum duration of UI was 2.27. In several cases, the extensions cut escapes to employment and out of the labor force. The cut in benefits for the childless significantly increased employment. The author notes that many of the effects are implausibly large.
Carling, Edin, Harkman and Holmlund (1996). The hazard of leaving unemployment (to any alternative) is modeled using an unrestricted baseline hazard, and is estimated semiparametrically. Explanatory variables include indicators for receiving UI benefits, or KAS (cash assistance, which gives smaller benefits for a shorter period of time) age, education, training, gender, citizenship, and the regional unemployment rate.	Sweden. Non-disabled unemployed workers under 55 registered at public employment agencies in 3 months of 1991. Identification from variation in claimant status across individuals. UI recipients were members of a UI fund for at least 12 months, and had worked for a certain number of days in the past 12 months. KAS provided compensation for those not covered by UI, and who met work or school requirements and included labor force entrants.	Elasticity of exit to employment with respect to the benefit level is estimated at –0.06.

continued on next page

Table 2.6, *continued*

Empirical specification	Data and identification	Findings
Roed and Zhang (2000). Flexible hazard rate model.	Norway. Register data on all unemployment spells between August 1990 and December 1999. Benefit variation due to changes in indexation over the year is used for identification.	Elasticity of hazard with respect to benefit of −0.35 for men and −0.15 for women.
Carling, Holmlund and Vejsiu (2001). Flexible hazard rate model of exits to employment and competing risks model of exits to employment, labour market programmes, and non-participation.	Sweden. Register-based longitudinal data from 1994 to 1996. Data from before and after cut in replacement rate from 80% to 75%.	"Our implied elasticity of the hazard rate with respect to benefits is about 1.6 …."

from benefit changes, but the estimates probably suggest moderate effects of UI. Individuals clearly were able to change the speed with which they went back to work when faced with financial incentives to do so, but the effects were not particularly large. The experiments also indicated that job search assistance and reporting requirements have a substantial effect on unemployment duration.

2.5.4. Unemployment insurance spillovers

An important issue on which more evidence is needed is the degree of spillover effects from UI recipients to other unemployed individuals. Might the spells of non-recipients become shorter, if UI recipients cut back on search activities and thus competed less strenuously for available jobs? The possibility of such spillovers has been emphasized by Atkinson and Micklewright (1985) and others. Levine (1993) examines this question empirically using the CPS and the National Longitudinal Survey of Youths. He finds that increases in the generosity of UI benefits appear to decrease the unemployment of those who do not receive UI. This is important work that suggests that previous work on UI and unemployment durations may have overestimated the overall effects of UI on unemployment rates. There is little other direct evidence on the question of whether general equilibrium effects of UI are much smaller than partial equilibrium effects. We should note that it is also possible that the adverse unemployment effects of UI will be magnified in general equilibrium. Carling, Holmlund and Vejsiu (2001) argue that UI will raise wage pressure in economies where wage bargaining is pervasive, thus reinforcing its adverse incentive effects on job search.

2.5.5. Other labor supply effects of unemployment insurance

Table 2.7 summarizes two studies of other aspects of labor supply that are affected by UI. Cullen and Gruber (2000) find that higher unemployment benefits are associated with less work by the wives of unemployed men. The authors find that there is substantial crowd-out of this form of family "self-insurance". Their estimates suggest that for every dollar of UI received by the husband, wives earnings fall by between 36 and 73 cents. McCall (1996) examines the effects of UI on part-time work. He finds that the level of the disregard (the amount of earnings allowed before benefits are reduced) has a significant effect on the probability of part-time employment during the first three months of joblessness. There is also some work on the extent to which the presence of UI shifts out labor supply of those who are employed [Anderson and Meyer (1997b)] and those whose benefits are about to run out [Katz and Meyer (1990)]. The first paper finds some support for potential workers' valuing the benefits (and labor supply thus shifting out), but the estimates are imprecise. The second paper finds little support for the hypothesis that higher UI benefits raise job-finding just prior to benefit exhaustion.

Table 2.7

Studies of other unemployment insurance effects on labor supply

Empirical specification	Data and identification	Findings
McCall (1996). The exit from unemployment to full-time or part-time work is modeled using a competing risks hazard model with explanatory variables including an indicator for UI receipt, the replacement rate, the disregard (amount that can be earned without reducing benefits) and interactions of these variables.	US CPS Displaced Worker Supplements from 1986, 1988, 1990, and 1992. Indentification from cross-state differences in disregard and changes in disregards (state fixed effects specifications).	Significant effect of disregard on probability of part-time employment during the first three months of joblessness.
Cullen and Gruber (2000). The labor supply of wives modeled as a linear function of potential UI benefits, demographic variables, the average wage of women similar to the wife, and lagged husband's job characteristics. Dependent variables are the share of months employed and average hours worked per month. OLS, Tobit and 2SLS estimates with benefits received instrumented for using potential benefits.	US SIPP data from the 1984–1988 and 1990–1992 waves. Married couples where both husband and wife are between 25 and 54. 2560 spells of unemployment.	Estimates of the implied income elasticity of labor supply for wives ranges from −0.49 using OLS to −1.07 using 2SLS. In a specification check, potential UI benefits also had a significant negative effect on the labor supply of women with employed husbands, suggesting that these estimates may overstate the true effect of UI benefits.

3. Workers' compensation

3.1. Main features of US workers' compensation programs

States have complete discretion in designing their workers' compensation (WC) programs. Nevertheless, state programs have many standard features. Coverage under workers compensation in the USA is about as universal as under UI. Approximately 97% of the non-federal UI covered workforce is covered, plus all federal employees. Unlike UI, a worker is eligible for WC benefits immediately when she starts work, even without a previous earnings history.

State WC programs cover the medical costs of a work-related injury or illness as well as four main types of cash benefits (also called indemnity benefits). First, 'temporary total' benefits are paid to workers who are totally unable to work for a finite period of time. All workers' compensation claims are initially classified as temporary total cases and temporary total benefits are paid; if the disability persists beyond the date of maximum medical improvement, the case is reclassified as a permanent disability[25]. About 70% of all claims are for temporary total disabilities. Second, if a worker remains totally disabled after reaching maximum medical improvement, she is eligible for 'permanent total' benefits. In most states, permanent total and temporary total benefits provide the same weekly payment, but in some states there is a limit on cumulative permanent total benefits. Benefits equal a fraction (typically two-thirds) of the worker's pre-disability average weekly wage, subject to a minimum and maximum payment. Figure 2.3 described earlier (p. 2345), displays a typical state benefit schedule. The maximum allowable benefit varies substantially across states, and is often linked to the worker's number of dependents. Approximately half of workers earned a high-enough wage that if they incurred a temporary total disability their benefit would be limited by the maximum level in their state. Third, workers who suffer a disability that is partially disabling but is expected to last indefinitely qualify for 'permanent partial' benefits. An employee who loses the use of a limb, for example, would receive permanent partial benefits. These benefits are typically determined on the basis of a schedule that links benefits to specific impairments. For example, an employee who lost the use of an arm in a work-related accident in Illinois in 2000 was entitled to a maximum benefit of $269 943. Finally, dependents of workers who are killed on the job are paid survivors' benefits.

Each state law requires a waiting period ranging from three to seven days before indemnity benefit payments begin. However, workers are compensated retroactively for the waiting period if their disability persists beyond a specified time period. Table 3.1 illustrates the interstate variation in workers' compensation benefit minima, maxima, replacement rates, waiting periods, and retroactive periods for twelve states. Comparing this table to Table 2.1, one will notice that WC has much higher replacement rates and

---

[25] The date of maximum medical improvement is the time at which a doctor determines that an injured worker will not recover further from an injury.

Table 3.1
Main characteristics of state workers' compensation programs in the USA[a]

State	Minimum weekly benefit ($)	Maximum weekly benefit ($)	Replacement rate (%)	Waiting period (days)	Retroactive period (weeks)
California	126.00[b]	490.00	$66\frac{2}{3}$	3	2
Florida	20.00	541.00	$66\frac{2}{3}$	7	2
Illinois	100.90–124.30[b,c]	899.81	$66\frac{2}{3}$	3	2
Massachusetts	149.93	749.69	60	5	3
Michigan	170.00	611.00	80[e]	7	2
Mississippi	25.00[d]	303.35	$66\frac{2}{3}$	5	2
Missouri	40.00	578.48	$66\frac{2}{3}$	3	2
Nebraska	49.00[b]	487.00	$66\frac{2}{3}$	7	6
New Jersey	151.00	568.00	70	7	8 days
New York	40.00[b]	400.00	$66\frac{2}{3}$	7	2
Texas	80.00	531.00	70[f]	7	4
Median State	100.00	529.00	$66\frac{2}{3}$	3	2

[a] Source: Analysis of Workers' Compensation Laws: U.S. Chamber of Commerce (2000).
[b] In California, Illinois, Nebraska and New York the minimum is actual earnings if less than the amount listed.
[c] Illinois' minimum benefit increases if additional dependents are present.
[d] In Mississippi the minimum does not apply in cases of partial disability.
[e] In Michigan the replacement rate is a percent of after-tax earnings.
[f] In Texas the replacement rate is 75% if earnings are less than $8.50 per hour.

maximum benefits than UI. A typical state has a WC replacement rate of two thirds, but a UI replacement rate of just over one-half. The typical state has a maximum WC benefit nearly twice that of its maximum UI benefit. Furthermore, workers' compensation benefits are not subject to income or payroll taxes.

The high replacement rates combined with the exclusion of WC from income taxation often leads to after-tax replacement rates near or above one. A couple of representative examples illustrate this point. Suppose an individual's taxable family income was under $43 850 in 2000 and she was subject to a 5% state income tax. Then, the combination of state income, federal income, and OASDHI payroll taxes implied a 27.65% total marginal tax rate. For someone whose benefit was not limited by the maximum benefit and who had a pre-tax replacement rate of two-thirds, the after-tax replacement rate was 92%. If income was over $43 850, the family was in a higher federal income tax bracket with a total marginal tax rate of 40.65% and the implied after-tax replacement rate was 112%. When a worker has higher take home pay not working than working, there is a strong disincentive to work.

These sharp work disincentives also apply to those who were working full-time, but are considering part-time or temporary work after their injury, likely leading a fifth type of benefits, 'temporary partial benefits', to be uncommon. A WC recipient with low earnings upon reemployment typically loses two dollars in benefits for every three dollars earned. Given that WC is not subject to income or payroll taxes, the return to working part-time or at a much lower wage than previously earned is negligible or even negative.

3.2. Workers' compensation financing

Workers' compensation is mostly financed through insurance premiums paid by firms. WC experience rating is much tighter than UI experience rating, with large firms almost perfectly experience rated. The premium rates as a fraction of payroll range from .1% in banking to over 20% in construction and trucking in some states. To determine its premium, a firm is placed in one or more of 600 classifications that are a mixture of industry and occupation codes. These classifications determine manual rates, which when multiplied by payroll, give the premium for a small firm. A large firm's rate is a weighted average of the manual rate and the firm's incurred loss rate, typically over a 3 year period in the past. The weight put on the firm's incurred loss rate increases with firm size, with the weight equaling one for very large firms.

3.3. Comparisons of unemployment insurance and workers' compensation program costs in the USA

Some striking patterns are evident in Table 3.2, which reports aggregate benefits and revenues for UI and WC during the past twenty years. The cyclicality of UI benefit payments is pronounced, with benefit payments high in 1982–1983 and 1992–1993 in response to the downturns near the beginning of those periods. Any cyclicality is less apparent for WC, but a secular rise in WC benefit payments and costs followed by a decline after 1993 is evident. Why WC costs rose so quickly and then fell is only partly understood. The rise was likely associated with benefit increases and associated behavioral responses, as well as the rise in medical costs, while the recent fall is partly due to a decline in injury rates.

3.4. Workers' compensation outside of the USA

We should emphasize that there are often very different institutions in other countries to compensate those injured on the job. Moreover, programs for the injured are often combined with other programs, and those eligible for one type of benefit are often eligible for another in certain circumstances. In particular, there is often no easy translation from the US workers' compensation program to an equivalent in another country, since the USA lacks national health insurance and WC provides medical benefits.

Table 3.2
Financial characteristics of workers' compensation and unemployment insurance programs [a,b]

Year	Workers' compensation		Unemployment insurance	
	Benefit payments ($ millions)	Costs ($ millions)	Benefit payments ($ millions)	Tax Collections ($ millions)
1980	13618	22256	14070	15010
1981	15054	23014	15580	15630
1982	16407	22764	21240	15950
1983	17575	23048	28850	18010
1984	19685	25122	16340	24060
1985	22470	29320	14360	24450
1986	24647	33964	15700	22880
1987	27317	38095	15080	24180
1988	30703	43284	13280	23820
1989	34316	47955	13500	21750
1990	38237	53123	16860	21360
1991	42170	55216	24420	20630
1992	45668	57394	36770	23010
1993	45330	60820	35070	25230
1994	44586	60475	26220	27960
1995	43373	57054	20990	28900
1996	42065	55057	22000	28550
1997	40586	52040	20300	28200
1998	41693	52108	19410	27370
1999	–	–	20720	26480

[a] Sources: Nelson (1988a,b, 1991); Mont, Burton and Reno (2000); U.S. House of Representatives Committee on Ways and Means (1990, 1998, 2000).
[b] Note: All amounts are in nominal dollars.

In Canada, WC is fairly similar to the USA, with substantial variation in programs across provinces. Replacement rates are typically 90% of earnings net of income taxes, pension contributions, and UI contributions. The waiting period and retroactive period are typically just one day, and firms in most cases must purchase insurance through a provincial fund.

In the United Kingdom, those who suffer an industrial accident or contract an industrial disease are generally eligible for the industrial injuries disablement benefit (IIDB), about half of whom also receive an additional allowance for reduced earnings. These benefits vary with the degree of disablement, but do not vary with previous earnings. The benefits are capped at a low level: IIDB benefits in 2000 were a maximum of £109.30 ($161) per week. As a result, these benefits provide little insurance to middle and upper income workers in the UK. The program appears to be more of a backstop akin to US welfare programs, and expenditures are fairly modest.

3.5. Theoretical responses of labor supply to workers' compensation

Workers' compensation affects at least four dimensions of labor supply. First, WC can affect the likelihood of an on-the-job injury. Much research on the labor supply effects of WC has focused on this issue. Second, program characteristics affect the likelihood that workers will make a claim given an injury. Once a claim has been made, we expect that labor supply will be affected by the adverse incentives of WC. Third, once on the program, WC can extend the time a person is out of work. Finally, the availability of compensation for on the job injuries can shift labor supply by changing the value to a worker of various jobs. We discuss these four effects in turn.

There is an extensive literature on how the provision of benefits can possibly make the occurrence of an injury more likely. This research is motivated by the idea that workers (and firms) will take fewer actions to prevent an injury when the injury becomes less costly due to the availability of benefits that compensate workers. Krueger (1990a) provides a simple model of this situation. Let expected utility on the job be written as

$$E[U] = [1 - p(e)]U(W) + p(e) V(B) - e, \tag{3.1}$$

where $p(e)$ is the probability of an injury, and e is the workers' effort devoted to injury prevention (care taken, or use of ear plugs, etc.), $U(W)$ is utility when working at wage W, and $V(B)$ is the utility of the WC benefit B when injured. The first-order condition for the choice of e that maximizes utility, assuming an interior solution, is

$$p'(e)[V(B) - U(W)] - 1 = 0. \tag{3.2}$$

By differentiating Equation (3.2) and using the second-order condition, one can show that

$$\frac{\partial e}{\partial B} = p'V'/p''(U - V) < 0, \quad \text{assuming } p' < 0, \ p'' > 0, \text{ and } U - V > 0. \tag{3.3}$$

Thus, the provision of workers' compensation benefits may reduce effort at injury reduction (a dimension of labor supply) and increases the probability of an injury. On the other hand, we should note that more generous WC benefits could decrease injuries through their effect on firm incentives, as discussed by Ruser (1985) and Ehrenberg (1988).

Second, the generosity of WC benefits may affect the probability that a person claims benefits conditional on having an injury. As the generosity of benefits rises, it is more likely that the benefits of receiving WC will outweigh the costs, which consist of lost earnings plus the transaction costs of establishing eligibility and possibly the stigma of WC receipt. As a result of higher benefits, there may also be more claims in marginal cases where it is unclear whether the injury is work-related and more cases involving outright fraud[26]. Furthermore, whether someone initially receives WC is partly related to how long they are out of work. A WC claimant cannot receive benefits until after a waiting period of typically 3 days. It is more likely that an injured worker will be out of work longer than this waiting period when benefits are high. Once a person is then on the WC rolls, they become subject to the implicit taxes on work and the consequent work disincentives. Therefore, additional claims will lead to a labor supply response as well as higher costs.

Third, the duration of time out of work is affected by WC. Like UI, this issue is one on which a substantial part of WC research has focused. The duration of time out of work while receiving WC can be thought of as determined by a sequence of decisions. Each period following an injury, an individual compares the benefits received from WC (and the leisure time when not working) to the earnings received when working. A worker's decision would also reflect the disutility of working with an injury (which would tend to fall as an individual recovers) and the increase in productivity with recovery. An additional factor in a person's decision is that a longer stay out of work might facilitate a full recovery, reducing future pain and increasing future productivity. In this setting, higher WC benefits would tend to delay a return to work, but make a full recovery more likely, just as higher UI could lead to a better job match.

One should note that permanent benefits under WC have an income effect, but no substitution effect. Permanent partial benefits, which are frequently paid as a lump sum settlement, also do not affect the marginal incentives to return to work; they only reduce work by increasing income.

One additional labor supply response is the extent to which labor supply shifts out in response to WC benefits because they make employment more attractive. This issue is examined theoretically and empirically in Gruber and Krueger (1991)[27].

3.6. Labor supply effects of workers' compensation: empirical evidence

There are excellent surveys that include summaries of the labor supply effects of WC, such as Ehrenberg (1988), Krueger (1990a), Moore and Viscusi (1990), and Kniesner and Leeth (1995). The empirical research on the labor supply effects of workers' compensation, while extensive, is probably less developed than the research on UI. Furthermore, while European researchers have recently produced many convincing studies of UI, research on WC outside the USA has lagged.

---

[26] For anecdotal evidence that higher benefits may also lead to fraud and overstated claims see the New York Times, December 29, 1991, p. 1.

[27] Also see Holmlund (1983).

3.6.1. The incidence of injuries and workers' compensation claims

Table 3.3 summarizes a large number of studies that examine the effect of workers' compensation program parameters on the incidence of injuries or the incidence of WC claims. Most of these studies, especially the early ones, examine aggregate data at the state-by-year level, or industry by state-by-year level. These studies tend to find that more generous WC is associated with higher injury rates, but the effect is usually small. This may be an accurate estimate or a result of the use of aggregate variables and proxies that are required when researchers use state or state by industry data. These studies also tend to find higher claims elasticities than injury elasticities, a result that is expected given the additional effect of higher benefits on claims conditional on an injury. The estimated benefit elasticities cluster around 0.2 or 0.3, though the only studies that use individual microdata, Krueger (1990a) and Butler, Gardner and Gardner (1997), find appreciably larger elasticities of the claims rate with respect to benefits. There is also a short literature examining whether claims for hard to diagnose injuries and injuries for which treatment can be delayed are more common when benefits are higher and on days when the injury is more likely a non-work injury (such as Mondays). The evidence on these issues is quite mixed [28].

3.6.2. The duration of time out of work after an injury

Most work on incentive effects of workers' compensation has focused on the program's effect on injury rates or the number of claims rather than the duration of claims. However, there has been a great deal of recent research on the effects of WC on the duration of time out of work that we summarize in Table 3.4. Early work by Butler and Worrall (1985) examined low-back injuries in Illinois. They found elasticities between 0.2 and 0.4, depending on the statistical technique used. When they examined data pooled from 13 states, however, they did not find a consistent relationship between the level of benefits and the length of spells.

Meyer, Viscusi and Durbin (1995) examined data from a natural experiment provided by two very large increases in benefit levels in Kentucky and Michigan. This natural experiment enables them to compare the behavior of people who are injured before the benefit increases to those injured after the increases. By using the approach outlined in Section 2.5.1., the paper provides a test of the effect of benefit changes on the duration of claims where the sources of identification are readily apparent. Meyer, Viscusi and Durbin (1995) find that a 60% increase in the benefit level is associated with an increase in spell duration of approximately 20%. The elasticities range from .27 to .62, with most clustering between .3 and .4. Overall, the elasticity estimates are very similar in the two states. These results suggest substantial labor supply effects of workers' compensation benefits. Subsequent papers which have followed this natural

---

[28] See Smith (1990), Card and McCall (1996) and Ruser (1998).

Table 3.3
Studies of workers' compensation and the incidence of injuries or claims

Study	Unit of observation and sample	Dependent variable	Benefit elasticity
Chelius (1982)	US State by two-digit SIC manufacturing industry; 36 states from 1972 to 1975.	Injuries per 100 full-time workers.	0.14
Ruser (1985)	US State by three-digit SIC manufacturing industry;	Injuries per 100 full-time workers.	0.062
	Unbalanced panel of 41 states from 1972 to 1979.	Injuries with lost workdays per 100 full-time workers.	0.116
Butler (1983)	US Manufacturing industries by year; 15 industries over 32 years in South Carolina.	Closed workers' compensation cases reported in the fiscal year per worker.	0.290
Butler and Worrall (1983)	US State by year; 35 states from 1972 to 1978.	Temporary total claims of non selfinsured firms per worker.	0.344
Krueger (1990a)	US Individuals in 47 states in 1984 and 1985.	Workers' compensation claims.	0.45
Krueger and Burton (1990)	US state level data for 29 states in 1972, 1975, 1978, and 1983.	Premiums per employee or manual rate.	Not significantly different from zero.
Butler and Worrall (1991)	US state level data for 1954–1981.	Workers' compensation claim costs.	0.68
Butler, Gardner and Gardner (1997)	US Individuals at a large nationwide firm during 1990–1993.	Frequency of disability claims. Indemnity cost per worker.	−0.45 to 1.24 (median 0.78) 0.06 to 2.90 (median 1.27)

Table 3.4
Studies of workers' compensation and the duration of claims

Study	Unit of observation and sample	Dependent variable	Benefit elasticity
Butler and Worrall (1985)	Low-back injuries in Illinois.	Length of claim using hazard models.	0.2–0.4
Worrall, Butler, Borba and Durbin (1988)	Low-back injuries in 13 states.	Length of claim using hazard models.	0.0
Meyer, Viscusi and Durbin (1995)	All injuries in Kentucky (1979–1981) and Michigan (1981–1982).	Length of claims; comparisons of means and Log(duration).	0.3–0.4
Krueger (1990b)	All injuries in Minnesota in 1986.	Length of claims; comparisons of means and Log(duration).	>1.5
Gardner (1991)	All injuries in Connecticut in 1985–1990.	Mean length of claims.	0.9
Curington (1994)	All injuries in New York 1964–1983	Severe impairment durations. Minor impairment durations	0.7–1.3 0.1–0.2
Aiuppa and Trieschmann (1998)	France. Administrative region level data from Caisse Nationale for years 1973–1991.	Indemnity costs per injured employee.	0.78
Neuhauser and Raphael (2001)	California Workers' Compensation Institute Administrative Data from 2 years before and after 1994 and 1995 benefit increases.	Duration of temporary disability claims.	0.25–0.35, but much larger with selection correction.

experiment approach and examined the effects of benefit increases have found large effects. Krueger (1990b), Gardner (1991) and the Curington (1994) results for severe impairments all imply duration elasticities over 0.7. On the other hand, the minor impairment results in Curington (1994) and the recent work of Neuhauser and Raphael (2001) suggest smaller effects, though that latter paper argues that the elasticities are understated due to claim composition changes.

Again, note that the elasticity of lost work time with respect to benefits is the sum of the injury or claims elasticity and the duration elasticity as we indicated in Section 2.5.3. Combining the injury or claims elasticity estimates with the duration elasticity estimates suggests an elasticity of lost work time with respect to WC benefits of between .5 and 1.0. This elasticity is probably slightly smaller than the UI elasticity, but implies large effects on work time.

3.6.3. Other labor supply effects of workers' compensation

Gruber and Krueger (1991) examine the extent to which WC makes employment more attractive for those currently not receiving benefits, leading labor supply to shift out. They find a substantial shift in their study, concluding that workers value a dollar of WC benefits at about a dollar. This increase in labor supply may dampen the labor supply reductions of WC, particularly for high injury jobs that would otherwise be less desirable.

4. Social Security retirement program

The Social Security system in the United States originated during the New Deal in the 1930s. Old Age Insurance, which in 1939 became Old Age and Survivors Insurance, is now the largest source of retirement income in the United States. Disability Insurance was added in 1956 and Medicare (HI) was added in 1965. In 1998, 90% of those age 65 or older received OASDI benefits[29]. For 18% of beneficiary families, Social Security was the sole source of income, and for 63% of families it was responsible for more than half of family income. Social Security benefits accounted for 38% of aggregate income of the elderly population in 1998 – nearly twice as much as labor earnings. The poverty rate among older individuals has fallen substantially since the advent of Social Security; in 1998 only 9% of beneficiaries were in poverty. Excluding Social Security income, an additional 39% of beneficiaries would have income below the poverty line. It would be surprising if a program of this magnitude did not have a substantial impact on the economy.

Social Security can affect labor supply in a myriad of ways. First, and most obviously, by providing benefits to eligible workers after the age of 62, the program has

---

[29] The statistics in this paragraph are from Social Security Administration, Office of Research, Evaluation and Statistics (2000).

a "wealth effect" which induces some individuals to retire. Unanticipated increases in benefits that are granted close to retirement age – which were common when Congress adjusted benefits on an ad hoc basis – would be expected to have a particularly large effect on retirement because individuals would not have adjusted their earlier consumption and work plans. Second, because the benefit formula specifies greater benefits for those who delay retirement from age 62 to age 70, the program could induce (or discourage) some workers to remain employed longer than otherwise would be the case. The actuarial non-neutrality of benefits associated with retiring at different ages has changed over time. Third, the program is financed by a pay-as-you-go payroll tax on the working population which would be expected to affect labor supply, although in an ambiguous direction, through traditional income and substitution effects, or through an "entitlement effect" resulting from the prospect of becoming eligible for benefits. In 2000 the OASDHI tax was 7.65% of earnings for both employees and employers – a combined tax rate of 15.3%. The OASDI tax applied to the first $76 2000 of annual earnings, while the Medicare component of the tax (1.45%) is not capped. Most workers pay more in Social Security payroll taxes than they do in federal income taxes[30].

Social Security can have other, less obvious, but important impacts on labor supply as well. For example, benefits for spouses are set to half of the primary earner's primary insurance amount, unless the spouse's benefits are higher on his or her own account. Thus, Social Security could reduce the incentive for spouses to join the labor force. In addition, Social Security can affect the incentive for partial employment after individuals begin receiving benefits. The Social Security "earnings test" reduces current benefits for beneficiaries whose earnings exceed a threshold level after they begin receiving benefits, although benefits are increased subsequently to compensate. Finally, because only 40 quarters of covered employment are required to become eligible for Social Security, and because the Social Security benefit formula is progressive, Social Security can influence the incentive of individuals to "double dip" – that is, move from the uncovered to the covered sector – toward the end of their career[31]. Moreover, the progressive benefit formula could possibly increase the likelihood that some individuals accept jobs with relatively high nonpecuniary compensation.

Most of the research on Social Security and labor supply has focused on the first two effects outlined above – the wealth effect and the substitution effect caused by benefits depending on retirement age. In addition, a recent thrust of research has focused on the impact of the earnings test.

---

[30] This statement assumes that employees bear the incidence of the payroll tax.

[31] The expansion of mandatory coverage to the public sector, self-employed sector, and non-profit sector over time reduced the incentive for double dipping. Workers currently excluded from coverage mainly include: federal civilian employees hired before January 1, 1984; railroad workers; employees of state and local governments who are covered under a retirement system; and household workers, self-employed workers and farm workers with very low earnings.

Some have attributed the long-term downward trend in labor force participation among older men to the availability of Social Security and Disability Insurance. This conclusion, however, hinges on what the labor force participation rate would have been in the absence of Social Security. Such a counterfactual is suggested, in large part, by the labor force participation trend prior to the advent of Social Security in 1935. Perhaps the post-1935 downward trend is just the continuation of a pre-existing trend. The data in Figure 1.2 suggest that labor force participation declined steadily throughout the 20th Century, including the pre-Social Security era. Using a different definition of labor force participation, however, Ransom and Sutch (1986) find that the labor force participation rate of men age 60 or older was fairly stable in years prior to the start of Social Security. Costa (1998), Lee (1998) and Margo (1993) question the historical data used by Ransom and Sutch[32]. In any event, attributing causality depends on the counterfactual trend in labor force participation in the absence of Social Security. It is possible that labor force participation would have declined more slowly in the post 1935 period absent Social Security, regardless of whether it was declining prior to 1935. The historical data, though interesting, are unlikely to shed compelling evidence on the impact of Social Security on labor force participation.

Table 4.1 summarizes several studies of the effect of Social Security on labor supply. The set of studies reviewed in the table is not exhaustive; rather, studies were selected because they illustrate a particular approach to the problem and/or because they have been particularly influential. Studies of the impact of Social Security on labor supply can be divided into two types. One group relies primarily on time-series variation in the law to identify the effect of changes in benefit levels or other parameters of the Social Security system on labor supply. The other group relies on cross-sectional variation in benefits (i.e., differences across workers at a point in time) to identify the effect. Studies that analyze longitudinal data are a hybrid, potentially drawing on both time-series and cross-sectional variation in benefits.

In one of the more influential papers in the literature, Hurd and Boskin (1984) estimate the effect of Social Security wealth on retirement using longitudinal data on men age 58 to 67 from the Retirement History Survey. They model retirement in the years 1969, 1971 and 1973, and report many alternative ways of measuring the impact of Social Security on labor supply. Cross tabulations of retirement rates by age, assets, and Social Security wealth indicate: (1) a large increase in the retirement rate at age 62, when individuals become eligible to receive Social Security benefits; and (2) a higher retirement rate for those who would qualify for greater Social Security benefits.

They also provide a series of logistic estimates of the probability of retiring at a given age. Their Social Security wealth variable corresponds to the present value of benefits that the individual would receive if he retired in that year, given his earnings history, family status, life expectancy, and the prevailing Social Security law at that

---

[32] Ransom and Sutch assume that anyone who is unemployed for 6 months or more in 1900 is out of the labor force.

Table 4.1
Summary of selected studies of social security and labor supply

Study	Description	Analysis and identification	Findings
Hurd and Boskin (1984)	Examine the effect of Social Security benefits in 1969 on retirement rates of older men. The cohorts under study experienced a largely unanticipated 52% increase in Social Security Wealth between 1968 and 1972.	Examine conditional retirement rates for birth cohorts over time, and estimate logit models of whether men retire in a particular year as a function of Social Security wealth, wages, and wealth, and interactions of these variables. Sample consists of white married men age 58–67 with non-working spouses. Identification from cross-sectional nonlinear differences in the Social Security benefit.	Based on cross-sectional estimates, the increase in Social Security benefits can account for the entire 8.2 percentage point fall in labor force participation of older men from 1968 to 1973. Evidence also suggests that liquidity constraints cause a substantial number of men to retire upon reaching age 62, when they initially qualify for benefits.
Krueger and Pischke (1992)	Examine effect of Social Security benefit generosity and the growth in benefits from delaying retirement one year on labor force participation, weeks worked and retirement.	Identification is based on the Social Security benefit notch, which lowered benefits for the 1917–1921 cohort. Use cohort level data on men from Current Population Survey, 1976–1988.	A decline in Social Security wealth for the notch cohort did not significantly affect labor supply, although the increase in benefits from delaying retirement is significantly related to labor force participation. Social Security wealth effect is less than onesixth as large as Hurd and Boskin find.
Burtless (1986)	Proposes a model of retirement behavior for anticipated and unanticipated changes in real social security benefits and how the retirement decision is affected by unanticipated changes.	Use Retirement History Survey to analyze unanticipated SS benefits from 1969 to 1972 on male workers who still have to make a retirement decision. Unlike previous work, the econometric model accounts for non-linear relationship between goods consumption and retirement age.	Finds that the long-run effect of the unanticipated increases in benefits decreased the average retirement age by 0.17 years and increased the probability of retiring between age 62 and 65 by 2 percent. Also, found that the effect would have been greater had the benefit increase come sooner.

continued on next page

Table 4.1, *continued*

Study	Description	Analysis and identification	Findings
Rust and Phelan (1997)	Examines whether liquidity constraints and lack of access to health insurance can explain spike in retirement rate at age 62 and 65. Also consider the effect of actuarially unfair benefits after age 65 on retirement at age 65 for their sample low-income men.	Estimate a dynamic programming model of the labor supply and participation in Social Security decisions, with incomplete loan, annuity and health insurance markets. Use data on a panel of individuals initially aged 58–63 from 1969 to 1979 from the Retirement History Survey.	For a sample of men whose only retirement income is Social Security, they find that liquidity constraints can account for the spike in retirement rates at age 62 and 65. They also find that the fact that individuals do not qualify for Medicare until age 65 induces some individuals to work longer than otherwise to be covered by employer-sponsored health insurance.
Blau (1997)	Examines the impact of social security benefits, specifically the spouse benefit provision, on the labor supply behavior of older married couples.	The model accounts for the features of the differing labor force decisions of the joint labor force behavior of older married couples. The analysis looks at the transitions of these joint labor force decisions.	
Moffitt (1987)	Examines impact of changes in social security wealth on labor supply of four broad age groups of men (25–34, 35–44, 45–64, 65+).	Uses time-series data to estimate the wealth elasticity of labor supply from variations in unexpected changes in net social security wealth over the life cycle. Aggregate data are constructed from the March Current Population Survey, 1955–1981.	Finds that although there is a negative relationship between social security wealth and labor supply, the timing of the labor supply response does not correspond well to changes in social security wealth.

continued on next page

Table 4.1, *continued*

Study	Description	Analysis and identification	Findings
Diamond and Hausman (1984)	Studies the effect of bad health, unemployment and permanent income on retirement behavior. Focuses on the impact of uncertainty.	Estmate hazard models of the retirement decision, probit models of whether involuntary unemployed workers become retired, and competing risk hazard models of retirement or reemployment using data from the National Longitudinal Survey of Older Men.	Emphasizes that cross-sectional studies of the effect of retirement income on retirement status overstate the substitution effect of retirement income because people may have retired prior to being eligible for benefits. Both social security and private pensions have a positive effect on the probability of retirement.
Gordon and Blinder (1980)	Examine the determinants of the retirement decisions of white men age 58–67.	Estimate a structural model of the retirement decision using data from the 1969, 1971, and 1973 waves of the Longitudinal Retirement History Survey. Jointly estimate via maximum likelihood structural models of the reservation wage and the market wage. Use these estimates to predict an individual's retirement decision, under the assumption that men retire when their reservation wage exceeds their market wage.	Find that the Social Security system has little or no effect on retirement decisions. Instead, retirement is driven primarily by the effects of aging on market and reservation wages and by the incentives set up by private pension plans.

continued on next page

Table 4.1, *continued*

Study	Description	Analysis and identification	Findings
Baker and Benjamin (1999)	Examine the effect of the introduction of early retirement provisions in Canada's public pension plans on pension receipt and labor market behavior of men age 60–64.	Exploit the fact that early retirement provisions were introduced sequentially – in 1984 in Quebec and in 1987 in the rest of Canada – to estimate a difference-in-difference model of the effect of the policy change. Data are from the individual files of the 1982–1983 and 1985–1990 Survey of Consumer Finance.	Find that the introduction of early retirement provisions led to significant increases in benefit take-up among men age 60–64 but did not increase incidence of early retirement.
Gruber and Orszag (2000)	Examine the impact of the social security earnings test on the labor supply behavior of older men and women. The earnings test reduces immediate payments to beneficiaries of certain ages who are still working and whose current labor income exceeds a given threshold, although benefits are subsequently increased to compensate for any reduction.	Identification based on changes in the parameters of the earnings test between 1973 and 1998. Data on earnings, hours worked, and social security receipt of men and women ages 59–75 are from the March Current Population Survey, 1974–1999.	Find that the earnings test exerts no robust influence on the labor supply decisions of men. Find some evidence of an effect on women's labor supply decisions.

time. Although they use panel data and 'study a period during which benefits were rising rapidly, variation in benefits is primarily a result of cross-sectional differences in individual circumstances because they control for cohort effects and estimate separate models by age (which has the effect of absorbing any time-related variable that cuts across individuals). Their estimates imply that a $10000 increase in Social Security wealth (in 1969 dollars) is associated with an increase in the retirement rate of 7.8 percentage points. Hurd and Boskin further predict that, based on this cross-sectional estimate, the 52% increase in Social Security benefits between 1968 to 1972 would lead to a decline in labor force participation of older men of 8.4 percentage points. This slightly exceeds the actual decline of 8.2 points. If this conclusion is correct, then Social Security has had a major impact on the decline in male labor supply.

Studies that examine cross-sectional data – or exploit cross-sectional variability in benefits in panel data by absorbing time effects – necessarily estimate how the *prevailing* Social Security law in a given year influences behavior [examples include Hurd and Boskin (1984), Boskin (1977) and Pellechio (1979, 1981)]. Moffitt (1987, p. 185) raises a fundamental concern about the econometric identification of Social Security effects in such studies:

> For social security, the law is the same for all people at any given time; consequently, all cross-sectional variation in social security benefits or any other measure of the system must arise from cross-sectional variation in earnings received over the lifetime, in family size and the number of dependents, in marital status, and in other such variables.
>
> That is, there is no variation in the law itself. The potential difficulty of course is that the variables for which variation is available may have independent effects on labor supply; hence there is a fundamental identification problem in cross-sectional data, a problem that can only be overcome by making restrictions in functional form of one kind or another.

Consequently, the impact of Social Security can only be untangled from the impact of other variables if functional form and exclusion assumptions are made, such as the assumption that marital status or past earnings do not directly influence labor supply[33]. In many cases, these assumptions are untenable. For example, if one considers two workers who qualify for different Social Security benefits because one of the workers earned higher earnings throughout his career by dint of hard work, motivation and innate talent, it is difficult to believe that those very characteristics would not influence the likelihood that the workers would retire at different ages, apart from their Social Security wealth. In this situation, the Social Security wealth variable would confound the effect of one's past earnings history on labor supply and the effect of Social Security wealth on labor supply. Notice, however, that *conditional on* earnings or non-Social-Security wealth, in all likelihood the worker with history of higher earnings has lower Social Security wealth because the benefit formula is progressive. That is, the positive unconditional relationship between Social Security wealth and past earnings is reversed if one conditions on past earnings, or uses the replacement rate as a measure of benefit

---

[33] Quinn (1987) makes a similar point.

generosity. Therefore, the estimates will be highly sensitive to the other variables included in the equation.

Panel data that follow individuals over time and time-series data provide a means to allow changes in the Social Security law to influence the benefits that individuals receive. The difficulty here, however, is that variables often trend together. Many of the papers that rely on time-series variation in benefits, for example, are based on the Retirement History Survey, which follows individuals over the years 1969-1979 [examples are Hurd and Boskin (1984), Burtless (1986), and Anderson, Burkhauser and Quinn (1986)]. During these years Social Security benefits grew rapidly owing to *ad hoc* changes to the Social Security Act and the over indexation of benefits. Most of the analyses of data from this time period conclude that more generous Social Security benefits reduce labor force participation, induce earlier retirement, or induce individuals to retire earlier than they had previously planned. But the negative association between Social Security wealth and labor supply in these studies may spuriously reflect the coincidence of two trends: rising benefits and falling labor supply, which were due to unrelated causes.

Indeed, the long-term time-series studies mentioned previously (see Figure 1.2), and Moffitt's (1987) cohort-level study of labor supply in the years 1955–1981 suggest that the timing of the decline in labor supply does not correspond well with changes in Social Security wealth. These results suggest that estimates that are identified by continually rising benefits over time may reflect secular time trends in labor force withdrawal, rather than a response to Social Security.

Krueger and Pischke (1992) seek to avoid this problem by examining cohort-level data for a period in which benefits rose and then fell for succeeding cohorts. Specifically, because benefits were over indexed for inflation in the 1970s and then corrected abruptly by legislation passed in 1977 for cohorts born between 1917 and 1921, the so called Notch Babies, there were large, unanticipated differences in benefits for otherwise identical individuals depending on whether they were born before or after 1917. This situation creates a natural experiment that can be used to identify the effect of Social Security wealth apart from general time trends. Figure 4.1 summarizes Krueger and Pischke's main findings. They used March CPS data from 1976 to 1988 to create a panel of labor force participation rates by single year of age for men aged 60–68. Social Security wealth was calculated for a man with average earnings in each birth cohort at each age and year. The data reported in the figure are the average labor force participation rate and Social Security wealth for each cohort, after removing age effects from both series. Benefits exhibit a sharp zig-zag pattern as a result of over indexation and the subsequent correction for the notch cohort. Labor force participation, however, displays a steady downward trend, which is largely unrelated to the sharp movements in Social Security wealth [34]. Logistic regressions that control for other variables, including

---

[34] Peracchi and Welch (1994) who also analyze CPS data, reach a similar conclusion concerning trends in labor force participation of older men, although they do not directly measure Social Security benefits.

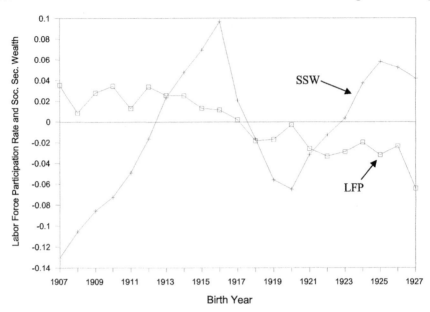

Fig. 4.1. Labor force participation and Social Security wealth. Average cohort effects after removing age effects.

the growth in Social Security wealth that is associated with delayed retirement, yield a similar conclusion: labor force participation rates of older men are unrelated to movements in Social Security wealth generated by the benefit notch.

There is considerable disagreement in the literature as to the magnitude and direction of the effect of Social Security on labor supply. For instance, after reviewing the past literature Aaron (1982) concludes there is little evidence showing Social Security has reduced the labor supply of elderly workers, whereas Boskin (1986, p. 62) concludes, "the acceleration in the decline of the labor force participation of the elderly from 1969 to 1973 was *primarily* due to the large increase in real Social Security benefits". Anderson, Gustman and Steinmeier (1999), Quinn, Burkhauser and Myers (1990), Hurd (1990), Ippolito (1998), Parnes (1988) and Danziger, Haveman and Plotnick (1981) reach more of a middle-ground conclusion, attributing a portion of the observed decline in labor force participation of older workers to Social Security. In our opinion, studies that use a more plausible identification strategy – for example, using variability in benefits due to legislated changes that cause breaks in the steady trend toward more generosity benefits – tend to find a very modest impact of Social Security wealth on labor supply in the United States.

Evidence from other countries is also mixed. For example, Baker and Benjamin (1999) find that the introduction of early retirement benefits in Quebec in 1984 led to significant increases in participation in the pension program for men age 60–64, but no greater increase in early retirement than that found in the rest of Canada, which adopted early retirement benefits later. This finding suggests that men who participated in the early retirement pension program would have retired anyway, and serves as a useful reminder that just because there is take-up of benefits in a social insurance program, the program may not affect behavior. On the other hand, the studies in Gruber and Wise (1999) suggest that Social Security systems have contributed to labor force withdrawal in many countries, particularly in Germany and France.

4.1. Automatic benefit recomputation

When a worker delays retirement after becoming eligible for Social Security, his or her Social Security wealth changes. Benefits are automatically recalculated to reflect the worker's current experience. Social Security wealth changes because (1) the worker typically displaces a year of low earnings with a year of high earnings, which raises the primary insurance amount, as emphasized by Blinder, Gordon and Wise (1980); (2) the worker grows older and therefore has less expected time left to collect benefits; (3) the actuarial adjustment to benefits may or may not be fair[35]. Moreover, because workers can self-select their retirement age based in part on their expected life expectancy, an actuarial adjustment to benefits based on unconditional lifetables is likely to be favorable to workers.

As Blinder, Gordon and Wise (1980) have noted, the *ad hoc* changes in Social Security benefits enacted by Congress prior to 1975 and double indexation typically resulted in more than actuarially fair growth in Social Security wealth for workers under 65 years old who postponed their retirement. They also noted that the 1977 amendments to the Social Security Act would substantially reduce the relative wealth advantage of delaying retirement. As a consequence, prior to the 1977 amendments, one would expect the Automatic Benefit Recomputation to induce some workers to delay their retirement. Krueger and Pischke (1992) report some evidence of this effect.

4.2. Liquidity constraints

Perhaps the most noticeable feature of retirement behavior is that a high proportion of people tend to retire immediately upon turning age 62 or age 65. Figure 4.2, taken from Rust and Phelan (1997), illustrates the spike in the retirement rate at ages 62 and 65. Using data on men from the Retirement History Survey, the figure shows the fraction of workers who begin receiving Social Security benefits at various ages. Nearly a quarter of workers first receive Social Security benefits in the year they turn 62, the very first year they are eligible, and almost as many start to receive benefits in the year they turn 65, the "normal" retirement age. A number of authors, including Crawford

---

[35] The first factor has less of an effect currently because a worker's past earnings are now indexed to overall earnings growth in the calculation of benefits.

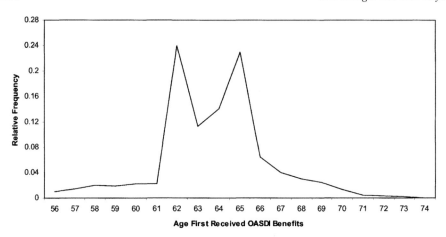

Fig. 4.2. Retirement age distribution [Rust and Phelan (1997)].

and Lilien (1981), Hurd and Boskin (1984), Boskin (1977), Kahn (1988) and Rust
and Phelan (1997) have concluded that the jump in the retirement rate at age 62 is
a result of liquidity constraints. That is, workers cannot borrow against their future
Social Security wealth and many lack access to other forms of credit, so they wait
until age 62 to receive retirement benefits, even though they would prefer to retire
earlier and borrow to finance their consumption.

Rust and Phelan (1997) provide a dynamic programming model of the retirement
decision, specifically modeling the effects of Social Security in a world with
incomplete markets for loans, annuities and health insurance. Their simulation results
suggest that liquidity constraints can account for the spike in retirement at age 62.
During the period they studied, the actuarial adjustment for delaying retirement beyond
age 65 was unfair – which would have encouraged workers to retire at age 65 – but they
conclude that the actuarial penalty for working longer only partially explains the spike
in retirement at age 65. More importantly, they suggest that eligibility for Medicare is
the main reason for the spike at age 65. That is, workers become eligible for Medicare
at age 65, so the value of employer-provided health insurance drops discretely at
this point. Interestingly, they find that workers who have employer-provided health
insurance but no access to retiree health insurance are four times more likely to retire
at age 65 than are those who lack health insurance or have coverage independent of
employment. And workers who lack health insurance or have coverage independent
of employment are much more likely to retire at age 62 than are those who rely on
employer-provided coverage. Thus, they find evidence that the spike in the retirement
rate at age 65 is largely due to "health insurance constrained" individuals[36].

---

[36] See Gruber and Madrian (1995) for related evidence showing that the likelihood of retirement is higher
for older workers in states that mandate that individuals have the right to purchase health insurance from
a previous employer after leaving the firm.

Two additional factors might contribute to the discrete jump in the retirement rate at age 65. First, many private pensions penalize workers who continue working after age 65. Second, until 1978, the United States permitted companies to maintain mandatory retirement policies, which enabled them to mandatorily retire workers upon reaching age 65. The mandatory retirement age was lifted to 70 in 1978, and then eliminated for most occupations in 1987.

A test of the impact of the Social Security program on the jump in the retirement rate for 65 year olds will soon be possible. In 1983 the Congress approved legislation that will gradually raise the normal retirement age from 65 to 67. The normal retirement age will rise by two months a year from 2003 through 2008, and then after a 12 year pause, it will rise again by two months a year from 2020 through 2025. It will be interesting to see if the retirement spike moves up by two months a year along with the normal retirement age, especially because the age of eligibility for Medicare will not increase with the normal Social Security retirement age. This program change should provide fertile research ground in the future.

4.3. Earnings test

Since it was founded, Social Security has included some form of a retirement earnings test, intended to limit benefits to retired individuals. Under the earnings test, Social Security recipients who have labor earnings in excess of a certain threshold lose part or all of their benefits in the year of their earnings. The particulars of the earnings test have varied considerably over time. The original Social Security Act of 1935 required that no benefits be paid to beneficiaries who received earnings from regular employment. Before it was repealed, in 2000 beneficiaries under the age of 65 could earn up to $10080 without any benefit offset, but benefits were reduced by $1 for every $2 of earnings above that threshold. The earnings test was less stringent for beneficiaries age 65 to 69: in 2000 they were allowed to earn up to $17000 without a benefit offset, and then faced a $1 reduction in benefits for every $3 of earnings above that threshold[37]. Since 1983, beneficiaries age 70 and older have not been subject to an earnings test.

A delayed retirement credit was provided to compensate workers age 65 to 69 whose benefits were offset by the earnings test. The delayed retirement credit increased workers' retirement benefits by 6% for each full-year-equivalent of benefits that were lost because of the retirement test. The 6% increase was not actuarially fair, but it was close to being actuarially fair. Similarly, beneficiaries age 62 to 65 who lost benefits because of the earnings test received an actuarial adjustment to their benefits later on (at age 65) to compensate for the earnings test.

---

[37] To be more precise, the lower age level pertained to people age 65 in the calendar year in which they turned 65.

Legislation passed unanimously by the House and Senate and signed by President Clinton in April 2000 eliminated the earnings test for workers age 65–69. For benefit computation, the earnings test was repealed retroactively to the beginning of the calendar year. The earnings test remained in place for younger beneficiaries, however. Because of the delayed retirement credit (which was already almost actuarially neutral, and slated to become actuarially neutral in the near future), the elimination of the earnings test was not expected to increase expenditures in the long run.

Policy makers including Alan Greenspan and Bill Clinton said they expected the elimination of the earnings test to increase labor supply of elderly workers. This argument probably relies more on psychology than economics, because the earnings test had an approximately actuarially neutral effect on workers' Social Security wealth. Nevertheless, if workers who were potentially affected by the earnings test did not realize that their benefits would subsequently be increased to compensate for benefit reductions for earnings above the threshold, or if they acted as if they were liquidity constrained or myopic and put greater weight on present benefits than future benefits, then eliminating the earnings test is like eliminating a payroll tax. In this case, for workers on the margin of working enough hours to exceed the threshold, the elimination of the earnings test would be expected to lead to an increase in labor supply. For workers above the threshold, the elimination of the earnings test in this setting would have opposing income and substitution effects.

Empirical evidence on the labor supply effects of the earning test is mixed, although the strongest evidence suggests that eliminating the earnings test will have at best a modest effect on labor supply. Friedberg (2000) finds evidence suggesting that some workers do respond to the earnings test because the earnings distributions of 63–69 year old workers tend to display excess clustering just below the relevant earnings thresholds. Moreover, the mass in the distribution just below the threshold moves when the threshold moves. It is unclear whether this clustering signifies an important labor supply response, however, because the number of workers who are clustered just below the threshold point is relatively small compared to total labor supply of older workers; the response of workers above the threshold level is potentially of more importance for overall labor supply. Friedberg (2000) estimates the impact of the earnings test on labor supply by estimating the parameters of a labor supply function by maximum likelihood assuming utility maximization over the piecewise linear budget constraint created by the earnings test. She predicts that eliminating the earnings test would raise the aggregate work hours of 65–69 year old men by 5%. Friedberg's estimates imply a larger labor supply response than most of the rest of the literature on the earnings test.

Gruber and Orszag (2000), for example, examine the impact of past changes in the earnings test on the labor supply behavior of elderly men and women in a less structural way. They directly examined how various measures of labor supply of older workers changed in years when parameters of the earnings test changed between 1973 and 1998. Specifically, they use data on the previous year's earnings, hours worked, employment status, and Social Security receipt of men and women age 59 to 75 from

March Current Population Surveys conducted from 1974 through 1999. They conclude that the earnings test exerts no robust influence on the labor supply decisions of men, although they find some evidence of an effect for women. The apparently weak impact of the earnings test on labor supply is probably more a result of a relatively inelastic labor supply response to a perceived tax, than a result of a rational calculation by the elderly that the discounted actuarial present value of their benefits is unaffected by their labor supply.

An obvious direction for future research is to use the elimination of the earnings test for 65–69 year olds that was enacted in 2000 to test the impact of the earnings test on labor supply behavior. For example, changes in the aggregate hours worked by 65–69 year olds before and after 2000 can be compared to the corresponding changes for 62–64 year olds and 70–74 year olds to control for business cycle effects. It is rare that economists can examine the effect of such a large and sudden change in a program parameter.

5. Disability insurance

To qualify for the Disability Insurance (DI) program, insured individuals must be unable "to engage in substantial gainful activity, by reason of a medically determinable physical or mental impairment that is expected to result in death or last at least 12 months". There is also a five-month waiting period before an applicant to DI can start receiving benefits. This is a strict standard. In essence, applicants must be unable to work in any job that exists in the US economy. The Social Security Administration (2001) advises prospective applicants: "If you cannot do the work you did in the past, we see if you are able to adjust to other work ... If you can adjust to other work, your claim will be denied"[38]. To qualify as covered for disability insurance, individuals age 31 or older must fully meet the insurance coverage requirements under Social Security and have worked in covered employment in at least 20 of the last 40 calendar quarters. The coverage requirement is less stringent for individuals younger than 31 because they have less time to satisfy the Social Security eligibility requirements[39].

A worker who qualifies for DI before reaching the normal Social Security retirement age can receive a benefit equal to 100% of his or her primary insurance amount. The spouse and unmarried children (under the age of 18, or 19 in the case of full-time students) of a disabled worker can also qualify for benefits. There is a cap on the total amount of benefits a family can receive, however[40].

---

[38] See http://www.ssa.gov/dibplan/dqualify6.htm.

[39] The blind are exempt from the requirement that they have considerable covered work in recent calendar quarters (i.e., 20 out of the last 40 quarters requirement for workers older than 30). Those who do not meet the employment history requirement for DI can apply for the Supplemental Security Income program, which pays less generous benefits but has no past employment requirement.

[40] For program details, see Rejda (1999) or Bound and Burkhauser (1999).

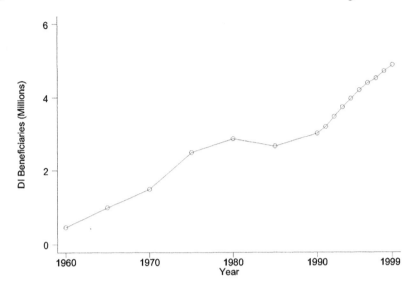

Fig. 5.1. Number of disability insurance beneficiaries, 1960–99. Source: U.S. House of Representatives Committee on Ways and Means (2000, Table 1-41).

Despite the official criteria, it is important to bear in mind that the assessment of a disability is inherently a subjective decision[41]. As Bound and Waidman (2000) stress, the standards used to evaluate whether individuals meet the DI disability test have varied over time, and are a major determinant of the number of participants on the DI program. For example, in 1980 Congress required more frequent eligibility reviews to check if beneficiaries continued to have a disability. Then in 1984 Congress loosened eligibility requirements, by, among other things, shifting the burden of proof to the Social Security Administration to demonstrate that the beneficiary's health had improved sufficiently to return to work, and placing more weight on the claimant's own medical evidence. In addition, the Social Security Administration changed its treatment of claims involving mental illness, by emphasizing the ability of the claimant to function in work or a work-like environment. As a consequence, by 1988 mental health became the most prevalent disabling condition among new beneficiaries, increasing from 11% of all cases in 1982 to 22% in 1988, and peaking at 26% in 1993[42]. In 1996 alcoholism and drug addiction were removed as disabling conditions, but mental impairment continues to be the most prevalent disabling condition, accounting for 22% of beneficiaries granted benefits in 1999.

Figure 5.1 illustrates the number of disabled workers receiving DI benefits in selected years since 1960. The number of disabled workers on DI was less than

[41] See Diamond and Sheshinski (1995) for a model of the optimal structure of DI benefits in a world with uncertain and imperfect evaluations of applicants' disability status.

[42] See *Green Book,* U.S. House of Representatives Committee on Ways and Means (2000, Table 1-43).

0.5 million in 1960, and then grew rapidly in the 1960s and 1970s, reaching 2.9 million in 1980. The number of beneficiaries fell slightly between 1980 and the mid 1980s, and then began to grow rapidly again beginning in the mid to late 1980s. The steady rise in the number of DI beneficiaries in the 1990s is rather surprising in view of the strong labor demand in the USA in that period. The unemployment rate, for example, fell from 7.5% in 1992 to below 4% at the end of 1999. DI participation usually follows a counter cyclical pattern[43]. Part of the explanation is simply that mortality decreased among the stock of DI recipients (because new recipients had longer life expectancies), which caused the number of people on the rolls to grow [see Autor and Duggan (2001)].

Another curious development is that the employment rate of people with a self-reported disability fell in the 1990s, especially for men. For example, Bound and Waidman (2000) find that the employment rate of 30–44 year old men with a work limitation fell from just over 40% in 1990 to below 30% in 1999. Employment rates of other workers increased or remained constant over this period. The distinct downward trend in employment for people with disabilities has stimulated new research into the DI program that is described below.

The earliest studies of DI examined the relationship between the generosity of DI benefits and participation in the DI program[44]. Perhaps best known and most controversial, Parsons (1980) estimated a probit model to explain labor force participation using data on 48 to 62 year old men from the 1969 cross-sectional wave of the National Longitudinal Surveys[45]. The key independent variable was the ratio of each individual's potential Social Security benefit to his hourly wage three years earlier. The results indicated an elasticity of labor force participation with respect to the potential benefit replacement rate of −.63, with a *t*-ratio of −2.5. The elasticity is even larger in magnitude for those in poor health, as proxied by their subsequent mortality probability. An issue that we have stressed repeatedly in this chapter arises in interpreting these probit estimates: the Social Security benefit is a deterministic function of past labor market behavior, so it is impossible to identify the effect of benefits separately from the effect of past behavior that might be related to present labor supply for reasons having nothing to do with DI. Had a more flexible function of past earnings been included in the model, the effect of the benefit variable would not have been estimable. Indeed, there is an indication that identification of the benefit elasticity apart from the effect of past wages is a problem in this analysis as Parsons reports in a footnote that the replacement ratio was used because of collinearity programs if

---

[43] See Black, Daniel and Sanders (1998) for compelling evidence that economic conditions influence participation on DI. Using exogenous shocks to local economic conditions resulting from swings in the coal industry in four states, they find that the elasticity of DI payments with respect to local earnings is −0.3 to −0.4. Similar results are obtained when they use shocks due to the collapse of the steel industry in six other states.

[44] See Bound and Burkhauser (1999) for a comprehensive summary of research on many aspects of DI, including labor supply.

[45] See also Leonard's (1979) related study.

wages and benefits were entered as separate variables. Because the potential Social Security benefit relative to the wage is lower for those with higher wages or more steady employment, there is a real possibility that the inverse relationship between the replacement rate and labor force participation is merely a reflection of the positive relationship between employment rates and earnings potential.

This problem aside, Parsons (1980) provides a rather useful check on the plausibility of his benefit elasticity. Specifically, he uses the estimated cross-sectional model to predict the labor force nonparticipation rate each year from 1948 to 1976. This is accomplished by combining the cross-sectional parameter estimates with values of the replacement rate and mortality index each year to generate predicted nonparticipation rates. This exercise reveals a fairly tight correspondence between predicted labor force nonparticipation and the actual nonparticipation rate. Because other variables not captured by the cross-sectional model may change over time (e.g., disability assessment standards could change), and the parameters in the cross-sectional model may also change over time, there is no guarantee that the predicted values will closely mirror the observed values, even under the best of circumstances. So this test does provide some additional information. (Another way of performing this same type of comparison would be to estimate a nonparticipation rate model with aggregate time-series data, and test if the benefit elasticity is the same as in the cross-sectional model.) It is certainly possible, however, that the similarity of the time trends in the predicted and actual nonparticipation rates is just coincidental, a reflection of rising benefits and declining participation in this period for unrelated reasons. Nevertheless, if the prediction diverged substantially from the actual data, then one would have even more reason to be skeptical of the cross-sectional estimate.

Bound (1989, 1991) challenges Parson's conclusion that DI is responsible for the decline in male labor force participation in the post-World War II period. He presents two types of evidence. First, he documents that among prime-age male applicants to DI who were rejected from the program because they were not judged to have a medical disability in 1972 and 1978, less than one half subsequently returned to sustained employment. He argues that the experience of these individuals, who presumably are healthier than DI beneficiaries, provides a natural upper bound estimate for the employment rate of DI beneficiaries had they been denied access to DI[46]. Because the drop in labor force participation has more than matched the rise in the proportion of older men on DI, he concludes that "DI accounts for substantially less than half of the postwar decline in the participation rates of older men". Second, and related,

---

[46] Parsons (1991) questions whether the employment experiences of denied applicants to DI provide a natural control group for successful applicants, because denied applicants may refrain from working because they are appealing their rejection from the program or plan to reapply to DI and would like to strengthen their case, or because they face obstacles returning to work because they spent time out of the labor force while applying to DI. In other words, in the absence of the program their employment rates might be higher. Similar arguments could be applied to Bound's logit equation described below. See Bound (1991) for a reply to this critique.

he estimates a nonemployment logit equation similar to the nonparticipation equation in Parsons (1980), except he uses a sample of individuals who never applied to DI, as well as a sample that closely parallels the one used by Parsons. The estimated elasticity of nonemployment with respect to the benefit replacement rate is similar in both samples. He infers from this that Parsons's estimate of the DI benefit elasticity is biased upwards because the non-applicants could not have been affected by DI. Although Bound acknowledges that DI does influence labor supply incentives, he questions whether the availability of the program is a major reason for the decline in male labor force participation, and he suggests that benefits are well targeted towards those who would not seek employment even in the absence of the program.

More recent studies have sought to explain both the rising number of DI participants and declining employment rate of individuals with self-reported disabilities since the late 1980s. Ironically, this rise in DI participation occurred during a time when the overall employment-to-population rate increased to a historically high level. Nevertheless, the employment rate fell considerably for male high school dropouts in the 1990s. Moreover, the declining labor force participation of people with disabilities is of concern if individuals with disabilities desire to work, and the expanding DI rolls in a period of strong growth in employment demand raises concerns about possible labor supply disincentive effects caused by the program. Although several hypotheses have been proposed to explain the fall in employment of people with disabilities and the rise in DI participation in the 1990s, a fair assessment is that this is an area where a consensus on the causes of these developments has yet to emerge.

Bound and Waidman (2000) attribute the decline in employment among people with a self-reported work disability mainly to increases in the availability of DI due to changes in disability assessment standards. Their evidence is rather circumstantial, however. Looking across states between 1989 and 1999, they find that the change in the fraction of the population that has a work limitation and is out of work tends to increase almost one for one with the proportion of the working-age population on DI. This suggests that many of the self-reported work-limited individuals who left employment received support from the DI program, perhaps because access to DI was relaxed.

Autor and Duggan (2001) attribute the rise in participation in the DI and SSI programs since the mid 1980s to the reduced stringency in screening applicants *and* to the interaction between growing wage inequality and the progressive benefit formula in these programs. The effective benefit replacement rate increased because the earnings of less-skilled workers fell, and the benefit formula is progressive and linked to average earnings. For example, between 1979 and 1999 the replacement rate increased from 56% to 74% for a 40–49 year old man at the 10th percentile of the earnings distribution. The addition of Medicare or Medicaid benefits could raise the effective replacement rate above 100%. Autor and Duggan also present cross-state evidence showing that the share of the population applying for DI benefits has become more responsive to employment shocks since the early 1980s. Thus, the declining job opportunities for less skilled workers, together with the progressive DI benefit formula and more liberal screening rules, may account for the increased participation in disability programs.

Acemoglu and Angrist (2001) and DeLeire (2000) look at another policy as a possible cause of the decline in labor force participation of those with a self-reported disability, the Americans with Disabilities Act (ADA) of 1990. This Act requires employers to accommodate disabled workers (e.g., by providing physical access) and outlaws discrimination against the disabled in hiring, firing, and compensation. Although the ADA was intended to increase employment of the disabled by reducing discrimination and increasing access, it also increases costs for employers. Acemoglu and Angrist, for example, find evidence that the employment of disabled workers declined more in states where there have been more ADA-related discrimination charges[47].

A final factor may be welfare reform. Even before Aid to Families with Dependent Children was repealed in 1996, states had tightened their welfare laws. It is possible that an increasing number of people sought DI because they were no longer eligible for welfare, or because welfare became less generous. Because state welfare programs primarily affect women, this might also help explain why the relative number of male to female workers who joined the DI rolls increased from 2 to 1 in 1985 to 1.2 to 1 in 1999[48]. The proportion of women who reported having a health limitation or disability that restricts them from working increased in the 1990s, after declining in the 1980s [see Bound and Waidman (2000)]. It is also possible that the changing mores concerning welfare may have affected responses to Census questions on disability status. It seems reasonable to speculate that during the 1990s because of the stigma associated with welfare it became socially less acceptable for an able bodied individual to report that he or she did not work. So a growing proportion of people who were out of the labor force might have reported a health-related work-limitation as the reason why they did not work because of changes in social norms.

6. Conclusion

The empirical work on unemployment insurance and workers' compensation insurance reviewed in this chapter finds that the programs tend to increase the length of time employees spend out of work. Most of the estimates of the elasticities of lost work time that incorporate both the incidence and duration of claims are close to 1.0 for unemployment insurance and between 0.5 and 1.0 for workers' compensation. These elasticities are substantially larger than the labor supply elasticities typically found for men in studies of the effects of wages or taxes on hours of work; such estimates are

---

[47] Bound and Waidman (2000), on the other hand, point out that the rise in disability applications began in 1989–90, prior to the passage of the ADA.

[48] *Green Book,* U.S. House of Representatives Committee on Ways and Means (2000, Table 1-43). The growing labor force participation of women might also help explain the change in the sex ratio of DI participants.

centered close to zero [see, e.g., Killingsworth (1983) and Pencavel (1986)]. They are also larger than the consensus range of estimates of the labor supply elasticity for women, which is highly dispersed but centered near 0.4. These seemingly disparate results may, in part, be reconciled by the likelihood that elasticities are larger when a labor supply response can easily occur through participation or weeks worked, rather than adjustments to the number of hours worked per week. Labor supply responses to WC and UI benefits occur mainly through decisions about weeks worked, and labor supply responses of women mainly concern participation and weeks worked. Male labor supply elasticities by contrast are primarily determined by adjustments to hours worked per week, a margin on which employees may have relatively little flexibility. These observations suggest that it would be misleading to apply a universal set of labor supply elasticities to diverse problems and populations.

Temporary total workers' compensation insurance benefits and the UI program also may generate relatively large labor supply responses because these programs lead to only a short-run change in the returns to work. For example, individuals are not eligible to receive UI benefits for an indefinite period; there is a maximum number of weeks benefits can be received. Thus, workers may inter-temporally substitute their labor supply while benefits are available, generating larger work responses than predicted by long-run labor supply elasticities. The window of eligibility for Social Security and Disability Insurance benefits is more permanent, so such inter-temporal considerations are likely to be less important.

In addition, receipt of UI and temporary total WC benefits makes the net wage (after-tax wage minus after-tax benefits) very low, often close to zero in the case of WC benefits. This situation is different from a typical cut in wages for two reasons. First, the income effect does not counterbalance the substitution effect to the usual extent because benefits are provided and income often does not fall appreciably. In the case of a replacement rate of 0.8, for example, the net wage falls by 80%, but short-run income falls by only 20%. In the usual case of wage variation, a drop in the wage dramatically lowers income, and thus, the income effect tends to mitigate the substitution effect. Second, the level of the net wage may be so low that it is out of the range of typical variation in cross-section wages or wage variation due to taxes. Thus, estimates based on other sources of wage variation may be less applicable to UI and WC.

Despite labor supply responses to social insurance programs, we would emphasize that the desirability of social insurance depends on the *intended* as well as unintended effects (or, more appropriately put, undesired side effects) of the programs. Thus, a finding of labor supply responses to incentives is not necessarily cause for abandoning a program. The undesired side effects must be balanced against the improved welfare from providing income maintenance to those in need. Moreover, for some programs, such as UI, it is quite likely that the adverse incentive effects vary over the business cycle. For example, there is probably less of an efficiency loss from reduced search effort by the unemployed during a recession than during a boom. As a consequence, it may be optimal to expand the generosity of UI during economic downturns (assuming the initial starting level was optimal). Unfortunately, this is an area in which little empirical research is currently available to guide policymakers.

A final point worth highlighting is that less research has been conducted on WC and DI than on UI, despite the large magnitude of the programs. In our view, WC and DI are under-researched relative to their importance to the economy and merit further study. These programs exhibit substantial variability over time or across states, and large data sets are available that can be analyzed, so there is potential for many valuable research projects on WC and DI. Another fruitful area for research involves the overlap among programs. For example, individuals who receive both WC and DI benefits have their DI benefits reduced if their combined level exceeds a certain threshold. Little research has been done on the incentive effects caused by the interactions among social insurance programs. Also, while the UI literature for Europe is rapidly catching up to the American literature, relatively little work has been done on WC-like programs outside the USA.

References

Aaron, H.J. (1982), Economic Effects of Social Security (Brookings Institution, Washington, DC).

Abbring, J.H., G.J. van den Berg and J.C. van Ours (2000), "The effect of unemployment insurance sanction on the transition rate from unemployment to employment", Working Paper (Free University, Amsterdam).

Acemoglu, D., and J. Angrist (2001), "Consequences of employment protection? The case of the Americans with Disabilities Act", Journal of Political Economy 109:915–957.

Adams, J. (1986), "Equilibrium taxation and experience rating in a federal system of unemployment insurance", Journal of Public Economics 29:51–77.

Agell, J. (1999), "On the benefits from rigid labour markets: norms, market failures, and social insurance", Economic Journal 109:F143–164.

Aiuppa, T., and J. Trieschmann (1998), "Moral hazard in the French workers' compensation system", Journal of Risk and Insurance 65(1):125–133.

Anderson, K.H., R.V. Burkhauser and J.F. Quinn (1986), "Do retirement dreams come true? The effect of unanticipated events on retirement plans", Industrial and Labor Relations Review 39(4):518–526.

Anderson, P.M. (1993), "Linear adjustment costs and seasonal labor demand: evidence from retail trade firms", Quarterly Journal of Economics 108:1015–1042.

Anderson, P.M., and B.D. Meyer (1993), "Unemployment insurance in the United States: layoff incentives and cross-subsidies", Journal of Labor Economics 11:S70–S95.

Anderson, P.M., and B.D. Meyer (1994), "The effect of unemployment insurance taxes and benefits on layoffs using firm and individual data", Working Paper 4960 (National Bureau of Economic Research, Cambridge, MA).

Anderson, P.M., and B.D. Meyer (1997a), "Unemployment insurance takeup rates and the after-tax value of benefits", Quarterly Journal of Economics 112:913–938.

Anderson, P.M., and B.D. Meyer (1997b), "The effects of firm specific taxes and government mandates with an application to the U.S. Unemployment Insurance Program", Journal of Public Economics 65:119–144.

Anderson, P.M., and B.D. Meyer (2000), "The effects of the Unemployment Insurance Payroll Tax on wages, employment, claims and denials", Journal of Public Economics 78(1-2):81–106.

Anderson, P.M., and B.D. Meyer (2001), "The distributional consequences of unemployment benefits and taxes", Working Paper (Dartmouth College, Hanover, NH; Northwestern University, Evanston, IL).

Anderson, P.M., A.L. Gustman and T.L. Steinmeier (1999), "Trends in male labor force participation and retirement: some evidence on the role of pensions and Social Security in the 1970s and 1980s", Journal of Labor Economics 17(4, part 1):757–783.

Atkinson, A.B. (1987), "Income maintenance and social insurance", in: A. Auerbach and M. Feldstein, eds., Handbook of Public Economics, Vol. 2 (North-Holland, Amsterdam).

Atkinson, A.B., and J. Micklewright (1985), Unemploment Benefits and Unemployment Duration (Suntory–Toyota International Centre for Economics and Related Disciplines, The London School of Economics and Political Science).

Atkinson, A.B., and J. Micklewright (1990), "Unemployment compensation and labor market transitions: a critical review", Journal of Economic Literature 29:1679–1727.

Autor, D.H., and M. Duggan (2001), "The rise in disability recipiency and the decline in unemployment", Working Paper 8336 (National Bureau of Economic Research, Cambridge, MA).

Baily, M.N. (1977), "On the theory of layoffs and unemployment", Econometrica 45:1043–1064.

Baker, M., and D. Benjamin (1999), "Early retirement provisions and the labor force behavior of older men: evidence from Canada", Journal of Labor Economics 17(4, Part 1):724–756.

Besley, T.J., and A. Case (1994), "Unnatural experiments? Estimating the incidence of endogenous policies", Working Paper W4956 (National Bureau of Economic Research, Cambridge, MA).

Black, D., K. Daniel and S. Sanders (1998), "The impact of economic conditions on participation in disability programs: evidence from the Coal Boom and Bust", Working Paper (University of Kentucky, Lexington, KY; Monitor Company, New York, NY; Carnegie Mellon University, Pittsburgh, PA).

Blank, R.M., and D. Card (1991), "Recent trends in insured and uninsured unemployment: is there an explanation?", Quarterly Journal of Economics 106:1157–1190.

Blau, D.M. (1997), "Social Security and the labor supply of older married couples", Labour Economics 4(4):373–418.

Blinder, A.S., R.H. Gordon and D.E. Wise (1980), "Reconsidering the work disincentive effects of Social Security", National Tax Journal 33(4):431–442.

Boskin, M.J. (1977), "Social Security and retirement decisions", Economic Inquiry 15(1):1–25.

Boskin, M.J. (1986), Too Many Promises: The Uncertain Future of Social Security (Dow Jones-Irwin, Homewood, IL).

Bound, J. (1989), "The health and earnings of rejected disability insurance applicants", American Economic Review 79(3):482–503.

Bound, J. (1991), "The health and earnings of rejected disability insurance applicants: reply", American Economic Review 81(5):1427–1434.

Bound, J., and R.V. Burkhauser (1999), "Economic analysis of transfer programs targeted on people with disabilities", in: O. Ashenfelter and D. Card, eds., Handbook of Labor Economics, Vol. 3C (Elsevier, Amsterdam) pp. 3417–3525.

Bound, J., and T. Waidman (2000), "Accounting for recent declines in employment rates among the working-aged disabled", Working Paper 7975 (National Bureau of Economic Research, Cambridge, MA).

Burdett, K. (1979), "Unemployment insurance payments as a search subsidy: a theoretical analysis", Economic Inquiry 17:333–342.

Burtless, G. (1986), "Social Security, unanticipated benefit increases, and the timing of retirement", Review of Economic Studies 53(5):781–805.

Burtless, G., and A.H. Munnell (1991), "Does a trend toward early retirement create problems for the economy?", in: A.M. Munnell, ed., Retirement and Public Policy (National Academy of Social Insurance, Washington, DC).

Butler, R.J. (1983), "Wage and injury response to shifting levels of workers' compensation", in: J. Worrall, ed., Safety and the Workforce (Cornell University Press, Ithaca) pp. 61–86.

Butler, R.J., and J.D. Worrall (1983), "Workers' compensation: benefit and injury claim rates in the seventies", Review of Economics and Statistics 50:580–589.

Butler, R.J., and J.D. Worrall (1985), "Work injury compensation and the duration of nonwork spells", Economic Journal 95:714–724.

Butler, R.J., and J.D. Worrall (1991), "Claims reporting and risk bearing moral hazard in workers' compensation", Journal of Risk and Insurance 49:191–204.

Butler, R.J., B.D. Gardner and H.H. Gardner (1997), "Workers' compensation costs when maximum benefits change", Journal of Risk and Uncertainty 15:259–269.

Card, D., and P.B. Levine (1994), "Unemployment insurance taxes and the cyclical and seasonal properties of unemployment", Journal of Public Economics 53:1–29.

Card, D., and P.B. Levine (2000), "Extended benefits and the duration of UI spells: evidence from the New Jersey Extended Benefit Program", Journal of Public Economics 78:107–138.

Card, D., and B.P. McCall (1996), "Is workers' compensation covering uninsured medical costs? Evidence from the 'Monday effect' ", Industrial and Labor Relations Review 49:690–706.

Card, D., and W.C. Riddell (1993), "A comparative analysis of unemployment in Canada and the United States", in: D. Card and R.B. Freeman, eds., Small Differences That Matter (University of Chicago Press, Chicago, IL) pp. 149–189.

Card, D., and W.C. Riddell (1997), "Unemployment in Canada and the United States: a further analysis", in: B.C. Eaton and R.G. Harris, eds., Trade, Technology and Economics: Essays in Honour of Richard Lipsey (Edward Elgar, Cheltenham, UK) pp. 47–97.

Carling, K., P.-A. Edin, A. Harkman and B. Holmlund (1996), "Unemployment duration, unemployment benefits, and labor market programs in Sweden", Journal of Public Economics 59:313–334.

Carling, K., B. Holmlund and A. Vejsiu (2001), "Do benefit cuts boost job finding? Swedish evidence from the 1990s", Economic Journal 111:766–790.

Chelius, J. (1982), "The influence of workers' compensation on safety incentives", Industrial and Labor Relations Review 35:235–242.

Classen, K.P. (1979), "Unemployment insurance and job search", in: S.A. Lippman and J.J. McCall, eds., Studies in the Economics of Search (North-Holland, Amsterdam) pp. 191–219.

Corson, W., and W. Nicholson (1988), "An examination of declining UI claims during the 1980's", Unemployment Insurance Occasional Paper 88-3 (US Department of Labor – ETA, Washington, DC).

Costa, D. (1998), The Evolution of Retirement: An American Economic History, 1880–1990 (University of Chicago Press, Chicago, IL).

Crawford, V., and D. Lilien (1981), "Social Security and the retirement decision", Quarterly Journal of Economics 96(3):505–529.

Cullen, J.B., and J. Gruber (2000), "Does unemployment insurance crowd out spousal labor supply?" Journal of Labor Economics 18(3):546–572.

Curington, W.P. (1994), "Compensation for permanent impairment and the duration of work absence: evidence from four natural experiments", Journal of Human Resources 29(3):888–910.

Danziger, S., R. Haveman and R. Plotnick (1981), "How income transfer programs affect work, savings, and the income distribution: a critical review", Journal of Economic Literature 19:975–1028.

DeLeire, T. (2000), "The wage and employment effects of the Americans with Disabilities Act", Journal of Human Resources 35(4):693–715.

Devine, T.J., and N.M. Kiefer (1991), Empirical Labor Economics: The Search Approach (Oxford University Press, New York, NY).

Diamond, P.A., and J.A. Hausman (1984), "The retirement and unemployment behavior of older men", in: H. Aaron and G. Burtless, eds., Retirement and Economic Behavior: Studies in Social Economics Series (Brookings Institution, Washington, DC) pp. 97–132.

Diamond, P.A., and E. Sheshinski (1995), "Economic aspects of optimal disability benefits", Journal of Public Economics 57:1–24.

Ehrenberg, R.G. (1988), "Workers' compensation, wages, and the risk of injury", in: J.F. Burton Jr, ed., New Perspectives in Workers' Compensation (ILR Press, Ithaca, NY) pp. 71–96.

Feldstein, M. (1974), "Unemployment compensation: adverse incentives and distributional anomalies", National Tax Journal 27:231–244.

Feldstein, M. (1976), "Temporary layoffs in the theory of unemployment", Journal of Political Economy 84:837–857.

Feldstein, M. (1978), "The effect of unemployment insurance on temporary layoff unemployment", American Economic Review 68:834–846.

Feldstein, M., and J. Liebman (2002), "Social security", in: A.J. Auerbach and M. Feldstein, eds., Handbook of Public Economics, Vol. 4 (Elsevier, Amsterdam) Chapter 32, this volume.

Friedberg, L. (2000), "The labor supply effects of the Social Security Earnings Test", Review of Economics and Statistics 82(1):48–63.

Fuchs, V.R., A.B. Krueger and J.M. Poterba (1998), "Economists' views about parameters, values, and policies: survey results in labor and public economics", Journal of Economic Literature 36(3): 1387–1425.

Gardner, J.A. (1991), Benefit Increases and System Utilization: The Connecticut Experience (Workers Compensation Research Institute, Cambridge, MA).

Gordon, R.H., and A.S. Blinder (1980), "Market wages, reservation wages, and retirement decisions", Journal of Public Economics 14(2):277–308.

Gruber, J. (1997), "The consumption smoothing benefits of unemployment insurance", American Economic Review 87(1):192–205.

Gruber, J., and A.B. Krueger (1991), "The incidence of mandate employer-provided insurance: lessons from Workers' Compensation Insurance", in: D. Bradford, ed., Tax Policy and the Economy 5 (National Bureau of Economic Research, Cambridge, MA) pp. 111–143.

Gruber, J., and B.C. Madrian (1995), "Health-insurance availability and the retirement decision", American Economic Review 85(4):938–948.

Gruber, J., and P.R. Orszag (2000), "Does the Social Security Earnings Test affect labor supply and benefits receipt?", Working Paper 7923 (National Bureau of Economic Research, Cambridge, MA).

Gruber, J., and D.A. Wise (1999), "Social Security and retirement around the world: introduction and summary", NBER Conference Report (National Bureau of Economic Research, Cambridge, MA).

Gustman, A.L. (1982), "Analyzing the relation of unemployment insurance to unemployment", in: R. Ehrenberg, ed., Research in Labor Economics 5 (JAI Press, Greenwich, CT) pp. 69–114.

Ham, J.C., and S.A. Rea Jr (1987), "Unemployment insurance and male unemployment duration in Canada", Journal of Labor Economics 5(3):325–353.

Hamermesh, D.S. (1977), Jobless Pay and the Economy (Johns Hopkins University Press, Baltimore, MD).

Holmlund, B. (1983), "Payroll taxes and wage inflation: the Swedish experience", Scandinavian Journal of Economics 85(1):1–15.

Holmlund, B. (1998), "Unemployment insurance in theory and practice", Scandinavian Journal of Economics 100:113–141.

Hunt, J. (1995), "The effect of unemployment compensation on unemployment duration in Germany", Journal of Labor Economics 13(1):88–120.

Hurd, M.D. (1990), "Research on the elderly: economic status, retirement, and consumption and savings", Journal of Economic Literature 28:565–637.

Hurd, M.D., and M.J. Boskin (1984), "The effect of Social Security on retirement in the early 1970s", Quarterly Journal of Economics 99(4):767–790.

International Labour Organization (2001), Cost of Social Security (International Labour Organization, Geneva, Switzerland). Available from www.ilo.org/public/english/protection/socsec/publ/css/cssindex.htm.

Ippolito, R.A. (1998), "Disparate savings propensities and national retirement policy", in: O.S. Mitchell and S.J. Schieber, eds., Living with Defined Contribution Pensions: Remaking Responsibility for Retired Men (University of Pennsylvania Press, Philadelphia, PA) pp. 247–272.

Kahn, J.A. (1988), "Social Security, liquidity, and early retirement", Journal of Public Economics 35(1):97–117.

Katz, L.F., and B.D. Meyer (1990), "The impact of the potential duration of unemployment benefits on the duration of unemployment", Journal of Public Economics 41:45–72.

Killingsworth, M.R. (1983), Labor Supply (Cambridge University Press, New York).

Kniesner, T.J., and J.D. Leeth (1995), Simulating Workplace Safety Policy (Kluwer Academic Publishers, Boston, MA).

Krueger, A.B. (1990a), "Incentive effects of Workers' Compensation Insurance", Journal of Public Economics 41:73–99.

Krueger, A.B. (1990b), "Workers' Compensation Insurance and the duration of workplace injuries", Working Paper 3253 (National Bureau of Economic Research, Cambridge, MA).

Krueger, A.B., and J.F. Burton Jr (1990), "The employers' cost of Workers' Compensation Insurance: magnitudes, determinants, and public policy", Review of Economics and Statistics 72:228–240.

Krueger, A.B., and J.-S. Pischke (1992), "The effect of social security on labor supply: a cohort analysis of the Notch Generation", Journal of Labor Economics 10:412–437.

Krugman, P. (2001), "Outside the box" (The New York Times) July 11, p. A17.

Lee, C. (1998), "The rise of the welfare state and labor-force participation of older males: evidence from the pre-Social Security era", American Economic Review 88(2):222–226.

Leonard, J.S. (1979), "The Social Security Disability Insurance program and labor force participation", Working Paper 392 (National Bureau of Economic Research, Cambridge, MA).

Levine, P.B. (1993), "Spillover effects between the insured and uninsured unemployed", Industrial and Labor Relations Review 47:73–86.

Margo, R.A. (1993), "The labor force participation of older Americans in 1900: further results", Exploration in Economic History 30(4):409–423.

McCall, B. (1996), "Unemployment insurance rules, joblessness, and part-time work", Econometrica 64(3):647–682.

Meyer, B.D. (1990), "Unemployment insurance and unemployment spells", Econometrica 58:757–782.

Meyer, B.D. (1992a), "Using natural experiments to measure the effects of unemployment insurance", Working Paper (Northwestern University, Evanston, IL).

Meyer, B.D. (1992b), "Quasi-experimental evidence on the effects of unemployment insurance from New York State", Working Paper (Northwestern University, Evanston, IL).

Meyer, B.D. (1995a), "Natural and quasi-experiments in economics", Journal of Business & Economic Statistics 13:151–162.

Meyer, B.D. (1995b), "Lessons from the U.S. unemployment insurance experiments", Journal of Economic Literature 33:91–131.

Meyer, B.D., W.K. Viscusi and D. Durbin (1995), "Workers' compen-sation and injury duration: evidence from a natural experiment", American Economic Review 85:322–340.

Moen, J. (1987), "The labor of older men: a comment", Journal of Economic History 47(3):761–767.

Moffitt, R. (1985), "Unemployment insurance and the distribution of unemployment spells", Journal of Econometrics 28:85–101.

Moffitt, R. (1987), "Life-cycle labor supply and Social Security: a time-series analysis", in: G. Burtless, ed., Work, Health, and Income among the Elderly (The Brookings Institution, Washington, DC).

Moffitt, R., and W. Nicholson (1982), "The effect of unemployment insurance on unemployment: the case of federal supplemental benefits", The Review of Economics and Statistics 64:1–11.

Mont, D., J.F. Burton Jr and V. Reno (2000), Workers' Compensation: Benefits, Coverage, and Costs, 1997–1998, New Estimates (National Academy of Social Insurance, Washington, DC).

Moore, M.J., and W.K. Viscusi (1990), Compensation Mechanisms for Job Risks: Wages, Workers' Compensation, and Product Liability (Princeton University Press, Princeton, NJ).

Mortensen, D.T. (1977), "Unemployment insurance and job search decisions", Industrial and Labor Relations Review 30:505–517.

Mortensen, D.T. (1986), "Job search and labor market analysis", in: O.C. Ashenfelter and R. Layard, eds., Handbook of Labor Economics, Vol. 2 (North Holland, Amsterdam) pp. 849–919.

Mortensen, D.T. (1990), "A structural model of UI benefit effects on the incidence and duration of unemployment", in: Y. Weiss and G. Fishelson, eds., Advances in the Theory and Measurement of Unemployment (St. Martin's Press, New York).

National Foundation for Unemployment Compensation and Workers' Compensation (2000), Highlights of State Unemployment Compensation Laws (NFUCWC, Washington, DC).

Nelson Jr, W.J. (1988a), "Workers' compensation: coverage, benefits and costs, 1985", Social Security Bulletin 51(1):4–9.

Nelson Jr, W.J. (1988b), "Workers' compensation: 1980–84 benchmark revisions", Social Security Bulletin 51(7):4–21.

Nelson Jr, W.J. (1991), "Workers' compensation: coverage, benefits and costs, 1988", Social Security Bulletin 54(3):12–20.

Neuhauser, F., and S. Raphael (2001), "The effect of an increase in worker's compensation benefits on the duration and frequency of benefit receipt", Working Paper (University of California, Berkeley).

Nickell, S. (1998), "Unemployment: questions and some answers", Economic Journal 108:802–816.

Parnes, H.S. (1988), "The retirement decision", in: M. Borus, H. Parnes, S. Santell and B. Seidman, eds., The Older Worker (Industrial Relations Research Association, Wisconsin).

Parsons, D.O. (1980), "The decline in male labor force participation", Journal of Political Economy 88(1):117–134.

Parsons, D.O. (1991), "The health and earnings of rejected disability insurance applicants: comment", American Economic Review 81(5):1419–1426.

Pellechio, A.J. (1979), "Social Security financing and retirement behavior", American Economic Review 69(2):284–287.

Pellechio, A.J. (1981), "Social Security and the decision to retire", Working Paper W0734 (National Bureau of Economic Research, Cambridge, MA).

Pencavel, J.H. (1986), "Labor supply of men: a survey", in: O. Ashenfelter and R. Layard, eds., Handbook of Labor Economics, Vol. 1 (Elsevier, Amsterdam) pp. 3–102.

Peracchi, F., and F. Welch (1994), "Trends in labor force transitions of older men and women", Journal of Labor Economics 12(2):210–42.

Quinn, J.F. (1987), "Life-cycle labor supply and Social Security: a time-series analysis: comment", in: G. Burtless, ed., Work, Health, and Income Among the Elderly. Studies in Social Economics series (Brookings Institution, Washington, DC) pp. 220–228.

Quinn, J.F. (1999), "Has the early retirement trend reversed?", Working Paper (Boston College, Chestnut Hill, MA).

Quinn, J.F., R.V. Burkhauser and D.A. Myers (1990), Passing the Torch. The Influence of Economic Incentives on Work and Retirement (W.E. Upjohn Institute for Employment Research, Kalamazoo, MI).

Ransom, R.L., and R. Sutch (1986), "The labor of older Americans: retirement of men on and off the job 1870–1937", Journal of Economic History 46(1):1–30.

Rejda, G.E. (1999), Social Insurance and Economic Security (Prentice Hall, Upper Saddle River, NJ).

Riddell, W.C. (1999), "Canadian labour market performance in international perspective", Canadian Journal of Economics 32:1097–1134.

Riddell, W.C., and A. Sharpe (1998), "The Canada–US unemployment rate gap: an introduction and overview", Canadian Public Policy 24:1–37.

Rodrik, D. (1998), "Why do more open economies have bigger governments?", Journal of Political Economy 106:997–1031.

Roed, K., and T. Zhang (2000), "Does unemployment compensation affect unemployment duration", Working Paper (Frisch Centre for Economic Research, Oslo).

Ruser, J.W. (1985), "Workers' Compensation Insurance, experience-rating, and occupational injuries", Rand Journal of Economics 16:487–503.

Ruser, J.W. (1998), "Does workers' compensation encourage hard to diagnose injuries?", Journal of Risk and Insurance 65:101–124.

Rust, J., and C. Phelan (1997), "How Social Security and Medicare affect retirement behavior in a world of incomplete markets", Econometrica 65(4):781–831.

Smith, R.S. (1990), "Mostly on Monday: is workers' compensation covering off-the-job injuries?" in: P.S. Borba and D. Appel, eds., Benefits, Costs, and Cycles in Workers' Compensation (Kluwer, Boston, MA) pp. 115–128.

Social Security Administration (2001), Social Security Disability Planner (Washington, DC); available from www.ssa.gov/dibplan/dqualify6.htm.

Social Security Administration, Office of Research, Evaluation and Statistics (2000), Fast Facts and Figures about Social Security (Washington, DC); available from www.ssa.gov/statistics/fast_facts/index.html.

Solon, G. (1985), "Work incentive effects of taxing unemployment benefits", Econometrica 53:295–306.

Summers, L.H. (1989), "Some simple economics of mandate benefits", American Economic Review, Papers and Proceedings 79:177–183.

Topel, R.H. (1983), "On layoffs and unemployment insurance", American Economic Review 73:541–559.

U.S. Chamber of Commerce (2000), Analysis of Workers' Compensation Laws, 2000 (U.S. Chamber of Commerce, Washington, DC).

U.S. House of Representatives Committee on Ways and Means (1990), Green Book, Background material and data on programs within the jurisdiction of the Committee on Ways and Means (U.S. Government Printing Office, Washington, DC).

U.S. House of Representatives Committee on Ways and Means (1998), Green Book, Background material and data on programs within the jurisdiction of the Committee on Ways and Means (U.S. Government Printing Office, Washington, DC).

U.S. House of Representatives Committee on Ways and Means (2000), Green Book, Background material and data on programs within the jurisdiction of the Committee on Ways and Means (U.S. Government Printing Office, Washington, DC).

Welch, F. (1977), "What have we learned from empirical studies of unemployment insurance?", Industrial and Labor Relations Review 30:451–461.

Worrall, J.D., R.J. Butler, P. Borba and D. Durbin (1988), "Estimating the exit rate from workers' compensation: new hazard rate estimates", Working Paper (Rutgers University, NJ).

Chapter 34

WELFARE PROGRAMS AND LABOR SUPPLY*

ROBERT A. MOFFITT

Johns Hopkins University; and NBER

Contents

* The author would like to thank the participants of a Handbook conference in Berkeley, December 1–2, 2000, for comments and Kara Levine for SIPP tabulations.

Handbook of Public Economics, Volume 4, Edited by A.J. Auerbach and M. Feldstein

Abstract

The labor supply and other work incentive effects of welfare programs have long been a central concern in economic research. Work has also been an increasing focus of policy reforms in the USA, culminating with a number of major policy changes in the 1990s whose intent was to increase employment and earnings levels of welfare recipients and other disadvantaged individuals. This chapter reviews the economic research on this topic, covering both the theoretical models that have been developed as well as the empirical findings from econometric studies of the effects of existing welfare programs on labor supply.

Keywords

welfare programs, labor supply, work incentives

JEL classification: I3, J2

Introduction

The work incentives of programs which provide means-tested transfer benefits to the low-income population has been a subject of increasing concern to voters and policy-makers in the USA. Interest in work incentives first arose in the 1960s, when caseloads in the Aid to Families with Dependent Children (AFDC) program rose dramatically, and Congress lowered the tax rate on earnings in the program to encourage work. Increased interest in encouraging work among welfare recipients gradually grew in the 1970s and 1980s, with a shift in focus toward work requirements rather than lowered tax rates. In the 1990s, major new policy developments occurred whose focus was on increasing work, including 1996 legislation introducing major new work requirements into the AFDC program as well as the expansion of the Earned Income Tax Credit (EITC), an earnings subsidy program. Increased interest in encouraging work simultaneously has occurred in disability programs and the Food Stamp program. Similar reforms have developed in Europe, particularly in the United Kingdom with the recent introduction of the Working Families Tax Credit and with the welfare reform there termed the "New Deal".

Research on work and labor supply issues related to welfare reform has also long been the subject of attention by economists. In the 1960s, both James Tobin and Milton Friedman noted that the 100% marginal tax rates which were, at that time, imposed by some welfare programs discouraged work and that a negative income tax (NIT) with tax rates less than 100% was one solution [Friedman (1962), Tobin (1965)]. The NIT is now a staple of undergraduate textbooks. The economics profession conducted an enormous amount of research on the NIT in the 1970s, with much of the focus on the development of new econometric techniques for the analysis of work incentives, as well as a focus on the analysis of several random-assignment experimental tests of a negative income tax. After something of a research lull in the late 1970s and 1980s, there has been a resurgence of research interest in the 1990s in these issues which is still underway. Econometric methods have shifted toward more reduced form methods which make identification more transparent but whose results are less convenient for generalizability than the older structural methods. Much of the analysis has likewise shifted from the estimation of underlying models of behavior to the impact estimation of specific programmatic reforms.

1. US policy and institutional background

Table 1 shows some of the major welfare programs in the USA and their characteristics relevant to labor supply – who is eligible, the form of assistance, average transfer amounts, and marginal tax rates. The most well-known cash program, the Temporary Assistance for Needy Families (TANF) program, provides benefits primarily to single mothers and their children; the Supplemental Security Income (SSI) program serves low income aged, blind, and disabled individuals and families; the Earned Income

Tax Credit (EITC) serves only those with positive earnings, albeit all individuals and families in that category; child-care programs likewise serve only those who are working and with children; and the Medicaid program serves the aged and disabled as well as single mothers and their children, the latter overlapping heavily with the TANF population. Only the Food Stamp program and housing programs are universal in eligibility (aside from low income and assets), and even the latter is unique because it is rationed in quantity and hence not universally eligible in that sense. That leaves the Food Stamp program as the only truly universal means-tested transfer programs in the USA.

This categorization of the population raises two issues. One is whether individuals can alter their eligibility status and change their labor supply in the process by making themselves eligible for a higher level of benefits. In some cases this might be desirable, as in the case of the EITC or child care where individuals might increase their labor supply to make themselves eligible for subsidies, while in other cases it might not be, as in the case of TANF or Medicaid where individuals (primarily women) might take actions to become, or remain, single mothers in order to retain eligibility for benefits, in most cases reducing their labor supply in the process[1]. A second issue is whether, even if eligibility status is unalterable or at least alterable but exogenous to labor supply, the set of eligibility categories, benefit levels, and marginal tax rates assigned to the different groups in the population makes sense from a normative point of view. Answering this question requires a framework to assess normative issues and will not be discussed in this review, although it is a key design issue for the transfer system as a whole.

The form of assistance varies as well, from cash to in-kind transfers for food, medical care, housing, and child care. This is a particular feature of the US system not present in some European countries, where there are no specific food programs and where health care is more typically covered by a universal program. The labor supply effects of in-kind transfers differ from those of cash transfers because they subsidize a good which may be a complement or substitute for leisure, and because the in-kind transfers typically provide minimum or fixed quantities of the good in question and hence have the potential to constrain the consumption choices of the family. What evidence there is on the cash-equivalent value of in-kind transfers suggest that Food Stamps are very nearly equivalent to cash while Medicaid, housing, and child care are not [Smeeding (1982)].

Expenditures vary tremendously across programs, with Medicaid being the dominant program in this respect. However, the bulk of Medicaid expenditures go for the aged and disabled; single mothers and their children, the group of most research focus in the literature, constitute only a little over 10% of total Medicaid expenditures. Among

---

[1] In all cases, of course, because benefits are only eligible for those with incomes below specified amounts, there is a labor supply disincentive. This is the standard labor supply effect to be discussed in Section 2 below.

Table 1
Characteristics of major means-tested transfer programs in the USA[a]

Program	Main eligible population[b]	Form of assistance	Annual expenditures[c] (FY2000)	Average monthly expenditure for family of 3 (FY2000)	Marginal tax rate on earnings
Temporary Assistance for Needy Families	Mostly single-mother families	Cash	14490	600	Ranges across states from 0 to 100%
Supplemental Security Income	Aged, blind, and disabled individuals and families	Cash	35066	1326	50%
Earned Income Tax Credit	Individuals with positive earnings	Cash	30000[d]	135[e]	Ranges from −40% to 21%
Food Stamps	All individuals and families	Food coupons	20341	279	30%
Medicaid	Families with dependent children, disabled, elderly	Health care services	207195	2238[f]	0% or >100%
Subsidized Housing[g]	All individuals and families	Housing units	22498	422[h]	Ranges from 20% to 30%
Child Care					
Child Care Block Grant	Working parents of children under 13	Child care assistance	6934	861[f]	Sliding fee scale set by states (can be zero)
Dependent Care Tax Credit	Working parents of children under 13	Nonrefundable credit in federal income tax	2200	75[i]	Credit is 20% to 30% of eligible expenses

[a] Sources: Blau (2003), Burke (2001), Rowe and Roberts (2002), U.S. House of Representatives (2000).
[b] In addition to low income and assets.
[c] Combined federal and state and local; in millions.
[d] Includes tax reduction as well as refundable portion.
[e] Per filing unit, tax year 2000.
[f] FY1999.
[g] Combined Section 8 and public housing.
[h] Family or dwelling unit.
[i] FY1998, for 2 children in child care.

the other programs, most are in the same general range except for child care, which is considerably smaller. The expenditures shown in Table 1 have changed dramatically over the last three decades, as TANF expenditures (equal to Aid to Families with Dependent Children, AFDC, prior to 1996) have declined from the largest in the late 1960s to one of the smallest today; as Food Stamps and Medicaid have grown, particularly the latter; and as the EITC and SSI expenditures have mushroomed [for more discussion of the history, see Moffitt (2002)].

The last two columns in the table, showing average expenditures per family of 3 (a rough measure of benefits) and the marginal tax rate, give some indication of the magnitudes of income and substitution effects on labor supply, respectively. Medicaid has the largest average benefits but, again, are much smaller for a family of three consisting of a single mother and two children, which are approximately $427 [2]. This makes SSI the largest average benefit program, perhaps not surprisingly since it serves a population which is capable of much less labor supply than the eligible populations for the other programs. Transfers for in-kind programs are generally smaller than those for TANF, necessarily because they are intended to subsidize only part of consumption. An exception is the child care block grant program, although benefits in this program are poorly measured. The EITC, despite its relative high expenditure level, has, on average, very low benefits because its recipient base is so large. As for absolute amounts, the TANF, Food Stamps, and housing programs (ignoring child care) are sizable relative to full-time minimum wage work of $893 per month.

The marginal tax rates (MTRs) in the programs vary greatly. Those in the TANF program are now set by the states, and range from 0 to 100% (a zero percent MTR is possible only if the state imposes a maximum income level, which by itself imposes a cliff, or notch, in the benefit schedule). SSI imposes a 50% rate, Food Stamps imposes a 30% MTR, and public housing and Section 8 programs typically impose double MTRs, one on income net of deductions and one on gross income, ranging from 10 to 30%. The Medicaid program is the most extreme form of a cliff, or notch, program, which is available in its entirety (i.e., full subsidized care) until eligibility is ended – such as income exceeding a fixed amount [3]. The EITC is an earnings subsidy program which has negative MTRs as long as –40% in its initial subsidy range and positive MTRs up to 21% in its phaseout range.

Virtually all of these rates are the same as they were when the program was created, with occasional important exceptions. The MTR in the TANF–AFDC program was 100% from its inception in 1935 to 1969, when it was lowered to 67%; the MTR was

---

[2] This estimate equals the average expenditure per adult plus two times the average expenditure per child. It is larger than the amount for many single-mother Medicaid families off TANF, for whom only the children are eligible.

[3] Medicaid has many different subprograms and a few currently require copayments, but they are the exception.

raised back to 100% in 1981, where it remained until the 1996, when states were given freedom to set it at their discretion[4]. The EITC rates were increased in 1993 as well.

Employment rates in transfer programs generally vary with MTRs in the direction one should expect. In TANF, the average employment rate is currently approximately 30%, and is higher in those states with lower MTRs. Prior to 1996, when MTRs were closer to 100%, employment rates among AFDC recipients were approximately 9%. As will be discussed below, this relationship does not prove that there is an effect of MTRs on labor supply because a lower MTR has a higher "breakeven" level of hours-worked (i.e., the level at which eligibility ends) and thus more workers are eligible in that case. But it does show that the MTRs are actually enforced and do affect the numbers of recipients combining work and welfare. The employment rate in SSI is only 6.7%, no doubt reflecting the high rates of disability in the program. Food Stamp employment rates are 24%.

The actual MTRs in most programs differ in significant ways from the "nominal" MTRs shown in Table 1, complicating the picture. Virtually all have exemption amounts of earnings, below which benefits are not reduced and hence the MTR is zero. The TANF program, Food Stamps, Medicaid, and child-care programs also all have maximum income limits that create notches, as benefits and eligibility go to zero for earnings that cause income to exceed those levels. In the TANF program, states are allowed to reduce calculated benefits by a fixed percentage, thereby reducing the MTR by that percent, as well as putting maximums on the benefit, which effectively creates a region of zero MTR. Most programs also allow deductions for work-related expenses and others for consumption items like housing or rental costs, which vary to some degree with income and hence lower the effective MTR[5]. A further wrinkle in some programs, such as TANF and SSI, is that a different MTR is applied at initial application for the program as is applied thereafter. In most cases a 100% MTR is applied at eligibility – that is, earnings are counted directly against the benefit – and then the lower nominal MTR, shown in Table 1, is applied after eligibility is established and recipiency has begun. These types of rules are designed to discourage entry into the program by workers. Their theoretical effects will be discussed below.

The MTRs may be considerably higher for families participating in more than one program, for the individual MTRs may add up to a considerably higher cumulative MTR. Table 2 shows multiple benefit receipt among nonelderly single-mother families in 1997, excluding the EITC and child-care programs. Around 16% of all single mothers received AFDC, Medicaid and Food Stamps and possibly one other program. About 32% of all single mothers who receive benefits from any program at

---

[4] Under so-called waiver programs, states began to be allowed to set their MTR in the early 1990s. See Moffitt (2003) for a detailed discussion.

[5] Work-related expense deductions are somewhat ambiguous because, if they do reflect true costs of working, they do not lower the MTR if the latter were calculated on net income in the first place. But the deductions vary considerable from state to state, from program to program, and over time, and are unlikely to represent true costs of working.

Table 2
Multiple benefit receipt by nonelderly single-mother households, 1997[a]

Source of benefit	Percent distribution
No Program	48.0
AFDC, Food Stamps, Medicaid, and another program	10.4
AFDC, Food Stamps, and Medicaid only	6.0
AFDC, Medicaid, and another program	1.1
AFDC and Medicaid only	0.7
Medicaid only	6.2
Food Stamps only	1.8
Other cash transfers only	4.9
Other	18.0
Total	100.0

[a] Source: Tabulations from the Survey of Income and Program Participation by Kara Levine, University of Wisconsin.

all are in this multiple receipt category; thus about a third of all welfare recipients in this group have significant multiple benefit receipt. This is thus the major multiple recipient category among the programs listed in Table 1.

The cumulative MTR for families receiving these three benefits is not as high as might be thought, however. The MTR for Medicaid is zero until the eligibility point for AFDC is reached (Medicaid eligibility is automatic with AFDC receipt). Also, the Food Stamp program includes AFDC benefits as income. As a result, the cumulative MTR for TANF and Food Stamps combined is $[t + 0.3(1 - t)]$ where t is the TANF MTR. Prior to 1996, when $t = 1.0$, the cumulative MTR was thus simply 1.0, not 1.3.

Cumulative MTRs after 1996 are shown in Table 3 for 12 states. The income calculations include the EITC and positive tax payments as well as TANF and Food Stamps, but not Medicaid. In the absence of the EITC, moving from 0 hours to part-time hours at the minimum wage results in MTRs ranging from 34% to 71%. While these rates are less than 100%, they are not low by most standards (e.g., the positive income tax faced by most US families). Moving from part-time work to full-time work results sometimes in higher MTRs and sometimes in lower ones, depending on the state. Higher MTRs typically occur when the individual hits the TANF income eligibility cliff and loses all benefits, while lower MTRs typically occur when the individual hits that limit in the neighborhood of part-time hours, implying that earnings obtained by moving to full-time work are taxed at lower, nonwelfare rates. Moving from minimum wage to $9/hour at full-time generally results in somewhat lower MTRs because usually the individual is off welfare by that point and hence only the nonwelfare rates almost always apply. The nonconvex budget set created by

Table 3
Cumulative marginal tax rates for recipients of TANF and Food Stamps in 12 states, 1997[a,b]

State	From no work to part-time work at minimum wage		From part-time work to full-time work at minimum wage		From minimum wage to $9 hourly wage at full-time work	
	w/o EITC	with EITC	w/o EITC	with EITC	w/o EITC	with EITC
Alabama	46	6	33	9	24	58
California	50	9	67	33	67	89
Colorado	57	17	71	39	29	59
Florida	46	6	59	28	35	63
Massachusetts	57	13	64	28	64	87
Michigan	63	23	84	47	35	63
Minnesota	55	8	65	27	69	89
Mississippi	34	−6	32	7	24	55
New Jersey	64	23	62	30	41	67
New York	65	16	67	27	55	84
Texas	50	10	24	0	25	57
Washington	71	30	67	33	50	76

[a] Source: Coe, Acs, Lerman and Watson (1998, Tables 4, 5).
[b] Income includes earnings, TANF and Food Stamp benefits, federal and state EITC amounts, less employee payroll and federal and state income taxes. Minimum Wage is $5.15 per hour. Family size of three assumed.

this pattern of rising then falling marginal rates tends to drive labor supply decisions to either extreme (i.e., either down to part-time work and up to an earnings level considerably above eligibility), a result to be shown formally below[6].

The EITC has drastic effects on these rates[7]. Moving from no work to part-time work or from part-time work to full-time work, rates are lowered by as much as 40%, which is the largest subsidy rate in the EITC. The resulting MTRs are quite low, no more than 30% in the first case and 47% in the second. However, when moving from the minimum wage to $9/hour at full-time work, the EITC actually increases the cumulative MTR because the individual is in the phaseout range of the EITC by that point. Cumulative MTRs are never lower than 55% and are often in the 80% range when moving to this higher earnings level. Thus, the EITC effectively convexifies the budget set, which should be expected to drive labor supply decisions toward the middle

---

[6] Adding Medicaid into the calculation would increase MTRs greatly in the second and third categories, where TANF eligibility is lost.
[7] After 1996 states are allowed to count the EITC in TANF income calculations but they generally do not do so.

point. Thus, there is an incentive to increase earnings from no work to full-time work but also to decrease earnings from high-wage work to lower-wage work, with expected ambiguous effects on labor supply (see below).

Finally, it should be emphasized that the benefit formula is not the only source of labor supply incentives in many US transfer programs, for work requirements have an additional, perhaps stronger, effect. In the TANF program, recipients are required to work some minimum number of hours (usually 20 per week or more) after some minimum stay on the welfare rolls, and sanctions (i.e., benefit reductions) are applied vigorously if recipients fail to meet the requirements. The Food Stamp program also has work requirements for all recipients and particularly strong requirements for non-disabled single individuals. Models of work requirements will be considered below.

2. Theoretical models and issues

2.1. Introduction

The basic static model of labor supply familiar to undergraduate textbooks has been the workhorse of the literature on work incentives of welfare programs for over thirty years. Despite the clear importance of dynamics, human capital, job search, and other considerations in the study of the effects of welfare programs, the endurance of the static model is testimony to its usefulness for the analysis of a wide range of types of welfare program alternatives and the analysis of the comparative statics of an equally wide range of effects of simple changes in program parameters. Its ease of graphical analysis increases its usefulness as an analytic tool.

Relative to the same model used for the work incentives of income and payroll taxes, the welfare application has some unique features, however. One is that the means-testing inherent in a welfare program necessarily creates a nonconvexity in the budget set somewhere over the range of earnings, at the very least at the point where income rises to the point of ineligibility. Changes in welfare reform parameters inevitably either change this eligibility point or change the incentives for individuals to locate above or below it, and this sets off work incentives which greatly complicate the analysis relative to that of income and payroll taxes. A related unique feature of welfare program analysis is that participation in welfare itself is a choice variable, partly because of the decision to locate above or below the eligibility point but also, it turns out, because even some of those whose income is below that point choose not to go onto welfare. This also adds some complexity to the model and to the analysis of labor supply effects.

These unique features have important ramifications for normative questions concerning optimal design of welfare programs. It turns out that almost all changes in welfare program parameters have labor supply effects that differ for different individuals in the distribution, and the desirability of implementing those changes requires a social welfare function or some other public choice mechanism which explicitly or implicitly assigns weights to distributional objectives. Almost no program reforms have unambiguously desirable labor supply effects on their own. Even a program as well-known and popular among economists as the negative income tax shares this feature, and its normative advantages in terms of labor supply are quite questionable without such an analysis. While the exposition presented below will stick fairly closely to positive analysis, normative issues will necessarily be referred to in appropriate places.

A final feature of the welfare model also relating to optimal design arises from the above-noted feature that welfare program participation is a choice and that some choose, voluntarily, not to participate. This necessarily self-categorizes the eligible population into those on welfare and those not, which implies that modifications of the welfare system in the form of adding new programs – e.g., for food, housing, medical assistance, or job training – must confront how those programs should be made available to those on the initial welfare program (e.g., cash) and those not. Both equity considerations play a role in that decision as well as efficiency ones, for if the different programs are at all tied together, incentives to join the various programs will be altered. A universalist policy which keeps all programs separate and makes all of them available to all of the low-income population is one extreme, but one that has been rarely chosen by US policy-makers.

2.2. Basic static model

The canonical static model of labor supply considers an individual with well-behaved preference function over hours of leisure (L) and consumption (C) which we denote as $U(L,C)$ and budget constraint $N + W(T - L) = PC$, where N is exogenous unearned income, W is the hourly wage rate, P is the price of consumption goods, and T is the total time available in the interval. With normalization by P we may relabel C as income, Y. With hours of work defined as $H = T - L$, we can equivalently consider a preference function $U(H,Y)$ maximized w.r.t. $N + WH = Y$. A generic welfare program provides benefit $B = G - t(WH + N)$, where G is the guarantee amount given to those with zero income and t is the marginal tax rate. With benefits added into the budget constraint, we have $W(1 - t)H + G - tN = Y$.

Figure 1 shows the familiar budget constraint so created as segment CD, where the intercept with vertical distance AC represents G and where the slope of segment CD is $-W(1 - t)$. The nonwelfare constraint is AE with slope $-W$ and intercept N (assumed to be zero for illustration). The arrows labeled 1 and 2 denote the two types of labor supply response to the creation of the welfare program, and both result in reductions in labor supply unambiguously.

The nonconvexity of the budget set clearly is a defining characteristics of Figure 1. It could be argued that individuals can convexify that constraint by moving on and off the program over time, thereby achieving an average hours of work and average income that lies above the constraint CDE. Put differently, they could "build" a constraint to bridge the nonconvexity. Ignoring preference discounting, higher utility could be

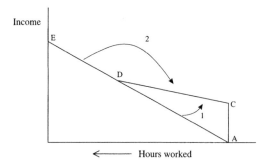

Fig. 1. Generic welfare program.

gained in that way than by choosing a fixed hours along CDE. One theory of welfare turnover is that it is induced precisely by this feature of the constraint, explaining why many individuals alternate between not working at all and being on welfare with working and not being on welfare, treating the two as mutually exclusive alternatives.

The existence of nonparticipating eligibles as a complicating factor may be mentioned at this point. For virtually all welfare programs, some individuals are observed to locate on segment AD in Figure 1, in a location which would appear to be inferior to being on welfare. One rationalization for this behavior is to assume that being on welfare carries some disutility, possibly arising from the stigma of being on welfare [Moffitt (1983)]. This can be modeled by inserting a welfare participation dummy, P (equal to 1 if on welfare and 0 if not) into the preference function as in $U(H, Y, P)$, where P has negative marginal utility. With heterogeneity of preferences w.r.t. P across the population of a sufficiently wide range, some individuals will choose not to participate despite the income and leisure gains to doing so. An alternative rationalization is to assume that there are fixed costs of going onto welfare in the form of time, money, or "hassle" costs of complying with the myriad rules of welfare and requirements to visit the welfare office periodically. With heterogeneity of such costs across the population, and with a sufficiently wide range that for some individuals the costs will exceed the utility gains of welfare participation, some individuals will again choose not to go onto welfare. These two models are observationally equivalent without some further structure imposed on them or some actual data on stigma or participation costs[8].

The labor supply implications of such nonparticipating eligibles are, at this stage, straightforward, for participation in welfare is more likely, the greater the utility gains from income and leisure, holding the stigma or fixed costs constant. Whether labor supply falls or rises upon joining the welfare program depends on the substitutability

---

[8] One approach in the literature to the stigma model is to consider stigma to be a function of how many other families are on welfare. This sets up a social interactions model with interdependent choices in the population. See Besley and Coate (1992a), Lindbeck, Nyberg and Weibull (1999) and Nechyba (1999).

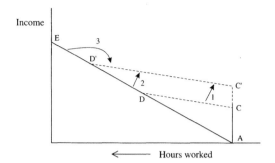

Income

Fig. 2. Effect of an increase in G.

or complementarity of P and L in the preference function, but if P is separable then labor supply will fall, as illustrated in Figure 1 by the arrow 1.

The most important two comparative statics of the model are those involving the effects of a change in G and a change in t. Figure 2 illustrates the effect of an increase in G. All three types of labor-supply effects, shown by the three arrows, are negative. Note that the change in labor supply is not a measure of traditional pure income effects because those represented by arrows 2 and 3 experience substitution as well as income effects, though these operate in the same direction as the income effects. Not shown in the figure are the effects on nonparticipating eligibles, for some individuals will move from segment AD to C'D' because the utility gains will now outweigh the costs of participating.

A reduction in t is illustrated in Figure 3, where the pre-change constraint is shown to have $t = 1.0$ (segment CD). Again, there are three types of response illustrated in the figure, but in this case the second two are opposite in sign to the first, resulting in an ambiguous net change in hours worked. The average change depends on the sizes of the different responses as well as the relative numbers of individuals at different initial points along the constraint. Those represented by arrow 2 are made newly eligible by the reduction in t and hence reduce their labor supply whereas those represented by arrow 3 now find the higher benefits available over the positive hours range to be sufficiently great as to reduce labor supply to join the program[9]. Because the region around points D and D' often falls in the part-time hours range, it can be said that this reform essentially subsidizes part-time work.

Among other things, this result shows why the employment rates or hours of work of those on welfare may be correlated with the level of t even if there is no labor supply response. For example, if arrows 1 and 3 are zero and arrow 2 is vertical (i.e., labor supply does not change when going onto the program for these individuals),

---

[9] Ashenfelter (1983) termed the arrow-2 response a "mechanical" change and the arrow-3 response a "behavioral" change. This interpretation is useful but is complicated by the presence of nonparticipating eligibles, some of whom in the range DD' will choose not to go onto the program despite the potential income and leisure gains.

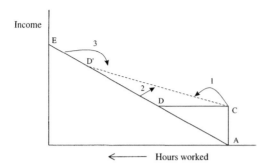

Fig. 3. Effect of a decrease in *t*.

then employment rates and mean hours of work of those on welfare will rise after the reduction in *t*, but this is just a compositional effect resulting from the addition of a group of high-hours workers to the welfare rolls.

The implication of this analysis is that the negative income tax, and general reductions in *t*, do not necessarily increase average labor supply [Levy (1979), Moffitt (1992)]. A corollary of this result is that it is possible that 100% tax rates maximize average labor supply. However, the distributional impacts of the tax rate reduction must be considered. The reform does achieve its objective of encouraging the lowest-labor-supply individuals to work more, but at the cost of some labor supply reduction among higher-labor-supply individuals, many of whom are in the group termed the "working poor". Incomes are increased among the latter group (at least for those represented by arrow 2) as well, representing a shift in the income distributional impact of the welfare program away from the lowest-income individuals and toward somewhat higher-income individuals, at least in relative terms[10]. Much of the policy debate over the desirability of a negative income tax and similar reforms revolves around the relative distributional weights assigned to the very poorest (sometimes called the "target efficiency" of the program) versus the "working poor", who receive no assistance in a *t* = 1.0 program.

In the US TANF program, states have tried at least two measures to avoid the labor-supply-reducing effects of *t* reductions. One is to disallow the lower *t* when considering initial eligibility, and to allow the lower *t* only for those individuals who have established eligibility under the stricter standard. In a world without transactions costs, these barriers would have no effect and individuals who wished to locate in the region DD' in Figure 3 would simply reduce their labor supply to point C to become eligible and then increase their labor supply to the preferred point[11]. With costs to entry and application, this process will be slowed but not eliminated. A second strategy

---

[10] An expenditure-constant change in *G* and *t*, for example, would rotate the segment CD' in a direction increasing the slope, showing more clearly the existence of such a distributional shift.

[11] Random shocks to labor supply would achieve the same result, e.g., if every individual has a probability *p* of being laid off or losing her job each period, after which labor supply can be freely chosen until the next layoff occurs, individuals will eventually end up at the global utility maximum regardless of the stricter eligibility rules.

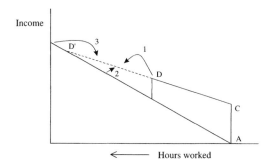

Fig. 4. Welfare program with a notch.

by states is simply to impose an upper limit on income independent of the benefit formula, as illustrated in Figure 4. In that figure, the notch occurs at point D and the segment DD′ is eliminated, discouraging workers above that point from coming onto the welfare program. However, some will still reduce their labor supply to point D in any case, and labor-supply gains that might have been experienced by those initially on welfare who would have otherwise increased work into the DD′ region are lost, so there is a cost to this approach. However, a number of states have taken this approach to its extreme by setting $t = 0$ at the same time as imposing such an eligibility limit.

Figure 4 also illustrates notch constraints in general, as occur in the Medicaid and other programs. The dashed line from D to D′ represents the effect of removing the notch and allowing a gradual phaseout of benefits. This change has ambiguous effects on labor supply for the same reason that a general reduction in t does. While it is true that those initially at D are encouraged to work more (arrow 1), those represented by arrows 2 and 3 experience labor-supply reductions. Thus, the labor-supply effect of eliminating welfare-program notches is ambiguous in sign.

A different method of providing work incentives is by increasing the rewards of being off welfare rather than on welfare. Whereas the reduction in t attempts to provide incentives by encouraging individuals to combine welfare and work, increasing subsidies for those who are off welfare and work could seemingly provide greater labor-supply increases. Figure 5 illustrates one real-world case of such a reform, in this case one in which Medicaid is offered to low-income families off welfare up to some maximum income point (the dashed line C′D′). An increase in child-support income off welfare has similar effects, but without the notch. Arrow 1 represents the labor-supply increases generated by this reform as some individuals move off welfare and receive Medicaid while off. However, labor-supply reductions also occur, as shown by arrows 2, 3 and 4 (arrow 4 arises as some of those who did not want to participate in the initial welfare program find Medicaid acceptable). Thus, the labor supply effects of this reform are again ambiguous in sign.

Of course, providing a new form of welfare "off welfare" is just a matter of semantics, for in essence this reform just adds another layer onto the initial welfare system. Ignoring the possible responses of nonparticipating eligibles or different stigma

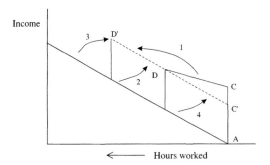

Fig. 5. Medicaid expansion.

effects of the programs, the effect of this reform is no different than simply extending Medicaid eligibility for those initially on welfare up to point D′, which is very similar to a reduction in t. Alternatively, simply combining the two programs and having one program with the constraint CDD′ would be equivalent. The popularity of some of these reforms to the general public appears instead to be based on the idea that Medicaid, child support, and other forms of welfare represented by the constraint C′D′ are preferable to cash welfare possibly represented by CD. But that requires bringing voter preferences into the model, which has not been done here. In the recipient-oriented model used here, there is no important difference between "on welfare" and "off welfare" reforms if they are all essentially welfare, and it is merely a matter of government form whether assistance is provided in one program or multiple programs so long as the eligibility groups are identical. The fundamental design issue of how to construct the overall constraint, where assistance should be given across the income and labor-supply distribution, and where labor-supply incentives and disincentives are preferred to occur, remains and requires addressing the same distributional questions already discussed.

2.3. Dynamics

We shall consider three separate topics in this section: (1) welfare-program effects on labor supply in a life-cycle context, (2) effects of welfare programs on human capital investment, (3) effects of welfare-based human capital investment programs, and (4) time limits on welfare receipt. There has been relatively little research on these issues so this section will be necessarily briefer than the last.

Life-cycle labor supply models are generally considered to be separable in order to apply two-stage budgeting techniques familiar from the literature on consumption [Blundell and MaCurdy (1999)]. If an individual is on welfare in all periods, the analysis of labor-supply effects of welfare programs is simple because those programs just reduce the net wage and increase nonlabor income. This leads to reductions in labor supply in all periods and to intertemporal wealth effects which also reduce labor supply. If the individual is on welfare in some periods and off in others, this also can be accounted for within the framework by the use of virtual income and virtual net wage formulations (Blundell and MaCurdy). Intertemporal asset allocations can be, as before, separated from the within-period decisions, and the latter are essentially the same as those in the static model with an adjustment in full income to take account of the asset flows. Thus, the net result of these models in the life-cycle labor-supply literature is that there is little if any alteration in the basic labor-supply effects found in the static model.

Two different types of effects are possible, however. One is the possibility of "building" a convexified constraint over the nonconvex budget set by moving on and off the program in different periods, as mentioned previously. This case has not been analyzed in the literature. Another is the effect of the income floor in transfer programs, which reduces precautionary saving and hence labor supply, as noted by Hubbard, Skinner and Zeldes (1995).

Effects of welfare programs on human capital investment have also been little studied[12]. Kesselman (1976) analyzed the effects of a welfare program on human capital, assuming that the individual was on welfare both before and after the human capital investment decision. Under this assumption, the effect of welfare programs is to reduce the incentive for human capital investment because both the opportunity cost of time changes from W to $W(1-t)$ and the return to investment changes from W to $W(1-t)$; thus the rate of return is simply reduced to $(1-t)$ of what it is in the absence of the program. This result is identical to that of the effect of a proportional income tax on human capital investment in an equally simple model. Income effects play no role, as is typical in human capital investments which assume perfect capital markets.

However, an investment in human capital which has a sufficiently high return as to move the individual above the income eligibility point and hence off welfare has a higher return than this, because the return, at the margin, remains W rather than $W(1-t)$. Thus, human capital investment is encouraged relative to what it would be in the absence of the program. This is entirely the result of the nonconvexity of the budget set, which leads to a type of increasing returns to investment.

The effects of human capital investment programs, or job training programs, for welfare recipients has been discussed by Moffitt (2003). The relevant case is that in which a recipient is required to undergo training as a condition of welfare receipt, and thus human capital investment becomes a type of work requirement. In this case the net present value of the investment opportunity becomes part of the welfare package. In a two-period model, that net present value is

$$\text{NPV} = -W_1(1-t)I$$
$$+ \frac{1}{1+r} \{ P_2 \left[(W_2 - W_1)(1-t) H_2 \right] + (1-P_2) \left[(W_2 - W_1) H_2 - (G - tW_1 H_2) \right] \},$$
(1)

---

[12] See Miller and Sanders (1997) for an exception.

where W_1 is the wage if the recipient were not to undergo the training program, W_2 is the (higher) wage in period two if she does, I is the amount of investment time required in period one (assumed to come out of work time rather than leisure), H_2 is hours worked in period 2, and P_2 is a welfare participation dummy in period 2 if the recipient undergoes the program [13]. The investment cost is represented by the first term and the return by the term in curly brackets, which depends on whether the individual is still on welfare after the wage increase. If not, the return is equal to the earnings gain minus the welfare benefit lost. If this net present value is positive, the welfare program is enhanced in value because it offers a training program with a positive return which is not available elsewhere, leading to an increase in welfare participation; but if it is negative, the value of the welfare program is enhanced and welfare participation will decline.

If the program is voluntary for welfare recipients, then the value of welfare cannot decline and welfare participation will ambiguously increase. Both of these cases illustrate the issue of tied transfers discussed previously, for a universal human capital program available to all low-income individuals would not have an effect on the welfare caseload as it does in these cases, when the program is only offered, or mandated, to welfare recipients.

Time limits on welfare receipt have dynamic effects that are more interesting than their long-run static effects. The long-run static effects of time limits are simply to eliminate welfare completely, and this should be expected to increase labor supply for the same reasons that welfare decreases labor supply in the first place. Supporters of time limits sometimes argue that mandatory human capital investment programs of the type just discussed would, if required during all available years of welfare receipt, increase potential wages enough that a former welfare recipient could be better off after the end of the time limit by working than he or she would have been on welfare. The empirical evidence on the rates of return to these programs does not support this conjecture, at least on average. Instead, time limits are best interpreted as simply a desire to reduce redistribution [14].

There are two types of dynamics effects that could arise from the presence of time limits. One would occur if individuals on welfare anticipate the approach of the limit and begin to leave welfare and accept job offers at an increasing rate as the limit nears. This behavior has been noted for unemployment insurance recipients approaching the point at which their benefits will be exhausted [Moffitt (1985)]. In the UI case, this behavior is generally explained by the randomness of wage offers and the desire to accept an attractive offer when it arrives even if it does so somewhat in advance of

---

[13] The change in H_2 resulting from the increase in the wage is ignored for simplicity.

[14] A more interesting question is why time limits would be preferred by the voters to simple reductions in benefit levels. This preference is probably based on the assumption that individuals experience a finite number of discrete negative shocks over their lifetimes and that full support should be given during those periods but not during others. A lower but permanent benefit level would simply lower the amount of support given during the periods during which negative shocks occur.

the benefit exhaustion date. The same may apply for welfare recipients approaching a time limit. The result is that labor supply will begin to increase in advance of the actual time limit, and that labor supply effects would be observed to occur even for those who do not actually exhaust their benefits [15].

A second response can occur if recipients "bank" their benefits by going off the rolls during good (labor market) times and saving their benefits for bad times (downturn in labor market, unexpected negative income shock, etc.). This result again requires the presence of uncertainty in future wage offers. A simple artificial model proves the possibility of this response. Suppose that the lifetime consists of two periods and that welfare can only be received in one of them. The per-period utility function is $Y - \alpha H$, where Y is income and H is a dummy equal to 1 if the individual works and 0 if not. Let B be the welfare benefit and suppose that an individual has a per-period probability p of a wage draw $W > 0$ and probability $1 - p$ of a wage draw $W = 0$. To make the comparison stark, let the positive wage draw equal B. Then, in the absence of any time limit, the individual will be on welfare both periods regardless of the wage draw because even if a positive wage is drawn, the disutility from working will make welfare participation the preferred choice. But with a time limit, an individual who has drawn a positive wage of B in the first period and is choosing whether to work and stay off welfare vs. going onto welfare and using up her entitlement compares utility for these two alternatives, which are, respectively

$$B - \alpha + \beta[pB + (1-p)B] \quad \text{if work in period 1,} \tag{2}$$

$$B + \beta[p(B - \alpha) + (1-p)0] \quad \text{if go onto welfare in period 1,} \tag{3}$$

where $\beta < 1$ is the discount rate. The value of working in period 1 is therefore

$$-\alpha(1 - \beta p) + \beta B(1 - p). \tag{4}$$

If $p < 1$ then this quantity can be positive if the second term is larger than the first. Thus the person will choose to work today and go onto welfare tomorrow even though the myopic decision today would be to go onto welfare.

2.4. Work requirements and tagging models

In several US welfare programs, work requirements have become an alternative means by which labor supply of welfare recipients can be increased. Figure 6 shows the effect of such a program which requires H_{min} hours of work on the part of the recipient. This eliminates the portion of the budget BC. Arrows 1 and 2 show possible responses, both of which lead to increases in hours of work. A work requirement, therefore,

---

[15] See Gottschalk (1988) for a model of the effect of welfare programs on job search and Krueger and Meyers (Chapter 33, this volume) for a review of the unemployment insurance literature.

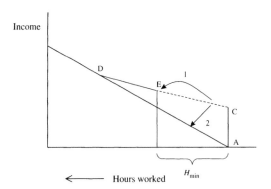

Fig. 6. Work requirement.

unambiguously increases labor supply. This should not be surprising because it is equivalent to eliminating welfare altogether over a certain hours range, and welfare is known to decrease labor supply unambiguously.

This favorable result is often contrasted by policy-makers with a reduction in t, which yields ambiguous effects on labor supply. However, the comparison is not appropriate because the conventional welfare program attempts to provide support to those who have sufficiently low wages (perhaps because of health reasons or very young children) that their hours of work are low or zero whereas a work requirement system provides no such support. Work requirement programs instead must necessarily be accompanied by a categorization of the welfare population into those who can work, who are given the budget constraint shown in Figure 6 with a minimum hours requirement, and those who cannot work, who are give support even at zero hours. Work requirements also stand in contrast to the idea of a negative income tax, which attempts to provide income support to those with low wages at the same time as providing some work incentives (through a reduced t). The favorable labor supply effects of work requirements are entirely dependent on the ability to adequately categorize the welfare population into the two groups.

There is a literature on tagging and related issues which considers the properties and desirability of these types of categorical systems. Akerlof (1978) showed that if individuals can be "tagged" as nonemployable, they can be given a greater G and lower t than they could under a noncategorical negative income tax. He, and others in this literature, directly dealt with the incentive problem to change categories by requiring that an incentive compatibility constraint be set that would discourage such behavior. Parsons (1996) extended the Akerlof model to consider what he termed "two-sided" error, meaning that not only are some of the untagged individuals truly nonemployable, but some of the tagged individuals are in fact employable. This leads to an optimal structure in which a positive G is given to both tagged and untagged individuals, but a higher G and lower t is given to the tagged group. More direct consideration of workfare as an alternative is considered in other papers. For example, Besley and Coate (1992b, 1995) showed that, under a different optimization criterion, workfare can be used as a screening device to ensure that higher-wage individuals do not take advantage of the program. In this rather different justification for work requirements, all recipients must undergo the cost of complying with work requirements, but benefits can be higher because high-wage individuals have been screened out [16].

The literature surrounding the negative income tax in the late 1960s and early 1970s emphasized the difficulties in tagging. It was generally argued that the administrative difficulty in assigning recipients to categories is too great for work requirements to avoid large error. It was also argued that work requirements would inevitably end up giving individual caseworkers in local welfare offices great discretion in deciding who is able to work and who is not, and that this would create an unacceptable level of inequitable treatment across individuals who are observationally identical [Barth and Greenberg (1971), Browning (1975), Lurie (1975)].

2.5. Wage and earnings subsidies

Wage and earnings subsidy programs have been discussed for many years as a means to increase labor supply incentives. In a wage subsidy, a government subsidy increases the hourly wage of an individual by $[\alpha - \beta W]$, where W is the individual's initial wage and $\beta < 1$. The resulting remuneration per hour for an individual is $\alpha + (1 - \beta) W$. The subsidy declines as W rises and reaches zero at $W = \alpha/\beta$. In an earnings subsidy, an individual receives a subsidy $S = sWH$ for earnings up to some cutoff level C, where $s < 1$, and after that cutoff level the subsidy is recalculated as $S = sC - r(WH - C)$, which declines at rate r for every dollar of earnings. The subsidy reaches zero at earnings equal to $[C(s - r)/r]$. The net wage up to C is $W(1 + s)$ while the net wage above C is $W(1 - r)$ [17].

Figure 7 shows how both types of subsidy affect the budget constraint. The wage rate subsidy creates the budget constraint AC while the earnings subsidy creates the constraint ABD. The labor supply responses are indicated by the arrows. The response for the wage subsidy is represented by arrows 1 and 2. While those entering work from nonwork clearly increase labor supply, the income and substitution effects of those initially at positive hours go in opposite directions, leading to a change ambiguous in sign. However, most of the groups made eligible for these subsidies have forward-bending labor supply curves, so the impact of the subsidy is generally expected to be positive. The earnings subsidy has the same effect in low ranges but a negative effect in the higher ranges of earnings and hours worked, where the earnings subsidy

---

[16] For other papers in this literature, see Beaudry and Blackorby (1998), Chone and Laroque (2001), Cuff (2000) and Immonen, Kanbur, Keen and Tuomala (1998).

[17] In some earnings subsidies, like the US EITC, there is a flat range of earnings in the middle over which the subsidy stays at its maximum, before starting to decline. There is a large literature on wage and earnings subsidies dating from the 1960s and 1970s. For some of the early discussions, see Barth and Greenberg (1971), Garfinkel (1973), Kesselman (1969, 1973) and Zeckhauser (1971).

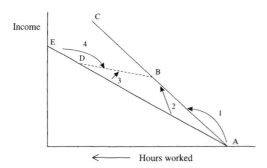

Fig. 7. Earnings and wage subsidies.

is reduced. Arrows 3 and 4 both represent reductions in labor supply. The net effect of the subsidy is ambiguous in sign. As for the welfare programs discussed earlier, the distributional impact of the program is important because the positive and negative labor supply effects occur in different ranges.

A simple comparison of the wage and earnings subsidies in the figure indicates that wage subsidies, because they do not have the taxback region BD, are more likely to increase labor supply than earnings subsidies. However, the wage-rate subsidy must nevertheless be phased out as the wage rises, and this creates a disincentive for human capital investment, job search, and other activities seeking higher wages. As it has turned out in the USA, wage-rate subsidies have foundered in any case on the administrative difficulties of measuring hourly wages and basing a transfer on them. Many individuals are not paid by the hour, for example, and even those that are often have an agreement with the employer for a stipulated number of hours of work, making the contract closer to an earnings agreement than an hourly wage agreement. Further, a wage-rate subsidy creates opportunities for fraudulent collusion on the part of the employee and employer to set the pay in terms of earnings rather than wages and then to overstate hours of work, pushing the reported wage rate down and the subsidy up. Preventing manipulations of the reported hourly wage would be quite difficult. For this reason, earnings subsidies, which are administratively simpler to conduct, are more common, even though they, too, have some incentives for overreporting of earnings [Hotz and Scholz (2003)].

The goal of wage and earnings subsidies is explicitly to increase earnings and labor supply. A secondary goal – though a primary one to some voters and policy-makers – is to increase government support for the "working poor", roughly meaning those families and individuals with significant hours of work but still low earnings. An earnings subsidy can be designed so that the maximum subsidy at point B in Figure 7 is in the middle of the range of earnings that define that group. This is a purely distributional goal that, in principle, could be at odds with the goal of increasing labor supply, particularly if the labor supply disincentives in the taxback region are significant. As has been demonstrated in several programs already in this review, subsidizing one part

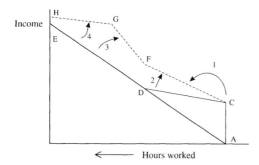

Fig. 8. Earnings subsidy plus welfare program.

of the hours or earnings distribution tends to draw individuals to that region from both above and below.

Earnings subsidies have also been proposed for those demographic groups who are eligible for an existing income transfer program, in the hopes that the earnings subsidy can counter the labor supply disincentives created by the tax rate of the welfare program. The combination of the two is illustrated in Figure 8, which is drawn on the assumption that the maximum earnings subsidy occurs at an hours level in excess of the hours level which ends the income transfer[18]. Compared to the income-transfer-only, the addition of the earnings subsidy has the same mix of positive and negative labor supply effects as the pure earnings subsidy, leading to ambiguous effects on labor supply. However, labor supply incentives for initial welfare recipients are all positive (assuming forward-bending labor supply curves) and it is possible as well that those recipients may "leave welfare" in some cases[19]. As illustrated in Table 3 discussed earlier, earnings subsidies have greatly reduced the cumulative marginal tax rate on earnings for welfare recipients, although they have also raised that rate at higher level of earnings. This effect is clear from Figure 8.

The shift in Figure 8 is the same as that created by a reduction in t in a welfare program at point F and below and differs only above F. The labor supply disincentives shown by arrow 4 are also the same as those created by the reduction in t. However, the labor supply disincentives represented by that arrow occur at a higher level of earnings than would occur from a reduction in t equivalent in magnitude

[18] In the USA, most welfare programs do not include the EITC as part of income. If they did, the effect of the earnings subsidy in pivoting the segment CD in Figure 8 around to CF would be much smaller. Indeed, if $t = 1.0$ in the welfare program, there would be no effect at all of the earnings subsidy on the slope of this segment if the earnings subsidy is included as income.

[19] As noted previously in the discussion of the Medicaid expansions and child support programs, many policy makers and analysts regard earnings subsidies as "not welfare" because they are not stigmatizing to the recipient and are more highly valued by the voter. This discussion ignores those effects. If stigma is less for the earnings subsidy than for income transfers, it is also possible that an individual on welfare may move off the welfare rolls to segment AD in Figure 8 and receive only the earnings subsidy, becoming an eligible nonparticipant for welfare.

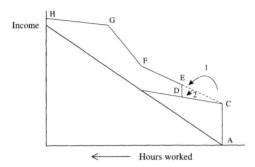

Fig. 9. Earnings subsidy with a work requirement plus welfare program.

to that created by segment CF (i.e., if CF were extended upward, as in the case
of a *t* reduction). In this sense, the earnings subsidy simply pushes the labor
supply disincentives further up the earnings and hours distribution than they would
be under a reduction in *t*. Once again, the desirability of this shift depends on
the distributional weights assigned to the groups in the population. On the other
hand, if point G falls closer to point F than is shown in the figure, then there is
little difference in an earnings subsidy addition and a reduction in *t* in the first
place.

The comparison of the program shown in Figure 8 with a reduction in *t* in a
welfare program is also complicated by the fact that public expenditures are almost
surely higher for the Figure 8 earnings subsidy addition than by the reduction in *t*,
for subsidies are paid out at much higher earnings levels which are typically in
much thicker regions of the income distribution. This makes it appear as though
all individuals can be made better off and no one worse off. A fairer comparison
would be an expenditure-constant comparison of an earnings subsidy addition versus
a reduction in *t*, for in that case the level of *G* would have to be lower at the time the
earnings subsidy is introduced to reduce expenditures. This demonstrates more clearly
that the earnings subsidy addition is a regressive program relative to a program which
reduces *t*, for it shifts support, in relative terms, away from the worst-off families and
individuals and toward those who are better off. This is the underlying reason for its
favorable effects on labor supply.

Finally, Figure 9 shows the effect of offering the earnings subsidy only to welfare
recipients who work a minimum number of hours, a suggestion that has been made by
some welfare policy analysts. For the same reasons as work requirements in general,
this will result in an increase in labor supply relative to an earnings subsidy program
without any such minimum hours rule, as shown by the arrows in the figure. However,
some individuals who would have increased their labor supply by a smaller number
of hours will fail to do so under this program, so some labor supply gains will be
lost. Also, once again, the distribution of government support shifts in this case, in
relative terms, away from the worst off and toward the better off, in return for the
more favorable labor supply effects.

2.6. In-kind transfers

There is a small literature on the effects of in-kind transfers on labor supply relative to the effects of cash transfers [Gavhari (1994), Leonesio (1988), Murray (1980)]. At first glance, there does not seem to be any issue, given that in-kind transfers in developed countries like the USA do not subsidize the market price of the commodity directly, as in developing countries, but rather simply provide families with a fixed amount of the good. That fixed amount initially seems close to having the same effect as an increase in income. For example, suppose the utility function is $U(L, S, C)$ where L is hours of leisure, S is the quantity of the subsidized good, and C is the quantity of other consumption goods. Let the amount of the gift of the subsidized good be $pS^* = pG - t(WH + N)$, where p is the market price of S, G is the maximum amount of the good given, t is the MTR in the program, and W, H and N are as defined in the static labor-supply model ($H + L = T$). Then the resulting budget constraint is

$$W(1 - t)H + N(1 - t) + pG = pS + qC, \tag{5}$$

where q is the price of C. This constraint looks very much like the constraint for a cash transfer, for the relative prices of S, C and H (or L) are the same as they are in a cash transfer.

However, as the above-cited studies demonstrate, the more interesting case is when the optimal S resulting from the maximum problem presented by the budget constraint in Equation (5) is less than the S^* amount granted by the government. In this case the individual is constrained to consume more of the good than he would have if the transfer had been provided in the form of a lump sum cash grant. This distortion of the consumption of S has effects on the consumption of L and C. The basic result from the studies is that if S and L are Hicks–Allen substitutes, then the effects of such an "over-provided" in-kind transfer is to increase hours of work rather than decrease them, because L is reduced by the excess consumption of S. If S and L are complements however, the opposite is likely to occur.

There is no strong empirical evidence on this issue to date. The Food Stamp program in the USA is generally considered to be nearly equivalent to cash because the amounts of food coupons provided to families are generally less than they appear to spend, i.e., they are inframarginal [Currie (2003)]. On the other hand, Medicaid and housing subsidies have cash-equivalent values less than one because individuals would in almost all cases consume less than the quantities provided by the government if the transfer were in cash. But what evidence there is suggests that these programs have work disincentives, but there has been no strong comparison of those effects relative to those of cash transfers.

3. Empirical evidence: a short review

3.1. Introduction

The volume of research on the effects of welfare programs on labor supply has been cyclical over the last three decades. While there was a large amount of research in the late 1960s and 1970s, there was relatively little in the 1980s and early 1990s. There has been a resurgence of interest in these issues in the 1990s, however, accompanied by an increase in the volume of new work.

Methodological controversies have been a major focus in this literature and continue to be at the present time. One controversy has been over the relative merits of structural versus reduced-form estimation of the effects of policy variation, and another has been over the best sources of policy variation to use when estimating either structural or reduced-form models. This distinction is not always fully understood. The first issue concerns whether some particular source of policy variation – such as cross-state variation in welfare rules, for example – should be used to estimate black-box impacts of policy difference without using economic models in any formal sense and without estimating any underlying behavioral elasticities, such as income and substitution effects. The primary argument for structural estimation in this sense has always been that it affords a superior method of conducting out-of-sample forecasting of untested and unimplemented policies than can the estimates from reduced-form models [20]. While the evidence on this issue is not conclusive at this time, it is a fact that estimation of reduced-form impacts of policy variation has become more common than structural estimation in the literature. The second issue concerns whether the best source of variation to use is pure cross-sectional variation in policies across areas (when it is available), variation across areas in how policies change over time (e.g., the state-fixed effects model), or variation between somehow-defined "eligible" and "ineligible" populations, either in pure cross section or over time (the difference-in-difference method). The latter two sources of variation have been more heavily used than the first. When these different sources of variation are each used to estimate just-identified models, it is generally not possible to test them against one another, which is one reason for the continued disagreement on which source is preferable. But whatever source of variation is used, either structural or reduced form estimation can be applied to it [21].

The issue of the source of policy variation is the more important one in the analysis of the effect of welfare programs on labor supply. Some programs in the USA (TANF, Medicaid, child-care subsidies, housing programs) have considerable cross-sectional variation as well as variation over time that differs across areas, furnishing the opportunity for the use of more than one type for identification. Yet other programs (the EITC, Food Stamps, SSI) have essentially no cross-sectional variation because they are national in scope and the same rules apply to everyone. These latter programs must use some other source of variation for estimation and usually it is a source which will rest on more tenuous assumptions.

---

[20] See Heckman (2000) for a discussion.

[21] Using non-policy sources of variation to identify policy impacts is in a different class. The main argument for using such non-policy variation (e.g., variation in wages alone to identify the effects of $W(1-t)$ when there is no variation in t) is that it is the only alternative if there is no direct policy variation cross-sectionally or over time.

The review of the empirical literature below is divided into sections based partly on these issues[22]. The pre-1995 literature will first be reviewed, for that literature tended to estimate structural models and use certain types of sources of variation for identification. The post-1995 literature will then be reviewed, first covering structural estimation and then estimation of reduced-form policy impacts. For the most part, the labor supply literature in this area is much thinner than might be supposed and hence there are not many studies to review.

3.2. Pre-1995 estimates

There have been several major reviews of the pre-1995 literature on the effects of welfare programs on labor supply [Danziger, Haveman and Plotnick (1981), Moffitt (1992), Hoynes (1997)] which exhaustively cover the studies. That literature will therefore not be rereviewed here in detail but rather merely summarized. Most of the studies estimated the effects of the AFDC program and consisted of structural or quasi-structural models, using pure cross-state variation in AFDC benefits along with other sources of identification to obtain parameter estimates[23]. They found almost universally that the AFDC program reduced labor supply by from 10 to 50% of non-AFDC levels. The substitution and income elasticities estimated from the literature fell into the general range of those elasticities obtained from the literature on substitution and income effects estimated from wage and nonlabor income variation, respectively, suggesting that the simple static theory – which presumes these elasticities to be the same – is roughly verified.

This literature also addressed the effects of a reduction in t and the ambiguity of labor supply response noted in the previous section. In general, it was found that for single mothers, the primary eligibility group for benefits, average labor supply was quite inelastic with respect to changes in t holding G fixed, suggesting that the labor-supply-inducing and labor-supply-decreasing effects roughly cancelled each other out (see Moffitt (1992), for a discussion). While these effects were obtained by simulation, using structural estimates of substitution and income elasticities to forecast the positive and negative labor supply responses to a reduction in t over the income and hours distribution, they are consistent with reduced form estimates from the negative income tax experiments[24]. The NIT experiments tested multiple G and t combinations and hence it was possible to determine the average effect of a change in t, holding G fixed, by comparing treatment–control outcomes across different experimental groups. The results showed a very mixed pattern of results, with labor

---

[22] For reasons of length, and not because of any lack of inherent interest, the literature from countries other than the USA will not be reviewed.

[23] There was one state-fixed effects estimate from this literature [Moffitt (1986)].

[24] The results of the NIT experiments will also not be reviewed here. See Moffitt and Kehrer (1981) and Burtless (1987) for reviews.

supply levels sometimes higher and sometimes lower with no consistent pattern and with few significant differences [SRI International (1983, Table 3.9)].

Fortin, Truchon and Beausejour (1993) addressed the social welfare issue referred to previously by simulating the effects of different combinations of G and t on a variety of social welfare indices, most of them based on Atkinson-style inequality aversion scales. Using a calibrated model with assumed elasticities, and a data set of Canadian families, the results showed a large number of "perverse" effects of a reduction in t on labor supply, consistent with prior evidence. However, the programs that most often maximized social welfare were those with relatively low levels of both G and t. At these levels, the amount of redistribution is not very high and, further, they occur in a range where reductions in t tend to increase average labor supply. The paper thus presents a useful exercise on how to address this important question, even though the results may be specific to the data set used and to the income distribution in the Canadian data set used for the analysis.

A scattering of estimates were obtained for other programs. Estimates of the effect of the Food Stamp program showed very little labor supply response, possibly because the benefit amounts in the program are quite small relative to those of cash programs. There were a fairly large number of estimates of the effect of Medicaid on labor supply, with the majority indicating some significant work disincentives of the program, albeit concentrated among those in poor health [see Gruber (2003), for a review of these studies]. One study attempted to estimate the labor supply effects of housing programs using a very indirect method of identification, rather than variation in housing programs per se, and found the program to reduce hours of work by about 4% [Murray (1980)]. There were also a number of structural estimates of the effect of the price of child care on labor supply, both before and after 1995 and using similar methologies. These studies almost uniformly show negative price effects on employment, implying that child care subsidies will indeed increase employment [see Blau (2003), for a review of this literature].

3.3. Post-1995 structural estimates

Because of the decline in structural estimation in the labor supply literature, there have been few structural estimates of labor supply responsiveness. Table 4 shows four of the more well-known studies. Hoynes (1996) studied the AFDC-UP program and found it to have significant negative effects on the labor supply of husbands and wives, but that marginal reductions in t had little effect, consistent with prior work. Hagstrom (1996) estimated the effect of the Food Stamp program on labor supply and found it to have very small effects, even smaller than those found in the pre-1995 literature. This reinforces the sense that the Food Stamp program has little effect on work disincentives. Keane and Moffitt (1998) focused on the labor supply effects of participating in multiple programs, including not only AFDC but also Food Stamps, subsidized housing, and the Medicaid program. They showed that cumulative tax rates were generally greater than 100% in this case. Nevertheless, while their estimated

Table 4

Recent structural models of the effect of welfare programs on labor supply

Author and program	Data	Population	Dependent variable	Welfare variables	Results
Hoynes (1996) AFDC-UP	Survey of Income and Program Participation, 1983–1986	Low Asset Married Couples	Labor Supply and Participation in the AFDC-UP Program	AFDC Guarantee and Tax Rate evaluated at specific points	AFDC-UP has sizable negative effect on labor supply; marginal changes in G and t have little effect
Hagstrom (1996) Food Stamps	Survey of Income and Program Participation, 1984	Low Asset Married Couples	Labor Supply and Participation in Food Stamps	Food Stamp Guarantee and Tax Rate	Very small labor supply disincentives
Keane and Moffitt (1998) AFDC, Food Stamps, and housing	Survey of Income and Program Participation, 1984	Low Asset Single Mothers	Labor Supply and Participation in AFDC, Food Stamps, and Subsidized Housing	Guarantees and Tax Rates in AFDC, Food Stamps, and Subsidized Housing evaluated at specific labor supply points	Sub elast is 1.82 and total income elast is -0.21; marginal changes in t have no effect on labor supply
Meyer and Rosenbaum (2001) AFDC, Food Stamps, and EITC	Current Population Survey, 1984–1996	Single Mothers	Probability of Working	AFDC and Food Stamp Guarantee and expected benefits if work	Guarantees reduce employment probability and tax declines increase it

substitution and income elasticities were sizable, the net effect on labor supply of reducing the marginal tax rates to a level below 100% was negligible. Meyer and Rosenbaum (2001) focused on an attempt to explain the increase in employment rates among single mothers from 1984–1996. They found that AFDC benefits and tax rates (the latter affecting potential benefits if working) had expected effects on employment probabilities, but that the time series increase in single-mother employment was less affected by changes in those parameters and other welfare variables than a change in the generosity of the EITC over the period[25].

Some of the simulations of alternative programs conducted by Keane and Moffitt bore on one of the issues raised in the theoretical section above, which is whether wage and earnings subsidies are likely to draw welfare recipients off welfare and into the (subsidized) private labor market. Keane and Moffitt found AFDC and Food Stamps to have heavy stigma attached to them but they assumed that there would be no stigma associated with a wage or earnings subsidy program. As a consequence, they found the latter types of programs to have much higher forecasts of work incentives than reductions in the welfare tax rate t. Whether there would be any stigma attached to such programs is not clear, however [see also Keane (1995)].

3.4. Post-1995 reduced-form policy impact estimates

The literature on estimating the reduced-form impact of policy changes on employment and earnings is also exceeding modest. Yelowitz (1995) used the expansion of Medicaid in different states and in different age groups of children to estimate their impact on employment, and found those expansions to have a positive effect on employment rates. A number of policy-impact studies of the effect of the EITC on labor supply have also been conducted [e.g., Eissa and Liebman (1996), Eissa and Hoynes (1998)]. The results show that the EITC increases employment probabilities for single mothers but has no net effect on their hours of work, if working. This is consistent with the notion that labor supply is encouraged among initial nonworkers but that the taxback region of the program reduces labor supply enough to cancel out the effects among workers. As noted above, Meyer and Rosenbaum (2001) also estimated the effects of the EITC on single mothers and also found it to have significantly positive effects on employment probabilities. The results from the Eissa–Hoynes study shed light on the effects of the EITC on married men and married women. The findings were that the EITC increased the employment probabilities of married men but decreased those of married women, and that it decreased the hours of work of workers of both men and women. The results for married women may be because many of them are located in the taxback region because their husbands have significant earnings in and

---

[25] Because Meyer and Rosenbaum examined employment rather than hours of work, the "perverse" effect of a change in t could not occur. They briefly examined effects on hours of work as a sensitivity test but they noted that the model-independent variables were not set up for that dependent variable.

of themselves and the wives may be regarded as the marginal worker, even at the first dollar. The hours results for men may be a result of the same taxback region [26].

These constitute the main body of this type of work and is, as already noted, quite small in volume. There have been no studies of this type for the SSI program at all, nor any new studies of the Food Stamp or housing programs.

Many more studies have been conducted of the effects of the 1996 welfare legislation, the Personal Responsibility and Work Opportunity Reconciliation Act (PRWORA), which transformed the AFDC program into the Temporary Assistance for Needy Families (TANF) program by introducing time limits, work requirements, and devolved responsibility and block grant funding to the states [see Moffitt (2003), for a detailed review of its provisions]. There were also a number of studies of so-called "waiver" programs just prior to 1996 under which states undertook to test programs that were in most cases similar to the later national PRWORA legislation. Evaluating these waiver programs was made possible by the fact that different states tested different types of programs and did so at different calendar times, furnishing variation in policy which could be used to estimate impacts on labor supply and other outcomes. However, evaluating the 1996 legislation is difficult because it was implemented nationally and all states had to come into compliance with its main provisions. Thus there was no cross-state variation in the overall nature of the program.

As a consequence, difference-in-difference methods have generally been used for the evaluation of the effects of TANF. As Ellwood (2000) and Schoeni and Blank (2000) note, use of these methods is particularly problematic when other reforms, such as the EITC, were occurring roughly simultaneously, and when business cycle and economy-wide trends were occurring which could affect different groups differently. A further difficulty in evaluation has arisen because the separate impacts of time limits, work requirements, and other provisions has been difficult to determine even in the pre-1996 waiver period. This is partly because a state's choice of those components is correlated with other characteristics of the state and partly because their implementation was often significantly different than what would be expected from their formal definition. As a consequence, while there are a number of estimates of the overall impact of welfare reform in this period, taken as a whole, there are almost no credible studies of the impact of different individual components of reform taken individually [27].

Table 5 shows the main studies estimating the overall impact of the pre-1996 waiver programs and of TANF. With a few exceptions, the studies show waivers to have had

---

[26] See Hotz and Scholz (2003) for a more detailed review of these EITC studies and a number of others that used indirect estimation methods to simulate the effect of the EITC on labor supply. It should be noted that the Eissa–Hoynes study, while using direct policy variation for reduced form estimation, also translated their impacts into estimated income and substitution elasticities.

[27] An exception is Grogger (2000, 2001), who has attempted to estimate the independent effects of time limits by using age variation in children combined with assumptions that that variation does not interact identically with other welfare reform features. The validity of the assumptions needed for these methods to be unbiased is unknown.

Table 5
Studies of the overall effect of welfare reform on labor supply

Study	Program(s)	Dependent variable	Source of program variation	Estimated effect of welfare reform
Pre-1996 Waiver Programs				
Bloom and Michalopoulos (2001)	Waiver programs in Connecticut, Florida, and Vermont	Employment, earnings, income, AFDC participation	Randomized assignment on population of AFDC recipients	Positive effect on employment and earnings, no effect on income, small or zero effects on AFDC participation
Fein, Long, Behrens and Lee (2001)	Waiver program in Delaware	Employment, earnings, income, AFDC participation	Randomized assignment on population of AFDC recipients	Positive effect on employment and earnings, no effect on income or AFDC participation
Moffitt (1999)	All state waiver programs	AFDC participation rate, labor supply and earnings of less educated women	Cross-state variation in timing of waiver introduction	No effect on employment or earnings; positive effect on weeks and hours worked; negative effect on AFDC participation rate
Mueser, Hotchkiss, King, Rokicki and Stevens (2000)	Waiver programs in five urban areas	AFDC entry and exit rates, employment rate of welfare leavers	Cross-state variation in timing of waiver introduction	Negative effect on entry rate, positive effect on exit rate, positive but small effect on employment rate of leavers
O'Neill and Hill (2001)	All state waiver programs	Employment, AFDC participation	Cross-state variation in timing of waiver introduction	Positive on employment, negative on AFDC participation

continued on next page

Table 5, *continued*

Study	Program(s)	Dependent variable	Source of program variation	Estimated effect of welfare reform
Schoeni and Blank (2000)	All state waiver programs	Labor supply, earnings, income, AFDC participation	Cross-state variation in timing of waiver introduction combined with difference-in-difference using high-educated control group	Positive effects on labor supply, earnings, income; negative effects on AFDC participation
TANF				
Ellwood (2000)	TANF	Employment, earnings	Difference-in-difference with high-wage control group	Cannot separate effect of EITC and welfare reform
McKernan, Lerman, Pindus, Valente (2000)	TANF	Employment	Difference-in-difference with childless women control group	Positive
O'Neill and Hill (2001)	TANF	Employment, AFDC-TANF participation	Cross-state variation in timing of TANF implementation	Positive on employment, negative on AFDC–TANF participation
Schoeni and Blank (2000)	TANF	Labor supply, earnings, income, AFDC–TANF participation	Difference-in-difference with high-educated control group	No effect on labor supply or individual earnings, positive effect on family earnings and income, negative effect on AFDC–TANF participation

positive effects on most measures of labor supply and negative effects on measures of AFDC participation, as expected. These studies all control for the state of the economy, usually by controlling for the unemployment rate, so the estimated effects of welfare reform are all intended to be net of the strong economy.

Two entries in Table 5 are for experiments which made use of traditional random-assignment methods rather than cross-state variation in the presence of reform. These studies generally also find positive effects on employment and earnings and negative effects on welfare participation[28]. However, random-assignment methods are not well-suited for major structural reforms like the pre-1996 welfare waivers – or for TANF itself – because such structural reforms tend to cause changes in local labor markets and local communities that feed back onto the control group, and because structural reforms tend to have significant effects on entry into welfare. Experiments produce biased estimates of total reform effects under these circumstances[29].

The estimates of the effects of TANF are generally positive on employment and earnings but not always. Further, in some cases the effects of TANF cannot be separated from the effects of other policy changes occurring at the same time, as emphasized by Ellwood (2000); he concludes that these difficulties are sufficiently severe that the separate contributions of welfare reform, the EITC, and the economy cannot be identified. McKernan, Lerman, Pindus and Valente (2000) and Schoeni and Blank (2000) are the other two studies using difference-in-difference methods, one of which finds TANF to have increased employment while the other finds it not to have done so but to have affected family earnings, income, and AFDC participation. The two studies used different control groups so this may be the source of the difference. What evidence there is, therefore, indicates some TANF effects in the expected direction but the small number of studies and problems in statistical inference make the conclusions rather uncertain.

4. Summary

The labor supply and other work incentive effects of welfare programs have long been a central concern in economic research. Work has also been an increasing focus of policy reforms in the USA, culminating with a number of major policy changes in the 1990s whose intent was to increase employment and earnings levels of welfare recipients and other disadvantaged individuals. This review of the theoretical and

---

[28] There have been many more random-assignment studies in this period but those listed in Table 5 are those which had all of the main features of PRWORA, namely, time limits, work requirements, sanctions, and enhanced earnings disregards, and which made these reforms within the AFDC system rather than outside of it.

[29] Another difficulty in the use of experiments for evaluating structural welfare reform is that the control group is often contaminated by the general atmosphere of reform which changes the expectations of the eligible population as a whole.

empirical literature on this issue reveals that there is much that remains to be done to gain a full understanding of these programs. Many issues relating to the optimal levels of welfare program parameters and the social desirability of labor supply effects in different parts of the income distribution remain to be studied, a key issue. New policy initiatives in the area of work requirements, time limits, and other topics have been understudied, as have dynamic models of labor supply response. The proper integration of the complex multi-program environment in the USA is also a needed area of research.

Even more on the empirical side, more research is needed in a number of areas. While traditional studies of the effect of AFDC guarantee and tax rates are reasonably plentiful, structural or quasi-structural models of the effects of welfare reforms in the 1990s are rare and yet are needed to understand the mechanisms by which effects of that reform have taken place as well as to forecast the effects of new policies. Many programs other than TANF are quite understudied, especially the SSI program but also including the Food Stamp and Medicaid programs. Even the EITC, which has seen a considerable amount of research attention, has at present been the subject of only a modest number of studies. Thus there are many areas of new research to be conducted on the effects of welfare programs on labor supply.

References

Akerlof, G. (1978), "The economics of 'tagging' as applied to the optimal income tax, welfare programs, and manpower planning", American Economic Review 68:8–19.

Ashenfelter, O. (1983), "Determining participation in income-tested social programs", Journal of the American Statistical Association 78:517–525.

Barth, M., and D. Greenberg (1971), "Incentive effects of some pure and mixed transfer systems", Journal of Human Resources 6:149–170.

Beaudry, P., and C. Blackorby (1998), "Taxes and employment subsidies in optimal redistribution programs", Working Paper 6355 (National Bureau of Economic Research, Cambridge, MA).

Besley, T.J., and S. Coate (1992a), "Understanding welfare stigma: taxpayer resentment and statistical discrimination", Journal of Public Economics 48:165–163.

Besley, T.J., and S. Coate (1992b), "Workfare versus welfare: incentive arguments for work requirements in poverty-alleviation programs", American Economic Review 82:249–261.

Besley, T.J., and S. Coate (1995), "The design of income maintenance programmes", Review of Economic Studies 62:187–221.

Blau, D.M. (2003), "Child care subsidy programs", in: R. Moffitt, ed., Means-Tested Transfer Programs in the U.S. (University of Chicago Press, Chicago) forthcoming.

Bloom, D., and C. Michalopoulos (2001), How Welfare and Work Policies Affect Employment and Income: A Synthesis of Research (Manpower Demonstration Research Corporation, New York).

Blundell, R., and T. MaCurdy (1999), "Labor supply: a review of alternative approaches", in: O. Ashenfelter and D. Card, eds., Handbook of Labor Economics, Vol. 3A (Elsevier, Amsterdam) pp. 1559–1695.

Browning, E.K. (1975), Redistribution and the Welfare System (American Enterprise Institute, Washington, DC).

Burke, V. (2001), Cash and Non-Cash Benefits for Persons with Limited Income: Eligibility Rules, Recipient and Expenditure Data, FY1998-FY2000 (Congressional Research Service, Washington, DC).

Burtless, G. (1987), "The work response to a guaranteed income: a survey of the experimental evidence", in: A. Munnell, ed., Lessons from the Income Maintenance Experiments (Federal Reserve Bank and Brookings, Boston) pp. 22–52.

Chone, P., and G. Laroque (2001), "Optimal incentives for labor force participation", Working Paper 2001-25 (Institut National de la Statistique et des Études Économique (INSEE), Paris, France).

Coe, N., G. Acs, R. Lerman and K. Watson (1998), Does Work Pay? A Summary of the Work Incentives Under TANF (Urban Institute, Washington, DC).

Cuff, K. (2000), "Optimality of workfare with heterogeneous preferences", Canadian Journal of Economics 33:149–174.

Currie, J. (2003), "Food and nutrition programs", in: R. Moffitt, ed., Means-Tested Transfers in the U.S. (University of Chicago Press, Chicago) forthcoming.

Danziger, S., R. Haveman and R. Plotnick (1981), "How income transfers affect work, savings, and the income distribution: a critical review", Journal of Economic Literature 19:975–1028.

Eissa, N., and H. Hoynes (1998), "The earned income tax credit and the labor supply of married couples", Working Paper 6856 (National Bureau of Economic Research, Cambridge, MA).

Eissa, N., and J. Liebman (1996), "Labor supply response to the earned income tax credit", Quarterly Journal of Economics 111:605–637.

Ellwood, D. (2000), "The impact of the earned income tax credit and social policy reforms on work, marriage, and living arrangements", National Tax Journal 53(Pt. 2):1063–1105.

Fein, D., D. Long, J. Behrens and W. Lee (2001), The ABC Evaluation: Turning the Corner: Delaware's A Better Chance Welfare Reform Program at Four Years (Abt Associates, Cambridge, MA).

Fortin, B., M. Truchon and L. Beausejour (1993), "On reforming the welfare system: workfare meets the negative income tax", Journal of Public Economics 51:119–151.

Friedman, M. (1962), Capitalism and Freedom (University of Chicago Press, Chicago).

Garfinkel, I. (1973), "A skeptical note on 'the optimality' of wage subsidy programs", American Economic Review 63:447–453.

Gavhari, F. (1994), "In-kind transfers, cash grants and labor supply", Journal of Public Economics 55:495–504.

Gottschalk, P. (1988), "The impact of taxes and transfers on job search", Journal of Labor Economics 6:362–375.

Grogger, J.T. (2000), "Time limits and welfare use", Working Paper 7709 (National Bureau of Economic Research, Cambridge, MA).

Grogger, J.T. (2001), "The effects of time limits and other policy changes on welfare use, work, and income among female-headed families", Working Paper 8153 (National Bureau of Economic Research, Cambridge, MA).

Gruber, J. (2003), "Medicaid", in: R. Moffitt, ed., Means-Tested Transfer Programs in the U.S. (University of Chicago Press, Chicago) forthcoming.

Hagstrom, P. (1996), "The food stamp participation and labor supply of married couples: an empirical analysis of joint decisions", Journal of Human Resources 31:331–358.

Heckman, J.J. (2000), "Causal parameters and policy analysis in economics: a twentieth century retrospective", Quarterly Journal of Economics 115:45–97.

Hotz, V.J., and J.K. Scholz (2003), "The earned income tax credit", in: R. Moffitt, ed., Means-Tested Transfers in the U.S. (University of Chicago Press, Chicago) forthcoming.

Hoynes, H. (1996), "Welfare transfers in two-parent families: labor supply and welfare participation under AFDC-UP", Econometrica 64:295–332.

Hoynes, H. (1997), "Work, welfare, and family structure: what have we learned?" in: A. Auerbach, ed., Fiscal Policy: Lessons from Economic Research (MIT Press, Cambridge, MA).

Hubbard, R.G., J. Skinner and S.P. Zeldes (1995), "Precautionary saving and social insurance", Journal of Political Economy 103:360–399.

Immonen, R., R. Kanbur, M. Keen and M. Tuomala (1998), "Tagging and taxing: the optimal use of categorical and income information in designing tax/transfer schemes", Economica 65:179–192.

Keane, M. (1995), "A new idea for welfare reform", Federal Reserve Bank of Minneapolis Quarterly Review 19:2–28.

Keane, M., and R. Moffitt (1998), "A structural model of multiple welfare program participation and labor supply", International Economic Review 39:553–589.

Kesselman, J.R. (1969), "Labor-supply efffects of income, income-work, and wage subsidies", Journal of Human Resources 4:275–292.

Kesselman, J.R. (1973), "Incentive effects of transfer systems once again", Journal of Human Resources 8:119–129.

Kesselman, J.R. (1976), "Tax effects on job search, training, and work effort", Journal of Public Economics 6:255–272.

Leonesio, M. (1988), "In-kind transfers and work incentives", Journal of Labor Economics 4:515–529.

Levy, F. (1979), "The labor supply effects of female heads, or AFDC work incentives don't work too well", Journal of Human Resources 14:76–97.

Lindbeck, A., S. Nyberg and J. Weibull (1999), "Social norms, the welfare state, and voting", Quarterly Journal of Economics 114:1–35.

Lurie, I., ed. (1975), Integrating Income Maintenance Programs (Academic Press, NY).

McKernan, S.-M., R. Lerman, N. Pindus and J. Valente (2000), "The relationship between metropolitan and non-metropolitan locations, changing welfare policies, and the employment of single mothers", Mimeo (Urban Institute, Washington, DC).

Meyer, B.D., and D.T. Rosenbaum (2001), "Welfare, the earned income tax credit, and the labor supply of single mothers", Quarterly Journal of Economics 116:1063–1114.

Miller, R., and S. Sanders (1997), "Human capital development and welfare participation", Carnegie-Rochester Conference Series on Public Policy 46:1–43.

Moffitt, R. (1983), "An economic model of welfare stigma", American Economic Review 73:1023–1035.

Moffitt, R. (1985), "Unemployment insurance and the distribution of unemployment spells", Journal of Econometrics 28:85–101.

Moffitt, R. (1986), "Work incentives in transfer programs (revisited): a study of the AFDC program", in: R. Ehrenberg, ed., Research in Labor Economics, Vol. 8 (JAI Press, Greenwich, CT).

Moffitt, R. (1992), "Incentive effects of the U.S. welfare system: a review", Journal of Economic Literature 30:1–61.

Moffitt, R. (1999), "The effect of pre-PRWORA waivers on AFDC caseloads and female earnings, income, and labor force behavior", in: S. Danziger, ed., Economic Conditions and Welfare Reform (Upjohn Institute, Kalamazoo, MI) pp. 91–118.

Moffitt, R. (2002), "Economic effects of means-tested transfers in the U.S.", Tax Policy and the Economy 16:1–35.

Moffitt, R. (2003), "The temporary assistance for needy families program", in: R. Moffitt, ed., Means-Tested Transfer Programs in the U.S., (University of Chicago Press, Chicago) forthcoming.

Moffitt, R., and K. Kehrer (1981), "The effect of tax and transfer programs on labor supply: the evidence from the income maintenance experiments", in: R. Ehrenberg, ed., Research in Labor Economics, Vol. IV (JAI Press, Greenwich, CT).

Mueser, P., J. Hotchkiss, C. King, P. Rokicki and D. Stevens (2000), "The welfare caseload, economic growth and welfare-to-work policies: an analysis of five urban areas", Mimeo (University of Missouri, Columbia, MO).

Murray, M. (1980), "A reinterpretation of the traditional income-leisure model, with application to in-kind subsidy programs", Journal of Public Economics 14:69–81.

Nechyba, T.J. (1999), "Social approval, values, and AFDC: a re-examination of the illegitimacy debate", Working Paper 7240 (National Bureau of Economic Research, Cambridge, MA).

O'Neill, J., and M.A. Hill (2001), Gaining Ground? Measuring the Impact of Welfare Reform on Welfare and Work (Manhattan Institute, NY).

Parsons, D.O. (1996), "Imperfect 'tagging' in social insurance programs", Journal of Public Economics 62:183–208.

Rowe, G., and T. Roberts (2002), Welfare Rules Databook Tables: State Policies as of July 2000 (Urban Institute, Washington, DC).

Schoeni, R., and R.M. Blank (2000), "What has welfare reform accomplished? Impacts on welfare participation, employment, income, poverty, and family structure", Working Paper 7627 (National Bureau of Economic Research, Cambridge, MA).

Smeeding, T. (1982), "Alternative methods for valuing selected in-kind transfer benefits and measuring their effects on poverty", Technical Paper 50 (Bureau of the Census, Washington, DC).

SRI International, Inc. (1983), Final Report of the Seattle/Denver Income Maintenance Experiment, Vol. I (SRI International, Inc., Menlo Park, CA).

Tobin, J. (1965), "On improving the status of the negro", Daedalus 94:878–897.

U.S. House of Representatives (2000), Background Material and Data on Programs Within the Jurisdiction of the Committee on Ways and Means (Government Printing Office, Washington, DC).

Yelowitz, A. (1995), "The Medicaid notch, labor supply, and welfare participation: evidence from eligibility expansions", Quarterly Journal of Economics 105:909–940.

Zeckhauser, R.J. (1971), "Optimal mechanisms for income transfer", American Economic Review 61: 324–334.

AUTHOR INDEX

Aaron, H.J.   1816, 1843, 2233, 2279, 2301, 2303, 2304, 2374
Abbring, J.H.   2351
Abel, A.   1926, 1927, 2304, 2309
Ablett, J.   1903
Acemoglu, D.   2055, 2066, 2384
Achilles, C.M., *see* Word, E.   2096, 2097
Acland, H., *see* Jencks, C.   2057
Acs, G., *see* Coe, N.   2401
Adamache, K.W., *see* Sloan, F.A.   2181
Adams, J.   2343
Adler, M.   1949, 1961
Advisory Council on Social Security   2313
Agell, J.   2332
Aigner, D.J.   2100
Aiuppa, T.   2364
Akerhielm, K.   2091
Akerlof, G.   2220, 2412
Akin, J.S.   2056, 2071
Alber, J., *see* Flora, P.   2254, 2255
Alberini, A., *see* Krupnick, A.   2162
Alesina, A.   2036
Alexander, K.L., *see* Entwisle, D.R.   2092
Alsalam, N., *see* James, E.   2048
Altig, D.   1820, 1855, 1917–1919, 1922
Altman, D.   2203
Altonji, J.G.   1926
Altonji, J.G., *see* Hayashi, F.   1926
Altshuler, R.   1967, 1971, 1973, 1974, 1978
Anderson, G., *see* Vroman, S.   2181
Anderson, K.B.   1828
Anderson, K.H.   2373
Anderson, M.C., *see* Mendro, R.L.   2106
Anderson, P.M.   2334, 2337, 2342, 2346–2348, 2354, 2374
Anderson, R.M.   2001
Anderson, S.P.   1830, 2027
Angrist, J., *see* Acemoglu, D.   2055, 2066, 2384
Angrist, J.D.   2091, 2114
Antos, J.R.   2104
Argys, L.M.   2079
Armor, D.J.   2071, 2072, 2080, 2106, 2111

Arnott, R.   2026, 2027, 2034
Arrau, P.   1917
Arromdee, V., *see* Coughlin, C.   1968
Arrow, K.   2165, 2166, 2168
Ashenfelter, O.   2405
Ashford, B.G., *see* Hatry, H.P.   2105
Atkinson, A.B.   1789, 1807, 1942, 2279, 2283, 2334, 2342, 2343, 2351, 2354
Auerbach, A.J.   1789, 1820, 1832, 1840, 1847, 1855, 1856, 1858, 1864, 1889, 1901–1903, 1907, 1914, 1917, 1926, 1927, 1937, 1939, 1942, 1947, 1958, 1967, 1977, 1978, 1986, 2167, 2280, 2290, 2293
Auerbach, A.J., *see* Altig, D.   1820, 1855, 1918, 1919, 1922
Auten, G.   2263
Autor, D.H.   2381, 2383

Badawi, A., *see* Marsteller, J.A.   2209
Bagwell, K., *see* Bernheim, B.D.   1924
Baily, M.N.   2339
Bain, H.P., *see* Word, E.   2096, 2097
Baker, G.P.   2105
Baker, M.   2371, 2374
Bakija, J.M., *see* Steuerle, C.E.   2230, 2287, 2289
Ballard, C.L.   1820, 1852
Ballou, D.   2104, 2105, 2117
Baloff, N., *see* Griffith, M.   2202
Bane, M.J., *see* Jencks, C.   2057
Banks, J.   2247
Bardsley, P., *see* Olekalns, N.   2163
Barham, V.   2004
Barnett, W.S.   2049
Barro, R.J.   1789, 1835, 1878, 1923, 2050, 2055, 2059, 2280, 2281
Barsky, R.B.   1894
Barth, M.   2413
Barthold, T.A.   1862
Baumol, W.J.   2059
Baxter, M.   2308
Beaudry, P.   2413
Beausejour, L., *see* Fortin, B.   2420

I-1

SUBJECT INDEX

HANDBOOKS IN ECONOMICS

1. HANDBOOK OF MATHEMATICAL ECONOMICS (in 4 volumes)
   Volumes 1, 2 and 3 edited by Kenneth J. Arrow and Michael D. Intriligator
   Volume 4 edited by Werner Hildenbrand and Hugo Sonnenschein

2. HANDBOOK OF ECONOMETRICS (in 6 volumes)
   Volumes 1, 2 and 3 edited by Zvi Griliches and Michael D. Intriligator
   Volume 4 edited by Robert F. Engle and Daniel L. McFadden
   Volume 5 edited by James J. Heckman and Edward Leamer
   Volume 6 is in preparation (editors James J. Heckman and Edward Leamer)

3. HANDBOOK OF INTERNATIONAL ECONOMICS (in 3 volumes)
   Volumes 1 and 2 edited by Ronald W. Jones and Peter B. Kenen
   Volume 3 edited by Gene M. Grossman and Kenneth Rogoff

4. HANDBOOK OF PUBLIC ECONOMICS (in 4 volumes)
   Edited by Alan J. Auerbach and Martin Feldstein

5. HANDBOOK OF LABOR ECONOMICS (in 5 volumes)
   Volumes 1 and 2 edited by Orley C. Ashenfelter and Richard Layard
   Volumes 3A, 3B and 3C edited by Orley C. Ashenfelter and David Card

6. HANDBOOK OF NATURAL RESOURCE AND ENERGY ECONOMICS
   (in 3 volumes)
   Edited by Allen V. Kneese and James L. Sweeney

7. HANDBOOK OF REGIONAL AND URBAN ECONOMICS (in 3 volumes)
   Volume 1 edited by Peter Nijkamp
   Volume 2 edited by Edwin S. Mills
   Volume 3 edited by Paul C. Cheshire and Edwin S. Mills

19. HANDBOOK OF SOCIAL CHOICE AND WELFARE (in 2 volumes)
    Volume 1 edited by Kenneth J. Arrow, Amartya K. Sen and Kotaro Suzumura
    Volume 2 is in preparation (editors Kenneth J. Arrow, Amartya K. Sen and
    Kotaro Suzumura)

FORTHCOMING TITLES

HANDBOOK OF RESULTS IN EXPERIMENTAL ECONOMICS
Editors Charles Plott and Vernon L. Smith

HANDBOOK OF ENVIRONMENTAL ECONOMICS
Editors Karl-Goran Mäler and Jeff Vincent

HANDBOOK OF THE ECONOMICS OF FINANCE
Editors George M. Constantinides, Milton Harris and René M. Stulz

HANDBOOK ON THE ECONOMICS OF GIVING, RECIPROCITY AND ALTRUISM
Editors Serge-Christophe Kolm and Jean Mercier Ythier

HANDBOOK ON THE ECONOMICS OF ART AND CULTURE
Editors Victor Ginsburgh and David Throsby

HANDBOOK OF ECONOMIC GROWTH
Editors Philippe Aghion and Steven N. Durlauf

All published volumes available

Printed and bound by CPI Group (UK) Ltd, Croydon, CR0 4YY

08/05/2025

01864967-0005